The Tragic Week
A Study of Anticlericalism in Spain, 1875-1912

The Tragic Week ❧

A Study of Anticlericalism in Spain, 1875-1912

JOAN CONNELLY ULLMAN

HARVARD UNIVERSITY PRESS

Cambridge, Massachusetts

1968

To Gladys Frances Connelly

Preface

ANTICLERICALISM is a central concern of Spaniards, in their private conversation and in their politics. To Americans reared in a secular society it seems a remote issue in light of the other truly serious problems confronting Spain. Even within the context in which anticlericalism took form as a popular political issue — in the context of the nineteenth-century liberal's concern for civil rights — it is not readily apparent why the Spanish *worker* would react so passionately. The traditional explanations, that he is by temperament committed to fight any institution that restrains his individual liberty or that he has turned against an institution which failed to live up to its ideal, appear to be more of those ipse dixits which obscure rather than clarify Spanish history.

However fascinating, anticlericalism did not seem to have a specific content that could be studied historically. This book started as an analysis of Spanish conservatism in the person of Antonio Maura y Montaner (1853–1925) and as an analysis of what Walter Lippmann has described as the true conservative's "respect and concern for the social order as a living body." Along this path anticlericalism intruded, for it was at the heart of the crisis of Maura's career: the rebellion in Barcelona in July of 1909 and the execution of Francisco Ferrer. This, then, was the first thread in the study: the political function of anticlericalism in relation to the problem of public order. The second thread, disclosed by research and reinforced by years of residence in that country, was the involvement of the clergy in every aspect of society; the four political regimes that have governed Spain in this century have affected only superficially the role of the clergy in the economy, public welfare institutions, and educational system. This explains both the difficulty of any political solution, and the worker's frustrated belief (encouraged by agitation) that the problem can be resolved only through force.

During the writing of this book countless Spanish friends, of varying political convictions, talked with me at length about the role of the clergy; even those most devoted to the Church believed the time had come to re-evaluate clerical activities on the basis of facts and of objective criteria. To that end they tried to help me gain access to archives: that the doors of most of those archives remained firmly closed indicates how delicate a matter anticlericalism continues to be.

I am very grateful to the American Association of University Women, which awarded me a fellowship that enabled me to devote the academic year 1961–1962 to research in Barcelona. Professor Felix Gilbert of the Institute for Advanced Study in Princeton gave generously of his time, insisting upon the importance of a chronological approach in a study such as this: it yielded immeasurable benefits in delineating cause and effect. Professor José Ferrater Mora, in the writing of this book as in my years of study with him, helped me to discern motivation behind eloquent Spanish rhetoric. To him, as to Professor Juan Marichal of Harvard University, I want to express my appreciation for their encouraging belief that this study could make some contribution to an understanding of a tangled problem. Professor Juan Linz of Columbia University and Professor Richard Herr of the University of California at Berkeley made invaluable suggestions that led to a sharper focus on sociocultural factors. Professor Caroline Robbins, Professor Roger Wells, and Dean Dorothy Nepper Marshall of Bryn Mawr College made important suggestions regarding detail and content. Sr. José Antonio M. Bara of the Archivo Histórico Nacional of Madrid has time and again supplied me with copies of public records or checked a reference. Dr. Pedro Voltes Bou, Director of the Instituto Municipal de Historia de Barcelona, has aided me on numerous occasions. And finally I want to acknowledge the contribution of my mother: through the three years of an academic administrative position that devoured my time, she convinced me that there were still some hours to devote to the completion of this study.

Joan Connelly Ullman

University of Washington, Seattle
June 1967

Contents 𝕽

Part Three:
The Prelude to the Tragic Week:
May to July 1909

Part Four:
The Tragic Week

Part Five:
Conclusions

The Tragic Week
A Study of Anticlericalism
in Spain, 1875-1912

BARCELONA 1909

SCALE IN MILES
0 1 2 3 4 5

IMPORTANT BUILDINGS

1 City Hall
2 Governor's Office
3 Headquarters of Captain General
4 Radical Republican Party Headquarters
5 Auto Factory where general strike begins, July 26.
6 Barracks of the Veterans of Liberty
7 Military Prison

NORTH

IX

San Andrés
San Martín

X

Clot

IV
Ensanche

VIII
Gracia

VI
Universidad

VII
Corts de Sarriá

AVE. MERIDIANA
DE SAGRERA
FRANCIA
CARRETERA
A

TRAVESERA
DIAGONAL
DE GRACIA
GRACIA
PASEO DE
PL Cataluña
ST. TRAYN
RAMBLA
AVE. DE LAS CORTS
RONDA SAN PABLO
PARALELO

I
Barceloneta

Pueblo Nuevo

Pequín

II
Parque

III

Puerto

V
Atarazanas

•4

•5

•6

•1
3•

•7

MEDITERRANEAN SEA

Introduction

*We are not persecuting the Church, nor has it entered our minds
to de-Catholicize* [decatolizar] *Spain . . . What I do say is that
the Catholic religion is a factor in the political life of my country,
and that a statesman who attempts to govern by de-Catholicizing
Spain may be a philosopher or a writer, but not a statesman.*

— *Melquíades Alvarez,
a republican deputy,
in December 1908*

DURING the last week of July 1909, the industrial workers of Barcelona seized control of the streets and held at bay the police and military forces of the Spanish state. The movement had started as a protest against sending conscript soldiers to fight a colonial war in Morocco, yet within twenty-four hours it developed into a ferocious attack upon the property of the Catholic Church. The fires set by the workers destroyed forty convents and twelve parochial churches. To a lesser degree these events were repeated in manufacturing cities throughout Catalonia. The threat to the established order constituted by the events of this Tragic Week (*la Semana Trágica* as it is known in Spanish history), together with the harsh government repression that followed, marked the end of an era of economic, political, and intellectual reform movements through which Spain had sought to make the adjustment demanded by the end of one century and the beginning of a new one.

During this decade there had been other and perhaps more critical problems confronting Spain than the clerical issue. These included the transition from a rural to an urban society, from an agricultural to an industrial economy, and from an authoritarian to a representative government — essentially the same process confronting all contemporary Western European nations, although many factors operated to make the Spanish situation unique. The most significant were that the economy of Spain remained agrarian,* that rural interests dominated the political structure, and that 43 percent of the adult population was illiterate; these factors combined to foster a highly traditional society wherein change was difficult.

A further obstacle to the modernization of Spain was the concentration of industry on the periphery of the Iberian Peninsula; efforts of industrialists to gain the sweeping reforms needed for expansion were hampered by the historic prejudice in Madrid against Catalonia and the Basque Provinces. A final major factor differentiating the Spanish fin du siècle within the European context was the death of the nation's leading statesmen, architects of the Restoration Settlement under which the Bourbons had returned to govern, ostensibly at least, as constitutional monarchs. The assassination of Conservative party leader Antonio Cánovas del Castillo and the death of his Liberal colleague, Práxedes Mateo Sagasta, not only deprived Spain of her most experienced politicians but also provoked a struggle for party leadership. This coincided with the implementation of the Universal Suffrage Law of 1890, which would have constituted a major undertaking in itself. It was unfortunate that these political developments should have coincided with a national crisis that transcended partisan considerations.

But the single most distinctive feature of the Spanish situation, the catalyst that precipitated the crisis in the nation's politics and economy, was the War of 1898 and consequent loss of the last major colonies (Cuba, Puerto Rico, and the Philippines). The government's inefficiency and corruption during the war incited industrial and professional groups to demand immediate drastic reforms. Unable to secure the support of either major party, these groups sought votes among the two social classes not directly represented in Cánovas' Restoration Settlement: the lower middle classes and the workers. Such an appeal for mass support constituted a threat to vested economic interests and to the social structure; therefore,

* In 1900, 68 percent of the Spanish labor force was employed in agriculture while 16 percent worked in industry and 16 percent in services. Ten years later, 65 percent of the labor force was employed in agriculture, 17 percent in industry and 18 percent in services. (María José Sirera, A.C.J., "Obreros en Barcelona, 1900–1910" [unpublished thesis for the degree of licenciatura, College of Philosophy and Letters, University of Barcelona, 1959].)

the defenders of the established order bcame more intransigent in opposing reforms. This action and reaction constituted the first political consequences of the Spanish-American War.

Another consequence was the intrusion upon the political scene of a militant Catholicism, militarism, and Catalan regionalism. Excluded from active politics by Cánovas, these forces had expended their energies in the colonies but after 1898 they returned to play a major role in Spain and to demand compensation for their losses. They had an immediate and profound effect upon the parliamentary regime, either because they constituted a powerful force or because the system, apparently viable, was actually weak and inflexible.

Demands for renovation were intensified by the intellectual ferment that called in question the fundamental values of Spanish society. Defeat served as a catalyst for a brilliant group of writers, known as the "Generation of 1898," whose work was the culmination of a long period of cultural achievement. Their immediate precursors, Joaquín Costa and Angel Ganivet, had detected the national crisis before the war exposed it. But it was defeat, tragic because it was so decisive a rout, that served to unleash and orient deep creative energies that might have been delayed or dispersed. These writers were forced to analyze Spain's greatness and the causes for her decline; they debated whether she should seek a solution for the crisis in her own traditions or should adopt measures more widely European. Pío Baroja's novels gave dignity and perspective to workers and middle-class politicians experimenting with European movements such as anarchism and socialism. Although he dabbled in these movements, Baroja was unwilling to commit himself and remained an observer. Even more intellectual was Antonio Machado, who gave poetic insight to the national plight. Essayist Azorín (José Martínez Ruíz) was the activist of this Generation; after some left wing experimentation, he plunged into politics in defense of the program of national regeneration propounded by Conservative Premier Antonio Maura y Montaner. Although elected deputy in 1907, Azorín aided Maura most effectively through his newspaper articles during the succeeding two years.

The demand for the "Europeanization" of Spanish culture was met by an impassioned defense of traditionalism. Yet even this concept was controversial. A neo-Catholic like Alejandro Pidal[1] defined traditionalism to mean simply established political, religious, and social practices. Miguel de Unamuno, the great philosopher of the Generation of 1898, agreed that the resolution of the crisis must be sought within Spain's tradition, but he argued that the authentic realities (which he termed "intra-history") assumed different forms in each historical period.[2]

The literary argument for change and its refutation by articulate defenders of the established order were echoed in newspaper editorials throughout the nation. This cultural ambiance of criticism and rebuttal served to sharpen the political controversy of the decade. Given the traditional nature of Spanish society, it served as a detriment insofar as reforms were discussed in ideological and not political terms. This was particularly true with respect to the clerical issue.

In Spain, any desire for reform leads inevitably to a critical review of the Catholic Church because the Church is involved in every aspect of national life. Catholicism has been identified with Spanish nationalism since the medieval reconquest of the land from the Muslims. This has enabled conservatives to construe any criticism of the Church as a threat to Spanish society and to national unity, an effective argument in a traditional community and one that the clergy has too often used in order to resist legitimate demands for reform.

But in 1898 clerical responsibility in the revolt of the Philippines made it possible to discuss in patriotic terms the old demand for state control of religious orders and a new plea for a state-supported school system. Some few politicians and intellectuals went so far as to argue that the only remedy for the civic and cultural lag in Spain was to develop a secular society.[3] There were others, however, who believed that a revitalized Church could inspire the nation to carry out social and intellectual changes and that it could provide the basis for collective action in a society rent by regional and social divisions. Juan Maragall, a leader in the Catalan renaissance movement and a devout Catholic, denounced the egotism of the bourgeois society and urged the Church to exert moral leadership in the crisis.[4] Severino Aznar worked pertinaciously to promote social action within the Catholic Action movement.[5] But the voices of Christians like Maragall and Aznar were muted by those of reactionary clergy and laymen. The hierarchy rejected even a moderate reform program, fearful that it might be but the first step to the complete separation of Church and state as had been the case in France. Even the challenging precepts in the encyclical of Pope Leo XIII, *Rerum Novarum,* were rarely cited in Spain and never implemented. This intransigence in intellectual and social matters was one contributing factor to the growth of anticlericalism in Spain from 1900 to 1909.

During this decade the Church was not the only institution in need of reform, nor were the wealth, the attitudes, and the political power of the clergy the only obstacles to the industrialization of the nation. Church spokesmen claim that anticlericalism became an issue solely because Liberal politicians, contending for the position of party leader, viewed anticlericalism as a means of garnering votes.[6] This is as obvious a simplification as is the opposing contention that the Church was exclusively responsible for the dire national plight of Spain.[7] The causes of anticlericalism must be sought in the developing urbanization and industrialization, and in their effect on politics. The unfortunate consequence for Spain was that the clerical issue obscured the decisively important problems constituted by a lack of industrial and financial initiative among the haute bourgeoisie, by the enormous land-holdings of the aristocracy, and by the political ambitions of army officers; these were the critical groups in the attempt to modernize the nation. Yet it was the clergy who became the primary, almost the exclusive target for reformers in Spanish politics during the twentieth century, a development that the events in Barcelona of July 1909 first dramatized and subsequently symbolized.

The Tragic Week of 1909 gains new importance today for the historian and the politician, who share an interest in the mechanics of mobilizing urban masses. Not only Spaniards may find it of value to study the sequence of events whereby an antiwar protest was transformed into a large-scale destruction of church property and to analyze the motives of the individual participants.

In the years since the convent burnings of July 1909, and during the harsh repression of educational and labor institutions that followed, republican politicians identified the modernization of Spain with the specific project of establishing state control over the wealth and constitution of religious orders. Intellectual and political anticlericals influenced workers. Miserably underpaid and overworked, denied political representation and alienated from the society in which he lived, the Spanish worker became convinced that he would gain justice or at least recognition of his existence through an assault upon the religious orders. This conviction was to persist, gaining new and tragic momentum during the Second Republic and the Civil War.

The present authoritarian regime in Spain has definitely not resolved the problem of the clergy in a modern Catholic state. A careful reading of the official *Boletín del Estado* discloses that despite the public affirmations of a traditional Catholicism, there continues on the administrative level a quiet sparring as some officials of the Franco Regime attempt to maintain their right to inspect Catholic schools and to demand of teachers an advanced academic degree. In private conversations, Spaniards still discuss with some acrimony the extent and nature of the income and the political influence of the clergy. A new and disquieting element in this old problem is the obligation to implement the reform decrees of the Vatican Council that may possibly make obsolete all concordats, the means by which the Church has traditionally defended its special interests in countries such as Spain.

It is a fact that the Catholic Church in Spain is a powerful institution. Therefore, in the politics of any future representative government the role of the clergy is certain to be as dramatic an issue as it was during the first decade of the twentieth century. But unless the inevitable anticlericalism is to end once more in the same futile violence as in the Tragic Week, politicians must analyze with crystal clarity the components of this problem in order to prepare a realistic program of reforms. It is to be hoped that these will be regenerative reforms so that in this lustrous moment of the ecumenical movement, the clergy will play a constructive role in the Spaniards' search for a new and more enlightened national identity.

Part One

The Social and Political Milieu in Spain:
1875–1909

CHAPTER I

The National Crisis

EVEN before the War of 1898 the urban worker had begun to demand representation in the Restoration Settlement.[1] Reinforcing his demand for implementation of the Universal Suffrage Law of 1890 was a major socio-economic development: the first authentic industrialization of Spain, carried out during the Restoration years (1876–1898), had concentrated workers in cities where they were accessible to politicians eager for their votes, and to labor organizers. This phenomenon was particularly marked in the region of Catalonia and to a lesser degree in Vizcaya and Asturias.

Fearing that this organized urban labor force might play an active and disruptive force in politics as it had during the First Republic (1873–1874), Catalan and Basque businessmen did not openly work for the protective laws that they needed but instead quietly negotiated compromise legislation with the agrarian-oriented governments in Madrid. The defeat of 1898, however, left businessmen no alternative: publicly they demanded drastic general reform legislation because of the imperative need to pay for the war and to re-establish Spanish prestige by stabilizing the peseta on the world market. In Catalonia particularly, cotton manufacturers experimented with mobilizing workers in political reform movements but turned almost immediately to working as a pressure group in competition with the Army and the Church in order to secure compensation for their losses in the colonies. Professional politicians, engaged in intraparty conflicts for the vacant posts of party leader, competed for the support of these interest groups; more tentatively, they appealed for worker support. The weight of political power is clear from the fact that the worker and the peasant bore the brunt of both the fiscal reforms and the industrial readjustment in the following decade.

The end result of all these forces was that, between 1899 and 1910, there was a profound change in the Restoration Settlement.

The Restoration Settlement: 1875–1898

Antonio Cánovas was the principal architect of the system whereby two political parties automatically rotated in power through the mechanism of contrived elections. "Anything which is not possible in politics is false," [2] he asserted, making little attempt to dissimulate the cynical conviction, born of his long political career, that nothing great was possible in Spain in 1875. The urgent need was for domestic peace in order to assuage the tensions engendered by civil war and social revolution. Believing it impossible to resolve the basic conflicts, Cánovas prepared a constitution of general principles. Spain was identified as a Catholic nation, yet the Constitution of 1876 also provided for liberty of individual worship. Provisions such as this enabled almost all groups to support the Monarchy in the expectation that in the Cortes they could defend their interests through the implemental legislation.

Behind this constitutional façade, Cánovas skillfully subordinated the King, the Church, and — above all — the Army to the Cortes.* His major achievement has been almost completely obscured: through the Cortes, Cánovas gradually provided representation for all social and economic groups (with the exception of the workers). His own Conservative party was dominated by Andalusian landowners, interested in maintaining their great properties and in exporting olive oil.[3] Soon after taking office as President of the Council of Ministers, Cánovas began negotiations for a rapprochement with the powerful commercial and banking oligarchy, whose spokesman was Práxedes Mateo Sagasta, and with Castilian wheat growers whose interests were de-

* Under the Constitution of 1876 legislative power was exercised jointly by the King and the Cortes. The Cortes was the national legislative body composed of two chambers with coequal powers: a Congress of Deputies and a Senate. The 409 deputies of the Congress were elected popularly, theoretically one for each 50,000 inhabitants grouped in approximately 316 electoral districts; in each of these an electoral commission supervised the election and officially designated the deputy. The Senate was composed of three groups (360 senators in all): 1) ex-oficio members (sons of kings and their descendants, the grandees of Spain, specified high-ranking officials of the Church, the Army, and the administration); 2) senators appointed by the King, to serve for their lifetime, in honor of outstanding achievement; 3) senators elected by corporate institutions (universities, academies, college of lawyers, etc.) and by the major taxpayers (voting through the legislatures of the provinces).

fended by the Liberal party. Although agreeing to collaborate, the Liberals refused to accept responsibility for the constitutional monarchy until the premature death of Alfonso XII, on November 26, 1885, threatened to revive old enemies: republicanism and Carlism. The King had left no male heir (Alfonso XIII was born after his father's death) and only a young queen, María Cristina, to act as regent for two infant daughters. Whether or not the Liberals actually signed the Pact of the Pardo at Alfonso's deathbed is immaterial. The fact is that after 1885 the Liberals assumed with Conservatives the joint responsibility for maintaining the Restoration Settlement.

Yet quietly during those same years, industrial pressure groups secured from the Liberal and the Conservative parties the legislation necessary to carry through the first authentic industrialization of Spain. No study in depth has yet been made of the intrigues and maneuvers by which industrialists (particularly in Catalonia, Vizcaya, and Asturias) secured laws protecting them against foreign competition and assuring them domestic and colonial markets. Spain gradually abandoned the Free Trade Policy of 1869 under which she had begun the industrialization and moved toward "integrated protectionism," symbolized by the decree of 1892 establishing a semiprotectionist tariff schedule.[4] Thus the Cánovas formula was to work out conflicting interests quietly among the politicians in the Cortes and not in debates open to the electorate. The rhetoric of politicians obscures (perhaps purposely so) this function of the Cortes.

While he consolidated this rapprochement with major business interests, Cánovas negotiated with other dissident groups. In 1888 he persuaded one faction of the Carlist movement, led by Alejandro Pidal, to sit in the Cortes. Pidal's *mestizos,* or "neo-Catholics" as they became known, defended clerical interests.

The only significant social group that still remained outside the settlement (excluding the workers, who were not even considered) was the professional and commercial middle class, the backbone of the republican parties.[5] For over a decade they had believed that a republic could be established through an army coup but lost all hope after the failure of Brigadier General Manuel Villacampa in 1886, the last of a series of abortive coups. Some republicans accepted seats in the Cortes from leaders of the major parties carrying out a "policy of attraction." The more scrupulous politicians did so as a means of keeping the republican ideal before the electorate. Others viewed it simply as a means of keeping their hand in the patronage till. The "attraction" of republicans culminated in the formal pledge of support for the Monarchy by Emilio Castelar, one of the presidents of the First Republic. Castelar exacted a high price: enactment of the Law of Universal Suffrage (1890) as the basis for the elections to national, provincial, and municipal legislatures stipulated in the Constitution of 1876.*

Cánovas agreed to the law only because he was confident of controlling all elections through *caciques* (political bosses).[6] Since the 1850's, politicians had used the cacique system as a means of fulfilling the requirement that a constitutional monarchy have at least the appearance of popular sovereignty. The purpose was not only to protect the oligarchy but to resolve a problem created by the Carlist civil wars (1833–1839; 1845–1848; 1872–1876), during which agricultural areas had fought to defend not only traditional and Church interests but regional independence. With the defeat of the Carlist branch of the Bourbons, Spaniards gradually lost the habit of — and interest in — local government, as politicians in Madrid decided administrative appointments and policy. When it became clear that these politicians would not implement the liberal tenets they had proclaimed in order to defeat Carlist regionalism, a volte-face took place: the left wing advocated local government. The cause was the growth (albeit limited) of cities throughout Spain. The Federalist party of Francisco Pi y Margall, essentially the urban middle class outside of Madrid, attempted during the First Republic the first large-scale decentralization of governmental functions: this effort was discredited by its simultaneous attempt to incorporate "the people" into the body politic, as potential voters for the Federalist program and in accord with the republican concept of their redemptive force in politics. When the Republic collapsed, power was restored to a small body of men in Madrid. "The 2,000 political personages of the Restoration,"[7] as Antonio Maura described them, were relatively free to make all political and administrative decisions through their control of the Cortes.

When there was a crisis in the Cortes — that is to say, when Cánovas or Sagasta decided to resign or was forced to do so by one of the interest factions

---

* The first electoral law of the Restoration (1877) imposed a property qualification: voters had to own property and to pay taxes, 25 pesetas annually in land taxes or 50 pesetas in industrial taxes. This law was superseded by the law of 1890 which provided for universal male suffrage, stipulating only that the voter be 25 years old, a resident for two years in the district where he voted, a registered voter, and in full possession of his civil rights. The law of 1890 was, in turn, superseded and slightly modified by the Electoral Law of August 8, 1907 (prepared by Antonio Maura), which remained in force until the end of the constitutional monarchy.

— he returned his powers to the monarch, who was theoretically free to call upon any member of the Cortes to govern. Alfonso XII made little use of this prerogative and his widow, Queen María Cristina, was at first too deferential to Cánovas and Sagasta to exercise much independence of judgment; however, toward the end of her regency she showed ability and discretion in counseling politicians in the formation of cabinets and in advising her son, Alfonso XIII, in his first years as King. Alfonso XIII later developed this royal prerogative into a means of playing a decisive role in politics.

But until 1902 the royal practice was to call only upon the head of the party (or his designee) to form a government. The newly appointed president of the council immediately appointed a minister of the interior; together they prepared a list of the candidates to be elected (*encasillados*) that would assure a proper majority for their own party, provide a few places for republicans, and grant the opposition suitable representation. As a courtesy, the key politicians (*cuneros*) of both parties were regularly returned to the Cortes. Generally these were professional politicians, resident in Madrid and rarely natives of the area that they represented. The interior minister appointed new civil governors to direct the elections in each of the fifty provinces.

The actual precinct work was carried out by the cacique: a prominent lawyer, a moneylender, or in rural areas a landowner or, as in Andalusia, the manager for the absentee landowner. In most regions there were caciques of both parties, but in Galicia or Extremadura, there was only one and he served all interests in his constituency. In most rural districts there was little need for a cacique to do more than send in favorable returns for his party; if the peasants had not voted as desired, the official returns showed they had. Such absolute control was never possible in urban districts, where caciques assured themselves a political following through the use of patronage, a powerful weapon in the centralized bureaucracy of Spain. A change of party in office was followed by a thorough change in the bureaucracy until, toward the end of the nineteenth century, this process was corrected slightly by the establishment of civil service examinations.

Cánovas did not invent the cacique system but merely refined an old electoral technique. Defenders of the system declare it was the result, and not the cause, of civic apathy and therefore a necessary link between the government and the apolitical citizen. But reformers such as Joaquín Costa and Valentí Almirall charged that Cánovas, by his blatant and skillful use of this technique, prevented the development of a citizenry adept in the practices of democracy. Their claims are supported by a study of cacique practices after the passage of the Universal Suffrage Law in 1890 enabled urban republican politicians (formerly dependent upon benevolent Liberal or Conservative governments) to win elections by a majority vote. Caciques of both parties adopted drastic measures to prevent this: exclusion of many electors from the lists, substitution of the names of imaginary persons or dead men, organization of groups (sometimes policemen dressed as civilians) to go to the polls and vote under those names, use of violence to prevent workers from voting.* Such measures indicated that the government obviously did fear public opinion, organized by republican parties.

The discrepancy between the theoretical universal suffrage and its negation in practice profoundly disillusioned the Spaniards in general, and workers in particular, concerning the efficacy of any political action whatsoever. In 1914 José Ortega y Gasset delivered a now famous lecture entitled "Vieja y nueva política," in which he eloquently described the divorce between what he termed "la España oficial" and "la España vital." The divorce was not quite that complete. The interests of the oligarchy and of most of the middle class were served by the parliamentary system, and by an elaborate network of personal and family contacts in the bureaucracy and the legislature which supplemented and to some degree supplanted the electoral system. It was the worker who remained outside the political structure during the Restoration era.

Politics and the Spanish Worker during the Restoration Era

The absence of the Spanish worker from the political scene was due to a complex of factors. Most obvious was the unwillingness of either major party to incorporate the worker into the body politic. In line with their policy of pacification, politicians authorized only that measure of activity which would prevent the labor movement from becoming subversive; the Law of Associations (1887) legalized trade unions, but police action curbed this right.

* These practices were very similar to those of professional politicians in Italy during the Giolittian era who, in collaboration with industrialists and landowners, attempted to prevent workers and the lower middle class from gaining control of the political parties (Arcangelo William Salomone, *Italy in the Giolittian Era: Italian Democracy in the Making, 1900–1914*, 2 ed. [Philadelphia, 1960], introductory essay by Gaetano Salvemini, pp. xviii–xix). Although the purpose was different, the cacique practices also resembled those of contemporary American political bosses who incorporated the waves of immigrant workers in the cities into the two-party system.

Far more decisive factors were the limited number of urban centers and their location along the periphery of the Peninsula. The roots of the failure of Spanish democracy may be found in this period when, under the auspices of the Constitution of 1876 and the Universal Suffrage Law, urban workers might have been organized into an effective electoral force and thereby have gained parliamentary representation. But the population remained predominantly rural,* and the few large industrial centers (Valencia, La Coruña, Bilbao, Cádiz, and Barcelona) were far away from Madrid. This made it easier for politicians in the Cortes to ignore the workers. As late as 1902 Francisco Romero Robledo, the most famous cacique of the Restoration, could brag of not knowing anything about "the social problem." [8]

After 1902 the situation changed slightly. Politicians made some attempt to integrate the worker. Liberal politicians jockeying for the position of party chief sought popular support, while Catalan industrialists appealed to workers to make common cause with them in defense of regional autonomy. Not only were these attempts faltering, mostly through fear of the potential violence of the masses, but they were combated by leaders of the labor movement. Both socialists and anarcho-syndicalists refused to participate in politics on principle.

SPANISH SOCIALISM

During the Restoration era, Pablo Iglesias organized both a Socialist party (1879) and a national trade union movement (1888)[9] and he directed them almost up until his death in 1925. In order to avoid any obligation to the bourgeoisie, Iglesias imposed upon the Socialist party a policy of "blessed intransigence" that precluded any electoral coalition with republican parties. Although motivated primarily by his disgust with Restoration politics, Iglesias' political exclusivism was in accord with the purest Marxist doctrine. He regularly attended the congresses of the Second International, where he was profoundly influenced by Jules Guesde's fight to defend the ideal of a workers' party, and he strengthened this conviction in subsequent correspondence with Guesde.

Because of Iglesias' policy, Socialist party candidates were elected to only a few city councils (for example, in Bilbao; not until 1905 did they win a

* In 1900, only 21 percent of the Spanish population lived in towns of over 20,000, while 51 percent lived in villages of less than 5,000 (figures cited by architect Fernando Chueca in a speech reported in *ES: The Week in Spain,* published by the Spanish Information Service [Madrid], no. 227 [February 13, 1967], p. 4).

seat in Madrid). No socialist sat in the Cortes until Iglesias was elected in 1910 and then only because, for the first and only time, he participated in a coalition with republicans. Even more significant was the slow growth of Socialist party membership; by 1907 the party had only 100 local sections with a total membership of 6,000.[10] This situation is usually ascribed to the fact that Catalan workers, the largest group within the Spanish labor force, preferred anarcho-syndicalism. Another equally important but neglected cause is that the type of worker to whom the Socialist party appealed — skilled workers interested in improving their position, inspired by ideals of civil and political liberties — still voted for republican parties.*

The membership figures of the socialist trade union affiliate, the Unión General del Trabajo (UGT), are only slightly more impressive. At the time of its Seventh National Congress in 1905, the UGT reported 351 member organizations with a total of 43,665 members; yet only 77 delegates attended the Congress.[11] Nor is it clear to what degree the member unions accepted direction from the UGT National Committee (where Pablo Iglesias presided); perhaps they functioned as independent labor organizations that participated in the UGT congresses and maintained a formal membership in the national confederation.[12]

Until 1901 Spanish socialism consisted of little more than the group of able men who collaborated with Iglesias in Madrid. However, with the enactment of major social legislation, socialism entered a new and more active phase. Iglesias still refused to join any electoral bloc but he did work closely with both major parties in setting up the Institute of Social Reforms (Instituto de Reformas Sociales) to administer the new legislation, and socialists sat on the board of directors as the official labor representatives.** Although certain labor groups denounced this policy of "collaboration" with

* To the Socialist Party Congress of 1902, only 73 labor organizations sent delegations. Yet to the National Republican Congress of 1903, which led to the organization of Unión Republicana, 84 labor groups sent representatives (Renée Lamberet, L'Espagne: 1750–1936, in the series, Mouvements ouvriers et socialistes: Cronologie et bibliographie, eds. Edouard Dolléons and Michel Crozier [Paris, 1953], p. 73, and Antonio Ramos Oliveira, Politics, Economics, and Men of Modern Spain: 1808–1946, trans. Teener Hall [London, 1946], p. 156).

** The Institute of Social Reforms (organized on April 25, 1903 to replace the Commission of Social Reforms, established in 1883), was an official agency responsible for advising the government on labor policy and for recommending new social legislation. The Institute's board of directors was composed of representatives from agriculture, big industry, small industry, and labor. In addition there were provincial and municipal boards, responsible for enforcing social legislation.

the Monarchy, Iglesias persisted because he believed that the Socialist party could not recruit more members until workers were better paid and protected against illness and unemployment.[13]

THE ANARCHISTS AND THE CATALAN LABOR MOVEMENT

The Spanish anarchist movement is the result of the alliance late in the nineteenth century of two groups: a small elite of anarchist theoreticians and activists, preaching a revolution leading to the destruction of the state; and the officials of Catalan trade unions* who were convinced that the only effective labor policy was direct, violent action, divorced from all political action. In 1870 and again in 1900 these groups joined forces to organize and dominate a national labor federation. It is important to understand the historic circumstances and the divers socioeconomic factors that consolidated this alliance.

The persistence of this resolute anarchist elite (composed of petite bourgeoisie and workers) — articulate in defense of its ideology, reinforced by contacts with anarchists abroad — was one factor in the formation of this alliance. To the extent that they planned for the future, anarchists wanted a new social order in which men would freely organize, not as a body politic, but as an association of producers in an economy geared to need and not to profit.[14] They easily converted Andalusian peasants, but however impressive the revolts of impoverished and isolated peasant villagers, they are not decisive in the making of a revolution in a modern nation.**

The key factor is the mass force of city workers, and one way to mobilize this force is through a labor movement. When the traditional anarchist ways of mobilizing workers failed (that is, through terrorism and propaganda), then they sought control of labor unions. Their rivalry with the socialists

* In the nineteenth century, particularly in Catalonia, the most common term for a union of all the workers in any one trade (carpenters, typesetters, etc.) was "sociedades de resistencia al capital." This term persists into the twentieth century but about 1900, in imitation of the French, "sindicato" was used. The English word "syndicate" does not mean trade union and furthermore, when used in this way in English it often has the connotation of a revolutionary labor union. In order to emphasize the primary characteristic of these unions, as a means of obtaining higher wages and working conditions, the terms "trade union" and "syndicate" have been used interchangeably in this discussion of the labor movement.

** Gabriel Jackson has summarized the elements of rural traditions (collectivized institutions and decentralization, coupled with opposition to Castile) that made anarchism so attractive to Andalusian peasants in "The Origins of Spanish Anarchism," *Southwestern Social Science Quarterly* 36 (September 1955), 135–47.

has often been described. Far less publicized and far more significant is the anarchist struggle with Catalan labor union officials to dominate the labor force in that region — the largest and most concentrated group of industrial workers in Spain.

By 1870, when the first national labor federation was organized in Spain, the officials of the Catalan trade unions had decided not to use these unions as a means of mobilizing support for republican parties but as an independent force which they could use in negotiations with the government to secure legal recognition of the right to bargain collectively, and in negotiations with employers to secure better wages and working conditions.[15] Catalan labor leaders found ready allies among labor leaders of other regions: after fifty years of liberal politics that had benefited only the propertied classes, workers in general rejected parliamentary democracy as the principal means to redress their grievances.

Anarchists and Catalan labor officials thus agreed on tactics — direct, violent action by the workers — but they did not agree on the need for a revolution; labor leaders considered this a last resort. But on the basis of tactics, the anarchists and Catalan labor leaders allied temporarily in order to organize the first national labor federation. This alliance ended four years later (1874), as much because of dissension between anarchists and Catalan labor leaders as because of government repression.

During the early years of the Restoration, particularly from 1881 on, there was no alliance because there was no need even to consider revolution: the initial conciliatory policies of the Restoration governments and the prosperity of an expanding Catalan textile industry gave reason to believe that workers could secure their major demands within the established order. By 1890, writes Catalan historian Jaime Vicens Vives, "the situation was completely favorable to a professional and political orientation of syndicalism."[16] It even appeared possible that the Catalan textile unions would affiliate with the socialist UGT.

Exactly the opposite occurred. In 1899 the UGT moved its headquarters from Barcelona to Madrid, signifying its failure to enroll the most important sector of the Spanish labor movement. And in 1900 Catalan syndicate officials helped to organize a new national labor federation to rival that of the socialists.

What were the real factors in the commitment of Catalan labor officials (and of Catalan workers in general) to the tactics of direct, violent, apolitical labor action — a position summarily described by many historians,

Spanish and foreign, as "anarchism"? It is often attributed to the individual-istic temperament of the Catalan, as against the authoritarian Castilian who more readily accepted socialist discipline. This exaggerates the importance of an undeniable factor. Catalan workers, however, did not object on prin-ciple to working through organizations or to paying dues.[17] It was simply that they did not have the money to sustain a labor organization, especially during the decade 1900–1910 when the Catalan economy suffered a severe depression.

This is only one of the many real factors that prevented labor from de-veloping an effective bargaining agency in Catalonia. It would be simplistic to say that intransigent employers forced the Catalan labor movement to become revolutionary. The chapter on regionalism will discuss the conse-quences for the labor movement of the Catalan economy's inability to ex-pand. In terms of anarchism, the most important consequence was the in-ability of Catalan factories, even before the defeat of 1899, to absorb the waves of workers moving into the cities from rural areas.* These unskilled laborers ("*los miserables*," to use Vicens Vives' term) constituted a social group par-ticularly vulnerable to demagogic ideologies, anarchist or whatever; possess-ing nothing they listened to anarchists who promised everything after "the revolution."

After 1899, and the loss of their major source of foreign exchange, Catalan industrialists used this constant surplus of labor to advantage; they acquired capital in order to purchase machinery through the reduction of labor costs. Their refusal to bargain collectively and their use of the lockout forced labor union officials to abandon negotiations in favor of violent labor tactics.

A final major factor in the orientation of Catalan syndicalism to violence, and to a new alliance with the anarchists, was the action of government offi-

---

* Contrary to a prevailing theory, anarchist influence on the Catalan labor move-ment cannot be ascribed to workers from Andalusia who emigrated to Barcelona. They constituted a tiny minority within the total labor force (by 1920 they were only 2.82 percent of the work force). Workers born in Catalonia constitute an over-whelming majority (69 percent in 1900, 66.5 percent in 1910). The largest group of non-Catalans came from the Levant (Alicante, Castellón, Valencia, and Murcia); the next largest group from Aragon (Huesca, Saragossa, and Teruel). (Jaime Alzina Caules, "Investigación analítica sobre la evolución demográfica de Cataluña," *Cuadernos de Información Económica y Sociológica* [Barcelona, June 1955] pp. 28, 33–34.) Theo-reticians and activists from Andalusia did, however, play an active role during the formative years of the anarchist movement in Barcelona, and in this way influenced the Catalan labor movement (Jaime Vicens Vives, *Cataluña en el siglo XIX*, trans. from the Catalan by E. Borrás Cubells [Madrid, 1961] p. 250).

cials who considered labor agitation strictly from the viewpoint of a threat to public order, a position they made very clear in the trials at Montjuich (Barcelona) in 1897. During the preceding decade a wave of terrorism had swept Barcelona, coinciding with terrorism in Italy and France; like workers in those countries, the workers of Barcelona suspected that police agents provoked this agitation in order to justify suppressing the labor movement. Their suspicions seemed to be confirmed by the trials at Montjuich* when union officials were tried on a par with anarchist terrorists, and when the trials were followed by a general repression of the labor movement. In order to defend themselves, Catalan labor officials saw no other recourse than to form a working alliance with the anarchists and to collaborate with them in the organization of a new *national* labor federation.[18]

The constituent congress of the new federation (Federación de Sociedades Obreras de la Región Española) was held in Madrid in October 1900; 150 labor and anarchist groups sent delegates and 50 more sent pledges of support. The delegates were openly antagonistic to the Socialist party, and opposed to political activity of any kind. They wanted an eight-hour day and a higher wage scale, and they planned to achieve these goals through independent violent action against employers and, if need be, against the state. They considered the general strike a necessary weapon in their economic struggle (although anarchist delegates managed to insert the possibility of using the general strike for any case of open police brutality or blatant social injustice).[19] The Congress openly acknowledged its debt to the anarcho-syndicalist ideology of Emile Pouget and Fernand Pelloutier, and to the recently organized French Confederation Generale du Travail.[20] The Federation announced plans to contact syndicalist groups in Italy, England, and North America. In 1900 approximately 52,000 workers were affiliated with the Federation, and by the time of the congress held the following year there were 73,000 affiliated workers — more than the socialist UGT national membership, but still only a small fraction of the total industrial labor force.

---

* The Montjuich trials established the image of "la Espagne inquisitorial" in the twentieth century — a Spain where freedom of conscience and of association was curtailed by the clergy and the Army. Ignoring the obvious parallels with the repression of terrorism elsewhere (as for example, the French terrorist trials of 1894), European liberals and labor leaders organized a protest against the Montjuich trials, on the ground that men were being prosecuted for their ideas. The campaign was so forceful that the Spanish government dared to execute only 8 of the 28 men sentenced to die by military tribunals. In 1909, using the same image of "la Espagne inquisitorial," European liberal opinion would again act as a force in Spanish politics.

The Federation began to disintegrate almost immediately because of the failure of the general strike in Barcelona in 1902, and because of crop failures and resulting famine in Andalusia after 1904. Still another cause for failure was that anarchists and Catalan trade union officials had still not resolved their differences. The latter group continued to consider the labor movement as a means of forcing the state and the employer to grant them justice and a living wage, and they continued to consider revolution only as a last resort.

Within the context of the national political crisis during the decade 1900 to 1910, the significant factor is that the labor movement in Catalonia, the most industrialized region of Spain, rejected politics and advocated violence, while in Madrid, the mining areas of Asturias, and Bilbao, socialists refused any compromise through which they might have gained representation for workers within the political structure.

Politics and Finances: Aftermath of the War of 1898

Against this background of industrial crisis, of labor leaders who boycotted politics, and of a controlled electoral system, politicians began to work out the problems caused by the Spanish-American War. The most serious were financial in nature. The expenses of the war and of the subsequent reintegration of returning military personnel, bureaucrats, and missionary orders posed a serious problem for an economy as poor and as rigidly organized as that of Spain. Between 1899 and 1905 the government carried out a program of severe economies that relieved the treasury of its heavy debts; it imposed higher excise and business taxes and thereby favored the agrarian interests with which Raimundo Fernández Villaverde, the architect of the retrenchment policy, is usually associated. However, although Fernández Villaverde refused the Catalan manufacturers' request for fiscal privileges and for subsidies to compensate for the lost colonial markets, he did favor industrial as well as agricultural exporters by stabilizing the peseta and thus achieving an improved exchange rate. The increased value of the peseta compensated for the loss of foreign exchange from the colonial trade and enabled industrialists to buy machinery (which they imported without paying duty) in order to modernize their factories. Meanwhile, political deals were made to ensure increased protection for national industry, culminating in the Liberal party law of 1907 establishing such high tariffs that it has been described as "a China wall, that closed off the Spanish market to foreign competition." [21] In short, the industrialist bought cheap abroad with pesetas that had increased in value, and sold at a high price in his protected market at home. The economically vulnerable classes, workers and lower middle class, bore the major costs of this industrial adjustment.[22]

Although in the decade from 1900 to 1910 politicians were fairly successful in resolving financial problems, they found that the political consequences of the defeat constituted a far more serious threat to parliamentary government. Religious orders, Catalan textile manufacturers, and army officers did not work through either of the two parties but functioned as pressure groups. The result was the debilitation of the parliamentary system, either because these militant groups were so strong or because the parliamentary system was so weak.

The Army

THE ARMY OFFICER IN POLITICS

After the War of 1898 the army officer returned to active politics, resuming the nineteenth-century role that Cánovas had attempted to eliminate in the Restoration Settlement. Cánovas' successors could not resist the attempts of officers to recoup in Spain and Morocco the prestige, pay bonuses, and promotions that they had formerly earned through service in the colonies. The ideology with which army spokesmen justified political intervention differed greatly from that of officer-politicians prior to the Bourbon Restoration. Although still professing to serve the national will better than did politicians, officers tended to consider themselves a privileged caste. Secondly, the voice had been stilled of officers like Bartolomeo Espartero who in the nineteenth century had defended classic liberal tenets of expanded personal liberty and civil rights (while carefully eschewing social reforms). The causes for this change in the military ideology were the establishment of military academies during the Restoration era and the resounding failure of republican military coups.

From 1875 to 1887, Progressive Republican party chief Manuel Ruíz Zorilla assiduously cultivated officers. Convinced that the First Republic had failed largely due to the alienation of the Army, Ruíz Zorilla believed that the Second Republic must come through a military coup. In the 1880's he organized the Republican Military Association (Asociación Republicana Militar). A principal recruiting agent was Nicolás Estévanez, Minister of War in the First Republic and a perennial conspirator who would wander back and forth from his exile in Paris to Barcelona until 1913, carrying materials for explosives and plans for a revolution.[23]

Another channel through which Ruíz Zorilla probably contacted army officers was Freemasonry. From 1870 until his exile in 1874, Ruíz Zorilla was the *Gran Comendador* of the Grand Orient of Spain. Republicans and anticlerical army officers may well have conspired in masonic lodges to establish a secular state, as some officers did in France. However, the evidence of a military Grand Lodge in Spain is meager and likely to remain so because the antireligious connotations of Freemasonry have made it difficult to consult any archival material that might exist.[24]

Therefore, it is not clear on what terms some army officers collaborated with Ruíz Zorilla in the clandestine Republican Military Association. The ineptness of the conspiracies, together with betrayals, culminated in the fiasco of the Villacampa coup of 1887 that dispelled any immediate hope of establishing a republic and tended to discredit republicanism among officers. It also discouraged officers from conspiring, particularly when the government kept Brigadier General Villacampa in prison until his death in 1889. After 1900, Alejandro Lerroux y García would try to renew this tradition of military republicanism.

The role of the academies in forming a conservative army corps is far clearer. Realizing that hope of promotion was a prime cause for military intervention in politics, Cánovas encouraged the development of professional academies that restricted officer candidates to members of the middle and upper classes who could finance the years of study; this almost completely eliminated the promotion up from the ranks and incorporation of militia officers that had characterized the Spanish army prior to the Restoration.* Military academies developed a caste spirit that encouraged officers to consider their interests as separate from those of their troops or of the body politic. They also instilled in cadets a strong sense of patriotism that was basically a loyalty to the established order; thus after 1900 officers increasingly considered social agitation as seditious, particularly when organized

---

* This was true in the artillery, cavalry, and engineers corps; under a policy of "closed ranks," a man graduated from the academy and was subsequently promoted by strict seniority. Only in the infantry corps could commissions and promotions be manipulated by politicians, causing resentment among infantry officers. (See letter from Alfonso XIII to Antonio Maura (1909) in Gabriel Maura y Gamazo and Melchor Fernández Almagro, *Por qué cayó Alfonso XIII: Evolución y disolución de los partidos históricos durante su reinado* [Madrid, 1958], p. 134. See also Emilio Mola Vidal, *Obras completas* [Valladolid, 1940], pp. 997–1000.)

labor, in Spain and abroad, became antimilitarist. Officers were further convinced that movements for regional autonomy (especially in Catalonia) were unpatriotic. Their humiliating rout in 1898 made officers particularly sensitive to their obligation to defend national honor, even if it were only by storming the offices of a Catalan humor magazine.[25]

Ideological and psychological conditions aside, the army officer after 1900 was faced with a far more pressing problem: how to maintain a standard of living consonant with his status, in the face of rising prices and decreased income.[26] Although officers' salaries constituted a major part of the military budget, the amount received by each individual was small.* With the loss of the colonies and with no military action in sight, officers could not hope to supplement their pay with battle bonuses or overseas duty. Junior officers could not even hope for promotion until the highest ranking officers retired; compulsory retirement at a certain age was included in every military reform project. After 1900 officer-politicians aimed at a higher pay scale and a more active policy in Morocco. They found an unexpected ally in Alfonso XIII, who began to rule in 1902 at sixteen years of age. He far preferred to spend his time in military garrisons and helped officers to gain a larger voice in national affairs. Eventually, army officers worked out an alliance with the Liberal party, a process dramatized in the *Cu-Cut* incident of 1906 and the resulting Law of Jurisdictions that granted the Army greater jurisdiction in civil affairs. This does not mean, however, that officers defended the interests of the conscript soldier in the Cortes.

THE CONSCRIPT SOLDIER

The Spanish Army has been described as "simply the permanent officers' corps imposed upon a conscript soldier unwilling to serve." [27] Since the mid-nineteenth century the worker had bitterly resented the fact that he alone was conscripted. His initial enthusiasm for the First Republic (1873–1874) had been based upon his hope that conscription would be abolished; when the government had to call up new conscripts in order to fight Carlists, the soldier had joined the officer in welcoming back the Monarchy. During the Restoration era, the Spanish worker made common cause with those in other

---

* In 1909 there were 60 division generals but only 16 divisions; 30 lieutenant generals but only 8 army corps; 3 colonels for every regiment; 14,920 lower ranking officers (Joaquín Sánchez de Toca, *Discurso . . . en apoyo de su enmienda a la base 1.ª de la letra B del proyecto de ley de servicio militar obligatorio*, Sesión del Senado, 16 de noviembre de 1910 y 10 diciembre de 1910 [Madrid, 1910], p. 36).

European nations in supporting the antimilitarism of socialists and anarchists.

In some ways the position of the conscript in Spain was worse simply
because of the administration of the system. The Law of 1885 (amended in
1896) provided for a standing army of 80,000 men; theoretically, by calling
up reserves, this could be doubled to a force of 160,000 men within ten days.
The annual army appropriation, approximately 168 million pesetas, represented a substantial portion of the national budget but did not cover the expenses of an 80,000 man army. The attempt to economize led to chaos, injustice, and military inefficiency.

Although 45,000 men were annually eligible for induction, only 30,000
were actually called up; selection led to numerous abuses.[28] Secular and
regular clergy were exempted, a provision attacked by military reformers
as well as social critics. The wealthy automatically escaped military service,
paying an exemption fee of 1,500 pesetas, while workers and petite bourgeoisie joined mutual insurance plans providing money for exemptions in
the event that they were called to serve; these fees constituted an important
source of income to the government. Furthermore, there were not sufficient
funds to keep on active duty the 30,000 men inducted into the army. Men
were called up in February, given three months' instruction, and then
granted leave for the summer months or sometimes for the balance of their
tour of duty. For nine months of a year an infantry battalion would often
be reduced to 200 and a line regiment to 300 men. In an emergency, delays
and expense occurred as men were summoned back to duty.

Theoretically, a recruit served three years on active duty although in practice he served only a maximum of two years. He was then placed on active
reserve for three years (in practice, four) and on the inactive reserve for six
years. Because he was assigned to the same battalion throughout his twelve
years of service, whether he was called back to active duty depended upon
whether his particular battalion was mobilized. In the event that he should
be called back, there was no statutory provision for the maintenance of his
dependents, nor for compensation in case of death or disability; in wartime
a law had to be passed for both contingencies.

Military mismanagement of the conscription system was abetted by politicians who feared that an efficient standing Army would prove a constant
temptation to politically ambitious officers. The result was important for
national defense and for social unrest: the Army was maintained at skeleton

strength (excluding, of course, the top-heavy officer contingent) until an emergency arose, and then reserves had to be called up.

Thus army officers, like Catalan regionalists, came in contact with only a limited number of workers. Of the three pressure groups active in national politics during the decade 1900–1910, only the clergy was in daily contact with people throughout the nation. This is one thread in the complex of reasons why the clerical issue eventually dominated national politics.

CHAPTER II

The Clerical Problem and the Politicians

A LATENT force in any Catholic society is the layman's natural resentment of the clergy's privileged position, a resentment that intensifies if he suspects that the clergy is abusing its privileges or if he believes that it is not fulfilling its vocational ideals of poverty and religious duties.* At tense moments in national life this animosity can be mobilized politically as an anticlerical movement whose exclusive objective may or may not be reform of clerical excesses.

At the turn of the century popular animosity focused on the regular clergy:** on its reputed great wealth (contrasting with a vow of poverty) and on its political influence, exercised directly over lawmakers or indirectly through the schools where they educated the propertied classes. During the preceding decades, in Spain as in France, the number of religious orders had increased and their total membership expanded. In France this provoked a campaign (1879–1889) to impose state control over clerical income and education; because of the political vicissitudes of the Third Republic, the campaign exceeded its original objectives and achieved the separation of Church and state in 1905. Despite obvious parallels, Spanish anticlericalism was autochthonous, both in its immediate and its long-range origins. The results, therefore, were very different.

* For many of the sociological and psychological aspects of anticlericalism discussed in this chapter, I acknowledge my indebtedness to Professor Juan Linz of Columbia University. My conversations with him helped to clarify impressions garnered from reading and from seven years residence in Spain.

** The term "regular clergy" is used in the strict dictionary sense to refer to those clergy who belong "to a religious or monastic order or community." "Secular clergy" is used to designate clergy "living in the world as distinguished from in a monastery or religious community; not bound by monastic vows or rules."

The occasion for the eruption of the clerical issue in Spanish politics was the widespread belief that abuses by missionary orders had led to the colonial revolts in 1898.[1] Clergy were even held responsible for mismanagement of the war: an ex-soldier told an Englishman in 1909 that "it was all the fault of the Jesuits at home, who stole the money which the nation gave for the Army." [2]

The causes of Spanish anticlericalism were far deeper. By 1900 statesmen in both parties were convinced that a sovereign state had no recourse but to impose upon the large and wealthy entity constituted by the religious orders the same conditions as those imposed on any other private organization. Amid the many factors in the subsequent campaign, one underlying cause should be emphasized. Consciously or not, anticlerical politicians were attempting to incorporate workers into the body politic on some issue other than social problems and thus to avoid the class struggle. As in France, there may be some basis to the charge that politicians were attempting to divert public attention from needed social and economic reforms to the more dramatic cause of clericalism.[3] Yet reformers argued convincingly and continued to do so through the Second Republic (1931–1939) that no progress was possible until a laic state was established in Spain.[4] To understand the passion of their conviction, we must view anticlericalism in the context of the three ways in which the Church affects secular life in Spain. The first is the historic role of the Church in Spain, which has lent credence to the belief, quasi-mythical in content, in clerical omnipotence in national affairs. Second is the function of Catholic schools within the educational system of Spain. Finally, there is the process through which the clergy necessarily finances its activities in an urban industrial society.

Church and State Before the Restoration

Spanish national unity was forged over a six-hundred-year period by the reconquest of Spain from the Muslims.[5] Because this acquired the aura of a Holy Crusade, the concept of the nation merged with that of the Catholic religion in a way that occurred nowhere else in Europe. In the sixteenth century, when Spain built an empire in America and Europe, the evangelical mission served as a motive power that compensated for the weakness of the governmental structure and of the economy. The empire began to disintegrate, yet in Spain the Church remained a powerful institution, reinforced through association with the nation's Golden Century. Catholicism was transformed from a dynamic force to a traditional one which opposed any reform movement as an attempt to change the nature of Spanish society.

This traditionalist character proved a major obstacle to the attempts of Bourbon kings, beginning with Carlos III (1759–1788), to subordinate the Church to the state. Carlos did expel the Jesuits and thereby established state control over the universities. Yet neither he nor his successors, plagued by expensive wars and the specter of the French Revolution, were able to execute agrarian reforms that would have weakened the basis of clerical power — the Church's hold upon extensive lands in mortmain.

In 1833, when the Church and specifically the religious orders openly espoused the cause of the pretender Carlos against Isabel II, the proposal to enact disentailing legislation became a political possibility.[6] Albeit tenuously, anticlericalism could be identified with loyalty to the Monarchy by arguing that church lands should be sold in order to finance the war against the Carlists. The patriotic motive was reinforced by urban riots. In July 1835, for the first time in Spanish history, convents were burned in Madrid and Barcelona. Cathedrals and parish churches were untouched. Significantly, these burnings did not occur in the countryside, where the property of religious orders was concentrated and where there were abuses, but in cities where mobs could be more easily mobilized.

The disentailing legislation was only *occasioned* by the war and the urban riots. The objective of ministers like Juan Alvarez Mendizábal was to amass the capital necessary for industrialization, in the belief that the only rapid way to do this was through the sale of the Church's enormous landholdings. Therefore they rejected a moderate solution more consonant with the realities of a traditionally Catholic nation, such as limiting the right of clergy to acquire property and subjecting all clerical holdings to state supervision and taxation.

The disentailing measures (contained in decrees of July, September, and October 1835) abolished all orders except those engaged in educational, charitable, or missionary work deemed essential to the national welfare; they thereby abolished the juridical right of the clergy to hold property as a collective entity. In the case of the service orders excepted from these decrees, there was no clear plan of how they were to finance their activities: through their own income, state subsidies, or a combination of both. Two subsequent decrees (February and March 1836) authorized the sale of lands belonging to the abolished orders. On July 29, 1837, a law was enacted that ordered the sale of all clerical holdings, to begin in 1840. Although the law abolished the right of religious orders to form communities in Spain, individual clergy were granted full civil rights.

The procedure was for the state to take possession of the property of abolished orders and of the secular clergy, and to issue government bonds paying three percent perpetual annual interest. This property was then sold, not to peasants (as in France) but to those who could pay cash — to wealthy men who then became firm supporters of Isabel's cause. Because sales were mishandled, only speculators profited; although proceeds did not reach the national treasury, the state continued to be responsible for the compensation for all clerical property that had been sold.

The attempt to resolve the clerical problem by abolishing the right of orders to organize communities in Spain and to hold property was ended by the Concordat of 1851. This was a compromise, based on the existing situation, and not intended to resolve the basic issues. The Spanish state declared Catholicism to be the official religion and therefore obligated itself to maintain from the national treasury the secular clergy, parish churches, and cathedrals. As for regular clergy, the state recognized its right to organize and acquire property of any kind. With regard to the sensitive matter of church lands already sold, the Vatican recognized such sales as valid with the understanding that the state would pay interest on the property.

In the Concordat the state recognized specifically three religious orders as official institutions, with the understanding that these religious would assist the hierarchy in pastoral duties. These orders were to be maintained at state expense, exempt from taxation: the Congregation of Priests of the Mission of St. Vincent de Paul (Vincentians), the Congregation of the Oratory of St. Philip Neri (Oratorians),* and a third order to be determined at a later date by mutual agreement between the papacy and the state. The failure

---

* The exact title in English of a Spanish religious order has not been easy to determine, unless the order has a community in the United States. In this case, the title used is the one cited in Oliver L. Kapsner, O.S.B., ed., *Catholic Religious Orders: Listing Conventional and Full Names in English, Foreign Language, and Latin. Also Abbreviations, Date and Country of Origin and Founders,* 2 ed. (Collegeville, Minnesota, 1957). I have also consulted the *Official Catholic Directory of the United States for the year 1966* (New York, 1966). For those orders which do not have a community in the United States, the title in English has been determined after consultation with Father Robert B. Sáenz, S.J., of the faculty of Seattle University, on the basis of information from the *Annuario Pontificio Per l'Anno 1966* (Città del Vaticano, 1966). I wish to acknowledge Father Sáenz' generous help.

to specify this order complicated all subsequent attempts to establish state control over religious orders.

In addition the state agreed to subsidize certain orders in exchange for specific services. Members of the Franciscan, Dominican, and Augustinian orders were to serve as missionaries in the colonies. The Congregation of Clerks Regular of the Schools (Piarists) was to receive payment for the free education of poor children. The Order of Brothers Hospitallers of St. John of God and the Congregation of Sisters of Charity of St. Vincent de Paul were to be paid for nursing the poor in public institutions. However, these and all orders (except the three specifically exempted) were considered private associations subject to civil jurisdiction and to taxation. But these provisions were not enforced, in part because of the loophole provided by the failure to name the third official religious order.

The *Progresista* faction of Liberals did not accept the Concordat of 1851 as prohibiting further disentailing legislation. Having failed to abolish religious orders or to deny their right to hold property, reformist ministers now proposed that the state administer their property — that is, they proposed to make the regular clergy (like the secular clergy) financially dependent upon the state. The disentailing legislation of May 1, 1855, and July 11, 1856, instructed religious orders to sell their property to the state and receive in exchange government bonds. This legislation was annulled by a *convenio* between the Vatican and the Spanish state (signed on August 25, 1859, and published as a law on April 4, 1860). After the Revolution of 1868, there was a new but largely unsuccessful attempt to implement the Progresista program.

In the short run, the disentailing measures caused many convents to close and clergy to disperse.[7] The long-range effect was to force religious orders to move from the country to the town, and to transform agricultural into industrial investments. This process was carried out quietly, in divers ways. Many orders were exempted from the legislation, either because they were educational and charitable institutions or because of special laws enacted from 1841 on. Probably some of the orders affected by the measures legally transferred property to individual members to hold until such time as the order had the right to own property collectively. Some orders whose property was sold may have then sold the government bonds and invested the proceeds. In fear of disentailing legislation, other orders probably sold their lands and invested the money in stocks which would be harder to nationalize.

From a political viewpoint, the disentailing legislation did curtail the power of the clergy and therefore removed the issue from the political arena. Although the influence of individual clergy in the palace of Isabel II was one among many provocations for the Revolution of 1868, it was not a popular cause. During the First Republic (1873–1874), despite the absence of effective police force, convents were not burned nor clergy killed.[8]

The Restoration Era

Following the restoration of the Monarchy in 1875, Spanish religious began to recover from the blows inflicted by the disentailing legislation. Old orders began to establish new communities and new service orders were established, particularly during the regency of the devout Queen María Cristina (1885–1902). Beginning in 1900 the number of regular clergy increased sharply as French clergy fled to Spain from the proscriptive legislation of the Third Republic, and as thousands of Spanish clergy returned from Cuba and the Philippines. The dramatic growth is shown in the accompanying table.

Year	Population of Spain	Secular clergy	Regular clergy	Men in orders	Women in orders
1767	9,308,804	65,823	83,118	55,453	27,665
1833	12,286,941	50,507	56,893	31,279	25,614
1859	15,464,340	38,563	a	a	a
1861	a	a	15,093	1,746	13,347
1900	18,753,206	33,403	54,738	12,142	42,596
1910	19,995,686	34,420	68,901	22,224	46,677
1920	21,389,842	29,969	67,812	16,700	51,112

Source: The figures for 1900, 1910, and 1920 are taken from the official census of Spain. The figures for 1767, 1833, 1859, and 1861 are from William Ebenstein, *Church and State in Franco Spain,* Research Monograph No. 8 of the Center for International Studies, Woodrow Wilson School of Public and International Affairs, Princeton University (Princeton, 1960), pp. 21, 25.
ᵃ Not available.

Although some of these religious settled in the rural areas where the Catholic Carlist movement had found its greatest support (in Navarre, the Basque countryside, and rural Catalonia), great numbers settled in three major cities (Barcelona, Madrid, and Valencia).[9] Despite the official rhetoric of a traditional Catholicism, the truth was that after 1875 the Church had to assert her political and intellectual force in an urban setting and to secure income from business or by performing services for the government. The struggle between the clergy and their opponents, therefore, tended to concentrate on the school and on the marketplace.

The Church and Society at the Beginning of the Century

RELIGIOUS VERSUS SECULAR EDUCATION

By the end of the nineteenth century there was tension in Europe at large as educators either incorporated or refuted the new ideas of scientists, historians, and sociologists. But in Restoration Spain it happened that a group of brilliant educators presented the daring proposal of a secular progressive education just at the very moment when the religious orders began an intensive drive to win back the propertied middle class. Two poles were established in the struggle: the Institución Libre de Enseñanza, founded in 1876 by Francisco Giner de los Ríos, and the schools of the Jesuits. The conflict did not primarily concern subject matter (although the *Institucionistas* would have preferred that it did) but rather the values that should be instilled in the citizenry from childhood.[10]

From the beginning the dispute was bitter but restricted. In the Institución Libre in Madrid, Giner de los Ríos was frankly concerned with educating only the middle class which would produce the leaders of society.[11] He believed that politics would remain sterile until politicians acquired new ideas and civic values for the formulation and execution of reforms. Therefore he created a learning situation that encouraged creativity and spontaneity, that instilled a respect for Spanish folk lore (not the tawdry, stylized "España de la pandareta") and a love for the countryside, as well as a knowledge of contemporary European thought and scientific research. The Institucionistas have been dismissed as an elite, isolated from the masses.[12] Giner's ideas apart, the realities of the situation left them little choice. That sector of the middle class interested in such an education was so limited in numbers and in funds that it could not finance many schools for its own children, much less endow schools for workers.*

* In 1909 there were 5,000 private Catholic schools in Spain. There were only 107 lay private schools and 43 of these were in Barcelona. (*El Heraldo* [Madrid], as cited in Rafael Shaw, *Spain from Within* [London, 1910], p. 190.)

Although openly secular in orientation, the Institucionistas were not anti-religious; nevertheless they became the target for attack by ultraconservative groups who realized that although only a small group of students was educated in the Institución, Giner's ideas had influenced a generation of intellectuals and of educational reformers.

The Catholic schools also concentrated their efforts on the middle class, especially the propertied groups from whom they had been alienated when the latter purchased disentailed clerical lands.[13] In one sense, to talk of the clerical problem is to talk of the Catholic schools: 294 of the 597 male religious communities in Spain were engaged in teaching, as were 910 of the 2,656 women's communities.[14] Although some of these orders taught only workers, the orientation of the movement — led by Jesuits, Piarists, and Marists (Institute of the Marist Brothers of the Schools) — was to develop an elementary and secondary education that would assure them not only a source of income but a tutorial role among the propertied classes. Part of the intensity of the subsequent clash between clericals and anticlericals is due to the success of Catholic schools in preparing men to defend the Church.

After 1900 the educational issue took on a new dimension as politicians debated how best to educate the illiterate masses, a problem of overwhelming proportions. In 1900, 43 out of 100 Spanish individuals over seven years of age were illiterate; only 15,000 of the nation's 45,000 towns had a public school.[15] Some statesmen recognized the implications: that an illiterate population possessing the right to vote was cause for political instability, vulnerable to demagogues. Farsighted businessmen realized that an ignorant, unskilled labor force was an obstacle to economic expansion. However, the loudest demand for schools came from the workers themselves. Since the First Republic their cry had been "Guerra al hambre y al analfabetismo." Politicians appealing for workers' votes always included some provision for schools. Even conscription into the Army was presented as a means for men to learn to read.[16]

Because of all these pressures, in 1900 responsibility for public primary schools was taken from the Ministry of Development and assigned to a newly created Ministry of Public Instruction and Fine Arts. But before funds were allocated or personnel employed, politicians argued about the type of education to be offered in the schools. Laymen educated by the clergy competed with those inspired by Giner's ideas (or simply by European movements) for the right to influence public school education. Now that the conflict between religious and secular education affected not just the middle classes but workers (the only ones who would attend public schools), the matter ceased to be a cultural affair and became a major political issue.

This was the background for the impassioned support of, as well as opposition to, the educational measures of Liberal politician Alvaro de Figuerola, Count of Romanones. He prepared the Royal Decree of July 1, 1902, whereby the Ministry of Public Instruction assumed payment of the salaries of primary teachers in public schools, thereby relieving their poverty and vulnerability to control by the local cacique. A decree of September 4, 1902, established provincial and municipal boards responsible for carrying out ministerial educational policy on the local scene. Romanones then moved on to establish state jurisdiction over private Catholic schools. A Royal Order authorized Ministry officials to inspect all private (that is, religious) schools and to force them to comply with the same health and educational requirements as public schools. Another order deprived the clergy of the right to examine and grant degrees on behalf of the government and thereby deprived them of the substantial fees paid for that service.[17] From 1901 on, Liberal governments would try to implement these measures while Conservative governments would neglect or actually suspend them. Insofar as they took an active interest in worker education, Conservatives favored the practice of granting government subsidies to religious orders who ran schools for the poor or admitted a certain number of poor children into their regular schools. As the urban population increased, such subsidies became an important item in the budget of many religious orders.[18]

The result was that in 1909 there were only 25,000 public schools in all of Spain and these were understaffed and miserably furnished. The national problem of teaching the masses to read, write, and count was almost forgotten in the conflict over cultural and social values.

THE INCOME OF THE CLERGY

After 1900 a primary target for anticlerical attacks was the industrial wealth of the clergy. Joaquín Aguilera, the secretary of the powerful Catalan manufacturers' association, (Fomento del Trabajo Nacional) reported in 1912 that religious orders "controlled, without exaggeration, one third of the capital wealth of Spain." [19]

As in the field of education, so in that of capital investment the Jesuits were the prime target. Reputed to enjoy the special favor of Queen Regent María Cristina, their economic ventures spread and diversified. The powerful shipping line, La Transatlántica, was reportedly their property; its ostensible owner, Claudio López y Bru, Marquis of Comillas, was deemed nothing more than a business manager for Jesuit interests. When Comillas invested heavily in Moroccan mines and port works, anticlericals declared that the economic development of Morocco would not benefit Spain but only the Jesuits.[20]

Jesuits were held responsible for the high cost of living. The sale of sugar, the one luxury of the poor, and of tobacco, both government monopolies, were farmed out to companies popularly believed to be owned by the Jesuits. Even more inflammable was the widespread conviction that the Jesuits put up the capital for the syndicates that collected the excise tax (known as *el consumo*) which urban dwellers paid on every item they consumed: food, drink, fuel, and timber.[21]

To move out of the rather rarefied realm of capital investments and into the observable activities of commerce and industry, middle-class businessmen resented the fact that most orders did not pay the heavy industrial taxes nor customs duties. This enabled the clergy to sell at a lower price than their lay competitors. So did the fact that labor costs were low, for products were made either by the religious themselves or by inmates in their institutions.

The Marists offer a good example of clerical enterprise. This religious order had entered Spain from France late in the nineteenth century for the purpose of teaching and directing workers' organizations. In 1909, the Marist brothers of Barcelona completed construction of an enormous complex of buildings, valued at millions of pesetas, where food and clothing for all members of their order in Catalonia were prepared (thereby depriving businessmen of this income). The Marists also ran a bisulphate factory on a commercial basis.

But only a few orders, like the Jesuits, had large capital to invest, and only a few orders, like the Marists, ran large-scale business ventures. The problem confronting Catholic clergy everywhere was how to support the increasing numbers of religious who no longer lived in autarkic communities, raising their own food and weaving their clothes as in the Middle Ages. The problem of financing clergy in urban areas, in Spain as elsewhere, greatly concerned Pope Leo XIII and the Sacred Congregation of

Religious who recommended that the government employ the clergy to perform the services demanded by an expanding urban society.[22]

The service orientation of religious orders in Spain can be seen in the following statistics for 1900:

Orientation	Female communities	Male communities
Education	910	294
Welfare	1,029	39
Contemplative	717	75
Priests	—	97
Missionaries	—	92
Total	2,656	597

Source: Luis Morote, Los Frailes en España (Madrid, 1904), pp. 15–16, 25.

In Spain as in France, the clerical monopoly of welfare and education antagonized the urban petite bourgeoisie, its competitor for government employment; this was a significant factor in mesocratic Spain. But the worker had direct cause to dislike the clerical staff of Catholic schools and asylums for they affected his personal life as did no other official agency except the police.

THE WORKER AND THE RELIGIOUS ORDERS

In workers' neighborhoods there were few parish priests, and they tended to live as poorly as did their parishioners. In contrast, members of religious orders usually inhabited large buildings that were only partially open to the public. This practice created an element of mystery that anticlerical propaganda exploited to good effect.[23]

To these buildings the worker went for the only education offered to him and to his children (excluding some few public or private secular schools). The aged and the orphan received asylum, and all charity (food, money, and clothing) from public and private sources was distributed by churches or convents. The clergy ran employment bureaus for men and women and industrialists preferred to hire through these bureaus. Clergy staffed juvenile and adult correctional institutions.

Postulants in the orders that cared for workers usually came from traditional family backgrounds, often from rural areas; they sometimes lacked the flexibility and sophistication necessary to work in a tense social situation. Furthermore, the large number of religious leads to the delicate question of vocations. Certainly some of the men and women who entered convents did so because of personal frustrations, which in turn made their difficult work with the poor even more tense. These sociological and psychological pressures often made nuns and friars authoritarian; they were "doing their duty" and exacting religious devotion in return. Ironically, the type of dedicated man or woman who did the most for the poor was precisely the kind of self-righteous individual most disliked by the workers. These undeniable tensions between workers and clergy were aggravated by constant anticlerical propaganda that urged laborers to resent the religious even though they were forced to accept their charity.

Because the financing of the clergy's welfare and educational institutions was not understood, it was deeply resented. Excepting those few instances where members of the religious orders administered the sacraments, their contacts with the workers had little to do with spiritual obligations. The two groups met to exchange a service, the costs of which had to be paid in some way. The clergy charged with the responsibility for the workers' welfare insisted that they could not meet the expenses out of their capital (although anticlerical propagandists insisted that they could). Nor did they receive sufficient subsidies from the government nor donations from the wealthy. Although the claims of the clergy were probably exaggerated, they undoubtedly needed additional income. Therefore they made and sold products such as pastries or painted postcards, or else they performed services such as laundry or embroidery. Often this work was done not only by the religious but by inmates in asylums or by poor children in a school; this was the basis for the popular charge that the orders deliberatedly exploited their charitable institutions in order to make money.[24]

There was still another reason why this activity aroused antagonism: this type of work was also done by wives of laborers in their home as an attempt to eke out the family income. In an urban proletariat that was overworked and underpaid, the women who laundered or sewed at home constituted the most wretched group. They labored fifteen hours a day for a pittance; undernourished and working in miserable conditions, they had the highest incidence of tuberculosis of any category in the Spanish population.[25] The business activities of the nuns, while never a major factor in the Spanish economy, caused great resentment among these working-class women who were thereby compelled to lower the already meager prices they charged for sewing and laundry.

Politics and the Church: 1900–1905

THE RELIGIOUS ORDERS ENTER POLITICS: 1900–1903

The clergy were undoubtedly troubled by angered workers but felt more threatened by the politicians' attempts to limit Church activities, for they had watched uneasily the course of events in France. Concluding just as the Spaniards began, the successful campaign of the French anticlerics profoundly influenced events on the Iberian Peninsula. In one way it helped to dignify the cause by convincing many in the Liberal party that anticlericalism was "a virtuous, honorable, intelligent" defense of civil power that respectable politicians could support with every expectation of success.[26]

Beginning in 1900, both the Church hierarchy and the anticlerical politicians mobilized their forces for open combat in the Cortes. To some extent the clergy precipitated the fight because of the urgent need to provide for the numerous religious returning from the colonies. Realizing the limited efficacy of Pidal's neo-Catholic parliamentary group, churchmen organized sympathetic laymen through the Catholic Action (Acción Católica) movement. In its Sixth National Congress, held at Santiago in 1902, Catholic Action members agreed that the religious orders were "irreplaceable auxiliaries in the resolution of the social conflict" and should therefore be employed by the state to teach and care for workers. Laymen were urged to organize a Commission for the Defense of Catholic Interests (Junta de Defensa de los Intereses Católicos) in each diocese to promote and protect clerical activities.[27]

At Santiago in 1902 the Church consolidated her alliance with the propertied middle class, initiated in Catholic schools during the Restoration, with results that were decisively important in the struggle between labor and capital. Thus at Santiago, to supplement the primarily political activities of Catholic Action, clergy and laymen decided to reactivate the National Council of Catholic Workers' Corporations (el Consejo Nacional de las Corporaciones Católica-obreras, first organized in 1893), and to urge that a branch be organized in each diocese. For this purpose three regional assemblies were held between 1905 and 1907. Yet the measures discussed were extremely conservative, as for example that of workers' circles: theoretically a "mixed union" of employers and employees through which workers would receive welfare and pensions, such organizations had long since proved ineffectual in France as in Valencia. Despite the strong recommendation of

Pope Pius X that Catholic workers be organized into craft unions (called *uniones profesionales* in Spain),[28] and despite the plea of prominent Catholic laymen and priests for a more dynamic means of confronting the new urban labor situation, the Spanish National Council of Catholic Workers' Corporations continued to favor workers' circles.[29] Yet relatively few were organized, and these earned no sympathy from the labor force which considered them merely as an agency for the recruitment of scab workers.[30]

What Catholic labor activities did accomplish was to force the socialist labor movement to adopt an active policy of anticlericalism. Until 1900, neither workers nor union officials had considered the clergy as a major threat.[31] Socialists believed that the Church, like the state, would disappear in the future workers' regime, and that anticlericalism was a halfway measure, more attractive to the middle class than to the proletariat.[32] But after 1900, the socialist attitude changed as membership in trade unions declined. Catholic labor circles constituted a serious rival for they appealed to much the same worker population as did the socialists — to those interested in peaceful resolution of labor difficulties and to funds for old age and illness. Catholics had the advantage of having more money to subsidize such programs. Therefore, beginning in 1902, labor leaders formed a tenuous alliance with middle-class republicans on the issue of anticlericalism, which crossed class borders as few other issues could do.

By 1903 those who defended clerical interests, acknowledging the extent and intensity of the anticlerical program, saw that Catholic Action was but a palliative: direct representation in the Cortes was necessary. They found an unexpected opportunity to intervene in the intraparty struggles for leadership; because the Liberals had already introduced anticlerical legislation, the clergy sought an ally within the Conservative party.

The decision of the clergy to enter politics made it difficult for those politicians in both parties who desired a realistic solution of the clerical problem, using existing legislation to control abuses. The swirl of politics took the clerical issue from the hands of moderate men and swept it into the center of the competition for the posts left vacant by Cánovas' assassination and by Sagasta's approaching retirement. The point must be stressed: politicians did not manufacture anticlericalism but merely used it to political advantage.

THE LIBERAL PARTY AND THE CLERICAL ISSUE: 1902

Bowing to public opinion and party pressures, Práxedes Sagasta in April 1902 authorized the administrative measures needed to implement the moderate program of forcing religious orders to register under the 1887 Law of Associations, a measure designed originally to regulate all non-official organizations (including labor unions).* It seems right that the last of the great Restoration politicians should have sponsored the first major attempt to venture out from behind the façade of Cánovas' constitutional monarchy and attempt the resolution of an issue that deeply divided Spaniards.

Sagasta's measures were contained in a Royal Decree of September 19, 1901, and an implementatory Royal Order of April 9, 1902.[33] The decree stipulated the conditions for legal authorization of religious orders, on the assumption that these were included under the 1887 Law of Associations. One of the provisions of the Royal Order instructed all clergy engaged in industry to register immediately on the tax lists. The other three provisions stipulated the procedure for legal inscription. Those religious associations already authorized by the state had only to present their papers to the governor; those not authorized must apply, including information about their members and finances. All orders having foreign nationals, permanently or temporarily, were to comply with the special legislation concerning alien clergy. In addition, Sagasta's government presented Romanones' proposals for education reforms, which have already been described.

Secretly Sagasta began negotiations with the Vatican for a new agreement authorizing the Liberal program, in accord with the cautious tactics characteristic of the Restoration era. But politicians were no longer free to make policy in this fashion for there was now, at least in theory, a franchised population. José Canalejas was the first major politician to grasp the importance of this innovation. And therefore in May 1902, when he learned of Sagasta's negotiations (which he considered a betrayal of the publicly announced policy), he took the issue to the electorate in a series of speeches throughout the country, and summoned republicans and socialists to support his program.

* The politicians' objective in requiring the clergy to register under the Law of Associations was to force them to acknowledge the right of the state to permit, or prohibit, the establishment of any given religious order in Spain. As a matter of fact, most of the religious orders were already registered with the state under the terms stipulated by the Concordat of 1851, through which the Pope had secured from the state a privileged position for the clergy in Spain. In 1904, of the 2,656 women's religious communities in Spain, 2,274 were registered in accord with the Concordat: 507 of the 597 men's religious communities were registered. (Luis Morote, *Los Frailes en España* [Madrid, 1904], p. 25.)

Sagasta expelled Canalejas and his group of "Demócratas" from the party on November 5, 1902, but this weakened his government. He left office in December and died one month later. The race for the position of party leader began; obviously the most dramatic issue was the program of clerical controls. Elderly politicians Montero Ríos and Segismundo Moret wanted a compromise in order not to alienate the moderate Catholic vote. Canalejas and his "Demócratas" remained on the fringes of the Liberal party.

THE CONSERVATIVE PARTY AND CLERICAL INTERESTS: THE FIRST ADMINISTRATION OF ANTONIO MAURA, 1903–1905

Confronted with the controversial measures of the outgoing Liberal government, no Conservative prime minister could ignore the clerical problem. The new head of the government in 1903, Fernández Villaverde, would probably have preferred to do so for he had already shown his sympathies with the Liberal program by proposing moderate fiscal controls on clerical property.[34] This proved to be a disadvantage during the following two years as he struggled for the post of party leader in competition with Antonio Maura, who publicly defended clerical interests.

Maura had only left the Liberal party for the Conservative party in 1902. He was abruptly brought to the front ranks in October 1903 when Francisco Silvela, nominal party leader since the assassination of Cánovas, unexpectedly retired from politics. In the following two years Maura wrested effective party control from his rival, Fernández Villaverde, because of his ability and because of his ambitious plans for naval and administrative reforms. But another cause for Maura's success was his alliance with powerful Catholic laymen like the Marquis of Comillas, leader of the Catholic Action movement, and Alejandro Pidal, chief of the ultraconservative Catholic faction in the Cortes. This was not simply a political maneuver: Maura sincerely hoped a pro-Catholic policy would encourage the apathetic propertied classes to participate as actively in politics as did the anticlerical sector of the middle class.[35]

In December 1903, upon becoming Prime Minister for the first time, Maura established himself as a "clerical" politician by appointing Friar Bernardino Nozaleda, former Archbishop of Manila, to the archbishopric of Valencia, a stronghold of republicanism in Spain. "All the shame and ignominy of 1898," protested the Madrid newspaper El Liberal, "are incarnated and reunited in the sinister figure of the ex-Archbishop of Manila." [36] Critics considered Nozaleda, a Dominican, to be a collaborator with the Americans, because he had remained in the Philippines under American rule to defend the schools of his order; his defenders replied that he could not abandon his flock merely because of a change of governments. Despite the opposition, the Cortes approved Nozaleda's appointment.*

Maura's government then proceeded to negotiate and sign an accord with the Vatican (June 19, 1904). Again the Vatican and the state failed to specify the third religious order that, together with the Vincentian and Oratorian fathers, was to be exempted from all civil and fiscal controls; this loophole was used by other orders to escape registering. Moreover, although the Vatican agreed that all religious establishments were subject to taxation except those devoted to teaching or welfare, it did not specify that the *business* activities of the latter orders were taxable. In effect, this secured fiscal protection for the two most important groups of religious orders.

Although Maura gained control of the Conservative party through Catholic support, he always resented the charge that he was a "clerical" politician; he conscientiously abstained from any act of personal favoritism and insisted that his government enforce all legislation concerning religious orders. Yet his opposition to any new restrictive laws, together with acts of open sympathy by subordinate officials, meant in effect a policy of protection for the clergy.

The Final Round in the Anticlerical Struggle: 1905–1907

THE CHURCH VERSUS THE ASSOCIATIONS BILL

The Liberals returned to office in June 1905 without having reached an agreement on who would succeed Sagasta as party chief or what would be the party's policy on the clerical issue. This uncertainty is reflected in the six cabinet changes that occurred during the two and one half years they remained in power. The intraparty struggle, together with clerical intransigence and growing public anticlericalism, meant that by the end of 1906 moderate solutions were rejected in favor of the more radical policy of José Canalejas — that is, that special legislation was needed, that the Restoration Settlement must be amended.

For this purpose Alfonso XIII did not ask Canalejas to form a govern-

* When Fernández Villaverde returned to office in January 1905 and was confronted with new incidents in Valencia, he persuaded Father Nozaleda to renounce the appointment.

ment but chose instead an elderly general, José López Domínguez, to preside; when the new government launched its program with a Royal Order legalizing civil marriages, Catholic laymen and the hierarchy immediately organized protest rallies and a newspaper campaign. Thus the Catholic sector was not only aroused but organized when, on October 23, 1906, Bernabé Dávila, Minister of the Interior, read to the Cortes a new and drastic Bill of Associations to be enacted without prior approval of the Vatican. Moderate politicians of all parties hoped that the issue could be solved in accord with Cánovas' formula: legislators should quietly work out a compromise to correct any abuse that might cause civil strife. Maura refused. He warned that the proposed Associations Bill would lead to a break with the Vatican: "For us the rupture constitutes war and you are the prologue of the civil war." In the perspective of Spain's history since that debate in 1906, Maura's warning takes on a symbolic importance. So does the reply of moderate republican Gumersindo Azcárate, who protested the implication that only the Conservatives were "Catholic." Azcárate declared that "when one speaks as Sr. Maura has spoken today, when the spirit of the nineteenth century is so disregarded, then it is not possible to govern." [37]

The Catholic Action movement took the protest against the Bill of Associations out of the Cortes into the public arena. Under the direction of its President, the Marquis of Comillas, rallies were held throughout Spain to protest the bill. Popular reaction for and against the bill was so intense that moderate Liberal politicians took fright. López Domínguez resigned and when Moret was unable to form a cabinet, the King asked Antonio Aguilar y Correa, Marquis of Vega de Armijo, to form a government in order to pass the annual budget. When the Marquis announced that he would support the Associations Bill despite Catholic opposition, it was obvious that his term in office would be brief.

However, during his short term, the Liberal government of the eighty-year-old Marquis sponsored an educational reform project of transcendental importance in the cultural history of Spain. In order to comprehend the magnitude of this achievement, it must be understood that educational reform had become associated with terrorism through a curious set of circumstances.

EDUCATIONAL REFORMS AND ANARCHIST TERRORISM

European intellectuals considered the Escuela Moderna, founded by Francisco Ferrer in Barcelona in 1901, a model for educational reform, an opinion due to Ferrer's contacts with international civil rights and educational reform movements and to a lack of knowledge about the Spanish situation. Ferrer's school was neither the first nor the most distinguished of the libertarian schools established late in the nineteenth century in Catalonia and Andalusia. Like Ferrer and his collaborators, the founders of these schools lacked academic degrees. On principle they refused all contact with the public education system and sought to educate workers for a more dignified and more prosperous future.[38] For Spanish authorities these schools, like the Escuela Moderna, were merely a subterfuge for the teaching of anarchist doctrine. By fortuitous circumstances, their accusations gained credence through the involvement of Ferrer and his Escuela Moderna in the attempted regicide of Mateo Morral.

On May 31, 1906, as Alfonso XIII and his bride, Victoria Eugenia of Battenberg, were returning to the palace after their wedding, Mateo Morral threw a bomb in the path of their carriage. The royal couple escaped unharmed but twenty-four spectators and soldiers were killed; another 107 were wounded. Police quickly traced the crime to Morral, a young Catalan employed by Ferrer in his publishing firm in Barcelona (not a professor in the Escuela Moderna, as commonly reported). Morral committed suicide before he could be captured. On June 4, 1906, Francisco Ferrer was arrested and indicted by judges who hoped to prove him guilty of planning the crime and inducing Morral to carry it out.[39]

As a result of the extensive publicity accorded the trial in Western European countries, Ferrer acquired international notoriety as a martyr for the cause of secular education in "la Espagne inquisitorial" (a propaganda campaign built on the one for the Montjuich prisoners organized six years earlier). The Escuela Moderna and its founder will be discussed within the context of Catalan politics in a later chapter. The concern at this point is the effect that Ferrer's trial for complicity in a crime of regicide had upon educational reform.

In the months following Ferrer's arrest (the same period in which the Liberals presented their Bill of Associations), reactionaries sought to associate the cause of secular education with sedition. Ferrer was still in prison awaiting trial when, on December 14, 1906, a group of militant Catholics introduced a resolution against lay schools:[40] "That the anarchist propaganda carried on in the lay schools in Barcelona is contrary to the Constitution and to the law, and should therefore be repressed by the government."

Amalio Gimeno, Liberal Minister of Public Instruction and a close friend of Canalejas, boldly protested the implications of the motion and praised secular education; he stated that only certain libertarian schools might be considered illegal. The Catholic deputies' motion failed to pass the Cortes but their opposition to secular education was unabated and the numerous violent, pro-Catholic rallies held throughout the nation in protest against the Bill of Associations showed that a large and organized sector of public opinion supported the ultraconservative faction.

JUNTA PARA AMPLIACION DE ESTUDIOS

In such a milieu it was all the more remarkable that one month later (January 12, 1907) the King would sign a decree establishing two royal commissions charged with educational reform. Liberal education minister Amalio Gimeno prepared the decree establishing the famous Junta para Ampliación de Estudios e Investigaciones Científicas, an innocuous title for a major enterprise: the preparation of a new generation of scientists and humanists by subsidizing university studies, postgraduate research, and study abroad. The decree established a second Junta (Junta para el Fomento de la Educación Nacional), to direct the reform of the curriculum and personnel of the public elementary school system. José Castillejo, the able secretary of the Junta, and his collaborators conceived of these as technical secretariats that would institutionalize educational experiments, until then carried out in private schools. But reactionary groups claimed then, and continued to do so for the next thirty years, that the Junta was merely using government channels to impose the program of Francisco Giner de los Ríos' Institución Libre, as well as other secular, European-oriented ideas that were insidious for traditional Spanish values.[41]

Because the Vega de Armijo government fell two weeks after the decree was published, the Juntas began under an ultraconservative, extremely devout Minister of Public Instruction, Faustino Rodríguez Sanpedro. The Deputy Minister was Cesar Silío, one of the Catholic deputies who had sponsored the motion against lay schools; having failed to secure prescriptive legislation, he achieved the same results through harassing administrative measures.

The Junta for primary education was abolished. But the Junta responsible for university studies (and therefore affecting only the propertied middle class) was allowed to continue its program of apolitical, professional reforms that served as a cultural stimulus of immeasurable importance.

CLERICALISM IN THE ELECTORAL CAMPAIGN

On January 25, 1907, the Marquis de Vega de Armijo acknowledged the lack of parliamentary support for his government and resigned. When the King asked Antonio Maura to form a government for the second time, he carried out the task in twenty-four hours. Although his government was an assurance that the Bill of Associations would not become law, the Church intervened actively in the elections in April to guarantee this: the Archbishop of Santiago and the Bishops of Zamora and Salamanca issued pastoral letters prohibiting the faithful from voting for candidates who did not honor their obligations as Catholics above all political considerations. In León priests went from house to house, declaring that salvation was impossible unless the devout voted for Catholic candidates; in Barcelona religious orders reportedly marched inmates of their asylums to the polls.[42] Whether Maura was prepared to acknowledge the designation or not, the elections had clearly established the image of his government as "clerical."

CHAPTER III

Reforms versus "Clericalism" in the Government of Antonio Maura

A G A I N S T a background of national crisis, amid cultural turbulence, Antonio Maura's "Revolution from Above" seemed for a moment the dramatic movement that would rouse the Spanish nation from her lethargy.[1] The stereotype, elaborated by politicians who declared (and perhaps sincerely believed) that Maura was a reactionary — placing public order above all other considerations, blindly serving the clergy — has obscured the fact that he proposed the only concrete, comprehensive reforms presented during the decade 1900–1910 and that his proposals had been carefully worked out in experimental legislation over a long career.

When he became President of the Council in January 1907 as the undisputed leader of the Conservative party, Maura apparently held the power to execute his reform program. The obstacles he encountered provide a case study of the interweaving interests that determined Spanish politics and eventually enervated all reform movements. Above all, they demonstrated the unwillingness of the propertied middle class (Maura's target audience) to participate in politics, even to defend its most cherished ideals.[2]

Maura's Reform Program

NAVAL AND MILITARY POLICY

Maura appealed to national pride with his plans for an enlarged combat and maritime fleet that would enable Spain to compete in the international naval race then in progress.

Spanish nationalism in 1907 was a complex matter.[3] Except for army officers, Spaniards rejected a militant foreign policy. A legislative investigation in 1906 into the conduct of the War of 1898 had reminded the nation of mismanagement and corruption and revived memories of defeat, of maimed and ill soldiers returning from the colonies. Yet the Spanish did not want to believe that their nation would not again figure as a great power. Maura astutely provided for these contradictory sentiments; he opposed an active foreign policy, and prepared for future action in the Bill of Maritime Organization and Naval Armaments, presented to the Cortes on November 20, 1907. Joaquín Costa, one of the few to oppose the bill, protested that Spain could not afford a navy and should spend the money on schools. Yet only seven days after the bill had been introduced into the Congress of Deputies, it was passed in what is known in parliamentary annals as "The Glorious Session." The deputies proved far less enthusiastic about appropriating the necessary money. Critics charged that the naval construction program was merely a device to increase state subsidies to Comillas' Transatlántica Company, reputedly owned by the Jesuits. Charges of corruption in the awarding of contracts provided an opportunity to attack the general integrity of Maura's government.[4]

Maura's attempts to achieve greater military efficiency met with even less success. War Minister Primo de Rivera prepared a small, well trained task force composed of two divisions (Orozco, and Cazadores de Gibraltar), totaling 16,000 men, in a permanent state of war readiness; this was the type of force many professional officers had proposed for years. But Primo de Rivera's irascible temperament annoyed both Maura and the King, so in March 1909 he was replaced by General Linares who immediately sent to the Cortes a bill proposing the opposite policy to that of his predecessor: Linares' bill would call up more men annually and prolong their service; it passed the Senate but not the Congress of Deputies. Thus by the summer of 1909, the nation had no effective military force at its command: for reasons that he never explained, Linares failed to maintain Primo de Rivera's special divisions at full strength until his own plan for reorganization was enacted.[5]

National defense formed an important but not central concern of Maura's program. The issue on which he staked his prestige was administrative reform.

ADMINISTRATIVE REFORMS

Believing that political apathy and the cacique system were the results of overcentralization, Maura proposed the gradual extension of autonomy in certain fields (taxation, education, and welfare) to local legislatures and administrations. He was convinced that the national evils of "adulterated parliaments" and "sterile governments" would disappear once the citizens participated directly in, and were responsible for, the political system. Specifically Maura appealed for direct participation in politics by the *fuerzas vitales* — not only the great industrialists and landowners, who had no tradition of public service, but the conservative urban and rural middle classes, essentially the rentiers, whom he termed "the neutral mass." These groups normally remained on the margin of politics, changing their party allegiance on each issue as it affected their interests. Maura urged them to adopt a party affiliation and through it to work in the Cortes to carry out necessary economic and political changes. Maura threatened them with the obvious: if responsible citizens did not carry out a "Revolution from Above," then change would come through a violent upheaval from below that would endanger the entire social structure.

On June 7, 1907, just a few days after the newly elected deputies assembled, Maura proudly presented his "bill to uproot caciquismo." ("Bill Establishing the Bases for the Reform of Local Administration"). From 1907 to 1909 it was the major political issue, occasioning 5,511 speeches in the Congress of Deputies and the Senate; 2,813 amendments were proposed.[6] Yet when Maura left office in October 1909 the bill had not been enacted into law. A description of the reasons why it failed will show the difficulties with which any reformer had to contend in the Spanish political situation.

Obstacles to Reform

A major obstacle was the control exercised by vested economic and social interests over the Conservative party. As a result of Interior Minister La Cierva's blatant manipulation of the electoral machinery, Conservatives dominated the Cortes; thus if the Administrative Reform Bill had been a party measure, it would have become law. Gabriel Maura, who served as his father's political secretary, sadly admitted that it was not. He reported that the oligarchy which controlled the party opposed reform of the cacique system because they considered it a bulwark of their interests. By 1907, Gabriel Maura would later conclude, the Conservative party was "too old and too sclerotic" to carry out any program of reforms.[7]

But Antonio Maura had staked his political prestige on the administrative reform issue and was determined to succeed. Therefore he decided to go outside the two-party system and to bid for the votes of the Catalan bloc of deputies, Solidaridad Catalana, elected on a program of regional autonomy. Maura respected the political potential of regionalist movements as a Castilian politician probably could not have done; he was a native of Palma de Mallorca and he had served continuously as its representative in the Cortes (in contrast with most deputies, residents of Madrid who had little if any contact with the constituents of the districts they represented). In the case of Catalan regionalism, he believed it might regenerate the two-party system; concretely, he planned to incorporate at least its wealthier industrial sector (the Lliga, represented by Francisco Cambó) into the Conservative party. Objectively considered, the plan might have benefitted all Spain: the politicians of Catalonia, the most industrialized and urbanized region of Spain, might have used their autonomous powers under Maura's bill to carry out a controlled experiment in the many problems with which the national parties would have to deal in the twentieth century. But the historic hostility of Castile to other regions, and specifically to Catalonia, obscured such rational considerations. Taking advantage of this hostility, and that of army officers who considered regionalism as an insult to the Spanish nation, Liberal politicians denounced Maura for being willing to trade national unity in exchange for a few votes. Thus the association of Maura's reforms with Catalan regionalism proved a major obstacle to passage of the bill.[8]

A second major factor in defeating the bill was the conservative nature of the reforms proposed by Maura and by the big Catalan industrialists who supported him. As Catalan essayist Gaziel aptly describes it, Maura proposed a "revolution without a revolution."

Revolutions from above, that is to say, carried out peacefully by the wealthy and conservative classes of a nation, may bring prosperity to business and increase profits, but they do nothing more . . . They do not constitute an authentic revolution but an evolution, more or less effective, more or less profound, but one that definitely does not disturb anything essential.[9]

Maura made no provision for the incorporation into the body politic of urban workers and peasants, undoubtedly convinced that they were not yet ready to participate.

Moreover, his provision for a "corporate vote" was interpreted as a direct attack upon the suffrage. To counterbalance the high degree of autonomy accorded local legislatures, Maura had proposed restrictions on election of local representatives. Voters would continue to elect a majority of the city councilmen; however, each civic and business organization (theoretically, labor unions as well as associations of property owners) would also have the right to elect one councilor to protect its own interests. As for provincial deputies, currently elected by popular vote, Maura's bill provided that instead they were to be elected by the city councils.

Because of these undemocratic provisions, Liberal and republican deputies opposed Maura's bill. Even Catalan republican deputies, tempted by the hope of regional autonomy, opposed it. To them it seemed that just in the moment when the 1890 Universal Suffrage Law was becoming a reality (in urban areas at least), Maura proposed to limit the suffrage.* Understandably they were reluctant to give up any of their hard-won rights. Yet they refused to admit that the illiterate, politically inexperienced masses were not ready for the responsibilities contained in the bill, or to consider the possibility that devolution of powers to local governments was the more important achievement, that a prepared electorate would later reclaim its rights in new legislation.

A final major obstacle to Maura's Administrative Reform Bill was the conflict inherent in the decision of who should staff the educational and welfare institutions subsidized by local legislatures: laymen, appointed through party patronage, or regular clergy. Since the time of the First Republic, in Spain as in France, the middle class had presented a demand through the republican parties for more government jobs. This had become an increasingly important issue, as urban areas necessarily expanded their welfare and educational institutions; concurrently, religious orders increased their membership and financed their activities by staffing these institutions. With specific reference to Maura's bill: if provincial and municipal governments were suddenly asked to administer these services, the logical response would be to support the existing institutions staffed by clergy. Therefore, a grant of power to local government in 1907 would diminish hopes for increased government jobs for laymen. Left wing opposition to Maura's bill,

---

* Maura secured passage of a new electoral law almost immediately upon entering office (signed into law in August 1907). It superseded the original Universal Suffrage Law of 1890, introducing some slight restrictions on the franchise and stipulating that a majority of the seats in a district should go to the party or bloc with the most votes. This law was not widely discussed, either because the restrictions were not noted or because there was simply a lack of interest. It remained in force until the end of the constitutional monarchy (1931). In 1909 still another law made voting obligatory, but it provided for exceptions.

therefore, was due not only to a belief in democracy but to a very real concern about political patronage.[10]

The Elements of Maura's Clerical Policy

Beyond the tangible problem of patronage lay the threat of an increase in clerical power under Maura's benevolent government. His opponents denounced him for attempting to organize a Catholic party similar to those in Belgium, Italy, and Germany.[11] They ignored the fact that the so-called Catholic groups constituted an important sector of the electorate, and that their support was as basic to the stability of the constitutional monarchy as was that of the working class masses. Instead, republican and some Liberal politicians attributed to Maura sinister motives, such as plotting to establish a theocratic state. During Maura's two years in office, the small but militant Carlist movement encouraged such suspicions. What anticlericals did not perceive, or did not want to perceive, was that the Carlists considered Maura far too liberal for their tastes; he was not, commented a Carlist laconically, "un santo de nuestra devoción." [12]

Maura's association with clerical interests was attacked not only on principle but in more concrete (and more disparaging) terms of business deals with "clerical" enterprises. A good case in point was the sugar monopoly, awarded by a government contract to a company whose president was Alejandro Pidal, a Maura associate and leader of the neo-Catholic group in the Cortes. In 1907 Pidal was denounced for attempting to bribe legislators to continue the monopoly. Workers protested the fact that there should be a monopoly on sugar at all and lamented the high price of this, their only luxury. So did pastry and candy manufacturers, an important interest group in Solidaridad Catalana (and this constituted yet another reason why Maura was unable to work out an alliance with the Catalan bloc). Another case involved the Vascocastellana Railroad which received a large government subsidy. In 1909 republican deputies accused a company director, the "Catholic General" Camilo Polavieja, of stock manipulations and "abuses and deceits" in the use of national funds under the protection afforded by the Maura government.[13]

Aside from these rather nebulous but highly publicized charges, Maura's government did favor the clergy through administrative measures. The most important problem received little public attention because of its complexity. This was the indemnification for the church property that had been sold.

There was general agreement that once and for all the total amount of the state's debt to the Church be determined and that plans be made to liquidate it; however Liberals demanded that it be done in the Cortes, not through bureaucratic decisions by Maura's officials who were certain to favor clerical interests.[14] In the end, nothing was done: the state simply continued to pay interest.

Opposition newspapers preferred to concentrate on decrees such as that of September 12, 1908, denying the right of state inspectors to enter cloistered convents in order to inspect a corpse before issuing a death certificate (and to collect for this service); these nuns were the only religious group exempted from internment in a public cemetery. The decree heightened the mystery surrounding cloistered nuns who were traditionally believed to be martyred and then buried in the cloister.[15]

As for the business activities of the clergy, Maura refused even to take them seriously. In one Cortes debate, employing the sarcasm that brought him so many enemies, Maura declared he could not believe "that the economic expansion of the Spanish nation, the continued prosperity of Spanish industry" was threatened by exempting from taxation "the pastries of the nuns." [16] By reducing clerical business activities to a trifling instance, Maura ignored a real concern of urban public opinion. Maura's manner as much as his policies enabled his opponents to charge him with being autocratic, a charge used to good advantage in their campaign against the so-called "Bill of Terrorism."

Maura and Civil Rights

The campaign against Maura's Terrorism Bill demonstrates (as did that against his Administrative Reform Bill) how difficult it is in a traditional society such as Spain to correct any abuse. Rhetoric prevents even an open discussion of the issue.

The problem was the mysterious explosion of bombs in Barcelona that had been occurring for almost two decades: set off in isolated places at unusual hours, the bombs did little harm but they had created an appearance of lawlessness in the Catalan capital. In an effort to deal with this situation, Interior Minister Juan de La Cierva presented to the Cortes on January 24, 1908, a bill consisting of one article that amended the 1894 Law on Assaults by Means of Explosives. It granted to the cabinet (the council of ministers), upon the recommendation of the authorities in the province concerned, the authority to close anarchist centers and newspapers and to exile anarchist leaders; this limitation upon the constitutional right of Spaniards to form associations was justified on the ground that anarchists formed associations for the purpose of committing a crime.

Politicians concerned with civil rights opposed the bill because they feared the way an ultraconservative government would interpret "anarchist" and they held an open legislative hearing on the bill, undoubtedly pleased by the opportunity to criticize Maura. Fears for civil rights seemed justified when the official representative of the reactionary Committee of Social Defense (Comité de Defensa Social), composed of Catholic lawyers, told the investigation committee that secular schools for workers in Barcelona should be closed as anarchist centers.[17] The association of secular education and social disorder, established at the time of the Ferrer trial, was revived.

Having established the impression that the Maura government was seeking dictatorial powers, opposition politicians carried the charge to the nation in a series of rallies during May and June 1908. Sensing the general discontent, they decided on a bold experiment: to break the sterility of the Restoration system (the automatic rotation in office of two parties) by organizing a popular protest against the Maura government. Under the leadership of Liberal politicians Segismundo Moret and José Canalejas, a *Bloque de Izquierdistas* was organized to direct the campaign; this was the first formal, public alliance between a dynastic party and the republicans.

One tactic of the campaign, launched on November 18, 1908, was to attack Maura's alliance with Solidaridad Catalana. "It is a case of Castilians against Catalonia," Santiago Albó told an audience in Segovia.[18] But the major issue upon which the Bloc appealed for popular support was anticlericalism, although it moved carefully, as demanded by a traditional society, and defended Catholicism while attacking the clergy. Melquíades Alvarez, a republican deputy, told a rally in Granada in December 1908,

We are not persecuting the Church, nor has it entered our minds to de-Catholicize (*decatolizar*) Spain . . . What I do say is that the Catholic religion is a factor in the political life of my country, and that a statesman who attempts to govern by decatholicizing Spain may be a philosopher or a writer, but not a statesman.[19]

However, other members of the Bloc were more blunt. Spain, said Santiago Albó in the Granada rally, "is a pontifical state, a religious colony of the Vatican, a source of embarrassment to the world."[20] Speakers distinguished between secular and regular clergy: Moret declared that "parish priests are dying of hunger while the religious orders live in luxury, absorb industry, and take the bread from the mouths of workers."[21]

By February 1909, when the Bloc concluded its anti-Maura campaign, the unpopularity of Maura had been amply demonstrated. But Liberal party officials were still not ready to demand office, partly because a leader had not yet been agreed upon. More important was the fact that with the single exception of José Canalejas, Liberal politicians were not willing to take office on the popular issue of anticlericalism.[22]

The Workers

TROUBLE BETWEEN WORKERS AND CLERGY

Denied political redress of their grievances, workers resorted to direct, violent action in opposing the religious orders whom they believed were encroaching upon their rights.

A minor factor was the socialists' decision to abandon their neutralist position on the clerical issue. The occasion was the demand of Catholic workers' organizations to supplant the socialists as representatives of "labor" in the Institute of Social Reforms, the Socialist party foothold in the power structure. Protection of the socialist position was crucial, for party membership in 1908 was declining. Therefore, beginning in March 1908, socialists such as Matías Gómez Latorre, socialist delegate to the executive board of the Institute, bitterly attacked Catholic groups. He charged that "not content with taking over large financial and industrial enterprises, banks, the most powerful business concerns, education, commerce," and thereby achieving the right to represent employers in the Institute, clerical and re-actionary interests now wanted "to monopolize the labor delegation."[23]

In cities, rumors about the clergy were rife. The clergy were reportedly preparing an armed uprising to overthrow the Alphonsine Bourbons and to install a Carlist pretender, a rumor credible only in a critical situation and by an illiterate population. In December 1908, the anticlerical press publicized a circular sent by gun salesmen to religious orders urging them to buy arms.[24] In northwestern Spain, this clerical-worker tension finally erupted into violence.

The townspeople of Osera, Galicia, were proud of a tiled altar, all that remained of the once handsome monastery now in ruins.[25] In April 1909 the Bishop of Orense ordered that the altar be removed reportedly with the intention of selling it; when men in Osera refused to do the work, he recruited through a Catholic workers' circle in nearby Orense and requested from the Governor a Civil Guard escort. In Osera the carpenters were opposed by angry men and women; Civil Guards fired, killing ten men. Public indignation was so high that the Bishop left Orense. When he returned quietly a few nights later, workers stoned his palace and then attacked the Catholic workers' circle where from a window, someone (reputedly a priest) fired. The mob then attacked the residence of the Marist Brothers, administrators of the workers circle, and the convent of the Congregation of Handmaids, Adorers of the Blessed Sacrament and of Charity (the Adorer Sisters), a group that cared for wayward girls. Civil Guards finally restored order.

In the spring of 1909 politicians were concentrating on charges of corruption in the Maura government's awarding of naval contracts. Thus neither Liberal nor Conservative politicians noted the serious implications of Orense, where workers had translated into action the anticlerical speeches of politicians.

MAURA AND THE WORKERS

The true cause for workers' discontent, expressed in such incidents as that of Orense, was their financial plight. Between 1900 and 1910 the national economy steadily recovered from the loss of the colonies but the worker did not share in the benefits. Prices rose gradually but steadily through the decade, yet workers' salaries remained almost stationary; thus from 1907 to 1909, when prices increased somewhat more sharply, their situation grew worse.

Rising prices affected more the cost of clothing, furniture, and housing than the cost of food; nevertheless, by 1910, 75 percent of a worker's salary went for food alone. The minimal average cost of food and housing for a family with two children was 112.33 pesetas a month; thus a family could not live on the salary of the father, whether he was a day laborer (paid on the average 60 pesetas a month, or approximately $26.82)* or a plasterer (paid 96 pesetas, or approximately $42.91), or a metallurgical worker (paid 108

---

* The conversion of wages paid in pesetas to dollars is based upon the official international exchange rate of pesetas to £ sterling in 1905 (32.913 pesetas = £1), and then converted to the purchasing power of a dollar wage scale as of 1960 (using the index 44.7).

pesetas, or approximately $48.28). Marginal income was secured through the employment of the wife and children (paid respectively, on the average, 48 and 24 pesetas monthly, or approximately $21.46 and $10.73).[26] Unskilled and illiterate, the worker had no prospect of increasing his earnings.

In accord with the paternalism that characterized the Conservative party's social policy, Interior Minister La Cierva energetically attempted to enforce legislation governing factory working conditions and the employment of women and children.[27] A new law (April 1909) did grant workers the right to strike under specified conditions (such as informing the police eight days before a proposed strike, avoiding all disorders), but it simultaneously granted employers the right to a lockout.[28] Maura further strengthened employers through the Law for the Protection of National Industry (February 1907), another major advance in the protectionist policy firmly entrenched by the high tariff law of 1906; significantly, this was the only major legislation enacted by the Cortes during Maura's administration (aside from the law for the construction of a fleet).

When the Cortes closed in June 1909, Maura remained in office even though he had been unable to enact his reform programs into law. This stalemate would be broken during the legislative recess, not by politicians in Madrid but by the workers of Barcelona.

Part Two

The Catalan Problem in the Framework of National Politics

CHAPTER IV

The Region and Its Politics

IN 1909 Barcelona was the motive force of the politics, the culture, and the economy of Catalonia.[1] Early in the nineteenth century the historic Principality of Catalonia had been divided into four provinces: Barcelona, Gerona, Lérida, and Tarragona. Each had its own Civil Governor and administration but for all practical purposes, Catalonia continued to function as a region and events in the metropolis of Barcelona continued to determine the course of events throughout Catalonia.

By 1909 Barcelona had acquired a new distinction — as a mecca for terrorists during the preceding three decades. Two causes for the terrorism were discovered (and these soon constituted an indelible stereotype): the region's centuries-old struggle to become independent of Madrid, and the anarchists' control of the Catalan labor movement.

Regionalism and anarchism were but the expressions of an inability to resolve the problems of Catalonia's complex society and economy through the national political structure. Many of the obstacles were those common to all Spain, such as the cacique's control over elections. Others were peculiar to Catalonia, as for example the refusal of industrialists to incorporate the rights of workers into their program for regional autonomy and thereby to gain more strength in the struggle with Madrid for autonomy. This was directly linked to the character of Catalan industrialization: its inability to expand and to diversify, together with its emphasis upon production of a low-price cotton textile that required minimal labor costs. A worker in these conditions, denied political redress of grievances as well as the right to bargain collectively with employers, had no recourse but the violent direct action extolled by anarchists. Violence, in turn, justified the contention of national politicians, and of industrialists throughout Spain, that the "labor problem" was merely one of public order.

During the second Maura administration, 1907–1909, Catalonia was represented in the Cortes by Solidaridad Catalana — a comprehensive and truly representative regionalist bloc, or so it seemed. But once again, as in 1901, the industrial situation would destroy the political unity, pitting Catalan employer against Catalan worker. And the clerical issue further divided Catalans.

The inability of Barcelona — and therefore the inability of Catalonia — to achieve a representative regional movement and thereby to resolve its problems legally can be traced, almost exclusively, to the structure of Barcelona's society and economy

The Ecology

Barcelona had 587,411 inhabitants in 1910, second only to Madrid which had 599,807. Of equal significance for its politics and economy, the city's population had expanded rapidly during the preceding decade (from 533,000 in 1900), almost entirely the result of an influx from rural areas.

Because Barcelona was a major seaport, and located near the frontier, it was in close contact with the rest of Europe as Madrid was not. The cosmopolitan orientation enriched Catalonia's indigenous *Renaixença* (expressed in books, theater, and opera). This splendor was offset by the fact that 48 percent of Barcelona inhabitants over seven years of age were illiterate, one of the highest urban illiteracy rates in Spain.[2]

To supplement its political importance as the historic capital of Catalonia, Barcelona could mobilize its economic strength — as the region's port of entry and as the center of the cotton textile industry, the pivot of the Catalan economy. Although agriculture remained an important element in the region at large, Barcelona's urban and industrial interests were reinforced by Catalonia's many other textile centers; the city was not isolated in a rural area as were Bilbao or Oviedo.

The city's topography reflected its multiple activities. The central district (dating back to a Roman encampment) fanned out from the waterfront. All government offices, including military and Civil Guard headquarters, were located in this district, as were the principal commercial and banking institutions. To relieve the congestion, late in the nineteenth century the City Council encouraged people to move by installing a sewage system and paving streets in an adjoining district (known as the *Ensanche*). Investment in companies which built these public works under contract to the city, companies such as Fomento de Obras y Construcciones, S.A., brought excellent returns. The appropriation of the necessary funds constituted a major issue in municipal politics; gas and electric companies lobbied among city councilmen to secure contracts. Although the Ensanche project was limited in scope, the population of the central district did decrease sharply between 1900 and 1910. Persons with money went to live in the Ensanche, while workers had to find a place in the already crowded slums or in the industrial suburbs.

The slum area bordering the waterfront, the Atarazana district, had the large percentage of prostitutes and criminals that abound in any seaport. Beyond this lay the Paralelo, a district of factories and of the homes of the most impoverished workers; they crowded into tenements or built hovels (*chavolas*) where there was room.[3]

Bordering the city were suburbs that until 1897 had been independent towns. Some, like Corts and San Gervasio, were residential areas of large estates. Others — Gracia, San Andrés, and San Martín — were old industrial centers where an established skilled artisan class, although fighting a losing battle against the mechanization of the textile industry, provided an element of stability in the labor force. Suburbs such as Clot and Pueblo Nuevo had no such ballast. Men and women who worked in the large factories and inhabited the tenements of Clot or Pueblo Nuevo were unskilled and illiterate; a majority had only recently arrived from rural areas outside of Catalonia.

Barcelona's extensive terrain proved profitable to streetcar companies (owned by Belgian capital), and to drayage firms that carried goods from the port and central market to suburban stores and factories. In order to assure these profits, company officials refused to negotiate with unions of teamsters or of streetcar employees.

Apart from the intracity transportation (an economic need), there was little attempt to incorporate workers — constituting 64 percent of the population — into the Barcelona community. Some people even believed that workers *should* live apart.[4] City authorities did not pave the streets nor provide sewage systems for workers' suburbs. Lack of housing,* and the re-

---

* Between 1900 and 1910, the population of Barcelona increased officially by 55,000 (probably closer to 61,000 in fact). Yet the number of new residences increased only by 5,864 (from 31,884 to 37,748). (Sirera, "Obreros en Barcelona.")

sulting health problem, were ignored.[5] There was no serious plan to combat illiteracy. While clergy and republican anticlericals quarreled over the personnel to be employed in the schools, the situation grew worse. In the older residential neighborhoods, the proportion of illiterates varied between 23 percent and 29 percent; in the slums it ranged from 46 percent in San Martín, and 47 percent in the port district, to 55 percent in the Paralelo, 57 percent in outlying Clot, and 57 percent in Pueblo Nuevo.[6] This alarming proportion of illiterates conditioned the politics and threatened the social structure of Barcelona.

The Middle Class

The society of Barcelona was composed of a large industrial labor force, a substantial middle class of professionals and businessmen, and an upper stratum dominated by industrialists and financiers. This society was very like that of Valencia and Bilbao, but vastly different from that of Madrid (composed of a traditional nobility, a rentier class, a bureaucracy, and a labor force employed primarily in services).

The middle class of Barcelona was employed rather than living on income — a reflection of the Catalan respect for work as well as of the greater opportunity for employment than was offered, for example, in Madrid. Obviously there were some bureaucrats, employed by the national as well as by the municipal and provincial government. Technically, army officers on garrison duty in Barcelona (numbering some 496) might be classified as bureaucrats; however, they usually came from other regions and were thus hostile to the Catalan bourgeoisie, the backbone of the regionalist movement. Most of the middle class were businessmen (17,817) although there was a strong professional group, including engineers or architects (496), doctors (1,532), journalists (2,631), lawyers (1,307), and teachers (1,179).[7]

Another distinctive feature of Barcelona was that many teachers were employed by the forty-three secular schools (outside of Barcelona there were only sixty-seven lay schools in all of Spain). A small group of teachers held posts in the official high school (*instituto*) or in the University of Barcelona which, despite the prestige garnered since the mid-nineteenth century, was still a very small institution.

Far more influential in Catalan politics were the journalists.[8] Newspapers attracted bright young men who, because they lacked a university degree or could not pass rigid state examinations, could find no other professional employment.* But newspapers sold few copies, in part because the high illiteracy rate meant a small reading public. The newspapers' lack of financial independence had important consequences. In order to reduce costs, the twenty-four or so newspapers in Barcelona used coverage provided by an agency in Madrid instead of employing correspondents. Newspapers differentiated themselves on the editorial page, written by Barcelona journalists in accord with the dictates of those who subsidized the paper. Ultra-conservative Catholics read *El Correo Catalán*. Anticlericals read the old-time *La Publicidad and El Diluvio,* or Lerroux' newer *El Progreso.* Three major newspapers were written in the Catalan language: businessmen preferred the rather dull *La Veu de Catalunya,* although a large number read the more interesting, republican-oriented *El Poble Català.*

Lawyers constituted by far the most influential professional group in Barcelona. They were profitably employed in business litigation and were elected to national or local legislatures. These lawyer-politicians were articulate and efficient in defending business interests, civil and regional causes. They also protected their own professional interests; under the regionalist banner they opposed the incorporation of Catalan jurisprudence within the national civil law code.

Barcelona's middle class suffered from the rising cost of living that affected its standard of living, widened the breach between it and the upper class, and — in monetary terms, brought it closer to the workers. In the tight caste system of Barcelona, this troubled the middle class and made it wary of a political alliance with workers; its reluctance to join forces with workers became a debilitating factor in the Catalan republican movement.

Every social group organizes institutions to safeguard its interests, both economic and spiritual. During that troubled decade Barcelona's bourgeoisie put to new use institutions organized in the nineteenth century: the Athenaeum, which sponsored literary and civic programs, and the Lyceum, the stage for Catalonia's famed musical activities. In these semiprivate, municipally subsidized institutions, bourgeois politicians and intellectuals mingled socially with great industrialists and financiers, and together they formulated the program of Catalan regionalism.

Catalan businessmen had other organizations to protect their interests

* In 1912, Barcelona newspapers or publishing firms employed 2,631 individuals as writers, artists, or typesetters; in all of Spain there were only 20,516 individuals so employed ("Censo electoral de Barcelona," *Anuario estadístico de la Ciudad de Barcelona,* X [1912]).

such as the League of Industrial Defense, the Mercantile Union and — by far the most important — the Fomento del Trabajo Nacional, a euphonistic name for the powerful association of cotton industrialists who negotiated with the Restoration parties for legislative favors such as high tariffs. In any emergency, government officials summoned representatives of these organizations, as well as elected political representatives, to seek a solution. From the workers' viewpoint, the salient aspect of these organizations (and of the network of trade employers' associations) was that capital could ably defend its interests in politics and in any conflict with labor syndicates.

Industry and Labor

THE COTTON TEXTILE INDUSTRY AND THE DEPRESSION OF 1898

The Catalan economy depended upon the prosperity of the cotton textile industry, and therefore ultimately upon the policies set by a small group of entrepreneurs: the twenty to thirty families, tightly knit through inter-marriage, that controlled the production of yarn through which they had accumulated great capital during the nineteenth century. Their policies were seconded by the textile manufacturers; this was a larger group for in contrast with the concentrated production of yarn, cotton textile manufacturing was characterized by small-scale, individually or family-owned factories.[9]

More than any other segment of the national economy, Catalan industry was affected by the consequences of the War of 1898: by the loss of colonies and the depression in Spain. The reason for this profound impact is that the defeat of 1898 merely accelerated a crisis already apparent in the Catalan economy. The crisis was particularly acute in the textile industry for a complex of reasons: the high price and scarcity of raw cotton on the international market, the lack of an over-all rational organization of the industry, of modern machinery, and of skilled personnel. Manufacturers had staved off a recession only through special legislation that increased the duty on all imported textiles and exempted Catalan cloth from all duties in the Antilles.

They had also staved off a recession through rigid control of labor costs in the production of yarn, which was centered in the Ter Valley. Beginning in the 1880's, the factories where yarn was spun, doubled, and finished were moved from Barcelona to this valley where coal could be replaced with the cheap hydraulic power furnished by the Ter, Treser, and Llobregat rivers. Because of the proximity to the port of Barcelona, the cost of transporting raw cotton was negligible. Within a few years there were more factories in the area than in any other within Spain. These were the years of "cotton euphoria" when countless fortunes were amassed. Workers did not share in the profits. They lived in colonies established by employers under a special tax arrangement and were required to purchase in factory-owned stores.

This artificially stimulated "cotton euphoria" (from 1876 to 1898) had obscured the general crisis in the Catalan economy that began about 1890, the result of a failure to move from the first phase of industrialization (of individual and family units) to a second phase of highly concentrated, large-scale enterprises. Here again the causes were many: an inability to develop a metallurgical industry because of the inaccessibility of raw materials, the lack of major banking facilities, and of a foreign market.

This general crisis intensified after the War of 1898. The Spanish consuming public, at best a poor market because of the poverty of rural inhabitants, was now further restricted because of unemployment and high taxes. The loss of Cuba and of Puerto Rico, and the need to share the market in the Philippines with the United States, affected Catalonia directly: although these markets had absorbed only a small part of the total Catalan textile production, they had constituted 95 percent of the sales abroad. The loss of Catalonia's major source of foreign exchange was keenly felt because manufacturers needed to buy equipment abroad in order to modernize the industry and thereby to compete more successfully in the world market.

Textile manufacturers mobilized all forces to resolve the postwar crisis. They demanded from Conservative party Finance Minister Fernández Villaverde compensation for their losses in the form of fiscal exemptions. When rebuffed, they transferred their support to the regionalist movement. Alberto Rusiñol, a magnate of the cotton textile industry, became president of the new Catalan party, the Lliga Regionalista, which demanded from the government in Madrid administrative and fiscal autonomy for the Catalan provinces.*

On the business front, cotton manufacturers realized that to survive they must find new markets. They began a serious effort to penetrate the Near East and South America, where English merchants were entrenched, competing on the basis of an inexpensive and therefore necessarily low-grade

---

* Woolen cloth manufacturers in Catalonia stayed in the Conservative party, perhaps because they had not been so decisively affected by the postwar crisis (See Aurelio Joaniquet, *Alfonso Sala Argemí, Conde de Egara: Visión de una época. Debelación del nacionalismo catalonista. Progreso de la técnica textil* [Madrid, 1955], pp. 161–64).

fabric. The cost of imported raw cotton was beyond their control. Therefore, they concentrated on reducing labor costs through further mechanization of the industry and through imposition of new working conditions and
lower wages. Of necessity this involved breaking the force of the textile
syndicates, the key element in the Catalan labor movement. In 1901 the
manufacturers launched their attack on organized labor in the Ter Valley,
the center of yarn production. In 1902 organized labor made a desperate
effort to retaliate in a General Strike in Barcelona.

Wages and working conditions in the Ter Valley prevailed throughout
the cotton industry, a uniform scale being enforced through the manufacturers' association (Fomento del Trabajo Nacional). Therefore, in 1901,
when manufacturers decided to impose a new wage scale and to substitute
women (paid 2 pesetas a day, approximately 89 cents a day — half the wage
of a male employee) on the new electric automatic spinning machines, they
had merely to wield the powerful weapon of a lockout in the enormous
yarn-producing factories in the Ter Valley.[10] Textile unions organized a
stubborn resistance movement known as the "hunger pact"; workers suffered heavy casualties when they attacked strikebreakers, brought in from
other areas under police protection. In 1902, when the factories reopened,
employers could claim only a partial victory; the unions in the yarn factories
had been almost completely destroyed but not all men had been replaced
by women. Manufacturers now set out to augment the productive capacity
of the new machinery by maintaining an eleven- to thirteen-hour workday.
Children were extensively employed, including those under twelve years
of age, despite legislation prohibiting it.

Following the example of the yarn producers in the Ter Valley, cotton
fabric manufacturers in Barcelona and in cities throughout Catalonia attempted to impose a lower wage scale and harsher working conditions. So
did employers in other industries, confronted with the same economic crisis.
Recognizing the threat, the large and relatively well-organized labor movement of Barcelona decided to pit its strength against employers in the
General Strike of 1902.

BARCELONA'S LABOR MOVEMENT VERSUS THE LABOR FORCE

On the eve of the confrontation between capital and labor in Barcelona,
some 45,000 workers were reported to be members of labor syndicates.[11]
But even this figure (probably too high an estimate) represented less than
one third of the city's total labor force. Some of the difficulty of organizing

workers was due to the conflict among labor leaders, divided among themselves into socialists, anarchists, and pure syndicalists. The greatest difficulty was due to the composition of the Catalan labor force.

In 1905 the total number of workers employed in the industry or commerce of Barcelona was estimated to be 155,828 (a figure that excluded domestic servants, delivery boys, and day laborers). This labor force was composed of 99,190 men, 35,333 women, 13,509 boys, and 8,796 girls.[12] In order of descending importance, they worked in the textile and allied clothing industry, transportation, building construction, metallurgical and vehicle construction, and maritime enterprises. The municipal labor census provides a detailed breakdown of these categories:

Category	Total	Men	Women	Boys	Girls
Textiles and allied clothing industry	52,744	17,665	27,098	3,475	4,516
Textile production	32,265	10,200	16,868	2,831	2,376
Cotton and linen	20,741	3,808	13,219	1,924	1,800
Wool	1,855	402	1,346	37	70
Silk	1,991	262	1,325	49	355
Bleachers, dyers	7,678	5,728	978	821	151
Clothing industry	20,479	7,465	10,230	644	2,140
Transportation workers (teamsters, streetcar employees, dockworkers, etc.)	17,890	17,704	—	186	—
Construction workers	15,229	13,544	—	1,685	—
Metallurgical and transport construction workers	11,149	9,229	420	1,343	157
Metallurgical workers	8,943	7,201	420	1,165	157
Transport construction	2,206	2,028	—	178	—
Maritime employees (sailors, cooks, workers, etc.)	4,437	4,377	60	—	—

Labor organizers in each of these industries faced certain common problems. One major difficulty was the continuous influx into Barcelona of unskilled workers from rural areas. Despite unemployment and lack of housing, they continued to come, in the belief that anything was preferable to the misery of the countryside. Previous waves of rural inhabitants had been absorbed into the labor force, the more ambitious ascending to the ranks of skilled workers and some very few becoming small-scale manufacturers. But between 1900 and 1909 such a process of assimilation was difficult because of two factors. The first was that a majority of the immigrants since the 1880's had come from outside Catalonia (Aragon, Valencia, Castellón, and Teruel); they did not even speak the same language as the native Catalans, who continued to form the majority of the labor force until 1910. A far more important factor was the postwar depression that made it impossible for Catalan industry to absorb a majority of the labor force except for certain months of peak production or for certain prosperous years (such as 1905). Desperate for work, able to perform the simple tasks of a relatively primitive industry, these men and women constituted a constant source of scab labor that led to the failure of collective bargaining and peaceful strike action. Concurrently an alarming number of more skilled workers, the backbone of any labor movement, left for South America, France, and Algeria.[13]

A successful labor movement in Barcelona was synonymous with an effective organization of cotton textile employees, who constituted one third of the city's total labor force. The ideal of labor organizers was the nineteenth-century union, Las Tres Clases de Vapor, that had not only incorporated both skilled and unskilled workers from the three branches of the industry (spinners, weavers, and dyers) but had organized the unions of each city into a regional federation; the objective was to mobilize all textile workers in Catalonia through one syndicate, capable of confronting the industrialists' organization, el Fomento del Trabajo Nacional.

In the organization of textile workers, labor organizers encountered serious obstacles. Most important were the availability of scab labor and the dispersion of textile workers among 742 factories scattered throughout the urban area. Still another obstacle was the growing employment of women and children. Male bleachers and dyers organized a relatively strong union during the decade (Sociedad Obrera Ramo del Agua) but they could not hope to achieve an eight-hour day nor a wage increase until the weaving machine operators, mostly women, could be organized in a union (which was eventually formed under the name Sociedad Obrera Arte Fabril). Finally and most importantly, the strength of the textile unions in Barcelona depended upon conditions in the yarn factories in the Ter Valley.

Thus the Ter Valley lockout of 1901 decimated not only the unions of workers in the yarn factories but textile workers' syndicates throughout

Catalonia. They could no longer lead the protest against the industrialists' attempt to make labor bear the major costs of the postwar adjustment. It was the metallurgical workers of Barcelona who organized labor's last desperate protest that was, simultaneously, a defense of their right to organize and to bargain collectively.

THE GENERAL STRIKE OF 1902 AND ITS CONSEQUENCES

In the fall of 1901 the strong metallurgical workers' syndicate demanded that the workday be cut from ten to eight hours, to alleviate unemployment by providing work for more men.

Employers rejected the demand and threatened a lockout. On December 6, 1901, all metallurgical workers in Barcelona went on strike, and they stayed out during the following three months despite the absence of strike funds. Employers refused all offers to mediate, even those of municipal officials; they ignored the warning of the republican newspaper, *El Diluvio,* that if the workers were defeated, labor would interpret it as "a good indication of what it can expect from peaceful strikes." [14]

By mid-February 1902, other syndicates decided that the success of the metallurgical strike was important to the entire Catalan labor movement. Under the auspices of the recently organized municipal federation (a branch of the national labor federation organized in Madrid in 1900), a general strike was organized. Anarcho-syndicalists may have provided the doctrine and the tactics but these were effective only because violence seemed the only way to break the impasse between labor and capital.

The General Strike began on Monday morning, February 17, and lasted through Saturday, February 22nd. No program was announced, and there were no acknowledged leaders. Neither factories nor commercial establishments were attacked. As soon as owners realized that the Army could not protect them, they closed their businesses, sending workers into the streets and thereby increased the dimensions of the strike. In accord with the shibboleth of labor movements, soldiers were expected to remain faithful to their class and therefore to make common cause with workers. Instead, troops obeyed their officers' order to fire on the strikers. Some street fighting did ensue, but the strategy of military authorities was to wait for the strike to exhaust itself. On Monday, February 24, workers returned to the factories.

Although neither workers nor their syndicates had gained anything, the General Strike did constitute an impressive display of worker solidarity which, if organized, could be a major force in Barcelona society. Anarchists and socialists in one way, government and industrialists in another, reacted to this latent power. Anarchists redoubled their propaganda to convince workers that the "sole object of the general strike is the revolution." They scoffed at its use for "utilitarian or sentimental reasons," such as solidarity with striking workers, and urged Barcelona labor not to miss another opportunity to overthrow the existing regime.

To socialists, the events confirmed their official policy of rejecting the general strike as an effective labor weapon. In 1903 the National Committee of the UGT issued a manifesto pointing out the vicious circle in which the Catalan labor movement had become entangled. By acts such as the General Strike of 1902, that posed a threat to public order, the labor movement provided employers and government officials with an excuse for suspending constitutional guarantees without which syndicates could not bargain collectively. The manifesto discreetly implied that the reliance of the Barcelona labor movement upon violence created a milieu in which agent provocateurs could provoke disorder in order to justify a harsh repression.[15] The socialist analysis was substantiated by developments in Barcelona.

Employers used the General Strike of 1902 as justification for carrying through their policy of reduction of labor costs through destruction of the labor movement. A collaborator was Governor Carlos González Rothwos, appointed in 1903 by a Liberal government; on the grounds that the labor movement was a threat to public order, he closed the most important labor centers and arrested 371 "agitators."

Workers fought back. In 1903, the year following the General Strike, they staged seventy-four strikes in behalf of improved wages and working conditions, but won only six. This led to new violence during which workers killed five strikebreakers. Police fired upon them in defense of "the right to work." [16]

Apart from receiving official support, employers were well prepared to oppose workers' demands through their trade associations. During 1903 they openly organized five company unions (sindicatos amarillos*) to replace those out on strike. But the new director of the streetcar company, Mariano de Foronda, would not tolerate even this pretense at labor organization; he deliberately set out to suppress the streetcar workers' syndicate.

* In Spain as in France, both company unionists themselves as well as their opponents used the term "yellow syndicalism" to refer to their syndicates. The term originated with the yellow paper which members of a French mining company union had pasted on the windows of its offices after strikers smashed all the panes. (Val R. Lorwin, The French Labor Movement [Cambridge, Mass., 1954], p. 19.)

Both labor and management knew that control of the streetcar workers was basic to control of the Barcelona labor force. A simple streetcar strike could prevent other workers from reaching their factories. In any general strike the action of streetcar employees, in touch with workers throughout the city, was decisively important. Police charged that officials of the streetcar syndicate were revolutionaries. Yet these same officials, in 1903, led three peaceful strikes in support of such moderate demands as a request that the workday be reduced to ten hours; that drivers not be required to clean the cars in their free time; and that they be paid 5 percent interest on the mutual funds they were required to deposit with the company. None of these strikes were successful. In such an impasse, anarchist ideas found a ready audience.

Mariano de Foronda, appointed in 1904 as director of the Belgian-owned streetcar company (Compañia Anónima de Tranvías), "as amiable as he was decisive," [17] set out to control this situation by firing union members and replacing them with men brought from his native Cazorla in southern Spain. He compensated employees for the lack of a syndicate by granting them a slight salary increase, some type of health benefits, and a pension fund for accidents and old age.

In combat with employers such as Foronda, the Barcelona labor movement was finally defeated. Many syndicates dissolved or suspended activities. In 1904 there were twenty-five strikes involving 11,047 workers; in 1909 there were twenty-two strikes but only 987 individuals took part. Yet despite the obstacles, certain key syndicates maintained their organizations and even, in 1904, reorganized the municipal federation dissolved after the General Strike.[18] Though powerless to act, these organizations enabled labor leaders to maintain contact with one another.

The Church

THE CHURCH AND POLITICS

The Catholic Church might have used its great prestige in Catalan society to mediate between employers and employees. Its failure to do so was the result of many factors.

Primary among these was the hierarchy's involvement in politics in defense of Catalan regional as well as clerical interests.[19] Workers and middle-class republican politicians interpreted this as a continuation of an alliance formed during the Carlist wars when clergy fought in battle to defend

Catalan autonomy and to oppose the anticlerical measures of the Liberal government in Madrid. Late in the nineteenth century priests such as José Torras y Bages, later Bishop of Vich, modified the Church's position vis-à-vis regionalism, yet it remained basically authoritarian. Concurrently, during the Restoration, clergy established closer ties with the upper classes as part of their plan to win back groups who had profited from the sale of church lands; for workers this spelled clerical support for the economic interests of industrialists, who were also supporting regional autonomy after 1900. The alliance between industrialists and the clergy was consolidated by the anticlerical campaign; under the direction of Salvador, Cardinal Casañas, appointed Bishop of Barcelona in 1901, the Church began a vigorous political campaign in defense of religious orders and turned to regionalist politicians for support.

In accord with the instructions of the Catholic Congress in Santiago, the Cardinal announced on June 22, 1903, the formation in Barcelona of the Junta Diocesana de Defensa de los Intereses Católicos, composed of representatives from all Catholic political or civic organizations.

In December 1906, when the Catholic protest against the Liberals' Associations Bill was being organized, the Junta proved too large to be efficient. Therefore in June 1907 a permanent executive commission was appointed to act for the plenary Junta.[20]

But this organization was not conservative enough to please one group of Catholic lawyers, essentially old-time Carlists. Sometime around 1907 they organized the Comité de Defensa Social that openly advocated closing secular schools, workers' organizations, and newspapers because they constituted a threat to "religion, authority, the family, and property." Vehemently, they defended the interests of religious orders.[21]

Regular clergy found another strong ally in the revived Carlist movement. "Where the Jesuits are, there are the Carlists," a Spanish worker told an English visitor in 1909.[22] During the Restoration, Carlism had lost ground because its extreme proposals found no place in the milieu of public order and national unity created by Cánovas. After 1905 Carlism began to revive in Catalonia in response to the growing extremism of the anticlericals. Carlos VII, the pretender, and Jaime, his nephew (both of whom lived abroad), received more newspaper publicity. Youths were organized in militia and gathered in rallies (aplechs) where orators talked aggressively of replacing the liberal Bourbon monarchy with an autocratic Catholic sovereign. During election time these armed Carlist youths served a necessary strong-arm function in those unruly times, harassing anticlericals and defending the "purity" of the vote. Although the reactionary ideology of Carlists constituted a cause of some appeal in a traditional society, it was not an effective political force. At best Carlism was a rural movement with no strength in the cities, where conservative businessmen and middle-class professionals supported the new party, Lliga Regionalista.

THE CHURCH AND THE WORKER

Thus political commitments and a need to defend clerical interests prevented Cardinal Casañas from defending the interests of the workers. Between 1903 and 1907, despite the tense labor situation, the Diocesan Council organized only two workers' circles: the Jesuits administered the Centro de San Pedro Claver in Clot, while the Marists were in charge of the Centro de San José in Pueblo Nuevo.

Located in the two industrial suburbs where workers were most isolated from contact with the Church, these centers were financed by private benefactors; they offered schooling, recreational facilities, mutual benefit funds, and cooperatives. Theoretically employers and workers would meet in these centers to break down the class barrier through their common religious bond; thus religious obligations were rigorously enforced. But the privileged class refused extensive contact with, much less responsibility for, workers. And the latter considered these centers merely as agencies for recruiting scab labor, and associated them with the unpopular Marquis of Comillas (reputedly the figurehead for Jesuit investments), whose industrial empire was centered in Barcelona, and who was prominent in the national Catholic labor organization.[23]

By 1907, when syndicalists and socialists reactivated the Barcelona labor movement, the need for a change became imperative. On June 13 (five years after it had been recommended at the Catholic Congress in Santiago), Casañas announced the formation of the Diocesan Council of Catholic Labor Corporations, and of a three-man commission to act for the plenary council. One appointee was a Jesuit priest, Gabriel Palau, who had studied Catholic labor organizations in European capitals; he advocated (as did Pope Pius X) the formation of unions of Catholic workers in each industry (the exact term used by the hierarchy for these unions was unión profesional). In an attempt to circumvent the traditionalism of existing Catalan Catholic labor organizations, Father Palau organized Popular Social Action (Acción Social Popular), modeled on the German Volksverein. Late in 1907,

under its auspices, the first Catholic trade union in Spain was organized —
composed of clerks and commercial employees, it was hardly a union to affect
the fortunes of Catalan industry.[24] Most clergy and laity were indifferent or
outright opposed to Father Palau's innovations.[25]

Cardinal Casañas had thus failed either to satisfy the workers' needs or
to provide them with an effective organization to defend themselves. He
could not even meet their spiritual needs because here, as elsewhere in
Spain, there was a dearth of secular clergy.[26] The poorly paid duties of a
parish priest held little attraction, even for those with a religious vocation.
There were few students in the seminary and they were usually unable to
finance their studies; the Bishop regularly solicited funds for scholarships.
Boys who could pay for their studies entered religious orders. This meant
that Cardinal Casañas could not provide a religious ministry for the thousands of workers who lived in the Paralelo or in the industrial suburbs. The
Bishop tried to fill the vacuum by requesting religious orders of priests to
assume pastoral duties and requesting that all orders open to the public
the chapels in their convents. He also made an effort to utilize more effectively the parish priests he did have, through the Association of Ecclesiastics
for the Popular Apostolate (established in 1905), that urged priests to consider social work as part of their parish duties and provided them with instruction.

BARCELONA AND THE CONVENTS

In contrast with the secular clergy, Barcelona had a great number of
regular clergy and they were relatively prosperous. According to Luis
Morote, an anticlerical but a responsible journalist, the city had 348 convents
(as against 187 in Madrid and 153 in Valencia).[27] This may have been the
result of special legislation that favored the orders in the old Crown of
Aragon, or it may have been Barcelona's proximity to the frontier; religious fleeing from France undoubtedly settled there.* Or the explanation
for the large number of clergy may have been simply the need to live in a
metropolitan area where the clergy could more easily finance their activities.

During the Restoration, some clergy had returned to Barcelona and rebuilt their convents (burned in the riots of 1835) in the center of the city;
for example, the Franciscan teaching sisters and the Capuchin monks. The

---

* In Barcelona 206 members of male religious orders were foreign, and 879 were
Spaniards. Only 235 members of the women's orders were foreign, while 3,882 were
Spanish. (Morote, *Frailes en España*, pp. 14, 24.)

more prosperous clergy built residences in the new Ensanche district or in suburbs such as San Gervasio. The more modest orders who served the poor went to live in the industrial suburbs.

According to figures published in 1903, the functions of the various religious orders in Barcelona were as follows:[28]

Function	Male communities	Female communities
Education	41	147
Welfare	9	117
Contemplative	2	17
Priests	7	—
Missionaries	8	—

Barcelona's impressive number of welfare institutions and charity schools was financed by subsidies from the municipal government, by gifts from the laity, and by business activities. Republicans ridiculed these clerical institutions as mere "trading concerns" and proposed the alternative of secularized public institutions, a proposal they sought to implement through the regionalist movement.

The Regionalist Movement

THE LLIGA REGIONALISTA

Between 1899 and 1900 Catalan politicians tried to organize a movement independent of both the Liberal and the Conservative parties, a movement that would elect native deputies who would work in the Cortes for specific regional interests. The immediate objective was to eliminate the farce of the Restoration, the cacique-contrived elections through which two parties alternated in power. A spontaneous citizens' protest against Madrid for losing the war in 1898 and the presence of a new generation of politicians and intellectuals were potential catalysts for change. However, politicians were unable to transform this energy into an effective political movement. Catalan interests were too contradictory: an articulate and influential clergy was determined to protect its interests in opposition to the professional and commercial middle classes who wanted more jobs in public institutions for laymen and more taxes on the religious orders. Far more debilitating was the conflict between industrialists, who viewed regionalism as a means of reforming the agrarian-oriented state established by Cánovas, and the workers, forced to bear the brunt of the postwar adjustment.

Nevertheless, twice within the decade, Catalan politicians thought they had found a viable formula. Their first effort was to channel the anti-Castilian feeling into support for a new party, la Lliga Regionalista, whose moderate program of political and fiscal autonomy was prepared by Enrich Prat de la Riba. In the election of deputies in May 1901, the Lliga's four candidates were elected; all were presidents of powerful businessmen's associations, including Alberto Rusiñol of the textile manufacturers' Fomento del Trabajo Nacional. The 1901 elections definitively destroyed the Liberal and Conservative parties in Barcelona.

But popular enthusiasm for the Lliga was short-lived; in Maura's "fair elections" * two years later, the Lliga did not win even one seat. Part of the cause was that the Lliga had presented a joint slate with the newly organized Junta Diocesana de Defensa de los Intereses Católicos; this was unacceptable not only to workers but to those middle class members of the Lliga whose political and economic interests ran counter to those of the Church.

Equally important a factor was Prat de la Riba's willingness to compromise on the issue of Catalan autonomy as the result of pressure from industrialists who did not want an open break with Madrid. During these years cotton manufacturers were negotiating with the government for a new and highly protective tariff law; there was some suspicion that their support for regionalism was merely a device to force the government to grant their demands. This was the background of the apparently trivial controversy that flared up in April 1904 on the occasion of the first state visit to Barcelona by Alfonso XIII. The trip had been arranged by Maura (with the help of the Marquis of Comillas); it was intended as the first step in his campaign to win back Catalan industrialists from the regionalist movement to the Conservative party. A majority of the Lliga politicians, the idealists who demanded absolute autonomy for Catalonia, voted to boycott the visit but the young and ambitious Francisco Cambó presented a petition

---

* Antonio Maura took great pride in the fact that the elections of deputies which he directed in April 1903, as Minister of Interior in the Conservative cabinet of Francisco Silvela, were generally considered the most honest elections of the Restoration period (for a good account of his activities as Interior Minister see José María de Bedoya, *Don Antonio Maura, ministro de la Gobernación: 1902–1903* [Madrid, 1940]) The 1903 "Fair Elections" were in sharp contrast with those of April 1907, managed expertly by Interior Minister Juan de La Cierva, during Maura's second administration.

of grievances to Alfonso in the name of the Lliga, thereby recognizing the authority of the Monarchy.

The Catalan nationalists withdrew and immediately founded a newspaper, *El Poble Català;* they found it more difficult to organize a political movement because the leaders differed among themselves. Ildefonso Suñol and Jaime Carner stressed greater administrative autonomy for Catalonia. Antonio Rovira y Virgili focused on other tenets, the classic ones of Federal Republicanism such as supremacy of civil over military jurisdiction and civil rights.

But the major reason that the Catalan republican movement (which finally organized the Centre Nacionalista Republicà in 1906) did not become a major force in Catalan politics, and thus gain independence from the Lliga, was that it was afraid to organize the workers. Remembering the violence during the First Republic, middle-class politicians avoided social questions and tried to win elections on civil and political issues (opposition to Maura's Terrorism Bill or to the corporate vote in his Administrative Reform Bill). They also attacked the companies holding monopolies on municipal utilities, on the grounds that they were responsible for the high cost of urban living. However, workers failed to respond, except to the issue of anticlericalism. Claudi Ametlla recalls that 40 percent of the republican program was pure anticlericalism and that speeches on this subject were always applauded far more than any others.[29] Nevertheless, Catalan republicans did point out the complexities of the clerical issue and thus lost votes to Radical Republican Alejandro Lerroux, who claimed it was a simple matter to eliminate the clergy, the evil genius of Spain. From 1907 to 1909, clericalism would become a divisive issue in the second (and last) attempt to incorporate all Catalan interests into one political movement.

SOLIDARIDAD CATALANA

Far more vigorous and representative than the movement created in the postwar period, the new Catalan regionalist movement developed out of a series of fortuitous circumstances touched off by the electoral victories of the Lliga party in the fall of 1905. In the city of Barcelona twelve Lliga candidates were elected to the city council (one hundred Lliga candidates were elected to city councils throughout the four Catalan provinces) and a total of seven Lliga candidates won election to the Congress of Deputies from the Catalan provinces. This was the Lliga's greatest electoral victory and won despite the fact that the elections were managed by the Liberal party, hostile to the regionalist movement. The Lliga considered it a triumph not only against the Liberals and their Radical Republican allies, but against army officers who had opposed regionalist aspirations. The Catalan humor magazine, *Cu-Cut,* printed a cartoon that bragged of the Lliga victory and taunted the Army for its defeat in war. In reply, on November 24, 1905, a group of approximately 250 officers burned the offices of the *Cu-Cut* magazine and of the daily newspaper, *La Veu de Catalunya.* The Governor of Barcelona, a Liberal party appointee, made an appearance during the attacks to show approval of the officers' action.[30]

In Madrid, officers supported their colleagues in Barcelona and demanded from the Liberal government a law that would grant their tribunals the jurisdiction over all cases involving any offense to the nation as well as to the Army. Segismundo Moret, head of the government, announced his loyalty to the principle of "the supremacy of civil power above all others," but the pressures from army officers for a law to avenge their honor forced him to reverse himself. In January 1906 Moret presented to the Cortes the famous Bill of Jurisdictions.

Catalan politicians immediately organized a protest. In a giant rally held in Gerona in February 1906, representatives of all Catalan parties formed a bloc, Solidaridad Catalana, to direct a propaganda campaign designed to prevent passage of the bill; only the Radical Republican party, led by Alejandro Lerroux, refused to join. One month after the Gerona rally (on March 20, 1906), the Bill of Jurisdictions was enacted into law.*

Solidaridad Catalana did not dissolve and one year later, in March 1907, it reorganized as an electoral coalition and presented a single slate of candidates in the election of deputies throughout the four Catalan provinces, in order to capture the entire regional representation. Although they insisted upon repeal of the Law of Jurisdictions, their political ambitions went far beyond this goal; they wanted to defend Catalan interests in Madrid and to enact a new national reform program. Enrich Prat de la Riba wrote the platform (*el Programa de Tivoli*) that demanded recognition of the "regional personality" of Catalonia through certain specific measures: the creation of a new regional government, financed by its own fiscal system, with jurisdiction over the four Catalan provinces in matters of public works, social wel-

---

* Three days after the King signed the Law of Jurisdictions the Cortes passed a new tariff law that was extremely favorable to textiles. The coincidence suggests some type of political deal whereby Catalan industrialists were persuaded to accept the Law of Jurisdictions.

fare, and education. Municipal governments were also to be given new and more significant powers.

This program purposely stressed the mechanics of local government and did not specify doctrine or detailed proposals. This was necessary in order to secure support from the completely disparate political groups within Solidaridad Catalana, united only in loyalty to the region and opposition to military intervention in government. Nicolás Salmerón, one of the Presidents of the First Republic, presided over the bloc; in a dramatic gesture he embraced the Carlist leader, the Duke of Solferino, to mark a symbolic end to the nineteenth-century wars between republicans and Carlists. But this did not resolve the conflict between these groups, which were divided not only by ideas but by the interests of their party members — the middle-class professionals and merchants who supported Salmerón found little in common with the conservative, rural followers of the Carlist Duke of Solferino.

The Lliga Regionalista was at the center of the bloc, between the extremes of Carlists and republicans. The powerful business interests of the Lliga were skillfully deployed by the most adept politicians in Solidaridad Catalana; Prat de la Riba stayed in Barcelona while Francisco Cambó went to the Cortes in Madrid.

Grouped around the center Lliga were the various republican groups. On the slate, Republican Nationalists were represented by Ildefonso Suñol and Jaime Carner. The small group of Federalist Republicans sent to Madrid the elderly José María Vallés y Ribot.

Solidaridad Catalana won forty-one of the forty-four deputy seats for the Catalan provinces in the elections of April 1907. These elections were remarkably honest, in contrast with the blatant maneuvering in other regions under the direction of the Conservative Minister of the Interior, Juan de La Cierva. The popular enthusiasm which swept the coalition into office came from a deep sense of regional loyalty that temporarily outweighed ideological and social differences, based on a conviction that Catalan cultural and economic needs were different from those of the nation at large and must be vigorously defended. In terms of national politics, Solidaridad Catalana represented a breakthrough in the effort to end the artificial representative system of the Restoration.

As soon as the deputies had taken their seats in the Cortes and had finished the initial round of oratory in defense of Catalonia, they began to work on specific legislation. Differences glossed over in elections now reappeared and intensified. The two issues that divided and finally destroyed Solidaridad Catalana were clericalism and Maura's Administrative Reform Bill.

The reformation of Solidaridad Catalana had, unfortunately, coincided with the national crisis occasioned by the new anticlerical Associations Bill. Politicians had agreed not to discuss the issue during the elections, and in return the Church endorsed the entire bloc. The fact that anticlericalism was not a major issue in Maura's Cortes covered over the deep divisions within the bloc. While Carlists absolutely defended the religious orders, the Lliga was eager to avoid the issue; publicly committed by the votes of the Catholic middle classes, Lliga politicians were sensitive to industrialists who resented clerical business activities. Republicans suffered from this enforced silence, for Lerroux denounced them for allying with Carlists and abandoning their most cherished principles of liberalism and anticlericalism.

Republican politicians suffered a new blow to their pride when Maura began an open courtship of the Lliga through its ambitious leader, Francisco Cambó. In October 1907 Ildefonso Suñol left Madrid with the angry comment that "I have made a fool of myself, intervening in the Maura-Cambó duet, which is the only duet now being sung." [31] Suñol was talking not only of a personal affront but of the realization that national politicians were interested solely in the Lliga, and that they dismissed Catalan republicans in the belief that they represented neither a great electoral force nor a major economic interest. In the following months republicans sought to recoup some of their lost popular support in Catalonia by attacking Maura's Administrative Reform Bill, seeking to rally worker support with their cry of "one man, one vote" in opposition to Maura's provision of a corporate vote. The idealistic Amadeo Hurtado sadly reported that workers were not interested in the issue.[32]

Although Solidaridad Catalana never formally dissolved, its effective collective action ended with the death in 1908 of Nicolás Salmerón, the only individual capable of holding the bloc together. In the by-elections of December 1908, member parties presented independent candidates.

Throughout this decade, 1900 to 1910, the worker in Catalonia had no institution through which to seek redress of grievances. Solidaridad Catalana had not even promised to present his demands for higher wages and job security, both because these ran counter to the industrialists of the Lliga and because middle-class Catalan republicans feared such campaigning might invoke new violence. The worker had no effective labor movement, for the repression that followed the General Strike of 1902 decimated the syndicates and federations built up during the nineteenth century in the face of police repression and employer intransigence.

Thus the realities of the situation, as much as his touted independence of temperament, made the worker in Catalonia vulnerable to revolutionary doctrines. By historic accident, perhaps by design, he had a number of ideologies among which to choose: anarchist terrorism, anarcho-syndicalism, libertarian education, and — most attractive of all — Lerroux's Radical Republican party.

CHAPTER V

Personalities and Forces for Revolution

IN 1901 Francisco Ferrer and Alejandro Lerroux appeared in Barcelona and began to prepare workers for an eventual revolution. They had collaborated for a decade in the Progressive Republican party, Ferrer in Paris as Ruíz Zorilla's close associate[1] and Lerroux from his newspaper in Madrid.[2] Both men had become disillusioned with Spanish republicanism, enervated by Cánovas' policy of "attraction" and by an endless quarrel over a federal versus a centralized republic.

Within a few years they could marshal all potentially revolutionary forces in Catalonia. Lerroux built a party of petite bourgeoisie and of workers; he also contacted army officers and thus revived the tradition of military republicanism cultivated by Ruíz Zorilla. Concurrently, Ferrer established a school and a textbook publishing firm designed to promote libertarian education. He maintained contact with the traditional anarchist movement but was far more interested in the new French-inspired anarcho-syndicalism, particularly after 1907 when syndicates began to form municipal and regional confederations.

Lerroux and Ferrer directed all these forces against the clergy (whom they personalized as the "Jesuits"), because they considered them the major obstacle to progress. Lerroux told workers that if they wanted schools, they must "demolish the Church, or just close it, or at the least reduce it to an inferior position."[3] These qualifying remarks characterized Lerroux's opportunistic politics and distinguished him from Ferrer, the doctrinaire anticleric, who spared neither expense nor effort in attacking the clergy whom he considered the evil genius of Spain.

Alejandro Lerroux and the Radical Republican Party

From their first meeting in 1892, Ferrer considered Lerroux the only republican able to rally both military and worker groups for a revolution.[4] Both men agreed with Ruíz Zorilla that army support was decisive, a position that separated them from the mainstream of Spanish republicanism and its cardinal principle of the supremacy of civil jurisdiction. Lerroux, the son of an army officer and himself a frustrated aspirant to the military academy in Toledo, openly courted army officers. Undoubtedly his masonic membership served as another means of contacting officers sympathetic to his ideas. However Lerroux, like Ferrer, realized that in order to establish a republic in the twentieth century, a military pronunciamiento would not suffice.

Indeed the conviction that the Progressive Republican party desperately needed the support of an organized working class was the basis for the initial collaboration of Lerroux and Ferrer. Throughout the 1890's they tried to attract workers by changing the Party's emphasis from political to social revolution; but their party proved an inefficient vehicle for any revolutionary action, especially after it was split into two factions at the death of Ruíz Zorilla in 1895. For Ferrer, as for Lerroux, the events of 1899 dissipated the last vestiges of the nineteenth-century republican myth of a spontaneous revolution by the masses. Despite the opposition to the Bourbon Monarchy for its role in the disastrous war of 1898, a republican revolution did not occur. A drastic change in republican tactics was necessary in order to gain mass support. From Paris, Ferrer wrote to Lerroux suggesting that he seize control of the Progressive Republican party. But Lerroux replied that an entirely new program of action and ideals was necessary and went on to outline the program that he was, in fact, to pursue during the following ten years.[5]

What is necessary is to carry out propaganda campaigns on one pretext or another, in the city rather than in the country; to organize committees or commissions, societies or juntas, depending on the individual case; and to maintain contact among all of these, to have ready a kind of tacit federation, with no written pact, of all revolutionary forces. And one day, taking advantage of some occasion, in one way or another, to [revolt in] the street.

Even as he wrote the letter, Lerroux had begun to put his program into effect. By participating in the protest against the brutality and dubious legality of the Montjuich trials in 1897, Lerroux gained access to the Catalan labor force. His fiery editorials and speeches earned him a short jail term and the fervent gratitude of workers.

Thus in 1901 soon after the formation of the Lliga Regionalista, when the disorganized republican parties in Barcelona sought a candidate who might successfully oppose the powerful Lliga candidates, it seemed natural to select the 37-year-old Lerroux. With good grace or bad, Catalan republican politicians agreed to support his candidacy. So did Segismundo Moret who was directing the elections for the Liberal party; viewing Lerroux as a means of frustrating Catalan regionalism, Moret supported him generously from the secret funds of the Ministry of the Interior.[6] Lerroux was elected deputy on May 19, 1901, with a popular vote of 6,000. In Maura's "fair elections" of 1903, conducted under Conservative party auspices, Lerroux was re-elected deputy by a vote of 35,000, while the Lliga did not win even one seat. The remarkable expansion of popular support was due in large part to the fact that Lerroux had consolidated his personal victory by organizing a new party — the Radical Republicans, a strong force not only in Barcelona but in industrial cities throughout Catalonia.

THE LERROUXISTA PARTY MACHINERY

The causes that Lerroux proclaimed were anticlericalism and a defense of Spanish honor against unpatriotic regionalists who, under the guidance of religious orders, were plotting to overthrow the Bourbon monarch and install an autocratic regime.[7] These issues enabled him to appeal not only to workers and petite bourgeoisie from other regions resident in Catalan centers who resented Catalan nationalism, but also to natives whose hatred of the clergy outweighed regional loyalty. To the workers, constituting two thirds of the party membership,[8] Lerroux talked of a future "social revolution," urging them to abandon syndicates and collective bargaining as useless instruments.

Lerroux was a master of propaganda media. Long years as a journalist enabled him to write effective editorials in the Radicals' daily newspaper, *El Progreso*. Yet Lerroux knew that a predominantly illiterate population was primarily dependent upon oral communication. In the era before the radio, the rally was the principal means of organizing public opinion as well as offering workers a source of recreation. A dramatic orator and a flamboyant personality, Lerroux organized impressive rallies; in warm weather he took the crowd to the country for his famous picnics (*meriendas*).

As the Radical party grew, it acquired a platoon of semiprofessional speakers. Some were workers with natural oratorical skills, like José Matemala. Others were lower-middle-class lawyers, university graduates with a grievance, such as the Ulled brothers or journalists like "Pierre" (Domingo Gaspar).

Rallies, however, required big auditoriums or public fields. In the long run it was the republican center, located in each neighborhood, that served as the principal means of communication with the worker. When Lerroux arrived in 1901, there were only ten centers in Barcelona belonging to any republican party and only one hundred in all Catalonia.[9] By 1909 the Radicals alone had more than fifty centers in Barcelona alone. In some cases the "center" consisted solely of a bar which the owner, for business reasons, was willing to allow the political group to use as a meeting place. With time, the Radical party added additional services such as inexpensive theatrical productions; cooperatives where food was sold at reduced costs; mutual benefit funds for illness and old age; and day and evening classes for workers and their children.

Late in 1904, after a trip to Brussels, Lerroux placed the first stone of a big building in the prosperous Ensanche district which he called the Casa del Pueblo in imitation of the Belgian socialist center he had visited.* Inaugurated in 1906, the Casa del Pueblo was a source of enormous pride to Barcelona workers.

The Casa del Pueblo and the centers also served to assure electoral victories for Lerroux by registering voters and seeing that they turned out on election day.** According to the electoral census of 1907, there were 129,362 registered voters (approximately one fifth of the city's population). Lerroux's Radical Republicans mustered a maximum vote of between 30,000 and 35,000. Given the fact that one third of the Radical votes came from the middle class, it is apparent that Lerroux actually recruited less than twenty-five percent of the 99,190 male workers in Barcelona (not all of whom, of course, were eligible to vote). It was a tribute to Lerroux's ability to maneuver, that under these conditions the party won elections.[10]

In recruiting workers, Lerroux secured the collaboration of one faction

---

* The socialists did not open a Casa del Pueblo in Madrid until September 28, 1907. They financed it by renting space to syndicates, most but not all of whom belonged to the UGT. (Fernando Soldevilla, *El Año político,* XIII: *1907* [Madrid, 1908], 363–64, 439.)

** For the legal conditions which a voter had to fulfill, see page 12.

of the Barcelona anarchist movement. He welcomed such ex-anarchists as Luis Bertrán who justified his defection on the grounds that he had become convinced that to make the present moment "better and more humane was perhaps more revolutionary and transforming than to carry out something for the future, for other men." [11] In Madrid, Lerroux bragged to the Cortes that his party was strengthening public order by domesticating these anarchists.[12]

But as with so much in Spain, the reality was far different from the ideal; within the Radical party these "domesticated" anarchists continued to plot a revolution. Like many other anarchists, in Spain as in France and Italy, they had become convinced that the traditional tactics of provoking a mass revolution by acts of terrorism were ineffective in the twentieth century; some members penetrated and manipulated labor movements, espousing the new principles of anarcho-syndicalism. Only in Barcelona did the anarchists find a republican party sympathetic to their ideas. They founded *El Descamisado* and *La Rebeldía,* far more extreme than the official Radical newspaper *El Progreso.* Even more significant was the control they established over the youth movement Juventud Republicana Radical (known familiarly as *Jóvenes Bárbaros*) which had branches in all worker districts of Barcelona. Composed of youths from sixteen to twenty-five years of age, the primary function of the Juventud Radical was to act as an armed militia (analogous to the function of Carlist youth groups), breaking up opposition rallies and protecting the "purity" of the vote at election time. Lerroux inflamed these "Barbarian Youths" with crude editorials such as the oft-cited "Rebeldes! Rebeldes!" published in 1906:[13]

Young barbarians of today, enter and sack the decadent and miserable civilization of this unfortunate land: destroy its temples; throw over its gods; tear off the veil of its novices, and elevate them to the category of mothers in order to invigorate the species; penetrate property registrar offices and make a bonfire of the papers so that the flame will purify the infamous social organization; enter the homes of the humble and raise legions of proletariat so that the world will tremble before its awakened youth.

Such exhortations began to embarrass Lerroux when he focused his ambitions on a national career through the republican movement in Madrid.

Lerroux had worked in Barcelona within the framework of the national republican movement, which had drawn new strength from the popular reaction to defeat in 1898. In 1903 Nicolás Salmerón had been able to revive

Unión Republicana, an electoral coalition of all republican factions in Spain (bitterly divided doctrinally into Centralists, Federalists, and Progressives) that had first been created ten years earlier. In Maura's "fair elections" of 1903, Unión Republicana won forty seats in the Cortes (twenty in Catalonia alone); Lerroux's victory in Barcelona was due in part to the national campaign of Unión Republicana. But the republicans' success in the elections did not satisfy Lerroux (at least in that stage of his political career), and so in 1904 he collaborated with Valencian republican leaders Vicente Blasco Ibañez and Rodrigo Soriano in the creation of the semiclandestine Federación Revolucionaria. Late in 1904 he accompanied Blasco Ibañez and Soriano to Paris and Brussels in a quest for arms and money. The trip was unsuccessful, largely because adverse publicity made European politicians reluctant to collaborate with them, but it did enable Lerroux to establish contact with sympathetic republican and civil rights groups in Europe.[14]

In 1906 Lerroux abandoned these revolutionary projects in favor of conventional party politics. Using as his power base the well organized Radical party in Barcelona he prepared to challenge Nicolás Salmerón's control of the national republican movement, Unión Republicana. Events in Barcelona served Lerroux's purpose. Salmerón, as a result of the crisis created by the *Cu-Cut* incident, had agreed to become the titular head of Solidaridad Catalana on the ground that military intervention in civil affairs warranted the formation of a common front of all political groups. Although he was supported by most republican politicians in Catalonia, the rank and file considered Salmerón's famous embrace of the Carlist Duke of Solferino not as a symbol of civic unity against the Army, but as a betrayal of the democratic and anticlerical principles he had always advocated. These men flocked to Lerroux's party, and in their bitter disillusion exalted the violence of the Jóvenes Bárbaros.[15]

The *Cu-Cut* incident and its consequence, the organization of Solidaridad Catalana, ended the uneasy collaboration between Lerroux and the other republican politicians in Barcelona, who had always considered him a *farsant* yet admired his political skills. Lerroux openly flaunted his support for the Army in an editorial, "El Alma en los labios"; he had not been in Barcelona the night that the *Cu-Cut* office was burned (a talent for missing such compromising situations was to mark his entire career) but if he had, Lerroux wrote in his editorial, "we would have gone — the people and I — to burn some convents, the schools of separatism." Vaguely but menacingly Lerroux added that he would have gone on to the barracks to persuade the soldiers they must fulfill their obligation "to the conscience of mankind."[16]

In June 1907 Lerroux carried his attack on Catalan regionalism, and his defense of the Army, to the national assembly of Unión Republicana. He proclaimed the need for a revolution, "but today the initiative must come from the workshop, the school, the furrow; the people must carry it out and the Army must second it." On the grounds that Salmerón had failed to carry out a revolution, Lerroux asked that he be ousted. With dignity the leader of Unión Republicana rebuked Lerroux and his opportunistic politics: "It is repugnant to evoke constantly and in vain the holy name of revolution."[17] In the ensuing vote of confidence, Salmerón received ninety-three votes as against twenty-three for Lerroux.

This defeat could be attributed partially to the fact that in the elections of April 1907 Lerroux failed to gain re-election for the first time. Maura's Conservative party had made no secret of its hopes of eliminating Lerroux from active politics. During the elections, it sought to alienate his middle-class support by describing him as a politician who condoned violence, and for this purpose it deliberately dramatized the implications of an incident in the Hostafranchs district of Barcelona, where some Radical extremists had recently shot at Salmerón and Cambó, seriously wounding the latter. The Maura government was not content with having Lerroux lose his seat in the Cortes; it wanted him to leave Spain before he could carry out his plans to organize a national Radical Republican party (announced on January 6, 1908). In February 1908 it revived an old charge against him for a seditious newspaper article; with no parliamentary immunity, Lerroux had to flee the country. Despite his absence, the Conservatives were unable to defeat the Radical party in Barcelona. In the December 1908 by-elections, Lerroux (in absentia) and two other party candidates were elected to the Cortes, while only one Solidaridad Catalana candidate (Ramón Albó, who ran as a Catholic) was elected. This was followed up in the municipal elections of May 1909 when the party won a large majority of the seats in the City Council. These triumphs demonstrated that Lerroux represented an authentic force in Catalan politics, independent of his own personality.

Lerroux's enforced absence proved to be of enormous benefit, a further tribute to his political skills. He went first to France, and then to Argentina where he collected funds from Spanish emigrees for the Radical party and also made a personal fortune through business deals. Meanwhile in Catalonia, the official policy of the Radical party — annunciated in *El Progreso* and defended in the Barcelona City Council — became more tempered, more attractive to the middle class, whose support Lerroux needed for a successful national political career. When Lerroux returned to Spain, he was able to initiate a markedly middle-class policy in the Cortes although his personal prestige as a rebel was unimpaired, at least among the masses. But his longtime collaborator Francisco Rivas recorded with regret that "Lerroux went to America one person and came back a very different one." [18]

During Lerroux's exile (February 1908 until October 1909), Juan Sol y Ortega represented the Radicals in Madrid. He was an old man, returning to politics after six years' enforced retirement; as a Restoration republican, bred to the cacique system, he saw nothing incongruous in accepting a seat in the Senate from a monarchist, the Count of Romanones. But his presence in Madrid assured a national audience for the anticlerical, anti-Catalan oratory of the Radicals.

The actual task of keeping the party going in Barcelona was performed by Emiliano Iglesias who acknowledged with some pride that workers considered him "the representative of the bourgeois policy in the party." [19] He served as editor of *El Progreso* and directed the activities of the Radical minority in the City Council. After the Radical triumph in the municipal elections of May 1909, he efficiently dispensed the all-important patronage, the cement of any party.

The direction of workers' activities was left to a fairly anonymous group of party leaders in the Casa del Pueblo, old-time republicans such as Luis Zurdo Olivares and Lorenzo Ardid. The task was an important one because, for the first time since the demise of the labor movement in 1903, Radical control over Catalan labor was being challenged. In July of 1907 labor leaders had revived the old municipal federation of all trade syndicates under the new title of Solidaridad Obrera. Radical leaders contended with anarchists, socialists, and syndicate officials for control of Solidaridad Obrera. In the fall of 1908, when the labor federation appeared well on the way to becoming an independent and effective organization, the Radical high command tried new ways of recruiting workers. It tried to organize a rival labor federation, Unión Obrera, but this was a resounding failure.[20]

Radical officials were, however, extremely successful in their campaign to incorporate into the party a large number of working class women, primarily machinery operators employed in textile factories. Emiliano Iglesias scornfully reported that he and other party intellectuals considered the women's organizations (Damas Radicales and Damas Rojas) "somewhat ridiculous." [21] But those in the Casa del Pueblo viewed the matter quite differently. Although these tough, semiliterate women could not vote, their support did assure the Radicals a hold on an important sector of the labor force that could be mobilized in an emergency. In mob action, for example, women attracted the sympathies of the general public; when placed at the head of a group, they could prevent police from firing.

Therefore, late in 1908, the Damas Radicales was expanded from its founding group in the industrial suburb of Gracia into a municipal organization. Its legal advisor was Alfredo García Magallones, a retired army officer prominent in the Radical party. But the Damas Radicales proved too conservative for those women who wanted to emphasize civil (that is anticlerical) marriages and funerals. In the spring of 1909 they organized the Damas Rojas, with headquarters in the Casa del Pueblo and a branch in the worker district of Clot. Their legal advisor was ex-anarchist Luis Bertrán.

By 1909 Lerroux and his lieutenants firmly controlled the key sectors of the industrial labor force of Catalonia. This enterprise had required not only skill but financing far beyond any that Lerroux could command through journalism or through the party. And money was important to Lerroux. One of ten children of an indigent army officer, he was a poor man who desired to live luxuriously; in later years his taste for diamonds and cars became the butt of political attacks.[22]

The question then is how Lerroux financed his political activities in Barcelona between 1901 and 1909. Funds were supplied by Liberal politician Segismundo Moret, either from the budget of the Interior Ministry (when the Liberals ran the elections) or from the party's coffers, in the hope that Lerroux would alienate workers from the Catalan regionalist movement and thereby debilitate it. According to Catalan syndicate officials, Lerroux was also financed by industrialists who hoped that workers would join his party and thus weaken the labor movement in Barcelona, the keystone of a successful labor movement in Spain.[23]

The most significant fact is that Lerroux had gained worker support by promising a "social revolution" that would, above all, involve destruction of clerical property, and that he had within the party an extremist faction that was merely biding its time for action. Despite his own ambitions for a national career, despite his own second thoughts on his work, Lerroux could not extinguish the revolutionary fervor that he had built up. In an editorial entitled "Revolución y República," Lerroux admitted that "at times men may precipitate its release but contain it, never." [24]

Francisco Ferrer and la Escuela Moderna

Ferrer shunned the limelight as assiduously as Lerroux sought it, and therefore his part in the creation of a revolutionary milieu in Barcelona is more difficult to describe. Upon his return to Barcelona from Paris in 1901, he announced that his objective was to propagate rationalist education through the establishment of a model school, la Escuela Moderna, and through a textbook publishing firm. His role as an educational reformer was suspect to government authorities, both because of Ferrer's past career and because of the cause he advocated.

In that decade of tension created by the Liberals' anticlerical campaign, any secular experimental school would have aroused opposition, particularly if it proposed, as Ferrer's did, to educate workers. Moreover, Ferrer had just returned from sixteen years' residence in Paris, and in the context of France's Third Republic rationalist education assumed another dimension: it was part of that complex of civil rights and educational reform movements that in France had not only secured anticlerical legislation but had promoted the establishment of a secular state, a campaign that led eventually to the separation of Church and state in 1905. In Spain such a campaign had revolutionary implications.

FERRER AND THE MASONS

In Spain as in France, pro-Catholic groups accused Freemasonry of being the occult force behind anticlericalism, to which Masons responded that they were simply a fraternal organization. If pressed, they would admit that during the nineteenth century Latin Freemasonry had semiofficially adopted a positivist philosophy, a naturalistic and mechanistic concept of the world, and had thereby abandoned the eighteenth-century masonic idea of a Supreme Being (still central to the ideas of the Scottish Rite).

In France during the Third Republic a group of anticlerics had worked through Freemasonry (as through many organizations) to secure laic laws; a scholarly study has detailed the way they exploited the secret, well organized masonic fraternity with its branches throughout France and con-

tacts in many intellectual circles.* By 1900 some French Masons were prepared to promote anticlerical activities in other Catholic nations; an international congress in that year was followed by another in 1902, at which
time delegates voted to set up an international bureau in Switzerland. In
1904 many of these same delegates met in Rome for an international congress of freethinkers where the delegates (including Francisco Ferrer) approved a resolution calling for the overthrow of the Catholic Bourbon
dynasty in Spain.[25] As yet there has been no historic study of whether the
Freemasons and affiliated groups were actually willing to contribute funds
to carry out such a resolution — for example, to subsidize the propaganda
work of Francisco Ferrer — and even more importantly, whether they were
willing to go to the extreme of contributing funds for a revolution.

Quite apart from any revolutionary potential, Ferrer's masonic membership, together with his close ties to the Grand Orient in Paris, made his
plans to establish a school in Spain suspect. In the Grand Orient Ferrer
had attained the rank of a Thirty-first-Degree Mason, and in its evening
classes he began his career as an educator by giving a course in Spanish.
Privately Ferrer was said to have considered the Freemasons as basically a
reactionary organization,[26] and to have found more congenial affiliated organizations such as the Free Thought Society (for which he had entered
Spain on special missions), and the League of Human Regeneration.
Through the League he met Paul Robin, the founder of rationalist education. Although he apparently never visited Robin's school at Cempuis, the
model for his own Escuela Moderna, Ferrer corresponded with Robin and
was deeply influenced by his ideas for educating boys and girls together in
a spontaneous fashion, rejecting all formal methods and doctrines.[27]

FERRER AND ANARCHISM

Ferrer's relationship with anarchists, openly acknowledged in France
but shrouded in mystery in Barcelona, is another complicating factor in the
picture of Ferrer as an educational reformer.**

In the 1890's Ferrer had contacted exiled Spanish anarchists in Paris as part

---

* Mildred J. Headings, *French Freemasonry under the Third Republic,* The Johns
Hopkins University Studies in Historical and Political Science, LXVI (Baltimore, 1948).

** The association of Ferrer, a Mason, with anarchism has a European dimension.
From the time of the First International, through the person of Michel Bakunin,
Freemasonry had maintained contact with anarchism. George Woodcock has com-
mented that this relationship deserves further study, in *Anarchism: A History of
Libertarian Ideas and Movements* (Penguin Books, 1963), p. 310.

of his and Lerroux's project to recruit workers for the Progressive Republicans. He was a delegate to the memorable congress held in London in 1896, where anarchists were definitively excluded from the Second International.[28] He was a party to anarchist discussions where arguments for the traditional agitation and terrorism by individuals lost ground to those for anarcho-syndicalism and libertarian education. Yet from the time of his return to Barcelona, Ferrer denied any association with anarchist organizations and described himself merely as an *acrata,* a philosophical anarchist.

Thus Spanish authorities viewed Ferrer's Escuela Moderna, not as an independent experimental school, but within the context of libertarian education. In Spain this tapped a wellspring of workers' enthusiasm for anarchism: Ferrer was but following in the footsteps of Elías Puig in Catalonia and José Sánchez Rosa in Andalusia, honoring the desire of Spanish workers for independent schools that, however modest they might be, would satisfy their need for dignity and for learning on their own terms.

However, this old tradition of libertarian education in Spain responding to a deep need, was offset by the European context. In France and Italy, anarchists had begun to stress the importance of the school as an agency for preparing individuals who would replace the authoritarian state with a new society. This was part of the general reorientation of anarchism which coincided with a rapprochement with the bored intellectuals of the fin du siècle, eager for a cause requiring dramatic action. In practical terms, this meant that the revolutionary implications of libertarian education were often played down in favor of an emphasis upon the need to free all men from traditional concepts of society, family, and property. Thus Ferrer's Escuela Moderna and adult education program had their counterpart in the movements centering around Luigi Fabbri's *Università Populare* journal in Italy, and Sébastien Faure's La Ruche school and Universités Populaires in France.[29] These parallels reinforced the opposition to Ferrer within Spain; to the charge that he was an anti-Catholic mason was added the more serious one that he bred sedition in his schools.

Ferrer's association with Freemasonry and anarchism prejudiced his educational endeavor in Barcelona even before he began. To counter this he could present no academic or intellectual credentials. From the diverse movements in which he had participated during his years in Paris, Ferrer had selected ideas at random but he did not reformulate them into a new ideology. He wrote only two books: a Spanish grammar textbook and a collection of essays on rationalist education that was published posthumously.[30]

The general opinion of those who worked with Ferrer was that his abilities were mediocre, but that he was passionately dedicated to a secular educational system which stressed antiauthoritarian and anticlerical ideas rather than knowledge itself.

FERRER'S CURRICULUM VITAE

Ferrer's personal life constituted still another obstacle to his acceptance in Catalan society.[31] Most obvious were his marital arrangements, a factor of significance in a traditional society where change is believed to lead inevitably to a relaxation of moral standards. Ferrer's marriage to Teresa Sanmartí, by whom he had three daughters, became so stormy that it, as well as involvement in a republican coup, caused him to flee to Paris in 1885. His wife joined him, but their quarrels grew so violent that she shot at him on the street, an incident that was publicized, discrediting him among more conservative acquaintances. His wife then formed a liaison with a Russian aristocrat and went to live in the Ukraine, while in 1899 Ferrer entered into a common-law marriage with Leopoldine Bonnard, a teacher of some renown in the Parisian free thought movement; a son, Riego, was born in 1900. Mlle. Bonnard returned with Ferrer to Barcelona and taught in the Escuela Moderna, although with time her heavy accent proved too great a handicap for her to teach.

To add to his lack of academic stature and to his marital complications, Ferrer's acquisition of wealth was open to criticism. A poorly paid railroad employee when he left Barcelona, Ferrer failed in the wine business in Paris. However he turned out to be a shrewd speculator in stocks. He acquired some capital from Leopoldine Bonnard, who deposited her fortune to their common account, but his windfall came from the legacy of an elderly Parisian spinster, Jeanne Ernestine Meunié, to whom he gave Spanish lessons. She grew fond of Ferrer and Leopoldine Bonnard, whom she believed to be legally married, and traveled with them to Italy and Barcelona. Although a practicing Catholic, Mlle. Meunié attended social functions in the masonic Grand Orient. Thus she knew of Ferrer's anticlerical ideas (if not of his anarchist associations) when she agreed to provide the collateral for the school that Ferrer proposed to establish in Barcelona. In March 1901 she died quite suddenly, leaving to Ferrer one half of her estate, consisting of bonds and a prosperous commercial property in Paris. Ferrer mortgaged this property and bought stock in the Fomento de Obras y Construcciones, S.A., the firm holding the municipal contract for public works in Barcelona.

The stock's value was increased through the award of additional contracts, a task performed by Lerroux's Radical Republican councilmen. Through clever manipulation of these stocks and a spartan simplicity in his private life, Ferrer amassed a substantial fortune, the income from which he spent on educational and labor activities. He insisted that the Meunié legacy, reportedly worth 1,300,000 francs, was his exclusive source of capital;[32] reactionary Catholic groups claimed he was heavily subsidized by Freemasonry. In either case, Ferrer was doubly dangerous, not only as a radical reformer but as a wealthy one.

Yet without his fortune, Ferrer could not even have begun a school. He wrote Odón de Buen, a professor at the University of Barcelona, to ask about requirements; de Buen replied the only thing necessary to found a school in Spain was "money, money, and money." [33]

LA ESCUELA MODERNA

On September 8, 1901, the Escuela Moderna opened its doors to a class of thirty boys and girls. The board of directors, Ferrer candidly admitted, was composed of "people with advanced ideas but not identified as members of any party . . . to defend the school from the attacks that clericals will not fail to lavish upon them." [34] Ferrer had been assured of the special protection of the Rector of the University of Barcelona,* Rodríguez Méndez.[35]

The high tuition at the Escuela Moderna excluded the workers whom Ferrer professed to educate. Although his daughter admitted this involved a certain "snobbishness," his supporters argued that workers were too deeply involved in the class struggle to be educated as teachers of rationalist principles. The Escuela Moderna was to serve as a normal school, training the middle class to educate workers; hopefully this middle-class elite would volunteer to lead the masses when the time arrived for revolutionary action.[36]

Ferrer's rationalist education enjoyed a vogue. On Sunday afternoons intellectuals came to give lectures to well-dressed audiences. During the five years of its existence, the Escuela Moderna grew steadily from the original seventy pupils to approximately 175. On October 15, 1905, Ferrer opened a branch of the Escuela Moderna in Villanueva y Geltrú, a neighboring textile-manufacturing center. Because the Liberal government in office advocated

---

* The law granted to the rector of each of the ten universities in Spain the responsibility for supervising all public and private schools in his district, and thus granted the rectors the right to determine educational policy. Rodríguez Méndez' tolerance of secular education is demonstrated in the large number of secular schools in Barcelona.

a radical anticlerical policy, Dr. Rodríguez Méndez dared to preside at the inauguration ceremony.[37]

By 1906 approximately 1,000 students in some thirty-four schools in Catalonia, together with some in Valencia and in major Andalusian cities, were directly or indirectly influenced by the Escuela Moderna and its textbooks. Many of these "schools" consisted of little more than a sparsely furnished room located in a political or labor center, and were taught by a teacher with little or no professional training. The success of such schools was a reflection of a desperate need and desire for education among workers, to which organizations of every type attempted to respond.

With Ferrer's help, Lerroux began to compete with Catholic schools by organizing inexpensive classes in the Radical centers located in each neighborhood, primarily as a means of attracting new members.[38] Political opponents charged these classes were little more than a pretext for obtaining municipal subsidies to private education, and that the money was actually spent on Radical party activities. Lerroux denied this accusation and defended his schools, claiming that they were on a par with the public schools. He defended them also in terms of a principle, of a means by which workers — free of middle-class domination — would prepare for their political responsibilities "after the revolution." Thus Radicals, like clericals, attacked the public school system in Barcelona. Ferrer considered the classes in the Radical centers a more effective means of reaching workers than the independently organized schools he had originally planned. He not only helped to appoint and instruct some of the teachers in Radical centers; his publishing firm provided cheap textbooks. As a good businessman, Ferrer made some profit, but in many cases he declined payment in order to propagate rationalist education.[39]

The high point (admittedly in poor taste) of the rationalist education movement was reached on Good Friday, April 12, 1906, when Ferrer led some 1,700 schoolchildren in a demonstration on behalf of secular education.[40]

L'AFFAIRE FERRER

Ferrer's career as an educator was cut short the following month, May 1906, when he was implicated in the attempt of Mateo Morral to assassinate Alfonso XIII. In this affair, Ferrer's personal life merged with his ideas to arouse impassioned criticism even among erstwhile supporters. Late in 1905 he had begun to live with Soledad Villafranca,* twenty-two years his junior, who was the director of elementary studies in the Escuela Moderna. A beautiful and very competent woman, she came from a family of brothers and sisters active in secular education.

Mateo Morral was also in love with Soledad Villafranca: apparently ignorant of her secret liaison with Ferrer, he was encouraged by her open flirtation. A compulsive young man, the son of a prosperous textile industrialist in Sabadell, Morral had first met Soledad when he enrolled his sister in the Escuela Moderna. In December 1905 he quarreled with his family about his radical political ideas and went to work in Ferrer's publishing firm in Barcelona. He suddenly left for Madrid on May 20, 1906, where he rented a room in a pension on the Calle Mayor. On May 31 he threw a bomb at the royal wedding party as it passed his pension and then escaped, committing suicide a few days later. Morral had reportedly been driven to this desperate act by unrequited love for Soledad Villafranca.[41]

On June 4, 1906, Ferrer was arrested. On two previous occasions police had tried to implicate Ferrer in political assassination attempts. Now they attempted to prove that Ferrer had planned the Calle Mayor attack, in conjunction with Nicolás Estévanez, the perennial conspirator and an expert in explosives, who had arrived from Paris several days before Morral left for Barcelona. Judges retained Ferrer in prison for one year while they sought evidence for these charges. On June 12, 1907, they ordered his release, admitting that they had not been able to find evidence of the link between "the teaching and publicizing of a baneful doctrine . . . and its natural and terrible consequences in the present case." [42]

A major cause for Ferrer's release was the publicity abroad, fomented by such organizations as the International Federation of Free Thought and the League of the Rights of Man, that presented their fellow member as a martyr in "la Espagne inquisitorial" for the cause of secular education. "From a *self made* [sic] man of culture," wrote Ferrer's daughter, he had become "the great Vedette of the avant garde." [43]

But to his anarchist supporters, Ferrer's release was a disappointment. Pío Baroja, the Spanish writer, was in London at the time, visiting anar-

* This occasioned a separation, apparently amicable, from Leopoldine Bonnard, who had just returned from lecturing in Holland on rationalist education, under the sponsorship of the famous anarchist, Domela Nieuwenhuis. She continued to live with their son on Ferrer's farm until she testified on his behalf in 1906 and then went to London to live.

chists Errico Malatesta of Italy and Fernando Tarrida del Marmol, a Spaniard who had lived abroad since the time of the Montjuich trials. Pío Baroja reported:

We talked of Spain. Malatesta had just learned that Ferrer had been absolved and said, with a certain air of sadness, "That's a fine turn of affairs. I don't know what I'm going to do now, after having prepared a protest movement." "In all truthfulness," murmured Tarrida, "that absolution represents a failure for you. There's nothing to do but to see if we can't have him stuck back in jail." [44]

In Spain, there was no pro-Ferrer campaign. Anarchists suspected that through Soledad Villafranca, Ferrer had used Mateo Morral. Republican politicians did not try to convert this into an "affaire Dreyfus," in part because Ferrer had refused to collaborate with them on the grounds that he had given up politics, in part because they considered him guilty.[45] Ferrer's only support came from Alejandro Lerroux, from Emiliano Iglesias who served as his lawyer, and from Rodrigo Soriano's republican newspaper in Madrid, *España Nueva*.[46]

Spanish educators remained aloof. Although abroad Ferrer claimed that the Escuela Moderna and the Institución Libre jointly defended the cause of secular education, there was actually no contact between them. Ferrer disdained the Institución as an instrument of "the right and the aristocracy," while the Institucionistas considered Ferrer an agitator who was exploiting the cause of education.[47]

FERRER'S ACTIVITIES FROM 1907 TO 1909

As a means of protecting his work in Spain, Ferrer and Soledad Villafranca left on July 22, 1907 (one month after his release from prison) to visit European capitals and to project the image of himself as a victim of the "Jesuits" in the cause of secular education. Although quite willing to exploit Ferrer's case for domestic politics, European politicians would not entertain him personally. Aristide Briand, an old acquaintance, urged him to leave Paris, and Terwagne and Paul Gilles in Brussels were similarly unreceptive.[48] However, during his frequent trips in the following two years, Europe's left wing leaders did meet privately with Ferrer.

One project that Ferrer carried out was the reorganization of the Catalan masonic organization. Because he considered the Spanish Grand Orient in Madrid and its Master, Miguel Morayta, too conservative, Ferrer had long tried to bring the Catalan Grand Lodge under the doctrinal and administrative jurisdiction of the French Grand Orient. After his release from prison, he decided that this purpose would be best served by forming a new masonic entity; in 1908, together with certain Radical politicians, he founded a new lodge, Los Siete Amigos, with headquarters in the Casa del Pueblo.[49]

Ostensibly, Ferrer concentrated during these two years on promoting rationalist education in Europe. On April 15, 1908 he began publication (first in Brussels and then from January 23, 1909, in Paris) of a magazine entitled *L'Ecole Renovée* that was to serve as a medium of communication among European educators; Ferrer paid for articles published here and in his *Boletín de la Escuela Moderna de Barcelona,* one way of securing the collaboration of intellectuals abroad. Concurrently, he organized the International League for the Rational Education of Children. Anatole France was honorary president of a board of directors that constituted a roster of the most progressive educators of Europe.

But in Barcelona Ferrer's educational movement lagged. He did not reopen the Escuela Moderna, closed at the time of his arrest. Rationalist education was carried on in a new school entitled Colegio de la Place, directed by José Casasola who had been a professor in the Escuela Moderna. With the help of the Rector of the University of Barcelona, Rodríguez Méndez, Ferrer reopened his publishing firm, which he named Publicaciones de la Escuela Moderna. He contracted writers for new textbooks and added a series of translations of writings by radical European authors. But Ferrer was unable to renew his contacts with Catalan educators. The Barcelona Branch of the League for Rationalist Education was not organized until February 1909 and then it included only Ferrer's relatives and close associates. The independent rationalist schools, ill-equipped and staffed by barely literate teachers, fared badly; in March 1909 four schools closed because of the competition offered by public schools.[50]

Ferrer's only hope for continuing his work was through the classes operated in Radical centers. The Casa del Pueblo now had a school with three teachers and one hundred pupils who studied in modern, well-equipped rooms. Ferrer expected to be appointed director of this school, but he was disillusioned, for during his imprisonment Radicals had preempted the cause of rationalist education and had modified it to fit the new moderate orientation of the party. They were reluctant, however, to use the term "rationalist education" because the ambiance was such that even moderate educational reform programs were defeated.* Ferrer was restricted to an occasional visit to schools in the Casa del Pueblo or in other Radical centers.[51]

THE SHIFT TO ANARCHO-SYNDICALISM

As early as the fall of 1907, Ferrer realized that the notoriety of his trial had cut him off from any hope he had seriously entertained of influencing secular education in Spain and that it was now impossible for the Radical party to collaborate openly with him. In part because of this isolation, in larger part because of his old enthusiasm for anarcho-syndicalism, Ferrer increasingly turned his attention to the reorganized Catalan labor movement. Ferrer had been in Europe when the syndicates of Barcelona had revived their municipal federation under the name Solidaridad Obrera.

Despite the conservative orientation of the Maura government in Madrid, the official attitude in Barcelona was one of tolerance for labor organizations. The individual responsible for this policy was Governor Angel Ossorio y Gallardo.

* The prime example was the defeat in the spring of 1908 of the Special Budget for Culture, whereby the Barcelona city government would have sponsored a fine experiment in primary education. The Council voted the budget, but the mayor vetoed it after Cardinal Casañas issued a pastoral letter condemning the project because it provided for coeducation and did not require attendance at religious classes. A Catholic publicist denounced the budget "as one more artifice of the very devil himself, represented by Masonry." (Joseph de Peray March, *Barcelona en 1908: Nueve impresiones* [Barcelona, 1909], p. 19.)

CHAPTER VI

The Governor and the Terrorists

THE personality of Angel Ossorio y Gallardo,[1] whom Maura chose to represent his government in the sensitive post of governor of the province of Barcelona, turned out to be an enormously complicating factor both in the politics of Catalonia, and in the relations between labor and management.

Ossorio owed his appointment to an intimate friend, Gabriel Maura y Gamazo, the son and political secretary of the Premier. He was only thirty-six years of age when he arrived in Barcelona to take up the duties of this, his first public office, and was confronted with problems that would have frustrated a far more seasoned politician. The most pressing task was to end the mysterious bomb explosions that had increased in number each year since 1902. The second was to facilitate the rapprochement of Maura and the Lliga, composed primarily of textile industrialists, and to do so at a time when the Catalan labor movement was recovering from the harsh repression that followed the General Strike of 1902. In dealing with these problems, Ossorio was caught between his ambition to advance his political career and his sincere respect for the rights of labor.

The political expectations of this energetic, intelligent young lawyer were enhanced by his privilege of communicating directly with Antonio Maura, bypassing and thus antagonizing his immediate superior, Juan de La Cierva, who was Minister of the Interior. La Cierva complained bitterly that his authority extended only to 48 of the 49 governors — for all practical purposes, Ossorio as Governor of Barcelona, acted as a "Viceroy."[2] To a large extent the feud between the rather pompous Minister of the Interior and the cocky young governor was due to a personal antagonism. But it was also a reflection of the significant, albeit latent, animosity that still existed between the

"Old Guard" of the Party (that is, those who had supported Fernández Villaverde) and the small group of Maura's collaborators.

The appointment of "Old Guard" member La Cierva to an important post was an obvious bid by Maura for party harmony. During the Maura biennium, La Cierva proved himself to be an autocratic and ultraconservative administrator, with a passion for public order that discounted any political expediency. Therefore he gave Ossorio unlimited support in the search for terrorists, from an enlarged police force to money from his ministry's secret funds; he even defended Ossorio's actions in the Cortes. But La Cierva was always conscious of the fact that Ossorio wanted his job, and he carefully watched for an occasion on which he could assert his authority over the young man.[3]

Aside from his political ambitions, Ossorio was committed to a certain plan of action by the reputation he had established as a lawyer in Madrid, where he had defended socialists in several key cases. Through his work in the Institute of Social Reforms, he had acquired a good knowledge of the labor situation. During his years as Governor, he visited factories where he investigated working conditions and then reported them in pamphlets, published at government expense, which criticized employers as well as government inspectors for failing to enforce the law.[4] Nevertheless, Ossorio was obligated by the policies of the Maura regime to collaborate with the manufacturers of the Lliga, particularly on such important matters as the bomb explosions.

The Problem of the Bombs

The mysterious bomb explosions constituted the most controversial issue in Barcelona politics, reviving the image of a lawless city that had first been created thirty years earlier. The explosions of the late nineteenth century had been directed by anarchist terrorists against the wealthy or against those in authority, but the bombings that began anew in 1902 had no apparent political purpose: they were set off in the streets of the poorest neighborhoods at odd hours, as though every effort were being made to protect human life.

Catalan politicians, deeply concerned by this problem, used provincial and municipal funds to set up an Office of Special Investigation and hired a Scotland Yard detective Charles Arrow to direct the investigation. In an article published in England, Arrow reported that, appearances to the con trary, a citizen was safer on the streets of Barcelona than on those of Paris or London.[5] The detective's investigation led to no convictions, however, and his assertions did nothing to dispel the ugly air of suspicion created in Barcelona.

There was ominous talk of the anarchist menace to society that lay behind the bombs. But the depleted anarchist ranks could cause little concern to anyone who took the trouble to investigate. By 1907 most of the activists (and workers in general) had abandoned anarchism for the Radical party, or they had become anarcho-syndicalists and were trying to penetrate the executive secretariat of the newly created labor federation, Solidaridad Obrera.

The financial plight of the remaining anarchist elite was precarious. Until 1908 it maintained a headquarters (Centro de Estudios Sociales) largely through a subsidy from Francisco Ferrer.[6] When forced to close for lack of funds, the anarchists used the offices of their newspaper, *Tierra y Libertad;* editors Juan Basón and Francisco Cardenal provided the small amount of direction that anarchists required.[7] Members of this group were regularly imprisoned for the bomb explosions and it is to be assumed that they were guilty of at least some of the incidents. For dedicated anarchists (such as the members of the "Grupo 4 de mayo") terrorism was necessary, for it demoralized the leaders of the existing social order and inspired the oppressed, specifically the workers, to revolt. To such activists, wage negotiations and social legislation only domesticated workers and postponed the revolution. Therefore, on the premise that the immediate end served by terrorism was immaterial, impoverished anarchists may have accepted fees from groups interested in provoking disorder for whatever cause. The suspicion that anarchists served the authorities as agents provocateurs disillusioned many workers and served to diminish the group's support still further.

In this context, the issue of the bombs took on a metaphysical quality as politicians discussed the "moral authors" of the bombings — that is, those responsible for inspiring, or for hiring, the terrorist who set the bombs.[8] Groups such as the Comité de Defensa Social, composed of ultraconservative Catholic lawyers, argued that the responsibility belonged to "anarchist" labor leaders, and to secular educators who failed to teach a respect for authority; therefore lay schools and unions should be closed as centers of terrorist sedition.[9]

To these charges, various republican groups replied that the bombs constituted "industrial terrorism," paid for by manufacturers eager to defame the labor movement and to justify the arrest of union officials.[10] Catalan politicians charged that certain Liberal politicians, working within the Radical party, subsidized terrorism in order to malign the regionalist movement.[11] The Radicals asserted that terrorism was paid for by the religious orders in order to provoke a revolt that would justify a harsh repression; bolder party orators went so far as to charge that the bombs were prepared in convents for a future Carlist rising.[12]

By exploiting the issue in this way, Catalan groups increased the importance of the bombs and encouraged the image of lawlessness against which they protested as loyal regionalists. Their efforts to solve the mystery were singularly ineffective. In the City Council sessions, Radicals charged the sole function of Charles Arrow's Office of Special Investigation was not to detect and convict bomb terrorists, but to arrest labor leaders.

Concurrently, and completely independently, Governor Ossorio ordered the arrest and conviction of a group of professional terrorists led by Juan Rull, who had served as an informant to three governors (including Ossorio). Rull, his brothers, and his mother had been preparing explosives for years, collecting from police for information on bombs they set. But in the Rull case, which dominated Barcelona politics for more than a year (from Rull's arrest in July 1907 until his execution in August 1908), government prosecutors tried to prove Rull had also been collaborating with Radical party conspirators all the time. Radicals refuted these charges with the aid of Police Inspector León Tressols, an astute and experienced detective who had been forced to resign and leave Barcelona because he knew too much about the Rull affair. The Radicals accumulated impressive evidence to prove their claim that Rull's terrorism was subsidized by Catalan and clerical politicians such as Eusebio Güell. As for Juan Rull himself, he went to his death without disclosing who, besides the police, had paid him.[13] On the day that he was executed, August 8, 1908, a bomb exploded on a main boulevard; police found a message announcing that Rull was innocent and that bombs would continue to explode.[14]

The Consequences of the Bomb Explosions

Despite the energy and funds expended on the project, Governor Ossorio did not solve the mystery of the bombs. During his two and one half years in office, thirty-one explosives and ten Orsini bombs went off in the streets; five persons were killed and twenty-seven injured.[15] And this despite the fact that by the spring of 1909 Ossorio had at his command a police force of 7,224 persons, maintained at an annual cost of 850,000 pesetas.[16] His action had been erratic, largely because he acted impetuously on each report from police informants. First he urged Maura to secure new legislation against terrorists, and then he abruptly persuaded him to withdraw when the protest began. Ossorio's failures made it highly improbable that he would advance to the post of Minister of the Interior: La Cierva's position seemed secure. The smoldering feud between these men and, even more importantly, Ossorio's desire to erase any impression of administrative incompetency by acting quickly and brutally, would constitute important causative factors in the events of July 1909.

Of equal import was the fact that the failure to stop the bombs contributed to the tension, to the sensation of an impossible impasse in all the fine civic reform movements launched two years earlier by Maura in Madrid and by Solidaridad Catalana in Barcelona.

This was reflected in a loss of momentum within Solidaridad Obrera, the labor federation. Ossorio had protected it by refusing to use the terrorist threat as a pretext for suppressing the labor movement (as previous governors had done). But this would not suffice. An active gubernatorial policy of conciliation and arbitration would have encouraged workers to concentrate on negotiated wage agreements and enforcement of factory legislation as effective means of redressing their grievances. The Governor's inability to execute such a policy, because of Maura's commitment to the Lliga, constituted one more factor in the eventual triumph of the revolutionary element within the labor movement.

CHAPTER VII

The Struggle for the Masses

The Syndicalists: Solidaridad Obrera

"INSPIRED exclusively, egotistically, by the interests of labor,"[1] offi
cials of Barcelona trade unions (or syndicates, as they were now called'
revived their municipal federation under the new name of Solidaridac
Obrera (obviously in imitation of Solidaridad Catalana, the political coali
tion).* Labor leaders acted because of the change in the Catalan economy
industry had emerged from the crisis of the postwar years and faced a rela
tively secure future under the protection of the new high tariff law. I
workers were to share in the profits they needed a strong organization t
negotiate for them. Individual syndicates would not suffice, even if the
had a national organization to back them (as did the metallurgical worker
and the typesetters). Therefore labor officials resorted to the strategy formu
lated forty years earlier of working through a federation composed of a
syndicates in Barcelona: the objective was to assure collective assistance, pe
haps even financial aid during a strike, in support of the demands of an
one group of workers.[2] The textile workers constituted a critical concer
for they had not been able to rebuild their strong syndicate, which had bee
destroyed in the Ter Valley lockout five years earlier. As the largest grou
in the labor force, their reincorporation into the labor movement would n

* The federation of Barcelona trade syndicates that had been organized in 1900 und
the name Unión Local de Sociedades Obreras had disbanded after the General Stri
of 1902. In 1904 it was reorganized but served primarily to maintain contact amor
syndicate officials. (Miguel Sastre y Sanna, *Las Huelgas en Barcelona y sus resultad
durante el año 1904* [Barcelona, 1905], p. 77; *Huelgas de 1905* [Barcelona, 1906], p. 5
Huelgas de 1906 [Barcelona, 1907], p. 93; and *Huelgas de 1909* [Barcelona, 1911
p. 22.) See also letter from socialist Arturo Gas in *El Socialista* (Madrid), March
1909.

only determine the success or failure of the new federation but the ability of any sector of workers to secure higher wages or a shorter working day.

To create an élan, labor leaders began to talk of a fight by workers and for workers. They specifically rejected "the tutelage of any political party, or of either of the two branches of socialism" and proposed instead to concentrate "exclusively on the class struggle" and to use the member unions "as schools of training for the struggle." [3] By describing their program as "the purest syndicalism," the organizers of Solidaridad Obrera acknowledged their debt to the ideas set forth in the eloquent *Carte d'Amiens* of the Confédération Generale du Travail, published just one year previously (1906); the *Carte* had proclaimed the independence of the French labor movement from all doctrines (including anarchism), and its dedication to economic warfare. Catalan labor leaders had been in contact with French CGT officials, but this was not the only reason they accepted syndicalism. Their traditional municipal federations of syndicates were analogous to the French Bourses du Travail, while the CGT's apolitical doctrine of direct economic action, resorting to violence when necessary, was similar to the ideas that had permeated the Catalan labor movement since the middle of the nineteenth century.

This was the context of events and ideas in which officials of Barcelona's key unions gathered in early June 1907 in the offices of the store clerks' union, Dependencia Mercantil, to reorganize the municipal labor federation. The commission included representatives of the metallurgical workers, typesetters, painters, bakers, and store clerks — the unions that had borne the brunt of labor's defense since the demise of the textile workers' syndicate.

On August 3, 1907, following a lengthy and turbulent meeting of union officials, the establishment of Solidaridad Obrera was formally announced in a manifesto that pleaded for worker solidarity, free of all political obligations, "for a direct march along the path of our social emancipation." [4] The manifesto was signed by representatives of thirty-five of the seventy unions in Barcelona. Solidaridad Obrera immediately launched a campaign against an employer who symbolized resistance to organized labor: Mariano de Foronda, director of the Belgian-owned streetcar company, whose employees had no organization (not even a company union) and who were among the poorest paid workers in Barcelona.

In the organization of Solidaridad Obrera, Socialist party officials such as Antonio Badía Matemala, of the store clerks' syndicate, and Arturo Gas had been extremely active. Socialist collaboration in an apolitical labor organization, described as "approximation without confusion," was neither new nor uniquely Catalan.* Although admitting that such a policy was controversial, Arturo Gas insisted that it "is noble and loyal, and that it does not *compromise in any way or for any purpose the independence that syndicates must possess."* [5] Socialists hoped to hold Solidaridad Obrera to the principles announced in its original manifesto, a constructive program to improve working and living conditions. "Workers conscious of their position emerge from strong syndicates," wrote Arturo Gas, "and from such workers emerge good socialists." Obviously the expectation was to fulfill the party's old aspiration (frustrated during the nineteenth century) of capturing the support of the Catalan labor force.

In this period Solidaridad Obrera enjoyed the special favor of Governor Ossorio who held in high repute its socialist members. Continuing the friendly contacts begun in the Institute of Social Reforms in Madrid, he went so far as to publish at government expense a pamphlet in which he lamented the absence of a strong socialist party in Catalonia.[6] Ossorio's motives for supporting the socialists and Solidaridad Obrera were impugned by Radicals who claimed his only purpose was to centralize labor activities in order to be able to keep them under closer surveillance.[7] And Badía Matemala, an executive of Solidaridad Obrera, was described as an "informer on a luxury scale." [8] Behind these bitter attacks by the Radicals, lay the recognition that Ossorio's support was decisively important in this, the formative period of Solidaridad Obrera.

In October 1907 the labor federation began publication of a newspaper, *Solidaridad Obrera*. But after this first burst of enthusiasm, activity lagged perceptibly. In December 1907 an editorialist writing in the *Boletín* of the typesetters' union declared that "it would be better for a new [Governor] González Rothwos to come and dissolve the unions; then we would have the excuse of saying that they died by violent means." [9] The editorialist was too impatient. After the years in which the labor movement had been quiescent, union officials needed time to convince workers that collective bargaining and strikes were an effective means of defending their rights.

In the spring of 1908 Barcelona labor leaders decided that the only means

---

* Catalan socialists had initiated this policy in 1904, the nadir of the labor movement, as a means of salvaging the syndicates. The same policy was advocated by Jean Jaurès in France where he urged the French Socialist party to collaborate with the CGT, a policy he described as one of "a free cooperation . . . without confusion or subordination or suspicion." (As quoted in James Joll, *The Second International: 1888–1914* [London, 1955], p. 132.)

of strengthening Solidaridad Obrera was to expand from a municipal federation into a regional confederation; they argued that its success depended ultimately upon coordinating the activities of the entire Catalan labor force. Therefore, on March 25, 1908, delegates from seventeen Barcelona labor unions, together with representatives from sixteen unions in other Catalan cities, gathered in the city of Badalona. They agreed to discuss the formation of such a confederation at a labor congress to be held in Barcelona in September. From March until September 1908, Catalan labor activities revolved almost exclusively around the preparations for this congress.

Needing a dramatic cause to promote worker solidarity in anticipation of the congress, labor leaders fell with alacrity upon Maura's Terrorism Bill. Speakers traveled through Catalonia to warn that the bill was not directed against terrorists but against "the liberty and action of labor societies." Asserting that only a strong labor organization could offer protection against such acts of tyranny, they urged workers to join syndicates and urged syndicate officials to affiliate with Solidaridad Obrera.[10]

Delegates to the Labor Congress assembled in Barcelona on September 6, 1908, in the newly acquired headquarters of Solidaridad Obrera. There were 142 delegates, representing 112 labor syndicates or municipal federations of syndicates, from industrial cities throughout Catalonia, with a total membership of between 20,000 and 25,000 workers. The delegates reaffirmed their apolitical policy:[11]

The Congress understands that those propagandists who speak in the name of Solidaridad Obrera must situate themselves always in the terrain of the class struggle, excluding all political and religious tendencies and procuring always to stimulate in the proletariat the will to fight against capital.

The report on strike tactics, prepared by socialist Antonio Fabra Rivas, justified their use for economic objectives only. During the three days of the Congress (September 6-8), delegates discussed problems of direct interest to workers: provision of adequate, decent housing; a minimum daily wage of five pesetas; the organization of the textile workers, a matter of concern to the entire labor movement.

The most important achievement of the Congress was the unanimous vote to organize a regional confederation. The Barcelona federation agreed to relinquish the title Solidaridad Obrera to the new labor confederation. A motion was also made to organize a national labor confederation, but delegates voted to postpone debate on this item until the congress scheduled for the following year (September 1909). In accordance with a vote of the Congress, the officials of the Barcelona federation prepared the statutes outlining a program of "pure syndicalism" for the new confederation and registered them in the Governor's office three months later (December 17, 1908).[12] The secretariat of the regional confederation had much the same membership as that of the Barcelona federation, a development due in part to maneuvering but also to the lack of money for officials to commute to meetings in Barcelona from out of town. The new secretariat was elected on December 29, 1908; José Román, who conferred occasionally with Francisco Ferrer, became secretary general. Socialist Badía Matemala was elected treasurer.[13]

The dignity and the constructive proposals of the Labor Congress had enhanced the prestige of Solidaridad Obrera, apparently presaging a new era for the Catalan labor movement. Despite the opposition of employers, and the suspicions of police that the confederation was plotting sedition, Solidaridad Obrera had become an important force on the industrial scene, working strictly in defense of workers' interests. In the closing session of the Labor Congress, representatives of the three political groups collaborating in Solidaridad Obrera had shared the platform to voice their approval of an apolitical program: Jaime Anglés Pruñosa spoke for the Radical Republicans, Antonio Fabra Rivas for the socialists, and José Rodríguez Romero for the anarchists. Nonetheless the situation changed immediately after the Congress, as each of these groups sought to control Solidaridad Obrera.

The Catalan Socialist Federation

Socialists had realized they could not continue indefinitely their policy of participating in Solidaridad Obrera. The proposal for a new national confederation constituted a direct threat to their own organization, the UGT. So did the revitalized Catholic labor activities in Barcelona. However, before they could carry out any concerted defensive action, socialists had to revitalize their party organization in Catalonia.

The taskmaster was thirty-year-old Antonio Fabra Rivas,* who resigned his job on the Paris newspaper *L'Humanité* and returned to his native Cata-

---

* Born in Reus (Catalonia), Fabra Rivas studied in the University of Barcelona before going to live in Germany, Scotland, and France, where he taught Spanish and worked on socialist newspapers. An excellent linguist, he earned his living in Barcelona by giving English language lessons. Fabra Rivas never sympathized with the regionalist movement, refusing always to speak in Catalan and insisting on an international approach to the labor movement.

lonia.[14] He was an inflexible socialist, well-disciplined in party doctrine and in sociology, who worked and studied long hours. Yet men as diverse as Claudi Ametlla who admired him, and Emiliano Iglesias who did not, believed he lacked that spark of perceptive intelligence that would have made him a truly effective party leader.[15]

In 1908 Fabra Rivas' youth and new ideas served as a catalyst for the moribund socialist organization that he found in Catalonia upon his arrival. Fabra Rivas had been deeply influenced by his French mentor, Jean Jaurès, and particularly by his concern with the need for a closer relationship between socialist parties and labor movements. Jaurès had been in contact with Catalan socialists for some years, sympathizing with their desire for a less doctrinaire, more militant policy than that decreed by party leaders in Madrid. Fabra Rivas' return to Barcelona* served to strengthen these ties; in turn, they reinforced his own position within the Catalan socialist movement.[16]

At the time of Fabra Rivas' return, the socialist group of Barcelona (Agrupación Socialista) had a central headquarters and branches in worker neighborhoods, but the entire membership was very small. During the summer of 1908 new officers were elected and a program of action worked out. These tasks, intended to complement the socialist action within Solidaridad Obrera, were barely completed by early September when the Labor Congress was held. Fabra Rivas made his first appearance in Catalan labor circles in the Congress, which he found an excellent forum for his ideas.

At the same time as the Labor Congress was held in Barcelona, the Socialist party had held its Eighth National Congress in Madrid. Pablo Iglesias was quite optimistic in reporting on the Catalan socialist movement; admitting its inactivity during past years, he promised that it would "soon play a brilliant role in the socialist movement as a result of the work now being carried out by our colleagues." [17]

In Barcelona, immediately after the Congress, Fabra Rivas met with delegates from socialist groups throughout Catalonia and planned the revival of the old Catalan Socialist Federation (Federación Socialista Catalana). The delegates agreed to publish a weekly organ, *La Internacional,* as a means of combating the newspaper *Solidaridad Obrera,* which they considered to be controlled by the anarchists; the first issue appeared on October 15, 1908.

---

* Governor Ossorio was not enthusiastic about Fabra Rivas, declaring that he had returned to Spain "to represent revolutionary socialism in opposition to the evolutionary socialism led by Pablo Iglesias" (July 13, 1910, *Diario de las Cortes,* III, 592).

As secretary of the Federation and as editor of *La Internacional,* Fabra Rivas labored diligently during the following months to strengthen the socialist organization but he made little headway. Catalan workers preferred either an apolitical labor organization or a demagogic party such as the Radical Republicans. Apparently socialists could influence Catalan workers only by working through Solidaridad Obrera.

Even this avenue was threatened in the fall of 1908 when Radicals and anarchists (working independently of one another) attacked the socialists as informants of the Governor. They claimed that Antonio Badía Matemala, an official of the Catalan Socialist Federation, was secretly maneuvering to gain control of Solidaridad Obrera for his party. Badía replied that in his role as treasurer of Solidaridad Obrera (which he had helped to organize), he acted strictly as a labor negotiator. Although colleagues defended his integrity both in the confederation and in his store clerks' syndicate, Badía remains an enigmatic figure; he was willing, for example, to borrow money from Francisco Ferrer for Solidaridad Obrera[18] — perhaps as a means of strengthening it in the fight against the Radicals. For in the following months, Fabra Rivas' socialists fought hard, in alliance with trade union officials, to preserve Solidaridad Obrera as an independent labor organization. Their major opponent was the Radical party.

The Radical Party versus Solidaridad Obrera

From the fall of 1908 until the summer of 1909, the Radical party fought to retain its hold over the Catalan labor force, either by dominating the labor confederation (in opposition to socialists, anarchists, or trade union officials), or by destroying it. "Solidaridad Obrera will become *lerrouxista* or it will cease to exist," Emiliano Iglesias had boasted as early as the spring of 1908, on a trip to Madrid.[19]

Being the prudent politician that he was, Iglesias delayed his campaign against Solidaridad Obrera until after the Labor Congress (in which the Radicals participated). During the six months following the Congress, the Radicals joined battle with Solidaridad Obrera on two occasions — first, in the citywide strike of teamsters, and then in the strike of typesetters employed by the Radical newspaper, *El Progreso.*

The labor issue was clear in the teamsters' strike, which lasted from October through November 1908.[20] The men demanded a new contract with agency owners to replace the one negotiated in 1902, a contract more often ignored than honored. They initiated the strike in the important Ayxelá agency, a strike considered both by workers and employers as a test case. Management refused to negotiate and employed scab labor. Workers killed one strikebreaker and police responded with violence, whereupon all teamsters in Barcelona went out on a sympathy strike. Governor Ossorio, with a group of businessmen, finally negotiated an agreement between teamster syndicate officials and the owners of the agencies, and thereby won the support of the teamsters' president Enrique Ferrer. Ossorio justified his intervention on grounds of public order, stating that there were reports that labor officials planned a general strike and that Ferrer was promoting it.[21] This is possible, for it would be in accord with the syndicalist policy of a general strike as an economic weapon. However the factor that counted historically was not such speculation but the excellent impression that the Radicals had made on teamsters by holding giant rallies in the Casa del Pueblo.

The second battle was joined over the strike of typesetters employed by the Radical newspaper, *El Progreso*. Labor officials dramatized this essentially petty dispute as "a fight between a bourgeois enterprise and a society of resistance [that is, labor union] which, because it was a member, was supported by the Confederation." [22] Implicit in the long and acrimonious campaign (December 1908 to March 1909) was the charge by syndicate officials that the Radicals had deliberately debilitated the labor movement not only to build their party but to serve bourgeois interests.

In mid-December 1908 Radical administrators suddenly promised to meet all the typesetters' demands. As soon as the elections were over, in which Radicals won three of the four seats for Congress, party officials announced they would not honor their agreement with Solidaridad Obrera. "We have blown up Solidaridad Catalana," exulted Alejandro Lerroux from his exile in Buenos Aires, "and now we will blow up Solidaridad Obrera." [23]

Throughout the following spring of 1909, the two organizations fought for the right to represent the Catalan worker. Solidaridad Obrera officials took the initiative, campaigning among syndicate members for a boycott of *El Progreso*. Teams of speakers traveled through the province to urge the labor movement "to defeudalize itself, once and for all, from bourgeois tutelage and to strengthen itself as an independent, international, and revolutionary movement." [24] Finally they succeeded in having a boycott declared, in an assembly held in Barcelona on March 21, 1909, attended by 104 delegates (almost as great a number as had attended the Labor Congress held the previous September). The victory was a hollow one.

The Radical party had retained control over the Catalan labor force. In the spring of 1909, in its second year of existence and at the moment of its moral victory in securing the boycott, Solidaridad Obrera had only 15,000 members in all Catalonia. Yet in Barcelona alone, in the May 1909 elections for city councilmen, Radical candidates were elected by 20,000 workers.[25]

The Anarchists and Ferrer

Concurrently, within Solidaridad Obrera, anarchists fought for control even more desperately than did the socialists, for they had no independent organization upon which to rely. In later years they would succeed in controlling the labor movement (as they did not succeed in the French CGT); the factors leading to their success have been obscured or misinterpreted.

Foremost was the inability of the labor confederation to gain employer recognition as a collective bargaining agency, a situation due to the dominant textile industry that employed mostly unskilled men, women, and children. Assured of a plentiful labor supply by the continuing influx from impoverished rural areas, employers had no need to negotiate. Thus labor leaders could point to no success in justifying a strict syndicalist policy and in refuting the argument of anarcho-syndicalists that the only alternative was revolution.

Spanish conservatives would scoff at such reasoning, for to them Solidaridad Obrera was nothing more than a façade. They pointed to the coincidence in time of the formation of Solidaridad Obrera (August 3, 1907), the international congress of anarchists in Amsterdam (August 24–31), and Ferrer's trip abroad (July 22 until late September) as proof of a complot: Ferrer created Solidaridad Obrera at the instigation of international anarchism.[26]

The accusation can be factually refuted. As early as June 8, 1907, a newspaper in Madrid, *España Nueva,* reported that Barcelona labor leaders had begun a series of meetings to prepare a new federation to be entitled Solidaridad Obrera; Francisco Ferrer was still in prison and was not released until June 12, 1907. Secondly, the formal organization of Solidaridad Obrera was completed and announced on August 3, 1907; Ferrer had left Spain on July 22. Thirdly, the international anarchist congress did not begin until August 24. Ferrer did not attend: according to his daughter, European anarchists asked him not to attend lest the notoriety of his trial cause the government to suspend the congress, their first major assembly in twenty-s years.[27] And at the Amsterdam meeting, anarchists did not agree unanimously to work through labor movements; a large group enthusiastically supported Errico Malatesta, who cited the experience of French anarchists in the CGT as proof that a labor movement was not a satisfactory vehicle for an anarchist revolution, and who urged a return to the traditional "propaganda by word and deed."[28] Admittedly, if Ferrer had been present in Amsterdam he would have espoused the cause of anarcho-syndicalism which excited him.

As soon as he had returned to Barcelona late in September 1907, Ferrer met with anarchists and urged them to participate in Solidaridad Obrera. He thus renewed a policy he had initiated in 1901, when he collaborated with certain labor leaders in the federation of that period and subsidized a newspaper, *Huelga General*. With the demise of the federation after 1902, Ferrer had concentrated exclusively on education. Now, in 1907, isolated from educational circles and from the Radical party, he tried again to impose his ideas through the medium of the labor movement.[29]

Remaining discreetly in the background, the full extent of his activities unknown not only to the membership at large but to many of the officers, Ferrer worked through men like José Rodríguez Romero of the typesetters' syndicate, and Leopoldo Bonafulla (Juan Esteve), the anarchist publicist. Ferrer could also call upon the prestige of Anselmo Lorenzo, the "grandfather" of Spanish anarchism, who had deeply influenced him for almost twenty years; he employed Lorenzo as a translator and maintained constant, albeit formal, contacts.[30] Ferrer agreed to subsidize the newspaper *Solidaridad Obrera*. Just before the Labor Congress of September 1908, he lent Solidaridad Obrera the money to rent a headquarters (a site to hold meetings and to rent office space to member syndicates) that was so necessary a basis for the independence of the labor movement.[31]

Yet even though some labor activists accepted Ferrer's money, they can not be considered ipso facto as agents who did his bidding. And Solidaridad Obrera can definitely not be considered as Ferrer's creature. In the words of national socialist leader Pablo Iglesias: "A labor movement is not created in such a manner, simply because one gentleman should have a whim; it is created by virtue of a genuine need."[32] Like so many other groups in that taut and inflexible Catalan society, Ferrer and the anarcho-syndicalists whose ideas he shared simply exploited every means to defend their cause. To them, the intensifying symptoms of a political and economic crisis were encouraging.

CHAPTER VIII

Mounting Tension: Plans for a General Strike

TENSION mounted through the spring of 1909 as Catalans realized that all the reforms launched with such enthusiasm two years earlier were stalemated. In Madrid, Maura's Administrative Reform Bill was deadlocked in the Cortes. Solidaridad Catalana's glowing promise to make a reality of representative government and to defend the region's multiple interests in the Cortes had ended in the isolation of the republicans and in new power for the industrialist-controlled Lliga. In Catalonia, the attempt of Catalan republicans to constitute a third force (between the Lliga and the Radicals) through projects such as educational reform had failed because of clerical intransigence and lack of worker interest. And Solidaridad Obrera as a strong labor organization able to bargain collectively was still only an ideal.

The frustration was intensified by a business recession that began late in 1908 and worsened in the spring of 1909 when several important factories and brokerage firms went bankrupt. Textile sales declined sharply, especially abroad, where one third of the total output was normally sold. Forty percent of the men and thirty percent of the women employed in the factories in Barcelona and the Ter Valley were discharged. The future promised more hardship as a result of the expiration of a ten-year agreement negotiated in 1899, by which Spain and the United States had shared the market of the Philippine Islands under a special tariff arrangement; Catalan textiles would now face stiffer competition in this important market.[1]

The recession was due in part to international conditions: the high price of raw materials, stiff competition among nations, and excessive stockpiles. But beyond this immediate situation lay the more important question of why

Catalan textiles could not compete effectively in the world market created by European imperialism. Economic analysts, one French and the other a Spanish government official, described basic deficiencies: the failure to integrate the entire process of textile production and thereby to avoid ruinous competition through a rational system of costs and prices; the lack of concentrated capital necessary to modernize the industry; the absence of management or of a work force skilled in new industrial techniques.[2]

One remedy, a novel one for the era and all the more so because proposed by a government economist, was that the state direct a reform of the national economy that would increase the productive capacity and therefore the acquisitive power of the domestic consumer.[3] Instead, textile manufacturers preferred the classical solution: reduction of labor costs by reducing wages and maintenance of a ten- to eleven-hour work day.

To oppose this project, textile workers did not have a strong labor organization. Textile syndicate officials had welcomed the support promised by Solidaridad Obrera and had collaborated in its formation. One month later (September 1907) they merged their syndicates: the stronger one of male bleachers and dyers (Sociedad Obrera Ramo del Agua) and the weaker one of female spinning- and weaving-machine operators (Sociedad Arte Fabril). The next step was to organize, with help from Solidaridad Obrera, a federation of all textile workers from Barcelona and the Ter Valley, a project on which syndicate officials worked from December 1908 until March 1909. Although only moderately successful, labor officials had at least established the machinery for consultation on common action by the time of the depression in the spring of 1909.[4]

The Case of the Alcalá del Valle Prisoners

SOLIDARIDAD OBRERA AND THE ALCALA DEL VALLE PRISONERS

In this context of political tension and a business recession, Solidaridad Obrera officials decided to push ahead with plans for a new *national* labor confederation as proposed in their First Labor Congress. This was the major item on the agenda for the second congress, scheduled for September 1909. For the preparatory campaign of agitation and propaganda, Solidaridad Obrera officials again (as in the previous spring when they attacked the Terrorism Bill) did not choose a labor issue to dramatize the need for worker solidarity but chose instead a civil rights issue: that of six peasants from the

Andalusian town of Alcalá del Valle, who were still imprisoned for their part in an uprising in the summer of 1903.[5] There had already been extensive publicity both in Spain and abroad about the tortures applied to the prisoners, in accord with the image of "inquisitorial Spain" given modern currency in the Montjuich trials. The concept of Maura as a dictator, established during the 1908 campaign against the Terrorism Bill, was refurbished, for Maura had been Premier when the Alcalá prisoners were tried and convicted.* Thus in the spring of 1909 Solidaridad Obrera joined other groups in demanding an amnesty, considering this an excellent means to arouse enthusiasm for a new national labor confederation.[6]

FERRER AND THE ALCALA DEL VALLE PRISONERS

Ferrer also worked on behalf of the Andalusian prisoners, but his objective was different: confident that Maura would reject demands for an amnesty, he hoped that the campaign would lead to a revolutionary general strike. His experiences in Spain since 1901 had either confirmed his belief in revolution or converted him to this belief. Lerroux commented on Ferrer's brusque change of ideology circa 1907 from republicanism to anarchism "with all the faith, the ardor, and the enthusiasm of a neophyte."[7] To Claudi Ametlla, who had known him since his return, Ferrer was "an anarchist, a revolutionary, and a fanatic; therefore unrealistic, dangerous, and intolerant," yet he tempered his judgment with admiration for "the courage of a man who believes, who is not performing a comedy, who lives only for one passion, who knows how to die for his ideas."[8]

It must be stressed again that Francisco Ferrer was not a charismatic leader. From behind the scenes he could prod and finance, he could travel abroad and use his extensive contacts to secure promises of support in the event of a revolution. But he definitely did not direct the Radical party or Solidaridad Obrera, through which he worked. As a theoretician Ferrer had devised a scheme whereby these two organizations would collaborate in the establishment of a republic, but this was incompatible with the realities: both the Radical party and Solidaridad Obrera fulfilled a function in Catalan society independent of Ferrer's machinations, a function that brought them

---

* In the summer of 1903, in this tiny village near Cádiz, peasants had demonstrated on behalf of Spain's political prisoners (possibly at the instigation of the anarchist-dominated Federación de Sociedades Obreras, which disintegrated a year or so later). Provoked by the brutality of Civil Guards, the peasants attacked officials and merchants; the uprising was harshly repressed.

into open conflict in the months following the 1908 Labor Congress. Ferrer was seriously disturbed by this quarrel;[9] his only hope for success would be the continued collaboration among former anarchists, of whom some had entered the Radical party and others had penetrated Solidaridad Obrera.

Meanwhile, from the fall of 1908 to the spring of 1909, Ferrer labored to secure French CGT support for a revolutionary general strike. He also wanted to persuade them of the need to collaborate with Radicals but because of their own experience with the bourgeois Third Republic, French syndicalists were reluctant. Therefore in October 1908, immediately after the Labor Congress, Ferrer financed the trip of a long-time collaborator, José Miquel Clapes, to Marseilles where he attended the national congress of the French CGT as an official representative of Solidaridad Obrera. Yet in his speech (reportedly prepared under Ferrer's direction) Clapes spoke not so much of Solidaridad Obrera as of the Radical party: he promised that workers would respond to a call for revolution even if party leaders should oppose it and then asked CGT support in vindicating oppressed Spanish workers.[10] Sometime during the fall, Ferrer published an article in southern France (reprinted in the Radical newspaper, *El Progreso,* on December 29, 1908), in which he explained the collaboration that he envisioned between the labor movement and Radical Republicans:[11]

> We are organizing as far as it is possible to do so, forming syndicates and federations in order to achieve the establishment of the General Confederation of Spanish Labor, so that when the republican party decides [to act], we may take part in the struggle and exert the weight of our force, so that the Spanish republic will be, as far as possible, a social, communist, and libertarian republic.

In February 1909 Ferrer made a well-publicized trip through urban centers in Andalusia under constant police harassment;[12] he then went abroad. In Paris he attended a meeting in the offices of Gustave Herve's *Guerre Sociale* (to which he contributed heavily) together with representatives of the CGT, the socialist newspaper *L'Humanité,* and the League of the Rights of Man. The Frenchmen agreed to sponsor a rally to demand that the Maura government release the Alcalá del Valle prisoners. The CGT delegate promised to obtain approval from their executive council for a boycott by French dockworkers of all Spanish goods if the prisoners were not released.[13] Moral support was all that the CGT could promise in the spring of 1909, for it was a weak organization and was currently divided by disputes between reformist and revolutionary syndicalists.[14]

Ferrer sent reports of his activities to Miguel Villalobos Moreno in Barcelona, a member of the committee for Alcalá del Valle prisoners and of the staff of the newspaper *Solidaridad Obrera*.[15] Ambitious and clever, the handsome Murcian was only twenty-eight years of age when he acted as Ferrer's factotum; he earned a modest living as a teacher in one of Ferrer's rationalist schools.* For a brief period he would play an important role in the shadowy world of interlocking revolutionary groups in Barcelona.

In April 1909 the campaign for the Alcalá prisoners entered a more intense stage, as Solidaridad Obrera officials began in earnest to prepare for their congress. Early in this month the confederation issued a manifesto threatening serious action if the prisoners were not released. On April 15 delegates from member syndicates met in Barcelona to discuss the campaign and voted to seek support of workers abroad; in a news release, spokesmen said that if their pleas were unanswered they would carry out "a decisive action" in conjunction with foreign labor organizations (presumably the French CGT). Four days later these spokesmen reported they had received promises of support from foreign workers.[16]

In May the campaign for the Alcalá del Valle prisoners gained new momentum when on May 8 one of the men died in prison, reputedly because of cruel treatment. In Madrid as in Barcelona, politicians of all parties joined in demanding that Maura grant the remaining prisoners an amnesty.

On June 13, Solidaridad Obrera held an assembly of delegates from member syndicates. By a vote of sixty-three in favor and fifteen opposed, they approved a circumspect use of the general strike "as an essential weapon in the struggle, without prejudice to the possibility of recurring to other weapons, depending upon the circumstances." The delegates may have been primarily concerned with the concurrent textile lockout when they took this major step in the direction of revolutionary syndicalism, a step they had rejected in the Labor Congress only nine months earlier.[17] However by the late spring of 1909 political and economic conditions made it difficult to adhere strictly to the trade union policy of the First Labor Congress.**

---

* Moreno, whose real name was reportedly José Sánchez González, was born in Cartagena, finished secondary school in Murcia, and then went to teach in a mining village, where he publicized anarchist doctrines in his free time. He corresponded with Ferrer during this period. When forced to leave the village, Moreno went to Barcelona, where in 1907 Ferrer found him a job in a school.

** The same turn toward revolutionary syndicalism was occurring simultaneously in France, although for different reasons. On May 28, the reformist syndicalist L.

Two days after this vote for revolutionary syndicalism, amid the furor of an intensified campaign on behalf of the Alcalá del Valle prisoners, Ferrer suddenly returned to Barcelona from London because his sister-in-law and his niece were ill; on June 19 little Layeta Ferrer died of tubercular meningitis. Despite unfinished business in England, Ferrer remained in Barcelona.[18]

The plans for a revolutionary general strike on behalf of the Andalusian prisoners had been calculated upon Maura's famed intractability. But the problem of national security caused Maura abruptly to reverse his position. In Morocco, skirmishes between Spanish troops and Riffian tribes threatened to erupt into heavy fighting. Spain governed in Morocco under an international mandate, and Maura did not, therefore, welcome a new campaign against "la Espagne inquisitorial" at such a difficult moment. He used the occasion of the birth of the Infanta Beatriz on June 22, 1909, to recommend that the King pardon three of the Alcalá del Valle prisoners and reduce the sentences of the other two men.[19]

Claiming the victory as its own, Solidaridad Obrera decided this was the propitious moment for the formal announcement of a second labor congress. On June 29 it published the agenda for the congress, scheduled for September 24, 1909: the major item was the expansion of Solidaridad Obrera from a regional confederation into a national organization, thereby formalizing the contacts already existing among labor groups throughout Spain.[20]

In mid-July the Alcalá del Valle prisoners were released and went to Barcelona for a series of rallies organized in their honor by Solidaridad Obrera. Francisco Ferrer or Miguel V. Moreno accompanied them to these public celebrations, which were poorly attended, in Barcelona and in Sabadell. The prisoners were not invited to any Radical centers, perhaps because the party was celebrating the acquittal of party members involved in the shooting of Lliga politician Cambó two years earlier.[21]

The poor reception accorded the Andalusian peasants suggests that their cause was far removed from the interests of Barcelona workers and therefore that the possibility of a general strike on their behalf had actually been quite remote. Yet the propaganda within Catalonia and abroad had con-

Niel resigned as secretary general of the CGT because of opposition to his policies by revolutionary syndicalists. A member of the latter faction, Léon Jouhaux, was elected secretary general on July 12. (Bernard Georges and Denise Tintant, *Léon Jouhaux: Cinquant ans de syndicalisme*, Vol. I: *Des origines à 1921* [Paris, 1962], pp. 11–19. I am grateful to Professor Val Lorwin of the University of Oregon for this reference.)

tributed to the creation of a revolutionary élan among the workers. And in
early July Solidaridad Obrera began to mobilize this élan in support of a
cause that directly affected the existence of the labor movement.

Solidaridad Obrera and the Textile Workers

The immediate concern of syndicate officials, and of Catalan workers in
general, was the deepening crisis in the textile industry and its consequences
for the labor movement. These were clearly spelled out on May 15, 1909,
when Senator Alberto Rusiñol closed his factory in Manlleu in the Ter
Valley and discharged 800 employees. Labor leaders interpreted this action
by Rusiñol, who presided over the Lliga and was one of the leading cotton
manufacturers, to mean that industrialists would once again — as in 1901 —
confront a business recession with the powerful weapon of the lockout.
Rusiñol denied this and stated that the factory had changed hands, to which
labor leaders replied that it had merely been transferred to Rusiñol's brother.
Their suspicions were confirmed when one week later the Rusiñol brothers
met with local authorities to inform them of the new wage scale and working conditions and to explain that workers would have to apply for re-
employment. When workers in Manlleu, acting under the guidance of textile syndicate officials, refused to accept the new conditions, Rusiñol sent
agents to recruit in other areas. The lockout in Manlleu was imitated by
leading manufacturers in other textile cities.[22]

Textile syndicates prepared to give battle. On May 30 and May 31, delegates from all Catalonia met in Barcelona and approved a resolution stating
that a reduction in working hours was basic to all other demands and voting
support for Manlleu workers. Late in June tension grew with reports of
an international meeting of cotton manufacturers in Milan; Catalan industrialists returned to report that the consensus was to follow the British
example — namely, to reduce production (and thus employment) until the
current stockpiles were depleted.[23] Catalan textile syndicate officials were
determined at least to try to prevent factory owners from forcing workers
to bear the brunt of the recession.

At this point, on the eve of action, officials realistically reviewed their
potential supporters. From the moment of its foundation, they had participated in Solidaridad Obrera, but in late June 1909 — recognizing the fact
that the Radicals still controlled factory employees — they sought a reconcili-

ation with the party; when Radical leaders demanded a public recantation of errors, the textile unions publicly abandoned the boycott of *El Progreso*. In reply to accusations that they had betrayed Solidaridad Obrera, textile syndicate officials replied that their aim was to protect the worker and for this purpose they would make whatever alliances were necessary.[24]

This was a critical juncture for Solidaridad Obrera. The defection of textile syndicate officials deprived it of members precisely at a moment when officials were planning its expansion into a national organization. The Manlleu lockout constituted a direct threat to these plans, and even to the continued existence of Solidaridad Obrera, as the labor confederation officials explained in a manifesto to Catalan workers.

Once more bourgeois machinations are directed toward the destruction of our weak organization by means of the "Hunger Pact" of sad renown . . . The lockout and the employment of scab labor are an attempt to make the worker forget his class consciousness and his dignity as a free man.[25]

Solidaridad Obrera officials summoned delegates from member unions throughout Catalonia to discuss the Manlleu lockout in an assembly to be held in the textile center of Granollers.

During the two day assembly, held on July 10 and July 11, 1909, in Granollers, orators declared that the outcome of the Manlleu lockout would affect the wages and working conditions not only of textile workers but of all sectors of industry. According to these speakers, the only recourse was a general strike: there was general assent, which Solidaridad Obrera officials interpreted and announced as a vote of approval, but there was no immediate attempt to prepare a general strike, even though the Radical party newspaper abandoned its former hostility and urged workers to support the labor confederation's plans to oppose textile manufacturers.[26] In part the failure to act was because of the continuing struggle among anarchists, socialists, and Radicals for control over the Catalan labor force. A still more important cause was worker apathy, as textile syndicate officials discovered when they tried to get non-textile workers to implement the enthusiasm they had shown at Granollers. Socialist Fabra Rivas, extremely active in the campaign, would have described it as a lack of class solidarity among Catalan workers.

The significant aspects of this campaign were that in mid-July textile workers in cities throughout Catalonia were discussing the possibility of a general strike and that Solidaridad Obrera officials, in collaboration with Radical party leaders, had made tentative arrangements to carry out the strike.

On the same day as the Granollers assembly, July 11, 1909, the government *Gaceta* published a Royal Decree authorizing the calling up of army reserves because fighting had begun in Morocco. This decree provoked an intense reaction among workers in a way that neither the campaign for the Alcalá del Valle prisoners nor that of the textile manufacturers lockout could hope to equal. All political and social problems in Catalonia, as throughout Spain, were eclipsed by the antiwar protest.

Part Three ❧
The Prelude to the Tragic Week
May to July 1909

CHAPTER IX

Public Opinion and the "Moroccan Adventure"

I N 1909, because he sent a military expedition to Morocco, Antonio Maura was assailed and eventually turned out of office. This was an ironical turn of events (as José Ortega y Gasset pointed out in a perceptive essay), for throughout his long career Maura had opposed an active policy in Morocco on the grounds that Spain must replenish her resources before embarking upon any new international venture.[1]

But by the spring of 1909 Maura could no longer ignore the demands of army officers and financiers for punitive action against the unruly tribes in the Rif. Leading spokesmen for the policy were Catalan magnates Eusebio Güell and the Marquis of Comillas, together with the Liberal politician Romanones; politically at odds, the three men were united by their investment in the Riffian iron mines and in Melilla harbor facilities. In May 1909 the problem assumed international proportions, and it was this which forced Maura to act. French businessmen who had invested in a rival mine in the Rif warned that unless the Spaniards immediately subdued the tribes that threatened the railroad leading to the port of Melilla they would export ore through neighboring Algeria. Aside from pure trade considerations, Maura was afraid that France might absorb the Spanish protectorate in Morocco on the grounds that Spain was unable to fulfill her obligations to maintain order as stipulated in the Algeciras Convention of 1906.[2]

Maura was forced to authorize a military campaign in the Rif but he still hoped to avoid unilateral action which might lead to a government crisis at home and to an international imbroglio. He therefore sent a special ambassador to the new Sultan of Morocco, Mulai Hafid, asking that he join Spain in a military police expedition in the Rif. But as so often happened, Maura failed in his choice of personnel. The arrogance and ill temper of Ambassador Alfonso Merry del Val angered the Sultan, as did the Ambassador's close association in Tangier with Franciscan monks, one of the missionary orders subsidized by the Ministry of Foreign Affairs. In Madrid, Maura's political adversaries spoke with contempt of a "mission of Friars" [3] led by an ambassador who was the brother of the Papal Secretary of State. In mid-May Merry del Val broke off his diplomatic talks and returned to Spain, whereupon Mulai Hafid announced that he would send a special mission to Madrid for direct negotiations with the Foreign Ministry. Maura replied that the mission would be received with pleasure.

In reality the moment for negotiations had passed. Whatever the results of the Madrid talks, the skirmishing between Riffian tribes and Spanish troops (led by officers eager for action and for battle pay) seemed inevitably to lead to war. Far more serious was the threat of French action: late in May Maura was troubled by a mysterious military expedition that suddenly appeared in the Riffian mine area and then abruptly returned to French Algeria, and this incident crystallized his determination to act. [4]

On June 4, the Premier closed the Cortes in order to deprive his opponents of a public forum where they could attack his measures with immunity and with the assurance that their speeches would be reprinted by newspapers throughout the nation; obviously he hoped to prevent the opposition from capitalizing on the unpopular policy of sending troop reinforcements to Melilla. There were no constitutional means by which he could be forced to reopen the Cortes, which did not even possess absolute control of the allocation of funds — the safeguard of constitutional government. Maura obtained a three-million-peseta credit from an emergency body entitled the Council of State, composed of former ministers. Even if war should break out, he could not be forced to convoke the Cortes. The Constitution stated that the responsibility for declaring and carrying out a war rested exclusively with the King, the only condition being that he give an account to the Cortes upon the conclusion of hostilities.

The Liberal party, Maura's adversary, was not really anxious to have the Cortes open. Liberal politicians were greatly influenced by army officers, who favored the expedition, and by financiers with interests in the iron mines, such as the Count of Romanones. Moreover, they were still too divided on party leadership and policy to demand that the government be turned over to them. However this did not prevent Liberal politicians from harassing Maura for political advantage all through June. Deftly avoiding the charge of being unpatriotic, an accusation they could not afford because of their army associations, Liberal politicians declared they were not protesting the defense of Spanish rights in Morocco, but rather that Maura was subordinating the national welfare and the honor of the Army to the interests of a private mining company.[5] Journalists, far more strongly than legislators, attacked Maura's lack of planning and his ulterior motives in Morocco.[6] The editor of the independent *Correspondencia de España,* Leopoldo Romero, bluntly warned of the consequences in an article published in Madrid on June 11, entitled "Ir a Marruecos es ir a la revolución"; the article was reprinted in all major cities.

The Conservative government made no effort to rally public opinion by a clear statement of its objectives in Morocco. Throughout June official communiqués stated that only a limited police action was planned, information intended primarily for the French and British governments and only incidentally for the Spanish people. Maura spent a great deal of time on vacation in Santander or conferring with the King in the summer capital of San Sebastián, oblivious to newspaper criticism that he should have remained in Madrid to deal with the crisis. In his absence, Interior Minister La Cierva acted as de facto head of the government; his dictatorial administrative measures, together with his flaunting manner, caused even more antagonism than did Maura's arrogance.* La Cierva acted always on the premise that public protests were potentially subversive.

This, then, was the political background for the situation in July 1909: a public opposed to the war but lacking a constitutional means of influencing national policy, an opposition Liberal party not ready to take office, and a government of men unwilling to compromise in their rigid ideas of public order. Confronted with this situation, politicians and journalists gradually ceased their opposition after the outbreak of heavy fighting on July 9. Although there was good reason to believe that army officers had provoked the Riffian tribes into attacking, politicians were convinced the nation had no recourse but to re-establish order.

* La Cierva's strained relations with the press reached a climax in the oft-cited interview of July 22, 1909. "In the summer I am going to be the only correspondent and you can rest," he told the press, "because in the winter you can get back at me." For one among many editorials criticizing La Cierva for this interview, see *España Nueva* (Madrid), July 23, 1909.

The Workers' Antiwar Protest

At this point, just as journalists and politicians abandoned the antiwar protest, workers began to agitate because only they were affected by the Royal Decree, published in the official *Gaceta* on July 11, that recalled reservists to active duty. The injustices of the conscription system were heightened by the failure to subsidize the families of soldiers called back to duty or to make provision for a soldier's death or disability.

Much of the popular protest could have been avoided if War Minister Arsenio Linares had maintained at full strength the special divisions prepared by his predecessor, General Primo de Rivera. Men assigned to these divisions would have been on active duty, psychologically prepared to fight because they knew they constituted an emergency force. This was quite a different matter from calling back to duty men who were in their homes, susceptible to family pressures and to the antiwar propaganda of newspapers and political speakers. Disregarding such considerations (if indeed they occurred to him), War Minister Linares mobilized the Third Mixed Brigade, stationed in Catalonia — that is, precisely the area of Spain where urban workers were most unruly as a result of two years of intensive political and labor agitation. General Linares knew about this situation because until March 1909 he had been Captain General in Barcelona. Perhaps such concerns were outweighed by Linares' desire to demonstrate the capabilities of the Third Brigade, for whose training he had been personally responsible.* Or perhaps Linares chose the Brigade simply because it was stationed close to the port of embarkation.

The Third Brigade included more men from Aragon and Valencia than from Catalonia, and therefore protests against the war spread all through northeastern Spain as reservists were recalled. It spread to the central regions in mid-July when Linares ordered mobilization of the First Mixed Brigade, stationed in Madrid. Despite Maura's continued assurances that only a police action was contemplated, the dispatch of so many troops presaged heavy fighting.[7]

Two national political organizations might have transformed the workers'

---

* Even before he was authorized to act, indeed even before hostilities began, General Linares had prepared the Third Mixed Brigade. On June 30 he canceled all leaves and ordered the Brigade to prepare for duty in Morocco. On July 8 he called up all reserves assigned to the Mixed Brigade. (See *El Progreso* [Barcelona], June 30, July 9, 1909; and *El País* [Madrid], July 9, 1909.)

protest into political action: the republican movement or the Socialist party. Republican politicians were in the better position to act, for they sat in the Cortes and might at least have demanded publicly that the legislature be opened for a discussion of national policy. Or they might have acted to carry out the threat they had been uttering for the past thirty-four years: to lead a revolution that would replace the Monarchy with a republic. Instead, republican politicians confined themselves to conferring about possible courses of action.[8]

Socialists, scornful of republicans' pusillanimity,[9] were eager to lead the antiwar protest, in fulfillment of their obligations both as a branch of the Second International and as a Spanish political party. Antimilitarism had been a major concern at the Seventh Congress of the Second International, held in Stuttgart just two years earlier (1907); Jean Jaurès went so far as to urge member parties to declare a general strike if all other means of opposing a war should fail, while Edouard Vaillant boldly declared, "Plutôt l'insurrection que la guerre." Because war seemed most imminent in Morocco, French and Spanish socialists had received a special mandate to prevent their governments from waging aggressive action; the first antiwar campaign, carried out in the fall of 1907, did not kindle the enthusiasm of Spanish workers, who were reassured by Maura's cautious policy in Morocco.[10] But in July 1909 Spanish workers welcomed Socialist party direction.

Pablo Iglesias, however, sought broader support for the antiwar protest, asserting that the Moroccan campaign satisfied no national interest and pointing out that not even all Spanish capitalists supported it. By protesting the war, Iglesias said his party was defending the national interest and giving proof of its "citizenship."[11] This orientation explains broad initial support for the socialist campaign, both in Madrid and in Barcelona. Only slowly and under pressure did the socialists adopt extreme measures.

In their first major antiwar rally in Madrid, on Sunday, July 11, socialist leaders were still obviously reluctant to abandon their traditional moderate policies, and this despite the outbreak of fighting two days earlier and the publication that same day of the decree calling up reserves. The situation changed drastically during the following week as soldiers embarked from Barcelona amid increasingly violent public protests. At the second rally in Madrid, one week later (July 18), Pablo Iglesias abandoned the caution of his lifelong career and suggested that the target for the soldiers' rifles should not be the Rifs but the government itself. "If it is necessary," he said, "workers will go out on a general strike with all the consequences."[12] This

threat was echoed in socialist rallies in Bilbao and Santander and was reported in the national press.

But it was the Barcelona Socialist party that proved to be the dynamo of
the antiwar campaign, in part because of the violent demonstrations in that
port city, in larger part because of Antonio Fabra Rivas. Like his mentor,
Jean Jaurès, he was convinced that the cause of antimilitarism would achieve
a new and enthusiastic rapport between workers and the Socialist parties.
Claudi Ametlla writes that Fabra Rivas was sincerely convinced that the
antiwar protest of July 1909 had provided the socialists with a means of
finally securing control over the Catalan labor force.[13]

Through the agency of the newly revived Catalan Socialist Federation,
Fabra Rivas was able to organize not only in Barcelona but throughout the
region. By good fortune, the Federation had scheduled its second congress
for Sunday, July 18 (the same day on which Pablo Iglesias in Madrid was
threatening a general strike). The twenty-two delegates, representing socialist groups in thirteen Catalan cities, began by voting enthusiastically to
continue support for striking textile workers in the Ter Valley (the contacts made during this campaign and the support it engendered for the idea
of a general strike were a prime factor in the subsequent successful organization of a general strike to protest the war). The central issue in the
two-day congress was the war in Morocco. Delegates approved a bold resolution that described the war in Morocco in strict Marxian terms as a product of the class struggle, provoked by Maura's government, "the enemy of
the proletariat and the representative on this occasion, even more than on
any other, of bourgeois interests." [14] Three antiwar rallies were planned by
delegates before they dispersed to their home towns throughout Catalonia to
stimulate worker support for the campaign.

During the following week, Fabra Rivas worked feverishly to maintain
the Socialist party leadership of the campaign to end the war in Morocco by
resorting to the "supreme" weapon of the general strike. This meant that
his group had to restrain anarchists in Barcelona who wanted immediate
action, while persuading the hesitant Pablo Iglesias to declare a general
strike for the first time in the party's history.* Within the context of the

* As early as 1902 the Spanish Socialist party went on record as favoring the general
strike as a "political act," with the proviso that it last no more than two days; only as
an economic weapon did the party reject the general strike (report on the sixth congress
of the Socialist party, El Liberal [Madrid], August 30, 1902, as reprinted in Fernando
Díaz-Plaja, ed. La Historia de España en sus documentos, Vol. IV: El Siglo XX, new
series [Madrid, 1960], p. 55).

events in Catalonia, Fabra Rivas' overly optimistic promise that the socialists could organize a national strike served as an incendiary spark within an already explosive situation.

The Antiwar Protest in Barcelona

The demonstrations that began in Barcelona on Monday, July 12, were expected to be the vanguard of a national protest, which started in Barcelona only in part because Catalans were among the first to be mobilized; as a matter of record, Catalans constituted a majority in only three of the six battalions of the Third Brigade.[15] Far more significant was the fact that Barcelona was the port of embarkation. Antimilitarists had learned through experience that the effective elements in such a demonstration were civilians. All predictions to the contrary, mobilization of a civilian army had not proved difficult; a sufficient number of soldiers appeared voluntarily or under force, and once in the barracks they offered no serious threat to military discipline. But their families and friends, or simply a sympathetic public, could be used to good advantage in a protest.

This process was clearly discernible in Barcelona during the week of July 12 through July 18. The ceremonies attendant upon the embarkations seemed calculated to excite the populace, not least because they conjured up sad memories of soldiers leaving for Cuba eleven years earlier; the transport ships were the same, the property of the "clerical" Marquis of Comillas. Government officials, accustomed as they were to formulating public policy with no regard for public opinion, made no conciliatory gesture toward the reserve soldier nor toward his family, left with no means of support. Instead officials gave speeches on patriotism, while socially prominent women, whose own sons were able to pay the 1,500-peseta fee necessary for exemption from conscription, distributed religious medals.

Public resentment in Barcelona reached an explosive climax on Sunday afternoon, July 18 (at the same time as the socialist rally in Madrid and the socialist congress in Barcelona). Anarchist Leopoldo Bonafulla, an enthusiastic participant in the demonstration, insisted that it was completely spontaneous.[16] Yet it seems quite probable that purposeful men could skillfully provoke violence, given the conditions that prevailed on that hot and sultry Sunday afternoon — the tension created by the anti-war protest during the preceding week, the enormous antagonistic crowds in the streets, and the blind intransigence of public authorities.

Even though a majority of the soldiers in the Reus Battalion scheduled to embark were Catalan, authorities made no concessions to aroused public feeling in Barcelona. Troops were marched to the wharf right through the center of town, heavily populated by workers, just at four-thirty when Barcelona residents customarily take a stroll on their day off. The crowd encircled the soldiers, who soon broke formation to walk arm in arm with relatives or friends. Officers merely guided the throng to the docks where Governor Ossorio and the Captain General were waiting. Ossorio had assembled an enormous police force, which went into action as the crowd approached and forced the soldiers to march directly onto the ship.

The spark that set off the violence was the distribution of medals and cigarettes by the society ladies.[17] Some of the soldiers disgustedly threw the medals into the water, as men and women in the crowd began to shout "Throw away your guns." "Let the rich go; all or none." "Let the friar go." "Down with Comillas." Military authorities ordered the gangplank raised and the *Cataluña* sailed out to sea, while the police dispersed the crowd by firing into the air and arresting key individuals. The events of Sunday, July 18, had aroused the workers of Barcelona to a fever pitch of excitement.

During the following week, Catalan labor leaders and politicians debated whether to allow the excitement to dissipate or to channel it into support of a political program. Fabra Rivas' socialist group supported the latter course of action, as did the Catalan Nationalist Republican faction led by Antonio Rovira y Virgili. Through a curious set of circumstances, these two groups acted and reacted upon one another in planning the mobilization of Catalan workers (each for its own purpose). The doctrinaire young socialist and the Catalan patriot were thinking only in terms of effecting change in national policy. Not until ten days later, under the pressure of events, did either man even consider the possibility of revolution.

Catalan Nationalists and the Antiwar Protest

The antiwar protest coincided with a crisis within the Catalan Nationalist Republican party which, five years after it had separated from the Lliga Regionalista, still had not achieved a definite identity. This was particularly important in the summer of 1909, for now that Solidaridad Catalana had disbanded, Catalan Nationalists had to distinguish themselves from the other republican groups. Jaime Carner was the leader of the Catalan Nationalists; a distinguished lawyer whose oratorical skill had been expected to attract the Catalan masses, Carner had proved to be an apathetic political leader. But in July 1909, within the party headquarters, el Centre Nacionalista Republicà, a faction of dynamic young Catalans had just been elected to a policy-making board (Secció d'Estudis i de Propaganda).[18]

The leader of this faction was Antonio Rovira y Virgili, the editor of *El Poble Català*. Articulate and hardworking, deeply versed in the politics and culture of his native Catalonia, he did not disdain the demagogic tactics necessary in that era. Although he had not yet been elected to office, either because of his youth or because of his extreme ideas on Catalan autonomy and anticlericalism, he seemed on the verge of a brilliant political career. In July of 1909 Rovira y Virgili welcomed the antiwar protest, reported his devoted colleague Claudi Ametlla, because he thought it might be used to satisfy "the everlasting obsession of attracting the working population" * to the Catalan Nationalist party.[19] Even before the dramatic events of July 18 Rovira had called together party officials from the entire city to consider the possibility of sponsoring a popular demonstration. Cooler heads prevailed, and the group decided to organize a series of antiwar lectures in Catalan Nationalist centers.

Through a curious coincidence, Rovira and Ametlla had been taking English lessons during the preceding year from Fabra Rivas. While some language knowledge was imparted, the classes turned out to be "interminable political and social discussions." [20] In July 1909 Fabra Rivas' enthusiasm about the political possibilities latent in the antiwar protest further inspired Rovira y Virgili who, on the basis of past experience, thought it highly unlikely that the Socialist party would gain through the antiwar demonstrations. And so, to back up the lectures in Nationalist centers, he began a dramatic campaign in *El Poble Català*. Rovira's actions met resistance among the cautious leaders of his party. In the Radical party, an extremist group was experiencing the same difficulty.

---

* In March 1908 Catalan worker opinion had been mobilized against *El Poble Català* by the striking typesetters' syndicate. Rovira y Virgili attempted to satisfy their demands (in contrast with Emiliano Iglesias at the Radical newspaper), but some antagonism may have lingered and have acted as a further stimulant for Rovira's attempt to secure worker support through an antiwar campaign. (For the typesetters' strike, see Sastre, *Huelgas: 1908*, pp. 13–15, and *Huelgas: 1909*, pp. 6–7; also *La Internacional* [Barcelona], December 11, 1908.)

The Radicals and the Antiwar Protest

The Radical party was the logical group to lead the workers in their protest. But Lerroux was still in Buenos Aires (due to return the following month, August 1909), and thus a second echelon of party leaders was left to resolve the most serious dilemma of the Radicals' very complicated career. One horn of the dilemma was the fact that their electoral strength depended upon workers, who opposed the war. The other horn was the party's desire to retain the support of army officers, a group whose friendship the Radicals had cultivated since the *Cu-Cut* incident, and who now demanded an expansion of the war. At first (June 1909) the party left the matter to *La Rebeldía,* the newspaper of the extremist youth movement (Juventud Republicana Radical, or "Jóvenes Bárbaros" as they called themselves), which opposed the war "not because of a lack of patriotism but precisely because we are sincere patriots." [21] Such sophistry did not suffice for an aroused worker population and so the Radicals, with *La Rebeldía* again leading the way, began to force the protest into the familiar groove of anticlericalism they protested that poor soldiers were being asked to fight for "little Gabriel Maura, Comillas, and other pals (*amigotes*) of the Pontiff." [22] By mid-July editorials were no longer enough and so party leaders began a series of those violent, rowdy rallies at which they were past masters. On Thursday, July 15, these rallies culminated in a massive assembly (reportedly 6,000 men and women) outside the Casa del Pueblo. Emiliano Iglesias, although long estranged from the demagogic activities of the party, now joined in the scurrilous attacks on "the interests of Comillas, Güell and Maura, all three of whom bow down before the Pontiff." Iglesias ended, however, on a cautious note: the Radicals had declared "war on the government, not on the nation." [23]

The purpose was obvious: to direct the discontent into the established channel of anticlericalism. The question was whether this strategy would enable Emiliano Iglesias, acting Radical party chief in Lerroux' absence, to contain the revolutionary impulse assiduously cultivated by Radicals during the past eight years — "In Barcelona a revolution *does not have to be prepared,*" reported Governor Ossorio, speaking of the Radical activities, "for the simple reason that it is *always prepared.*" [24]

An action group was necessary to mobilize the workers, but this too stood ready, in positions of command within the Radical party. It consisted of the "domesticated anarchists" about whom Lerroux had bragged, "the obscure fanatics of the perennial anarchism, allied with Lerroux because they had no other milieu in which to move," in the words of Catalan essayist Gaziel.[25] This was the same group that maintained contact with Ferrer (or at least, accepted his money). Its leading figures were Luis Bertrán, a onetime anarchist now a rationalist professor in a Radical center located in the industrial suburb of Clot, and the legal advisor of the Damas Rojas;[26] Ignacio Claría, who ran the presses at El Progreso and basked in his glory as a martyr of the 1902 General Strike;[27] and Juan Colominas, an official of the Juventud Radical movement both in the municipal organization and in the branch in Pueblo Nuevo, and active also on behalf of rationalist education in his position as director of the school in the Casa del Pueblo.[28] These men were joined by veteran revolutionaries, dedicated republicans like the sixty-year-old Lorenzo Ardid [29] and enthusiastic officials of the youth movement like the lawyer José Ulled.[30] These individuals, with contacts in Radical centers throughout the city and in the most extremist factions within the party, began excitedly to prepare for action. The role of Emiliano Iglesias was to resist their demands or, should that prove impossible, to use their services in a movement designed principally to release pent-up revolutionary furor.

The Governor and the Antiwar Protest

In July 1909 personal factors rather than strict considerations of public order conditioned the policies of Governor Ossorio y Gallardo. Despite frequent trips to Madrid, a ministerial portfolio had eluded his grasp; as an avid collector of newspaper clippings, he must have been deeply affected by those that mocked his frustrated ambitions. He had not solved the mystery of the bombs, and he had antagonized the business community both by defending the teamsters at the time of the Ayxelá strike and by enforcing the Law of Sabbath Rest. Ossorio had angered another equally vociferous sector of the community: the owners of the brothels and gambling halls in the waterfront districts. In the spring of 1909, perhaps to improve his image as a public administrator, Ossorio decided to apply immediately and harshly a series of measures against prostitutes and gamblers, measures he had previously refused to implement because they had been prepared by his arch-opponent, Interior Minister La Cierva.[31] And finally, to compound his unpopularity, the Governor quarreled with the new Captain General who arrived in June; instead of helping General Luis Santiago Monescán, whose ineptness was immediately apparent, Ossorio remained aloof until the two men met in the ceremonies that marked the troop embarkations.[32] When the protest disorders began, Ossorio ignored their import as an expression of opinion and considered them from the viewpoint of public order; their successful repression might well enhance his career.

Personal ambitions, ideologies, political aspirations — such were the forces that motivated the events in Barcelona during the week beginning on Monday, July 19. But it was the action and counter-action of events that determined the final result.

CHAPTER X

From Street Demonstrations
To General Strike

ON MONDAY, July 19, Maura's government attempted to abate the public protest by announcing that there would be no further troop embarkations from Barcelona. Politicians were forced to find some new means of sustaining the antiwar protest, so on Monday night the demonstrations that had taken place on the wharf moved uptown to the central city boulevards. Though obviously propelled from behind the scenes by "*lerrouxistas* from the Casa del Pueblo and young members of the Centre Nacionalista Republicà," as Governor Ossorio reported,[1] the occasion for the public protest was both authentic and serious.

The military expedition to Morocco became a full-scale war with the battle on Sunday, July 18, when for the first time since their initial assault, Riffian tribes attacked the supply lines. The Spanish troops were routed and suffered heavy casualties, a development that added a desperate quality to the antiwar protest; despite eight years of experimentation, Catalans had still not devised any effective means of influencing national policy. Unable to halt the embarkations, they now resorted to street demonstrations, the only means of expression available to them, in attempting the more serious project of forcing the government to end hostilities in Morocco.

During the week of July 18 through July 25, the events in Barcelona were still considered the vanguard of a national protest. In fact they gained new importance when on Tuesday, July 20, demonstrations began in train stations in Madrid and other cities of central Spain, as battalions of the First Brigade left for Morocco.

Monday Evening, July 19

The demonstrations in the streets of Barcelona began in an apparently spontaneous fashion.[2] Cabled reports of Sunday's battle had arrived too late for inclusion in the Monday evening newspaper, but the news circulated orally in cafés and political centers.* By 8:30 P.M. a group of young workers had gathered on the Ramblas to shout "Down with War," the slogan adopted by the Radical party. A crowd assembled and soon began to move in a compact mass, pausing before the Marquis' palace to proclaim "Long Live Spain and Death to Comillas" before moving on to the offices of Rovira Virgili's *El Poble Català,* where employees leaned out of the windows to applaud and demonstrators responded with approving shouts. The crowd emerged on the Plaza de la Universidad, where a special police detachment was waiting; the police quickly dispersed the crowd by firing into the air and arrested eight young men. This was the pattern for the demonstrations that occurred nightly until Friday, July 23.

The wisest course might have been to allow the demonstrations to take place, under police surveillance, as an escape valve that would have eased the tensions. But Ossorio refused such advice, claiming that the protest was not an expression of public opinion but the work of republican agitators. When he made elaborate plans for a direct confrontation with the demonstrators, he endowed them with an importance out of proportion to their numbers and contributed to the pervading violence.

Tuesday, July 20

The morning newspapers printed reports of the rout in Morocco two days earlier. Reinforcing the news coverage, Emiliano Iglesias in *El Progreso* and Antonio Rovira y Virgili in *El Poble Català* began their decisively important editorial campaign. "The war is now a fact. Neither the clamor of the people in the street nor the press have been able to impede it," commented *El Progreso.* "From his summer hideaway in Santander, Maura has decreed war." Workers were urged to demand a speedy and honorable peace. The Nationalist Republican paper echoed these sentiments. A wide sector of the Catalan political spectrum welcomed the editorial campaign and considered it "sanctified and patriotic." [3]

---

* Only those who have lived in Spain can appreciate the efficacy and rapidity of this channel of communication, undoubtedly developed as one means of combating regimes that limit the standard channels of the press and meetings.

The City Council, assembling that evening for its regular Tuesday session, might have played a constructive role, serving as a forum for public discussion and mediating the confrontation between an aroused public and government officials bent on restoring order. But city councilors had only taken office on July 1, so they lacked both experience and cohesion. The presiding officer was Mayor Juan Coll y Pujol, a professor of penal law in the University of Barcelona and long active in Conservative party politics; he was an elderly man in poor health, who had only been appointed late in June to fill the post left vacant throughout the previous year.*

The Radical party constituted the majority in the City Council, and the extremist faction tried to use this for political gain. On Tuesday evening Santiago Valentí Camps rose to defend both Spain and the Army, as a preface to his proposal that the Council send a respectful request to Maura that he not "expend more lives on behalf of private enterprises." [4] Although spectators applauded, none of Valentí's Radical colleagues seconded the motion and it was finally referred to a committee. In this Council session, Radical party leaders began the dichotomous policy that they followed during the next two weeks. As befitted responsible public servants, Radical councilors advocated moderate measures leading to a rapid restoration of order. But in their newspaper, and even more in violent speeches in Radical centers, officials urged the workers to resort to violence in demanding an end to the war.

Meanwhile, members of the Juventud Radical ("Jóvenes Bárbaros") participated in the street demonstrations. On Tuesday evening the police tried hard to control them; they patrolled the central district and arrested those who shouted "Down with War," brutally mistreating the prisoners, according to Radical accounts. At 9 P.M. Governor Ossorio appeared and walked up the Ramblas, the central boulevards, "surrounded by his general staff"; by the time he reached the Plaza de Cataluña, the catcalls and shouts were so offensive that he decided to seek refuge in a hotel.

These street demonstrations, still very minor affairs, accumulated momentum daily as workers grew bolder and police more exasperated. One very serious consequence of these nightly street encounters was that they impaired the authority of the Governor. Both *El Progreso* and *El Poble Català* exploited the events for comic effect, juxtaposing the dramatic image

---

* Barcelona had been without a mayor since the late spring of 1908 when Mayor Juan Sanllehy resigned because of the bitter criticism of his veto, in response to clerical pressures, of the Special Budget for Culture.

of a city under siege with the ludicrous image of "the obese Ossorio" as "el General Bum-Bum," who took refreshments as well as precautions while he prepared for battle.[5] More importantly, although the Governor assembled a large police force in the streets, he could not end the disorders; the police were not skillful enough to prevent mobs from forming nor able to disband them permanently. Ossorio bragged (and with good reason) that despite all provocations, the police obeyed their orders not to fire upon the crowd. Yet to employ so many armed police in so unsuccessful a manner only served in the long run to incite further violence.

The street encounters had other consequences. They forced merchants to close their shops early in the evening, appreciably decreasing sales. Merchants, already irritated by the Governor's prohibition of work on Sunday, were infuriated by his inability to reestablish order; at this critical time Ossorio thus lost the support of an important sector of the middle class. However, the single most significant consequence of these demonstrations was that they encouraged Catalan politicians — and specifically the workers' duly elected representatives to the Cortes — to support the antiwar movement.

The Catalan Nationalist Republican deputies initiated the action: they met and decided to send a telegram to Maura, demanding that he open the Cortes in order "to give parliamentary stature to the question, and to make public the aspirations of the Republican Nationalist movement in Catalonia." Such a move would have pleased Rovira y Virgili, editor of the group's official organ, but calmer voices prevailed. The deputies decided that the telegram would have little effect if sponsored only by their party, a minority within the Catalan electoral bloc; therefore they decided to seek the support of the other republican parties in Solidaridad Catalana. A meeting was arranged for the following day with deputies from the Federalist and Republican Union parties which had, independently, announced earlier that same afternoon that they were reviewing their policy in view of developments in Morocco.[6]

Those in direct contact with workers knew that such measures would not assuage their intense anger at an unjust conscription and a war. By Tuesday night certain officials of Solidaridad Obrera had decided to schedule for the following Friday a meeting to discuss the possibility of forcing Maura to end hostilities.[7] Given the tense situation and the mobilization of workers begun in the campaigns for the Alcalá del Valle prisoners and against the

Ter Valley lockout, the anarcho-syndicalist faction hoped that Solidaridad Obrera would decide at the meeting to call a general strike.

For Fabra Rivas and his group of collaborators, the plans for a Solidaridad Obrera meeting posed a serious problem. The socialists had a minority voice in the labor confederation, as in the Catalan labor force in general. The only way that their party could hope to benefit from the workers' anti-war protest was to incorporate it into a national general strike convoked by the Socialist party. Two days earlier Pablo Iglesias had publicly threatened such a move. Barcelona socialists intended to force him to make good on this threat; in the name of the Catalan Socialist Federation they prepared a petition asking that the National Committee immediately organize a congress in Madrid of all labor groups, who would authorize and prepare a general strike. Lacking money for railroad fare, they mailed their petition to Madrid. Preparations for a nationwide general strike would take at least ten days: Fabra Rivas' group set Monday, August 2, as the target date. In the interim, its concern was to maintain the Socialist party in the vanguard of the protest. One means was to publicize the petition for a national congress, even though it had not been formally approved by Catalan socialists as yet. Because the next issue of Fabra Rivas' own newspaper, *La Internacional,* would not appear for another three days, he decided to ask that the petition be published in the paper of his friend and language student, Antonio Rovira y Virgili.

Wednesday, July 21

On Wednesday morning, *El Poble Català* published as a news item a report of the petition of the Catalan Socialist Federation: concrete plans to prepare a national general strike were thus publicly announced for the first time, not in a small labor publication but in a metropolitan daily newspaper. *El Poble Català* also published the announcement of the Solidaridad Obrera meeting to be held on Friday to discuss the war. Finally, *El Poble Català* published an editorial assuring the workers of its support in their antiwar protest "not only in the name of Catalonia, but also in the name of humanity and of the proletariat." The Catalan Republican Nationalist paper was the only one that day to publish news of the activities planned by labor groups. Perhaps Rovira y Virgili included this news as a means of prodding Catalan republican deputies into taking action on behalf of their labor constituents.

At 3:30 P.M. deputies of all republican groups represented in Solidaridad Catalana met in the home of José María Vallés y Ribot to consider the telegram proposed by the Catalan Nationalists demanding that Maura open the Cortes. Republican deputies incorporated into the demand the workers' grievance against the conscription system. But again republican deputies hesitated before acting, perhaps because they realized (with whatever sadness) that their request would have no effect upon Maura unless it were signed by the powerful Lliga Regionalista. It was probably as great a surprise to them as it was to Governor Ossorio that Lliga leaders, contacted the same afternoon, signed the telegram. This signified an end to Maura's effort to work out an alliance between the Conservative party and the Lliga.*

Considered from another viewpoint, the decision of the industrialists of the Lliga to join with workers, middle class republicans, and journalists in Catalonia to demand that the Cortes be opened, made it appear for one moment that these duly elected representatives to the Cortes might secure through *legal* channels a change of government policy — that is, an end to hostilities in Morocco. But from Governor Ossorio's viewpoint, the telegram to Maura merely signified Solidaridad Catalana's support for a "slanderous protest movement." [8] And workers probably interpreted the telegram in much the same way, as support for them in a violent street protest against the Maura government rather than an actual attempt to change policy — a sad commentary on representative government in Spain.

Although Catalan deputies, labor leaders, and the demonstrators were acting independently of one another in protesting the war in Morocco, each acted and reacted upon the other. The result was to transform the encounters between workers and police into a serious threat to public order.

One indication was that shots were fired in an encounter late Wednesday night. Governor Ossorio had briefly reviewed his police forces and then retired with his officers to the fashionable Maison Dorée Restaurant. While they were dining, police skirmished with demonstrators down in the Atarazana district near the wharves. Shots were fired and a policeman was injured slightly in the leg. There were no further casualties, surprising in view of

* Francisco Cambó, the Lliga leader who had collaborated with Maura in working out this alliance, was not in Barcelona in July 1909. Temporarily disillusioned with politics when a jury freed the Radicals who had shot at him during the election Cambó was taking a leisurely trip abroad. Had he been in Barcelona he probably would have supported Maura, for he was the only Catalan politician who had publicly defended an active policy in Morocco. (Jesús Pabón, *Cambó: 1876–1918* [Barcelona, 1952], pp 326–28.)

the fact that many Radical rowdies carried guns, which (according to Lliga deputy Juan Ventosa[9]) they were able to buy for cash or even on credit at the Casa del Pueblo.*

A far more serious indication that the antiwar protest had entered a new phase was that on Wednesday night the workers drew up a formal statement of their grievances in a rally held in Tarrasa, which is located thirty-one kilometers from Barcelona.

The rally at Tarrasa resembled the Solidaridad Obrera rally held on behalf of the textile workers in Granollers just three weeks earlier. Again, plans for a general strike were not announced in Barcelona but in another city. And, as had happened at the earlier rally, the resolution adopted at Tarrasa did not actually announce a general strike but simply warned workers to prepare for such an eventuality.

At Tarrasa, Fabra Rivas was a featured speaker, at the side of Mariano Castellote, an anarchist famed because of repeated arrests as a terrorist, and José Prat, who had helped to publicize anarcho-syndicalism in Catalonia. The young socialist was desperately bidding in competition with the anarchists for the allegiance of the workers, as he joined in harsh condemnation of the government. The police agent assigned to report on the meeting tried but failed to suspend the proceedings. Ignoring the police, the assembled group of perhaps 2,000 workers went on to approve, by acclamation, a resolution that was a strange mixture of the class struggle and the anti-clericalism so dear to the Catalan worker. Fabra Rivas had reportedly prepared the text of the resolution:[10]

Considering the fact that war is a fatal consequence of the capitalist system of production;

Considering, also, the fact that under the present Spanish system, only workers go to fight the war which the bourgeoisie declare:

The Assembly protests energetically:

1. Against the action of the Spanish Government in Morocco;

* The government entered as evidence in the trial of Radical politicians an anonymous letter reporting that Browning revolvers were distributed or sold on credit in the Casa del Pueblo during this week by Joaquín Vila, a city councilman, and reporting that the capital to buy the arms had been supplied by Juan Rovira Palau, a wealthy Argentine elected in May 1909 on the Radical ticket to the City Council (Ministerio de la Guerra, *Causa contra Trinidad Alted Fornet, Emiliano Iglesias Ambrosio, Luis Zurdo de Olivares y Juana Ardiaca Mas por el delito de rebelión militar. Ocurrió el hecho desde el 26 al 31 de julio de 1909. Dieron principio las actuaciones el 29 de julio de 1909. Terminaron el 5 de julio de 1910* [Madrid, 1911], I, 166–67.)

2. Against the proceedings of certain ladies of the aristocracy who insult the suffering of the reservists, of their wives and children, giving them medals and scapularies instead of providing them with the means of sustenance which is wrenched from them by the removal of the head of the family;

3. Against sending to war citizens useful to production and in general indifferent to the triumph of the Cross over the Half Moon, when they could form regiments of priests and monks who, besides being directly interested in the triumph of the Catholic religion, have no family nor home nor are they of any service to the nation; and

4. Against the attitude of the republican deputies who have not taken advantage of their parliamentary immunity in order to take their place at the head of the masses in the protest against the war:

And it demands that the working class concentrate all its forces in the event that it should become necessary to declare a general strike in order to force the government to respect the right of Moroccans to preserve intact the independence of their nation.

In Madrid, Interior Minister Juan de La Cierva interpreted the Tarrasa resolution, the only published statement of the causes and objectives of the general strike in Catalonia, as confirmation of his contention that the antiwar demonstrations was merely a pretext for a seditious political movement. La Cierva was determined to forestall any such movement, particularly in view of the crisis in Morocco, where a major battle seemed imminent.

Thursday, July 22

Therefore early Thursday morning, La Cierva instructed all governors to implement emergency measures of public order because of threats from "revolutionary elements in Madrid and Barcelona." [11] Through these measures he achieved, albeit with no legal authorization, a suspension of constitutional guarantees.

Barcelona was a matter of particular concern to La Cierva. He had received reports from the secret Spanish police assigned to the embassy in Paris that anarchists in the French capital were talking of plans for a revolution in Barcelona. Therefore, early Thursday afternoon, La Cierva followed up his original telegram to all governors with a message to Ossorio warning him to keep all Radicals and anarchists under close surveillance, noting especially if they took a trip abroad. La Cierva did not share the

Paris reports with Ossorio but merely expressed his own fears as cause for action.[12]

La Cierva's instructions refired his dormant feud with Ossorio, the "Minister-Governor" of Barcelona. To Ossorio, battling for his position and perhaps his career, La Cierva was merely using the antiwar demonstrations as a pretext for reasserting his authority and for enhancing his prestige as an efficient administrator. Ossorio planned to use the opportunity for his own political advantage. On the basis of reports from his own paid informants in Barcelona, Ossorio was convinced that the workers' protest movement was not seditious in intent; at the most he thought it would be simply another of the explosions of worker violence that characterized Catalonia. He had begun to prepare for a confrontation with the workers.

On Thursday morning a proclamation by Governor Ossorio had been posted throughout the city. Referring solely to the wounding of a policeman on the previous night (and not to the national emergency), Ossorio prohibited groups from gathering on public thoroughfares and threatened that police would not continue to show the restraint of previous days.[13] Although he stated that the disorders were the work of professional agitators, he made no arrests. The city, which sympathized with the demonstrators, took affront at Ossorio's "infamous proclamation." Even the normally reserved Juan Caballé, writing in *El Liberal* on the following day, protested that "through this draconian edict, Ossorio had carried martial law into effect without actually proclaiming it."

But Ossorio persisted. La Cierva had prohibited the circulation of all seditious news, so Ossorio went still further: at 2 P.M. he informed newsmen in Barcelona that he was suspending all long-distance calls to Madrid and all direct telegraph communication.[14] This drastic measure cut Barcelona off from factual reports of the disorders in Madrid and of the war; the city's newspapers carried speculative, dramatized accounts, while exaggerated rumors circulated in cafés and political centers, based on the premise that such severe government measures must indicate a serious crisis.

The struggle for power and prestige between the Governor and the Minister of the Interior added a new factor to the tense situation in Barcelona. However Antonio Maura was still in Madrid to arbitrate this quarrel as he had done for the previous two years; not until he left the capital over the weekend did the feud between Ossorio and La Cierva assume great, perhaps even tragic consequences.

The effect of Ossorio's harsh measures was to make workers even more determined that the government should heed their demand to end the war. On Thursday two more papers (*Las Noticias* and *El Progreso*) published the Solidaridad Obrera invitation to all labor syndicates, whether members of the confederation or not, to send representatives to the meeting scheduled for the following night. The Radicals' *El Progreso,* erstwhile foe of Solidaridad Obrera, urged "all labor societies, without distinction, to work on behalf of the campaign that is to be initiated."

El Poble Català devoted an entire editorial to the general strike which the workers were preparing. Fabra Rivas' influence was to be discerned in the curious statement that the protest would force the government to change its policy in Morocco and yet would involve no violence. "As Catalans and as human beings," *El Poble Català* pledged its support.

Newspapers had announced the Solidaridad Obrera meeting and posters had been put up throughout the city. Yet it was not until Thursday morning that labor leaders applied for the necessary permit. José Rodríguez Romero, a longtime associate of Francisco Ferrer and a minor official of Solidaridad Obrera, went to the Governor's office, where he was told that all antiwar rallies were now prohibited. Ossorio ordered that Rodríguez Romero be detained for several hours, informed him that he would be prosecuted for planning an illegal meeting, and sent the posters to the court as proof of sedition.[15] The Governor appeared to be deliberately taunting the labor movement, which, prodded by a small group of agitators, was quite willing to take up the gauntlet.

Catalan socialists still hoped that the National Committee would heed their request, and would convoke a labor congress in Madrid for the purpose of declaring a national general strike — before the anarcho-syndicalists launched a strike in Barcelona. But in reality, preparations from Madrid for a national strike were made almost impossible by La Cierva's censorship of telegraph and telephone lines. Ossorio had cut off all communication with Madrid, and Barcelona socialists did not even have the fare to send a representative by train to convince the National Committee of the need for a general strike. Aside from these technical difficulties, timid national party leaders delayed a decision until they could consult (evidently by mail!) leaders in various cities.[16]

By now the protest had grown far beyond a complaint against the recall of workers to military duty. The problem of how to provide for the conscript's family, however, had not yet been solved, and so somewhat belatedly on Thursday afternoon, prominent Barcelona citizens met to consider remedying this situation through private philanthropy.[17] The Board of Directors of the Chamber of Commerce, Industry, and Navigation met in a special session where its president, Pedro Maristany, urged his colleagues to continue paying the salaries of all reservists while on active duty. The board members agreed and promised to urge other employers to comply. On that same afternoon the Marquise of Castellflorite, a prominent philanthropist, presided over a meeting attended by civic and business leaders as well as by the Governor and other authorities. This group agreed to assume responsibility for paying the salary of a reservist out of funds to be raised by subscription or possibly through a loan from the provincial government.

Although the civic groups had tried to avoid a patronizing tone, workers resented the fact that this was relief offered by the wealthy to the poor (lest they forget, the Radical newspaper reminded them). Nevertheless on the following day, Friday, many families filed an application for aid. But the group actually had no funds on hand to meet the need. These measures might have had some impact on public opinion during the preceding week when reserve soldiers were first called up; but they were almost ignored by a worker population aroused by two weeks of street demonstrations and by the prospect of a general strike.

Reacting to these powerful stimuli, the workers in the Radical party showed their discontent with the cautious policy of their leaders. Their indignation reached its climax at an antiwar rally in the Casa del Pueblo, with Emiliano Iglesias scheduled to be among the speakers. But only a minor official, Juan Pich y Pons, appeared, with an obvious mission to pacify. Pich lamely excused the absence of the party leaders, proclaimed his fervent love for the Army, and assured the workers that he understood their desire for peace; however, their only hope was for Maura to decide to open the Cortes. The police agent assigned to the meeting reported that the audience, particularly the women, shouted and stamped on the floor to show their dissatisfaction. There were angry comments that "the other orators had not appeared because they were cowards."[18] Radical leaders could not delay for much longer a response to the workers' demand for action.

Friday, July 23

On Friday morning, Barcelona newspapers published the text of Maura's reply to the telegram of Solidaridad Catalana deputies. It dispelled any hopes they may have seriously entertained about influencing Maura's policies. The Premier refused to concede that the legislators had any basis for criticism of the Moroccan expedition, stating that he had not changed the established colonial policy but was merely repressing "a lamentable turbulence and aggression." Criticism of the conscription system was "inadmissible" in view of the fact the Cortes had failed to pass an army reform bill that his government had introduced. He did promise, however, that an "amelioration" of current difficulties was being prepared.*

On Friday afternoon Catalan republican deputies met in the home of Federalist Vallés y Ribot to discuss Maura's reply. The Premier's intransigence confused them; the answer seemed to be further consultation. The Catalan republican deputies decided to invite the entire parliamentary representation of Catalonia to meet with them — that is, not only the Carlist and Lliga deputies of Solidaridad Catalana, but Radical deputies Hermenegildo Giner de los Ríos and Sol y Ortega. Vallés y Ribot mailed out invitations for a meeting to be held in his home on the following Tuesday afternoon. The Radicals showed no interest in the meeting, but Carlist and Lliga deputies promised to attend.[19]

The turmoil in labor circles contrasted sharply with the placidity of the Catalan deputies' deliberations. On Friday morning the socialist newpaper, *La Internacional,* was distributed. An editorial criticized republican politicians for their failure to act. Far more important was the announcement that the Catalan Socialist Federation had asked the National Committee of the Socialist party to organize a general strike of the entire country. But this paper probably reached only a small audience which would explain why *El Poble Català* felt it necessary to print the text.

On Friday, the day of the Solidaridad Obrera antiwar rally, workers were undoubtedly far more affected by the exciting news on the front pages of the commercial press. Public indignation focused on the report that, under orders from the Captain General of Barcelona, General Santiago, ten of the reserve soldiers in the Reus Battalion who had participated in the demonstration at the wharf on the previous Sunday had been summarily court-martialed; it was rumored that they would be executed. *El Poble Català* and *La Publicidad* printed the text of the Tarrasa resolution on the need for a general strike to oppose the war. But no newspaper reported that the Governor had prohibited the Solidaridad Obrera meeting.

Therefore at 9:30 on Friday evening, representatives of Barcelona's labor

---

* On Saturday, July 24, the official *Gaceta* in Madrid announced that families of reserve soldiers would receive fifty céntimos a day, cold comfort in an economy where the minimum existence wage was three pesetas fifty céntimos a day.

unions began to gather in the headquarters of the labor confederation.[20] They were met by a police agent sent by Ossorio, who informed them that the meeting could not be held. Union representatives were shown the Governor's order, which stated that the gathering was not intended to protest the war but "to disfigure events, excite passions, and stimulate the rebellious to produce serious disorders." They were also informed that the Governor intended to prosecute Solidaridad Obrera officials for convoking the meeting. Workers stayed on in the Solidaridad Obrera offices or went to the nearby cafés to discuss the situation. The element of a personal vengeance against Ossorio had been added to their protest, reported Anarchist Leopoldo Bonafulla; a general strike appeared to be the only means whereby "the militant proletariat could prove they would not blindly obey a man who described them to other men as enemies."[21]

Despite agreement among workers on the need for a general strike, the final decision had yet to be made. Officials of the member syndicates of Solidaridad Obrera opposed the move. From a judicious appraisal of the harsh repression that was certain to follow, or simply from fear, these officials refused to implicate the labor confederation in so hazardous an undertaking — first on Friday, and then definitively on Saturday night.

Throughout the weekend tension mounted. "The valves have been closed and steam is accumulating. Who knows if it will explode?" editorialized *El Poble Català* on Saturday morning, reporting Ossorio's suspension of the workers' meeting the previous evening. Conscious of its role in having fomented that tension, Rovira y Virgili's newspaper was now afraid that the protest would break out prematurely; workers were warned that if their protest was to affect government policy, they "must contain all impulses."

By now the movement had gone too far to be controlled by rational considerations or by moderate groups such as the Catalan Nationalists. The subsequent development of events in Barcelona resulted from the actions and interactions of a small group: the "domesticated anarchists" in the Radical party; the socialists and anarcho-syndicalists determined upon a general strike (albeit for different purposes); Governor Ossorio, who had the necessary force to control the situation; and Mariano de Foronda, director of the streetcar company, who had become the symbolic leader of management's resistance to labor demands.

Throughout the weekend, the Barcelona protest was still believed to be the vanguard of a national movement. Until censorship cut off their news, Catalan workers had read of demonstrations in Madrid and other cities, and they had no reason to believe the national protest would not continue. And on Saturday morning, despite the censor, workers read of the most severe battle yet fought: Riffian tribes had finally succeeded in their week-long attempt to break the Spanish supply lines. The fighting had taken place the preceding day (July 23) on the spurs of Mt. Ait-Aix, where a battalion of the First Brigade from Madrid had borne the brunt of the fighting; but Barcelona residents were angered by reports that untrained, seasick reserves were marched straight from the ship to the battlefield. The heavy fighting that continued through the next six days had two effects upon developments in Barcelona: it made workers even more determined to force the government to stop the war, and it was used to justify Interior Minister La Cierva's imposition of still harsher measures to maintain public order.

Saturday, July 24

By Saturday the Governor had the force he needed to forestall any large scale action by the workers. Police had complete dossiers on all Barcelona agitators; Ossorio could have ordered their arrest. He had brought into the city some 700 armed Civil Guards, some of whom were mounted troops, from throughout the province of Barcelona; he might have stationed this police force, the one most feared by Spanish workers, in the streets to intimidate the workers. The Governor chose not to take any action.

Long after the events, Angel Ossorio insisted that to have done so would have been interpreted as a provocation that justified violence. He admitted that men were planning a general strike but sarcastically pointed out that they were merely "corroborating a protest already formulated by newspapers, deputies, and senators."[22] Paid informants assured him that plans were still vague and syndicate officials reluctant to act. And in the event that the strike did occur, the Governor was confident he had the power to repress it. He was determined that an effective handling of the antiwar protest should redound to his political credit and not to that of the Interior Minister. Ossorio's position became more vulnerable on Friday morning when Antonio Maura left Madrid to join the King in Santiago de Campostella for ceremonies honoring the patron saint of Spain; Maura did not return until Tuesday morning, July 27. In the interim Ossorio was forced to deal directly with the officious La Cierva.

Mariano de Foronda, head of the Belgian-owned streetcar company and a powerful cacique of the Conservative party, complicated the difficult relationship between Ossorio and La Cierva. On business and political ground he felt personally responsible for preventing any successful labor demonstration. On Saturday evening Foronda went to talk with Ossorio about the possibility that a general strike might actually take place on the following Monday. The Governor dismissed the reports as unimportant rumors. Alarmed by this nonchalant attitude and by the proportions that the strike was assuming, Foronda telegraphed his information to La Cierva in Madrid; La Cierva immediately telephoned Ossorio who denied that there was an emergency, adding that if something unexpected should occur, he had the force to repress it.[23]

However by the late evening even Ossorio was beginning to have second thoughts. He had been so confident of his control over the situation that he had signed permits authorizing thirty-four dances in working class neighborhoods to honor the patron saint of Spain. Almost all political centers were holding special activities. In these large gatherings throughout the city, exaggerated accounts of the fighting in Morocco and attacks upon the Maura government circulated freely. Ossorio was sufficiently concerned by reports on these gatherings to call a press conference late in the evening and to denounce the "elements to whose advantage it is to keep alive public excitement, calmed to some degree by the censorship. . . . Following a preconceived plan, they divulge verbally what would be prohibited by any other means."[24]

Until late Saturday it was still true to say, as Ossorio contended, that there "existed the intention of going out on strike when it would be possible, and in the form in which it would be possible, but that no agreement had been reached."[25] The situation changed with the formation of an action group: the Central Committee for the Strike (Comité Central de Huelga).

About ten-thirty on Saturday night José Casasola, a professor long identified with Ferrer, concluded a lecture on "Science and Religion" in the Solidaridad Obrera headquarters and then reportedly left. Miguel Villalobos Moreno, another teacher associated with Ferrer, stayed behind to discuss with four or five individuals the possibility of holding the general strike on the following Monday. They immediately reported their plans to the Solidaridad Obrera officials and the delegates of the member syndicates who were on the premises. Most of them rejected the plan and they definitely refused to have Solidaridad Obrera officially sponsor the strike, some because they were convinced that the movement would be a failure.[26]

Thereupon Moreno and José Rodríguez Romero, an official of the printers' union long associated with Ferrer, constituted themselves the Central Committee for the Strike. Those Solidaridad Obrera officials willing to collaborate went immediately to cafés throughout the city and asked labor leaders to support the strike with the understanding that it would last only one day.[27]

About midnight Moreno and Rodríguez Romero went to invite the socialists, who were meeting in another section of Barcelona, to participate in the Committee. Fabra Rivas and his socialist group tried to persuade Moreno to postpone action until the following Monday (August 2), by which time they could organize a nationwide general strike. But Moreno was adamant and so the socialists agreed to collaborate, designating Fabra Rivas as their representative on the Committee. Moreno was to represent the syndicalists, and Rodríguez Romero the anarchists.[28]

The leadership provided by the three able members of the Central Committee was the determining factor in transforming a diffuse antiwar protest of Catalan workers into a general strike. Eusebio Corominas, a Catalan republican, was later to protest that the Committee "served for nothing more than to give the signal of how and when the movement was to begin, as any political element whatsoever could have done." [29] But that was the point: neither the Centre Nacionalista Republicà, nor the Radical party, nor even Solidaridad Obrera had been willing to take the lead. The Committee assumed the responsibility and began twenty-four hours of feverish organizational activity, planning to culminate this with a giant rally of Barcelona workers at midnight on Sunday, the eve of the strike.

One of the Committee's first tasks was to inform the newspapers. Leaving the socialist meeting, the three men visited the offices of newspapers in Barcelona that had protested against the war in Morocco to inform them of the Committee's existence. They claimed that Solidaridad Obrera officials were supporting the strike but that in order to avoid implicating either the labor confederation or the member syndicates, Solidaridad Obrera would not officially sponsor the strike. They assured newspapermen that they planned nothing more than "a general work stoppage as a protest against the war in the Rif, and even more than against the war, as a protest against the lack of prior planning on the part of the Government and against the conscription of reserve soldiers." Almost all the editors whom they visited expressed their sympathy with the strike.[30]

The next step was the actual organization of a strike, not only in Barcelona but in cities throughout the province of Barcelona and, if possible, in the other Catalan provinces. One of the Committee's decisions was to avoid all public association with men like Francisco Ferrer, anarchists Leopoldo Bonafulla and Anselmo Lorenzo, or Radical extremist Luis Zurdo Olivares. "We did this," explained a Solidaridad Obrera official "because of our fear that their influence might cause the failure of the movement, which was popular and of interest to all classes, without any specific political orientation." [31]

Another concern was to evade police detection. The Committee chose a secluded place for its headquarters and prepared an elaborate system of replacements so that the strike would not fail if a few individuals were arrested. The Committee then began the task of informing workers of the strike plans and coordinating those plans. The Sunday newspaper had not even mentioned the strike. The Committee published no leaflet. Two editors of *El Poble Català*, R. Noguer y Comet and Marius Aguilar, subsequently reported that the Committee asked them to contribute money for the publication of some propaganda leaflets, because Solidaridad Obrera had no funds and even if it had the money could not use it for the strike, which was not an official activity. The Catalan Nationalists agreed to contribute but the men never returned to collect the donation.[32] There was no other mention that leaflets were even planned.

The general strike was organized by contacting labor leaders throughout the city and the provinces of Barcelona and Gerona, in person or by letter.[33] It was reported that Moreno and Rodríguez Romero "stole" Solidaridad Obrera's official seal and used it on all correspondence connected with the strike;[34] certainly it would have dignified the letters mailed to Madrid and Bilbao. Several individuals went at their own expense to contact labor groups in Valencia and Saragossa. Fabra Rivas himself left sometime during the dawn hours of Sunday to persuade the textile workers in the Ter Valley (already alerted to the possibility of a general strike in protest against the Manlleu lockout) to support the antiwar general strike; he did not return until late on Sunday evening.[35] His absence from Barcelona at a crucial moment in the strike preparations may account for his failure to realize until too late that Moreno was maneuvering to turn the entire movement over to the extremist faction of the Radical party.[36]

Working in Barcelona, Moreno and Rodríguez Romero used to advantage the fact that on Sunday syndicate officials often used their free day to come in from the industrial suburbs of Barcelona and from nearby towns to consult with Solidaridad Obrera officials about business. A larger than usual number came because of the antiwar protest; they were informed of the general strike and given instructions for carrying it out in their districts. The Committee sent delegates to inform labor syndicates which were not members of

Solidaridad Obrera that the strike would not involve violence and would last only twenty-four hours; syndicates were invited to send representatives to the rally scheduled for late that night in which the final plans for the strike would be announced.[37]

During the afternoon Moreno and Rodríguez Romero canvassed newspaper offices, informing the editors of their preparations for the strike and reassuring them of its nonviolent character. They asked that the Monday morning editions carry editorials urging workers to support the strike.[38] At five o'clock the two men reached the offices of *El Progreso* and told Emiliano Iglesias' secretary, Bartolomé Calderón Font, of the latest details. They had met with Iglesias once on Saturday night and now sought a second interview; Calderón wished them good luck with their plans and said that Iglesias would be in the office later in the evening. The two men returned at seven o'clock but Iglesias had still not arrived; Calderón suggested they come back at eleven o'clock. Moreno and Rodríguez Romero concluded their visits to the other newspaper offices by nine o'clock and then went to invite Fabra Rivas, who had just returned from the Ter Valley, to attend the meeting with Emiliano Iglesias.[39] These two men realized better than Fabra Rivas did that the factor which would spell success or failure was the position adopted by the Radical party.

The Radical Party

Radical leaders had also been busy since Saturday evening, for they could no longer ignore the demands of the extremist faction within the party. As their editorials and speeches had indicated, anticlericalism would be the focal point of any action they planned. The moment could not have been more propitious, because the following day, Sunday, July 25, was the seventy-fourth anniversary of the first convent burnings in Barcelona. *El Diluvio,* a republican newspaper, commemorated the occasion by reprinting as usual "Recuerdos," an article by Francisco Pi y Margall first printed in 1892, in which the President of the First Republic had suggested that burning convents might once again, as in 1835, be the only solution for solving the clerical problem. On the front page of its newspaper, *El Progreso,* the Radical party carried an editorial with the English title, "Remember." Despite the parliamentary immunity from prosecution suddenly conferred on *El Progreso* the preceding day by Radical Deputy Giner de los Ríos, the editorial was cautious. It merely reminded readers that the occasion for the convent burnings of 1835 had been bad bulls and expressed a hope that the bullfight scheduled for that afternoon would not have a similar epilogue. When Interior Minster La Cierva later denounced the inflammatory nature of "Remember," Emiliano Iglesias blandly replied that insofar as the charge was true it merely incited workers to burn convents, which constituted a civil crime, and not a rebellion as La Cierva charged.[40]

The full legal implications of "Remember" had undoubtedly been discussed in the meeting held on Saturday evening in the Casa del Pueblo where lawyer Emiliano Iglesias conferred with three city councilmen of the Radical party.[41] Hundreds of workers, knowing of the meeting, gathered to await the announcement of whether or not the Radicals would participate in the general strike. One of these individuals was Baldomero Bonet, who had come to inquire what role his baker's union, affiliated with the Radical party, would be expected to play. Learning that the party leaders were still conferring, he left the building, but he returned later to dine in a private room of a café with the Radical politicians. On the basis of Bonet's subsequent activities, authorities suspected that the men had discussed the possibility of burning convents.

The following afternoon crowds thronged the Casa del Pueblo, as they normally did on a Sunday afternoon. Several meetings had been scheduled. Members of Juventud Radical, extremely active in the demonstrations of the previous week, met to consider the plight of their members who had been arrested. Far more important was a large rally of textile workers from all over Catalonia, the key element in the labor force, who had met to discuss the continuing lockout in the Ter Valley. In the Casa del Pueblo the Radicals' bold editorial "Remember" was the main topic of discussion, together with rumors of a general strike.

From the viewpoint of Emiliano Iglesias, the question was how best to coordinate the Radical antiwar protest (focused on anticlericalism by the editorial "Remember") with the plans of the Central Committee for the Strike. Over the weekend he met twice with Committee members to discuss the issue.

The Central Committee and the Radical Party

The first meeting of the Committee members and Emiliano Iglesias was held late Saturday night or in the very early hours of Sunday morning. Because a majority of the organized workers of Catalonia belonged to the

Radical party, it was imperative for the Committee to secure from Iglesias a statement of support for the general strike. As Fabra Rivas later reported, this was the sole reason why the Committee contacted Iglesias; at least he was under no illusion that the Radical politicians were actually sincere in their demagogic propaganda about defending workers' rights.[42]

Fabra Rivas used his eloquence and his knowledge of the congresses of the Second International to try to convince Iglesias that the general strike "would be a peaceful work stoppage, a sitdown strike and nothing more." His references to peaceful general strikes in other countries greatly annoyed the chauvinistic and pragmatic Iglesias who said flatly that in the tense Barcelona situation it was inevitable that police and workers would clash, shots would be fired, and street fighting would ensue.

A second objection offered by the Radical chief was the fear that the movement would be isolated and thereby defeated. But Fabra Rivas assured him that socialists in Madrid, Bilbao, and Saragossa — at the least — would immediately second the strike in Barcelona. In order to conclude this first interview, Emiliano Iglesias took refuge in the perfectly logical argument that the Radicals as a political party, could not sponsor a general strike, which was the function of a labor organization.

On Sunday afternoon Rodríguez Romero and Moreno wanted a second interview with Emiliano Iglesias. After two unsuccessful attempts, they finally succeeded in arranging one for eleven o'clock in the evening. Fabra Rivas returned from the Ter Valley in time to join them. By now the situation had changed drastically. Preparations for a general strike in the industrial centers of the Catalan provinces of Barcelona and Gerona had been completed, and worker enthusiasm was intense.[43] The rapidity of these preparations was possible because of the campaigns earlier that spring for a general strike (either for the Alcalá del Valle prisoners, or for the textile workers' lockout).

On Sunday night the Committee members (Fabra Rivas less insistently than Moreno and Rodríguez Romero) again asked the Radicals to support the general strike and invited Iglesias to become a member of the Committee. The serious situation in Barcelona and the midnight rally of Barcelona workers scheduled by the Committee made it necessary to talk of a matter that the doctrinaire socialist Fabra Rivas had possibly not fully considered: political participation in the Committee would give the general strike a revolutionary orientation. Iglesias asked bluntly if they had considered a change of government. Fabra Rivas had not: he continued to insist that he planned only a pacific general strike as an antiwar protest. But Moreno openly expressed his hope that the Radicals would take advantage of the movement and go on to revolution and the establishment of a republic. Iglesias answered that the Committee did not have the force to carry out such a movement and denied that the Radicals were in a position to act. "We have been counting on discontented army officers to carry out a revolution," Iglesias is reported to have said, "but we can't knock at that door because right now is precisely when they are being promoted." Fabra Rivas brusquely rejected such a suggestion: "We don't want anything to do with the 'sabers,' " whereupon Iglesias retorted that this was "all the more reason for not doing anything." [44] Moreno inquired why it would not be possible to mobilize the "revolutionary groups" within the party, but Iglesias disdained any contact with such groups, adding that in any event he did not have the authority to give orders until he had convoked a party council.

Annoyed by the Committee's insistence, Iglesias finally cut short the conversation. He assured them of his personal sympathy and promised to publish a report the following morning of the Committee's plans for a strike, with the understanding that it would last only one day; the Committee later denied having made any such promise. Iglesias' decision may have been discouraging to Moreno and to Rodríguez Romero, as to the extremists within the Radical party, who viewed the general strike merely as a stratagem for creating artificially the conditions for a revolution. But Fabra Rivas was probably satisfied with Iglesias' decision, particularly because it had been coupled with a promise not to oppose the strike. His studies of other general strikes had shown him the critical importance of middle class neutrality — if not support — in the initial stage of a workers' protest. [45]

Fabra Rivas' contacts with Catalan Nationalists also helped to neutralize the middle class. Later Sunday evening he talked with R. Noguer y Comet and with another editor of El Poble Català to report that, although Iglesias was opposed, "those in the Casa del Pueblo, who definitely want to support the strike, will force him to agree." And then, perhaps to offset the threat of a Radical-dominated Committee, Fabra Rivas invited the Catalan Nationalists to participate in the Committee. But Noguer refused, on the principle that a party should not participate in a worker protest. [46]

Shortly after midnight the Committee met with approximately 250 workers in a secret place, while police carefully watched the Solidaridad Obrera headquarters. [47] The purpose was to ask the assembled workers to ratify the plans for a general strike. Some delegates from other Catalan cities had remained in Barcelona to learn the outcome of the rally before returning home to organize the strike in their districts. Despite all the Committee's preparations there was still a heated debate about whether the strike should take place or not. The Committee was not able to announce the formal approval of the Radical party, but sometime during this rally (with or without Emiliano Iglesias' express approval) Radical workers decided to participate. After nearly three hours of discussion, a majority of workers finally voted to support the strike. Fabra Rivas sent a socialist colleague to inform the editors of *El Poble Català* that the strike would definitely take place, so that a last minute notice could be inserted in the newspaper.

Immediately after the rally, the president of the teamsters' union met — by accident or by design — Police Inspector Feliciano Salagaray and reported that his syndicate, a key element in a general strike, "had not agreed to it and there is no way of making us agree." President Enrique Ferrer told the Inspector that his men would report for work in the morning but expressed a fear that the Radicals "who dominated the syndicate, might perhaps prevent the wagons from leaving the barns or force them to return." The teamsters' president told Salagaray to advise the Governor to be "on his guard because . . . within a few hours, something was going to happen, but that there would definitely not be a general strike." [48] When Ossorio received the teamsters' report, he became more confident than before of his ability to suppress any violence that might occur.

The Governor and the General Strike

Like all other residents of Barcelona, Ossorio had read the editorial "Remember" in the Sunday morning edition of *El Progreso,* and so he sent numerous police forces to forestall any demonstration at the bullring such as had led to convent burnings in 1835, but there were no disorders. In the evening he ordered Civil Guards and police to patrol the central districts. A heavy layer of sand was thrown down on the boulevards in order to prevent galloping horses from slipping. This measure, adopted only in emergencies, convinced the populace that serious trouble was in store. Streets and theaters were almost deserted, an unusual occurrence on a Sunday evening in a Spanish city. But beyond these preventive measures Ossorio would not go; he made no arrests nor did he close the Solidaridad Obrera headquarters or the Casa del Pueblo, although he sent police agents to keep him informed on developments. He was still determined "to wait events, because if I had anticipated them with inopportune measures, it would have been said, with reason, that I had provoked the strike." His purpose now was to "have the general strike degenerate into a movement against me personally, before the Army should have to intervene." [49]

Whether streetcar executive Mariano de Foronda was in agreement with this policy or not, he had no recourse but to accept the Governor's plan. Both the Governor and Foronda announced on Sunday that, despite any opposition they encountered, they would personally guarantee that the streetcars would continue to run. As in the past, the streetcar would serve as the symbol of public order in Barcelona. [50]

In Madrid, La Cierva was still acting head of government in the absence of Maura. He had received new police reports from the Spanish Embassy in Paris warning that the strike in Barcelona would lead directly to a revolution. Shortly after midnight, La Cierva wired Ossorio to remind him yet again that a strike in protest against the war, whose purpose was "eminently political and revolutionary," could not be dealt with as would be a simple strike of workers against employers for higher wages. La Cierva wanted Ossorio to make every effort to prevent the strike from beginning. Ossorio wired back that he did not believe the strike had any revolutionary overtones, and that he had sufficient police to stop a strike. La Cierva was deeply concerned: he left the Ministry shortly after midnight and returned early Monday morning before breakfast. [51]

Shortly after midnight (just as workers began their secret rally), Ossorio sent instructions to all local police delegations reporting that certain individuals were "attempting to provoke a general work stoppage." [52] He ordered police to guard all factories, wharves, construction sites, and carbarns in order to prevent workers from being coerced by strikers. Offering no instuctions on how police were to execute so mammoth an undertaking, Ossorio retired to spend the night in his summer home on Mt. Tibidabo and left word that he was not to be disturbed until nine o'clock.

At four o'clock in the morning strike organizers took up their assigned posts along the highways and informed the men and women who were walking to the factories that the General Strike had begun.

Part Four

The Tragic Week

CHAPTER XI

Events: July 26 Through August 1, 1909

Monday, July 26

THE GENERAL STRIKE (to use Ossorio's graphic terms) "did not explode like a bomb but spread out like a string of firecrackers."[1] The fuses were set in the suburbs where the majority of workers lived and where the big factories were located. Not until all work ceased in those districts could the Central Committee for the Strike concentrate on developments in the center of Barcelona.

Beginning at four o'clock in the morning, strike organizers stopped men and women as they walked to work and urged them to strike for one day only as "a protest against the war and against the abuses of the government." Despite angered crowds, police arrested some organizers. Most workers entered the factories at the normal hour, between six and seven o'clock. A new tactic was necessary, for a sine qua non of a successful general strike was that it start on a Monday morning, before the work week began.

The next operation was so smooth that it may have been planned beforehand as part of the over-all strategy. At 8 A.M., the recess hour, delegations of strikers talked to crowds outside the factories or even forced their way past guards into the workrooms. The women in these delegations, wearing the white bow that had been adopted as the symbol for the strike, were usually the most violent and daring. Their agitation was effective, for many workers did not return to the factories after the morning break. Hesitant to strike as individuals, they were willing to walk out as a group.

The final stage followed swiftly. Owners closed their factories and sent employees to swell the ranks of strikers in the street; many of these employers closed simply because they realized that there was not a sufficient police force to protect their property, but at least some of them acted out of sympathy with the antiwar protest. For whatever motive, in the critical hours when the movement got underway, factory owners indicated they would not oppose the Committee's aim to paralyze the Barcelona economy. Governor Ossorio reported indignantly that it only became a *general* strike when factory owners "decided not to work." [2] By 9 A.M. the General Strike was a success in the industrial suburbs: Pueblo Nuevo, San Martín, Gracia, San Andrés, las Corts de Sarriá, and Sans.

The center of action moved toward the heart of Barcelona. At the city limits crowds had already burned the guard stations where the excise taxes (*consumos*) hated by all urban residents were collected — a regular occurrence in any public disorder — and had seized the rifles of many guards. Nevertheless they were unable to prevent farmers from taking produce into the city, because authorities had foreseen this contingency and had assigned sufficient Civil Guards to ensure a food supply for Barcelona.

Newspapers played no immediate role in launching the General Strike. Fearing inflammatory editorials, the Governor ordered police to seize all morning papers, at the presses or in the post office, on the ground that some contained uncensored reports of the fighting in Morocco.[3]

Ossorio had been unduly alarmed. Only the newspapers of the Radicals and of the Catalan Nationalists, together with a third republican organ, *La Publicidad,* mentioned the strike, and they merely printed reports that workers planned "a general work stoppage, in a pacific and orderly fashion, for the sole purpose of adding their protest to that of the general public." *La Publicidad* stressed there would be "no violence of any kind, which we would be the first to censure." *El Progreso* alone stated that the strike would last one day. It joined *El Poble Català* in reporting that, according to informants, a general strike would also take place in Madrid, Valencia, Seville, and Saragossa, as well as in additional major textile cities of Catalonia. By merely publishing reports of the workers' plans, the editors did not explicitly support the movement and thus guarded against prosecution for inciting to sedition.

The failure of the newspaper campaign (on which the Committee had worked so hard during the weekend) meant that neither the workers of Barcelona nor the population at large had a clear concept of the General Strike as a peaceful work stoppage intended to coerce Maura's government into ending the hostilities in Morocco.[4] No leaflets were distributed to fill this lacuna. The three relatively obscure members of the Central Committee for the Strike did not, probably could not, personify or dramatize this issue. Actually, the antiwar protest had been merely the catalyst for a mass reaction against the generally unpopular Maura government, a reaction that the Committee had precipitated. The question now was what would happen in the vacuum created by the lack of responsible leadership and of a formal program of action.

Francisco Ferrer, deeply concerned about this lack of political leadership and skeptical of the General Strike's success, came to Barcelona from his farm near Masnou in order to discuss the problem with Miguel Villalobos Moreno, who for more than a year had served as his contact with Solidaridad Obrera.* Throughout the previous week, Ferrer had followed the preparations for the antiwar demonstration through the enthusiastic reports sent to him by Moreno,[5] who had played a decisively important role in launching the General Strike. The socialist member of the Strike Committee, Fabra Rivas, either did not know about these contacts or he thought them unimportant.**

Moreno was waiting at the railroad station when Ferrer arrived on the 3:30 train. The two men talked about the plans for a new rationalist school, primarily for the benefit of Ferrer's police escort who stood nearby. Gradually Moreno and Ferrer moved to the far side of the station, where they discussed the strike. Moreno triumphantly showed the older man a copy of the editorial "Remember" as proof of the Radical willingness to collaborate in the movement. Ferrer, still skeptical, tried to "bring his friend to his senses." He reminded him of past deceptions practiced by the Radical party, and of its recent conflict with Solidaridad Obrera over the typesetters' strike, expressing doubts that the Radicals would now work with the syndicalists. "What if

* Ferrer had written to Moreno and asked him to come out to the farm over the weekend. Moreno replied that events were moving in "too rapid a fashion" and suggested Ferrer come to Barcelona on Tuesday morning. Fearing that the banks might be closed on Tuesday, Ferrer came instead on Monday. (Sol Ferrer y Sanmartí, *Le véritable Francisco Ferrer d'après des documents inédits, par sa fille* [Paris, 1948], pp. 80–81.)

** Shortly before his death in 1958, Socialist Antonio Fabra Rivas asked the distinguished Spanish historian R. Olivar-Bertrand to arrange an interview with Gabriel Maura, the son of Antonio Maura. In this interview Fabra Rivas continued to insist that Francisco Ferrer had played no part in the preparation of the General Strike, nor in the direction of the events that followed (information from Olivar-Bertrand, in a private conversation in 1963, in Washington, D.C.).

his [Iglesias'] secret purpose is to cause us to blunder?" Ferrer inquired, to which Moreno replied only that, for better or for worse, it had begun.[6] Ferrer concluded that "if it was a serious movement, that was going to lead to anything, it had all his sympathy; but if it were to be a mere flash in the pan, he regretted it."[7] The two men agreed not to meet again that day in order not to arouse police suspicions.

Ferrer went to his publishing firm where he discussed his doubts with Cristobal Litrán, his business manager and an official of the Radicals' Casa del Pueblo. He spent the rest of the morning visiting print shops and photo-engravers, undoubtedly concerned with the need to provide an alibi for his activities. He stopped repeatedly to discuss the day's events with acquaintances, for he still believed that there was not a proper "ambiance" for an uprising.[8] Ferrer may have thought this because events in central Barcelona were moving at a slower pace than in the industrial suburbs.

At 6 A.M. a large crowd had gathered in the Plaza de Cataluña, the heart of the commercial district, where Mercedes Monje Alcazar dramatically urged the men to prevent more troops from embarking for Melilla. A Civil Guard lieutenant, with a small detachment of men, ordered the crowd to disperse, but Mercedes Monje defied him, shouting that "Civil Guards always picked on the women." Undeterred, the lieutenant threatened to fire; the crowd obediently scattered, and Mercedes Monje was arrested.[9] Police could easily control demonstrations such as this; they were also fairly efficient in dealing with anarchist agitators.

According to police informants, anarchists had promised the Committee for the Strike to be responsible for organizing the protest in the waterfront districts.[10] Thus the police believed that to prevent serious trouble it was necessary only to detain anarchists like Tomás Herreros. By 8:00 A.M. they had located Herreros, an officer of Solidaridad Obrera, as he harangued a crowd that included reserve soldiers in uniform. Police caught him as he tried to escape and dragged him to prison as he continued to shout, "*Imbéciles!* Herds of sheep! They are trying to ship you off to war. Resist."

Even in this initial stage, anarchists were interested in far more than a peaceful work stoppage; as veterans of revolutionary action, they incited crowds to attack a powerful symbol of power of the status quo — the police station. Trinidad de la Torre was arrested, also before 8 A.M., just as he was mobilizing two hundred men and women for an attack against the station on the Calle Conde de Asalto in order to free a woman who had just been arrested. At 8:30 police detained Francisco Cardenal, business manager of the anarchist newspaper *Tierra y Libertad,* who was inciting a crowd to violence in the same Atarazana district; as he was taken to prison, Cardenal continued to abuse and ridicule the police.

On the Ramblas, the two best known anarchists in Barcelona, Francisco Miranda and his stepfather Mariano Castellote, urged another large crowd to attack police forces; both managed to escape when the police dispersed the group. Miranda made a second public appearance at 11 A.M., this time in the company of Jaime Aragó, and tried to organize a group on the Ramblas for an assault upon the police station. None of the men were armed, so police broke up the demonstration with ease, but Miranda again escaped arrest.

This was the sum and substance of anarchist activity. Despite their personal bravery and their fame as revolutionaries, they were only able to promote violence among groups already in the street. As Francisco Miranda confessed to Emiliano Iglesias later that day, his anarchist group "lacked the force to carry out any enterprise whatsoever." [11] Throughout the week anarchists evidently continued to operate from the offices of their newspaper, *Tierra y Libertad,* located on the Calle San Pablo.

The General Strike in Barcelona was actually launched by metalworkers, the same workers who had led the first General Strike seven years earlier.[12] Shortly after 8 A.M., the two hundred and fifty employees of the Hispano-Suiza automobile works on the Calle Floridablanca left the factory and spread out through the Atarazana district, persuading workers in fifteen or twenty plants to join the strike. Neither the unarmed Security Guards nor the few armed Civil Guard patrols could halt the proceedings.*

By 9 A.M. when Governor Ossorio arrived in his office, masses of workers had begun to fill the Paralelo and the Cortes, the main thoroughfares of the worker districts. Ossorio could have prevented this three hours earlier, employing all of the 700 armed Civil Guards at his command to reassure

* Both the Civil Guard (Guardia Civil) and the Security Guard (Guardia de Seguridad) are national police forces, subject to the jurisdiction of the Ministry of the Interior and therefore, within a province, to the Civil Governor. Of the two, the Civil Guards are the most rigidly disciplined and they alone, in the period under discussion, carried arms. In general, Civil Guards maintained order in rural districts and Security Guards in urban areas. But in major cities like Barcelona, some Civil Guards were stationed in the downtown area and in the suburbs. In an emergency, all Civil Guards would be brought in to the city from the province, or even from neighboring provinces.

factory owners and to intimidate workers. Realizing that he had lost the initiative, the Governor resorted to the extreme measure of sending out the Civil Guard cavalry. He went immediately to the barracks on the Calle Consejo de Ciento, where he worked with Colonel Ibañez Aranda, the commander of the Civil Guards in the province of Barcelona, and with Lieutenant Colonel Adolfo Riquelme Sánchez, in charge of the cavalry. Mounted Civil Guard patrols were dispatched to the trouble areas as these were reported by telephone. Ossorio instructed Civil Guards to fire "over the heads of the strikers." He then returned to his office and sent off the first telegram of the morning to his superior in Madrid, Interior Minister La Cierva. He made no mention of the strike's success in the industrial suburbs and reported only the events in central Barcelona. Ossorio asked La Cierva for "a rapid concentration of forces from Gerona [the adjoining province] or from the commandancy that seems best to you." He continued to insist, however, that the workers planned only a work stoppage.[13]

When the Governor telegraphed Madrid, he was right in stating that the work stoppage was not yet complete. At 10 A.M. most stores were still open, although those in working-class districts had taken the precaution of putting up big signs denouncing the war.[14] Most teamsters had reported for work as Enrique Ferrer, the union's president, had said they would. Carts transported coal from the wharves to the factories as on any normal work day, while public and private carriages circulated freely.[15] The streetcars, whose employees had been the first to stop work in the General Strike seven years earlier, continued to run. Nor had any violence actually occurred.

About 10 A.M., the situation gradually changed, then swiftly gained momentum. Storekeepers were among the first to succumb as groups of women and young boys, the women wearing a white bow as an emblem, came to demand that stores close. Amadeo Hurtado, a Catalan republican deputy, describes a group which he followed down the fashionable Paseo de Gracia.[16]

The operation was simple. A few steps ahead of me two youths, seventeen or eighteen years of age, abruptly approached the door of the first store and shouted in a loud voice: "Close for the sake of our brothers in Melilla." Immediately the personnel of the shop came out into the street, as if they were merely awaiting the order to close, and lowered the shutters. I slackened my pace in order not to miss the exploits of that authentic minority action group, seeing how all their orders were executed instantly with the same success. . . . In the Plaza de Cataluña we separated . . . and I began to understand that the acquiescence of the city in the protest and in the revolt was the factor which assured the extension of the strike.

The closing of the stores signified the support of the middle class, or at least its neutrality, in the General Strike.

This encouraged workers in the Atarazana port district, already elated by reports of the success in the suburbs, and they grew bolder in defying the Civil Guards sent by Governor Ossorio to patrol the area. Women played an important role, as they had in the suburban factory areas.[17] At least some belonged to the Damas Radicales or Damas Rojas of the Radical party, but others were women accustomed to street frays and delighted to engage police in the name of a political cause. María Llopis Berges, a notorious prostitute known familiarly as "Cuarenta Céntimos," led a band of men and women along the Paralelo; they broke furniture and plate glass store fronts of cafés that refused to close, then went on to overturn a streetcar and to charge a Civil Guard patrol.[18]

Wagons and carriages gradually disappeared from the streets as teamsters submitted to the demands of the crowds. Streetcar employees were not so easily intimidated.

As he had promised he would do, Mariano de Foronda traveled throughout the city in his automobile to force drivers to continue operating the cars despite threats from the crowds. He exercised an iron discipline over employees, many of whom he had brought from his native town in Andalusia as part of his publicly announced campaign against organized labor. On this Monday, July 26, Foronda again made the streetcar a symbol of the status quo power structure; workers took up the gauntlet.*

Street car employees and striking workers joined battle at 9 A.M. As might have been predicted, it began in an outlying industrial suburb where thousands of men and women factory employees thronged the streets and where there was less government control. The site was Pueblo Nuevo — with 41,758 inhabitants (many of whom were new arrivals from rural Aragon) crowded into 3,016 buildings and numerous shacks, with 57 percent of these inhabitants illiterate, served inadequately by one parish church and several

---

* During June and July the Radicals had bitterly denounced in their newspaper and in the City Council the powerful influence of Foronda in municipal politics. Workers already hated the streetcars because, among other items, they were equipped with bad brakes and regularly caused accidents in crowded neighborhoods. (*El Progreso* [Barcelona], June 16 and 21; July 9, 14, 21 and 23; and December 15, 1909.)

establishments of religious orders, but strongly influenced by a Radical party center and a rationalist school founded by Ferrer.[19] Pueblo Nuevo residents again and again during the week were the shock troops as the protest movement moved forward from one stage of violence to the next.

Early Monday morning, strikers in Pueblo Nuevo had been appeased by the promise of drivers to return their streetcars to the barns in central Barcelona; when they returned with the cars, workers attacked. The streetcar manager in Pueblo Nuevo telephoned Governor Ossorio for protection, and Ossorio sent the commander of the Civil Guard cavalry in person to restore order. But as soon as the cavalry left, strikers attacked anew, whipped into a fury as they saw streetcars continuing to arrive from downtown Barcelona. Civil Guards returned and dispersed the crowd, but they did not complete this task until noon.

In Barcelona proper, members of the Committee for the Strike were excited by news of this clash. They had counted on stiff resistance from most employers, as well as from Mariano de Foronda, so much so that they had not expected to achieve a complete work stoppage for at least two days. But by 11 A.M., the Committee realized that the streetcar was the only obstacle to a complete work stoppage and decided upon a dramatic measure. It ordered the men and women of Pueblo Nuevo, heroes of the morning assault upon the streetcars, to be brought into the center of Barcelona. They arrived shortly before noon, "to impose the strike on the traitors of the working class," as socialist Fabra Rivas described it.[20]

Governor Ossorio agreed with Committee members that the streetcars constituted the pivotal issue in a successful general strike. Therefore, shortly before noon he armed the Security Guards with short carbines and sent them to ride the cars in order to defend "the liberty to work." Whether this was a deliberate provocation to strikers (as Emiliano Iglesias charged)[21] or whether it was a natural development from the morning's events, the result was the same — a violent clash between armed police and workers. Ossorio had anticipated this and he intended to use it as justification for a full-scale suppression of the protest movement.

Ossorio's decision to arm the Security Police climaxed a morning of feverish activity, during which he had expended less time and energy in controlling developments in Barcelona than in refuting instructions issued by Interior Minister La Cierva.[22] Heavy fighting in Morocco engaged the national government's entire attention and served to justify La Cierva's most extreme measures. Ossorio could not count on support from Antonio Maura, President of the Council, who did not return to Madrid until the following day.

The issue that La Cierva and Ossorio debated all Monday morning, via teletype, was the purpose of the General Strike. The Governor continued to maintain, as he had the previous week, that it was simply a work stoppage in protest against the war and the conscription system. The Minister contended that the General Strike was but a prelude to armed insurrection and that its ultimate intent was to seize power. On Monday morning, La Cierva could point to events in Sabadell, a cotton textile center located thirty miles from Barcelona, as proof of his contention. Except for Barcelona, and the relatively smaller city of Badalona, Sabadell was the only city in the province of Barcelona where the General Strike had begun early Monday morning.

By 7 A.M. the General Strike was a success in Sabadell.[23] The strike organizers, having stopped all work in the city, led an attack upon a train carrying reserve soldiers, and this in turn led to armed conflict: workers fired with revolvers at Civil Guards and frontier guards (carabineros) who tried to protect the troop train. La Cierva considered these developments an ominous indication of events in Barcelona; to Ossorio he stressed not only the revolutionary potential of the armed conflict in Sabadell, but the fact that anarchists, socialists and Radicals there had been collaborating closely with their counterparts in Barcelona.* Therefore he urged the Governor to convoke a meeting of the provincial authorities (that is, the Captain General of the Fourth Military Region and the President of the Provincial Supreme Court, as well as the Governor) and to have them proclaim martial law. This would have meant that the Governor could use army troops as well as police in restoring order. But it also meant that the Captain General would temporarily become the supreme authority in the province. No one could doubt La Cierva's concern with public order, but neither could one ignore the satisfaction he would derive from circumscribing the authority of his old rival, Ossorio.

Ossorio fought this attempt by his old rival to diminish his authority. He was confident of his ability to restore order, but he needed time for police and workers to have an armed encounter over the streetcars, which he would

---

* On Friday night, July 23, two of the most prominent leaders of the Radical youth movement — Rafael Guerra del Río and Angel de Borjas Ruiz — went to Sabadell and addressed an antiwar rally of some 3,000 people (*El Progreso* [Barcelona], July 24, 1909).

use to justify issuing new orders to the Civil Guards that they use any and all means to suppress the disorders. Legally he could even have commanded army troops in such an emergency. He was also counting on "the conservative classes who up until then had been silent, thereby contributing to the success of the strike"; he believed that when workers fired at police, the middle class would rally to his support. Finally, Ossorio was calculating on the antagonism between the Army and Catalonia, convinced that civic and political groups interested in the re-establishment of order would prefer to collaborate with a civilian official than with a military officer. But all these calculations were based on being allowed leeway to work out the matter through his own authority. Therefore, in support of his argument that civil jurisdiction sufficed, Ossorio continued to assert that technically no "serious tumult" had yet occurred in Barcelona.[24]

La Cierva was not willing to grant him any leeway. He had already dispatched Civil Guard reinforcements from other provinces to Barcelona and was determined that Ossorio should not be allowed to use these troops to build up his personal prestige. And as Minister of the Interior, La Cierva could give orders to the Governor. Late in the morning La Cierva wired his decision. Although he personally recommended the declaration of martial law, he did not exclude the possibility of an "energetic and rapid action" such as Ossorio proposed. What he did insist upon was that the Governor meet immediately with provincial authorities to make the final decision about whether or not to declare martial law. "I shall do as you order," replied Ossorio, admitting later that "I should not conceal the fact that the order to convoke the Commission of Authorities mortified me."[25]

Ossorio had one last gambit to play. He and the other two provincial officials had the absolute authority to declare, or not, martial law. If the Governor could convince the Captain General and the President of the Provincial Supreme Court that he was able to repress the General Strike, he could defy La Cierva. But in order to suppress the riots, he must also obtain from General Santiago permission to use army troops in support of his police action.

Punctually at twelve noon, the Captain General and the acting President of the Supreme Court, Judge Elpidio Abril, arrived at the Governor's office, accompanied by their advisors.[26] This took Ossorio by surprise but he immediately sent for advisors of his own: the Civil Guard Commander, Colonel Ibañez Aranda, and the Chief of Police of the city of Barcelona, Enrique

Díaz-Guijarro. As soon as they arrived, the meeting began. Ossorio summarized strike developments and read aloud his teletype correspondence with La Cierva. He then described his plan "to quell the movement that same afternoon, employing — at whatever cost — the necessary violence." Ossorio eloquently argued against the use of the Army in suppressing domestic disorders.* He pointed out the danger of sending conscripted workers into the streets with orders to fire upon demonstrators who claimed to be defending soldiers from fighting in a war for "capitalist interests"; he reminded them that the morale of the soldiers had already been seriously undermined by the antimilitarist propaganda of recent years. Initially, the army officers were impressed by these arguments while the civilian officials, including police officers, opposed the Governor.

General Santiago's advisors "sounded the most accurate note of the meeting," reported Ossorio, when they supported his statement that troops could be used to restore order without the declaration of martial law. "Although this was discussed at length," Ossorio added with sadness that the two officers — General Ramón Pastor (Chief Military Advocate of the Fourth Military Region), and General Sánchez y Rodríguez Escalera (Chief of the High Staff) — did not make a firm offer of troops.

Judge Abril demurred, contending that the declaration of martial law was "the pacific solution of the conflict." Citing his experience in a general strike in Galicia, he said that the violence proposed by Ossorio would only aggravate the conflict. District Attorney Valdés corroborated this from his experience in Bilbao. Finally Captain General Santiago announced that he was impressed with Judge Abril's argument that the declaration of martial law would lead "to a more rapid establishment of normality," and was there-

---

* Ossorio was arguing for an important principle: the supremacy of civil jurisdiction. He declared that to have handed his powers over to the Army without first attempting to utilize the police "would have been a degradation of my function." Here in this meeting of authorities there was a clear example of the decisive interaction between historic forces and individual personalities that shape events. The predisposition of government officials to use military force in any civil disorder was intensified by their serious doubts about Ossorio's ability to suppress the riots, in view of his failure to act during the preceding week. A strikingly similar instance occurred at the time of the convent burnings in May 1931: conservative republican Miguel Maura and Socialist party leader Indalecio Prieto wanted to reinforce the prestige of the civil government by employing police — that is, Civil Guards — as the most efficient way to end the burnings. The Republican Premier, Manuel Azaña, insisted on using the Army because it would not so greatly "offend" the people (Miguel Maura, *Así cayó Alfonso XIII* [Mexico, 1962], pp. 253–54). The abdication of civilian responsibility in countless similar incidents led inexorably in time to military dictatorships.

fore willing "to assume command, if this were considered necessary for the public good and the avoidance of greater evils." The General voted with Judge Abril for a declaration of martial law; the Governor opposed it. Ossorio immediately informed La Cierva of the decision by teletype and announced his resignation "due to the poor state of my health, and not having any obligation to fulfill." The Minister replied at once, ordering him to remain at his post in order to assist General Santiago with the "police services the Governor knew so well." Ossorio abruptly cut off the teletype. "I should have ordered his arrest," commented La Cierva, "but what was one to do with that Governor who abandoned his post and *neglected* his duty at such a critical moment?" [27]

"I was not willing to be a governor with his authority delegated to someone else," Ossorio explained. At 1:30 P.M., having packed up his numerous personal papers, Ossorio departed under police escort for his summer residence on Mt. Tibidabo. "Did I do the wrong thing?" Ossorio wrote. "I probably did. But we men are what we are, [and] that is my idiosyncracy." [28]

Gubernatorial duties were taken over by Judge Mariano de Enciso, President of the Provincial Court, who returned to Barcelona late on Monday afternoon and stayed in the governor's office for the rest of the week. Judge Enciso devoted himself exclusively to administrative matters and took no part in political developments nor in the suppression of the General Strike.

At 1 P.M. General Santiago took over the government of the province of Barcelona for the specific task of suppressing the strike. Even if martial law had not been declared, the success of the General Strike depended in the last analysis upon the action and the attitude of the Army. And those individuals who hoped the strike would become more than a peaceful work stoppage were convinced the Army in Barcelona could not exert its full powers of repression.

The most salient feature was the faltering leadership of General Santiago. He had been in Barcelona less than one month, so he did not know the city's topography and much less its political nuances. On taking office, he had antagonized Catalans by a pompous military ceremony that made them all the more willing to believe the widespread report that he was incompetent. There are, however, many factors to explain his hesitancy in acting on July 26, 1909.

Most obvious among these was the fact that the Captain General had at his command only 1,400 men and officers, together with the 700 Civil

Guards.[29] War Minister Linares' plan had been to send all troops on active duty with the Third Brigade to Morocco, and to assign late-arriving reserve soldiers to duty in Catalonia. Because many of these reserves had not yet reported for duty, garrisons were at skeletal strength — a situation that had undoubtedly encouraged strike organizers to act immediately, before the garrisons were reinforced.

The doubtful loyalty of these troops in the face of an antimilitarist demonstration was another decisively important obstacle to effective military action. Santiago followed standard procedure in his initial order confining troops to barracks in order to isolate them from the protest movement, but this may have been a tactical error: strikers, together with the citizens at large, interpreted this to mean that the Captain General did not trust his soldiers. And this conviction further reduced the Army's ability to restore order.[30]

Even the loyalty of the officers on duty in Barcelona was a matter for concern. Their open opposition to Catalan regionalism, and their less open but no less real antagonism to the clergy, made it difficult for them to work with Barcelona's leading citizens to restore order. The officers' ambiguous attitude toward the popular uprising, or at least their doubtful loyalty to the Maura government, was in itself a positive factor for the strike organizers.

Confronted with these difficulties, General Santiago wired the War Minister for guidance; General Linares had just left Barcelona in March of 1909, after two years service as Captain General. But on Monday, July 26, Linares was concentrating exclusively on Morocco, where Spanish troops were engaged in heavy fighting; he therefore delegated his responsibility for suppressing the General Strike to Interior Minister La Cierva. Although General Santiago protested, he was forced to comply.[31]

Santiago's first move was to summon from neighboring provinces those army units that came under his jurisdiction in an emergency; his basic policy during the next three days was to bide his time until the reinforcements arrived. Late in the afternoon General Santiago's formal proclamation of martial law was posted throughout the city. His assertion that he would repress any disorder was meaningless in view of the continuing tumult in the street. So was the prohibition against citizens congregating on the streets, together with the stern warning that it would be strictly enforced. In the long run this prohibition proved to be a decided disadvantage in ending the disorders, as a Catalan republican deputy, Corominas, pointed out: its effect was to keep all peaceful citizens in their homes and to leave the streets to the militant workers who were not afraid of the warning that police would shoot. Corominas contended that if residents had circulated freely, there would have been less violence.[32]

The most important part of Santiago's proclamation was its warning about the crimes for which individuals might later be tried in military courts: sedition was defined as the publication of news that in any way threatened military discipline, and as any attack upon communication, transportation, or utility facilities. With the exception of the streetcars, no facilities had yet been attacked; Santiago dispatched Civil Guards to protect gas and electricity stations and to patrol workers' neighborhoods.

Late Monday afternoon the Captain General directed the embarkation of two ships, one carrying stragglers and one bearing ammunition.[33] The event passed almost unnoticed and unopposed; only one worker was arrested, as he clung to the reins of a horse in a futile effort to prevent the embarkation. This successful dispatch of reservists in the midst of an antiwar demonstration was General Santiago's one and only tour de force of the week. It undoubtedly comforted him as he dealt, far less successfully, with the violence now focused on two objects: the streetcars and the police stations.

The streetcar encounters turned out to be, all in all, a victory for the strikers. They occurred in the first hours of General Santiago's command, and he chose not to use them as an occasion to join battle with the strikers (as Ossorio had planned to do).

The workers from Pueblo Nuevo, who had arrived in central Barcelona about noon, led the attack on the streetcars. A numerous contingent of women, wearing the symbolic white bows and carrying large banners inscribed with the Radical party slogan "Down with War," had deliberately been placed at the head of the demonstrators in order to deter police from firing directly on the crowd.[34]

Employing the techniques that had been successful in Pueblo Nuevo, the workers attempted to block the streetcar lines, but they retreated when Security Guards, unused to handling carbines, fired often and aimlessly in an attempt to clear the tracks. Conductors answered all protests from the crowd by saying they were "obeying orders." Men and women began to throw stones, shattering the windows; they then tore up rails and pulled down cables. Finally, thoroughly enraged, they overturned and set fire to the cars, totally destroying two cars and severely damaging thirty-four.

Skirmishes, many of them organized in the Casa del Pueblo, became more frequent and more intense.[35] Leaving a humble job as manager of a doughnut (*churro*) shop, Esteban Roig y Roig, an enthusiastic Radical party member, took up a role as a street rebel; he and his band stopped streetcars on the Paralelo, forcing the police escorts to dismount. Farther up in the Ensanche area, a crowd stopped a streetcar and was fired upon by the police escort; a few men, carrying revolvers, returned the fire.

Inevitably these clashes led to bloodshed. Two streetcar employees were killed and eleven seriously wounded.[36] The most serious clash occurred at midafternoon on the Calle Aribau, near the Radicals' Casa del Pueblo. A gang forced passengers to dismount, then took the brake off and sent the car careening down the street. As Civil Guards approached, they were met by revolver fire. The Guards fired back, killing three workers and accidentally shooting a little girl. The Aribau incident, the climax of a tense afternoon, made General Santiago decide to stop the circulation of the streetcars. At 3 P.M. he telephoned Mariano de Foronda, who agreed to call in the cars; it was probably 4:00 before all the cars were back in the barns. Foronda issued instructions that all employees were to report for work daily, despite the strike, and his order was obeyed.[37]

Police stations now replaced the streetcars as the principal focus of attacks: ostensibly the objective was to free individuals arrested for participation in the General Strike. The first such attack, against the station on the Calle Conde de Asalto in the Atarazana district, failed when Police Chief Manuel Bravo Portillo fired on the mob and wounded one man.[38] Far more serious was the assault in the suburb of Clot (a district very similar to Pueblo Nuevo), between three and four o'clock in the afternoon, by workers armed with knives and revolvers. Prominent among them was Carmen Alauch Jérida, a fishmonger's wife and a member of a Radical party women's organization, who began at the police station in Clot her week's career as a street fighter. Of the rioters, two men and one woman were killed in the struggle, while two Civil Guards and seven Security Guards were seriously wounded. Reports of the fighting in Clot circulated throughout Barcelona and served as a stimulant for new violence.[39]

At 5:00 P.M. the mounting tension in central Barcelona finally erupted in a bloody incident that occurred in front of army headquarters on the Paseo de Colón, near the waterfront. Police were trying unsuccessfully to disperse a large crowd, including numerous women, as it marched down the Ramblas shouting "Death to War" and stopped in front of the Captain General's headquarters. Men and women cheered the Army and mocked the police who were guarding the building. Some of the men ostentatiously carried revolvers. When the crowd refused to disperse, Security Guards fired, killing at least three workers, but possibly as many as fifteen according to some accounts.[40]

Apologists for the strike, citing incidents such as this one, declared that the General Strike took a violent turn only because of police provocation. Actually, the gangs — armed with revolvers, cheering the Army, and taunting the police whom they disliked because of previous encounters — were more eager for a fight than were the harassed policemen. Throughout the week, Security and Civil Guards bore the brunt of the street fighting.

By Monday afternoon, far more rapidly and more completely than the members of the Central Committee had envisaged, the General Strike had paralyzed Barcelona's industry and commerce. More significantly, strikers had exceeded the Committee's announced objective of a work stoppage and had staged an armed attack against government authorities. Spontaneously or otherwise, workers had launched an uprising. Whether this would turn into an insurrection depended not upon the workers but upon politicians, and specifically upon the Radicals — the only party in contact with organized masses. And to be still more precise, in the absence of Alejandro Lerroux who had been exiled from Spain for over a year, the decision of whether or not the Radicals would use the General Strike as the prelude to the establishment of their "Social Republic" depended almost entirely upon the acting chief of the party, Emiliano Iglesias.

Francisco Ferrer was determined to find out for himself if Emiliano Iglesias intended to use the General Strike as the occasion for their long announced republican revolution. Since early morning Ferrer had continued a round of activities intended to establish him as a respectable and prosperous citizen. He ate lunch in the fashionable Maison Dorée; as he was about to leave, the French director of one of the subsidiary streetcar lines in Barcelona came up and cordially shook his hand. Having thus established himself as a respectable businessman, Ferrer felt that he could risk a meeting with Emiliano Iglesias. He asked his business manager, Cristobal Litrán, to make the arrangements.[41]

Emiliano Iglesias was eating a leisurely midday meal when the message arrived that Ferrer wanted to meet him in the Casa del Pueblo. Up until that point Iglesias — like Ferrer — had managed to remain aloof from the General Strike. Arising at his usual comfortable hour of ten-thirty, he had gone to the courts with a client who had been waiting for him to get up.

Iglesias started home on a streetcar, but strikers forced him to descend, so he had walked the rest of the way home. Iglesias, who had served as Ferrer's lawyer since his trial, was quite willing to meet with Ferrer. However, he decided to keep him waiting until he attended a meeting of the Public Works Commission. Iglesias left his home about 3:30.[42]

Ferrer had already been waiting for Iglesias more than thirty minutes. He had sat down at a table with Litrán in the café of the Casa del Pueblo. Because he had another business appointment at 4:00, Ferrer grew impatient when Iglesias failed to appear. Finally he stopped Lorenzo Ardid Bernal, the only Radical party official present at that moment. Ardid, who had known Ferrer for several years, invited him to sit at his table, but Ferrer suggested that they withdraw to a quiet corner. The approximately 400 party members who were swarming through the Casa del Pueblo knew that Ardid and Ferrer were conferring but they did not know what was being said.

Ferrer had already stated his position to several other Radical leaders while he waited for Iglesias: he expressed doubts that the violent disorders would develop into anything serious, and he insisted that the General Strike "would fail in its project" to stop the war. His own position was to wait to see what events developed, and to act only if a true revolution were possible. Ferrer now began his conversation with Ardid by asking whether he thought that the protest would develop into something more serious, to which Ardid replied that it was all over, "at least as far as the Radical party is concerned, since it has nothing to do with the matter . . . Now as for those who are directing this whole affair, they'll have to see what is to be done." [43]

Ardid's comment was undoubtedly an allusion to men like Miguel V. Moreno who had done so much, working through Solidaridad Obrera, to bring about the General Strike. Ferrer had brought with him to the Casa del Pueblo, or had met there, three members of Solidaridad Obrera who were to play a prominent role in the events of the week. They obviously did not share Ferrer's pessimism for while Ferrer was talking, they circulated through the Casa del Pueblo to talk with Radicals, "loudly declaring that opportunities must be used to full advantage."

There were, then, four positions among those present in the Casa del Pueblo on Monday afternoon, July 26. The Solidaridad Obrera members wanted to move on from a General Strike to a revolution. Francisco Ferrer was skeptical of success and wanted to know what the official Radical position would be, considering the party the keystone of success. The Radical party members, exhilarated by the armed encounters with police that had finally forced General Santiago to order the streetcars to stop circulating, were primed for revolutionary action. As a Radical party official, Ardid's position was to resist workers' demands for further action and to prevent Ferrer — intent upon a true revolution, and under police surveillance — from incriminating the party.

Excited Radical party members, overhearing Ferrer express his doubts, had interpreted them to mean that he was "a defeatist" and they protested against his presence in the Casa del Pueblo. They were already antagonistic toward Ferrer because for the past six months they had been told that he was financing Solidaridad Obrera's campaign against the Radical party. Ardid used the growing hostility of the Radical crowd to convince Ferrer that he should leave; he later reported that he was concerned about Ferrer's safety and wanted to avoid an unpleasant incident. Ardid advised Ferrer to keep his opinions to himself and then he suggested, or ordered, him to leave the building immediately through the false door that led on to la Calle Casanova. Not even Cristobal Litrán tried to protect Ferrer. "Ferrer obeyed immediately," Ardid reported, "and I did not see him again." Ardid then ordered that the three members of Solidaridad Obrera who had accompanied Ferrer be ousted from the building. In this as in all his activities during the week, Lorenzo Ardid made a conscious effort to dissociate himself from the protest movement — even parading in front of the Civil Guard barracks which made Lieutenant Colonel Riquelme, remembering Ardid's past revolutionary activities, so suspicious that he considered arresting him.[44]

In this encounter in the Casa del Pueblo, Ardid had formally stated the official position that the Radical party would maintain — both in talking with idealists who tried to force them to lead a rebellion (like Ferrer), or in talking with police. The Radical party position was that, despite all appearances to the contrary — despite the largescale participation of party members, and even of party officials — the Radical party had neither planned nor directed the disorders.

Radical party chief Emiliano Iglesias, at the city hall, was following an equally circumspect course of action as he conferred with municipal officials in his role as a responsible party spokesman. He could not, however, continue to avoid contact with the strike organizers.

Anarchist Francisco Miranda, in hiding since his public appearance that morning, sent two young workers to look for Iglesias at the city hall with an urgent message that he come to his home for a conference. Iglesias, accompanied by José Canals y Zamora, a wealthy shopowner and Radical city councilor, went to look for the address on the Calle Consejo de Ciento provided by the messengers. Unable to locate the exact apartment, and noting that "my presence aroused excessive interest among the people who were at the doors and windows," Iglesias was afraid he would lead the police to Miranda's hiding place. He went to the Casa del Pueblo and sent Bota, a young Radical, to look for Miranda. The anarchist came immediately and discussed with Iglesias possible courses of action, but confessed that he could offer no forces to carry out any plan.[45]

While Iglesias and Miranda conferred, young extremist Radicals were holding a meeting in another part of the Casa del Pueblo, determined to develop the General Strike into a revolt. According to a police informant, "the Ulled brothers, and especially the younger one, particularly distinguished themselves in inciting the masses to rebellion in an outrageous manner."[46] At 5 P.M., Civil Guard Lieutenant Juan Pérez Moreno and a small detachment arrived with orders to close the Casa del Pueblo. When several rash youths fired on the Guards, Iglesias abruptly broke off his meeting with Miranda, promising to meet him later. He then accompanied Lieutenant Pérez around the building, and urged party members to leave peacefully. Radical militants were furious at being forced to abandon their headquarters, the focal point of the disorders until then, and some openly called Iglesias a "traitor" to the Radical cause.[47] They obeyed, however. But by closing the Casa del Pueblo, General Santiago scored only an apparent victory. Despite the permanent guards stationed at the building, Radicals managed to enter the building throughout the week. Iglesias and other party leaders moved to the newspaper offices of *El Progreso* where they conferred freely with representatives of all groups.

While the Casa del Pueblo was being evacuated, a group of women party members approached Emiliano Iglesias to tell him they had decided that the convents should be burned. This was "the culminating event of the week," the Radical chief reported; unable to discuss details at that moment, he arranged to meet the women later that night.[48]

On Monday evening, despite the success of the General Strike, Iglesias would not consider the possibility of a revolt until he was assured of support from republican and labor groups in other cities. But he also knew that he could not withstand for much longer the demands of extremist factions within the Radical party, especially those of the Youth Movement, for action of some type. Members of the women's organizations had suggested one course of action, the burning of convents, but before Iglesias decided on this matter, he wanted to sound out the opinion of various groups.

At 7:00, Iglesias went to a meeting convoked by the editors of the republican newspapers *El Diluvio, La Publicidad,* and *La Tribuna.*[49] The purpose was to discuss whether the newspapers should continue to publish during the period of martial law. Subject to the limitations set by Santiago's edict, the press could have done much to restore order by printing editions that evening and the following morning — minimizing the events in Barcelona, reporting the arrival of additional troops, and stating that the rest of Spain had failed to support the movement.* If newspapers were not published, the strike organizers could continue to circulate rumors of government weakness and of the support of other cities.

Most editors were undecided. Those from the republican *El Diluvio* and the moderate *La Vanguardia* stated definitely that they intended to publish a morning edition in order to put an end to the strike by informing workers of the actual situation. Iglesias claimed he was the only editor present who openly supported the strike. When he declared he would not publish *El Progreso,* Catalan republican deputies Ramón Mayner, editor of *La Tribuna,* and Juan Caballé, editor of *El Liberal,* finally agreed to support him.

Immediately after this meeting, again accompanied by Radical Councilor Canals, Iglesias went in search of Miguel V. Moreno to warn the Committee for the Strike that some newspapers might publish a morning edition. He was startled to find that military authorities had closed the Solidaridad Obrera headquarters. When the porter was unable to tell him where to find Moreno, Iglesias decided to return to the offices of *El Progreso.*[50]

At 7 P.M., when Iglesias was beginning his meeting with the newspaper editors, Moreno was meeting with the members of the Committee for the Strike and with their collaborators. The group was elated by reports from

---

* Most of the typesetters were, of course, on strike, but there was a possibility that sufficient non-striking printers could have been found to publish one or more editions. Typesetters employed on the *Boletín Oficial,* for example, worked all week. (Letter from N. Belver in Ministerio de la Guerra, *Causa contra Francisco Ferrer Guardia, instruída y fallada por la jurisdición de Guerra en Barcelona: Año 1909* [Madrid, 1911], p. 150.) But there are no reports that any newspaper attempted to publish an edition until Sunday, August 1.

the province of Barcelona that the General Strike had been successful in Mataró, San Felíu de Llobregat, and Manresa, while street fighting was reported in Tarrasa, Badalona, and Sabadell. To the Committee, the General Strike appeared to be a success in cities throughout the province of Barcelona, and in a few cities in the province of Gerona. Some of the trade union officials present in the meeting insisted that this sufficed, that workers should return to work after their dramatic protest against the Maura regime.[51]

Some of the strike organizers, however, had already started to prepare a rebellion. Like good conspirators, they began with an assessment of the effectiveness of the Army and with plans to weaken or divert it. They were counting on a delay of several days before substantial troop reinforcements could arrive. During his first hours in office, General Santiago had shown that he did not possess the skill to deploy effectively the few troops at his command, and this encouraged the Committee. Plans were made to use more extensively the mechanism of fraternization — the only means that leaders of any unplanned uprising have "to promote an ad hoc disintegration of the armed forces." [52]

That afternoon, in the bloody incident on the Paseo del Colón, General Germán Brandeis ordered two companies of dragoons to fire on striking dockworkers, but soldiers had refused to obey when the workers shouted "Don't fire, companions; we are fighting for you." Now the Committee planned to extend the use of this strategy (including applauding and cheering troops) in order to "win the soldiers over to our cause."

The Committee made plans to isolate Barcelona so that it would be difficult for General Santiago to obtain troop reinforcements or instructions; it also wanted to prevent workers from learning that the revolt was not yet supported by cities outside of the provinces of Barcelona and Gerona. Committee members issued orders to tear up tracks at key points on all railroads leading into Barcelona and cut down telephone and telegraph poles. They also adopted "the necessary measures" to prevent any newspaper from printing a morning edition.

At 9:00, two representatives of the revolutionaries in Sabadell arrived with an offer to bring 1,500 armed men to Barcelona and place them at the orders of the Committee for whatever action judged necessary. The Committee politely declined, stating that the Barcelona workers sufficed to confront the few military forces that General Santiago commanded.[53]

The most important visit was that of certain extremist Radical leaders who wanted to arrange another meeting with Iglesias in order to force him into leading a rebellion; these were the same men who had engineered the participation of party members in the day's events, despite the official policy of abstention. Some of the strike organizers, especially socialist Fabra Rivas, were reluctant, but Moreno was enthusiastic. Finally the group voted to hold the meeting in the hope that Iglesias might still be persuaded to become a member of the Committee for the Strike, or at least to support the movement publicly.[54]

Moreno then presented to his colleagues a manifesto that he had prepared, demanding that Maura send no further troops to Melilla; if he failed to comply with the demand, then those who had signed the petition would lead a revolt against the government. The strike organizers decided to present the manifesto to Iglesias for his signature; in the event that he refused they hoped to obtain a promise that he would not take any action until it could be seen whether or not cities outside Catalonia would join the uprising.[55] The new meeting of the Committee members with Emiliano Iglesias was scheduled for later that evening in the offices of *El Progreso*.

Francisco Ferrer learned about this meeting from Moreno, for despite the agreement reached that morning in the railroad station, the two men did confer in the evening.

After leaving the Casa del Pueblo, Ferrer had spent the afternoon visiting printers. At 5:30, accompanied by two workers, Ferrer was seen talking with individuals in the crowd on the Paseo de Colón; the soldiers had to break up this excited mass by force.[56] By now Ferrer was convinced that this was an authentic uprising of workers which must not fail for lack of political leadership.

Moreno, when he met Ferrer, talked excitedly of the Committee's plans that were thwarted only by Emiliano Iglesias' continued refusal to support a revolt. When Ferrer asked what he could do to help, Moreno asked him to sign the manifesto. Ferrer agreed, even going so far as to promise that if a revolution took place and if a republic were estblished, he would serve for several days, if need be for several weeks, in a provisional government. Agreeing this was a strange decision for a man who had always evaded the limelight, Ferrer's daughter insisted that he acted from a sense of honor and a horror of bloodshed. Ferrer promised to help in persuading Iglesias to sign the manifesto, then the two men separated for the evening.[57]

Ferrer ate supper alone in a hotel on the Ramblas. At 9:30 P.M., as he was having coffee, Francisco Domenech, the barber from Masnou, the town near Ferrer's farm, and an ardent Radical party member, happened to walk by;

for the rest of the evening he accompanied Ferrer. They went first to the offices of *El Progreso,* where Ferrer left a message with the porter, asking Emiliano Iglesias to meet him in a café. Then they walked down the Calle Aribau to the Plaza de la Universidad where they met Cristobal Litrán, Ferrer's business manager, who was accompanied by his wife; the group sat down to have coffee in one of the cafés which were still open. Impatient for news about the manifesto, Ferrer asked Domenech to go to the Solidaridad Obrera headquarters. When the barber refused (probably because he was afraid), Litrán agreed to go, returning within a short time to report that military authorities had closed the headquarters and that he had escaped arrest only by posing as a French newspaper correspondent.[58]

Meanwhile, in the offices of *El Progreso,* Iglesias was conferring with Radical district chiefs from all sections of Barcelona. Most of the Juventud Radical leaders were also present, including twenty-year-old Porqueras who was to die later that week in an assault on an armory. Angrily the youths demanded that the Radical leaders prepare a rebellion. This demand was presented to the party directorate: Lorenzo Ardid, Radical Councilor Jorge Vinaixa, labor spokesman Luis Zurdo Olivares, and cautious Provincial Deputy Pichy Pons.[59] Emiliano Iglesias reported that in these meetings he was seeking a leader who would assume direction of the movement; instead, he found "enthusiastic youths, obscure soldiers in the revolutionary army, who revealed a spirit of sacrifice and proofs of valor." [60] But this was not sufficient basis for a rebellion.

Late Monday evening, deciding that he could not leave his office, Iglesias sent Calderón Font, his right-hand man, and Enrique Tubau, prominent Casa del Pueblo orator, to invite Ferrer to come to see him. Calderón and Tubau delivered the message to Ferrer in the café, then sat down briefly to discuss events.[61]

At that very moment Fabra Rivas, possibly accompanied by some colleagues, was arriving at the offices of *El Progreso*. Despite their differing ideas, Emiliano Iglesias found it easy to discuss matters with the learned young socialist. In turn, Fabra Rivas confided in Iglesias that he had taken "precautions against the anarchists in case they should try to create turmoil, in accordance with their custom." [62] In response to Iglesias' warning about the newspapers appearing the following day, Fabra Rivas said that the Committee had adopted the necessary preventive measures. He went on to plead with Iglesias to order party members "to hold the police forces at bay, in the expectation that other cities would second Barcelona." The Radical

leader argued that the wisest course would be to end the whole affair, ordering workers to return to the factories on the following day and, "above all,
searching for an elegant solution that would justify the withdrawal." Fabra
Rivas replied that the least the Radicals could do would be to cooperate in
preventing a troop ship from departing, as scheduled, on the following day.
Iglesias promised to meet again the following morning to discuss this
project.[63]

Between 10:30 and 11 P.M., while Iglesias was still conferring with Fabra
Rivas, Ferrer arrived in the offices of *El Progreso*. Because the socialist had
just told Iglesias that "if he even suspected that Ferrer had intervened in
the Committee, or in the strike activities, he would be the first to withdraw,"
the Radical leader wanted to avoid a meeting between the two men. Leaving the socialist to confer with Radical leaders in his own office, Iglesias went
out to meet Ferrer in the outer room, in full view of the many party members gathered there.* When Ferrer demanded to know if Iglesias had signed
the manifesto, Iglesias inquired sarcastically just what forces and armament
Ferrer could count upon for such a revolution. He told him, as he had told
Fabra Rivas, that the best thing would be to resume work. Concerned about
the fact that Ferrer was under police surveillance, Iglesias urged him to return home for his own safety.[64]

Ferrer left the offices, in the company of the barber Domenech. As they
walked down the street they happened to meet Moreno. Telling him that
the Radicals still refused to carry the strike beyond the original plans of a
work stoppage, Ferrer urged Moreno to go to the offices and find out the
final decision. Moreno assured him that the Radicals could not back out
because they were already heavily implicated. "And for anyone who fails
us," Moreno added, "we'll deal with him as they deal with traitors in
Russia." [65]

Ferrer remained in Barcelona until 1:30 A.M., when he learned that Iglesias definitely would not sign the petition. Deeply discouraged, he told
Cristobal Litrán, the director of his publishing firm, "Don't deceive yourself. No party is going to carry out a revolution. There's nothing here,
nothing. Believe me: drop all political adventures and devote yourself to
working seriously on behalf of education." [66]

---

* Iglesias later admitted that he met with Ferrer several times during the week — in
the offices of *El Progreso*, in Iglesias' home, and in an undisclosed site ("Campaña
revisionista: Lo que *no* dijo Emiliano Iglesias," *El Progreso* [Barcelona], March 26,
1911).

Ferrer decided not to spend the night in Barcelona. Because the trains had stopped running late in the afternoon, he and the barber Domenech set out to walk the fifteen miles to his farm near Masnou. Despite his desire to participate, Ferrer had been excluded from the events in Barcelona.[67]

At midnight on Monday, July 26, the forces of order and those of disorder had reached an apparent stalemate. On the one hand, although the General Strike had not ended the war, it had paralyzed Catalonia's economic life. Labor leaders, however, could not persuade Emiliano Iglesias to go one step forward to an insurrection. On the other hand, the Captain General had neither the skill nor the force to end the General Strike.

The respectable citizens of Barcelona harshly criticized General Santiago, echoing the statement of a Catalan republican deputy, Corominas, that the Captain General's failure to act during the first twenty-four hours "permitted what had been a closure of shops to become a real revolution." [68] To a large extent the criticism was justified. Santiago showed no dexterity in employing troops, even though reinforcements began to arrive at 10:30 in the evening. Instead, he decided at midnight to send for still more troops, preferring to postpone all fighting until soldiers outnumbered workers.

Criticism of General Santiago's ineptitude, however, must be tempered by recognition of the fact that he received no help whatsoever from responsible citizens in the community. In other Catalan cities prominent citizens immediately organized militias which by Monday evening had suppressed most of the disorders, but in Barcelona the middle classes remained in their homes. "With very few exceptions," commented a critic of Catalonia, "Barcelona society treated the events as if they constituted, exclusively, a dispute between the Government and the revolutionaries." [69]

In the vacuum created by Governor Ossorio's resignation, no other civilian official volunteered his services. Even the new Mayor, Juan Coll y Pujol, appointed by Maura's government for long services as a Conservative party cacique, deftly evaded the Captain General's plea for assistance. On Monday night, Santiago telephoned the Mayor to ask that he use his influence among merchants so that stores would open the following morning and citizens be encouraged to resume their normal duties. Mayor Coll replied it would be impossible to comply because the Captain General's injunctions against groups in the street intimidated peaceful citizens who might venture out to purchase.[70]

In part, the hostility of Catalans toward General Santiago was due to the traditional hostility toward the Army; in part it was due to Catalan sympathy for the workers' protest against an expensive and poorly managed war. Strike leaders counted on this sympathy as they prepared for new action on Monday night.

Shortly after midnight on Monday, July 26, the stalemate of power was broken when workers burned a Catholic school and thereby forced the protest movement into a new stage of violence. The idea, reported Fabra Rivas, originated with "groups of Freethinkers" and with the extremist faction of the Radical party.[71]

Once again it was the workers of Pueblo Nuevo who served as the catalyst. The agency through which they were mobilized was the Radical center in Pueblo Nuevo that housed an active chapter of the Radical youth movement, Juventud Radical, as well as a rationalist school closely associated with Ferrer.[72] The incendiaries chose with care the site in Pueblo Nuevo at which to launch their campaign against the Catholic clergy: the Workers' Circle of San José run by the Marist Brothers which offered its five hundred members financial help through mutual aid funds, a library, a free clinic, and a school.[73] This Workers' Circle symbolized many of the aspects of clerical activity that had aroused most antagonism. Trade union officials and republican labor politicians could not compete with the Marists, whose services to workers were subsidized by wealthy laymen; in Pueblo Nuevo they were reportedly financed by the Marquis of Comillas, whom Barcelona workers generally disliked, and particularly at that moment when ships owned by his Transatlántica company were transporting men to Morocco.[74] The Marist order itself was anathema to workers, in part because of its long association with workers' circles (which labor considered merely a device for recruiting scab labor). Furthermore, although the Marist order, French in origin, had worked in Spain for twenty years and so by 1909 most members were Spanish, it was still resented as a "foreign order"; it so happened that the director of the Workers' Circle in Pueblo Nuevo was Swiss. But from the viewpoint of the "groups of Freethinkers" and the extremist faction of the Radical party who planned the attack, the object of greatest animosity was the school which, because of its heavy subsidy, charged little or no tuition. This angered the Marists' competitors, the rationalist school in the Radical center in Pueblo Nuevo which was forced to charge, if only a pittance.

This rationalist school in Pueblo Nuevo was practically the only school still openly associated with Francisco Ferrer. Unlike most of the teachers who had once worked with Ferrer, the directors of this school — José Robles Layas and his wife, María Villafranca (a sister of Ferrer's mistress) — had continued to work closely with him after his release from prison.[75] In July 1909, at the conclusion of the Alcalá del Valle campaign, Robles had joined Ferrer in forming a new group to promote rationalist education.[76] This may well have been the group that organized the burning of the school in Pueblo Nuevo. The members of this group had contacts with all of the most extremist elements in Barcelona: José Casasola was the director of the successor school to the Escuela Moderna; Cristobal Litrán was Ferrer's business manager and an official of the Casa del Pueblo; Luis Bertrán, ex-anarchist turned Radical and the advisor of the Damas Rojas, was extremely active in the events of the following days.

This group of rationalist educators had contact with the Radical center in Pueblo Nuevo through Juan Colominas who not only served as an executive officer of the school in the Casa del Pueblo in downtown Barcelona, and as an editor of the Radical youth movement's extremist publication, *La Rebeldía,* but was president of the Juventud Radical in Pueblo Nuevo.[77] Just a few weeks earlier, Juan Colominas had presided at a meeting in Pueblo Nuevo where Casasola and Litrán had talked to these "Jóvenes Bárbaros" about rationalist education and about the need to eliminate their rivals — the schools run by religious orders.[78]

The time for action came at 11:30 on Monday night, July 26. With no prior announcement, men and women gathered in front of the Marists' Circle of San José and plunged the area into darkness by breaking all the street lamps around the Calle Wad-Ras. Police informed General Santiago of the impending attack and he immediately dispatched a cavalry detachment. But by the time it arrived, the Circle of San José was ablaze. In accord with the established policy, crowds wildly cheered the troops protecting the Marists as they left the building to spend an uneasy night in their nearby residence.[79]

Francisco Ferrer did not leave Barcelona for his farm until after the Workers' Circle of San José had been burned. Given his close association with the rationalist school in the Radical center in Pueblo Nuevo this seems particularly significant. If Ferrer could not have his revolution, at least he would have the satisfaction of knowing that a Catholic school was burning.

Emiliano Iglesias, however, would later *imply* that Ferrer left without knowing about the event in Pueblo Nuevo.[80]

No one seemed to sense that the event augured further burnings. Even
the Franciscan Sisters, whose school for girls was just a few blocks from
the Marist school, were not alarmed: "We did not believe it would go any
further," reported one sister, "because they told us that the hostility was
directed against the Marquis [of Comillas?] — and that establishment was
his doing." [81]

With the burning of the Marist school in Pueblo Nuevo, Barcelona ended
the first day of a general strike called in protest against conscription of
soldiers for a colonial war. The startling incongruity of these events did
not alert military authorities. Or at least they made no apparent effort to
forestall further attacks on church property.

Tuesday, July 27

The second day of the General Strike began in Barcelona with a mood
of portentous expectancy. The Central Committee for the Strike issued no
statement: workers simply did not report at factories and shops. The Captain
General made no effort to restore confidence in the government by posting
throughout the city an informative communiqué to fill the void created by
the silent newspapers. Barcelona residents, therefore, knew neither what had
happened nor what they could expect, but in the course of the morning
they did learn that transportation and communication had been cut off and
the city was almost completely isolated.

Strike organizers had done this deliberately, as the only possible strategy
for maintaining the protest movement in Catalonia as an example and as
a stimulus to workers elsewhere. Socialist Fabra Rivas continued firm in his
expectation of a national general strike that would not only force the government to terminate the fighting in Morocco but would immeasurably
enhance the prestige of the Socialist party; on Tuesday, in Madrid, Pablo
Iglesias finally signed the call for a national strike to be held the following
Monday (August 2). Anarcho-syndicalist Miguel V. Moreno had still greater
expectations: that the General Strike would lead to the revolutionary overthrow of the Bourbon Monarchy.

In the course of the day Fabra Rivas came to realize what Moreno had
understood from the beginning: if a popular protest movement succeeds,
it rapidly achieves a momentum that must be harnessed immediately by
political leaders or expend itself in futile violence. On Tuesday the future

course of the uprising was set, but this emerged clearly only in the course of the day's events.

The objectives of the Central Strike Committee in ordering the isolation of Barcelona on Monday night were more limited. They wanted to prolong the strike as a means of encouraging workers elsewhere to join the protest movement, but in order to do this they must prevent workers in Barcelona from learning that no city outside of Catalonia had yet seconded their protest. Isolating the city thus forestalled a demand for an end to the General Strike; it also crippled the armed forces.

All domestic railroad lines had been blown up at sites far from the city; only the line to France had been left intact.[1] Troop reinforcements brought in by train were forced to march some distance into the city. Meanwhile, telephone and telegraph lines were torn down in order to prevent authorities in Madrid and Barcelona from arranging effective punitive measures. Somehow the demolition teams overlooked the cable to Mallorca: either late Tuesday or early Wednesday, government officials discovered that they could communicate by sending messages to Mallorca, which were then relayed to Valencia and on to Madrid.[2] With this one exception, Barcelona was isolated from Tuesday until Thursday afternoon.

On Tuesday morning some few citizens tried to resume their normal activities, encouraged by the numerous police squads and smaller units of soldiers who patrolled the commercial district of Barcelona. Food markets opened early in the morning; housewives bought food, then quickly returned home and locked the heavy street doors behind them. In many districts, stores opened for business but were forced to close by roving bands of women and young boys. Some transport wagons and a few coaches circulated, withdrawing when stoned by strikers. Postal and telephone employees reported for work, as they did every day throughout the week. Although hostile crowds fired at them, some brave postmen walked out to the trains and brought back mail (which, however, was not distributed until Friday). Intra-urban telephone lines continued to function, despite the Committee's orders that they be cut in order to prevent police and military officials from conferring. But such timid efforts to restore order were of no effect within a vacuum of authority created by the resignation of the Civil Governor and the weakness of the Captain General.

While General Santiago waited for reinforcements, and the Strike Committee awaited messengers with news from cities outside of Catalonia, excited workers clashed with police — carefully applauding soldiers in accordance with the established pattern. The disorders took place in the three political strongholds of the Radical party: in the industrial suburbs of Pueblo Nuevo and Clot-San Martín, and in the slum district of Barcelona.

All Monday night, extremist factions within the Radical party had tried to persuade Emiliano Iglesias to proclaim the long-awaited Social Revolution.[3] Lest the élan of rebellion diminish, the mobs in Pueblo Nuevo (the first to attack the streetcars and to burn a religious building) were again mobilized on Tuesday morning.

The new violence was merely an extension of the burning of the Workers' Circle of San José the previous midnight.[4] At 9 A.M., men gathered in front of the Marist residence. The brothers, having changed to lay clothing, were preparing to escape when a workman forced his way into the building and promised to lead them to safety. Relying on the good relations they had maintained with their neighbors, the Marists confidently followed him out the door. Suddenly the worker ran ahead and shouted, "Here you have them: fire." Brother Lycarion, the Swiss-born Director of the Circle of San José, who was at the head of the group, was shot and killed instantly.[5] In the ensuing melee, the other brothers managed to escape.

One Marist took refuge in the police station and this occasioned further violence. When the crowd demanded that the brother be turned over to them, one clever policeman convinced them that he was dead by displaying the corpse of a workman killed during the previous day's fighting. Meanwhile the station chief had telephoned the Captain General; by the time the cavalry troop arrived, between 10 and 11 A.M., police had managed to disperse the crowd.

Armed assaults upon authority, the necessary ingredient of a revolt, were also launched in the heart of Barcelona, where Radical chief Lerroux ruled as "emperor" — in the Paralelo-Atarazana districts composed of industrial plants, slum dwellings, and the waterfront area common to every Mediterranean port.

Here the Central Committee and their elusive Radical colleagues could rely upon a vanguard of some 2,000 men and women. These included not only unskilled workers (as in Pueblo Nuevo and Clot-San Martín) but representatives from all branches of the underworld, adept at fighting police and already incensed against authority by Governor Ossorio's recent attempts to curb vice. Bravo Portillo, police chief of District V, reported that a group of prostitutes and criminals had been busy since Monday afternoon, "desirous of finding some spark to touch off a rebellion." [6] Anarchist Leopoldo Bonafulla commented defensively that "the allies of a revolution are neither prepared nor chosen"; he and his colleagues believed that once this action group launched the rebellion, workers would gain courage and join in.[7] So Salvador Lloret, a petty criminal, gathered a mob before the Atarazana police station to throw rocks and to shout "Death to the government," but the group disbanded when police closed the station doors. About 11:30 A.M., a Radical party member, teamster José Bel Pla, led a sortie against a Civil Guard platoon.[8]

The uprising slid almost imperceptibly into an armed revolt, a move signified by the erection of barricades. Conditions in District V were ideal: dark, narrow streets paved with loose stones, and tall houses where snipers could find refuge or a vantage point from which to fire. Throughout the district men and women piled up stones and sewer covers on street corners, apparently without being given instructions to do so. When patrolling Civil Guards ordered workers to desist, they were answered with jeers and whistles; Guards fired warning shots and armed men responded. This skirmishing continued intermittently until 11 A.M., when General Santiago sent five infantry companies across the district, from the Ramblas to the Paralelo, to clear the streets; yet even in their presence the crowds continued to pile up stones.[9] The inefficiency of the troops increased the revolutionary fervor.

By 1 P.M. an uneasy silence had settled over Barcelona. Rumors circulated that workers in Madrid, Valencia, and Saragossa had risen in arms; undoubtedly these were deliberately circulated to encourage Barcelona workers. The men and women in the streets awaited instructions.

The would-be leaders of the revolt hesitated to give the final order but had they known the situation in Morocco, they probably would have acted. The Army was fighting the heaviest engagement of the entire campaign. Brigadier General Pintos, a personal friend of King Alfonso, led untrained troops across unfamiliar territory to charge up Mt. Gurugú from which Riffian tribes dominated the region; according to official figures 1,238 men died in the battle of "el barranco del Lobo." [10] On Tuesday and Wednesday the government in Madrid could spare neither time nor reinforcements to help General Santiago in re-establishing order in Catalonia. Insurgent leaders in Barcelona had nothing to fear from national authorities, but the irony is that they did not know this. They had deliberately isolated Barcelona from news of the outside world in order to prolong the protest movement, but they had also cut themselves off from information about the war in Morocco.

Interior Minister La Cierva parlayed this lack of communication into a positive gain. He was convinced that the General Strike was simply a device to enlist and organize workers for a revolutionary movement. Unable to end the strike in Barcelona by force, he sought to discredit the movement among workers elsewhere in Spain. La Cierva was given free rein by Antonio Maura, President of the Council, who returned to Madrid shortly before noon on Tuesday but was glad to leave the domestic situation to the Interior Minister while he concentrated on Morocco.

On Tuesday morning, La Cierva issued a communiqué to Madrid news services that described events in Sabadell as "revolutionary," although admitting that the situation in Barcelona had not yet passed beyond the limits of sedition. When a journalist asked for comment on reports that the events constituted a Catalan separatist movement, the Minister implied the interpretation was correct. Admitting later there was absolutely no basis for this claim, La Cierva wrote that he deliberately encouraged the nation to consider it as a Catalan uprising so that "a sense of patriotism would impose itself on all other aspirations and passions" [11] — a subterfuge that was to prove extremely successful in preventing both Catalan politicians and labor leaders in other regions from supporting the Barcelona workers. And on Tuesday, July 27, any measure seemed justified to the government in Madrid, the only ones who knew the desperate plight of the Monarchy as it faced a military disaster in Morocco and a potential revolution in Barcelona.

Fortunately for the Maura government, Radical leaders — who held the balance of power — never seriously considered carrying out a republican revolution. They were unwilling to risk their benefits as a political party, such as access to government funds and the use of patronage, by leading a revolution they believed had little chance of success.[12] Therefore they parried the demands of Radical extremists for action, waiting until it should become evident (as they were certain it would) that Barcelona workers fought alone.

And in the interim, between Monday night and Tuesday morning, the energies and passions of the populace were enrolled in a great crusade: the burning of convents. For legal and political reasons, Radical leaders were always reluctant to recount details, and thus only the general configuration of motivations and preparations can be discerned. Most obviously, the incendiarism was a logical development of the propaganda of the Radical party during the preceding eight years: the clergy was the evil genius of the nation, and it was necessary to burn convents, symbols of clerical wealth and power. In this context, the convent was a symbol of the established regime — the "Bastille" of the Barcelona working class.* From the first moment of the antiwar protest of July 1909, the Radicals had focused the blame on the religious orders, and by the weekend of July 24, incendiarism was being discussed. Prosecutors later tried to prove that party leaders had talked about this in their Saturday night meeting with Baldomero Bonet in the Casa del Pueblo. In any case, the Radical editorial "Remember" had broadly hinted at the idea of incendiarism. Emiliano Iglesias said the idea had been proposed on Monday afternoon by a group of women party members.[13] But the definitive event was undoubtedly the burning of the Marist school in Pueblo Nuevo. Sometime between Monday night and Tuesday morning, Iglesias reached a compromise decision: Radicals could burn church property (he probably could not have prevented this in any case) but the Radical party itself would be completely divorced from the action. One factor that influenced Iglesias, as he later candidly admitted, was that incendiarism constituted a crime under the civil law code, and not an act of treason. Iglesias thus prepared against future prosecution.

The incendiarism prevented the popular uprising from developing into a revolution; it dissipated the stored-up revolutionary energies, while the lawlessness alienated potential middle-class allies, both civilian and military. Senator Sol y Ortega warned the incendiaries on Tuesday afternoon that "this is not the way to the republic, because no one would dare to proclaim it by the glare of a fire."[14]

This consequence of the incendiarism may not have been foreseen. In the first moments of the uprising there was some talk of a military coup, of using to advantage the many attempts that had been made to cultivate republicanism among officers. Sometime on Tuesday, Emiliano Iglesias told a group of members from various political parties that he thought the best solution would be to find an officer to head the uprising, the same thing he had told the Strike Committee over the weekend.[15] Republican Senator Sol

* Half a century later, Marist Brother Adaulfo Abaurrea, who fled from anticlerical mobs in Mataró, remembered specifically this aspect. Workers "were against the government, believing rightly or wrongly that it had not been effective in the war. They attacked all elements of order, including the Church." (Interview with Brother Abaurrea in Barcelona on October 31, 1961.)

y Ortega claimed he did secure the promise of two generals to lead a revolution, and that he was busy arranging automobiles and messengers when the convent burnings began and "paralyzed preparations for a coup."[16] Given Sol's braggadocio, the potential of these plans is difficult to assess.* The fact of historical significance is that the incendiarism eliminated the possibility of a military coup.

It did not, however, compel officers to redouble their efforts to suppress the revolt, but rather had just the opposite effect. Officers did not try to stop the convent burnings, a reflection of the latent antagonism toward the proclerical, pro-Catalan policies of the Maura government to which they were nominally committed. For the past three years, Radical politicians had openly sought an alliance with officers on the basis of these common antagonisms. Emiliano Iglesias had many friends in the Barcelona garrison[17] and he may even have sounded out certain key officers on their attitude toward a limited program of convent burnings. Whatever be the origin, the tolerance of the officers was an important factor in the events of the following days.

The official history of the Radical party (of which Emiliano Iglesias was coeditor) later reported that the order to begin the convent burnings was issued on Tuesday morning by "X" who acted "spontaneously" when he decided that the Central Committee for the Strike had lost control of the situation.[18] The Radical official who actually issued the orders for the convent burnings, according to Solidaridad Obrera spokesmen, was Lorenzo Ardid — an old-time republican noted for his ability in a street fray and the man who had assured Ferrer that the Radical party did not plan a revolution. Many of Ardid's orders were countermanded by Iglesias, reported labor leaders in an effort to emphasize Iglesias' pusillanimity.[19]

Military authorities believed that Rafael and José Ulled actually directed the campaign of convent burnings. Lawyers by profession and officers of the Juventud Radical, the Ulled brothers were reported as present at many of the convent burnings.[20] Juan Colominas,** also an official of the Jóvenes

---

* What is certain is that the aged Senator, true to the violent anticlericalism of his career, attended many convent burnings in the following days. He justified this on the ground that he had to show "he was not afraid" and in order "to avoid greater evils." (See the biography by his political secretary, Miguel Tato y Amat, *Sol y Ortega y la política contemporánea* [Madrid, 1914], pp. 479–80.) Army prosecutors charged Sol y Ortega with responsibiilty for organizing the attack on the Jesuit residence (described below on pp. 231–32); primarily because of his immunity as a senator, he was not convicted.

** Although only twenty-six years old, Colominas had been elected to the Barcelona City Council in May 1909, a post gained through extensive service to the Radical party

Bárbaros, and a city councilman, admitted many years later that he attended almost all of the burnings;[21] by reason of his background and of his contacts with the extremist factions within the Radical party, Colominas was undoubtedly a key figure in the organization of the convent burnings.

On Tuesday morning, according to the party history, "X" gave instructions to a group of ten youths, all under twenty years of age, and sent them to each of the city districts with written instructions "for the purpose of unifying the movement, orienting the great mass of fighters toward a specific object."[22] Messengers, usually on bicycles, carried to each district lists of convents to be destroyed. Many wore Red Cross armbands in order to divert the suspicions of policemen.

"Certain norms" were established by those who were worried about defending the convent burnings later, wrote a Jesuit observer, who defined the burnings as "a political conspiracy."[23] Aggression was directed against the wealth, not the person, of the clergy, which served to assuage the consciences of army officers and private citizens who failed to defend church property. Mobs were instructed not to kill. Many religious were warned of pending attacks and voluntarily left their buildings; others were urged to do so by army officers, or by the incendiaries themselves. This facilitated the arson while avoiding casualties.[24] Leaders directed that all jewels, bonds, and cash be thrown onto bonfires: apologists for the convent burnings maintained that looting was done by rabble who arrived after the idealistic incendiaries had departed; clergy claimed that both tasks were performed by the same group.[25]

As for the task of agitation, orators had merely to remind men and women of abuses, real or imagined, by the religious who administered charitable institutions. Crowds were promised proof that tombs of contemplative orders contained fabulous wealth and the corpses of tortured nuns. Workers were urged to destroy Catholic schools: in some towns in Catalonia this objective was openly announced, although in Barcelona it

---

in its schools and in its youth movement (particularly in Pueblo Nuevo). He and his group of young republican extremists had participated in the planning of the General Strike of 1902. Francisco Ferrer wanted to gain access to this extremist group, and so in 1907, he had appointed Colominas as his business manager. In the fall of 1908 Colominas resigned, stating publicly that he did so to protest Ferrer's support of Solidaridad Obrera in its attack upon the Radical party. But possibly Colominas continued to maintain contact with Ferrer through his wife, Angeles Villafranca, a sister of Ferrer's mistress; he definitely continued to work with Ferrer's associates on behalf of rationalist education.

was only occasionally scrawled on the wall of a burned school but often shouted by the incendiary groups. To these well-worn issues of anticlericalism, still another was added on Tuesday, July 21: the shibboleth that religious orders were preparing an uprising to replace the Alphonsine Bourbons with a Carlist pretender, for which purpose they had stored arms within the convents.* This gained new currency because some clergy, anticipating attacks and alarmed by military passivity, attempted to work out an arrangement with the armed Carlist youth militia to defend convents and churches.[26] And while the convent burnings were being prepared, Iglesias went to a meeting of city officials.

"From the first moment of the events, Emiliano Iglesias prepared his alibis with the ability befitting a lawyer," the chief military judge was to declare some months later.[27] Iglesias began his preparation at 11 A.M. on Tuesday, in the meeting called by Mayor Coll y Pujol to ask advice of representatives of the five political parties in the City Council.

Lliga Councilor Narciso Verdaguer commented to Iglesias on the widely circulated reports that Radical extremists had tried to force him to lead a revolution and expressed sympathy for his difficult position. "Friend Verdaguer," Iglesias replied demurely, "I could not, nor should I, nor would I want to take part in a movement that appears to have no practical purpose whatsoever and that has become discredited by this time." [28]

This sophistry offered and accepted, Iglesias moved on to the urgent matter of canceling the City Council's regular Tuesday evening session. Lliga Councilor Verdaguer insisted it be held as a means of securing the collaboration of the public in the re-establishment of law and order. Reluctantly Iglesias agreed but with two provisos: military authorities must guarantee the maintenance of order in the Plaza de San Jaime, outside the city hall, and a junta of civilian officials must be organized with authority to negotiate a settlement between striking workers and army officers. To set up the junta, Iglesias asked Mayor Coll to call a meeting, prior to the Council session, of all Catalan deputies and senators as well as representatives from business and civic organizations. He further suggested that officials of the most important labor syndicates be invited, so that they could exert "moral

---

* Just eight days earlier the Carlist pretender, Carlos de Borbón y Este, had died; he was succeeded by his son, Jaime (El Correo Catalán [Barcelona], July 20, 1909). The clergy were rumored to be aiding the Carlists to gather arms in preparation for Don Jaime's return to Spain (Shaw, Spain from Within, pp. 152–64, 169–72).

pressure, if it were indeed true that they had any influence on the elements who had organized the strike"; this suggestion was not implemented. Mayor Coll did agree, however, to arrange a meeting of the other individuals at 4:30 in the afternoon.

Beyond proposals for further meetings, not one of the five political leaders was willing to assist Mayor Coll to fill the vacuum of civilian authority created by Governor Ossorio's resignation. They merely voted that "the most proper thing would be to award a vote of confidence to the Mayor who, in accord with his own criterion, would study and carry out the most opportune measures."

The meeting not only enabled Iglesias to establish a reputation early in the week as a responsible public official, but also provided him with an alibi for the only incident linking him with the armed rebellion. Sometime between noon and 1:00 Iglesias left the city hall, accompanied by two friends. Either because he was forced to do so by party militants, or because he just happened to walk along the Calle San Pablo where barricades were being constructed, Iglesias stopped to greet the men at work. The well-dressed Radical politician, walking-stick in hand, was immediately recognized. Men took off their caps in admiration. "There goes Emiliano Iglesias," one worker called out. "Look at how he is willing to incriminate himself." Iglesias did not intend his presence at the barricades to be more than a gesture, and so he merely acknowledged the greetings and continued on his way.* His purpose was "to capture and have in my home the Committee for the Strike which later not even God was to see." [29]

Between 1:00 and 1:30 in the afternoon, the three members of the Central Committee for the Strike assembled in Iglesias' apartment located in the central business district. Also present were some few labor leaders, as well as representatives of the Juventud Radical. In short, this was a meeting of all those who had half-guided and half-followed the workers' antigovernment protest. Fabra Rivas, whose primary concern was still the antiwar

* Military judges later tried to use this incident to implicate Iglesias in the armed rebellion. The only three witnesses to testify were suspect because they were sponsored by the reactionary Catholic lawyer's group, el Comité de Defensa Social. Furthermore, the hour the witnesses specified was the hour when Iglesias was meeting with other city councilors. *Causa: Rebelión militar,* I, 449–50, 535; II, 27–30, 58–59, 242–43, 249–51. During his trial, Iglesias denied having been on the barricades, yet one year later he bragged of it in an article attempting to prove his bravery ("De la Revolución de Julio," *El Progreso* [Barcelona], August 6, 1910).

issue, persuaded the Radicals to promise help in preventing the embarkation of a troop ship, scheduled to depart at three in the afternoon.[30]

The central concern of the meeting was whether or not to use the uprising as the occasion to seize power. Once again Miguel V. Moreno asked Emiliano Iglesias to proclaim a republic, a proposal which was received in silence by the labor leaders and with enthusiasm by the Jóvenes Bárbaros.[31] Iglesias reiterated that he could not decide until word was received of support from outside Catalonia, to which Fabra Rivas replied that Madrid and Valencia would launch a supporting protest movement within a few hours. Those assembled agreed, at least in theory, to stage the rebellion that night and to meet again at 8 P.M., in the Café Mallorca, to work out the final details.[32]

Socialist Fabra Rivas left the meeting firmly convinced that Iglesias was "willing to occupy a place in the vanguard of the revolutionary troops." [33] But the Radical chief had no intention of becoming "the pawn of a Committee that did not represent anything, and that could not even offer him *forces* nor a *plan*." [34] Iglesias did not intend to appear at the Café Mallorca meeting until he knew that cities in other parts of Spain had declared a general strike, a development he doubted would occur.

By the time Febra Rivas and José Comaposada* (a fellow socialist and his constant companion during these days) left Iglesias' apartment, convents had begun to burn — a project about which the socialists had known nothing beforehand. "Such ignorance," Iglesias disdainfully commented, "was a reflection of the fact that, inflated by the importance of their role, they had not reconnoitered the city, nor were they in contact with those who were fighting and accomplishing things." [35] Because he had been able to deceive Fabra Rivas about the convent burnings, Emiliano Iglesias lost his respect for the socialist's ability as a revolution-maker.

The socialists realized that during their hour-long meeting with Iglesias the scene in the streets had changed from skirmishes with the police to "full revolution." [36] The stark realities were that the socialists had provided

---

* José Comaposada, a member of the Socialist party, had during the preceding few years been active in Catalan labor circles—in his own railroad workers' union, and in Solidaridad Obrera. He had worked closely with Fabra Rivas on the socialist newspaper, *La Internacional*. (*El Socialista* [Madrid], August 12, 1910. Sastre, *Huelgas: 1908*, p. 116. *La Internacional* [Barcelona], January 1, 1909). Comaposada later published a series of nine articles on the General Strike ("Sucesos de Barcelona," *El Socialista*, October 29–December 24, 1909). These were reprinted in book form: *La Revolución de Barcelona* (Barcelona, Biblioteca Acción, 1909), and *La Revolución en Cataluña* (Barcelona, Biblioteca Acción, 1910).

organizational leadership for the General Strike, which had gained them a place on the Central Committee, but they could provide neither members to man the barricades nor a party organization to direct the seizure of power. Even if Emiliano Iglesias and the Radical Republicans did fulfill the promises they had just made, Fabra Rivas and José Comaposada were unwilling to turn over to them the movement they had done so much to promote. At least they would try an alternative: to persuade the Catalan Nationalist Republicans to provide political leadership, alone or with other Catalan republican groups. On the basis of his personal contacts with Catalan Nationalist Republicans — and specifically with Antonio Rovira y Virgili, the editor of *El Poble Català* — Fabra Rivas had grown to respect their integrity and sincerity.

Fabra Rivas had already talked with Rovira y Virgili and with the other editors of *El Poble Català* in the newspaper office around noon on Tuesday, warning them that unless some well-known and distinguished politicians took hold, "the whole thing will slip out of our hands, the riffraff will take over, troops will arrive from other provinces, and everything will be lost." [37] But however sympathetic the young editors might be to Fabra Rivas' proposal, the power to act did not rest with them but with the Catalan republican legislators.

The legislators were to meet that very afternoon, Tuesday, July 27, in accordance with plans made the previous Friday after Maura had rejected their suggestions for ending the hostilities in Morocco. Although the Radical deputies had spurned the invitation of the Catalan republican deputies, all groups within Solidaridad Catalana had agreed to attend. Newspapers over the weekend had publicized the meeting extensively, so all Barcelona knew the time and place.

When the legislators assembled in the home of Federalist Republican Vallés y Ribot, in the very center of Barcelona, shortly after 2 P.M., they did not know that a Catholic church had already been ignited just a few blocks away.[38] Considering the movement strictly as a protest against the war, they enthusiastically supported it. "The unanimous state of subversion had penetrated the meeting," reported Catalan Republican Deputy Amadeo Hurtado, who added that the conservative politicians "were the most excited of all those of us who gathered." [39] The first action of the deputies was to send Lliga Deputy Puig y Cadafalch to the city hall to learn the latest news and to offer "assistance in any action deemed useful in those grave moments." Senators and deputies then discussed the proposal that had occasioned their meeting, the preparation of a second and more forceful protest to Maura about the fighting in Morocco. All agreed to sign a telegram warning Maura that unless he ended hostilities immediately they could not be responsible for the consequences.*

Vallés y Ribot's wife ran into the room to announce that the Piarist Fathers' school had just gone up in flames, and everyone crowded out on the balconies to watch. When they came back in, Hurtado reported, "the tone of our meeting had changed." Carlist Mariano Gomar "returned to being his usual reserved self, muttering . . . in a dull voice, 'This no, this no.' " [40] The group decided to disband as soon as Puig y Cadafalch returned from the city hall.

Suddenly the uprising penetrated the legislators' meeting. By now the movement had been clearly defined as revolutionary, reported Federalist Republican Deputy Joaquín Salvatella, and therefore workers — knowing their elected representatives were meeting — came to request *jefes ostensibles;* they came not as excited individuals, but as formal delegations with a request for instructions and for deputies to appear on the streets. Some identified themselves as Radical party members, informing Salvatella they were asking for instructions from Catalan republican politicians (their erstwhile enemies) "because at that moment they did not know where to find those who should have been their chiefs." [41] Six young Federalist Republicans, reporting that they had been present when convents were burned and that the "people wanted to fight . . . at all costs," demanded that their chief, Vallés y Ribot, give them "orders and arms for the revolution." Veteran of many an uprising, Vallés y Ribot deftly dispatched the amateurs with the admonition that such matters needed careful study before politicians could decide.[42] After some consultation, the deputies agreed that to involve their parties in so amorphous a movement would be risky. In their name, Salvatella repeatedly went into the street to warn, "We don't know what this whole thing is. Neither do we know who has organized this movement that is just beginning, nor the purpose . . . We cannot honorably sacrifice ourselves, nor should we sacrifice ourselves, and we advise you not to participate in a violent struggle in which you will inevitably have to succumb." [43] By now the terrified concierge had closed the street doors to prevent any more groups from entering the building, but opened it to admit Puig y

---

* On Tuesday evening, when deputies attempted to send the telegram to Maura, the telegraph office refused to accept it for transmission.

Cadafalch, who brought alarming news. Convents and churches throughout the city were burning, and municipal authorities had no means of defending themselves. Most importantly, Interior Minister La Cierva "in
order to prevent the insurrection from becoming contagious, had proclaimed
to the four winds that Barcelona had declared a separatist uprising." [44] Some
deputies had already left; the others hastily prepared to do so.

Reluctantly albeit firmly, the legislators — the middle-class politicians —
disengaged themselves from the workers' protest that they had done so
much to foment, because they were afraid to confront its profound social
implications; considerations of public order once more superseded the desire
for reform, as they had so often with Spanish politicians since the nineteenth century. Perhaps "someday we shall have to repent so much serenity,"
reflected Salvatella. [45] "Our position," wrote Hurtado, "had nothing splendid
about it." The saddest part, he added, was that Catalan politicians who had
boasted of replacing the traditional cacique-dominated parties with a truly
representative movement, found themselves in exactly the same position as
their predecessors of seven years before: "completely ignorant of the drama
that a people in revolt were living." [46]

The drama that the people of Barcelona were living was staged with a
fine sense of timing and of effect. Between 1:30 and 3:30 P.M., convents began to burn both in the city and in the suburbs, a remarkable degree of
coordination, given the extensive terrain and the difficulty of communication.

In Barcelona proper the spectacle started with the demolition of the
handsome buildings, four stories high and covering one city block, belonging to the Piarist Fathers. Both the site and the religious order had been
selected with care. The dignified old Royal College of San Antón was in
the heart of the city, on the edge of a slum area. Piarists had long been associated with the Carlist cause, which during the week was rumored to be
arming for a new uprising. [47] But according to the Piarists themselves, the
incendiaries had chosen this site to begin the burning of church property in
Barcelona because they were the principal religious order associated with the
education of the poor and received large subsidies from the state for this
purpose, a function they performed in addition to educating the propertied
classes; in recent years they had been a special target for attacks by lay educators, and specifically of Francisco Ferrer. [48]

The assault had been carefully prepared. Early Tuesday morning a group started to construct barricades designed to prevent mounted police or soldiers from charging the rebels. These were leveled by a detachment of sixteen mounted Civil Guards who remained to guard the building all morning, but suddenly, for reasons that were never explained, the Civil Guards withdrew at noon. Immediately a band of men, women, and boys began rebuilding the barricades, an enterprise that required at least one hour to complete.

It was probably for this reason that the first religious building ignited in Barcelona proper was the parish Church of San Pablo del Campo, located in the same area but closer to the waterfront.[49] The rapidly executed and spectacular attack may have been a diversionary maneuver. Since early morning the Gothic church had been encased behind stone barricades, but until 1 P.M., the would-be incendiaries had wandered aimlessly; as soon as "a young man, scarcely twenty-five years old, decently dressed, a gentleman," arrived and gave the order to "fire the church," two picturesque criminals went to work. Rafael Fernández ("Noy de la Veu") and Adela Anglada directed the burning of furnishings and the igniting of the building, then left to burn the nearby convent of the Hieronymite Nuns. An army officer and his soldiers, summoned to restore order, were able to salvage the church with the help of neighbors and firemen; the rectory, however, was left in ruins.

The individuals in charge of the assault upon the Piarist establishment had used to good advantage the hour from one to two o'clock (while the Church of San Pablo was being burned). One task was to secure arms. José Gomis Montells led twenty men to a nearby rifle shop and demanded that the owner, Roca, "open up so that they could provide themselves with arms in order to fight those who were persecuting them." Roca entreated the group, "among whom were many extremely well-dressed men," not to take his stock of arms that "represented my entire fortune." Realizing his pleas were futile, Roca fled with his family to a neighbor's home. Gomis and his men seized approximately 225 rifles, 500 revolvers, and 35,000 cartridges, then returned to the barricades around the Piarist buildings and distributed the arms among "the most aggressive individuals."[50]

At 2 P.M., a man arrived to give the signal for the attack.[51] He wore a business suit, not a worker's smock; some whispered he was a prominent pickpocket, while others said he was the son of a wealthy family, a former student of the Piarists. The man waved his walking stick in the air, shouted "Long live the republic and the revolution," and the attack began. A group of young boys forced open the wooden entry gates, leading from the main boulevard. Another group of young boys entered with long ladders, set them up against the building, and climbed to the second floor, while others forced open the ground floor doors. Hundreds, perhaps thousands, watched from the streets or from the balconies of nearby houses.

The spotlight focused briefly on the fifty Piarist Priests and Brothers who were still inside their residence. They had rejected all warnings to flee on the ground that because they educated the poor, their convent had been one of the few spared by the mobs in Barcelona in 1835 and would be spared again. Even if they were attacked, the Rector, Father Ramón Riera, had been convinced that "the entire neighborhood would line up at our side to defend us. How mistaken we were. No one came to our rescue." [52] For a while it appeared that not even the authorities would help, for only after the Rector made three frantic telephone calls to General Santiago did he get a response. At 2:30 P.M., while the main gates to the school were burning, the Captain General came in person in command of fifty infantry and twelve cavalry soldiers. In accord with the established tactic, the attacking mob applauded the troops, who merely escorted the priests from the residence to waiting carriages. General Santiago departed, but many of the soldiers went to the far side of the boulevard to watch the burning. The Piarists were firmly convinced that the Army had orders "to tolerate certain things." * [53]

By 3 P.M., some fifty to sixty boys were inside the Piarist school, tossing down objects for the bonfire built under the direction of Antonio Villanueva Cabo, who had a long prison record of theft and other crimes.[54] One youth found a rifle and waved it out the window as he shouted that the Piarists "were armed to the teeth." Scavengers found false money that the Brothers later explained was used in their commercial classes. They also discovered a machine which the youths claimed was used to mint false money that was then circulated to debase the currency;** the Piarists said it was used to

* So was the Mother Superior of the influential Adorer Sisters whose convent was attacked unsuccessfully three times. She informed the head of her order that a large number of the armed forces in Barcelona were united with the mob, that army officers tried to persuade clergy to leave the buildings so that the incendiaries could enter, and then that officers watched with pleasure while the convents were burned ("Carta-relación de la Rdma. M. Corazón de Jesús, Superiora de esta casa, a Rdma. Madre Superiora General," Crónica de la Casa de Barcelona: Instituto de las Adoratrices Esclavas del Santísimo Sacramento y de la Caridad. Quinta parte: 1908–1922. Vol. I, 175–76 [mimeographed]).

** Emiliano Iglesias later rose in the Cortes to defend this charge, stating that in the many cases for counterfeiting in which he had acted as a lawyer, the plaintiffs always make religious medals. Explosives were set off in the right wing of the school, so strong that they destroyed even the outer walls. Finally, the youths set fire to the building and fled. The flames from this fire could be seen by the Solidaridad Catalana deputies, meeting several blocks away in the home of Vallés y Ribot.

Incendiaries immediately went across the street to set ablaze the Piarists' school for poor children. However they permitted firemen to put out this fire because it endangered the adjoining homes of workers, but they forbade them to turn their hoses on the main school building. One band then left to continue their work elsewhere, but many incendiaries stayed behind to see flames consume the dignified old Royal College of San Antón. Despite scores of lesser victories during the next few days, the incendiaries were never able to repeat so dramatically successful a devastation.

An equally destructive assault had been carried out concurrently on a convent located across the street from the Piarist building — the Royal Monastery of San Mateo belonging to a cloistered order of Hieronymite Nuns.[55] The convent held a special attraction for anticlericals because these nuns were cloistered, and because they were then — and are today — rumored to be fabulously wealthy.

Although warned of the attack, the twenty-eight nuns remained inside the building until the incendiaries arrived. They fled out the back, through public laundries which they owned, to be met on the street by neighborhood women who threw stones and jeered at them. Army officers provided no escort, as they had for the Piarists. The nuns went to the home of a factory owner but the mob threatened to set fire to the building, so they dressed in lay clothing and scattered to private homes throughout Barcelona.

Neighbors enthusiastically joined in destroying the property of the Hieronymite Nuns — the church, the convent, and an apartment building despite pleas of its working-class occupants to spare their possessions. Amidst cheers stocks were thrown into a giant bonfire (although some were carried off to be sold later). From a nearby window, the nun who acted as treasurer watched; she calculated the stocks were valued at "considerably more than one million pesetas," explaining they constituted the capital accumulated from dowries of the Hieronymites over the four hundred years of their existence.[56] In addition, she said, "considerable funds" had been deposited

claimed that the dies were used for making medals (July 6, 1910, *Diario de las Cortes*, II, 406).

with them by private citizens.* In this foray, the wealth of the Hieronymite Nuns had been ably exploited for propaganda. The aura of mystery surrounding a cloistered order was not used in this way until the following day.

In contrast with this spectacular initiation, the burning of convents in the slum areas of Barcelona (the Paralelo, Atarazana, and Pueblo Seco) was performed in a rapid, almost perfunctory manner. In the course of one hour and a half, a total of seven Catholic schools, welfare institutions, and parish churches were burned.

In this area, as in the industrial suburbs, the incendiaries were usually residents in the neighborhood. At times the leaders had been educated or nursed by the clergy they attacked; they may have desired vengeance for some humiliation, real or imagined, or they may have resented the need to accept charity from foreign clergy. Or perhaps the reason was simply the frenzy of a moment, joining in with a group which appeared with gasoline and a plan to burn. These acts of ingratitude were balanced by the generosity of some few valiant families who, remembering past services or taking compassion on defenseless women, aided nuns to leave the convents and gave them refuge in their homes.

At 2 P.M. (the time when the Piarist school was set afire), the assault began on the unpretentious convent and school of the Franciscan Sisters of the Immaculate Conception in Pueblo Seco.[57] Working-class women believed that these sisters forced students to embroider goods which were then sold commercially. Neighbors gossiped about a pretty sister reputed to have been martyred in the convent and her body exposed in a glass tomb.** Therefore, on Tuesday when the Franciscans rang the bell for help, neighbors did not respond. The sisters left the building to face an abusive crowd agitated by three of their former students; one man tried to disrobe one Franciscan sister because "we want to see if you are carrying arms." Two well-dressed men intervened and enabled the sisters to reach private homes. They changed

---

* The claim that some of the stocks had been left on deposit was repeated in the case of another cloistered order, the Capuchin Nuns in San Gervasio (see page 235). Republican newspapers sarcastically pointed out the cheap rates for depositing funds in Barcelona's many banks (*El País* [Madrid], August 13, 1909).

** The Mother Superior stated that the tomb contained not a martyred sister but Leonor, daughter of a King of Aragon, whose mummy was venerated by the order. Mother Beatriz declared that the fifty elaborately embroidered communion dresses found inside the convent were the gift of society ladies, not made for commercial sale. Finally, she said the expenses of the school were paid by official subsidies and contributions. (*El Correo Catalán* [Barcelona], September 10, 1909.)

to lay clothing and went to other areas of the metropolis, while their building was totally destroyed.

The same efficient arsonist band went on to burn three additional buildings, a task facilitated by the fact that they were empty: the parish church of Santa Madrona la Nueva, which served the 70,000 workers of Pueblo Seco; the church and rectory of Santa Madrona la Antigua; a small and sparsely furnished school run by the Brothers of the Christian Schools, where 225 boys studied free of charge.[58]

Concurrently, another group attacked the convent of the Little Sisters of the Assumption, an extremely strict and austere French nursing order that had only recently been established in the diocese for the gratuitous care of the poor; fifteen of the sixteen sisters were French. The Mother Superior reported that their "neighbors comported themselves in an admirable manner" and showed their gratitude, even though they thereby exposed themselves to danger.[59] However, as in the case of the other nuns, they were forced to leave the neighborhood.

Gaining confidence from these successes, incendiaries moved westward from the section of narrow, dark streets to the wider avenues of the industrial sector of the Paralelo. Their target was the well-known asylum on Calle Aldana, run by the Daughters of Charity of St. Vincent de Paul, which included a school, day nursery for working mothers, and orphan asylum. Neighbors believed the sisters exploited these activities by requiring students and inmates to sew for private customers, thus earning money and harming small businessmen.

All day the Sisters of Charity had watched the excited mobs in the street and when at 3 P.M. they saw smoke rising from the Church of Santa Madrona, they guessed it would be their turn next. The Mother Superior and the fourteen sisters went down to open the door to the incendiaries who arrived one half hour later; in the crowd they recognized persons whom they had educated and some who were parents of children currently enrolled in their school. The Mother Superior boldly inquired what the crowd wanted. "We want to burn the convent," declared the leader. "Out, out! We have to burn. We want the republic." "And what is the republic?" inquired the Mother Superior. The spokesman began: "Well, it is . . . the republic, that's all." [60]

Overwhelmed by the force, not of the argument but of the throng, the Sisters of Charity agreed to leave. A Red Cross representative, who came to escort them through the streets, dissuaded them from carrying any valuable lest it provide the excuse for an attack in the street. The sisters went to the women's prison, staffed by members of their order, while their asylum was plundered and burned.

One more school was destroyed in this district that so desperately lacked educational facilities: the school of the Handmaids of the Sacred Heart of Jesus, who had only recently moved to Pueblo Seco to settle in a house belonging to a wealthy conservative Catalan Deputy Ignacio Girona. Although the school was relatively small, Antonio Camallonge, who led the incendiaries, was determined to make it the site of an exemplary anticlerical manifestation; not one item was to be stolen, everything had to burned. Camallonge was a man of some prominence in the Radical party, a neighborhood character who flew the flag of the First Republic over his home each Sunday. On Tuesday afternoon, July 27, he ordered that a huge bonfire be built and that all household furnishings, as well as the chickens and goats of the sisters, be consumed by the flames.[61]

By five o'clock the burning of religious buildings in the slum districts had ended; incendiaries were free to carry out their tasks in other neighborhoods.

On Tuesday afternoon, in Barcelona proper, only one other religious building was burned — the convent of the *Arrepentidas,* a reformed penitential cloistered order of nuns, whose convent was located in the University district of prosperous business and residential establishments.[62] These nuns had occupied the same site for three hundred years before the Radicals constructed their Casa del Pueblo on the same street.

At 2:30 (just as boys were entering the Piarist schools), sixteen-year-old Carmen Gabaldón led a crowd of women and young boys to the cloistered convent. Next came a large group of men carrying hatchets and long ladders, directed by Salvador Tourner who had served five sentences for robbery. "We have come," the spokesmen told the nuns, "to place you at liberty and to burn the convent." Followed by a shouting mob, the nuns took refuge in a nearby convent while their orchard was plundered; chickens and pigs were slaughtered on the spot. The fires set were so intense that they burned for eight days, during which time people returned to ransack the building.

Not until three hours later did a second attack occur in the University district, a respite necessary to bring in and to instruct mobs from slum areas.

The violence in the working-class districts of Barcelona was matched by that in the industrial suburbs of Pueblo Nuevo and in the adjoining Clot-

San Martín suburbs. All these districts had in common their poverty and the political control of the Radical party.

Pueblo Nuevo was quiet all Tuesday morning, the aftermath of the slaying of the Marist Director of the Workers' Circle of San José, yet it was apparently no secret that further burnings were being planned. A public works contractor, Grau, went to the Radical center on the Rambla del Triunfo in Pueblo Nuevo to secure protection for two factories; he was assured that the only project as of that moment was to burn clerical property.[63] The initial target was the parish Church of Santa María del Taulat.[64] Anticipating this, Father Ramón Riu and his vicar went to hide in the basement at 10 A.M. In the afternoon incendiaries burned all except the massive walls, for which task they may have used explosives; police dispersed the spectators but left the church to burn.

The arsonists had gone on to the school, located near the parish church, where a community of Franciscan Sisters taught working-class girls.[65] The sisters had already been taken to safe lodgings (escorted by a "foreigner," according to their account); no one threatened harm nor insulted them, a tribute to the good will they had gained in this rough neighborhood. As soon as the seditionaries burned the Franciscan school, they returned to the parish church to tear down the walls. In so doing they came upon the hiding place of the two priests. All afternoon men and women threw objects down on Father Riu and shouted abuse. For twelve years Father Riu had been the parish priest of Pueblo Nuevo, and yet on that Tuesday afternoon no parishoner attempted to save him. Shortly after 6 P.M. the elderly priest died of smoke suffocation, and possibly of shock; his body was dragged into the street and profaned.[66] By now the incendiarism had become a sideshow to the main act of an armed revolt.

In Pueblo Nuevo as in other working-class areas, crowds eagerly attacked police, a favorite pastime now heightened by the hope of destroying the police files of criminals. At 2:30 P.M. Pedro Ramón, together with the brothers Francisco and Salvador Sagarra, attempted to penetrate the station with the help of two hundred men and women.[67] An army detachment came immediately to relieve the besieged police and inflicted casualties on Pedro Ramón's group, which was forced to disperse. At 5 P.M., as soon as the soldiers left Pueblo Nuevo, the throng returned and forced its way into the station, looting and then utterly destroying it. Realizing the futility of resistance, police abandoned the stations located in workers' neighborhoods late on Tuesday afternoon; they would not fight while army officers waited for troop reinforcements. This withdrawal of police marked the passage of the movement from an uprising into an open rebellion, as soldiers and Civil Guards were left to defend the government.

The residents of Pueblo Nuevo looked forward to this confrontation. In midafternoon they had begun to construct barricades, the familiar nineteenth-century symbol of a popular rebellion. Women were in the vanguard (as they had been since the first moment of the General Strike), as for example Enriqueta Sabater, "La Larga," who directed the construction of barricades; she then went around with a saw and cut down electric light poles and telephone lines, but interrupted her work to take pity on a Franciscan nun whom she escorted to a safe refuge. Rosa Esteller, "La Valenciana," terrified local officials: she helped to build barricades before going to nearby houses where, by brandishing her revolver, she forced owners to leave the street doors open so that rebels could climb to the rooftops and fire on police. Then La Valenciana returned to the street, where she was later to distinguish herself in the fighting.[68]

In the neighboring industrial suburb of Clot-San Martín, men had begun at dawn on Tuesday to fire at police from houses along the highway leading from Barcelona. They continued all morning until casualties overflowed the clinic and the fire station. Clot was an older community than Pueblo Nuevo, with a more varied social grouping of artisans and skilled workers. Political activity was intense, as indicated by the many competing party centers; by far the most popular was the Radicals' Casa del Pueblo de Clot. Although police were convinced that this was where the insurrection was being planned,[69] they made no effort to close it.

At 3 P.M., men began to build a barricade on the Calle Mayor. Fishmonger Carmen Alauch, a member of the Damas Rojas and described by neighbors as a "notorious lerrouxista agitator," bullied neighbors into helping and recruited teenage boys for the fighting; she thus continued at the forefront of the rebels in Clot, a position established the previous day when she had participated in the armed assault on the police station.

Somewhat as a side affair, the new and spacious parish Church of San Martín de Provensals was burned. Father Miguel Roura had assumed that those who had contributed funds for building the church would be willing to defend it but was disabused by the chief of the local militia who advised him to leave. Dressed in lay clothing, Father Roura and his assistants were departing when they met the incendiaries, led by Gregorio Baltrina, who asked directions to the church; the priests courteously complied. Baltrina's group burned the furnishings but did little damage to the church, then went on to try to blow up a railroad bridge, at which they were equally unsuccessful.[70]

In the suburb of San Gervasio on Tuesday afternoon, anticlericalism remained the focus of the uprising. This was a district of luxurious estates (that escaped unscathed), with a small commercial area, around which were clustered working-class homes. In this rather unlikely setting, another religious was to be killed.

The assault upon the school run by the Sisters of the Society of the Holy Child Jesus (*Damas Negras*) was a half-hearted affair.[71] The large community of sisters was warned and left; a loyal gardener beat out the flames with the help of army troops who arrived almost immediately.

The residence of the Franciscan Fathers was the true target.[72] At 3 P.M. the monks, warned that the mob was on its way, left for private homes. Father Ramón María Usó, the Superior, and Father Francisco Bragulat waited until the rest were safe; at 4 P.M., they set out, wearing their habits because there was not sufficient lay clothing, and carrying the securities and cash of the community. They were sighted by an armed group who shouted at the Franciscans to drop their packages. The monks started to run and a man fired, wounding Father Usó. Father Bragulat dragged him around the corner and into a friendly house. One hour later the Red Cross took Father Usó to a clinic where he died the following day. He was the third, and the last, religious to die during the week. The slaying in San Gervasio had no impact upon the course of events. The decisive incident took place in the suburb of Gracia where residents fired on soldiers on Tuesday afternoon and thereby formally launched the armed rebellion.

In Gracia, a large manufacturing area only recently annexed to Barcelona, the General Strike had been primarily antimilitarist from the start. One reason was that two hundred reserve soldiers from Gracia had already left for Morocco, possibly a larger number than from any other city district.[73] Another factor was that the Radical party did not exercise the control over workers in Gracia that they held in other worker areas and could not therefore focus attacks upon police and convents. True, a group of armed incendiaries had gathered early in the morning to burn the residence of the Oratorian Fathers of St. Philip Neri (*Filipenses*), a missionary order; however no one came to give directions. The fathers climbed the wall and fled, while some individuals ransacked their residence and the crowd dispersed.[74]

In contrast with this haphazard affair, the construction of barricades was zealously executed. Beginning late in the morning, on the corners of streets intersecting with the main arteries of the Calle Mayor and the Traversera de Gracia, men constructed seventy-six barricades of metal bedsteads, railings, and paving stones (for which they tore up more square meters of street surface than anywhere else in Barcelona). In Gracia men would not fire from rooftops, as elsewhere in the metropolitan area, but fought in a manner reminiscent of nineteenth-century street battles. Appropriately, there were more shouts of "Viva la república" in Gracia than in all the rest of Barcelona.[75]

The uprising was as picturesque as it was intense. Elderly Esteban Sala Bonnany, "el Curandero," drank a goodly number of brandies to fortify him for his command of the barricades on the Calle León; waving his pistol, Sala announced he had fought for the First Republic and was highly pleased with this new revolution.[76] Ramón Giró, a poor sculptor, is a more puzzling rebel; Giró was a respected member of a Catholic organization. Nevertheless he became a leader of the street fighting, trying to badger neighbors into helping construct a barricade, and when they refused, he did it himself.* The efforts of José Alvarez Señalado, "el Gallo," proved more productive; the 27-year-old man led his band (including one Italian) into a firearms store where they seized 33 shotguns, 89 revolvers, and a large store of ammunition, all of which they distributed among the rebels on the barricades.[77]

The precise site of the street battle was the intersection of the main thoroughfare of Gracia with the central boulevard of Barcelona.[78] Rebels first engaged the mounted Civil Guards on patrol duty, who, when they were unable to disperse the crowds by firing over and around them, requested support from a cavalry detachment. Because the lieutenant and his troops were greeted with applause by the rebels, the officer was encouraged to believe he could persuade them to desist. But as soon as he left, the rebels began to pile their barricades higher.

By now it was twelve noon. The lieutenant returned and prepared to do battle; behind hastily devised barriers he arranged first the Civil Guards and behind them, his soldiers. At 1:30 P.M., he gave the order to fire; one

---

* Ramón Giró was one of only fifty individuals found guilty of rebellion. His sentence of life imprisonment was later commuted to permanent exile. In Perpignon the enterprising Giró was elected to the Committee for the Defense of Expatriated Spaniards, charged with obtaining a general amnesty. (*El País* [Madrid], October 9 and 11, 1909; *La Publicidad* [Barcelona], October 8, 1909; and *El Poble Català* [Barcelona], June 19, 1910.)

worker died instantly and several more were wounded. The rebels on the barricades responded with gunfire and continued to fire all afternoon. The lieutenant remained on duty but he was deeply resentful of having to suppress a civil revolt:* idly he wished that he could be transported immediately to Morocco where "at least I could die with glory and not be assassinated, as might occur here." [79]

At 2:30 P.M., General Brandeis arrived with infantry reinforcements; he soon sent for additional troops and late in the afternoon, he ordered artillery support. At 6:30 P.M., cannons were fired down the Calle Mayor, forcing the rebels in Gracia to abandon the barricades after five hours of fighting.

Workers in the streets had begun a rebellion. On Tuesday afternoon and evening politicians had to make their final decision of whether to support the rebels, and thus to lead a revolution, or to collaborate with officials of the legally constituted government in the suppression of the rebellion.

At 4:30 P.M., a small group of Barcelona's representatives to the Cortes and business leaders assembled in the city hall to discuss with Mayor Coll y Pujol the proposal that they form an ad hoc junta with powers to mediate between military authorities and rebels in order to end the conflict rapidly. The proposal had been made by Emiliano Iglesias in his meeting earlier that day with municipal officials, presumably on the ground that senators, deputies and businessmen had more authority than city councilors. But only some thirteen individuals had accepted Mayor Coll's invitation. The presidents of the all important business and civic organizations had come (Luis Muntadas for the Fomento del Trabajo Nacional, Pedro Milá y Camps for the Liga de Defensa Industrial, Manuel Raventós for the Instituto Agrícolo Catalán, José María Roca for the Athenaeum). Only three senators and three deputies were present; from Solidaridad Catalana, Senator Raimundo de Abadal and Deputy Puig y Cadafalch to represent the Lliga, and Federalist Republican Vallés y Ribot. Republican Senator Odón de Buen put in his only public appearance of the week, as did Radical Deputy Giner de los Ríos.

The meeting was dominated, and eventually frustrated, by elderly Republican Senator Sol y Ortega. The Senator attacked the proposal that the group act as an intermediary in the dispute.[80]

---

* Lerroux reported that one officer, mortally wounded in the fighting in Gracia, said that "what grieves me most is to die as a result of republican bullets, I who have been a republican all my life" (Alejandro Lerroux y García, *Mis Memorias* [Madrid, 1963], p. 529).

What could we tell the rebels? They have risen against the entire established order. Could we tell them that Maura has fallen? That there is no war? That an amnesty will be granted? Well then, if we can say nothing of all this, we run the risk of making ourselves ridiculous because they will pay no attention to us — and with good reason.

Someone suggested that the proposed junta could at least serve as an advisory group to the Captain General who was unfamiliar with Barcelona. "Let General Santiago resign his command to me," replied Sol y Ortega, "and I will be responsible for everything." He then went on to champion the revolt and to threaten that rebels would halt food deliveries into Barcelona: "on behalf of 'the people'" he addressed the group "stating the conditions of surrender in order for food supplies to enter the city." Lliga Deputy Puig y Cadafalch muttered that "now we know who the author of the movement is." [81]

Confronted by Sol with a potentially revolutionary situation, Barcelona's leading citizens conferred for two hours; unable to reach any agreement, they adjourned. Emiliano Iglesias, who had watched the proceedings as a spectator, was bitterly disappointed.[82] He had undoubtedly hoped to announce that civil leaders would mediate between the Army and the rebels, and thereby to forestall demands for a revolution which were to be presented at the session of the City Council that began only fifteen minutes later.

The session of the City Council was the climax of the rebellion in Barcelona. Leaders of the popular uprising marshaled all their forces in an effort to compel municipal republican politicians to lead a revolution, a role the Catalan republican deputies had rejected earlier in the afternoon.

Radical extremists, together with the groups led by the Committee for the Strike, planned to force Emiliano Iglesias to use the Council session as the occasion to take over the city government and to proclaim a republic. The Council would constitute a more authoritative basis for a revolutionary government than did the juntas which workers had organized in other cities in the province of Barcelona (Sabadell, Mataró, and Granollers).

According to Fabra Rivas,* the plan had been agreed upon in the morning

---

* Iglesias denied the plan of assembling revolutionary forces (*El Progreso* [Barcelona], August 13, 1911). Because Iglesias told so many conflicting tales and often admitted contradicting his earlier account, I have accepted Fabra Rivas' statements as accurate.

meeting between Emiliano Iglesias and the Committee for the Strike. Iglesias had promised to meet the members of the Committee in a café on the Calle Mallorca at 8 P.M., and to accompany them to the construction site of the Church of the Holy Family, where the rebel forces were to assemble; the crowd would then proceed to the city hall and seize power in Barcelona.[83]

Iglesias admitted that he had agreed to meet the Committee members in the café, but by Tuesday evening he knew that no city outside Catalonia had seconded the protest movement. Therefore, his objective was to end the rebellion in Barcelona or, failing that, to dissociate his party officially from any revolutionary plan.

In order for Iglesias to achieve these objectives, he had to find a way to ensure a food supply for Barcelona residents so that he could forestall a maneuver planned by the rebel groups in conjunction with the extremist faction of the Radical party. Councilor José Jorge Vinaixa, who spoke for the extremist Radicals, planned to make a motion that the City Council declare itself in permanent session to deal with urgent matters — such as food supplies for the city. Then, in the event that the City Council resisted the rebel attempt to make it the basis for a revolutionary government, the rebels had arranged to cut off food supplies until the City Council would agree to negotiate. Republican Senator Sol y Ortega had already publicly announced the terms under which rebels would permit provisions to enter the city.

Iglesias had hoped to counteract this plan, at least in part, by being able to announce that there was no need for a permanent session because the Mayor had already arranged food provisions. As part of a commission appointed by the Mayor, he had already met earlier in the afternoon with slaughterhouse employees to discuss meat supplies to asylums and hospitals. When told that both employees and employers were willing to work if the Army provided sufficient troops to protect them, Iglesias had informed Mayor Coll who sent a request for military protection to the Captain General. But at the time the City Council session began, no answer had yet been received from General Santiago.[84]

The mood of the crowd that filled the public chambers of the city hall, and of the 3,000 people who waited outside in the Plaza de San Jaime, was frankly revolutionary. It was a mood created by hopes and rumors so forceful that they momentarily prevailed over news reports. Saragossa, Valencia, and Bilbao were said to have seconded the Barcelona protest, despite reports to the contrary. The Maura government was said to have fallen. Because the news that General Brandeis had terminated the street battle with cannon shot had not yet reached the city hall, it was rumored that "the republic has been proclaimed in Gracia."

Having failed to convince the Catalan deputies to the Cortes gathered in the home of Vallés y Ribot to lead the rebellion, the extremists now tried to persuade members of the Barcelona City Council to lead it. The leaders of the Juventud Radical, Rafael Guerra del Río and José Ulled, assured Radical city councilors that the suburb of Gracia had been completely handed over to "the revolutionaries." The only Radical councilman who openly expressed his pleasure at the possibility of revolution was José Puig de Asprer of the extremist faction. "Now it's going well," he exclaimed in Catalan. "Are va be!" [85] Catalan republican councilors were subjected to the same pressures by excited youths who urged them to proclaim a republic; these youths were finally forcibly expelled from the Council chamber.[86]

The session began at 6:45 P.M. Thirty-one councilors were present, of whom eighteen were Radical party members. Presiding was Mayor Coll y Pujol who, with the experience born of a long career in Conservative party politics, sought to avoid all problems by ending the session immediately; councilors would agree, the Mayor said, that there was not a "sufficiently tranquil state of mind to deliberate on many of the matters on the agenda." [87] Iglesias seconded the motion, carefully straddling the line between "city hall" and "the street"; in the name of the Radical party, he wanted to go on record "in a clear and definitive manner, to state that although it lamented the events, it had the warmest sympathy for the people of Barcelona." Lliga and Catalan republican councilors also supported the Mayor's motion.

Vinaixa, a lerrouxista Radical, broke into the chorus of assent to declare that the situation in Barcelona "obligated the City Council to exercise a permanent function": the Council should merely suspend the session, not adjourn it, and thereby constitute itself in permanent session in order to deal with urgent problems such as food supplies. The Mayor cited legislation to prove that such administrative matters were the concern of commissions, and not of the plenary Council; he reported that a commission had already negotiated with slaughterhouse employees and that he was momentarily expecting the Captain General's approval of the agreement. When Vinaixa insisted that the City Council must remain in session to supervise food supplies, Lliga Councilor Federico Rahola moved that the session be temporarily suspended while they waited for General Santiago's reply.

Emiliano Iglesias used the recess to good advantage. He summoned to the city hall some of the key rebel leaders and persuaded them to assume responsibility for providing meat to hospitals and asylums, thereby eliminating one ostensible reason for keeping the City Council in permanent session. Iglesias then went down to the Plaza de San Jaime, in front of the city hall, where some 3,000 persons were waiting for the Council's decision. Many carried arms and were prepared to defend themselves against the Carlists, who were reportedly planning a bloody campaign to avenge the convent burnings. In full view of the crowd — probably as a gesture intended to please the Radicals in the crowd — the Radical chief conferred with Ramón Homedes and Enrique Pujol, ex-anarchist members of the Radical party who were among the leaders of the current rebellion; later, Iglesias was to brag of this as one instance of his bravery during the week.[88]

At 8:45 P.M., Mayor Coll again called the session to order. Lliga Councilor Rahola pointed out that the five members present did not constitute a quorum, and so the Mayor adjourned the session. Only four of the eighteen Radical councilors present in the earlier session had remained: either Vinaixa had not been able to persuade his colleagues to declare a permanent session, or Iglesias had dissuaded them.

Having successfully weathered the crisis of the Council session, Emiliano Iglesias still had to deal with the Committee for the Strike and the Radical extremists — the groups that persisted in the hope that a revolution was still possible.

Fabra Rivas, Miguel V. Moreno, and other rebel leaders had been waiting for Emiliano Iglesias in the café on the Calle Mallorca since eight o'clock in the evening. "The most select elements of anarchism, syndicalism, and Radicalism," meanwhile, had assembled at the rebels' rendezvous site. Furious at being detained "in a period of full revolution," they could not act before knowing Iglesias' plans.[89] After the Council session, at approximately 9:15, Iglesias sent a messenger to the café and invited Fabra Rivas and Moreno to confer with him at the city hall. He later reported that he had planned to show them the text of a manifesto he had prepared and sent to the printers, a manifesto in which he urged workers to end the General Strike. Because he did not want Committee members to think he was working "behind their backs," Iglesias had decided to read it to them before releasing it to the public.

Fabra Rivas and Moreno considered Iglesias' invitation to come to the city hall, "somewhat extraordinary and somewhat suspicious." Nevertheless, they set out immediately, "not without taking the precaution of summoning an escort of militants to accompany them in case it should turn out to be an ambush or a betrayal." They arrived sometime between 10 and 10:30 P.M., and leaving their escort in the plaza, the two men searched the entire building; but Iglesias had already departed without leaving any message. The would-be revolutionaries went to his home but could arouse no one with their shouts. They went to the offices of *El Progreso,* where Radical officials assured them they did not know Iglesias' whereabouts. By this time, Fabra Rivas reported, the forces assembled at the Church of the Holy Family had dispersed "without order, and without [making] any agreement." [90] Iglesias explained later that he had waited for the Committee members but finally left because he did not think they intended to come; Fabra Rivas charged that Iglesias left before the appointed hour. Whatever the truth, the fact is that Iglesias had succeeded in paralyzing the Committee's plans for a revolution. He had demoralized the rebel forces by keeping them waiting all evening. Whether it was his intention to do so or not, by making Committee members look for him all evening, he deprived the rebel forces of their leaders. It was almost inevitable that they would disperse.

Iglesias could avoid meeting the Committee for the Strike but he could not isolate himself from Radical extremists who demanded that he wait some hours more in the hope that Madrid and Valencia might still second the movement. He had left the city hall at 9:30 P.M., accompanied by Radical Councilor Arturo Jiménez and by Vinaixa, the spokesman in the Council for the extremist faction. Iglesias conferred again with Ramón Homedes, an ex-anarchist metalworker who had played a prominent role in the first General Strike seven years earlier and was one of the most active organizers of the current rebellion. On the Calle Carmen, Iglesias talked to Ramón Font, a minor Radical official who continued to direct street fighting in the heart of Barcelona until late in the week when he went out to continue fighting in the suburb of Horta. Everywhere Iglesias stressed "with deep regret the precipitated and entirely isolated situation in which they [the workers of Barcelona] found themselves." [91]

Even if Igliesas had persuaded these men to abandon the fight, an unlikely possibility, there was still a chance that a Catalan republican politician might be persuaded to take over the rebellion.

Late Tuesday night the deputies of the Catalan republican parties, the "left bloc" of Solidaridad Catalana, met again in the home of Federalist Republican Vallés y Ribot, presumably to learn the outcome of the evening's events: the meeting with the Mayor prior to the Council session, which Vallés y Ribot had attended, and the City Council session itself. In the course of their deliberations, Catalan Nationalist leader Jaime Carner was called out of the meeting to talk with Rovira y Virgili and Claudi Ametlla, editors of the party newspaper, El Poble Català.[92] They had come in the name of socialist Fabra Rivas and of other labor leaders to ask that Carner lead the other republican deputies in providing the rebellion with a political objective. Fabra Rivas confessed through his two delegates that he had intended only to organize a protest against a war, but it had turned out to be "a revolutionary movement." To Republican Deputy Amadeo Hurtado, reviewing these events many years later, the socialist and his colleagues were "obscure personages" who had given the order for the General Strike and had then taken fright at the ensuing course of events, believing themselves responsible when in reality the causes were far more profound.[93]

Denied this panoramic view of the events, Fabra Rivas on Tuesday night tried to impose some order on the havoc he had helped to create. Speaking through the editors of El Poble Català, Fabra Rivas, after expressing his astonishment at the revolutionary developments, went on to state that "we are in no position — it would be foolish to believe otherwise — to attempt a social revolution." Fabra Rivas offered Carner his own and his "friends'" unconditional support in return for only two promises: that Carner be the leader of the revolution, and that a republic be established — "the republic, nothing more than the republic. We won't demand any part of our social program." In characteristic fashion, Carner answered that "it was very serious, very serious, and that it was necessary to think about it a great deal."[94] Laureano Miró was the only one to pledge support, offering to go to his home district (San Felíu de Llobregat) and to recruit one thousand men to take over Barcelona. Hurtado gently mocked Miró and his "imaginary combat force," describing the young Deputy as one "whose knowledge of revolutions had come only through allegoric colored pictures."[95] According to Deputy Joaquín Salvatella, after further discussion the deputies as a group decided "we could not accept any direction of what might be a revolutionary event, whose origin we did not know and whose objective it was no longer in our hands to determine." Salvatella solemnly affirmed that this meeting ended the attempt of the republic bloc to organize a formal, joint participation in the uprising. But he admitted that later Tuesday night a small faction had acted on its own initiative and maintained contact with the movement, and that the entire republican bloc had assumed responsibility for the actions of the faction.[96]

Fabra Rivas was responsible for these contacts. He managed to obtain a personal interview with Laureano Miró, who offered his "troops," and with another "eminent person" — probably Jaime Carner, whom Fabra Rivas greatly respected. Although "cautious and reserved," Fabra Rivas reported, the "eminent person" indicated his willingness "to support and guide a revolutionary movement" as soon as he received news that revolts similar to that of Barcelona had occurred outside Catalonia.[97]

The basis for Fabra Rivas' belief that such revolts would occur was that on Tuesday night, in Madrid, Pablo Iglesias finally signed the formal declaration of a general strike to be held the following Monday, August 2. Iglesias signed for the national committees of both the Socialist party and the national trade confederation (UGT), and this declaration was published in the weekly newspaper *El Socialista,* normally distributed on Wednesday evenings (although bearing Friday's date). Socialist executives in Madrid dispatched messengers with strike instructions to Valencia, Aragon, Asturias, and Galicia in a desperate attempt to recover the ground they had lost the previous week. To Fabra Rivas in Barcelona, they sent a request that he keep the insurrection going as a stimulus and an example.[98]

By securing Carner's conditional promise of Catalan Nationalist support, Fabra Rivas indirectly prevented the Radicals from publicly abandoning the rebellion on Tuesday night. A police informant told Inspector Moisés Zapatero that Radicals and Catalan Nationalists had met and agreed to withdraw their party members (possibly because the letter refused to consider Iglesias' suggestion that they look for a military leader). But the Radicals "suspected that the Nationalists were taking advantage of this occasion to lure forces away from them"; in the opinion of this informant, the only reason why the rebellion continued beyond Tuesday night was that Radicals feared Catalan Nationalists might take over the movement.[99]

While politicians debated about a revolution, the burning of the convents continued all night long — "the Tragic Night" ("la noche trágica"), Spaniards entitled it. Socialist Fabra Rivas traveled through the city to view the burnings, condemning the act yet awed by its grandeur and stirred by the intense hatred of the clergy that it revealed.[100]

The wanton destruction carried out under the direction of persons who never identified themselves, for a purpose that was never announced, created a sense of terror. One nun whose school was burned (a Missionary Sister of the Immaculate Conception) tried to explain the fear: "No one knew what lay behind all those masses of people, one was fighting the unknown." She was convinced that had it not been so mysterious a movement, "many of those who abandoned us would not have done so." [101]

The entire city was not ablaze. Fires were concentrated in two districts within the city (the lower middle class Audiencia neighborhood, and the affluent Ensanche area), and in five suburbs (in highly industrialized Gracia, San Andrés, and Clot-San Martín, and in the residential suburbs of Corts and San Gervasio).

To initiate the evening campaign, incendiaries chose an order of reputed great wealth and influence: the Order of Handmaids, Adorers of the Blessed Sacrament and of Charity. But incendiaries were not to score the victory that their easy successes in the afternoon had led them to expect. The Adorers resisted three major attacks during succeeding days, due largely to the efforts of the Superior, Madre Corazón de Jesús, who employed common sense and personal bravery to supplement the prayers offered by the sisters.[102]

The Adorers had long been a favored target for Radical propagandists. In addition to educating poor children, the sisters rehabilitated wayward young girls. Inevitably they antagonized some of their charges, difficult working-class girls from slum neighborhoods, who constituted the type of woman participating in the convent burnings. Furthermore, their "bastille for young girls" was located just one block from the Casa del Pueblo; the sisters rang their bells at 11 P.M., drowning out the voices of speakers in the rallies held in the Casa, and in revenge Radicals threw stones or shouted abuses as they passed by. Thus the Adorers expected an attack. The arsonists arrived at 5 P.M. and quickly penetrated the grounds, but Madre Corazón de Jesús had organized the sisters and their eighty-four wards for defense. Army troops arrived almost immediately and the throng dispersed, but not before Madre Corazón de Jesús managed to bribe two of the incendiaries into helping put out the fire. She had only contempt for the army captain on duty, believing that he wanted the sisters to abandon the enormous building to the incendiaries. She refused at first to leave, but she was finally persuaded to do so. By means of threats and personal visits to the Captain General's office, the Mother Superior insured that army troops remained on duty all week.

The convent of the cloistered, penitential Sisters Magdalenes (the Order of Sisters of Our Lady of Charity of the Good Shepherd; the rule of St. Augustine) did not fare so well. At 6 P.M., the sisters were permitted to leave the convent, located just a few blocks from the Casa del Pueblo, and to take refuge in private homes. A neighbor who watched the attack on the convent reported that the assailants were primarily infuriated women who showed a "savage desire to destroy the convent and everything in it." They left intact certain rooms which they believed contained proof of the tortures perpetrated in cloistered convents. Hundreds of curious citizens later visited the tiny windowless cubicles and the "infamous martyrdom room," containing a metal bed whose frame consisted of perforated tubes connected with gas pipes. They viewed the opened tombs that revealed the corpses of nuns tied hand and foot, with heavy scourges beside them. The bodies of men and children were also found buried in the cloister.[103] No explanation by the sisters could dispel the sensation created by this cloistered convent.*

The incendiary group, their work completed at the convent of the Sisters Magdalenes, went on to burn the residence of a congregation of nursing sisters, the Servants of Mary. This was their fourth and last target in the immediate vicinity of the Casa del Pueblo. At first the sisters refused to leave, relying on gratitude for the services they had performed, but they fled over the back wall when they saw the smoke of neighboring convents. José Ulled, an officer of the Radical Youth Movement, reportedly came to direct the incendiaries. The 21-year-old lawyer, clad in a business suit, stood out sharply among workers dressed in blue cotton working smocks. His directions were obviously needed, for arsonists had brought the regulation hatchets and ladders, but no gasoline. Ulled sent men to demand that a nearby shop furnish it, "because the republic has been proclaimed in Madrid and it is

---

* Because the discoveries in the convent of the Sisters Magdalenes remained a topic of impassioned debate long after the Tragic Week, the Prioress of the Order finally granted an interview. The "martyrdom room" had been constructed to take care of a sister who was insane, whom they had not wanted to send to an asylum. The Prioress explained that in her order, as in the Hieronymite Order, a sister was buried with her scourge and with her hands and feet tied. Despite this interview, and additional proofs of Sor Teresa Bonsoms' insanity, tales of tortures in this convent lingered on. The republican newspaper Las Noticias presented all points of view, including the idea that the mobs had installed the gas pipes, that is, "planted" the evidence. The article ended with the comment that some orders did "martyrize themselves in order to consecrate themselves to God. Whether the bed, and the room, were or were not used for the purpose that the people supposed, only God and the nuns knew." (Las Noticias [Barcelona], August 2, 6, and 7, 1909.)

necessary to finish off all the churches and convents." As soon as the gasoline arrived, a fire was set that within one hour had reduced the convent to its outer walls.[104]

At the same time as these attacks, convents were also burned in the central Audiencia district, an area of modest homes and shops, poor but more respectable than the Paralelo. Men, women, and children had come from other neighborhoods and waited in the streets for the incendiaries to arrive. A neighbor described them: "feverishly excited, reflecting in their countenances that they were the owners of Barcelona; they appeared to be conquerors." [105]

They had six buildings to destroy and so they began with zeal as soon as the arsonists arrived. Their first target was the residence of an order of Friars Minors Capuchin whose members served as missionaries or taught in schools and reformatories. The friars had left, "wearing our holy habit, not saving even a single piece of paper," and so their building was quickly set ablaze, but neighbors on the crowded, narrow street persuaded the mob to allow firemen to wash down the walls of adjoining buildings. The fire smouldered inside the church for ten days and left it completely gutted.[106]

The arsonists moved down the street several blocks to the residence of the *Agonizantes,* the Camillians or the Fathers of a Good Death (of the Order of Clerks Regular for the Care of the Sick).* Unmoved by the neighbors' plea that the fathers "did great good for humanity, taking care of all kinds of ill people in order to help them to die a better death," the arsonists burned the Camillians' residence and adjoining church (Nuestra Señora de la Ayuda), and the public school installed on the second floor of the fathers' building. All books and blackboards were thrown onto a bonfire before the building was ignited. Firemen were not permitted to intervene until the interior had been burned out, but on the walls of the second-floor classroom they could still read the scribbled slogan, "Down with the Camillians. Long live Lerroux." [107]

A second team of arsonists, reportedly the ones who had led the attack on the enormous Piarist school and thus presumably an elite among incendiaries, had gone to burn the parish Church of San Francisco de Paula, where, for the first and only time throughout the entire week, Catholic laymen defended church property. Members of the local Carlist organization, with offices in

---

* This was the second time the Camillian Fathers were burned out. After the first fire, in 1835, they left Barcelona and did not return until 1900.

a building adjacent to the church, had been waiting with guns cocked; they killed or critically wounded three men.[108]

This did not, however, deter the burning of an additional three churches in the Audiencia district. At 10 P.M., the humble twelfth-century Chapel of Marcus was ignited.[109] Within a few minutes, the parish Church of San Cucufate was also ablaze; the throng found a large supply of stock certificates and money, which they burned or took away, despite the protests of the priest that these were to be used in the restoration of the ancient church.[110]

The last target was the handsome Church of San Pedro de las Puellas, a more formidable undertaking both because of the thick stone walls and because of a troop of soldiers who stood guard. The incendiaries left, but at 9:30 "some twenty men, led by a gentleman wearing a straw hat" returned to carry out the job amidst shouts of "Long live anarchy." This time the soldiers guarding the church fraternized with the crowd. Because the stone walls of San Pedro de las Puellas were so thick, it was necessary to return a third time, at 6 A.M., in order to complete destruction of the nave and chapels.[111]

In the affluent neighborhoods of the Ensanche district, incendiaries burned primarily the private schools run by the clergy. The residents of these neighborhoods, served by the schools, made no effort to defend them against the incendiaries who came from other districts. One Vincentian Father (of the Congregation of the Mission of St. Vincent de Paul), whose residence was destroyed, remarked with feeling that it was curious that "so many ladies and gentlemen, who had sworn to defend the Church, should permit this." [112] Even more embittering a complaint was that neighbors treated the burnings as an entertainment. Army Captain José Roca described the "peaceful and bourgeois" streets surrounding the Montesión Convent (belonging to the teaching Congregation of the Dominican Sisters of Charity of the Presentation of the Blessed Virgin Mary) where neighbors waited on their balconies of their apartment houses.[113]

Since night was coming on, and the rebels did not appear, the audience grew impatient, undoubtedly because they had to wait. So they whiled away the time; the sound of pianos could be heard in some apartments, while sardana dances were organized on various balconies, adding variety to the sound of shots that were to be heard every once in a while, both far off and close at hand.

Captain Roca used this incident to substantiate his claim that "honorable and peaceful citizens," by acquiescing in the incendiarism, had to accept a share of the responsibility. "One can say all one wants to about the events of the Tragic Week," added socialist Fabra Rivas, "but basically the bourgeoisie did not lament the anticlerical direction that the events had taken, keeping in mind that the attacks were against property while persons were always respected." [114]

Encouraged by this tolerance, incendiaries burned five buildings in the Ensanche area. At 7:30 P.M., they descended upon the provincial headquarters of the Vincentian Fathers, an order particularly disliked by workers: under the Concordat of 1851, the Vincentians received an official subsidy for services as auxiliary parish priests, but the poor claimed the priests devoted their time to the wealthy, only occasionally going to preach or to distribute charity in workers' neighborhoods. One neighbor of the Vincentian Fathers described a workman whose hatred was so intense that he continued with his frantic destruction of their residence even after he had been shot and wounded by a passing army patrol; he finally collapsed and died in the ruins. [115]

Late in the evening, amidst the piano music and the sardana dances, incendiaries tried to burn the Montesión Convent, belonging to Dominican Sisters who taught poor children and nursed in public hospitals, but they were unable to break through the armored entrance doors. The militants then went on to the buildings of the Missionary Priests of the Sacred Heart of Jesus. [116] By the time they arrived, at 10:30 P.M., the priests had left. Utilizing the considerable experience it had acquired, the group was able to build a fire that within one and a half hours destroyed the school, the church, and the residence.

At the fashionable school of the Sisters of the Immaculate Conception of the Blessed Virgin Mary, a group of ten incendiaries proved unable to burn the stone structure even though the sisters had left. In charge were four Casa del Pueblo officials, including Baldomero Bonet, the man with whom Radical party leaders were later accused of having discussed plans for incendiarism. Bonet's group abandoned the assault on the school for no apparent reason, but at 3 A.M. they returned to burn the church. The principal loss of the Conceptionist Sisters was in teaching materials and other provisions for their schools throughout Catalonia. [117] Incendiaries burned a total of five such provincial headquarters of educational religious orders where supplies for schools throughout the province were stored, thus crippling many schools in addition to the ones destroyed in Barcelona.

The real objective — destruction of the Catholic education system — was clearly stated in the last burning to occur in the greater Ensanche area. The site was the semi-cloistered convent of the *Beatas Dominicas,* one of the third orders of Dominican Sisters, who ran an elementary school for girls. Hours before the attack the sisters had left the building and found refuge with their neighbors. At 11 P.M. a group of thirty young boys, led by an older man, entered their building. They ate and drank everything they found, threw all items of value onto the bonfire, and prudently sold the hens for fifteen céntimos apiece.

The chaplain, Father Antonio Calvet, later described the frenzied activity he witnessed from a nearby balcony: "The supreme moment had arrived, the hour to liberate the poor sequestered women, the victims of religious fanaticism." [118] Fifteen tombs were opened, and the corpse of a sister dead only one week was dragged through the streets to be left on a corner. At 12:45 the boys set fire to the buildings, watching to see that the flames burned brightly before they departed. When the smoke cleared only the outer walls remained, and on these the rebels had proudly painted:

VIVA LA REVOLUCION Y LOS MAESTROS DE CATALUÑA

QUEMA DE LOS CONVENTOS — 27 JULIO 1909

This was one of the few times during the entire week when the incendiaries[119] identified their revolutionary cause with the destruction of Catholic schools not only in their shouts but by writing it down.

In Barcelona proper, the Tragic Night had begun with a thwarted assault upon the convent of the Adorer Sisters, and it ended with an even more resounding failure in two attempts to burn the formidable Jesuit residence on the Calle Caspe, symbol par excellence of clerical wealth and power.

Well aware of worker sentiments, the Jesuits had persuaded the Captain General to assign some of his few troops to guard their residence, one of the few religious buildings so honored. Rabid anticlericalist Sol y Ortega scoffed that "civilian and military authorities had special interest in protecting and defending the building of the Marquis of Comillas." [120] The Jesuits left for private homes, while armed laymen remained on duty inside the residence and on neighboring housetops. The building itself was almost impregnable: a stone structure set flanking the street, with no surrounding gate but with windows high off the ground and doors covered by metal sheeting. There were reflector lights that could be turned on groups who approached the building, making it easier to fire directly upon them.

Military investigators found that there "were considerable proofs to consider as author" of this attack Senator Sol y Ortega.[121] After his flamboyant claim to speak for the rebels in the meeting called by the Mayor, Sol went to sit in a café in downtown Barcelona where he loudly commented on the reports of developments as they were relayed to him. He did not go in person to the Jesuit residence. The assault was reportedly directed by José and Rafael Ulled, leaders of the Juventud Radical, and City Councilor José Vinaixa who had tried to force the Council to declare a permanent session. They led groups of approximately fifty boys to the building twice that night, and again the following night, but although they bravely returned rifle fire with revolver shots, the fighting was a useless gesture. The Jesuit residence was unassailable.[122]

Not all the working-class members of the Radical party joined in the mighty conflagration on the Tragic Night. Through lethargy or fear of prosecution, many stood aside (like the prosperous middle class), content to be spectators.

In a house located just two blocks from the Dominican school, late Tuesday night, Juana Ardiaca went up to the roof to visit with friends. A member of the Damas Radicales, Juana Ardiaca was indignant to find her fellow Radical party members passively watching the burnings. "What are you doing here?" she shouted. "If you have no arms, you can get some in the Center; I'll go with you." When no one showed a willingness to fight in the street, or even to burn a convent or two, Juana Ardiaca settled down to visit.[123]

In her attempt (albeit halfhearted) to encourage men to participate in the armed rebellion, Juana Ardiaca resembled the hundreds of women in Barcelona who had helped to launch the General Strike, attacked police stations, and now led the attacks on convents as well as the street fighting. With some exceptions, they were the products of a textile economy, women who started to work in factories at twelve or fourteen years of age and continued after they were married because the family could not live on the husband's salary. Usually illiterate, cut off from the traditional Spanish pattern of church-going and intense family life, these women sought social identification in labor unions or in the women's affiliates of the Radical party. Juana Ardiaca was a product of this environment.

At twenty-eight Juana Ardiaca was separated from her husband and worked in a factory to support her child and her parents. She joined the Damas Radicales because she wanted the health insurance that they promised but could not finance. Probably the Radicals' extremist policies also attracted her, to judge from the fact that her father had been disabled since his imprisonment in Montjuich in 1899 on charges that he was an anarchist. However, in general, her friends and co-workers considered Juana Ardiaca a frivolous, excitable young woman.

After visiting with her friends on Tuesday night, Juana Ardiaca returned home; she did not leave again, because her baby was ill. But Angela Santiago, former president of the Damas Radicales, who was present on the rooftop, later denounced Juana Ardiaca to military authorities for inciting others to participate in the rebellion.*

By midnight the incendiaries had burned some twenty-three churches and convents in the heart of Barcelona, where General Santiago had concentrated his meager troops. In the suburbs, bereft of army troops or Civil Guards, mobs were free to burn as they willed, yet they attacked only eight convents in five suburbs. One possible explanation is that the incendiaries needed direction that could not be supplied until the following days, when leaders finished in the center of the city or in other suburbs.

The groups in Pueblo Nuevo, having destroyed all the religious institutions in the neighborhood during the afternoon, went in the evening to the Pequín district of fishermen and day laborers, located farther up the shoreline. During the preceding seven years a zealous priest, Father Manuel Barguño, had provided this poverty-stricken area of hovels with the Church of San Pedro el Pescador, a clinic, a workers' circle, and an elementary school; they were completely destroyed by a fire that smoldered until Friday.[124] No Pequín resident tried to put it out, reportedly because of the threat that incendiaries would return from Pueblo Nuevo.**

The center of activity in this northwest corner of Barcelona on Tuesday night was the Clot-San Martín district. First on the agenda was the Asylum of the Daughters of Charity of St. Vincent de Paul, where eighty children of working mothers were cared for all day and five hundred girls were

* Together with Emiliano Iglesias and two other Radical officials, Juana Ardiaca was tried as "an instigator, organizer, and director of the events." See pages 292–93 for a discussion of the significance of the charges against Juana Ardiaca.
** In 1962 Pequín had only a makeshift school and church. Older residents nostalgically recalled Father Barguño's buildings, the best they have had in that neighborhood.

educated at little or no charge. The sisters had remained in the asylum and together with their neighbors they dissuaded the incendiaries on the basis of their charity. This infuriated one woman in the crowd who warned the men that "if you are too cowardly, I'll look for some who aren't." [125]

These arsonists were far more successful at the convent-school of the Sisters of the Piarist Schools, Daughters of Mary (an educational congregation affiliated with the Piarist Fathers). The sisters had left their residence, so throngs were free to rummage for objects before they burned. Antonio Eudaldo Plácido, with a record of petty thefts, found a wallet containing only a few coins, yet showed it gleefully to the crowd and shouted "Now we are happy." [126]

The direction of these and similar burnings in the suburbs was executed by minor Radical officials like Rafael Climent who came out from the city in an automobile — an expensive and rare vehicle — to direct the destruction of the isolated, relatively luxurious Convent of San Joaquín, belonging to the Minims (of the Congregation of Minor Clerks Regular), located in the Camp d'Arpa. When the fire was blazing in the residence of the friars, and in their church, Climent fired his revolver several times and then, in the words of a watching neighbor, "left hastily for some other site to continue his destructive task." [127]

While Climent was directing burnings, militants in Gracia were warning rebels that a republic could be established only after convents had been burned. Despite the crushing defeat in the street battle earlier that evening, crowds turned out to burn the parish Church of San Juan Bautista, the convent of the Oratorian Fathers (attacked but not burned early Tuesday morning), and the convent-school of the Discalced Carmelite Sisters. None of the fires burned when first ignited, thus incendiaries were forced to return at least three times to each building.[128]

In the far distant suburb of Corts, an area of large estates, incendiaries took advantage of the dark and isolation to burn three large buildings. The first was the orphan asylum of the Daughters of Charity of St. Vincent de Paul which, in the words of the Mother Superior, served "that so much neglected . . . long-suffering class, that of the bureaucrats." [129] The second was the modest trade school, Colegio-Taller del Niño Jesús, run by the Congregation of Sons of the Holy Family* as a semi-reformatory under a subsidy from the

* Two other buildings of the Sons of the Holy Family were attacked. Although their modest school on the Calle San Gil in central Barcelona was only sacked, their provincial headquarters in San Andrés was completely destroyed.

provincial government.[130] The last building destroyed in Corts was the school of Nuestra Señora de Loreto, run by the Congregation of Sisters of the Holy Family; crowds, lured by tales of the treasures to be found in this school for wealthy girls, carried off or destroyed every part of the luxurious estate during the night.[131]

The most spectacular incident in the suburbs on Tuesday night, the event that appealed most to the popular imagination, was the assault on the convent of cloistered Capuchin Nuns located in San Gervasio. This was the same neighborhood where Franciscan Father Usó had been shot in the afternoon. Excited crowds came dangerously close to repeating the violence in the evening.

At 11 P.M. a crowd gathered before the convent, excited by news that the nuns were still inside. Many men carried rifles they had seized from the local militia under the leadership of Luis Alferez, a prominent Radical extremist who had also directed the burning of the residence of the Franciscan Monks earlier that afternoon.[132] According to the Capuchin Nuns, however, the director of the assault upon their convent was a well-dressed gentleman who spoke Spanish with a marked foreign accent. Under his guidance the crowd entered the grounds, overpowering three monks who lived with the chaplain in a house separated from the convent. The presence of these monks excited in the crowd a curiosity that was not assuaged by the nuns' contention that they took care of the gardens and orchards. All night the nuns remained locked in a room while the crowd ransacked the residence. At daybreak they were released, but before they could leave the building women searched their habits to see if they were carrying off anything of value. One nun, who had tried to conceal a favorite statue of the Virgin, was told that "we can't let you. We have to destroy everything. It's our turn now." [133] The Capuchin Nuns sought refuge in the vicinity but no house would receive them because of the ferocity of the crowds. Finally they were given haven in the local clinic.

Back in the nuns' residence, the rebels finally stumbled upon the hiding place of the seventy-year-old Madre Eminencia, who had sought to conceal stock certificates and bonds of great value; she insisted that only part of them belonged to the nuns, while others had been left for safekeeping by families who were on vacation. On orders from the foreigner who was in charge, the bonds were thrown onto the bonfire.

Accompanied by one of the women, the Madre Eminencia was allowed to depart, but she got only as far as the Travesera de Gracia where she was stopped by a gang of women led by Francisca Norat, "La Gallinaire," who had been terrorizing the neighborhood all night. La Gallinaire forced the Madre Eminencia to disrobe, and when she found more stocks concealed in the habit she drove the elderly nun down the street, clad only in her petticoats, amid insults and jeers. In this inglorious fashion, the Tragic Night ended in Barcelona.

Wednesday, July 28

By Wednesday morning, a clearly defined modus vivendi had been established through a tacit agreement between the 526,000 residents of Barcelona and the approximately 30,000 individuals who shot, burned, or looted.[1] Insurgents were allowed to camp freely in the streets, while citizens remained behind the locked doors of their homes, except between the hours of 7 A.M. and 9 A.M. when housewives went to the markets for food.[2] They found a plentiful supply of dried goods and starches to compensate for the limited fresh produce. Some markets had a tiny meat supply because of the Captain General's determination to prevent rebel leaders from cutting off Barcelona's food supply as a means of forcing negotiation with government officials. Complying with the request of city councilors, Santiago had sent troops to guard the slaughterhouse and to protect the wagons transporting the meat to market; these troops had sustained a running battle all night long with rebel bands who tried desperately, but failed, to prevent this and other food supplies from reaching the markets.[3]

Apart from this minor triumph the Captain General remained inactive, even though infantry reinforcements arrived (a battalion from the Luchana Brigade of Tortosa, and a regiment from the Asia Battalion of Gerona). Possibly he did not trust the loyalty of these troops who had come from other Catalan cities, or even the loyalty of their officers.* All morning he devoted his time to the details involved in dividing the metropolitan Barcelona area into five zones. At dawn a senior officer had been placed in command of each of these zones and assigned some of the available troops. This division of responsibility in the task of restoring order was necessary because

---

* Charges were brought against a major of the Luchana regiment because of his "suspicious" refusal to act against the rebels. They were dismissed for lack of evidence, as were most charges against middle-class citizens. (See trial of M.A. [sic], *La Publicidad* [Barcelona], January 27, 1910.)

Santiago had found it impossible to direct operations from a central head-quarters, both because he knew so little of the city's topography and because of the crippled communication system.

Any merit in these long-range preparations was obscured by the Captain General's patent inability to control the troops in the heart of the city, the result of his own unwillingness to take disciplinary action as much as of the rebel strategy of courting the conscript soldier. Socialist Fabra Rivas described the scene in the central districts where soldiers strolled the streets, "not bothering to salute their officers." Even the infantry and cavalry detachments ostensibly assigned to patrol duty remained inactive, "their officers gathered to one side while the soldiers fraternized with civilians, embraced by the women and accepting tobacco from the men." [4] Civil Guards were utilized where action was necessary: in Gracia, for example, soldiers who patrolled the streets with their guns pointed toward possible snipers on roof-tops, were trailed by mounted Civil Guards who kept their guns trained on the soldiers.[5]

General Santiago issued his second edict of the week, in which he curiously continued to define the events not as a rebellion but as a breakdown in public order. In this document, posted throughout the city at dawn, he ordered citizens to withdraw completely from the streets and from balconies and rooftops, or to be fired upon without warning. Secondly, Santiago indirectly acknowledged the rebels' successful strategy (as well as the insubordination of his troops) by stating that shouts such as "Hail the Army" not only would not prevent troops from firing, but would lead to prosecution of all persons uttering such shouts, or persons renting property from which such shouts were uttered. He also threatened prosecution of the tenants of any property from which army troops were attacked.[6] In short, the Captain General warned Barcelona residents to disengage themselves in word and act from the disorders, or to be treated as combatants. However they, like the rebels, knew the Captain General could not enforce these measures.

The absence of effective authority, together with the heightened enthusiasm of the groups that fought on barricades and ranged at will through unprotected convents, provided optimum conditions for a revolution. So did the fact, unknown to the rebels, that national officials were still concentrating all their attention on the desperate battle in Morocco.

Conditions in many cities throughout the Catalan provinces of Barcelona,

Gerona, and Tarragona favored a revolution (the fourth province, Lérida, where there were fewer industrial cities, remained quiet). In the province of Barcelona, revolutionary juntas had already been formed in Sabadell, Granollers, and Palafrugell. Under the direction of three men from the city of Barcelona, a general strike was successfully launched on Wednesday in the major industrial city of Reus in the province of Tarragona, and in several less important cities in that province such as Montblanch and Valls. Although order was restored in most of these cities, authorities knew that they had not the force to repress a full-scale workers' revolt. Fabra Rivas reported that not only were there sufficient armed men in the city of Barcelona to seize power from the military command but that additional forces in the province awaited the signal to pour into Barcelona.[7]

The only element lacking for a successful revolution was political direction. Rebel leaders waited for the definitive answer of Radical and Catalan Nationalist politicians as to whether or not they would provide leadership and an ideology for the insurgent forces, either in the ambitious (and oft-vaunted) enterprise of replacing the Monarchy with a republic, or for the more modest task of ousting the hated Maura government. And in turn, Radical and Catalan Nationalist politicians waited all day Wednesday to see if any city outside Catalonia would support the Barcelona rebellion. Rebel leaders and politicians knew that Interior Minister La Cierva had already described the events as a Catalan separatist rebellion, thereby diminishing the possibility of support from national republican politicians.

All hope on Wednesday focused on the effort of socialist leaders to persuade urban labor organizations throughout the nation to support the workers of Barcelona. In one sense, this was the first of many attempts in the twentieth century to link the revolutionary potential of Catalan regionalism, a traditionally divisive force, with the new cohesive force of the national class struggle. Fabra Rivas realized that if the workers of Barcelona alone declared a revolution, it would be viewed in Spain "as a revolution not against the government or against the ruling classes, but against the Spanish people themselves." He pointed out "the risk of arousing the patriotic sentiments of workers in other regions," the result of which would have transformed "the antiwar, anticlerical, and truly revolutionary movement into an interregional fight, into a true civil war between individuals of the same class."[8] Fabra Rivas' analysis of the situation was more convincing to the higher echelon of the Radical party, where Emiliano Iglesias presided, than to the extremist faction that controlled the throngs in the street.

The Radical officials who controlled the Casa del Pueblo, men such as the 24-year-old lawyer Rafael Guerra del Río,* persisted in the illusion that "a social republic" could be established in Barcelona by sheer force, and that Lerroux would serve as the leader.

For weeks the Radical party had been planning a reception for Lerroux, scheduled to return early in August to Barcelona from his exile, under the immunity afforded by his election (in absentia) to the Cortes seven months earlier. In the interim he had conducted a highly successful fund-raising campaign in Argentina and Uruguay. Lerroux had sailed from Buenos Aires on July 23, apparently without foreknowledge of the General Strike, which began three days later in Barcelona. Judging from Lerroux's long political career, there is no reason to believe that simply because he had collected funds to establish a republic he therefore seriously intended to lead a revolution; this was not, however, clear to his followers in Barcelona. Guerra del Río sent a message to Las Palmas (the first port where Lerroux was to dock) reporting that the revolution in Catalonia lacked only a leader to be completely successful, and urging Lerroux "to speed to Barcelona" to assume that role.[9] For an answer, Guerra del Río would have to wait at least two weeks, until August 12 when Lerroux was due in the Canary Islands. While he was on the high seas, his young lieutenants had the task of promoting disorders without proclaiming any ideal or designating revolutionary leaders, marking time until socialists in other cities launched a general strike and until Lerroux reached Spain.** The coupling of such incompatible objectives is proof of their desperate position.

"Without a war cry, without chiefs, or a standard," † Barcelona rebels

* Guerra del Río, a native of the Canary Islands, was not only a vehement spokesman for the extremist faction of the Radical party, but an intermediary for big party contributors; during the elections of 1910 he presented Lerroux with a luxury car "on behalf of a friend" (Lerroux, *Mis Memorias,* pp. 258–59).

** By the time Lerroux reached the Canary Islands on August 12, 1909, the rebellion was over and the repression had begun. He therefore decided not to return to Barcelona but to go instead to Paris where he stayed until the Cortes opened in Madrid, thus assuring him of his parliamentary immunity. Lerroux returned to Spain in October.

† These oft-cited words of Alexis de Tocqueville to describe the revolution of 1848 in Paris are almost identical with those of ex-Governor Ossorio, who watched events in Barcelona from his house on Mt. Tibidabo. "The sedition had no unity of thought, nor homogeneity of action, nor a leader to personify it, nor a tribune to inflame it, nor a war cry to make it concrete. On each street they shouted different things and fought for different purposes" (Ossorio y Gallardo, *Barcelona, julio de 1909: Declaración de un testigo* [Madrid, 1910], p. 54).

burned convents and shot at police or army officers. "One cannot imagine anything more sinister, or more enervating," declared José Pijoan, the Catalan author who was in Barcelona during the Tragic Week, in a letter written shortly after the events.[10]

The rebels concentrated their activities in the slum districts of Barcelona and in the industrial suburbs of Pueblo Nuevo and Clot. The rest of the metropolis was relatively tranquil except for marauding bands that revisited convents assaulted the previous day, either to reset fires that had not been effective or to rummage in the ruins for objects of value. Peaceful citizens remained inside their apartment buildings, the street doors tightly shut. Only occasionally did an army or Civil Guard patrol stop the marauders and confiscate their revolvers, or disperse looters with a few, well-aimed shots. These roving bands kept the city in a state of tension and endowed the rebellion with an extent and an importance out of proportion to the relatively small number of individuals involved.

With no ideal to proclaim, these rebels could merely echo the essential nihilism of Mariano Portoles, down in the Paralelo district. "Long live Lerroux!" shouted Portoles, as he fired his gun in an aimless fashion. "Death to the police and to the Civil Guards." [11] On Wednesday afternoon Civil Guards arrested many men like Portoles, Radical party members who wandered through the streets, revolver in hand — with no leader and no objective.

The consular corps of Barcelona was deeply troubled by the failure of military authorities to act. On Wednesday morning, members gathered in the home of David de Gaetani, Italian Consul and Interim Dean of the Corps, to formulate a polite ultimatum. Under military escort, Gaetani then went to inquire formally if General Santiago could guarantee the lives and property of foreign residents. If not, the consuls were willing to request that their governments send warships to Barcelona to help the Captain General. Pride dictated that General Santiago decline such an offer: he assured Gaetani that his government had already dispatched reinforcements to suppress the insurrection immediately upon their arrival. The Italian Consul then reported back to his colleagues and added that he personally considered General Santiago a competent officer; after some discussion the consuls agreed to delay action for another day. As a goodwill gesture, General Santiago dispatched a few troops to guard the consulates.[12]

In the Paralelo district, the street fighting had both dramatic and comic elements. Radical party member Esteban Roig y Roig, a doughnut maker transformed by events into a rebel leader, continued to direct the band that had first achieved prominence in the streetcar fray; sometime Wednesday Roig was arrested, whereupon, according to malicious rumor, he fainted.[13]

Such incidents contrasted with the intense fighting of valiant rebels such as those on the barricades of the Calle Conde del Asalto. Early in the morning a detachment of Treviño cavalry attempted to dismantle the barricades but was driven back by gunfire; in the ensuing fight a corporal was killed and one soldier wounded, while rebels suffered several casualties. Simultaneously, a clash occurred at the police station in Pueblo Seco; a company of army engineers was dispatched to relieve the police beseiged by an angry crowd. Fighting became so intense that an artillery unit was summoned to the station; it was, however, unable to get beyond the barricades on the Calle Mediodía.[14]

The general staff of these barricades constituted a vivid example of the alliance that Radicals, criminals, and prostitutes had forged in this slum district. Josefa Prieto, "La Bilbaina," was undisputed commander-in-chief. The owner of one of the most notorious houses of prostitution, and veteran of countless jail terms for having assaulted policemen with knives, Josefa Prieto's great prestige in the Paralelo district enabled her to mobilize various criminals in the construction and manning of the barricades.* Her able assistant was Encarnación Avellaneda, "La Castiza." The men were relegated to a minor role although Domingo Ruíz, ardent Radical party member, was nominally in charge. The paramour of La Bilbaina, Ruíz indignantly denied Interior Minister La Cierva's charge that he and other street fighters were "apaches"; he insisted he earned a living as a construction worker. Rafael Fernández, "Noy de la Veu," made no such pretense; as his nickname implied, he took things as they came and lived comfortably with La Castiza. For the preceding few days, however, Radical party member Fernández had been very busy, enjoying the dubious distinction of having led the first church burning (San Pablo) in Barcelona.[15]

---

* Josefa Prieto was exiled by a military tribunal to Perpignon, France, where she further demonstrated her executive ability by being elected to the Committee for the Defense of Expatriated Spaniards, responsible for securing an amnesty from the government of José Canalejas. (*El Poble Català* [Barcelona], June 19, 1910.) Rafael Fernández offered to go to Morocco as a volunteer soldier but the court, unaffected by his elated patriotism, sentenced him to life imprisonment. Domingo Ruíz was sent to a maximum security prison. (*La Publicidad* [Barcelona], October 30, 1909.)

Behind the barricades on the Calle Mediodía, these four individuals utilized their vast experience to harass police and Civil Guards, but they did little more. According to the Civil Guard officer, they did not even wound any of the guards upon whom they fired. The value of damages to pavements and street lights was only 636 pesetas.[16] The function of groups such as that of La Bilbaina was merely to create disorder and to keep at bay the perennial enemy, the police. This situation, together with the insurgents' refusal to fire on soldiers, infuriated police, as the case of Eugenio del Hoyo clearly demonstrated.

On Wednesday morning a concealed sniper fired upon a detachment of the Ninth Mounted Regiment as it patrolled the Atarazana slum district. The commanding officer ordered soldiers to break open the doors of a house on the corner of the Calles Arco del Teatro and Montserrat, where they found two Security Guards alone in the building. Forty-two-year-old Eugenio del Hoyo had been firing from the window of his apartment; because he was tubercular, del Hoyo was on an official leave. His companion, Manuel Carrillo, had simply failed to report for duty that day. Under military escort, the two policemen were taken to prison and charged with armed rebellion.[17]

This incident dramatized the breakdown of civilian authority in Barcelona. Although del Hoyo was the only policeman who joined the rebels in firing upon the armed forces, one Security Guard officer (Lieutenant Izquierdo) abandoned his post at a critical moment. One municipal policeman (Tomás Rodríguez) was convicted of complicity in the convent burnings.[18]

Of more significance within the context of the Tragic Week is the clear demonstration, through the del Hoyo case, that the police deeply resented the role assigned to them. They had neither the discipline nor the indoctrination of the Civil Guards, which might have prepared them to quell a civilian uprising, particularly one designed to break down police morale. Rebels insulted the police and aimed their shots at police, at the very time they applauded soldiers. When Security Guards realized that army officers intended that they, and not soldiers, should confront the rebels, they abandoned the six stations located in worker neighborhoods and went home.* In par-

* Seventy-eight Security Guards were discharged at the end of the week for having abandoned their posts. They appealed to Interior Minister La Cierva, claiming that their superiors had ordered them not to return to work. Thirty-five guards were eventually reinstated. (*La Publicidad* [Barcelona], August 4 and 25, 1909, and *El País* [Madrid], September 18 and 24, 1909.)

this was because they would not risk their lives if soldiers were not compelled to do the same thing, but there was a second, more subtle explanation: the miserably underpaid Security Guards[19] were being asked to fire upon friends and neighbors, among whom they lived and with whose protest against the government they sympathized. Security Guard Santiago Guillén, for example, defended his refusal to report for work on the grounds that "I did not want to be an assassin."[20] Although Manuel Carrillo (arrested with Eugenio del Hoyo) denied he had fired at army troops, he did subsequently identify himself in the Radical newspaper as "one of those of the Glorious Week" and he boasted of not having reported for work, "of not having gone to seize a rifle and fire upon the people."[21]

The prolongation and intensification of the insurrection, therefore, was due not only to the disloyalty of troops on garrison duty in Barcelona but to the refusal of many Security Guards and other policemen to fire upon the insurgents. On Wednesday the rebels gathered new courage as they realized they had only to fight the Civil Guards.

Socialist José Comaposada reported that the only reason there was not more fighting in Barcelona was that there were not sufficient arms for all who wanted them.[22] The revolvers carried by Radicals were not effective for barricade fighting, nor for shooting from rooftops. This need was met in part by a raid on a militia headquarters in the Atarazana slum district.

The storming of the headquarters of the Veterans of Liberty, together with the fierce street battle that followed, constituted the most spectacular armed encounter of the week in Barcelona proper.

In the first phase, the storming of the militia headquarters, there were instances of true bravery, yet the action as a whole was but a pale imitation of the traditional revolutionary assault on the barracks. The militia consisted only of ten men who had fought with General Prim forty years earlier. However they were armed with eighty new rifles and an abundant ammunition supply, issued only the previous day by the Captain General when the veterans' commanding officer, Lieutenant Juan García Sabater, offered his "troops" in repressing the revolt.[23] In justification of issuing arms to a handful of elderly men, General Santiago probably would have pointed out that no other group of citizens had offered help.

News of the Veterans' arms cache had spread through the neighborhood and aroused sharp interest at the barricades on the Calle San Pablo commanded by Miguel V. Moreno, anarcho-syndicalist member of the Committee for the Strike.* Because the duties of "Captain Moreno" often kept him from the barricades, his orders were carried out under the direction of José Ginés Perea. A bookbinder by trade and a sometime executive officer of Solidaridad Obrera, Ginés also had to leave the barricades, as for example on Tuesday night when he went to burn convents.[24] At such times Ginés' young mistress, Natividad Rufo, proved to be a competent aide-de-camp. An active member of Solidaridad Obrera, she shared Ginés' anarcho-syndicalist ideas. Revolutionary propagandists later carefully distinguished between women like Natividad Rufo, who ironed to earn a living, and common prostitutes, like Concha Ortíz, who stood on the corner and recruited for Ginés. "You have no blood in your veins," Concha told neighborhood men, "if you don't go to defend the barricades."[25]

On Wednesday morning, about 10:00, Ginés and his followers went to the Veterans of Liberty headquarters on the Calle Sadurní.[26] They were joined by excited members of the Radical Jóvenes Bárbaros, the same group of hotheads who earlier in the week had forced Emiliano Iglesias to acquiesce in the insurrection; one of the group (Porqueras) was to die in the fighting. The ubiquitous Ulled brothers, officers of the Youth Movement, reportedly stood by and supervised.

By 10:30 Ginés' group and the Radical youths had attracted a large crowd. An observer, Radical party member Manuel Andrés, reported that finally "a gentleman, poorly disguised as a worker" led one group armed with revolvers across the street and into the building. Hundreds of shabby workmen brought up the rear, commanded by Natividad Rufo. This initial attack was repelled when the Veterans fired down the stairwell and from the windows.

This respite was used by municipal employees to flee from their offices on the ground floor of the building. The rebels made no effort to stop them, until they sighted José Regás Cardés amid the fleeing bureaucrats. Regás had repeatedly preached the doctrines of anarchism to Radical audiences in the Casa del Pueblo, but he had just recently secured a job as an apprentice clerk and so he tried to escape involvement in the rebellion. But he was detained by a man who shouted, "You're one of us. Grab a rifle." Regás then took his place in the vanguard of the attack.**

* The importance of the Calle San Pablo rebel group is shown in the fact that theirs were the first barricades constructed in Barcelona proper. The rebels behind them were the first to fire on the police. And the Church of San Pablo, enclosed behind the barricades, was the first religious building burned in the city.

** José Regás, José Ginés, and Natividad Rufo were tried and convicted by military

After several failures, the group entered the militia offices on the third floor. "In the midst of a terrible hysteria," the Veterans of Liberty fled over the rooftops, while the rebels located the rifles and returned to the street. An infantry detachment of some twenty-five soldiers, commanded by "a young, very pale lieutenant," was waiting on the far side of the barricades. "The soldiers burst out laughing," reported Radical party member Andrés, when they saw the ragged rebels awkwardly managing the Remington rifles. A Spanish flag belonging to the veterans was unfurled, whereupon soldiers and rebels applauded. Then a worker donned a militia uniform and blasted away on a trumpet. "If you were to insert a smile in the midst of that atmosphere of tragedy," Andrés wrote, "you would be reflecting the reality." The infantry soldiers then withdrew: "their presence had served as an occasion to fraternize with the public and for nothing more." [27]

Some of the men bearing rifles went to the police station on the Calle Conde de Asalto, where they fired at the walls, not because any one ordered them to do so — reported Andrés — "but we did so with tremendous enthusiasm." Abruptly the mood changed to drama, as police returned the fire and summoned an infantry detachment to support them; in this encounter one soldier died and four were critically wounded. [28]

Some insurgents went to housetops in the Atarazana district, while one group of Radicals joined the anarchists at Moreno's barricades on the Calle San Pablo. At 1 P.M., the Captain General sent Civil Guards, who were forced to fight "the most persistent and harshest battle of all those sustained during the week." [29] Three rebels were killed and at least five were critically wounded. Late in the afternoon General Mora ordered that two small cannon be set up on the Parelelo; four shots were fired at the barricades and four were aimed at a house where snipers had been firing all afternoon. The cannon fire cleared the streets. Although army units immediately occupied the rooftops of buildings along the Paralelo, they did not yet dare to penetrate the narrow side streets.

The rebels were only temporarily subdued. When General Mora rode out to inspect the district at dusk, he was fired upon by a sniper who wounded his horse and those of two aides. [30]

Incendiaries burned convents for the last time in Barcelona proper on

---

judges as the "authors" of the attack upon the militia headquarters. They were sent into "perpetual exile" in France.

Wednesday. The pace was slower and successes were fewer, because the groups had done the bulk of their assigned task the day before.

At 9 A.M., they destroyed two more educational institutions: the enormous buildings belonging to the Claretians (of the Congregation of the Missionary Sons of the Immaculate Heart of Mary),[31] and the very unpretentious school of the Sisters of the Society of St. Teresa of Jesus,[32] both located on the outskirts of the city. The religious had been warned and had left for private homes, so fires were easily set and booty carried off. This peaceful process was interrupted when a Claretian Father tried to re-enter the building in order to save some property; Padre Bérges was detected by the mob and although he managed to escape, he lost one eye from a bullet wound.[33]

About noon men gathered in front of the Seminary (Seminario Conciliar, where youths studied to become secular priests), which covered an entire city block. Unsuccessful at the convent of the Adorer Sisters and at the Jesuit residence, the Radicals reportedly tried to ensure success by sending Lorenzo Ardid of the Casa del Pueblo, as well as the Ulled brothers, to direct the burning. They had barely begun when cavalry troops arrived and dispersed the crowd, causing some casualties. The leaders decided to await the protection of nightfall before attacking again.[34]

Meanwhile a new type of anticlerical melodrama was organized for the pleasure of excited crowds in the Atarazana district. The secrets of cloistered convents, enjoyed by incendiary groups the night before, were now paraded publicly.* The stage was set by an excited woman who gathered a group of housewives in the Plaza del Padró and told them "her sister had been martyred" in the nearby convent of the Hieronymite Nuns. She urged them to discover for themselves the proof of how nuns tortured a member who displeased them, perhaps for nothing more than being prettier than the others. Swiftly the scene gathered momentum. A frenzied mob, composed almost entirely of women, entered the convent and pried open fifteen tombs where they found corpses buried with scourges and tied hand and foot.

The women now organized an expedition to the city hall; the corpses would be taken in their caskets to the authorities who must be forced to end the cruel practices of cloistered orders or, at least, the unhygienic custom of cloistered orders of burying their dead inside their convent walls. Emiliano

---

* The Hieronymites had always been an object of special curiosity and particularly since the open references to their convent in Jaime Piquet's popular play, "The Nun Buried Alive" ("La Monja enterrada en vida, o Secrets de 'Aquell Convent'"), first produced in 1866 (José Benet, *Maragall i la Setmana Tràgica,* 3rd ed. [Barcelona, 1965], p. 55).

Iglesias was in the city hall when the women arrived, accompanying the men who carried the caskets. Describing the scene later, Iglesias excused the error of the men and women who had believed the bindings were "clear proof of torture." He insisted that the corpses had not been profaned, and that the people had been guilty only of "an inquisitive zeal, an eagerness to find out the truth, perhaps a lack of prudence." [35] But if the scene had been planned as an orderly anticlerical demonstration (and there is every indication that it was), some of the actors got out of hand.

A few women dragged corpses to the barricades on the corner of the Calles Carmen and Roig where five rebels, enthused by the new diversion, set out to deposit the bodies in front of the homes of Eusebio Güell and the Marquis of Comillas, prominent Catholic laymen and Catalan regionalists. The scene was macabre as the group made its way along the Calle Carmen to the Ramblas. Twenty-two-year-old Ramón Clemente García, a handsome, dirty, simple-minded coalman, did an obscene dance as he carried a corpse to the home of Comillas; he considered it "an amusement, and he was delighted to find that he could be of use as a revolutionary." [36] Clemente and several others were arrested by Civil Guards a few hours later and were retained in prison, despite the efforts of Emiliano Iglesias to secure their release late Wednesday night.

The final round of convent burnings in Barcelona was concluded late Wednesday night. Civil Guards and army troops repelled with ease the attacks upon the Seminary, the Jesuit residence, and the convent of the Adorer Sisters.* Therefore, incendiaries had to content themselves with lesser victories scored at three institutions which, although important, were not as prestigious as the first group of target institutions. Two were schools, located across the street from one another, and run by orders affiliated with one another: a school for girls run by the Congregation of Salesian Sisters of St. John Bosco, and a school for boys run by the Fathers of the Salesian Society of St. John Bosco. The third institution was an orphanage, administered by Sisters of the Congregation of the Holy Family of Bordeaux. All three of

---

* A neighbor of the Adorer Nuns met one of the principal incendiaries in the street and inquired why they had left the convent only half burned. "Don't talk to me about it," the other replied. "If we don't burn the convent of those nuns, and the Jesuits, we really haven't accomplished anything at all. We have everything ready, all the signals prepared, for the moment when the troops leave. We'll be able to enter and destroy everything in half an hour, if not with fire then with dynamite." ("Crónica: Adoratrices," I, 175.)

these institutions operated under the official patronage of foreign consulates: the schools under Italian, and the orphanage under French protection. Ironically, they were attacked on the same day on which General Santiago had promised to protect foreign property.

The foreign origin of the Salesian orders aroused antagonism. So did the multiple activities of the Salesian Fathers in Hostafranchs: their school, workers' circle, and food cooperative would apparently make them a prime target for the incendiaries.[37] Yet there seemed to be some confusion about whether or not the building of the Salesian Fathers should be burned: the Superior overheard one incendiary challenge another on this point, insisting that the school was not on the list. This confusion, together with four effective Civil Guards, caused one attack to fail. On Wednesday night the Civil Guards abruptly withdrew, and the mobs entered the building of the Salesian Fathers and capered about in clerical vestments until midnight when they ignited the building. They also burned the extremely unpretentious school of the Salesian Sisters located across the street.[38]

Incendiaries were also successful at the Orphanage of San José of the Sisters of the Holy Family of Bordeaux, in a far distant sector of the Ensanche.[39] The Mother Superior had deterred one attack by convincing the crowd that the orphanage cared only for impoverished children. She was powerless in the face of the second assault, on Wednesday night, when enraged women urged the men to hold their lighted torches close to the habits of the sisters as they left the building. Fires were then set which destroyed the interior of the orphanage.

In the suburbs the incendiaries achieved no success on Wednesday night. In San Gervasio (where the Franciscan Monk had been killed and the Capuchin Nun abused), marauders looted the lovely old Royal Monastery of Santa María de Valdoncella, occupied by a cloistered order (the Cistercian Nuns of the Strict Observance) since 1670. The nuns found refuge in the local government offices, under the solicitous care of Radical city councilman Manuel Santamaría González, while incendiaries set a fire that did not burn.[40] Still another convent in San Gervasio was saved from destruction by neighbors who put out the fire: the Royal Monastery of Nuestra Señora de Jerusalén of the cloistered Clarisses (of a Second Order of Franciscan Nuns) escaped with minor damages.[41]

However, even the most important of Wednesday's burnings was eclipsed by the open rebellion that was taking place in Clot-San Martín and in San Andrés.

The fighting in Clot and in San Andrés, where the rebels could not be held back by politicians safeguarding against future prosecution, unequivocably constituted an armed rebellion characterized by bold and brave action. In these suburbs the men fought behind barricades, protected by snipers on rooftops.

In Clot, firing began at dawn and continued from housetops within the residential district. The snipers prevented Civil Guards from clearing away the barricades of telephone and lamp posts that blocked the streets. At noon a mounted Civil Guard detachment opened fire on one barricade; when the rebels fired back, the Guards dismounted to give battle. Soon they summoned infantry reinforcements from the Asia Brigade. Eventually General Brandeis (the officer in command of this entire northeast metropolitan zone) came in person to direct the action; he ordered soldiers to charge the barricade despite the continuous fire of insurgents. A sergeant died and six soldiers were wounded before rebels were forced to flee, leaving Civil Guards to dismount the barricades.[42]

Meanwhile, incendiaries were burning two important clerical institutions in Clot. One was the asylum of the Daughters of Charity of St. Vincent de Paul. On two earlier occasions, neighbors had dissuaded incendiaries from burning this asylum; on Wednesday afternoon they succeeded a third time in preventing the burning. However, the leader of the group warned the Mother Superior as he left "not to resist any more, for you are on the list and tonight you will be burned." [43] At 9 P.M., true to his word, fires were kindled that destroyed the interior of the building and all the furnishings.

Far more spectacular was the destruction of the well-equipped facilities of the Jesuit-run workers' circle in Clot (Nuestra Señora del Carmen y San Pedro Claver) which had a library, food cooperative, and restaurant.[44] In contrast with the neighbors of the asylum of the Daughters of Charity, workers in the vicinity of this institution made no attempt to defend it, showing that the Catholic hierarchy had failed in its objective of winning back the workers from republican parties through the use of workers' circles. The residents of Clot had resented the conditions for membership in the circle — obligatory attendance on Sundays and holidays, and participation in religious services. On Wednesday they joined in the large scale looting and burning, or watched passively as the buildings were destroyed.

In addition to the ferocious street fighting, the rebellion in Clot was distinguished by the efforts of Radical activists to incriminate party officials. Throughout the metropolitan area Radicals resented the attempts by politicians to direct the movement from the safety of their homes; only in Clot did they do something to remedy the situation. The effort to implicate Pedro Rovira, the president of the Radical center in Clot, was only relatively successful: when Juan Garrós' group seized the rifles of local militia they left behind a receipt signed by Rovira,* but he indignantly denied that the signature was his.[45] In contrast, the Radicals of Clot did succeed in compelling former city councilor Luis Zurdo Olivares to participate. Government prosecutors were to cite Zurdo's actions as their principal evidence for the charge that Radical officials were responsible not only for the convent burnings but for the armed rebellion.

In miniature, almost in caricature, Zurdo's activities during this period had exemplified the plight of all Radical politicians — demagogues actually forced to make good on the promises through which they had won political power.** Zurdo had laid special claim to the worker's vote because he was a self-made politician, in contrast with the middle-class lawyers who dominated the Radical party hierarchy. In addition to defending labor, Zurdo had won distinction as an anti-Catalan, anticlerical extremist; during the preceding week he had written articles in El Progreso attacking the Moroccan expedition as a clerical enterprise. Once the antiwar protest began, according to rumors, Zurdo had been largely responsible for transforming it into a conflagration of convents. But Zurdo, like his colleagues, intended to avoid direct involvement. On Tuesday night, from the balcony of his home, he had tried to bully his neighbors into joining the arsonists, by reminding them that the convents were the real power behind the Catalan separatist movement; neighbors ignored him and so Zurdo threw down buckets of water, a flamboyant gesture that failed to satisfy Radical members in Clot.[46]

On Wednesday men forced their way into Zurdo's home to say that "you implicated us in this; it's your obligation to go at the head of the group." [47] He went into the street to talk with the armed insurgents, who still hoped that the Radicals would establish a republic. One man assured Zurdo that "authorities are powerless to repress the insurrection for another seventy hours," while still another demanded that the "Captain General be made

---

* Military prosecutors asked the death penalty for Juan Garrós, later reducing it to life imprisonment. Pedro Rovira was merely detained for questioning and then immediately released.

** In central Barcelona, Radical rebels reportedly tried at gun point to force Jaime Anglés Pruñosa, another prominent worker-politician who had helped to launch the antiwar protest, to participate in the rebellion but they failed (Causa: Rebelión militar, I, 255–56, 346).

to turn his command over to them." [48] Zurdo's reaction was to stage an anti-clerical scene for the admiring mob: in full view of his neighbors he drank from a bottle allegedly containing the consecrated wine of the Mass. Then the group moved off, Zurdo walking in front between two rebels and followed by two armed men. A neighbor, Emilio Escoda, happened to meet the group in the street where he overheard one of the armed rebels express a fear that Zurdo would slip away and return home.[49] The Radical politician roamed through Clot, a rifle on his shoulder, but military authorities produced no evidence that he went near the barricades. He then returned home and remained there for the rest of the week. Because he was the only Radical politician to bear arms, Zurdo became a hero in party annals.

In the relatively comfortable industrial suburb of San Andrés de Palomar, where perfect order had been maintained until Wednesday afternoon, the rebels worked frantically as though to make up for lost time. Initially the convent burnings were subordinated to the armed rebellion, a development that may have been the result of the political orientation of the rebel leader in San Andrés: José Miquel Baró was not a Radical, as in other worker districts, but a member of the Catalan Nationalist Republican party.

Certainly all events had pointed toward an immediate confrontation with the clergy, particularly with the Marists whose school in Pueblo Nuevo had been the first building burned in Barcelona and whose Superior had been the first religious to be killed. A brother from that school had come immediately to warn the 110 residents in the provincial house in San Andrés, an enormous edifice just recently constructed at great expense.[50] The Marists prepared to defend themselves and by so doing may have provoked the very attack they feared: late Tuesday night, when the brothers heard a shot that they interpreted as a signal to the incendiaries, they fired from within the residence. A member of another religious order in San Andrés later expressed the opinion that these shots from the Marist residence constituted the spark that set off the violence in that district.[51]

A major obstacle to violence was the well-staffed Civil Guards barrack in San Andrés. When by Wednesday morning there had as yet been no disorders in San Andrés, authorities decided there would be none and dispatched most of the Guards to duty in Barcelona. Their departure created a void that the municipal police refused to fill; they stayed within their headquarters, insisting their orders were to protect criminal records and denying they had been intimidated by threatening mobs.[52] The head of the local militia —

Jaime de Moner, a wealthy Carlist lawyer — tried to recruit some of the militia members to defend clerical institutions, one of the few such attempts in metropolitan Barcelona (although a commonplace occurrence in cities elsewhere in the province). In the tense situation, Moner's action was interpreted as an effort to organize a Carlist Catholic insurrection; the reaction was so alarming that Moner decided to go into hiding.*

The result of all this was to leave San Andrés virtually unprotected, an opportunity immediately exploited by a group of agitators from other suburbs who appeared in the main Plaza del Comercio late Wednesday afternoon and incited residents to burn convents and build barricades.[53] The highest ranking municipal official in San Andrés, Teniente Alcalde Ignacio Iglesias of the Catalan Nationalist Republican party, sent José Miquel Baró to the Plaza for news of the gathering.[54] Once in the Plaza, Miquel took command of the rebellion: whether he did so with or without the consent of his party is not clear.

Miquel Baró had many qualifications for a revolutionary role. Most obviously, he looked the part. Tall and heavyset, the 44-year-old Miquel had a thick red beard and wore an extra-long blue worker's smock that made him stand out in a crowd. One would not have guessed from his appearance that he held a modest post as a porter, earned through faithful political service. A native of Aragon, Miquel Baró had for some reason espoused with enthusiasm the cause of Catalan regionalism; for the past sixteen years he had been a member of the Catalan Nationalist party. His extreme political ideas had convinced many of his neighbors in San Andrés that he was slightly mad. In short, José Miquel Baró — impetuous by nature, barely literate — was the type of man who could lead a revolt.

Assisted by 18-year-old Domingo Valls and by Pedro Duaso, Miquel armed his followers by seizing rifles from the guards who collected duties

---

* The mystery surrounding Moner's activities was increased by his subsequent refusal, at the conclusion of the disorders, to disarm the militia and turn the rifles over to General Brandeis. Moner was prosecuted for having abandoned his duties as chief of the militia when he went into hiding, the only civilian to be so charged or at least the only one whose case appeared in the newspaper. Dressed in a frock coat, Moner appeared in court accompanied by Carlist Deputy Leoncio Soler y March and made a speech "lamenting that his name had been mixed in with that of the wretches accused of rebellion." Moner was acquitted. (La Publicidad [Barcelona], October 12, 1909; La Tribuna [Barcelona], September 27, 1909; and El Correo Catalán [Barcelona], September 28, 1909. For the Carlists' attempt to defend clerical institutions see the letter from the Junta del Centro Tradicionalista de San Andrés, El Correo Catalán [Barcelona], September 28, 1909.)

on food entering the city. He then directed the construction of a barricade on the main highway leading in from Barcelona, and another in front of the Civil Guard barracks. At 6:30 P.M., he directed the burning of the parish church, first ordering that all items of value be thrown into the enormous bonfire. The fires completely destroyed the rectory but scarcely damaged the church. Meanwhile, the ubiquitous José Miquel had gone back to lead the firing from the barricades, directed against the Civil Guards still in the barracks.* Fighting began about 8:30 P.M. and continued for several hours, until a squadron of Montesa cavalry arrived to relieve the Civil Guards. Order was finally restored, but the throngs were exhilarated by their first taste of action and merely bided their time until a new opportunity presented itself.

In the prosperous residential suburb of Las Corts, incendiaries burned a Catholic school and a cloistered convent. They refused to burn a hospital run by the Order of Brothers Hospitallers of St. John of God, an incident that became a cause célèbre.

At the very unpretentious school belonging to the Christian Brothers,** José Llansá Bagés, a twenty-year-old construction worker and a Radical party member, ordered his accomplices to search the brothers for "weapons": when none were found, the religious were allowed to depart before the buildings were burned.[55]

A large crowd had already gathered at the hospital when at 8 P.M. Prior Lorenzo González opened the doors and asked the crowd to "help us carry out the innocent little children, and then you can do what you like with the building." Men and women entered to view the two hundred incurably ill children, cared for by twenty friars; there was no dissenting voice when the leaders agreed to leave the building untouched. Prior Lorenzo then tried to dissuade them from burning the neighboring convent of the cloistered order of Discalced Carmelites, lest the fire spread to the hospital. "We can't do that," they replied. "It must be burned."[56]

Their first act, once inside the empty Carmelite convent, was to drag the corpses from the tombs and out onto the street where they tossed the bones into wells and fountains, thereby contaminating the water supply for weeks.

---

* José Miquel Baró was tried by a military tribunal and was found guilty of armed rebellion. He was executed on August 17, 1909.
** Another school belonging to the Christian Brothers had been burned in Pueblo Seco on Tuesday afternoon (see page 212).

This same group then returned to place Red Cross banners on the roof of the hospital. During the rest of the week they supplied chickens and rabbits, probably stolen from some other location. Ordered to leave their doors open, the friars received a steady stream of visitors of all social classes who came to see the children and went away impressed with what they had seen. "This is all to our favor," reported Friar Andrés Ayucar in a widely publicized letter, adding that "no harm was done to us; no insult was uttered."[57] Republican newspapers would publicize this case as an illustration of their contention that when incendiaries found an order that was generously fulfilling a charitable function, they respected and aided the clergy.

On Wednesday insurgents were caught up in the momentum of convent burning and street fighting and therefore made almost no demands for leadership. This enabled politicians to spend the day waiting for news from other cities before deciding definitively whether or not to organize a republican revolution.

Several of the Catalan republican deputies established an informal headquarters in the fashionable café Maison Dorée in central Barcelona. Eduardo Calvet, Julio Marial, Juan Moles, and Joaquín Salvatella each set up a table, to which their followers came for news and advice. The Catalan republican councilmen made somewhat more of an effort; they even visited party members wounded in the street fighting who were in the hospitals.[58]

Radical chief Emiliano Iglesias was primarily concerned with his own safety. "I confess I was not born to be valiant," he wrote many years later;[59] and so he took a laxative that made it impossible for him to leave the house — or to go near the barricades. Gleefully, socialists and Catalan politicians dubbed him the "Laxative Hero."[60]

Safely ensconced at home, Iglesias conferred with Radical delegations from all over Catalonia who wanted to know whether they should prolong the rebellion, now that the convents had been burned. The Radical leader gave them minute instructions about what to do in case of a revolution or in case of a retreat.[61] He sent them away with the admonition that "if they received no further orders that day, it would be a signal that the movement had failed because of isolation [as a separatist movement]."[62]

Iglesias also conferred on Wednesday with Villalobos Moreno and Fabra Rivas: in this his last formal meeting with the ill-starred Committee for the Strike,* he again discussed plans for a revolution, contingent upon the sup-

* The third member of the Strike Committee, anarchist José Rodríguez Romero, is not mentioned as attending any meeting after Sunday, July 25. Military authorities, however, charged Rodríguez with aiding Moreno in directing the barricades on the

port of cities elsewhere in Spain. The men separated with the understanding they would send representatives to a meeting scheduled for 9 A.M. the following day (Thursday), at which time each would report what he had been able to organize during the night.[63]

At 5 P.M. Iglesias left his home to spend the night at the city hall. Solidaridad Obrera officials reported he made the trip in an ambulance although his malady was "no other than a desperate and malodorous case of fear-itis that prevented him from traversing the city streets." [64]

In contrast with Emiliano Iglesias, Francisco Ferrer was indiscreet — to say the least — in attempting to use the popular uprising as the occasion for a revolution. Excluded from events in the capital, Ferrer was limited to action in the small seaside towns of Premiá del Mar and Masnou.

At 10:00 on Wednesday morning he left his farm, Mas Germinal, for the first time since his trip to Barcelona. He went first to the neighboring town of Masnou, to the barbershop, which rapidly filled with people "who wanted to see and talk with me," reported Ferrer, "because the rumor had got around that I was the director of the movement." [65] The primary source of this rumor was barber Francisco Domenech who had recounted Ferrer's efforts to compel Emiliano Iglesias and Lorenzo Ardid to commit the Radical party to a revolution.

Ferrer and Juan Puig Ventura, president of the Radical group in Masnou, drew apart from the crowd to talk in private. They discussed the rebellion in Barcelona, the reports of an uprising in Madrid, Valencia, and Saragossa, and finally the possibility that from one moment to the next a republic might be proclaimed. Ferrer urged that Masnou join the rebellion. When Puig pointed out that the town had remained tranquil, Ferrer said they should "begin" by encouraging men to burn the local convent and church, that "this was indispensable for the triumph of the revolution that had developed." Puig objected that he "did not understand how this measure could bring about the republic," to which Ferrer replied that "the important thing was not the republic, the question was that there should be a revolution." [66]

Before taking action, the two men decided to walk to Premiá del Mar for

---

Calle San Pablo (*Causa contra Ferrer,* pp. 660, 665). Moreno said Rodríguez left Barcelona on Monday "before any violence occurred" ("Por la Verdad," *El País* [Madrid], November 2, 1909). Fabra Rivas corroborated this (letter printed in *El Socialista* [Madrid], November 12, 1909). Moreno and Fabra Rivas may have said this because they feared that Rodríguez, long associated with Ferrer, was still in Spain and subject to prosecution (see military summons to Rodríguez to appear, in *La Publicidad* [Barcelona], September 10, 1909).

a conference with Mayor Domingo Casas Llibre, whom Ferrer had met when a rationalist school was inaugurated in the Radical center of Premiá. Casas was a cautious man who from the first moment of the General Strike had juggled his responsibilities as Mayor and his obligations as the leader of a particularly extremist Radical center, which, in the words of a Guardia Civil officer, "might be considered the general headquarters of some incendiaries and seditionaries." [67] A conservative politician in Premiá said that Ferrer deliberately went to this center because he "believed he would be safe, and would be supported." [68]

Ferrer and Puig arrived in Premiá shortly after twelve noon, and went directly to the bar of the Radical center where they drank beer to ward off the humid heat as they talked of revolution with Casas and a few other Radical officials. Casas began by expressing surprise and concern that Ferrer should appear in public at such a dangerous moment.[69] The entire question of proclaiming a republic in Premiá was discussed in a meeting that lasted less than forty-five minutes — probably due to Mayor Casas' eagerness to have Ferrer leave as soon as possible.

As Puig and Ferrer walked back to Masnou, they talked about Emiliano Iglesias' refusal to commit the Radicals to a revolution. This, together with Puig's request for help in becoming a city councilman, prompted Ferrer to deliver a stern lecture on the vanity of political ambitions. "There you have what the republicans are; what they want is to get into the city government and into the Cortes, and that is not what they should want" said Ferrer: the desideratum should be "revolution and opposition to the government." [70]

Ferrer returned to his farm, Mas Germinal, "rather satisfied" with his four-hour excursion, reported his daughter. "Nothing gained, but he has the feeling that the situation is developing," Sol Ferrer summarized, "that the republic has a chance — to begin — and that the peasants do not misinterpret it." [71] Ferrer did not again appear in public.

Mayor Casas and his associates would later testify that Ferrer proposed the proclamation of the republic in Premiá, and that they opposed it.[72] And yet only a few hours after Ferrer's visit, Leopoldo Iglesias of the Radical center in Premiá organized a group of thirty to forty men prepared for action.[73] From the welter of details recounted by witnesses and participants, three important facts emerge. The men claimed to act in the name of Ferrer: Leopoldo Iglesias* and a colleague appeared on the balcony of the Masnou

* When Leopoldo Iglesias was arrested, he complained bitterly that only "unfortunate wretches" like himself were punished, while the "real culprits" like Mayor Casas es-

city hall to announce that Ferrer himself could not attend because he "had to take care of revolutionary matters in Barcelona." [74] Secondly, the townspeople of both Premiá and Masnou believed that Casas was involved from behind the scenes, for "his best friends were the visible leaders of the uprising." [75] Finally, and most significantly, the purpose behind Leopoldo Iglesias' activity was to assemble a large group of armed men from the entire region and then proceed to Barcelona to help their comrades who, beleaguered by cannon fire, were "imploring" aid. [76]

On Wednesday Ferrer, working through the Radical extremists of Premiá, obviously hoped to exert pressure upon Radical party chief Emiliano Iglesias so that the popular uprising would not die out, but would be the occasion for the proclamation of a republic. Throughout metropolitan Barcelona other Radical extremists, as well as socialists and anarchists, were striving for the same goal. But the success of these groups — working independently or in contact with one another — was conditional upon uprisings in other parts of Spain. All hope of outside support banished completely by Wednesday night.

In the province of Logroño a troop train was wrecked, while in Alcoy and Valencia the workers staged a noisy antiwar demonstration. [77] This was the extent of the protest movement outside of Catalonia. Valencia caused the most bitter disappointment, for republicans in Barcelona had counted heavily on support from the well-organized Valencian republican parties, one led by Blasco Ibañez and one by Rodrigo Soriano. The rank and file of the Valencian republicans were eager to participate, but party officials refused to issue any orders. [78] Interior Minister La Cierva, meanwhile, was in constant contact with developments in Valencia; he jubilantly reported that despite their militancy, Valencian republicans were "patriotic" and so "the suspicion that the Catalan movement was separatist in nature, combined with the well-known energy of the Governor, prevented them from supporting the republicans in Barcelona." [79] Yet even this failure paled in comparison with the ignominious defeat of the rebel cause in Madrid.

The national antiwar protest collapsed — stillborn — in Madrid as the result of government resolution and republican timidity. The Interior Minister continued firm in his original conviction: the antiwar protest was not a valid expression of popular opinion but a device whereby a faction op-

---

caped (*Causa contra Ferrer*, p. 270). Perhaps this explains why Iglesias' testimony was not included in the published transcript.

posed to the government sought to incite workers. On Wednesday he told
newsmen in Madrid that the General Strike of Barcelona was but the first
stage of a "seditious movement, revolutionary in nature, in all of Spain." [80]
From the King, La Cierva secured special powers to act: on Tuesday Alfonso had suspended constitutional guarantees in the four Catalan provinces,
and on Wednesday he suspended them throughout Spain. The latter decree
was published that same day (Wednesday, July 28) in a special edition of
the official government bulletin (*Gaceta*). La Cierva waited expectantly
for the opportunity to wield his special powers to arrest and to detain men
in prison.

National republican leaders gave him no opportunity to do so. At 5 P. M.
Benito Pérez Galdós, Julio Cervera, Julian Nougués and other republican
deputies met in answer to a letter from Nougués — sent two days earlier —
to discuss the possibility of concerted action to force Maura to open the
Cortes and there explain his government's Moroccan campaign. Although
deputies refused either then or later to disclose their conclusions, it is obvious
that they decided to refrain from any action whatsover.[81] Socialist leader
Pablo Iglesias was scornful: "The republicans have confirmed what we have
so often said of them, namely that they have neither the men to carry out
a revolution nor even the desire to do so." Iglesias reported it would have
been an "excellent occasion" to act, for the national antiwar protest launched
by the socialists threatened not only the Maura government but the Monarchy itself. "We would have achieved our objective," Iglesias contended,
if republican leaders had "fought firmly" at the side of the socialists, but
they were "cobardes y traidores" — cowards, because nowhere in Spain
did republican politicians act, and traitors, because in Barcelona they abandoned their members who took part in the uprising.[82]

"We were alone," reported a socialist editorial writer, "completely alone
in the moments of most danger; this gives us the right to claim exclusively
for ourselves any glory that might be involved." [83] Late Wednesday afternoon, July 28, socialists began to distribute copies of the weekly newspaper,
El Socialista, carrying the proclamation that Pablo Iglesias had signed of
a nationwide general strike on the following Monday, August 2, as a protest against the war in Morocco.

Armed with his special powers, La Cierva reacted immediately. La Cierva
did what Ossorio — two days earlier — had refused to do: he prevented the
strike from beginning by arresting the leaders. He sent police to the offices

of the socialist newspaper with orders to arrest Pablo Iglesias and National Committee members Francisco Mora and Francisco Largo Caballero. Iglesias' health was poor, and so La Cierva ordered that he be put under house arrest. When Iglesias insisted on going to jail, he and the other officials were taken there in an automobile — a great courtesy.

La Cierva's other acts to stop the general strike were far less cavalier. He had all copies of the newspaper, El Socialista, rounded up at railroad stations and post offices. Early the following morning (Thursday), La Cierva closed the socialists' Casa del Pueblo in Madrid. He ordered the arrest of labor leaders and republican extremists throughout Spain: some two hundred men were arrested, handcuffed, and harshly mistreated in what socialists described as a deliberate campaign of "terror." Pablo Iglesias ruefully acknowledged La Cierva's effectiveness in "decapitating" the national protest of workers.[84]

Late Wednesday night, rebel leaders and politicians in Barcelona learned of the confiscation of newspapers and arrest of the three socialist leaders. Socialist Fabra Rivas was bitterly disappointed that the attempt to organize a general strike — a dramatic departure from the traditionally conservative policies of the Spanish Socialist party — should have failed so utterly. "Most cities didn't even know about the [strike] decision, because the government intercepted the correspondence and newspapers that announced it," he wrote.[85] It was a foregone conclusion that Claudi Ametlla would inform him, late Wednesday night, that the Catalan Nationalist Republicans could not support a rebellion that had no support elsewhere in Spain.[86]

At 11 P.M., Emiliano Iglesias slipped away from his refuge at the city hall to confer in the offices of El Progreso with Miguel V. Moreno and his aide, Uruguayan anarchist Antonio Loredo. In "this somewhat tragic meeting," as Iglesias described it, the members acknowledged that Iglesias had been right from the beginning about the precipitateness of the revolt and the failure to coordinate beforehand with groups in other cities. They agreed that "isolated, without having achieved anything definite here, it would be inhuman to continue the struggle just for its own sake." In order to end the insurrection, they agreed with Iglesias that he and the Committee should prepare a manifesto.[87]

Fabra Rivas did not attend this meeting nor was he seen again in Barcelona, although he did not leave for France until two days later.[88] Emiliano

Iglesias and Moreno began to accuse the young socialist of personal coward-
liness, and of betraying a movement that had been launched largely because he had promised that socialists in other cities would support it.[89]

The withdrawal of Fabra Rivas on Wednesday made it impossible to
carry out Iglesias' suggestion that he and the Committee for the Strike
issue a joint concluding manifesto. Despite his subsequent calumniations
against the Committee, Iglesias had used it to advantage as a scapegoat —
as the entity nominally responsible for having organized and directed the
events.

From Wednesday night on, the Radical chief worked independently to
end the uprising and even more to dissociate his party from it. For assistance he turned first to Hermenegildo Giner de los Ríos, hoping to take
advantage of Giner's immunity as a deputy to the Cortes and his prestige
as a professor in the state secondary institute. Despite his post as president
of the municipal junta of the Radical party, and excepting only his attendance at the special meeting convened by the Mayor, Giner had remained
aloof from the events. Late Wednesday night Iglesias tried to involve him:
he sent Juan Moreno, a young extremist from the staff of *El Progreso,* to
talk with Giner in his home in Gracia, requesting that he use his "indispu-
table authority" to prepare a manifesto for the members of the Radical
party, "protesting in their name against the excesses and violences that had
been committed, and asking that all honorable people isolate themselves
from the events." Giner replied that he would be delighted to be of service
but must delay a decision until he received an answer from Mayor Coll
concerning a similar proposal he had already submitted.[90] In other words,
Giner declined any responsibility for ending the insurrection.

Without such a manifesto, Emiliano Iglesias found it impossible to clear
30,000 insurgents from the streets. The best he could do was to order all
Radical officials to withdraw now that the bulk of the convent burnings
had ended. Thus a Juventud Radical leader (possibly Juan Colominas),
when queried by a college classmate two days later, could answer truth-
fully: "We finished on Wednesday; now there are other elements who
are continuing." [91] For the Radicals, the convent burnings would stand as
an end in themselves, not a prelude to revolution as the extremists — and
as Ferrer — had conceived them.

By default the leadership of the uprising passed to the militants — to
"the people who really wanted to carry out a revolution," as Claudi Ametlla described them.[92] They were anarchist by conviction although nominally

members of the Radical party or of Solidaridad Obrera. All day Thursday these rebels would fire from housetops in the center of the city until troop reinforcements drove them out to the suburbs, where they would fight and burn convents for another two days.[93] In honor of these belligerents, the official position of anarchists and socialists would be that the revolt of Barcelona workers did not end until Thursday night.[94]

Thursday, July 29

Although the tacit agreement to suspend fighting between 7 and 9 A.M. was scrupulously observed Thursday morning, new tensions threatened to interrupt the routine. In working-class districts there was a serious food shortage, although markets in wealthier neighborhoods offered some fresh fish and meat, transported under the direct supervision of General Santiago. Medical personnel used the early morning truce to remove by ambulance all casualties from the streets of the Atarazana-Paralelo district, where, punctually at 9 A.M., shooting began anew. Rebels aimed at the Civil Guards, who once again rode out to bear the brunt of combat.[1]

At the barricades on the Calle San Pablo, where anarchists José Ginés and Natividad Rufo, acting on orders from Miguel V. Moreno, were in command, rebels initiated another day of fighting. Despite the previous day's savage battle, climaxed by the firing of cannons, men rallied to fight again. At noon rebels and soldiers clashed in front of the headquarters of the Captain General.

On the Calle Carmen, a sturdy Aragonese built a barricade of paving stones in front of the burned-out convent of the Hieronymite Nuns, where several policemen had taken refuge; perhaps for as long as sixteen hours, he fired while neighbors hung out the windows to shout encouragement and throw down food. When he had used all his ammunition, the Aragonese hoisted his rifle to his shoulder and left.[2]

Brave actions, yet they lacked the stimulus of a cause that would compensate street fighters for the physical exhaustion of fighting in extreme humid heat and for the casualties they suffered. Exhaustion and sleepiness began to take their toll. Anarchist Leopoldo Bonafulla described the morale of the men on the barricades: "It would have been madness to count on the total triumph of the revolution. This idea they had already discounted. But once they lost the hope of being supported by the very people who, at the beginning of the protest had declared themselves to be in favor of it, their sacrifice at that point would have been sterile."[3] This disenchantment enervated workers even before the troop reinforcements went into action on Thursday afternoon.

At noon on Thursday Radical extremists staged the last dramatic anti-clerical coup of the week, as if to provide a new stimulus for the waning enthusiasm of the crowds and to compensate for the end of convent burnings and street fighting. The site was the Piarist school, where they had scored their first and most spectacular success. Again Radicals exploited the popular association of the Piarists with armed Carlists fighting for a theocratic state.

Although nothing remained to carry off, not even the water pipes, men and women still swarmed over the smouldering ruins of the Piarist school.[4] About noon the cry went around that some Piarist Fathers were hiding in a liqueur factory across the street. The Piarists were reputed the true owners of the factory although Antonio Tortrás, a devout Catholic and Carlist, figured as the nominal owner. These tales prepared the way for the incident that occurred at 2 P.M.

As a patrolling infantry detachment passed by the liqueur factory, hidden snipers fired upon it. Almost immediately a Radical party extremist, Domingo Ferrer March,* appeared and told the crowd that priests hidden inside the factory had shot at the soldiers in order to provoke them into firing on the rebels. Ferrer, a shoemaker by trade, had brought with him a small team of men carrying gasoline and torches. He announced his plan to burn the factory as revenge for the priests' attack upon the soldiers, con-tinuing the rebels' policy of an alliance with the Army. The crowd followed Domingo Ferrer into the factory but found it empty; the explanation was that the priests had fled through a secret tunnel. Within half an hour the crowd had plundered and set on fire the factory, which, because of its highly combustible contents, burned rapidly. Domingo Ferrer emerged from the building carrying silverware and documents, but these were taken from him at the door by a man wearing a Red Cross arm band — a man who may have been a bona fide member of the Red Cross, or may have been a Radical party representative sent down to supervise the affair so that it did not get out of hand (as part of the Radical officials' general attempt to end the dis-

---

* Domingo Ferrer was one of the few incendiaries convicted by a civilian court (in contrast with the many armed rebels convicted by military tribunals) and was sen-tenced to life imprisonment (*El Progreso* [Barcelona], July 20, 1910; *La Publicidad* [Barcelona], November 17, 1909; and Leopoldo Bonafulla [pseud. Juan Bautista Esteve], *La Revolución de julio en Barcelona* [Barcelona, n.d. [1909]], p. 224).

orders despite the party extremists). Neighbors complacently watched the factory burn, according to the Radical newspaper, "pleased that so important a Carlist [as Antonio Tortrás] should suffer so considerable a loss."[5] Meanwhile a Carlist youth, reputed to have fired on incendiaries in defense of the Church of San Francisco de Paula, was dragged along the Paralelo to a horrible death.

The destruction of the Carlist's liqueur factory was the final scene in the anticlerical panorama that picturesque, brave but brutal men and women had staged for three days in the streets of Barcelona.

Even the excitement of discovering priests hidden in Carlist factories paled beside the major developments of the day: the arrival of troop reinforcements on Thursday morning, and the re-establishment of order in central Barcelona on Thursday afternoon.

The troops had come from Valencia and Saragossa, and even from as far away as Pamplona and Burgos. After days of procrastination, General Santiago finally felt strong enough to move against the rebels. His first act was to station the bulk of the newly arrived troops in the Atarazana-Paralelo district, the site of the only street fighting in central Barcelona. Santiago thereby gained an immediate psychological advantage: rebels were disheartened by the great numbers of reinforcements, and by the antagonism of the soldiers who had been told they were going to fight a Catalan separatist movement. The newly arrived soldiers were therefore well-indoctrinated against the argument that the conscript soldier should refuse to suppress a civilian insurrection fought on his behalf, the argument used to demoralize the troops garrisoned in Barcelona.[6]

But the harshest blow to the rebels' morale was dealt by the soldiers' report that workers outside of Catalonia had not declared a general strike. The residents of the Paralelo district were particularly disheartened to learn, from the troops who had just come from Valencia, that the tale of rebel leaders in Barcelona of a rebellion in Valencia was completely false. "The revolutionaries, . . . now considered their noble effort annihilated," wrote a Radical journalist. "Many of them returned to their homes."[7]

Emiliano Iglesias, beginning early Thursday morning, redoubled his efforts to dissociate his party from the rebellion. The first item on his agenda was a mere formality. At 10 A.M., he sent an emissary to meet one final time with the delegates of the Committee for the Strike; only Antonio Loredo, representing Moreno, was waiting. Fabra Rivas sent no delegate. The Radical messenger informed Loredo that Iglesias had "worked all night in vain, in communication, in search of what he did not find"[8] — in short, Iglesias insisted that he had really tried to organize a revolution but had found it impossible. This meeting between the emissary of Iglesias and Antonio Loredo formally terminated the uneasy collaboration between the Radical politician and the Central Committee for the Strike.

Meanwhile, the Radical chief had dispatched messengers to San Felíu, Tarrasa, Mataró, and "other cities" in the province of Barcelona. Informing party officials that the movement had failed outside of Catalonia, Iglesias instructed them to warn all individuals involved in the uprising so that they would have time to escape.[9]

The textile cities of Manresa and Igualada in the province of Barcelona, and Reus, Valls, and Montblanch in the province of Tarragona, were caught off guard by the sudden change of plans.[10] Insurgents began to act early Thursday morning, before messengers could arrive. Thus it was by a strange quirk that these cities, quiet since the initial disorders connected with the General Strike, began an insurrection complete with street fighting and convent burnings on the very day that the rebellion in Barcelona proper was definitively repressed.*

In Pueblo Nuevo, on Thursday morning rebels waged a bloody battle on the barricades with rifles (and presumably with ammunition) supplied by the porter of the Radical center, Juan Castells Santoña.[11] The timing suggests that the extremist element within the Radical party had once again mobilized the illiterate, unskilled workers of Pueblo Nuevo,** this time to compel reluctant politicians to turn the insurrection into a revolution. Located in the suburb farthest from party headquarters in central Barcelona, rebel leaders in Pueblo Nuevo either did not know — or chose to ignore — Emiliano Iglesias' decision to withdraw.

* The disorders in Manresa and Igualada, centers of the textile industry, were suppressed within the next two days with relative ease, both because of the disheartening news of the rebellion in Barcelona, and because in these cities the leading citizens and the local militia (somatén) cooperated closely with the Guardia Civil and the Army. Of the two, the events in Manresa were the more serious: two workers and a minor municipal official (Joaquín Cardona) were killed. The disorders in Reus, Montblanch, and Valls were very quickly repressed.

** Some wounded veterans of Thursday's battle in Pueblo Nuevo, while being treated later in the day in the public clinic, were overheard to say that "they would kill the *lerrouxista* chiefs, because they had deceived them" (*Causa: Rebelión militar,* I, 532–33).

The rifles had reportedly been seized earlier in the week from police and militia. They had been deposited in the Radical center, but the porter Castells had been unwilling to implicate the party and so had taken them to the home of a Radical official, Pedro Margalet. Now, on Thursday, Castells retrieved the rifles and distributed them to a band of rebels led by Radical party member Ramón Caballé Parsell. An impassioned party member and a teamster by trade, Caballé was a prime example of the type of worker mobilized by Radical extremists in Pueblo Nuevo. He had been "deprived of the bread of intelligence," to use the words of his defense lawyer who would seek thereby to justify his attacks upon a society that had never shown any concern for his welfare or his education.[12] Bravery, reinforced by vengefulness, compensated for any deficiencies in Caballé, a natural leader. He had never even held a rifle until Thursday when the Radical center porter Castells gave him one and showed him how to use it. Castells accompanied Caballé's band to the barricades, taking care not to carry a weapon.

Although acknowledging the nominal leadership of Caballé, one band took orders from 27-year-old Victoriano Segués Artigas. In normal times only a hired hand in his brother's stable, Segués had proved to be an articulate and resourceful rebel leader. He had led a band that burned convents, was possibly the killer of the Marist Superior, and now on Thursday would fight on the barricades under Ramón Caballé. There was friction between these two leaders, the result of personal and possibly political rivalries, and this would be important later during the trial.[13] But on Thursday such differences were forgotten as rebels in Pueblo Nuevo made one last attempt to achieve a full revolution.

For the preceding two days the district had been so quiet that troops had been able to dismantle the earlier barricades.[14] At dawn on Thursday these were hurriedly reconstructed, with lamp posts and stones covered over with barbed wire. By 7 A.M., when General Brandeis came to inspect the Civil Guard squadron as it took over patrol duties from the Montesa cavalry regiment, armed men were waiting on the barricades. When they ignored his order to disperse, the General commanded Civil Guards to dismount and prepare for action. At 11 A.M. some of the army troops who had just arrived in Barcelona came to reinforce the beleaguered Civil Guards. By 12:30 the skirmishing had assumed the proportions of a major battle. Rebels, forced to abandon the barricades, continued to fire rifles and revolvers from rooftops and windows. At 1 P.M., two cannons arrived and were set up, facing the Calle Mayor del Taulat. Only when householders hung out white cloths did General Brandeis order the cannon fire to cease. Rebels fled to houses throughout the district, forcing owners to open the street doors; they climbed to the rooftops, and occupants of the buildings hid in the cellars, while Civil Guards stormed the houses. In one struggle, handsome Lieutenant Daniel Gabaldon was killed and two Civil Guards seriously wounded. Victoriano Segués' band, which had been separated from Caballé's group, was finally subdued on the Calle Wad-Ras. Caballé's men forced their way onto the roof of a house on the Calle Dos de Mayo and fought until the moment of their arrest. The porter of the Radical center remained with Caballé's group until the end, although witnesses testified that Castells never uttered a threat nor carried a weapon.* In all, at least eight rebels had been killed and eighteen seriously wounded; there were probably many more, but friends and relatives hid the casualties. Officers arrested twenty-three men, forcing them to dismantle the barricades before transporting them to prison.

By midafternoon military authorities were in complete control of Pueblo Nuevo and were thus free to suppress the rebellion, simultaneously, at its other two focal points: the central Atarazana-Paralelo district and the industrial suburb of Clot.

Late Thursday afternoon General Santiago began his offensive in the Atarazana district, having first taken time to intersperse the newly arrived troops among his own garrison forces and Civil Guards. Punctually at 4:30 P.M., the troops, divided into three contingents, entered the district.[15] Contrary to all expectations, they met no resistance. "Revolutionaries abandoned this zone to the troops," wrote anarchist Leopoldo Bonafulla, "as if they were carrying out a maneuver."[16] Most simply withdrew to their homes, although fanatics like Radical party official Ramón Font retreated to the suburbs and kept on fighting.[17] Soldiers were left free to occupy the area, triangular in shape. On one side of the triangle, the Ramblas, General Bonet's forces stood guard. Their duties turned out to be the most onerous for they were subjected to constant sniping from rooftops, regulated by whistles that sounded just before and just after the shots were heard. One Security Guard was killed.

---

* Juan Castells, the Radical center porter, was released. Victoriano Segués was convicted of rebellion and sentenced to death, but this was commuted to permanent exile. Ramón Caballé was also condemned to death but his sentence was changed to a life term in a maximum security prison; he published an open letter to Lerroux and Emiliano Iglesias, thanking them for intervening on his behalf.

Meanwhile, General Mora's nine companies had entered the district from the Rondas and the Paralelo, the two boulevards that completed the triangle, and began to work their way across the district. They were immediately fired upon by a sniper in the vicinity of the Piarist school; a squad was dispatched to search for him, while troops continued to make their way toward the Ramblas. Despite the many barricades, General Santiago reported they encountered no further difficulties, "nor any person in the streets nor visible on the rooftops." After the entire area had been traversed, and guard posts set up along the way, General Mora ordered a house-to-house search for arms that uncovered numerous revolvers, but only twenty rifles.

Meanwhile, another contingent of soldiers and police had worked its way up from the waterfront to meet General Mora's troops. In these narrow streets, where fighting had been most intense, snipers occasionally harassed the troops, but because these shots did not interfere with their work, soldiers did not respond. They forced men lounging in the many taverns to tear down the barricades. This done, the troops began a search of suspicious houses.

Long before dawn troops succeeded in occupying the rooftops throughout the district. The narrow, dark streets fell silent for the first time that week.

Rebel leaders had obviously decided that their only chance of success was to concentrate their forces in the industrial suburbs north of the city. The task of restoring order in this, the most rebellious sector of the metropolis, had been given to General Germán Brandeis.[18] His assignment to the Radical strongholds of Pueblo Nuevo and Clot seems to have been a shrewd move by the Captain General, because Brandeis had been a hero to Radical party members since he had led army officers against Catalan regionalists at the time of the *Cu-Cut* incident. From the outset of the General Strike, Brandeis had been widely applauded each time he appeared on the street; at times he would graciously acknowledge the cheers before dispersing the crowds. However, he was first and foremost an officer; born in Germany and trained in his native army, Brandeis demonstrated his determination to restore order in the industrial suburbs, even if it were necessary to employ cannon fire to do so. On Thursday morning he had concentrated on the savage revolt in Pueblo Nuevo; once order was re-established, Brandeis went to Clot to direct operations there.

Mobs in San Andrés were therefore left to their own devices. Although they used this respite to build two more barricades, they proved far more interested in burning convents. Late in the afternoon they set so intense a fire in the parish church that it burned for thirty hours.[19] The Marists interpreted this as a warning; the 110 individuals left their handsome new building and sought refuge with the religious who staffed a nearby insane asylum. Refused admittance, the Marists set out in small groups to walk thirty-six kilometers to their residence in Garriga.[20]

By this time a group of incendiaries, led by Pedro Duaso and Francisco Queralt, had entered the Marist property.[21] When they came upon a flock of chickens, they halted their destructive task and went to a nearby tavern, where they waited while the chickens were roasted. Only after they had feasted, did Queralt lead his men out to a warehouse where they seized fifteen liters of gasoline. The group then returned to the Marist residence. One rebel leader, Pedro Duaso, laid aside the shotgun he had been sporting for the past few days in order to indulge his religious hatred. He fell with a frenzy upon the religious images, beheading them and quartering the bodies before he threw them onto a bonfire, which he stirred until no splinter remained.

Exhilarated, encouraged by their easy success, men in San Andrés prepared for another day of convent burnings just at the moment when elsewhere in the city such activities were being terminated.

In Clot, a district similar in social composition to that of Pueblo Nuevo, workers were far more serious in their attempt at rebellion. The fighting took on epic proportions as rebels fired from housetops; barricades were used only to obstruct the passage of troops.[22] Radical politician Zurdo Olivares could not be forced out upon the street again; yet even though they had no leaders, men fought intensely and bravely. Here as in Pueblo Nuevo, they fired directly at army troops and disregarded the nice distinction maintained by Radical leaders elsewhere that only police forces were to be fired upon. In the fighting, a sergeant died and six soldiers were wounded.[23]

In mid-afternoon, General Brandeis arrived to direct the troops in Clot, having concluded the military operation in Pueblo Nuevo. He ordered that the cannons be brought from that suburb. Meanwhile he ordered troops to enter and occupy houses along the highway. When the cannons first arrived they were fired against a house where rebels had been concentrated; afterwards they swept the highway. Yet even during the artillery fire, snipers continued to harass the Civil Guards. Before he left Clot, Brandeis stationed

Asia infantry troops on strategic rooftops. This was an unnecessary precaution for fifteen cannon shots had effectively ended the fighting in Clot.

It had not, however, ended the rebellion, despite the assertion of Interior Minister La Cierva in Madrid. Late Thursday evening he issued a communiqué on the fighting in the Clot-San Martín suburb and reported that "the principal leaders of the uprising" were among those who had fought in Clot, and had "finally surrendered with their arms." Announcing that this marked the end of the rebellion, La Cierva promised to supply the press with details. Newsmen smiled cynically as days went by and no report was forthcoming: the fighting in Barcelona had not yet ended.[24]

Friday, July 30

On Friday recalcitrant rebels fled first to San Andrés and then to Horta, where they concentrated on concluding the campaign of burning convents rather than on street fighting. This made it easier for General Santiago to restore order elsewhere in Barcelona. His task was further facilitated by the arrival of two more infantry companies (the Luchana Regiment from Tortosa, and the Mallorca Regiment from Valencia). Even more significant from the viewpoint of public order were the three hundred Civil Guards who immediately upon arrival were sent out on patrol duty.[1]

The arrival of these forces made it possible for the Saboya infantry regiment to embark for Melilla. Barcelona residents watched quietly as the troops marched down the Ramblas toward the wharf. The protest against the war, the ostensible cause of the insurrection, seemed forgotten after the holocaust of the preceding four days. One worker did remember. "It hardly seems possible that you, with rifles in your hands," shouted Ramón Escuder at the soldiers, "would let yourselves be led off to a slaughterhouse." Surrounded by an unprotesting crowd, army officers arrested Escuder.[2]

Numerous soldiers and Civil Guards continued to patrol the Atarazana district until midafternoon, even though there were no disorders; one brisk exchange of fire with unseen snipers ended as soon as it began. At the Piarist school, General Santiago stationed Civil Guards far in excess of those required by the smouldering ruins and regained thereby a site abandoned to the incendiaries on Tuesday afternoon; the action signified his reassertion of authority in the Radical domain.[3]

General Santiago made a concerted effort to restore public confidence. The Bank of Spain even opened a few hours for business. The Captain

General concentrated particularly on restoring public utilities, a difficult task because the rebels had done considerable damage. Streets had been darkened since Monday night, except in those few neighborhoods that enjoyed the luxury of electricity. Repairmen worked all day on gas mains but succeeded in restoring street lights only in the central district.

Streetcars could not resume service due to the numerous rails that had been torn up. As a gesture, late in the afternoon one streetcar made its regular run through working-class neighborhoods, up the Calle Balmes to Sarriá.

Shortly before noon citizens had returned to the streets, happy to be released from confinement after four hot and humid days. To Catholic propagandist Villaescusa, venturing out for the first time, it seemed that the public reacted splendidly; a few private carriages circulated up and down the main streets, apparently in an effort to encourage people to come out onto the streets.[4] Republican Deputy Amadeo Hurtado, characteristically independent, found something unpleasant in the scene as people "in great numbers went to visit the ruins of the fires with the usual delight [afforded by] a free spectacle."[5]

Among those who strolled the streets on Friday, for the first time that week, was Senator Odón de Buen, who had for years advocated establishing a republic through revolution. But when, in the course of his excursion, mysterious shots suddenly rang out, the dignified Senator took refuge in a public garden because, reported a gardener, he was "very frightened."[6] The republican politician was not the only one. "No one dared to stay out on the streets," declared Villaescusa, "because the firing did not cease."[7]

Some of these mysterious shots were fired by die-hard rebels who refused to give up without a struggle, as for example Antonio Terradés Caballé who had gained renown for his exploits during the week. On Friday morning the fifty-year-old Terradés had dutifully reported for work in the slaughter-house; when finished he went to a tavern where he drank heavily, then left to join an armed gang that had installed itself in the ruins of the convent of the Servants of Mary, located near the Radicals' Casa del Pueblo. At 4 P.M. a detachment of Alcántara cavalry surrounded and charged the convent, but heavy insurgent fire prevented them from entering the building until 6 P.M. They found Antonio Terradés, wounded and unarmed, watching over his three dead companions. He volunteered to lead the soldiers to the rebels' hiding place and set off across the Plaza de Letamendi, the troops following close behind. Suddenly a volley of shots rang out; three soldiers were killed.

Too late they realized they had walked into a trap. Muttering "Vengeance, vengeance," Terradés was led off to prison.[8]

Such incidents were rare. Most of the hidden snipers remained undetected.

From Thursday afternoon until Saturday night, these unseen snipers continued to fire from rooftops, harassing army troops who patrolled the streets where order had been restored. *Los tíos pacos** constituted the mystery of the week, in part because they went undetected, in part because these hidden snipers fired at soldiers and officers, abandoning the policy expressed in the shouts of "Viva el Ejército" (Hail the Army) that had marked the early stages of the uprising.

No mystery at all, snapped General Santiago and ex-Governor Ossorio.[9] The snipers were simply die-hard Radicals and anarchists who, defeated in the streets, continued their desperate fight from the rooftops. Socialists, anarchists, and republicans in general refuted this charge. They asserted that the "authentic" rebels had already begun to cross the frontier into France in order to escape arrest, and claimed that the hidden snipers were clergy or lay accomplices whose purpose was "to provoke and compel" the newly arrived troops into carrying out "a harsh repression." [10] This "very jesuitical maneuver of priests and monks" was successful, reported Fabra Rivas, and "the street encounters became more bloody than they had ever been before." [11]

Several incidents seemed to substantiate the charge, particularly those in the Ensanche district where workers did not live and where most of the sniping occurred. From a house on the corner of Aribau and Diputación, two friars reportedly fired on troops and on civilians, and one was detained when he attempted to flee, revolver in hand.[12] The Ensanche police chief, Antonio Andrade, filed an official report on "some priests dressed in civilian clothing [who] fired upon the troops" from a house at number 183 of the Calle Aragón; the police chief of Barcelona forwarded this report to General Santiago in the belief that he would want to prosecute the occupants of the buildings from which the shots had been fired (as Santiago had warned in his edict).**

---

* *Los tíos pacos* was a term first used to describe the sharpshooters of the Moroccan campaigns. The word *paco* represents an attempt to imitate the short, sharp sound of rifle fire.

** The disposition of the case, concerning the incident on the Calle Aragón, is not reported in the official trial transcript (for the police report sent to army prosecutors see *Causa: Rebelión militar,* I, 256). In the Cortes, Emiliano Iglesias reported that an

The authenticity of these and other incidents was difficult to verify in an atmosphere of such general suspicion. On the Calle Tapiolas in the slum district of Pueblo Seco, for example, a concealed sniper fired continuously all day Friday at patrolling soldiers. Neighbors were convinced it was an outsider attempting to provoke soldiers into taking reprisals against the workers. One republican source said the culprit escaped undetected, while anarchist Bonafulla reported that the sniper was arrested and found to be a wealthy member of a Catholic club, dressed in laborer's clothing.[13] The Catholic Carlists denied all these charges, countering with the claim that some snipers disguised themselves as clergy and fired in order to anger the Army against the religious and thus prevent it from defending clerical property.[14]

Whatever be the explanation, there were serious consequences of this mysterious sniping.[15] For the city at large, it embittered the restoration of order and prolonged the process until Saturday night. For Emiliano Iglesias, it complicated his negotiations to exonerate Radical party officials.

On Friday morning Iglesias intensified these efforts when military authorities made clear their intention to prosecute officials as well as the rank and file. Early that morning they had arrested a prominent leader of the Jóvenes Bárbaros, Rafael Guerra del Río, as he left a meeting with two other officials of the Juventud Radical, Angel de Borjas and Dr. Rafael Canales. Although he was generally believed to have played a major role in organizing the disorders, Guerra del Río had studiously avoided being seen on the streets during the uprising. Therefore his arrest, witnessed by a small crowd on the Ramblas, was based on the minor charge that he wore a false Red Cross arm band.[16]

Iglesias meanwhile, was meeting with a "commission of revolutionaries in order to study the means whereby the repression would not be carried out blindly." The commission told him — or threatened him? — that his continued presence in Barcelona would be "a guarantee for the tranquillity of all involved." [17] A large group of rebels from the suburb of Clot, where a fierce battle had been fought the previous day, secured from Iglesias a promise that "come what may, I will be in Barcelona to save myself and my men, or to suffer the same consequences." [18]

---

army officer (Lieutenant Rafael Santamaría) tried to secure an indictment in the Calle Aragón incident; Lieutenant Santamaría was not only unsuccessful, he was himself prosecuted (July 6 and July 11, 1910, *Diario de las Cortes,* II, 405, 508).

Their principal hope, Iglesias told one group of revolutionaries, was "to interest the corporations in a benign solution"—[19] that is, to have Barcelona's civic and business organizations request clemency for all those participating in the insurrection. Time was of the essence on Friday, so Iglesias decided first to persuade leaders of all political factions in the City Council to recommend clemency, a recommendation which could then be presented to the Captain General as a nonpartisan measure.

A Catalan Nationalist city councilor, Trinidad Monegal, agreed to co-sponsor this proposal. Both Monegal and Iglesias claimed they met at the city hall quite by chance on Friday morning, yet it seems more than coincidence that spokesmen for the political groups most active in the insurrection should most diligently seek protection against prosecution. The two men went to Mayor Coll y Pujol, requesting that he present their proposal to the business community, and that he approve a meeting of the same municipal politicians who had assembled on Tuesday morning. When he agreed to both measures, Iglesias and Monegal immediately issued a joint invitation to the politicians for a meeting that was scheduled for the following morning.[20]

Political attempts at pacification were complicated by the continuing disorders in San Andrés. In reality, these events were due more to an absence of effective law enforcement than to any revolutionary zeal. When General Brandeis was finally free to concentrate on San Andrés, he occupied the suburb with ease. In the interim, incendiaries completed their destruction of the Marist buildings early in the morning and went on to burn two additional educational institutions. Of their own largess they decided not to burn an asylum for the aged.

The attack upon the handsome new school for working-class girls run by the Sisters of the Congregation of Jesus and Mary, was a routine affair. Beginning at noon scavengers used hand carts to carry off the furnishings. The fire did little damage to the building, but a new one could not be kindled immediately because incendiaries were at work elsewhere.[21]

Beginning at 4 P.M., they looted and burned the provincial house of the Congregation of Sons of the Holy Family, the storehouse of books and supplies for the schools of this order throughout Catalonia. Lamenting that the attack "came toward the end of the disorders, when hope of salvation had already appeared," the fathers were still hopeful that neighbors would help. They did not, because incendiaries threatened to burn the home of anyone who did so.[22]

In the interval between the burning of the two schools, the incendiaries decided not to burn the large asylum run by sisters of the Congregation of the Holy Family of Urgel even though urged on by "several revolutionary women"; this was only the second such instance in Barcelona.* Some two hundred neighbors rallied to defend this shelter for numerous old people, while rebels left behind two armed guards, lest some other group try to burn the asylum.[23]

The incendiarism completed, activists had really no objection to allowing General Brandeis to occupy the suburb. Anticipating resistance, the General had arrived at the outskirts of San Andrés with several pieces of artillery and two squadrons. Ordering his men to rest, Brandeis stopped a passing cyclist and instructed him to tell the townspeople that if within one hour all barricades had not been torn down, he would bombard the town. When the hour passed, the General entered San Andrés with no opposition. What he saw apparently convinced him not to bombard the town. Residents had not even been near the barricades since José Miquel Baró attacked the Civil Guards barracks on Wednesday afternoon. General Brandeis' "presence alone calmed their spirits," reported the Radical newspaper; people surrounded Brandeis "lovingly, when he stopped his horse to converse with those individuals whose hearts had been inflamed with hatred of the war." [24]

However, incendiaries did not allow the affectionate reception of General Brandeis to interfere with their returning the following day (Saturday) to complete the burning of the school of the Sisters of Jesus and Mary. Only then did workers resume their duties in the factories of San Andrés.

The peaceful reconciliation between the Army and the workers of San Andrés was possible because the most militant fighters had fled to the nearby suburb of Horta, the site of the last fighting of the week.

Horta was an incongruous setting for the finale of a rebellion. Located far from the center of Barcelona, it did have a small commercial area inhabited by workers, but most of the suburb consisted of expensive summer homes

---

* Not one of the establishments of the Sisters of the Congregation of the Holy Family of Urgel (four in Barcelona and four more in the province) was attacked during the week. In contrast, all three establishments of the Congregation of the Sons of the Holy Family were burned. Both were Catalan orders, both were relatively new (the sisters had organized their community in 1866, the fathers in 1877), and both were primarily teaching orders. Apparently the Congregation of the Holy Family of Urgel had mastered the difficult task of caring for the poor in a more effective way than had the Congregation of the Sons of the Holy Family.

Horta had been quiet all week until the arrival of men fleeing from the troops.

Here as elsewhere, the Radical center was the focal point of the disorders.[25] Its president, Ramón Font y Folch, was an influential member of the party's extremist faction.[26] On Friday he returned to Horta to direct the revolt, having fought the previous three days in the Atarazana district where Emiliano Iglesias had gone out on the street to confer with him. Font could count on the help of Andrés Grau, the violently anticlerical porter of the Radical center, but found few other volunteers.

Therefore, it was necessary to hire incendiaries for a fee of seven pesetas, fifty céntimos per individual.* A mysterious Juan Alemán came on Friday night to dispense funds to a group composed of forty-nine individuals, including two boys fourteen years of age.[27]

At midnight they burned the lovely sixteenth-century parish Church of San Juan[28] and then went across the street to plunder and partially destroy a school run by a Third Order of Dominican Sisters.[29] The building was empty, for the sisters had fled on Tuesday; they undoubtedly found no compensation for their losses in the knowledge that theirs was the last convent to be burned in Barcelona during the Tragic Week.

Saturday, July 31

Barcelona "initiated tranquillity," to use General Santiago's phrase: government officials returned to work, most storekeepers did business, and banks opened for a few hours. Citizens were encouraged by the Captain General's third and final edict of the week, posted throughout the city at dawn, which authorized them to circulate freely through the streets.[1] The edict was reassuring only because city residents knew that there were sufficient forces to implement it: Santiago was rumored to have 10,000 men at his command,[2] which was at least three times as many as the actual number of troops in the city.

The bands of ragged men, women, and children evacuated the public thoroughfares of the city; their place was taken by ordinary pedestrians, as well as by public and private vehicles. Soldiers guarded market places, where housewives found plentiful supplies of fresh food.

Repairmen continued their work. Wagons cleared away the debris while laborers employed by the city dismantled the barricades and set the paving

* Military authorities tried but failed to prove that Francisco Ferrer had supplied the funds to pay the incendiaries; see pages 299–300.

stones back in place. Work continued on telegraph and telephone wires; however such extensive damage had been done that only official messages could be transmitted. By afternoon sufficient streetcar rails had been repaired to enable a few lines to function regularly.

City officials were anxious to cover over all signs of an insurrection before 170 German tourists were allowed to disembark from their ship, armed with cameras. They were the vanguard of hundreds of foreigners who visited Barcelona that summer in order to view the site of a popular uprising. Mayor Coll y Pujol did everything within his power to impress the Germans, receiving them in his office and accompanying them through the city hall. For the tour of historic sites, he assigned them an escort of municipal policemen (Guardia Urbana), arrayed in their new scarlet uniforms. Refusing to be distracted, the tourists stopped along the streets to photograph the burned convents and the few empty barricades that still remained.[3] And they may possibly have heard the shots that rang out at intervals during the day.

There were scattered pockets of resistance. At 1130 A.M., snipers fired from rooftops across the street from the San Agustino artillery barracks but fled immediately when pursued by an officer and a handful of soldiers. In the slum district of Pueblo Seco, a large mob completed the burning of the rectory of the Santa Madrona parish church. Up in the wealthy Ensanche area, a small band defiantly continued to occupy the residence of the Vincentian Fathers, and rang the chapel bells so that no one could say they were hiding.[4]

Throughout the Ensanche, mysterious snipers fired sporadically on passing army patrols. If the intent were really to provoke troops into carrying out a harsh repression, it was successful and particularly so in the case of Civil Guards who had borne the brunt of the week's fighting. They were inclined to fire and investigate later, a policy that had tragic consequences in an incident[5] occurring at the ruins of the convent-school of the *Beatas Dominicas,* where incendiaries had proudly painted upon the walls: "Hail the revolution and the teachers of Catalonia."

Since early morning hundreds had visited the ruins, even though nothing remained to carry off. The crowds were inspired by a macabre curiosity to inspect the corpses of the semicloistered order for evidence of torture, and to view the tremendous destruction. By midmorning there may have been as many as 1,500 persons within the block-wide grounds of the convent. The Civil Guards' repeated warnings to disperse were ignored. When more people entered the building, the Guards sent for reinforcements. At 11 A.M., they surrounded the building; what followed became a matter for controversy. Guards reported that they fired into the air in order to frighten the people, whom they considered merely scavengers, and that men inside the convent fired back. Labor spokesmen insisted that the Guards had fired without provocation on a defenseless crowd of sightseers. Both versions are possible; some men may have carried weapons and replied to the fire of the Guards.*

The shooting panicked the crowd which started to force its way out onto the street. Civil Guards shot and killed the first six men to emerge and wounded many more. They arrested approximately forty to fifty individuals whom they released, without charges, twenty days later. In the words of socialist José Comaposada, this was "the last episode, the bloody epilogue" of the Barcelona insurrection.[6]

Away from the street, up in the more rarefied realm inhabited by politicians, Emiliano Iglesias deftly maneuvered to restore order with as few recriminations as possible. The occasion was a meeting, in the home of Lliga politician Narciso Verdaguer, of those city councilors who spoke for the major political parties. All five men who had attended the Tuesday meeting in the Mayor's office were present: Verdaguer, Iglesias, Catalan Nationalist Monegal, Lliga Councilor Puig y Alfonso, and Republican Councilor Ramoneda. They were joined by Radical Councilor Valenti Camps, and by republican councilors J. Roca y Roca and Lacambra.

Iglesias took the initiative, his prerogative as the organizer of the meeting. His proposal was prefaced with an expression of deep regret about the events, and a fervent desire to cooperate in the re-establishment of order. Specifically he proposed that an ad hoc committee be formed, composed of representatives of all parties, which would impress upon General Santiago the urgency of having all factories and shops begin work on Monday morning. As a means of encouraging workers to return to their jobs, the ad hoc committee would ask General Santiago to issue a statement clarifying the legal distinction among the three types of crimes committed (burnings, lootings, and street fighting), and the penalty corresponding to each crime. According to Lliga Councilor Puig y Alfonso, Emiliano Iglesias recommended that the

---

* A Catalan journalist reported that after the Tragic Week, "The Browning is now more than a weapon for *lerrouxistas;* it is an ideal. A *lerrouxista* without his Browning is like a Catholic without his rosary." (*La Metralla* [Barcelona], March 10, 1910.)

full penalties stipulated by law be applied to those arrested for burning, plundering, or profaning convents, while benevolence should be shown toward crimes of a political nature* — that is, of those persons "dragged into the rebellion because of a political ideal." [7]

Verdaguer said that even if the Captain General were willing to consider the proposal, he was certain to inquire what municipal politicians intended "to contribute" to the re-establishment of order. Pointedly, the Lliga party leader asked Iglesias, "as chief of the local political party designated as the principal participant in the events in question, and as the director or advisor of the daily organ, to state whether he would be able to offer the use of those powerful media in an attempt to have all rebellion cease and the establishment of order guaranteed." Iglesias declared that he would "with pleasure, pledge his word to carry out those measures," although he wished to record officially his personal sympathy for the protest against the war. [8]

After further discussion the councilors agreed to recommend that the Captain General issue a statement defining the crimes and their punishments. They rejected the idea of a partisan committee and decided instead, as they had earlier in the week, that the Mayor should speak for the municipality. Verdaguer telephoned Mayor Coll y Pujol to ask that he present their proposals to the Captain General and to the business community. When he agreed to do so, the councilors scheduled another meeting for five o'clock that afternoon, at which time they would learn what the Mayor had been able to accomplish.

Emiliano Iglesias did not appear at the five o'clock meeting. On his way to the city hall he was arrested, to his great surprise, for he had counted on his immunity as an elected municipal official and on his painstaking effort to avoid direct implication. [9]

* Iglesias' rather surprising statement in this meeting merits a word of explanation for it indicates the strategy which the Radical party was to follow in extricating itself from the legal and political problems resulting from the uprising. By affirming that all felonies (looting and burning) would be punished, Iglesias was seeking the support of his colleagues and the middle class groups they represented in order to re-establish order rapidly in Barcelona. Yet Iglesias could comfort Radical party members who were prosecuted by pointing out that these crimes would be tried in civil courts, before popular juries, and that defendants would have the benefit of the Radicals' platoon of eloquent young lawyers. All those who had taken part in the armed rebellion (that is, those charged with the crime of treason) would be tried before tribunals of army officers; for these men, guilty of "political crimes" to use Iglesias' term, the Radical leader hoped to secure the help of all political parties in urging benevolence. For further details, see pages 285–87.

Army officers immediately began their interrogation. At most, Iglesias would admit he was a member of the Radical party, but he denied that he "formed, or had formed, part of any executive board or of any center." Iglesias declared that he had gone only three or four times to the Casa del Pueblo since Lerroux's departure, a year and a half earlier, "because of his antagonism towards three or four individuals who . . . acted as if they owned the building." Interrogators tried to make this a policy matter, and to have Iglesias identify as the extremist faction those "individuals" to whom he was opposed — "the Ulled brothers, Vinaixa, other persons of the tendency of such men within the Radical party." Iglesias refused to commit himself. Admitting that he had been elected to the City Council by Radical party members, Iglesias told interrogators that he was considering resigning because Radicals considered him "a traitor" for having collaborated with authorities during the week.[10]

In this interrogation, Emiliano Iglesias continued the devious and somewhat ignoble task of dissociating himself from the events of the Tragic Week. Only when it came time for elections in the following year, and when he was free from prosecution, did Iglesias extol the rebels and glorify the events.

Despite Emiliano Iglesias' absence, city councilors met with Mayor Coll y Pujol. Apparently General Santiago was unwilling to promise clemency or to specify the crimes and their penalties; at least no communiqué was issued.

The Mayor had been more successful in talks with representatives of the all-powerful "corporations" that controlled Barcelona society. Business leaders had promised to open the factories on Monday morning and to pay all employees who reported for work on that day their full salary for the preceding week. This could not be officially announced because it was only a recommendation and not legally binding on individual employers; yet word of this promise spread through all working-class neighborhoods. Observers generally agreed that the promise to pay workers' salaries, more than any other single measure, accounted for the pacific resumption of work on Monday morning.[11]

Horta was the last outpost of rebel resistance. Although the fifty or sixty men who looted and burned in this suburb were hopelessly outnumbered by army troops and Civil Guards, they continued fighting until subdued. Poor, deluded Alfonso Monreal insisted they were "going to carry out the revolution." [12] In the exchange of gunfire that continued all morning, one rebel was killed and two were critically injured, while the officer commanding the troops was seriously wounded.[13] As soon as the fighting was over, Radical leader Ramón Font fled to France.*

The rebellion in Barcelona had ended, its grand finale somewhat demeaned by the admission of some of the prisoners that they had accepted a fee for participating in the burnings.

Sunday, August 1

The day was scarcely to be distinguished from any normal Sunday. Not a shot was fired in Barcelona or in the suburbs. All streetcar lines were in operation, beginning early in the morning. Even flower vendors opened their stalls along the Ramblas.

Early in the morning the Mayor's edict, formally reporting the results of his negotiations with the business community, was posted throughout the city. He announced "with satisfaction" that all business establishments would open the following day, Monday, and expressed the "hope that workers will respond to this summons." [1]

Mass was said in all churches that had not been burned. Great numbers of friars and nuns whose own chapels had been destroyed were to be seen in parish churches. In Nuestra Señora de los Angeles, a church belonging to one order of Dominican Sisters that was located just a few blocks from the ravaged Piarist schools, a Te Deum was sung for the miraculous salvation of their convent.

Governor Ossorio left his mountain hideaway by ship for Valencia, en route to Madrid.** As he embarked, he overheard the Captain suggest to the ship's owner that he be put in the special luxury cabin. "For God's sake be quiet," replied the owner. "He isn't governor any more. Put the wine

---

* Ramón Font remained in France until 1911, when he returned and was elected a city councilor from Horta. In 1912 a military tribunal reviewed his case and unanimously condemned him to death, whereupon Font again fled to France. (*El Progreso* [Barcelona], November 11 and 12, 1911, January 3, 1912, and January 14, 1913; and Pedro Sangro y Ros de Alano, *La Sombra de Ferrer: De la "Semana Trágica" a la guerra europea* [Madrid, 1917], pp. 403–04.)

** Ossorio's behavior during the Tragic Week almost completely destroyed his political career. He was never again appointed a governor. He was a minister only once, in 1919 when Maura headed a coalition government for a few months. Not until the Civil War (1936) was he appointed ambassador. Ossorio did, however, retain his seat in the Cortes and remained active in Conservative party affairs; he led the faction that remained loyal to Maura.

merchant in the special cabin." Ossorio went off to his humbler quarters, consoling himself with "Sic transit gloria mundi." [2]

The leaders of the rebellion, who left Barcelona in an even more modest fashion, undoubtedly echoed Ossorio in sentiment if not in Latin.

On the previous afternoon, Miguel V. Moreno and anarchist Francisco Miranda had sent two messengers to Mas Germinal, Ferrer's farm near Masnou, with a request for funds. Soledad Villafranca received them and then allowed the men to talk with Ferrer, who was hiding in caves located on his property. He gave them 1,000 pesetas for the trip, together with instructions for Moreno about its distribution. Ferrer told Moreno and Miranda to wait for him in Marseilles. He himself planned to remain in hiding until the police had relaxed their vigil, when he could then slip over the frontier into France and direct a new campaign against the Maura government.[3] Reportedly disgruntled by the small sum of money,[4] Moreno and Miranda walked out to where the railroad tracks had been torn up, then took a train intending to leave Spain by ship from Valencia.*

In the afternoon, editors of all Barcelona newspapers gathered in the offices of *El Diluvio* and appointed a committee which went to request from General Santiago a policy statement on what he would permit them to report about the events. The Captain General replied that they could not report in detail. Thereupon the newspapermen selected the editor of *La Veu de Catalunya,* the Lliga organ, and the editor of *El Liberal,* part of the national chain of Liberal newspapers (Sociedad Editorial de España, known generally as the "Trust") to prepare a summary account of the events. General Santiago approved the summary and it was published by all newspapers in their Monday editions.[5]

The remarkably smooth transition from a rebellion to normality was threatened briefly by some of the indomitable women who had played so prominent a role throughout the week. Late in the afternoon these women marched through the streets of the northern suburbs — the battle area — and demanded that all prisoners be set at liberty; they warned that workers would not return to the factories until this was done.[6] Such a demand found

* After waiting several days in Graus, in the province of Valencia, the men decided the police cordon was too effective to leave by sea. With the help of Dr. Manuel Navarro Mingote (who was subsequently prosecuted because of this), they escaped to France across the Aragonese frontier. (*Causa: Rebelión militar,* I, 570. II, 12, 101–02, 135, 139–40. Constant Leroy [Miguel V. Moreno], *El Correo Español* [Mexico City], January 7, 1913.)

no response among crowds whose revolutionary fervor had completely burned itself out.

On Monday morning, at 6:30 A.M., men and women reported for work at the factories; no incidents of any kind were reported. The Tragic Week had ended in Barcelona.

CHAPTER XII

The Tally Sheet

THE REBELLION ended and the repression began — a repression that included not only the prosecution of individuals charged with crimes of treason or of felony, but the closing of lay schools and labor unions as institutions inculcating civil disobedience and violent anticlericalism.

On Monday, August 2, as workers returned to the factories, a military tribunal conducted its first trial under summary procedures: Ramón Baldera Aznar was convicted of armed rebellion for his part in the street fighting, and he was sentenced to life imprisonment.[1] Baldera was neither a politician nor a rebel leader; he was simply one of the countless, nondescript persons caught up in the rebellion because of a political ideal, or simply by the excitement of a battle.

Four days after Baldera's trial, Maura appointed a new Governor, Evaristo Crespo Azorín, who had no other political distinction than that of being a personal friend of Interior Minister La Cierva. Crespo's first decision was to continue the suspension of newspapers published by the Catalan Nationalists, the Radicals, the anarchists, and Solidaridad Obrera.[2] In order to gather evidence on the general origins of the rebellion, Maura sent to Barcelona the Attorney General (*Fiscal del Tribunal Supremo*), Javier de Ugarte, known as a "clerical politician." Ugarte arrived on August 8 and during the following two weeks consulted primarily with Catholic organizations.[3] On the day he left, August 24, Governor Crespo ordered the closing of 94 lay schools and 34 "centers of advanced ideas" in the province of Barcelona; two days later an additional 26 schools were closed.[4] These included some of the oldest and most distinguished private schools. Solidaridad Obrera and other labor organizations remained closed.

Martial law continued in force in Catalonia until November 7, and in the rest of Spain until September 27. Not until October 14, when Maura opened the Cortes, could his opponents begin the bitter debate — that continues today — of whether the harsh repression was justified by the crimes committed.

Therefore at this point, midway between the Tragic Week and its decisive national consequences, it is important to summarize the crimes actually committed, together with the sentences imposed by military and civilian courts. The concern is not only to see how closely the sentence fitted the offense in individual cases, but to see if those most responsible for the events were actually punished.

General Analysis of the Prisoners

In the month of August, 990 individuals were arrested (approximately one third of the total number detained).* Two generalizations about this initial group of prisoners have political significance: the minute foreign element, and the large majority of native Catalans.

Conservative groups contended that the insurrection had international connections and that foreigners had participated.[5] Yet only 13 foreigners were held for trial and none were charged with being leaders.** This number was insignificant in view of the fact that Barcelona was a seaport located near the frontier, and that numbers of Italian and French had come to work in the textile factories.

Far more decisive for domestic politics was the report issued by the Captain General, almost the only data he supplied voluntarily to the press, which encouraged the impression deliberately created by Interior Minister La Cierva — namely, that the events constituted a Catalan separatist movement. According to Santiago's report, 60 percent of the prisoners had been born in Catalonia; 18 percent in Valencia; 15 percent in Aragón; five percent in Castile; two percent in Andalusia.[6] To the report was added the comment that of the

---

* More than 2,000 individuals fled from Catalonia to France. However, many of these went to avoid conscription into the Army and not because of complicity in the events. (Circular published in the Boletín Oficial of Barcelona on August 13, 1909, as reprinted in Soldevilla, Año político, XV: 1909, 291; and General Linares, Minister of War, October 20, 1909, Diario de las Cortes, p. 76.)

** Of the 13 foreigners held for trial, six were Frenchmen, two Cubans, two Argentines, two Swiss, and one Algerian (El Correo Catalán [Barcelona], August 29, 1909). In addition, some 40 foreigners who were professional criminals or prostitutes were expelled from Spain (Salvador Canals, Los Sucesos de España en 1909: Crónica documentada, I [Madrid, 1910], 211).

40 percent non-Catalan prisoners, many had lived for years in Barcelona and had married there; they could thus be considered Catalans. Despite the angry protest of Barcelona politicians, led by Republican Deputy Laureano Miró, the erroneous impression persisted that the insurrection was inspired by Catalan separatism.

The predominance of Catalan workers among the prisoners had deeper significance. For years Catalan politicians had been saying that Lerroux had no real support in Barcelona, that he recruited exclusively among men and women who came from other provinces to work in the factories. Whether the Catalan prisoners were members of the Radical party, or whether they merely followed its lead during the Tragic Week, their participation indicates that social and religious issues had far more appeal to workers than did a program emphasizing only loyalty to Catalonia. The inability of Catalan republican politicians, either before or after 1909, to combine these forces — social and religious reform, and Catalan regional pride — into a positive political program left the workers of Catalonia vulnerable to demagogues.

The Crimes: Felonies versus Armed Rebellion

Spanish law divided into two categories the crimes committed during the Tragic Week. The bearing of arms and participation in the construction of barricades were construed as crimes of armed rebellion (*rebelión militar*) — that is, as crimes of treason. Attacks upon public utilities or transportation (including streetcars) were also included in this category. These cases were tried before military tribunals. The looting or burning of convents, together with attacks upon the person of the clergy, were classified as felonies and assigned to the jurisdiction of civil courts; unless individuals so charged had also participated in the street fighting, they were not tried until late in the fall when civil courts again began to function.

The attacks upon the convents had constituted the most extensive and most popular element in the uprising. Given the absence of effective forces of public order and the potential of large mobs agitated by years of anticlerical propaganda, casualties and damages were relatively low despite six days of convent burnings.

Only three clergy were killed, all on Tuesday at the outset of the campaign. Two of them were shot: Swiss-born Brother Lycarion (Francisco Benjamin Mey) of the Marist Workers' Foundation in Pueblo Nuevo, and the Franciscan Monk Ramón María Usó of San Gervasio. Both religious were directors of their residences. The third clergyman, Father Ramón Ríu, the parish priest of Santa María del Taulat in Pueblo Nuevo, died on Tuesday evening of suffocation and shock while hiding in the basement of the burned church.

In addition, Father Pedro Bergés of the Congregation of Missionary Sons of the Immaculate Heart of Mary was shot and blinded in one eye. Father Bergés, like the Franciscan Monk and the elderly Capuchin Nun in San Gervasio, was attacked while attempting to protect stocks and cash belonging to his religious community.

Considering that many in the crowds carried pistols, and that hatred of the clergy was intense, it is remarkable that only three members of the clergy were killed, only two of them deliberately. As a Jesuit observer noted, such a situation implied control exercised over the mobs by leaders who wanted a bloodless anticlerical demonstration.

The objective was to destroy the property — the wealth — of the clergy. The achievement was impressive: according to the official report of the acting Bishop of Barcelona, 12 churches and 40 convents or religious establishments were destroyed.[7] A few days earlier he had reported only 30 convents burned,[8] a discrepancy that reflects the difficulty of determining how many convents were assaulted but not burned, and how many fires did little or no damage. Other discrepancies must be ascribed to political and personal considerations.*

For obvious political reasons, the clergy published no estimate of the total value of property destroyed. In comparative terms, fewer than half the total number of religious establishments in Barcelona were burned.** Given the

---

* The Captain General, anxious to defend himself against charges of negligence, reported that only 27 churches and convents were burned ("Copia de las comunicaciones del Capitán General de la 4.ª Región dando cuenta de los sucesos ocurridos en Cataluña durante los días 26 al 31 de julio de 1909," dated August 20, 1909, page 7 of Appendix 1 to the fourth session [October 19] of the 1909 legislature, *Diario de las cortes*). Senator Sol y Ortega, concerned with exonerating Radical defendants, said only a total of 38 religious buildings were destroyed ("Una casi interviú," *El País*, August 4, 1909). Interior Minister La Cierva, in order to justify a harsh repression, said that 61 religious buildings had been burned (October 19, 1909, *Diario de las Cortes*, p. 61).

** Although their figures vary, most politicians estimated that less than one-half the total number of religious establishments in Barcelona had been attacked. Interior Minister La Cierva declared that 61 of a total of 148 churches and convents in Barcelona were burned, to which Catalan republican deputy Juan Moles replied that "the latter figure "underestimates while the former exaggerates" (October 19, 1909, *Diario de las Cortes*, p. 61). Liberal party leader Segismundo Moret said that 51 of 133 religious institutions were destroyed: 21 of the 58 churches and 30 of the 75 convents (October 18, 1909, *ibid.*, p. 25). The Captain General reported that 27 of 160 religious buildings were burned (p. 7 of Appendix 1 to October 19, 1909, *ibid*).

passivity of army troops and the failure of Catholic laymen to defend clerical property, more convents could have been burned if there were any serious intent to do so. A concluding chapter on anticlericalism will comment upon this aspect. It will also analyze the type of religious building assaulted (educational, welfare, and cloistered institutions, and residences of male religious orders) in relation to the general objectives of the incendiarism.

By December of 1909 most of the cases involving convent burnings had been turned over to civil courts. No figure was released of the total number tried for these crimes, but in April 1910 the government announced that a total of 1,967 individuals had been freed.[9] Government prosecutors grew desperate, for at the last moment witnesses would deny their earlier accusations; members of religious orders refused to testify or would not give details when they did, in an attempt to avoid intensifying the workers' antagonism toward them. The Radical party's platoon of lawyers defended the accused — Emiliano Iglesias in the most important trials, Rafael Guerra del Río and José Ulled in routine cases. Sympathetic juries acquitted even the notorious Baldomero Bonet, who had directed the burning and plundering of the Conceptionist Sisters' school, among others. La Rebeldía, the newspaper of the Radical Youth Movement, jubilantly reported that the acquittal of Bonet signified that "Barcelona applauds the revolution of July." [10]

The leniency of the civil courts was due in part to the fact that they did not begin to function until months after the insurrection. The military tribunals' most severe sentences were handed down between August 1 and November 25, the period immediately following the insurrection.

Armed Rebellion

The sentences meted out by military tribunals seem particularly harsh within the perspective of the limited damage and casualties despite five days of "urban guerrilla warfare," [11] as this type of street fighting has been described. The objective was clearly the harassment of government officials rather than the conquest of power.

Only eight police or army personnel were killed, while 124 were wounded.*

---

* Distribution of government casualties is as follows: two Civil Guards died, 49 were wounded; four army officers and soldiers were killed, 43 wounded; one Security Guard was killed, 23 were wounded; one municipal policeman (Cuerpo de Vigilancia) was killed, five wounded (La Cierva, October 19, 1909, Diario de las Cortes, p. 61, and July 8, 1910, ibid., II, 467).

In addition, four members of the Red Cross were killed and 17 were injured, most of these at night as they picked up casualties or took bodies to the cemetery for burial.[12] Rebel casualties are more difficult to determine because friends and relatives concealed them. Approximately 104 civilians (98 men and six women) were reported to have died, a figure that included spectators as well as rebels. Some 296 individuals were treated in clinics, but undoubtedly more were wounded.

Figures for the value of damage done to utilities and to transportation systems, or to the looted rifle shops, were not published. Municipal officials did issue a report on the cost of dismantling barricades and repaving streets; 17,768 pesetas were spent to reset the 5,927 square meters of paving stones torn up for the construction of barricades. This report did not include data on Pueblo Nuevo and Clot, site of the heaviest fighting, probably because few streets in those suburbs were paved. The district where the greatest number of barricades had been erected was the Atarazana slum district; however, to judge by photographs, most of these 113 barricades amounted to little more than stones piled up on street corners. Far more impressive were the 76 solid barricades constructed in the suburb of Gracia, which cost the city 10,148 pesetas to dismantle.[13]

These were the crimes of "armed rebellion" tried in military courts. La Cierva reported that 1,725 individuals, in a total of 739 different cases, were indicted by military prosecutors between August 1, 1909 and May 19, 1910, when the tribunals ceased to function. Of the 1,725 individuals indicted, 214 were never captured. Charges against 469 persons were dismissed, while 584 were acquitted. Army officers condemned 17 men to death, but only 5 were executed. The sentences of the other 12 men were commuted to life imprisonment, making a total of 59 individuals who received this sentence.[14]

The first four men executed for the crime of treason, that is, of armed rebellion, were — in order of their deaths — José Miquel Baró, leader of the rebellion in San Andrés (August 17); Antonio Malet Pujol, for burning the furnishings of a church in a remote village, and for firing against the armed forces (August 28); Eugenio del Hoyo, the Security Guard who fired on an army detachment (September 13); and Ramón Clemente García, the coalman who had danced with the corpse of a nun, for having helped to build a barricade (October 4). Not one of these men was accused of having killed anyone. Not one of the incidents had been of decisive importance in the rebellion. Not one of these individuals was prominent in political circles.

Only the porter, Miquel Baró, had gained some local albeit fleeting recognition as a leader.

The impression is that military judges — consciously or not — singled out one individual guilty of each type of crime perpetrated during the week for an exemplary punishment: one petty criminal who destroyed clerical property; one disloyal policeman; one man who profaned the clergy; and one municipal employee, a political appointee, one of the hundreds who participated in the rebellion.[15] This matter of exemplary punishments is particularly evident in the case of José Miquel Baró, the first man to be executed. His sentence must be considered in relation to the preceding trials.

On August 6, at the second of the five summary procedure trials, Antonio Capdevila Marqués was accused of having fired from the barricades on the Calle Mediodía commanded by Josefa Prieto. Capdevila, who owned a house of prostitution that was a business rival of Josefa Prieto's establishment, did not deny his presence on the barricades. However, he did indulge old business grudges to testify against Prieto and her paramour, Radical party member Domingo Ruíz; this probably accounts for his sentence to life imprisonment instead of death.[16]

On August 9 and 10, a military tribunal in Barcelona heard charges against 13 men from the town of Monistrol, including the notorious anarchist Timoteo del Usón. They were accused of having been members of a gang of forty men who, on Friday morning, July 30, had gone to the town of San Vicente de Castellet — which is on the main railroad line between Barcelona and Madrid — where they destroyed railroad tracks, burned 29 loaded boxcars that were standing in the station, and destroyed the telegraph lines. One defendant received a reduced sentence because he was a minor; he was sentenced to 17 years in prison while the others were condemned to life imprisonment. The reported leader of the attack, Santiago Alorba, had managed to escape, probably to France.[17]

José Miquel Baró, the first man to be executed for his role in the Tragic Week, had not done as much damage as the men from Monistrol, nor had he killed anyone. But there are certain factors to explain why he received a death sentence: most obvious was the fact that he had led the rebellion in San Andrés.[18] Equally important, from the viewpoint of the authorities, was the fact that Miquel Baró was openly identified as a member of one of the political parties whose members had participated in the rebellion — the Catalan Nationalist Republican party. The exemplary nature of this execution is shown in the rapidity with which it was carried out, three days after his trial (although Malet Pujol, the first man sentenced to die, was not executed until seventeen days after his trial). Newspapers did not play up Miquel Baró's exploits as a rebel (for after all, he had fired only at Civil Guards, in action that was far less serious than the battles of Pueblo Nuevo or Clot-San Martín), and stressed instead the poignant aspects of the case — that Miquel died professing himself to be a fervent Catholic, that his execution left a wife and three children destitute (Clemente García and Malet Pujol were not married, nor apparently was Eugenio del Hoyo). Even though Catalan politicians Pedro Corominas, Amadeo Hurtado, and Felipe Rodés had tried but failed to secure a pardon for Miquel from the Maura government, the Radical party tried to exploit the death by charging Catalan republicans had done nothing; the Radical newspaper reported that Lerroux had finally had to find a job for Miquel's impoverished widow.[19] Radical politicians did not say so but they must have taken pleasure in the knowledge that the only municipal employee to be executed was not a political appointee of the Radical Republican party, but a porter who had earned his menial post through the Catalan Nationalist Republican party.*

In terms of the maintenance of constituted authority, a principle deeply honored by the Maura government, the execution of Eugenio del Hoyo can also be explained: he was a former soldier, a former Civil Guard, and currently a Security Guard (albeit on temporary leave because he suffered from tuberculosis).[20] But for whatever personal or political reasons, Eugenio del Hoyo had fired upon army troops during a rebellion even though there was no charge that he had wounded anyone. His execution was quite pointedly a warning to other Security Guards: ten men from each of the seven companies in Barcelona were brought to the prison to witness del Hoyo's death before a firing squad.[21]

The executions of Antonio Malet Pujol and Ramón Clemente García are far more difficult to explain, even in the context of Spain in the wake of a rebellion. Malet Pujol was a 30-year-old bachelor who had been raised in an orphan asylum, had twice deserted from the Army, and had later served time in jail for robbery.[22] During the Tragic Week, he left the private estate

---

* Indeed, the political significance of the charge that hundreds of municipal employees had participated in the uprising is that opponents wanted to emphasize the responsibility of the Radical party. As head of the majority party in the City Council, Emiliano Iglesias had been able to secure jobs for many party members — so much so that Lliga Deputy Juan Ventosa said that "the register of municipal employees tended to be the same as the list of the members of the Casa del Pueblo" (July 16, 1910, *Diario de las Cortes*, III, 686).

in Clot where he worked as a handy man and accompanied by the son of his employer, he went to the neighboring town of San Adrián de Besós, where he organized a mob to burn the parish church. When neighbors convinced him that this would endanger their homes, Malet contented himself with building a bonfire in the plaza where he burned some church furnishings. In the Cortes, Catalan Republican Deputy Pedro Corominas cited the official engineers' report to prove that the total value of damages was 180 pesetas (very roughly, about $70). Yet in defending Malet's execution, Interior Minister La Cierva cited only the burning of church property[23] (which technically was not included in the indictment of armed rebellion).

However, some Barcelona newspapers reported that Malet led a group that destroyed a railroad bridge, seized the rifles of the guards who collected the excise taxes, and fired upon "armed forces" although there was no report that he wounded anyone. One fairly reliable newspaper stated that Malet did not deny these charges, that instead he proudly recounted the details at his trial, then listened stoically to the sentence and agreed to sign it — that is, to admit his guilt. If this account is accurate, Antonio Malet was the only individual whose case was publicized who admitted even participating in the rebellion. However, most newspaper accounts merely stressed that Malet was one of the many petty criminals — the *hampa,* the dregs of society — who come to the fore in any popular uprising.*

Far more difficult to explain is the execution of Ramón Clemente García, the simple-minded coalman, who had danced in the streets with the corpse of a Hieronymite Nun. He was tried and convicted, however, not for this act but for having helped to build a barricade and thereby participating in the armed rebellion. His three co-defendants — clerks, and thus presumably of more social status, and who had not touched the corpses — were merely sentenced to permanent exile from Spain. At his trial Clemente García sobbed that many others had done the same thing, while many who had committed far graver crimes had not even been arrested.[24] Politicians of all parties and spokesmen for numerous civic groups petitioned for clemency, but Clemente was executed on October 4. Various political groups claimed that Maura did not dare to pardon Clemente, lest it set a precedent for the trial of Francisco Ferrer y Guardia.[25]

* Fabra Rivas was defensive when he admitted the participation of the criminal element in the uprising. But he concluded philosophically that if the bourgeoisie with all their police force had not been able to eliminate this "plague", then the revolutionaries could not be expected to do so in just a few days (Magin Vidal [Fabra Rivas], "En pleine Révolution," *L'Humanité* [Paris] August 15, 1909).

At most, the first four individuals executed were mere participants in the rebellion. Military prosecutors would fail completely to prove the involvement of any organization in the rebellion, or to convict any political leader of having issued an order

Leadership of the Rebellion

Military authorities charged that officials of the Radical party, the Catalan Nationalist Republican party, and the anarchist movement had directed the armed rebellion in Barcelona.[26] However, they did not present evidence to substantiate the claim that Catalan Nationalists had tried to carry out their "crazy ambitions" and did not indict any party official. They did bring charges of being "instigators, organizers and directors" of the armed rebellion against four Radical party members* and seven anarchists.**

The charges against the anarchists were the first to be discounted. Four of the defendants (Arnal, Cardenal, Castellote, and Herreros) had been apprehended early Monday morning in the act of urging workers to support the General Strike, but this could not be construed as rebellion. Nor could military authorities prove their firm suspicions that anarchists had helped to prepare the General Strike. Therefore, on November 2, 1909, the senior military advocate in Barcelona ruled that the four men be turned over to civil courts for trial on the lesser charge of inciting to sedition.[27]

Radical party officials were left to defend themselves — and their party — against the charge of having organized an armed rebellion. Most curious was the charge against Juana Ardiaca as an instigator or organizer of armed rebellion. Although the version presented in the text (pages 232–33) is possibly not a complete account of what happened on that rooftop on the night of Tuesday, July 27, military prosecutors offered no other evidence: they did not even imply that she was present at a convent burning, much less a street barricade. The implication is that Juana Ardiaca was prosecuted as a repre-

* The four Radicals were Emiliano Iglesias, Luis Zurdo Olivares, Juana Ardiaca, and Trinidad Alted Fornet (a minor official who accepted the legal responsibility for the party newspaper, El Progreso).
** Of the seven anarchists charged, only four actually stood trial: Federico Arnal Angelet, Francisco Cardenal Ugarte, Mariano Castellote Targa, and Tomás Herreros Miquel. A fifth man, Trinidad de LaTorre Dehesa, was also accused of having collaborated with Ferrer during the rebellion; nevertheless, on the ground that he had formally withdrawn from the anarchist movement one year earlier, de LaTorre was granted provisional liberty. Two anarchists included in the indictment were never captured: Francisco Miranda Concha and Jaime Aragó García.

sentative of the many Damas Radicales and Damas Rojas who participated in the uprising. She may have been singled out for prosecution simply because military authorities found a witness willing to testify against her. They were, however, unable to prove that she had influenced any person to take part in the armed rebellion. Juana Ardiaca was released on November 10, 1909, although charges were not formally dismissed until March 4, 1910.[28] A far more typical Dama Roja was Carmen Alauch who helped to build a barricade; she was indicted for having "favored military rebellion," but no disposition of her case appears in the published transcript, perhaps because her neighbors in Clot would not testify against her.

Military authorities were forced to drop charges against another Radical official, Trinidad Alted, who had assumed responsibility for several articles that had appeared in *El Progreso* in the days preceding the strike — and specifically, the editorial "Remember" which authorities charged had incited the burning of convents, and "Rumores de ayer," the article published on July 26 reporting the rumors of a general strike, which authorities charged had incited workers to strike. However, there was no claim that Alted had actually written the articles, nor that he was in fact the editor of *El Progreso*. Alted was released on November 10, 1909, at the same time as Juana Ardiaca, and charges against him were dismissed on March 4, 1910.[29]

Army prosecutors were far more interested in the case against Emiliano Iglesias and Luis Zurdo.

ARMY OFFICERS AND RADICAL LEADERS

The published transcript of the military trial of the Radical politicians included extensive testimony concerning the incendiarism although the accusation of having directed the convent burnings was not formally included in the indictment of the Radical leaders. Probably the judge responsible for the case, Major Vicente Llivina y Fernández, had hoped to show that convent burnings and armed rebellion were but two phases of the same movement. But the official Radical position was that although they occurred during the same week, they were completely independent actions. Therefore, although they might possibly have been involved in convent burnings, the Radical leaders had not been guilty of armed rebellion.

Many army officers, albeit surreptitiously, helped the Radical leaders to maintain this position. The reason was obvious; during the Tragic Week, officers had tolerated the convent burnings, either because they had found it impossible to prevent the destructions, or because they sympathized with a campaign that spared the lives but destroyed the property of the clergy, their old rival for political sovereignty in Spain. The Church officially protested the fact that for two days, convents had been burned in the presence of army officers and police.[30]

Therefore, army officers, or some of them, were only too willing to discount any connection between the incendiarism and the armed rebellion against the state, and to dismiss charges against men accused solely of having participated in the burnings. An important factor in this development was the personal friendships between officers and Radical party members. "I am honored," Emiliano Iglesias later told the Cortes, when it discussed the trials, "with the friendship of many of the officers who have performed the duties of judges." [31] Iglesias even managed to ascribe the military prosecution to the clergy. He told the Cortes that it was being directed by the Military Advocates Corps, a recent and ignominious addition to the noble Spanish army, and one infiltrated by fanatical Catholics; the chief of this Corps, General Ramón Pastor, was reported to check in daily at the Jesuit residence for instructions on how to proceed. Iglesias' stratagem was resented by General Angel Aznar, the War Minister, who rose in the Cortes to say that Iglesias "lacked the gallantry to attack the Army directly." [32]

During these trials Iglesias was concerned, not only to secure the acquittal of as many of his party members as possible, but even more importantly, with the need to preserve the tenuous alliance forged between the Radical party and the Army. During his own interrogation he reminded officers that "the principal platform of the Radical party was the unity of the Nation and, therefore, the exaltation of the Army." [33] Behind this statement was the fear that the incendiarism had gone too far, that it had threatened not simply one institution but the existing society, and that this fear of social upheaval had alienated army officers who sympathized with the Radicals' tenets of republicanism, nationalism, and anticlericalism.* In short, the Tragic Week had endangered Ruíz Zorilla's nineteenth-century revolutionary ideal of a workers' party collaborating with army officers in the establishment of a republic.**

---

* One Radical Deputy, when questioned by army officers, insisted that the rebels had shouted "Viva el Ejército y abajo la guerra" to prove "the moral identification of the people with their honorable representative, the armed forces of the Nation" (Hermenegildo Giner de los Ríos, *Causa: Rebelión militar,* I, 100).

** Even Francisco Ferrer, onetime aide to Ruíz Zorilla, sought to exonerate his military prosecutors. In a letter published posthumously, he stated that if most Spanish people possessed the dignity and courtesy of army officers and soldiers, there would be

José Ulled Altamir of the Radical youth movement led the campaign to re-establish a working alliance between army officers and Radical party officials.* The effort was all the more difficult in view of the fact that initially José Ulled and his brother, Rafael, were charged by military officers with being "the presumed chiefs of the movement" in Barcelona.[34] Twenty-one year-old José Ulled, a lawyer, was also charged with having used the press (the extremist publication, *La Rebeldía,* of which he was an editor) to incite to sedition and disorder.[35] In early August authorities had sent out telegrams describing the discovery and detention of the Ulled brothers, both officers of the Juventud Radical, as "extremely important." [36]

José and Rafael Ulled fled to Paris where they participated with other exiles in public protests against the repression. In mid-November they returned to Barcelona and voluntarily appeared before a military judge to clear themselves of the charges against them. Officials prepared a report charging (but without evidence) that the brothers had participated in the burning of the convent of the Handmaids of Mary and in the attacks upon the Jesuit residence, the Seminary, and the barracks of the Veterans of Liberty. But there was no charge that they had participated in the armed rebellion and so they were released.[37]

José Ulled then turned to the most important task at hand: to achieve a new rapport with army officers. Three days after charges had been dropped against him, José Ulled published in *La Rebeldía* an interview with Nicolás Estévanez, onetime collaborator of Ruíz Zorilla, who had devoted his long conspiratorial career to securing army support for a republic. Ulled reported that Estévanez had told him in Paris:

> The movement in Barcelona merits all my sympathy, although I regret the fact that, misinterpreted by some individuals, it might create a certain divorce between the people and the Army — a divorce which, if it were to take place, would banish the hope of a free and progressive Spain.[38]

Developments in twentieth-century Spain have proven Estévanez' fears to be well-founded.

---

no need for the Escuela Moderna (*El País* [Madrid], April 2, 1911). Even if the letter is apocryphal, it was published by republicans and remains an instance of their effort not to estrange the Army.

* Lerroux claimed that after his return to Spain in the fall of 1909, he used the money collected in Buenos Aires to subsidize military as well as civilian republican conspirators. He cited specifically Lieutenant General Enrique Bages, General Maroto, and General Segura (*Mis Memorias,* pp. 528–29).

THE RADICAL DEFENDANTS

Authorities were unable to implicate in the incendiarism the group of young doctors, lawyers, and teachers who constituted the editorial staff of *La Rebeldía* through which they directed the Radical youth movement, Juventud Radical. Guerra del Río, Angel de Borjas, Rafael Canales, Colominas Maseras, together with the Ulled brothers, were merely interrogated or indicted, but not convicted.[39]

Government prosecutors were equally unsuccessful in pressing charges against Radical officials who reputedly had carried out the rebellion through other sectors of the party machinery — through the newspaper, or through the Damas Radicales and the Damas Rojas. In March 1910 Military Judge Llivina declared it had been impossible to prove the accusations and listed the reasons: civil authorities, including police, had made general charges but offered no evidence; all military judges throughout the city had been requested to contribute evidence from cases under their jurisdiction of rebels having received orders from Radical officials, yet not one had come forward; witnesses had been asked to volunteer but none had appeared. Major Llivina had finally summoned representatives of Catholic organizations, as the entities who had suffered the greatest damage, only to find that they talked in general terms about "moral inductors" without presenting any factual evidence. Therefore, on March 21, 1910, Emiliano Iglesias, Juana Ardiaca, and Trinidad Alted were acquitted of all charges that they had led the armed rebellion. Only Luis Zurdo was found guilty.[40]

Iglesias had been busy maneuvering behind the scenes in order to secure his own release, and had finally sought help from a minister in José Canalejas' Liberal cabinet. Later, explaining the matter to the famous novelist Pío Baroja, Iglesias said that the minister acted solely "because of affection for me"; however, since it would have been too "blatant" to release him alone, the minister also protected Zurdo and secured a commutation of the latter's sentence from life imprisonment to exile.[41]

Zurdo Olivares, the reluctant rebel who had carried a rifle through the streets of Clot yet menaced no soldier or police agent, was the only prominent Radical convicted of armed rebellion. But he had been convicted of having participated in the armed rebellion, not of having led it. On June 14, 1910, Spanish authorities set him down on the French side of the frontier.[42]

THE RADICALS AND FERRER

In addition to lack of evidence and to sympathetic army judges and cabinet ministers, there was another major cause for the exoneration of Radical party officials as the "authors" of the rebellion: the willingness of Radicals to testify that Francisco Ferrer was responsible for the rebellion,* and that he had used as his instrument Solidaridad Obrera — the archenemy of their party.[43]

The first members of the Radical party to testify were those in Ferrer's home district. On August 7 Francisco Domenech Munté told of Ferrer's activities in Barcelona on Monday evening, July 26; the young barber then mysteriously secured funds to go to Argentina where he remained four months.[44] Juan Puig Ventura and Mayor Domingo Casas of Premiá testified several days later about Ferrer's activities on Thursday, July 29.** At this stage, only Mayor Casas suggested that Ferrer was responsible for the entire rebellion in Catalonia.[45]

Late in August and continuing through September, Radical officials in Barcelona (Iglesias, Manuel Jiménez Moya, and Baldomero Bonet) testified that Ferrer had been one of the organizers of the armed rebellion.[46] Only Alfredo García Magallones, a retired army officer active in the Radical party and a sometime police informant, reported that Emiliano Iglesias, as well as Ferrer, had been "the promoters of the rebellion."[47] Lorenzo Ardid (under indictment for having presumably given orders for the burnings during the week) testified that although he could offer no proof, he "suspected him [Ferrer] of being one of the organizers," of the armed rebellion.[48]

"They are going to shoot me," said Ferrer, "simply on the word of a few Radicals."[49]

* The staff of *La Rebeldía,* embarrassed by the accusations of Radical officials against Ferrer and by the taunts of anarchists that they were *delatores,* published an open letter in several major republican newspapers asking Radical leaders to repudiate the informers (letter published in *El País* [Madrid], October 26, 1909. See also the anarchist newspaper, *Tierra y Libertad* [Barcelona], October 13, 1910).

** One reason why these accusations against Ferrer became so important was that Pedro Maristany, president of the powerful Barcelona Chamber of Commerce, also happened to be the Mayor of Masnou and the employer of Juan Puig Ventura. Maristany was able to have charges against Puig — accused of being coauthor with Ferrer of the rebellion in Masnou — dismissed after Puig testified against Ferrer (*Causa contra Ferrer,* pp. 29, 32–33, 117).

CHAPTER XIII

Francisco Ferrer:
"Author and Chief of the Rebellion"

FRANCISCO FERRER was apprehended on August 31, 1909, as he fled toward France. On October 9 a military tribunal studied the evidence gathered by army prosecutors and sentenced him to die as the "author and chief of the rebellion." Specifically it found him guilty of having "decisively influenced" the Radical party to intervene in the rebellion, directly through personal contacts and indirectly through his "subordinates" in Solidaridad Obrera, and guilty of having encouraged anarchists to burn convents and to act "as chiefs of the rebellion on one of the barricades which offered most resistance to the Army" (presumably the barricades on the Calle San Pablo where "Captain Moreno" was in command, but although this was mentioned it was not specified).[1] Antonio Maura refused to recommend a pardon to the King. Four days after his trial, Ferrer was executed by a firing squad in Montjuich Castle.

In the ensuing half century of impassioned debate on whether Ferrer was in fact "the author and chief of the rebellion," one matter has too often been obscured: no popular explosion of the magnitude and intensity of the Tragic Week is the work of one man. The complexity and savagery of the underlying causes frightened Spanish society, which sought relief by discussing the events in simplistic terms of good versus evil, of society versus anarchy, and by making one individual bear "at least the moral responsibility" for the events.

The Evidence

The true point at issue is the extent to which Ferrer had been preparing for a revolution in Spain, and the degree to which he worked with other men to use the popular uprising of July 1909 as the occasion for that revolution. Conclusive evidence — if it does in fact exist — remains locked within police and military archives. There should have been no question about what Ferrer did from the time of his return to Barcelona from London in mid-June 1909, for he was supposedly under constant police surveillance. Yet in the transcript of the military investigation, published one year after Ferrer's execution, the police report provides only vague references to his movements, a lack explained only indirectly through reports that Ferrer eluded his escort by driving off in an automobile.[2] The published transcript is a selected account of the investigation and testimony, and it definitely does not substantiate the charge that Ferrer's activities in Barcelona on July 26, and in Premiá and Masnou on July 28, constituted directing the rebellion.

Despite all assertions to the contrary, the case against Ferrer was based primarily on his *personalidad revolucionaria.** His activities during the Tragic Week are cited as but one example of the general charges: first, that a revolution in Spain had been the constant objective of Ferrer's long career, the ulterior purpose behind his educational, labor, and political activities both in Catalonia and abroad; second, that Ferrer's deliberate strategy was to remain in the background, influencing organizations through subsidies and contacts with key members. To substantiate their charges, military prosecutors relied upon evidence of Ferrer's career and writings, thus employing the same evidence and the same procedure that had led civil judges to acquit him in 1907.

Only indirectly did army prosecutors refer to the widely publicized charge that Ferrer had provided funds for the rebellion, a charge originating with Pascual Zulueta, Barcelona correspondent of Maura's newspaper *La Epoca,* published in Madrid: on August 4, Zulueta reported that shortly before the

---

* In 1912 a high army tribunal ruled there was no proof that any rebel acted "on direct orders" from Ferrer and therefore, that his estate could not be sued for damages. The ruling was occasioned by a test case in which the plaintiff sought compensation for damages caused by Timoteo del Usón, an anarchist long associated with Ferrer, who had been convicted of tearing up railroads leading into Barcelona (see page 289). ("Providencia del Consejo Supremo de Guerra y Marina, dictada en la causa seguida contra Francisco Ferrer y Guardia," December 29, 1911, in Sangro, *Sombra de Ferrer,* p. 386–89.)

Tragic Week, Ferrer withdrew 70,000 pesetas from his bank account and that this money was distributed among Radicals in the Casa del Pueblo.[3] Army officers investigated the charge, but the transcript includes no report on inquiries at the bank; it does include interrogations of the paid incendiaries in Horta, yet includes no statement linking them with Ferrer. Officers also interrogated Cristobal Litrán, Ferrer's business manager, about reports that he had hired men for the rebellion;[4] the transcript includes no reference to this part of Litrán's testimony.

Although he later became one of Ferrer's most eloquent defenders, Cristobal Litrán played an enigmatic role during the trial. An old-time Federal Republican journalist of some prestige, and a minor official in the Radical's Casa del Pueblo, Litrán had arranged the meetings between Ferrer and party officials on July 26. After being questioned for three hours, he was exiled to a small Aragonese town together with Ferrer's mistress, relatives, and friends (including famous anarchist Anselmo Lorenzo). Although these were the people with whom Ferrer had spent the Tragic Week, they were not called to testify. According to Soledad Villafranca, Litrán restrained them from contacting Ferrer's army lawyer until it was too late to enter testimony.[5] This is one of the many mysteries that still envelop the Ferrer trial.

Ferrer and the Stock Market

Another matter left unresolved was the report, widely circulated in Barcelona, that Ferrer and Radical politicians wanted a republic proclaimed in order to cause a decline in the value of the Monarchy's state bonds, and thereby to make money through speculating on a drop in the stock market. Ferrer's defense lawyer, Captain Francisco Galcerán, denounced this as an attempt to discredit the idealism of his client.[6] The accusation, however, is not so easily dismissed. As early as the fall of 1908, at the time of the teamsters' strike, an informant had told police that Ferrer was "apparently trying to carry out a stock market operation through certain revolutionary labor elements."[7]

In August 1909, the charge that the rebellion constituted a stock market maneuver was lodged originally against five Radical party officials: Iglesias

* Still another explanation of the mysterious snipers (los tíos pacos) was that they were professional gunmen paid to prolong the rebellion while politicians speculated in municipal securities (José Brissa, *La revolución de julio en Barcelona: Su represió sus víctimas, el proceso de Ferrer. Recopilación completa de sucesos y comentario con el informe del fiscal y el del defensor Sr. Galcerán* [Barcelona, 1910], p. 74).

Vinaixa, Juan Rovira Palau, José Mir y Miró, and Valdés. An anonymous letter to military authorities, dated August 2, 1909, supplied the names and addresses of the six brokers who had handled the transaction.[8]

In mid-August the charge was expanded to include Ferrer. "Pierre" [Domingo Gaspar Mata], a Radical journalist who had fled to France, was reported to have said that Ferrer met him in the street shortly before the Tragic Week and advised him to play the market on the basis of a drop in stock values. "Pierre" believed the rebellion was nothing more than an attempt by Ferrer and Emiliano Iglesias to make money.[9]

Ferrer, it will be remembered, had amassed his fortune through harsh economies and shrewd stock market operations, primarily with shares in the construction company that held a monopoly contract on Barcelona's public works (Fomento de Obras y Construcciones, S.A.);* the value of this stock was thus intimately related to municipal politics.

Army officers investigated the charges but found them difficult to prove or disprove. Stock prices had declined sharply, both because of the war and the disorders in Catalonia. When questioned about the possibility that individuals had profited from this decline, stock exchange officials could reply only that they had no record of a large-scale operation by registered brokers but they pointed out that the transaction could have been handled through unofficial stock agents in Barcelona or through exchanges located in other cities.[10]

Ferrer and Miguel V. Moreno

Ferrer's "subordinates in Solidaridad Obrera," to whom military judges referred, were José Rodríguez Romero and Miguel V. Moreno. Military au-

* These stocks were of such great concern to Ferrer that they led directly to his arrest. On August 16 a note came due in Barcelona on a bank loan for which Ferrer had pledged the Fomento stocks as collateral. Ferrer was hiding in caves on his farm, protected by reports published by friends in Paris that he was safe in France. He sent Soledad Villafranca to renew the note but she was told she must have Ferrer's signature. He committed the amazing indiscretion of signing it because he thought he could trust the bank manager, a personal friend. Military authorities, however, were informed; unable to locate his hiding place, they deported Ferrer's relatives on August 19 and waited for him to attempt to escape. On August 31 he was apprehended not far from his home, as he made his way toward France. (For details of the affair of the bank and of Ferrer's arrest see Sol Ferrer, *Véritable Ferrer*, pp. 198–200, and *Ferrer: Martyr*, pp. 141–42; La Cierva statement to the press, *El País* (Madrid), September 2, 1909; *Causa contra Ferrer*, pp. 43, 79–83, 419; Brissa, *Revolución de julio*, p. 218; Constant Leroy [V. Moreno], "Campaña humanitaria," *El Correo Español* (Mexico, D.F.), January 7, 1913.)

thorities stressed the manifesto announcing a revolution, which Ferrer and Moreno tried to have the Radical party issue. They also cited Moreno's activities in connection with the mainfesto prepared on Monday night and on the barricades of the Calle San Pablo in summarizing Ferrer's responsibility for the armed insurrection.[11]

As one socialist official later ruefully admitted, Moreno was the decisive member of the Central Committee for the Strike.[12] Fabra Rivas, in an angry confrontation with Moreno in Paris in October 1909, charged that Moreno had schemed from the start to turn control of the movement over to the Radical party.[13] Moreno's importance is further attested by the fact that Emiliano Iglesias had risked arrest by going to confer with him during the Tragic Week.

The question is whether Moreno was under instructions from Ferrer, simply kept him informed of his negotiations with Radical officials, or whether he acted on his own initiative. Ferrer's daughter wrote that Moreno acted on his own.[14] Yet he was only twenty-eight years old, a penniless teacher in one of Ferrer's rationalist schools, who achieved no subsequent distinction either in Spain or in exile politics. At first Moreno was welcomed by Ferrer's associates in Paris and played a prominent role in anti-Maura demonstrations. The following year (1910) he went to South America under the sponsorship of Ferrer's International League for the Rational Education of Children, and there began to recount details of Ferrer's activities during the Tragic Week. Cristobal Litrán, Ferrer's business manager, published an article declaring his "respect" for Moreno, but denounced him "for forgetting obligations contracted with all solemnity." [15]

Late in 1912 Moreno began to publish a series of articles in a newspaper in Mexico City, El Correo Español, under the pseudonym of Constant Leroy, in which he stated unequivocally that "Ferrer took an active part in the revolution of July, and promoted those events with his money and his personal action." Moreno reported that he himself had been "in a certain way the principal agent, in union with Ferrer and other individuals." [16] He promised to reveal all details but the newspaper series ended just as it began to describe the Tragic Week. Moreno subsequently (1913) published a book under the same pseudonym and again promised to reveal details of the revolution in a second volume, but this was never published.[17] There is little evidence, therefore, to evaluate the extent and nature of Moreno's role in the Tragic Week.

The Culpability of Ferrer

The nature of the charges and of the evidence in the military trial facili-
tated the contention of Ferrer's defenders that he had been executed *solely*
because of his activities as a secular educator in "la Espagne inquisitorial." [18]
The Maura government, speaking through the resolute Interior Minister
Juan de La Cierva, stated categorically that an impartial investigation by
army officers had proved Ferrer to be "the *chief* leader" of the rebellion.[19]
Neither of these extreme positions can be sustained by the evidence of
Ferrer's actions during the Tragic Week.

In his conversations with Radical leaders in Masnou and Premiá, Ferrer
urged a formula for action that initially coincided with the course of events
in Barcelona: to burn churches and convents as a means of creating a revolutionary milieu and then, when skirmishes with police began, to proclaim
a republic. This does not mean that Ferrer was the mastermind of the rebellion, but rather that this was an obvious formula for revolution in Catalonia
in 1909. At their trial, Radical politicians found it convenient to recall that
Ferrer had suggested this course of action, as though he were the only one
in those troubled days to urge that the popular uprising be used as the occasion for a revolution.

On July 26, and again on July 29, Ferrer had abandoned his position as a
"philosophical anarchist" (acrata). An old-time anarchist and a staunch
defender of Ferrer, Federico Urales, reported that Ferrer, "who subordinated
every other ideal to that of revolution, attempted to exploit that spontaneous
moment in order to effect a change of regime in Spain." [20] He failed for two
reasons. In the first place, his personality and notoriety had isolated him
from rebel leaders: Emiliano Iglesias would later write that because of "well-
known circumstances, Ferrer could not be either the chief, nor even a
director, nor even an advisor of those who carried out the protest." [21] Laureano Miró, a Catalan republican deputy active during the Tragic Week,
stated that Ferrer tried to intervene "but no one paid any attention to
him." [22] Second, Ferrer failed — as Urales bluntly explained — because the
revolutionary masses were firmly led by men whose objectives were solely
and exclusively to win elections. Ferrer's execution was more the result of his
past career than of his actions during the Tragic Week. As "an impenitent
revolutionary," wrote a Radical editorialist, two years after the events,

"Ferrer viewed that movement with pleasure and wanted to contribute to it.
. . . But what was pardonable in all others because of the suggestive revolutionary ambiance, in Ferrer was the greatest crime of the revolution." [23]

Yet however limited Ferrer's sphere of action, or however questionable the extent of his personal influence in Barcelona, his long-range contribution to the creation of a revolutionary atmosphere must be recognized. Through his subsidies, his textbooks, and his contacts with European labor and civil rights groups, Ferrer had helped to set the stage for an uprising such as the Tragic Week. The significant aspect of this affair is not Ferrer's activity per se, but rather the situation that he exploited: high illiteracy, a tense labor-management relationship, and a political stalemate.

In the half century that has elapsed since Ferrer's execution, Spanish politicians and historians have made few attempts to clarify the details of his career or of his trial. Losing its identity as an historic event, Ferrer's sentence has served as a rallying cry for both of the "Two Spains" — a sentence defended by advocates of the status quo and attacked by reformers.

Part Five

Conclusions

CHAPTER XIV

National Consequences of the Tragic Week:
1909–1912

THE EVENTS of the Tragic Week and, far more, the repression that followed decisively affected the development of three institutions in Spanish society: representative government, the educational system, and the labor movement.

The political consequences were most dramatic. The Ferrer case and Maura's restoration of order became the issues which determined alliances in the Cortes and, more importantly, which enervated the drive to reform Cánovas' Restoration Settlement in order to make of it a viable instrument for government in the twentieth century. After the crisis ended in 1912, politicians maintained the façade of a constitutional monarchy but they no longer claimed to use the legislature as a means of enacting profound reforms as they had done during the first decade of the twentieth century. Gone were the enthusiastic campaigns "to root out" the cacique, to build a navy, to reinforce civil jurisdiction over the Church and the Army, and to incorporate regionalism — campaigns in which workers had been urged to exercise their newly acquired right to vote. Politicians avoided general elections as often as possible. Lacking dynamic leaders like Maura or Canalejas, and lacking the discipline of party policy, they concentrated on forming and re-forming cabinets from among the many interest groups within the Cortes; they concentrated, that is, on the prerogatives rather than on the exercise of power.

Spaniards became increasingly cynical about the authenticity and effectiveness of politics. The general European crisis of parliamentary government undoubtedly helped to condition this cynicism, yet a more direct and vital factor in the Spanish situation was the specter of the Tragic Week that loomed again at the time of the 1917 General Strike — the specter of a mobilized urban labor force that haunted the middle class as well as the oligarchy and prevented them from working through the political machinery for redress of grievances as they had done in the aftermath of the War of 1898. They returned to the Restoration practice of making deals with government officials and with other interest groups. When this did not suffice, each group within the society sought to defend its material or ideological interests through force and, if necessary through violence, and not through legal or political channels; this is the general phenomenon of "direct action" (*acción directa*) that José Ortega y Gasset analyzed in his famous *España Invertebrada,* a book published in 1921 on the eve of the collapse of the constitutional monarchy and its substitution by a military dictatorship.

Thus the Cortes failed to fulfill its function as the agency through which interest groups met to compromise their differences in the formation of national policy. This, the pivot of the failure of the constitutional monarchy, was nothing more than a symptom of the national ill — of Spain's "social impotency" ("impotència social"), as Juan Maragall brilliantly epitomized the crisis of the autumn of 1909. "We have here a great conglomeration of individual energies that have not been able to create a social organism proportionate to its size," wrote the Catalan in an analysis of the crisis of Spanish society.[1] Maragall was asking not so much whether the social order could endure (for he recognized the force of police and laws) but whether it should endure in the form in which it was then constituted. This fundamental question will be considered in the final chapter; the following sections will describe the ways by which various groups adjusted and survived

The Ferrer Case in Spanish Politics

In the controversy following the Tragic Week, Spanish politicians, perhaps deliberately, did not focus upon the Tragic Week itself but on the Ferrer case. Even more specifically, politicians eschewed the complex issue of Ferrer's involvement in the rebellion and concerned themselves with the aspect of the case in which the Maura government was vulnerable: the juridical procedure under which Ferrer had been convicted and executed.

The issue of protecting the individual's freedom of conscience and thought against state interference was a matter of deep concern to European intellectuals and labor leaders in 1909. Therefore, immediately after Ferrer's exec tion, they mobilized mass demonstrations in the capital cities in order to exploit the execution for domestic political purposes; their task was facilitated by the image established during the trial of 1906 of Ferrer as a martyr for the cause of secular education in "la Espagne inquisitorial." On the very day of Ferrer's execution, French syndicalists and socialists put aside their differences and organized a protest in front of the Spanish Embassy in Paris that drew a crowd of 15,000. French novelist Emile Zola and his Belgian colleague Maurice Maeterlinck denounced this new injustice of "la Espagne inquisitorial." Within the next few days demonstrations were organized in Rome and Milan, Vienna, Trieste, Budapest, and Lisbon — that is, in countries where clerical power still appeared to pose a threat to individual liberty.[2]

Spanish republican and Liberal leaders were slow to follow suit. They could plead, of course, that they could not act because of the censorship and threat of imprisonment, but they were motivated by other considerations. One was the general conviction that, however vulnerable the military trial, Ferrer was guilty to some degree; not one prominent Spanish politician requested a stay of execution.[3] A second, more important reason was the threat of renewed violence. In October 1909 Liberal party leaders, including Segismundo Moret, told an English journalist that they deliberately chose not to exploit the Ferrer case as an anticlerical issue because they did not want to risk any repetition of the Carlist wars.[4]

Reports of militant Carlist activity, directed and encouraged by the Jesuits, circulated in Madrid and Barcelona. Although most politicians smiled at reports of a Carlist "army," they were concerned with the effect of these rumors upon the passionate anticlerical sentiments of urban workers — the powerful, latent force that politicians were determined to contain. Later in the fall, when they organized anti-Maura demonstrations, Liberals joined republican politicians in circulating instructions to demonstrators that they must resist any command to engage in violence, as a precaution against agents provocateurs who might cause new riots that would justify still more repressive measures.

This policy of left wing leaders responded to *ordenancismo,* Miguel de Unamuno's term to express that deep concern of the Spanish body politic with public order that outweighs social or intellectual considerations.[5] In rallying support for his government, Antonio Maura made an astute appeal to this powerful motivating force in Hispanic politics, yet there is no reason to doubt his sincerity as he described the national crisis in these simplistic terms:[6]

Spaniards concerned with public life can be divided into two groups. One includes all those who patronize uprisings and sackings, burnings and revolutions, as well as all those who sympathize with, or compromise with, such things. The other includes all of us who hold the deep conviction that without a strong social discipline, without a deep respect for authority and law, society — life itself — is not possible; they believe that in order to establish these principles firmly, it is absolutely necessary to take action against the first group of individuals.

Relying upon this appeal to members of the Establishment, the only ones who sat as representatives in the Cortes, Maura believed that legislators would vote the continuation in office of his government. He therefore dared to open the Cortes on October 14, the day after Ferrer's execution.

El Turno

The opening of the Cortes coincided with the pro-Ferrer demonstrations in European capitals. Although they were more extensive than Maura had foreseen, he was convinced that legislators — if not the general public — would rally to his support in defense of their honor as Spaniards in the face of "this insult to my nation." [7]

Liberal party chief Segismundo Moret might have responded to this appeal, both because he was afraid to exploit the Ferrer case and because he wanted the Conservatives to end the war in Morocco and conclude the trials in Catalonia before the Liberals took office. However, a group within his party, motivated by hatred of Maura or by a desire to return to office after more than two years without patronage, urged Moret to demand office. Maura's arrogance compelled Moret to act. On October 20, La Cierva rose in the Cortes to defend the Conservative government; he said that the Liberals' policy of subsidizing the Barcelona Radicals (see page 92) had led to the attempted regicide of 1906 and, by implication, to the events of July 1909. Maura rose and dramatically shook his Minister's hand. [8]

Moret now began to maneuver in order to force Maura to resign and to succeed him as the head of the government. True to the Cánovas system, the Congress would not be asked for a vote of confidence; even less probable at that troubled moment was the convocation of general elections. The professional politicians of both parties would be expected to resolve the matter privately and then to secure royal approval. But in 1909 a new element was introduced into the parliamentary procedure. Alfonso XIII intervened decisively, the first of many such actions.

Whether in subsequent years Alfonso weakened the political system by intervening in parliamentary affairs, or whether he was free to act only because the political structure was already debilitated, is an important question for future research — as Spanish historian Jaime Vicens Vives has pointed out.[9] The point here is that Alfonso's first major intervention occurred during the Ferrer crisis when he decided that the head of the Conservative party must leave office even though he still held a majority in the congress.

In October 1909 Alfonso acted from a complex of reasons. The 23-year-old monarch was not personally fond of the stern statesman, the only one with whom he never dared to use the familiar "tu." Influenced by the army officers with whom he spent much of his time, Alfonso wanted a more active Moroccan policy than Maura advocated. Furthermore, he was troubled by the possibility of new violence in Spain and by an aroused European public opinion. The King was therefore pleased when he learned that Moret was willing to form a Liberal government. On October 21, 1909, Maura offered to resign, confident that Alfonso would refuse to accept the offer; instead, Alfonso thanked Maura for resigning and formally asked Moret to form a government. But four months later Moret was forced out of office by his arch-rival, José Canalejas, who presided over Liberal governments from February 1910 until November 1912.

As Alfonso explained to Maura's son many years later, he had decided to "sacrifice" Maura because he could not prevail against "half of Spain and more than half of Europe." [10] Alfonso's personal inclination was confirmed in 1910 when he joined other reigning monarchs in London for the funeral of Edward VII, and they advised him not to recall Maura to govern. And yet despite this royal decision, Canalejas was quietly working to reincorporate Maura into politics as part of his statesmanlike policies, but the Liberal party leader was assassinated on November 12, 1912. This assassination ended any serious effort to secure major reforms through legislation. It also occasioned a year-long crisis through which Maura was definitively excluded from politics.

To succeed Canalejas, Alfonso asked another Liberal politician (Manuel García Prieto) to form a government. Angered, Maura resigned as Conservative party chief in December 1912; he published a letter accusing republicans and socialists, as well as those Liberal politicians who collaborated with them, of "morally coercing" the King in order to prevent him from returning to office.[11] Still hopeful that Maura might somehow return to power,

Conservative leaders persuaded him to rescind his resignation, but in the following year they realized clearly that to remain loyal to Maura was to abandon all hope of political office. Therefore, in October 1913, when Alfonso approached Conservative leader Eduardo Dato about the possibility of forming a government, Dato agreed and most of the Conservative politicians promised to support him.

Maura's effective political career had ended. Although Ossorio y Gallardo immediately organized a *Maurista* movement of men who admired his conservative principles, Antonio Maura refused to utilize this as the basis for political action. Rigidly orthodox, he waited to be recalled as chief of the Conservative party. This call never came although on a few occasions after 1918, in the last throes of the constitutional monarchy in Spain, Maura was asked to preside over several coalition governments.

Exiled to Rome in the 1930's, Alfonso XIII discussed this crisis with Maura's son and concluded that he had deprived himself of the services of one of the few politicians capable of defending the Monarchy.[12] During the years before and after the First World War, Spain suffered from a lack of political leaders and so the loss of Maura was particularly significant.

Within the political context, the exclusion of Maura is even more important because it signified an end to *el turno,* to the rotation in office of disciplined Liberal and Conservative parties. In the years that followed, the campaign of "Maura, no!" embittered and confused party politics. Factions of politicians, not national parties, alternated in office. The campaign of "Maura, no!" also diverted attention from the central fact of the political crisis created by the Tragic Week and the repression: the failure to incorporate the workers into the political structure.

The Workers and Political Power

To Socialist party leader Pablo Iglesias, the political crisis of 1909–1910 had seemed the perfect opportunity for organized labor to secure a place within the political structure.

Maura's concept of parliamentary government, very similar to that of Cánovas, had been that the two major parties would represent all national interests. With respect to workers, the Conservatives had enacted almost all of the laws governing health, working hours, and employment of women and children. Maura believed the party should do this because of a concern for national welfare and not because they were committed to this policy by workers' votes. But after 1909 this paternalistic system no longer satisfied workers, who demanded direct representation. Pablo Iglesias was explicit about this point in a speech on June 13, 1914. Acknowledging La Cierva's conscientious enforcement of the factory laws, Iglesias asked whether the Minister had seriously thought this would prevent the socialists from opposing him "on the day that you trampled on us in the field of political action." Labor's most earnest desire was to prevent the Conservatives from "erecting obstacles to the political action of the proletariat because through this action, the proletariat is going to increase its strength, which is the only positive guarantee of all its conquests." [13] In the belief that the closing of labor centers and of workers' schools by the Maura government in 1909 had signified just such an obstacle, Spanish socialists abandoned a fundamental party tenet and allied with the bourgeois republicans. Through this Conjunción Republicana-Socialista, Pablo Iglesias gained a seat in the Cortes in the elections of May 1910 and thereby became the first socialist deputy. The "political action of the proletariat" seemed just over the horizon. Yet somehow it never appeared.

For Maura, the willingness of the King and of the Liberal party to collaborate with the Conjunción Republicana-Socialista was "unconstitutional," and he called upon Alfonso to "rectify" the situation. Republicans and socialists were quick to seize upon the undemocratic implications; Maura did not look to the electorate for a mandate to govern, but to the King. Dato's Conservative faction entered office without making any attempt to clarify this or any other issue; Maura's term "the accommodating ones" ("los idóneos") perfectly described Dato's group who, in this case, were opposed to political power for the republicans or socialists but would not openly fight them.

Gradually, through the haze of the "Maura, no!" campaign, the socialists perceived that in a subtle and more effective fashion, the Liberals also opposed political power for labor. Liberals merely promoted an informal relationship with the Conjunción as a means of neutralizing the left wing, and made no effort to reform constitutional practices. Essentially the Liberals established a working entente with the republicans, whose leaders were even invited to the palace, but there was never any suggestion that a republican should enter the cabinet. At a critically important period in Spanish politics, this prevented republicans and socialists from realizing the full potential of their coalition as an independent force; it also prevented the consolidation of the alliance between the urban middle class and organized labor which was the key to any serious reform movement.

Socialists also became convinced that republicans did not really respect the rights of workers, and suspected they were being exploited — a warning repeated constantly by Fabra Rivas from his exile in Paris. "We have ceased to be socialists," wrote one party editorialist in 1914; "we are dupes and gulls." [14] From 1914 on, the socialists once again began to work independently although party leader Iglesias tried to prevent the UGT from breaking openly with the republican parties.

Meanwhile, the national problems defined by politicians at the turn of the century persisted, and because they were not resolved they intensified. The Catalan regional problem is an excellent case in point.

Catalan Politics

The reformist zeal of Catalan politicians, who had seemed the vanguard of a national reform movement, diminished sharply. There was no attempt to revive Solidaridad Catalana as a bloc through which all local parties would work in the national Cortes toward social and economic benefits for all Catalans. The three Catalan republican parties coalesced in the Unió Federal Nacionalista Republicana under the leadership of Pedro Corominas.[15] However, because the Unió (or the *Esquerra,* as it became known) never actively solicited workers' votes with a promise of social reforms, it remained a negligible factor in regional and in national politics.*

The Lliga definitively abandoned its nationalist and interclass character to become, in the words of Josep Benet, "conservador y clasista." [16] The Lliga returned to the Restoration practice of making private agreements with Madrid politicians, but after the Tragic Week its position was weaker. Despite all the evidence to the contrary, the suspicion lingered that the insurrection had been a separatist movement and thus a treacherous blow to national unity in wartime. The Lliga was further discredited for having failed to aid public authorities to suppress the rebellion. The Tragic Week seemed to confirm all doubts about Maura's attempt to incorporate regional aspirations into a national reform program. In 1918, when Francisco Cambó entered Maura's National Government in a desperate effort to save the constitutional monarchy, he tried to implement a well-planned series of public works and eco-

* It is the opinion of Alberto Pérez Baró, a socialist active in Barcelona labor circles from the time of the First World War, that if the Esquerra had not repudiated the events of the Tragic Week and the men who participated, it would have won the support of workers who were disillusioned with the Radicals but found no other party to defend them (interview with Pérez Baró on July 28, 1960, in Barcelona).

nomic reforms for the industrialization of Spain, but they were suspected of being merely a device to enhance Catalan power.

This was due in part to the continued demands of Catalonia for greater autonomy. In October 1912 Canalejas had presented to the Cortes a bill providing for an association (*Mancomunidad*) of the legislatures of the four Catalan provinces with limited jurisdiction. Canalejas had hoped to rise above partisan considerations and to resolve an urgent problem through legislation. After his death, his Liberal party proved incapable of such a statesmanlike policy; when the Count of Romanones pressed for a vote, the party split over the issue. Because the need was urgent, the Conservative government of Eduardo Dato abandoned the course of legislative reform and established the mancomunidad through royal fiat (December 18, 1913). By the following April the Catalans had organized their unified provincial assembly and yet, remembering the events of the Tragic Week, neither the Lliga (composed essentially of industrialists) nor the Esquerra (the middle class) were willing to use the full potential of this institution as a means to mobilize all Catalans, including urban workers, in order to secure "integral autonomy" [17] — that is to say, the autonomy of the four Catalan provinces, within the Spanish monarchy, in all matters except defense and foreign affairs. In the crisis of 1917 and again in 1918, Catalan politicians did not work through the mancomunidad; instead they tried to force the central government to concede autonomy to Catalonia by working with other dissident national groups. Catalan politicians' distrust of urban workers became an open fear from 1919 on, when industrialists and organized labor waged open warfare in the streets of Barcelona.

Within the framework of national politics, the failure to achieve representative government, through the mancomunidad, in Catalonia — the most industrialized area of the nation — dealt a crippling blow to the cause of Spanish democracy. Workers everywhere in Spain looked for salvation to the labor movements, not to political parties, and the labor movement functioned outside of the political structure.

The Labor Movement

On October 31, 1910, labor representatives from all over Spain met in Barcelona and voted to expand the Catalan Regional Confederation of Labor (Solidaridad Obrera) into a national confederation. On September 8, 1911, the Confederación Nacional del Trabajo (CNT) was officially inaugurated in a congress held in Barcelona; delegates voted to abstain from all political reforms and to move directly toward "social emancipation." The usual explanation of these developments is that Catalan workers, inspired by the power they had exercised during the General Strike of 1909 under the direction of anarcho-syndicalists, and disillusioned with the failure of the Radicals to establish a republic, enrolled enthusiastically in the CNT. This was not the case.

The Radical party, not Solidaridad Obrera, emerged as the hero of the Tragic Week and the martyr of the repression that followed. The same Radical politicians who had disclaimed any responsibility for the rebellion before the courts, boasted of their actions in the elections of 1910 and thereby won five of Barcelona's seven seats in the Cortes through workers' votes. Emiliano Iglesias, whose behavior had been perhaps the most ignoble, was elected deputy for the first time. But in succeeding years workers became convinced that politics in general, and Lerroux's Radical party in particular, were not the instruments through which to redress their grievances.* When they returned to the labor movement, they adopted without protest its policy of aggressive syndicalism — in part because the policy was well-articulated, in part because it met their needs in the complex labor situation that prevailed after 1917.

The CNT's policy of aggressive syndicalism was a result of the repression that followed the Tragic Week. The Maura government closed the Solidaridad Obrera headquarters, claiming that the labor confederation had been the instrument through which Francisco Ferrer, in collaboration with the French CGT and international Freemasonry, had carried out the rebellion. They did little to prove the charge beyond making a passing reference to a small loan from Ferrer, which had enabled Solidaridad Obrera to rent its offices, and to the assertions of Radicals that the labor confederation had no funds and therefore must have been subsidized by Ferrer.[18]

Solidaridad Obrera officials tried to refute the charges, insisting upon the facts that the confederation had refused to sponsor the General Strike and that no official had been prosecuted; the secretary general, José Román, was

---

* There is an oft-recounted anecdote that reflects the disenchantment of workers both with republican and with Liberal politicians after the Tragic Week. Anarchist Leopoldo Bonafulla and Radical Luis Zurdo discussed the situation in their jail cells in 1910. "We're now grist for the elections," said Bonafulla. When Zurdo lamented that Moret "has made fools of us republicans," using them to force Maura to resign, Bonafulla replied that "we all allowed ourselves to be deceived." (Bonafulla [Esteve], *Revolución de julio,* pp. 227–28.)

banished from Barcelona but allowed to return on November 11.[19] In a special assembly held in Barcelona in December 1909, delegates from trade syndicates voted to prepare a documented refutation of all charges; either this was not prepared or it was not published.[20] Despite these efforts, the image of the labor organization as one dedicated to the overthrow of the existing regime had been established in the public mind.

Membership in Solidaridad Obrera dropped from 15,000 in all of Catalonia to only 4,418.[21] Only 27 unions sent delegates to the special labor assembly held December 18, 1909, while 40 other unions sent pledges of adherence;[22] these figures are to be compared with those of the special assembly held in April of the same year, to which 108 unions had sent 104 delegates, who voted to boycott the Radical newspaper. Solidaridad Obrera had lost the few gains achieved in two years of harsh competition with the Radical party.

The repression caused not only a drop in membership but a change in the composition of Solidaridad Obrera. Moderate labor leaders, particularly officials of trade syndicates, withdrew from the Labor Confederation, either because of fear or because of a lack of class unity, which led them to negotiate independently with employers.[23] Another factor in the control established by the revolutionary elite over the Catalan labor force was the decision of the socialists to withdraw from Solidaridad Obrera as soon as it became a national organization. Disregarding the advice of Fabra Rivas, and of Jean Jaurès in France, Spanish socialists abandoned the major labor force in Spain to the anarcho-syndicalists, instead of trying to work within the CNT or at least to collaborate with it.[24]

The new aggressive attitude that prevailed in Solidaridad Obrera was already evident in the fall of 1910 when a small number of delegates from all of Spain met in Barcelona. The Catalan representatives now asserted that "Ferrer was shot for acts which we performed." [25] It was at this meeting that the vote was taken which led to the formation of the Confederación Nacional del Trabajo (CNT). The establishment of a nationwide labor confederation had been on the agenda for the 1909 congress, which had been postponed because of the Tragic Week. Thus the rebellion, and even more the repression that followed, did not so much instigate the formation of the national labor confederation as determine that it would be anarcho-syndicalist in orientation — that is, the confederation would be less a collective bargaining agency than a vehicle for organizing violent, lawless activity. Subsequent government persecution forced more and more workers to accept these policies.

After the formal inauguration of the CNT in September 1911, its first action — hardly one to allay suspicions about the labor movement — was to schedule a general strike for September 16.[26] It failed completely because police learned all the details from informants (particularly from the brother of Miguel V. Moreno), and because Lerroux cooperated with authorities in suppressing it.[27]

As a result of the repression that followed the General Strike of 1911, the three strongest syndicates in Barcelona were disbanded (stevedores, teamsters, and metallurgical workers), and the most active labor leaders were arrested or fled to France. Until the summer of 1914 the government did not allow the National Committee of the CNT (which had its headquarters in Barcelona) to function legally. Not until 1918 was the CNT able to establish formal contacts with member syndicates.[28] All of this served to convince workers that given the government policy of opposing organized labor — of suppressing the labor movement as often as possible, as a threat to public order — the only alternative was to defend their interests through violent direct action. Despite government prosecution (especially during the Primo de Rivera dictatorship) and lack of organizational machinery, the CNT had 800,000 members by 1928 and more than one and a half million during the Second Republic.[29]

The popularity of the CNT program of violence, together with the events of the Tragic Week, are cited as the basis for the contention that the Catalan worker is an anarchist by nature, who prefers to use the labor organization as an instrument for destroying by force the established state (be it monarchy or republic). The facts lend themselves to another interpretation.

The objectives of the CNT were not primarily political; they were economic. The policy of direct violent action was an effective response to the conditions of the Catalan industrial situation, where the economy could not expand with ease and where employers were not inclined to negotiate with labor. Even the CNT organization was a response to an urgent need: how to organize predominantly unskilled, semiliterate workers, and how to persuade more skilled workers to make common cause with the unskilled. The Solidaridad Obrera tactic, continued by the CNT, was to work through a confederation of member trade unions (*sindicatos*), of skilled workers' unions (for example, typesetters) and some unskilled (textile factory machinery operators, for example). Not until 1918 did CNT leaders experiment (in the *sindicatos únicos*) with incorporating into one union both skilled and unskilled workers.

The wisdom of the CNT apolitical policy, based on a long tradition of workers' distrust of politicians, was confirmed in 1917 — the very last moment in which the constitutional monarchy might have saved itself through legislative reforms. The failure of Catalan politicians to seek worker support for regional autonomy has already been noted. This was part of a general phenomenon: middle class republican politicians, gathered in an extraconstitutional Cortes, not only failed to press their demands, but rallied to support the government when workers declared a general strike (August 13, 1917) as a means of coercing the government into granting reforms which seemed otherwise unobtainable. That elusive alliance between the worker and the middle class, which Pablo Iglesias had pursued since 1910, vanished and did not reappear until the Second Republic.

Following the collapse of the reform movement of 1917, workers actually fought in the streets of Barcelona to defend their interests against intransigent employers and police. This conditioned the development of the entire Spanish labor movement, decisively influencing the policy of the CNT and affecting its relations with the socialist UGT. Further Catalan labor violence made the oligarchy even more determined to refuse all concessions and justified a government policy of harsh restrictions. An important element in this vicious circle, one locked within police and industrialists' files, is the role of the agent provocateur in inciting workers to violence or terrorism.

National Education

A prime objective of the incendiarism of the Tragic Week was the destruction of the Catholic school system. Together with the fact that Francisco Ferrer, presumed author of the rebellion, was a rationalist educator, the incendiarism has served as the basis for the argument of Spanish conservatives that secular education leads inevitably to atheism and violence; on the fiftieth anniversary of Ferrer's execution, Madrid newspapers still repeated this charge. These developments had direct consequences for the problem of educating a largely illiterate population and for the more subtle problem of what kind of secondary and university education — secular or Catholic — should be offered to the middle class.

The attempt to dissociate secular education from the incendiarism of the Tragic Week began immediately. On August 11, 1909, the Guild of Private Teachers of Catalonia (Gremi de Professors Particulars de Catalunya) issued a public protest: "It being public knowledge that the rebels, in their shouts and even graphically, have mixed the august name of education with the vulgarities of their revolution, the Guild protests the insult thereby inferred to the sacred ministry served by its guild members." [30]

Their protest was ignored in view of the tremendous damage to the Catholic school system. In Barcelona alone incendiaries had burned twenty-one schools run by religious orders, only two of which were schools for wealthy children. Both of the workers' circles burned had offered classes to workers. Three of the seven headquarters of male religious orders destroyed by fire were the property of clergy engaged in education; the buildings served as storage places for educational material used in their schools throughout the province.

In the trial of Francisco Ferrer, military prosecutors mentioned (although they did not make this a major element in the case against him) the charge that he had incited the Radical party members to armed rebellion through the teachers he had placed in schools located in Radical centers. The charge was made in the case of José Folch Dalmau, head of the rationalist school in Premiá and president of the Radical center; Folch took an active part in burning convents before fleeing to France.[31] In at least one other Catalan city, Calonge, teachers in schools associated with Ferrer participated directly in the burning of Catholic schools.*

Conservatives used these events to argue against educating workers, a viewpoint stated most forcibly in an editorial in the Carlist newspaper, El Correo Catalán, on August 16, 1909: "Between a worker who does not know how to read, and one who reads atheistic and anarchist newspapers that attack . . . all the fundamental principles of the social order, we would always and in any case prefer the first." Only some few men dared to argue that better-educated workers would not be so violent or so prone to believe the tales of anticlerical demagogues. Only a few statesmen recognized the possibility of stabilizing the Monarchy, of easing the social struggle, by preparing the worker to par-

---

* The events in Calonge directly influenced the career of Dr. Pedro Roselló, in 1963 co-Director of the International Bureau of Education in Geneva. Roselló's father, a laborer, sent him to a school associated with Ferrer in Calonge. The teacher was jealous of the school run by the Christian Brothers which, because it was subsidized, offered free tuition; with no outside funds, the rationalist school had to charge a pittance of five reales a month. During the Tragic Week, the teacher of the rationalist school participated in the burning of the Catholic school. Disapproving of this, Roselló's father sent him to be educated in France. (Interview with Roselló in Geneva, on November 24, 1960.) The events in Calonge became so notorious that the Rector of the University (Bonet) found it necessary to issue a public statement making it clear that no public school teacher had participated (La Publicidad, September 29, 1909).

ticipate in the political system and to perform a more remunerative function in the industrial structure. Education became a political issue, a means of indoctrination, and not a campaign for the development of the nation's most valuable resource.

This was clearly shown in the closing of the public schools in August of 1909 by the Conservative Governments of Antonio Maura. When Education Minister Rodríguez Sanpedro refused to issue the order, Interior Minister La Cierva did so on the grounds of "public order." [32] Despite opposition from Catholic groups throughout the nation, the Liberal government permitted these schools to reopen on February 3, 1910. This did not, however, end the opposition to secular education nor resolve the problem of an illiterate population.

In Madrid, lay educators, particularly those associated with the Junta para Ampliación de Estudios Históricos e Investigaciones Científicas, worked quietly in pursuit of their ideal of education as the realization of professional and cultural excellence, independent of ideologies and politics. They met intense opposition not only from extremists of the Right but of the Left. In 1936, at the outset of the Civil War, the Junta's experimental school — the Instituto Escuela — was closed by the Popular Front government as a bourgeois institution. It was not permitted to reopen by the Franco regime because of its reputed left wing associations.

The failure to expand primary education in order to achieve a literate population, and the reluctance to allow even private educators to experiment with new ideas, were prime examples of the stalemate of reform movements during the remaining years of the constitutional monarchy.

Spanish society weathered the crisis that followed the Tragic Week without reorganizing itself to resolve the fundamental problems involved in the Barcelona rebellion; it merely sought men who could hold office and still avoid the issues. When the need for reforms became critical, it was met from outside the established structure: in 1917 infantry officers tried to work through their newly organized juntas to demand that the King change the system, while Catalan and republican legislators tried to accomplish the same goal through an extra-constitutional assembly, and labor tried a revolutionary general strike. By playing one group off against another, the social and political system emerged intact from this crisis. And this in turn provided extremists with new grounds for arguing that only a revolution would bring about the necessary changes in Spain.

CHAPTER XV

The Function of Anticlericalism
in Spanish Politics

ON JULY 26, 1909, a general strike began in the industrial cities of Catalonia as an antiwar protest and developed into five days of convent burnings. This is the central fact in the Tragic Week.[1] The corollary illustrates the critical issue in Spanish politics: this insurrection led to no political reforms, not even to legislation controlling the fiscal and educational activities of the clergy. The anticlerical uprising had served exclusively to dissipate a potentially revolutionary movement.

In this context, anticlericalism is not considered as a religious issue, nor even as a matter concerning the Catholic Church as such. The Second Vatican Council demonstrated what Protestant leaders like John Bennett have been asserting for years, namely that it is not "a monolithic Roman Church, built somewhat on the lines of the Stalinist empire, that is controlled from the Vatican."[2] The character of the Church in each country is determined by its dynamic relationship with the society — by the way in which laymen perceive and carry out their religious obligations, as well as by the way in which the national clergy interprets its duties. The Confessional Catholic State of Spain, so often a contentious issue in modern history, is the product of a subtle merger of Church precepts and Iberian society.

In the forging of national unity and in the establishment of an empire, the Catholic Church has played a great and a creative role in Spain. But events since the late sixteenth century have tended to make the Church an instrument of state authority. It may be argued that the state benefited more than did the Church, and that the clergy has too often subordinated its spiritual obligations to its political function; there are, however, exciting indications that the clergy in the future may play a dynamic role in the reorganization of social power in Spain. But in 1909 most clergy, like most workers, considered the Church the keystone of the established order.

And in a subtle fashion, anticlericals served the same political function — "as the prop for the maintenance of institutions," said one editorialist writing of the Radicals' action during the Tragic Week of 1909.[3] Catalan labor leader Joaquín Maurín was even more explicit: "lerrouxismo directed the popular protest into the burning of churches and convents in order to leave intact the real foundations of the regime."[4]

The Chronology of the Tragic Week

The motor impulse of the General Strike — the cause that rallied men of all social classes — was not anticlericalism. It was the unpopular war in Morocco and the decision of the Maura government to call up reserve conscript soldiers. In this sense, Governor Ossorio and other government officials were correct in describing the General Strike, and the events of Monday, July 26, as an improvised, spontaneous movement.[5]

On Tuesday, July 27, convents began to burn, barricades were built, and street fighting began. Such activities presuppose organization. The socialists constituted a minute faction, the anarchists were an isolated group. Only the Radicals had an enormous worker membership, in the city and in the province — a membership gained in large part because of Alejandro Lerroux' promise to prepare a "social revolution." On July 27 the workers forced party leaders to carry out these plans. Or so it appeared when Radical leaders acquiesced in the burning of convents, mysteriously but efficiently organized by the extremist element from the Juventud Radical and the Casa del Pueblo.

For men like Ferrer, and for all those anarchists and Radical extremists with whom he had worked for so long, incendiarism was the way to a revolution in Spain. When Juan Puig of Masnou had asked Ferrer how the burning of convents could lead to a republic, Ferrer replied that "the important thing was not the republic, the question was that there should be a revolution." During the preceding year, Ferrer and his collaborators had tried to prepare a revolutionary situation through artificial means — through a general strike on behalf of the Alcalá del Valle prisoners. The antiwar General Strike afforded them a far better opportunity for action. But for the Radical leaders, the convent burning was an end in itself (particularly after they learned that no other city outside Catalonia had seconded the anti-war protest).

And so during the week of July 26, 1909, only convents and churches were attacked. Even though the uprising had started as an antiwar protest, no military garrison was attacked. Despite the economic depression, neither banks nor factories nor homes of wealthy industrialists were burned* — not even Rusiñol's factory where workers had been locked out.[6]

Army officers and the middle classes acquiesced in the incendiarism either through fear or inability to re-establish order, or because they secretly sym-pathized with the project.** Juan Caballé, a moderate Catalan republican deputy, explained that the propertied classes welcomed it as a "hygienic measure," for the excessive number of convents in Barcelona and its suburbs constituted "an epidemic that is asphyxiating us."[7] The incendiarism did not even cause permanent material damage to the Church; within a year most of the religious establishments had been rebuilt.

Why did the Radical extremists concentrate the uprising almost exclusively on church and convent burning. The answer may simply be that they con-sidered the incendiarism a means of dispersing the revolutionary fervor they themselves had cultivated through anticlerical propaganda; this was neces-sary in order to protect the Radical party's position within the established regime.†

* This anomaly is pointed up in the following anecdote. In the Catalan manufactur-ing town of Palamós during the Tragic Week, when a crowd demanded the keys of the church from the parish priest, he replied: "Let's burn the church but we'll also burn the factory. Both you and I will lose our daily bread. We'll begin with the fac-tory." The priest set out, but the crowd did not follow and it did not burn the church. (Brissa, Revolución de julio, p. 185.)

** When certain pro-Catholic deputies complained in the Cortes that only church property had been attacked, Interior Minister La Cierva replied that there had been attacks on jewelry stores but that they had been turned back by the armed guards on duty (La Cierva, July 8, 1910, Diario de las Cortes, II, 468). But this, of course, begs the question of why armed guards were not permanently stationed at convents and churches as well as at jewelry stores and banks. Fabra Rivas denies there were guards at banks, and affirms that incendiaries chose not to attack them or the homes of the wealthy, because the movement was directed entirely against the clergy (Magin Vidal [Fabra Rivas], "Réponse a des calomnies," L'Humanité [Paris] August 18, 1909).

† Burning convents as a diversionary maneuver in a general strike had been pro-posed three years earlier by Alejandro Lerroux. In his infamous article, "El Alma en los labios," Lerroux analyzed the General Strike of 1902 and concluded that in any popular uprising only two alternatives were possible within the realities of the Bar-celona situation: that "the blood of the people would flow," or that convents be burned. The choice between these two means of releasing pent-up antagonism —

It is also possible, as some of their republican opponents charged, that the Radical leaders acted in collaboration with government authorities and deliberately precipitated a general strike in Barcelona before the socialists had time to organize a national general strike. An editorialist writing in *La Publicidad* of Barcelona, on July 9, 1910, lamented that Socialist party leader Pablo Iglesias had lacked the documentation to prove this charge during the debate in the Cortes. Whether done deliberately or inadvertently, the effect was the same: precipitating the strike in Barcelona deprived the potential national labor protest of force. Moreover, it enabled La Cierva to discredit the protest as a Catalan separatist movement and thus to isolate it from other worker support.

There is still another possible explanation of Radical motivation. From the moment that Lerroux first arrived in Barcelona, labor leaders had suspected him of receiving subsidies from employers and accused him of trying to break the power of the labor movement. In the month immediately preceding the Tragic Week the socialists and labor leaders of Solidaridad Obrera were preparing a general strike of textile workers in protest against a lockout by key industrialists; this lockout continued throughout the fall of 1909, but because the government had closed both labor centers and newspapers, workers could expect little satisfaction. It seems more than mere coincidence that the General Strike of 1909, like the General Strike of 1902, should occur at a time when textile manufacturers wanted to reduce labor costs, a project that necessarily involved restricting or repressing the labor movement.

Whether the Radical extremists acted autonomously or under instructions, the result was the same: the burning of convents served as a safety valve for a tense society. This leads back to the fundamental question of why anticlericalism had served throughout that decade to divert attention from other and perhaps more serious problems, such as the industrial crisis or the growing power of army officers; why in 1909 did it serve as an automatic and a relatively harmless release for a potentially revolutionary force? To those concerned about the pastoral mission of the Church, and to those concerned about future disorders that may result from anticlericalism, an analysis of

---

Lerroux went on to state — would be made by the Army: in 1902 soldiers had fired upon workers; in 1906 Lerroux stated openly his hope to persuade soldiers to burn convents. The article, published in 1906, was reprinted in *De la Lucha* (Barcelona, n.d. [1909?], pp. 96, 98.) In 1930, looking back on his article, "El Alma en los labios," Lerroux concluded that he had "done the wrong thing" in publishing it, then added "but I wrote what I thought and felt at that moment." (*Al Servicio de la República,* p. 42).

the Tragic Week might help to clarify the conditions that enabled anti-clericalism to perform this function in Spanish society.

The Objectives of the Incendiarism

The causes for the workers' animosity toward the clergy are clearly revealed in the types of religious establishment they burned during the Tragic Week. Basic to the hostility was the adjustment made by the Church to the urbanization of society and the changes this involved in its relations with workers. One major problem was the clergy's need to finance its activities, and the corresponding resentment of the worker who had to pay for the services or who simply disliked the money-making activities of a religious institution. This very real conflict was complicated by semantics, by the clergy's attempt to defend its activities in terms of its historic role in feudal or imperial Spain.

The specific causes for worker antagonism are indicated in the following summary of religious institutions destroyed during the Tragic Week.

Type of institution	Number destroyed
School buildings	24
Schools in parish churches, or in welfare institutions	4
Schools in workers' foundations	2
Administrative centers of male educational religious orders	3
Total	33
Parish churches	14
Welfare institutions (orphanages, asylums for the aged, corrective institutions)	11
Residences, male religious orders (including the seminary)	8
Contemplative (cloistered) convents	8
Catholic workers' foundations (workers' circles)	6
Grand total	80

The destruction of educational institutions was the principal objective. Workers not only believed the clergy made a profit from their schools, but considered them an obstacle to the development of a free public school system. Articulate labor spokesmen, as for example socialist José Comaposada, declared that the ideas taught in Catholic schools were antithetical to the cause of workers' rights. Workers *"know,"* wrote Comaposada in 1909, "that every convent is a perpetual conspiracy against every principle of democracy, against all ideas of liberty, and all aspirations to progress." [8]

The attack upon contemplative orders was prompted by a macabre curiosity about life within a cloister; incendiaries took special delight in the mysterious room in the convent of the Augustinian Nuns. These orders were considered exceptionally wealthy, an opinion based largely on the fact that the nuns performed no remunerated service; the search for stocks and cash in fact proved relatively successful only in the convents of the Hieronymite and Capuchin Nuns. Finally, the antagonism toward contemplative orders was indicative of another constant in anticlericalism: the growing unwillingness of a secular world to admit the necessity for institutions entirely devoted to religious practices.

Incendiaries attacked Catholic workers' circles for more concrete reasons: because they considered them agencies for scab labor, or simply a means of attracting workers away from republican and socialist centers by promising them insurance benefits. In 1909 members failed to defend these circles, proving the contention of farsighted priests and laymen that workers felt no loyalty to these employer-sponsored institutions. After the Tragic Week, employers refused to finance new workers' circles and yet opposed the organization of Catholic trade unions. The Catholic labor movement remained a weak organization, neglected by the clergy, who thereby lost still another opportunity to reach the urban worker.

Some of these workers' circles had been located in the fourteen parish churches, situated in slum districts, that were destroyed completely or in part during the Tragic Week. These churches also served as agencies for the distribution of aid to the indigent and provided evening classes for workers. In these activities as community centers, parish churches were competing with the neighborhood centers of the Radical party which provided much the same services.

Welfare institutions constituted the third largest group of institutions attacked. These asylums, like the schools, were at the center of the dispute between clergy and Radical politicians about how the Spanish state should meet the demands of an urban population for expanded services. Between subsidizing religious orders and employing laymen in public institutions, the Radicals — always eager to expand their patronage — far preferred the second alternative.[9]

The desire of middle-class republicans for more jobs was reinforced by the workers' resentment of the clerical welfare institutions. They disliked the apparent hypocrisy and the exploitation of charity for profits involved in forcing inmates or orphans to prepare merchandise for sale. Furthermore, these clerical enterprises deprived workers of employment, indirectly by competing with secular businessmen (who thus employed fewer workers or paid them less in order to compete with clerical enterprises), and directly by performing more cheaply services such as laundry and sewing, often done by wives of workers to earn extra money. In short, workers tended to consider the clergy simply as businessmen who competed in favored conditions.

From a clerical viewpoint, the matter was quite different. In this decade of rising prices the clergy, particularly those faced with caring for the poor, had to augment their traditional sources of income: interest from capital constituted by the dowries of their members, various government subsidies, and the alms of the faithful. For many orders this involved only small-scale activities (candy-making or embroidery), while some few orders (such as Marists and Jesuits) had the capital for larger ventures. Although the figure has never been proven, the aggregate of clerical capital at this time was said to have constituted one third of the capital wealth of Spain.

These economic factors formed the basis for the workers' conviction that religious orders and great capitalists were closely linked, and for the popular identification of clericalism with capitalism. In 1909 Anselmo Lorenzo, a spokesman for the Spanish labor movement since the time of the First Republic, wrote that "the permanent cause" of anticlericalism among workers was the "existence of the plutocratic-clerical trust," formed in Catalonia by the cotton manufacturers and the Jesuits: "it sucks up the blood of workers and absorbs all wealth produced by labor." [10] This focus of worker hatred,* of the exploited toward the exploiter, has complicated the pastoral mission of the Church since the nineteenth century. In the long run the success of this mission depended not only upon the resolution of the Church's institutional difficulties but upon the health of Spanish society.

* As a further example of this climate of opinion that influenced workers, or at least labor leaders, Hippolyte Havel wrote in explanation of the Ferrer case: "No previous economic system has understood so well as capitalism to identify itself with the existing political form of a given country. In republican America it allies itself with corrupt politics, in autocratic Russia with Tsarism, in militaristic Germany with the aristocracy, in Spain with clericalism." (See Leonard D. Abbott, editor, *Francisco Ferrer: His Life, Work and Martyrdom. With messages written especially for this brochure by Ernst Haeckel, Maxim Gorky. Published on the first anniversary of his death* (New York: Francisco Ferrer Association, n.d. [1910]), p. 28).

Church and Society

Juan Maragall, the Catalan poet, saw with incisive clarity that the Tragic Week was but a manifestation of the malady that affected not only Catalan society but all Spain — "a social impotency higher than that of other people like ourselves." [11] The workers had chosen to attack the Church as a symbol of the Spanish social structure. For the uncivilized crimes committed, all sectors of society and most specifically the *classes dirigents* must bear the responsibility, argued Maragall. The attempt by the "lower mob" to demolish the social structure because of hatred was matched by the failure of "the other, the conservative mob" [12] to defend the structure, because of egotism; this indicated a crisis so profound that it was necessary to change the social patterns of the culture. No repression, no matter how severe, would make the *causes* of the Tragic Week disappear. Maragall's strongest article, "La Ciutat del Perdó," in which he berated the classes dirigents for allowing some individuals to be shot in Montjuich "for an evil that is in all of us" and begged that they demand a general amnesty, was never published; it was the eve of Ferrer's execution, and the policy of the Lliga newspaper (the only medium through which Maragall could reach the classes dirigents) was to support Maura.[13]

Despite his prestige as a writer and as a devout Catholic, Maragall's attempt to alert clergy and laity to the dangers — and to the possibilities — implicit in the Tragic Week were politely ignored. In 1963 José Benet published a scholarly work on the articles and letters written by Maragall in connection with the Tragic Week; his book was so popular that it has twice been reprinted, suggesting not only that the clerical problem is very much a contemporary one but that Maragall's solution is more acceptable to readers today.

Maragall's goal was the formation of a new social collectivity, the transformation of the Spanish population into a united people ("de població en poble"). In an article entitled "L'església cremada," published on December 18, 1909, he asked that the Church serve as the medium through which to effect this transformation; he urged laymen and clergy to welcome and retain within the Church those individuals who had had to burn the doors to get in.

As a poet, Maragall talked of "love" that would banish the "hatred" that divided society, but essentially he was urging the process that reformers today describe as community development: the incorporation of the workers, "the outsiders," into the political structure so that their presence can be felt and their vote count. Quite apart from any improvement in personal income or living conditions, a successful community develops only when — to use the expression of Frank Mankeiwicz — "the forgotten and ignored have been invited to 'join the parade.' " [14]

Maragall proposed that the Catholic clergy and laity take the lead in restructuring social power, but at least until now Spanish Catholicism has not met this challenge.* A less visionary goal was the correction of specific abuses that had led to the Tragic Week; in this instance, also, politicians failed to meet the challenge.

Incendiarism and Politics

The convent burnings of 1909 led to anticlerical legislation, as they had in 1835 and would again in 1931.** The difference is that the "Padlock Law" of 1910 concerned a very minor issue and had no long range significance.

This was not apparent at first. When critics dismissed the Tragic Week as "a sad and sterile revolt," a mere device to gain popular support, Radical Deputy Emiliano Iglesias declared with pride that it had made possible enactment of the so-called "Ley del Candado" ("Padlock Law"), presented by Canalejas to the Cortes on June 9, 1910, and rapidly passed into law on December 23, 1910. After ten years of campaigning, Spanish anticlericals had

---

* Reinhold Niebuhr remarks upon this phenomenon: "It may be significant that Catholicism is most creative in an environment of an industrial civilization, where it is historically least at home. . . . In the Rhineland and in France, it brings its ancient wisdom to bear on the problems of modern collectivism, and incidentally provides a haven for the imperiled individual in the technical togetherness of urban life. In Bavaria and in Spain, its ancient wisdom is not enough to cut through the ancient traditions of a feudal society" (Niebuhr, "A Plea for Tolerance," *The Atlantic,* 210 [August 1962], p. 75).

** Concerning the convent burnings in May 1931, which had so tragic an effect upon the politics of the Second Republic, Miguel Maura, Minister of the Interior in 1931, reported that they constituted "a simple sectarian manifestation," organized by a group of middle-class youths in the Ateneo of Madrid "as a protest against the leniency of the government in clerical matters." Prime Minister Azaña acquiesced when assured of the limited nature of the demonstration. Army officers were instructed not to interfere. (Maura, *Así cayó Alfonso XIII,* pp. 249–64. For a slightly different interpretation, see Indalecio Prieto, *Cartas a un escultor: Pequeños detalles de grandes sucesos* (Buenos Aires, 1961), pp. 46–55). These contrived, small-scale convent burnings for the purpose of securing anticlerical legislation are of a completely different character from the anticlerical violence during the Civil War when 7,937 clergy were killed (12 bishops, 283 nuns, 2,492 friars, and 5,255 priests) (Hugh Thomas, *The Spanish Civil War* [London, 1961], p. 173).

finally passed a law asserting the right of the state to establish controls on religious orders — the first such law since the Restoration of the Bourbons in 1875. Despite this assertion of an important principle, the law itself merely stated that no new orders could be established in Spain until the Cortes enacted a new law of associations; it was intended to be the first stage of a thorough legislative reform of the civil status of the clergy.

In line with the principle of civil supremacy asserted in the "Padlock Law," Canalejas did not believe it necessary for the state to negotiate a new concordat with the Vatican before it passed a new law of associations; for diplomatic and domestic reasons, however, he was willing to begin negotiations for a new concordat. However, when the Vatican refused to make any concessions, Canalejas broke off diplomatic relations and withdrew his ambassador. He persisted in his preparations of an Associations Bill, which he presented to the Cortes in 1911; his assassination the following year banished all hope of passing it. Canalejas' successor, the Count of Romanones, dealt with the associations bill as he (and the other politicians of his era) dealt with all reform legislation — he quietly abandoned the bill, lest it become an issue that aroused strong public reaction. Canalejas even retreated from the position established through the "Padlock Law" — the right of the state to legislate on matters concerning religious orders. In 1913 he negotiated an agreement with Rome concerning the establishment of new orders, and promised therein that there would be no new legislation on any clerical matter without the consent of the Vatican. Given the ultraconservative policies of Rafael Merry del Val, the Spanish Cardinal who served as the Papal Secretary of State, this spelled an end to resolving the problem through legislation.

Some part of this failure lies with the anticlerical politicians themselves. Anticlericalism served no political ideal. In France politicians established state control on clerical businesses and schools as a means of debilitating the monarchist cause and of strengthening the Third Republic. In Spain some anticlericals were monarchists, others republicans. Republicans were further divided over such basic issues as whether to organize a centralized or a federal state. Thus anticlericalism too often served to cover a general doctrinal confusion and lack of concrete projects for specific reforms — agrarian, educational, and industrial reforms.[15]

Still another factor in the failure to translate the violent protest of the Tragic Week into legislation was the fear of middle-class politicians to utilize the full potential of workers' votes. When Pedro Corominas, Catalan republican leader, lamented the violence and bloodletting of the Tragic Week, he revealed an uncertainty that explains why the Esquerra was an ineffective force in politics. In an editorial published on July 27, 1910, *La Tribuna* pointed out the inconsistency of Corominas' position: only through such disorders — "in which only the people, self-denying as always, take part" — could Corominas and his republican colleagues hope to take office.

During the remaining years of the constitutional monarchy, politicians in general succumbed to the argument that popular reform movements lead inevitably to violent disorder; there was no attempt to show how and why Radical extremists and anarchists had incited workers to burn convents. Such arguments have until now made it impossible to work out moderate proposals for the many problems that Spain must resolve before she can deal effectively with the economic and social conditions of the twentieth century. These are substantial, complex matters that must be analyzed realistically and not in terms of a traditionalism that only obscures the issues.

This is particularly true in defining the role of the Church in a Catholic nation such as Spain. The debate must avoid rhetoric and shibboleths, and must limit itself to specific issues: fiscal control of clerical business activities; the extent to which laymen or religious will be employed in public institutions; state control of Catholic schools and Church control of state schools; the legitimate competition between Catholic organizations and labor or political groups to enroll workers as members. At the turn of the century these matters were decided in France and Italy by compromise. In Spain they drifted along, only to flare up again in tragic fashion during the Second Republic and the Civil War. The victory of the Nationalist forces in 1939 merely suspended debate on the subject, while Franco's subsequent reliance upon the Church has aggravated a conflict whose resolution is left to future politicians.

Chronology
Bibliography
Notes
Index

CHRONOLOGY: 1833–1913

NB: Only those events are listed which are discussed in the text.

Bourbon Monarchy (1833–1868)

1833	September 29	Ferdinand VII dies and is succeeded by infant daughter Isabel under regency of her mother, María Cristina
1834		First Carlist War begins (Basques, Catalans, and some religious orders support the pretender, Don Carlos)
1835	July 25	Convent burnings in Barcelona and Madrid
	July 25 September 3 October 11	Royal Decrees, prepared by Juan Alvarez Mendizábal, providing for dissolution of religious orders and disposition of their property
1836	February 19 March 8	
1837	July 29	Law ordering sale of property of religious orders to begin in 1840
1839	August 31	First Carlist War ends (Peace of Vergara)
1845–1848		Second Carlist War
1851	March 16	Concordat between the Vatican and the Spanish state (granting religious orders right to form communities and to hold property in Spain)
1855 1856	May 1 July 11	New legislation providing for sale of property of religious orders
1859	August 25	Legislation annulled, in effect, by agreement signed by the Spanish government and the Vatican
1868	September 19	Military uprising against the monarchy
	September 30	Isabel II leaves Spain

Interregnum (1868–1875)

1869	June 1	New constitution approved by the Cortes
1870	January 2	Amadeo I of the House of Savoy begins to reign
	June 19–26	First National Labor Congress, held in Barcelona: approves organization of first national labor federation
	June 25	Isabel II abdicates in favor of her son, Alfonso XII
1872–1876		Third Carlist War
1873	February 11	Amadeo I abdicates
		Proclamation by the Cortes of the First Republic
1874	January 3	First Republic ended by a military *golpe de estado* (General Manuel Pavía)
	December 29	Pro-monarchist military uprising at Sagunto (General Arsenio Martínez Campos)

The Bourbon Restoration (1875–1899)

1875	January 14	Alfonso XII returns to Madrid
		Antonio Cánovas del Castillo, head of the government (until 1881)
1876	June 30	Constitution approved by the Cortes
		Industrialization of Spain begins (in Catalonia, "cotton euphoria" — until 1898)
1877		First electoral law
1879	May 2	Pablo Iglesias founds the Partido Socialista Obrero Español (PSOE)
1881	February 8	Práxedes Sagasta, Liberal party chief, heads a government for the first time (until 1883)
1885	November 26	Alfonso XII dies in the Palace of El Pardo (Madrid)
		Sagasta and Cánovas agree to share responsibility for the Monarchy — *el turno* ("Pacto del Pardo")
		Regency of Queen María Cristina (until 1902)
1886	May 17	Alfonso XIII is born
	September 19	Unsuccessful military uprising of Brigadier General Manuel Villacampa, in Madrid
		Republicans begin to accept seats in Congress of Deputies ("policy of attraction")
1887		Law of Associations (governing organizations of private citizens — cf. labor unions)

1888		Foundation of national socialist trade movement (Unión General del Trabajo — UGT)
1889	July	Second International Workingmen's Association founded, in Paris
1890	June 26	Law of Universal Suffrage
1893	September 24	Bomb thrown by anarchist Paulino Pallás at Captain General of Barcelona
	November 7	Bomb thrown into theatre by anarchist Santiago Salvador to protest torture of Pallás
1896	June 7	Bomb thrown into Corpus Cristi parade in Barcelona
1897	Spring	Trials at Montjuich Castle (Barcelona) of anarchist terrorists and labor leaders
	August 8	Cánovas assassinated by Italian anarchist, Michele Angiolillo, in revenge for Montjuich trials
1898	April 23	United States declares war on Spain
	July 26	Spain asks for peace terms
	December 10	Treaty of Peace signed in Paris (Spain renounces Cuba, Puerto Rico, Philippines, Guam)
1899		Socialist UGT national headquarters moved to Madrid

Decade of Reforms (1900–1909)

1900	March 13	Law governing factory working conditions of women and minors
	October 13–15	National labor congress held in Madrid
		Votes to organize a new national anarcho-syndicalist labor federation (Federación de Sociedades Obreras de la Región Española)
		Catalan industrialists begin to support regionalist movement
1901		Francisco Ferrer (1859–1909) returns from Paris to live in Barcelona
		Alejandro Lerroux (1864–1949) moves from Madrid to Barcelona to head republican movement
	May 14	National election of deputies
		Alejandro Lerroux elected in Barcelona
		4 Lliga candidates elected in Barcelona (presidents of four major business organizations, including Alberto Rusiñol)
	Spring	Textile manufacturers' lockout in the Ter Valley (Barcelona)

	September 8	Ferrer's Escuela Moderna opens in Barcelona
	September 19	Royal Decree, prepared by Liberal government of Sagasta, requiring religious orders to register under 1887 Law of Associations
1902	February 17–24	General Strike in Barcelona
	March	Sixth National Congress of Catholic Action, held in Santiago
	May 17	Alfonso XIII begins to rule (at 16 years of age)
		José Canalejas begins his anticlerical campaign among electorate
	July 1 ⎫ September 4 ⎭	Decrees prepared by Romanones strengthening primary public school system, and controlling Catholic schools
	December	Establishment of Ministry of Public Instruction (formerly, under the Ministry of Development)
	December 6	Francisco Silvela forms Conservative government, with Antonio Maura as Minister of the Interior
1903	January 5	Liberal party chief Práxedes Sagasta dies
	April 12	Reactivation of national republican movement (Unión Republicana) by Nicolás Salmerón
	April 25	Establishment of the Institute of Social Reforms
	April 26	Maura's "Fair Elections" (of Deputies)
	June 22	Junta Diocesana de Defensa de los Intereses Católicos organized in Barcelona
	Summer	Worker uprising in Alcalá del Valle (Cádiz)
	October 26	Silvela resigns as Conservative party chief, naming Antonio Maura his heir
	December 5	Maura forms a Conservative government (his first)
	December 31	Friar Bernardino Nozaleda appointed Archbishop of Valencia
1904	April 6	Alfonso XIII makes his first visit to Barcelona, accompanied by Premier Maura
	June 19	Maura government signs new agreement with Vatican on religious orders
	December 14	Antonio Maura resigns
1905	January 27	New Conservative premier, Raimundo Fernández Villaverde, finally agreed upon Persuades Friar Nozaleda to withdraw

June 23	Fernández Villaverde resigns Liberal party forms a government
September 10	National election of deputies
November	Nationwide election of city councilors
November 24	*Cu-Cut* incident (army officers attack Catalan regionalist magazine offices)
1906 January	Liberal party chief Segismundo Moret presents to the Cortes his draft Law of Jurisdictions
February 11	Catalan political groups hold first joint protest rally in Gerona against proposed Law of Jurisdictions
March 20	Cortes passes the Law of Jurisdictions
April 12	Good Friday: Ferrer organizes giant rationalist education demonstration in Barcelona
May 31	Marriage of Alfonso XIII to Victoria Eugenia of Battenberg, in Madrid Mateo Morral throws bomb at wedding party
June 4	Francisco Ferrer arrested as an accomplice of Morral
June 15	The Escuela Moderna, in Barcelona, is permanently closed
June 23	King signs new high tariff law
October 23	Bernabé Dávila, Liberal party Minister of the Interior, presents to the Cortes a draft of a new (anticlerical) Law of Associations
December–January 1907	Nationwide campaign against proposed Law of Associations organized by Catholic Action (Marquis of Comillas) In Barcelona, organization of Comité de Defensa Social (militant Catholic lawyers)
December 14	Militant Catholic deputies present resolution in Congress against private secular schools (re: Ferrer case)
1907 January 12	Royal Decree establishing Junta para Ampliación de Estudios e Investigaciones Científicas
January 25	Liberal government of General José López Dominguez resigns Antonio Maura forms Conservative government
February 14	Law for the Protection of National Industry
March	Catalan republicans, Carlists, Lliga form electoral coalition, Solidaridad Catalana, under presidency of Nicolás Salmerón

April 27	National election of deputies
June 7	Maura presents to the Congress his proposed Law for the Reform of Local Administration
June 12	Francisco Ferrer released from prison
June 13	In Barcelona, organization of Junta Diocesana de Corporaciones Católica-Obreras
June 23–26	National congress of Unión Republicana: Lerroux unsuccessful in attempt to oust Salmerón as President
July 6	Governor Ossorio announces arrest of terrorist Juan Rull in Barcelona
	Charles Arrow arrives in Barcelona to head Office of Special Investigation
July 22	Ferrer leaves for tour of France, Belgium, England
August 3	Municipal federation of trade unions reorganized in Barcelona under name, Solidaridad Obrera
August 8	New Electoral Law (supersedes Law of 1890)
August 24–31	International congress of anarchists in Amsterdam
August 18–24	Seventh Congress of Second (Socialist) International, in Stuttgart
	Antimilitarist resolution
September 28	Socialists inaugurate their Casa del Pueblo in Madrid
October	French, Spanish Socialist parties carry out joint antiwar campaign (re: Morocco)
	Publication begins of newspaper, *Solidaridad Obrera*
1908 January 24	Interior Minister Juan de La Cierva presents proposed Terrorist Law to the Cortes
February	Alejandro Lerroux leaves Spain to avoid prosecution for sedition
April	Ferrer organizes International League for Rational Education, and begins to publish *L'Ecole Renovée* in Brussels
Spring	In Barcelona, defeat of the Special Budget for Culture
May	Public hearings by Committee of Deputies on proposed Terrorist Law
May–June	Republicans and some Liberal politicians carry campaign against proposed Terrorist Law to the nation
August 8	Terrorist Juan Rull executed in Barcelona

Fall	Antonio Fabra Rivas returns to Barcelona to reorganize the Catalan Socialist Federation	
September 6–8	First Catalan Labor Congress held in Barcelona Votes to organize *regional* labor confederation under the name, Solidaridad Obrera	
October	CGT Congress in Marseilles Solidaridad Obrera is represented by José Miquel Clapés	
October–November	Teamsters' strike in Ayxelá agency in Barcelona	
November 18	*Bloque de Izquierdas* (republican and some Liberal politicians) launch campaign against Maura government	
December–March 1909	Strike of typesetters employed at *El Progreso*	
1909	February	*Bloque de Izquierdistas* concludes its anti-Maura campaign
		Francisco Ferrer makes a trip through Andalusia
1909	March	Ferrer leaves for France, England Alcalá del Valle campaign begins
	March 1	General Miguel Primo de Rivera resigns as War Minister General Arsenio Linares (Captain General of Barcelona) succeeds him
	April 23 and May 4	Anticlerical riots in Osera and Orense (Galicia)
	April 30	Law granting workers limited right to strike
	May 15	Lockout in Manlleu (Ter Valley) by textile manufacturer Alberto Rusiñol
	May 30–31	Meeting in Barcelona of Catalan textile union officials
	End of May	French expedition into Rif mining area of Morocco
	June	International meeting of textile manufacturers in Milan
	June 4	Maura closes the Cortes
	June 13	Solidaridad Obrera special assembly in Barcelona approves use of general strike as a labor weapon
	June 15	Francisco Ferrer returns from London to Barcelona
	June 22	Alfonso (at Maura's recommendation) pardons three of the Alcalá del Valle prisoners
	July 9	Fighting breaks out in Morocco between Riffian tribes and Spanish Army
	July 10–11	Solidaridad Obrera meeting at Granollers: resolution approving, in principle, a general strike against textile manufacturers' lockout

July 11	Official Gazette calls up army reserves for service in Morocco
	In Madrid, Socialist party holds first antiwar rally
July 18	In Barcelona, violent demonstrations as Reus Battalion embarks for Morocco
	Congress of Catalan Socialist Federation
	In Madrid, second antiwar rally held by Socialist party, and Pablo Iglesias threatens a general strike
July 26–August 1	In Barcelona, the Tragic Week

End of Decade of Reforms

August 2	Factory employees resume work in Barcelona
	First summary military trial for armed rebellion: Ramón Baldera Aznar, sentenced to life imprisonment
August 6	Second summary military trial: Antonio Capdevila Marques, sentenced to life imprisonment
	New Civil Governor, Evaristo Crespo Azorín, arrives in Barcelona
August 8	Attorney General Javier de Ugarte arrives in Barcelona to investigate uprising
August 9–10	Third summary military trial: 13 men from Monistrol (including anarchist Timoteo del Usón), sentenced to life imprisonment
August 11	Fourth summary military trial: Antonio Malet Pujol, sentenced to die
August 14	Fifth (and last) summary military trial: José Miquel Baró, sentenced to die
August 17	José Miquel Baró is executed
August 24	Attorney General Ugarte leaves Barcelona
	Governor Crespo orders the closing of 94 private secular schools, and 34 centers of "advanced" ideas, in the province of Barcelona
August 26	An additional 26 schools are closed in Barcelona province
August 28	Antonio Malet Pujol is executed
August 31	Francisco Ferrer Guardia is arrested
September 5	Military trial: Eugenio del Hoyo is sentenced to die
September 9	Military trial: Ramón Clemente García is sentenced to die
September 13	Eugenio del Hoyo is executed

	September 27	Constitutional guarantees reestablished everywhere in Spain except in Catalonia
	October 4	Ramón Clemente García is executed
	October 9	Military trial of Francisco Ferrer
	October 13	Execution of Francisco Ferrer
	October 14	Maura opens the Cortes
	October 21	Alfonso XIII accepts the resignation of the Maura government; asks Segismundo Moret to form a Liberal government
	November 2	Four anarchists charged with being leaders of armed rebellion turned over to civil courts
	November 7	Martial law ends in Catalonia
	November 10	Radical party members Trinidad Alted, Juana Ardiaca, and Emiliano Iglesias released, pending their trial
	December	Establishment of Conjunción Republicana-Socialista, to prepare for congressional elections
1910	February 9	Moret resigns: José Canalejas forms a new Liberal government
	March 21	Charges of being leaders of armed rebellion dismissed against Emiliano Iglesias, Trinidad Alted, Juana Ardiaca; Luis Zurdo found guilty and condemned to perpetual exile
	May 8	National election of deputies
	June 9	Canalejas presents "Padlock Law" to the Cortes
	June 14	Luis Zurdo set down in France
	July 30	Canalejas breaks off diplomatic relations with Vatican
	October 30–November 1	National labor congress held in Barcelona votes approval of new national labor confederation (Confederación Nacional del Trabajo — CNT)
	November 4 December 23	Senate ⎱ votes for "Padlock Law" Congress ⎰
1911	Spring	Canalejas presents his draft of a new Law of Associations
	September 8–11	CNT holds first congress in Barcelona
1912	October	Canalejas presents draft for a law for new regional associations (Mancomunidades)
	November 12	Canalejas is assassinated by an anarchist, Manuel Pardiñas Count of Romanones forms a new Liberal government

December	Antonio Maura resigns as Conservative party chief, then rescinds resignation
1913	Romanones negotiates agreement with Vatican on religious orders
October 27	Eduardo Dato forms a Conservative government
December 18	Dato Government prepares Royal Decree authorizing regional associations (Mancomunidades)

BIBLIOGRAPHY

I. DOCUMENTS

Barcelona. Ayuntamiento. "Actas del Ayuntamiento de Barcelona," vols. III, IV (1908–1909). Handwritten folios.

—— *Anuario Estadístico de la Ciudad de Barcelona, 1902–1912,* vols. I–X. Barcelona, 1903–1913.

Barcelona. La Iglesia Católica Romana, Diócesis de Barcelona. *Annuales Ordo recitandi ac celebrandi juxta noviss Rubr. Breviarii et Missal Romani. Decreta S.R.C. et ad Norman Kalendi perpetui hujus Dioecisos, noviter reformati et a S.R.C. die 10 decembris 1900 aprobati. Ad resum Almae Basilicae Barcinon Ejusq. Dioeces. Pro anno domini bissextile* (1908).

—— *Boletín Oficial Eclesiástico del Obispado de Barcelona.* Vols. 42–52 (1900–1910). Barcelona: Imprenta y librería religiosa y científica de Pablo Riera, 1900–1910. (Note: cited by issue number in notes.)

Madrid. Ayuntamiento. *Gaceta de Madrid,* vol. III. Madrid: Est. tip. Sucesores de Rivadeneyra, 1909.

Spain. Congreso de los Diputados. *Diario de las sesiones de las Cortes.* 1909, 1 vol.; 1910, 11 vols.; 1911, vol. II.

Spain. Ministerio del Fomento. Dirección General de Agricultura, Industria y Comercio. *Memoria acerca del estado de la industria en la provincia de Barcelona.* Madrid: Imprenta de V. Tordesillas, 1910.

Spain. Ministerio de Gracia y Justicia. *Causa por regicidio frustrado, 1906–1909. Atentado de 31 de mayo de 1906. Causa contra Mateo Morral, Francisco Ferrer, José Nakens, Pedro Mayoral, Aquilino Martínez, Isidro Ibarra, Bernardo Mata, y Concepción Pérez Cuesta.* Madrid: Sucesores de J. A. García, 1911. 5 vols. Se imprime la presente causa por acuerdo del Excmo. Sr. Presidente del Congreso y a requerimiento formulado en la sesión del 20 de diciembre por el señor diputado don Juan de La Cierva.

Spain. Ministerio de la Guerra. *Causa contra Francisco Ferrer Guardia, instruída y fallada por la jurisdicción de Guerra en Barcelona: Año 1909.* Madrid: Sucesores de J. A. García, 1911. Se imprime la presente causa por acuerdo del Excmo. Sr. Presidente del Congreso de los Diputados y a requerimiento formulado en las sesiones de 9 and 10 de diciembre de 1910 por los señores diputados don Juan de La Cierva y don Rodrigo Soriano.

—— *Causa contra Trinidad Alted Fornet, Emiliano Iglesias Ambrosio, Luis Zurdo de Olivares y Juana Ardiaca Mas por el delito de rebelión militar. Ocurrió el hecho desde el 26 al 31 de julio de 1909. Dieron principio las actuaciones el 29 de julio de 1909. Terminaron el 5 de julio de 1910.* Madrid: Sucesores de J. A. García, 1911. Se imprime la presente causa por acuerdo del Excmo. Sr. Presidente del Congreso de los Diputados y a requerimiento formulado en las sesiones de 9 y 10 de diciembre de 1910 por los señores diputados Don Juan de la Cierva y Don Rodrigo Soriano.

—— *Juicio ordinario seguido contra Francisco Ferrer y Guardia ante los tribunales militares en la plaza de Barcelona.* Madrid: Est. tip. Sucesores de Rivadeneyra, 1909. Contiene Acusación fiscal ante el Consejo de Guerra; Dictamen del Asesor del Consejo; Sentencia; Dictamen del Auditor General de la 4° Región.

United States. Roman Catholic Church. *The Official Catholic Directory of the United States for the Year 1966.* New York: P. J. Kenedy and Sons, 1966.

Vatican. *Annuario Pontificio per l'Anno 1966.* Vatican City, 1966.

II. NEWSPAPERS AND MAGAZINES

ABC (Madrid) August–December 1909. Daily publication. Monarchist.

Acracia [Suplemento de *Tierra y Libertad*] (Barcelona) 1908–1910. Weekly publication. Anarchist.

La Actualidad (Barcelona) August–December 1909. Weekly pictorial publication. Issue of August 28, 1909, completely devoted to the Tragic Week.

La Barricada (Barcelona) March 22, 1912. First issue.

Boletín de la Escuela Moderna: Enseñanza Científica y Racional (Barcelona)
    Primera época: 1901–1906. Published weekly by Francisco Ferrer's publishing firm, Publicaciones de la Escuela Moderna.
    Segunda época: 1908–1909. *Boletín de la Escuela Moderna: Enseñanza Científica y Racional. Extensión internacional de la Escuela Moderna de Barcelona: Eco de la revista L'Ecole Renovée de Bruselas.* Published weekly by Francisco Ferrer's publishing firm, Publicaciones de la Escuela Moderna.

Boletín de la Sociedad del Arte de Imprimir de Barcelona (Barcelona) Vols. X, XI: 1908–1909. Weekly publication of the typesetters' syndicate.

La Campana de Gracia (Barcelona) August 1909–July 1910. Weekly republican satirical publication.

El Correo Catalán (Barcelona) 1910–1912. Daily publication. Catholic-Carlist.

El Diluvio (Barcelona) 1909–1912. Daily publication. Republican, anticlerical, anti-Lerroux.

Les Documents du Progrès. See *The International.*

La Epoca (Madrid) August–October 1909. Daily publication. Catholic, monarchist; considered to be "Maura's organ."

España Nueva (Madrid) June 1906; August 1909–August 1910. Daily publication. Republican newspaper of Rodrigo Soriano. Only major pro-Ferrer publication.

Esquella de la Torratxa (Barcelona) Fall 1909. Weekly publication. Catalan republican, satirical.

La Forja (Barcelona) 1910–1912. Weekly publication of the Catalan republican coalition: Unió Federal Nacionalista Republicana.

Germinal (Barcelona) October 7, 1915. First issue. Editor: Emiliano Iglesias.

La Internacional (Barcelona) 4 scattered issues: December 1908–May 1909. Weekly publication. Organo del Partido Socialista Obrero: Federación Catalana. Editor: Antonio Fabra Rivas.

The International (London) Vols. IV–VI: December 1908–November 1909. Monthly socialist publication. The English edition of the magazine, published in France as *Les Documents du Progrès,* and in Germany as *Dokumente des Fortschritts.*

El Liberal (Barcelona) 1909–1912. Daily publication. Part of the national newspaper chain owned by the Sociedad Editorial de España (founded in 1906 by Rafael Gasset); the newspaper chain was called "el Trust," using the English word.

La Metralla (Barcelona) 1909–1910. Weekly publication. Catalan republican: l'Unió Catalana.

El Mundo (Madrid) September 1909–July 1910. Daily publication. Pro-Maura.

Las Noticias (Barcelona) 1909–1910. Daily publication. Ostensibly nonpartisan; in practice, pro-republican, anticlerical.

El Noticiero Universal (Barcelona) 1909–1910. Daily publication. Nonpartisan.

El Obrero Moderno (Igualada [Catalonia]) 1909–1915. Organ of syndicalist movement.

El País (Madrid) 1909–1912. Daily publication. Republican, anticlerical, pro-Lerroux.

El Poble Català (Barcelona) 1909–1912. Daily publication. Organ of republican, anticlerical Catalan Nationalists. Editor: Antonio Rovira y Virgili.

El Progreso (Barcelona) 1909–1911. Issues for the months of July–August, 1912–1930. Daily publication. Official organ of the Radical Republican party of Alejandro Lerroux.

La Protesta (Barcelona) September 14, 1912. First issue.

La Publicidad (Barcelona) 1909–1913. Daily publication. Anticlerical, anti-Lerroux: organ of La Unión Republicana.

La Rebeldía (Barcelona) Scattered issues, 1906–1910. Weekly publication. Organ of the Youth Movement of Lerroux's Radical Republican party. First issue published September 1, 1906.

La Rebelión (Barcelona) November 4, 1910. First issue. Published by extremist group dissatisfied with the official policy of Lerroux' Radical Republican party. Editor: Rafael Guerra del Río.

El Sindicalista (Barcelona) October 29, 1912. First issue. "Organo de los sindicatos obreros. Escrito por trabajadores y para los trabajadores."

El Socialista (Madrid) 1907–1912. Weekly publication. Official organ of el Partido Socialista Obrero de España.

Solidaridad (Barcelona) July 20 and 27, 1907. First two issues. Weekly publication of Solidaridad Catalana.

Solidaridad Obrera (Barcelona) Scattered issues: 1909–1910. After 1917, a daily publication. Official publication, first of the Catalan labor confederation, Solidaridad Obrera; then of the national labor confederation of the same name.

Tierra y Libertad (Barcelona) Scattered issues: 1910. Weekly publication. Anarchist.

La Tribuna (Barcelona) 1909–1912. Daily publication. Moderate, prorepublican.

La Vanguardia (Barcelona) 1909–1912. Daily publication. Moderate, pro-Catalan.

Veu de Catalunya (Barcelona) 1909–1910. Daily publication. Organ of the Lliga.

III. BOOKS AND ARTICLES CONTAINING DOCUMENTARY MATERIAL

Abbott, Leonard D., ed. *Francisco Ferrer: His Life, Work and Martyrdom. With messages written especially for this brochure by Ernst Haeckel, Maxim Gorky. Published on the first anniversary of his death.* New York: Francisco Ferrer Association, n.d. [1910].

———— and William Thurston Brown, eds. *The Detroit Francisco Ferrer Modern School.* New York: The Herold Press, 1912.

Albó y Martí, Ramón. *Barcelona: Caritativa, benéfica y social,* rev. ed. Barcelona: Librería "La Hormiga de Oro," 1914. 2 vols.

———— *El Pressupost extraordinari de cultura del Ayuntament y les escoles d'enseyenassa primaria que en el mateix es proposar.* Conferencia donada en el Ateneo Barcelones el 28 de mars de 1908. Barcelona: Librería "La Hormiga de Oro," 1908.

Ametlla, Claudi. *Memòries polítiques: 1890–1917.* Barcelona: Editorial Pòrtic, 1963.

Archer, William. *The Life, Trial and Death of Francisco Ferrer.* London: Chapman & Hall, Ltd., 1911.

Aznar, Severino. *La Cruzada social.* Barcelona: Acción Social Popular, 1913.

———— *Impresiones de un demócrata cristiano.* Madrid: Compañía Ibero-Americana de Publicaciones, S.A., 1931.

———— *Problemas sociales de actualidad: 1914. La Conquista del Proletariado. Para la historia del Catolicismo social en España. Hechos y criterios sociales.* Barcelona: Acción Social Popular, 1914.

Bertrán, Luis. *"Yo acuso": El Testamento de Ferrer.* Barcelona: Tipografía de Félix Costa, 1911.

Bonafulla, Leopoldo [pseud. of Juan Bautista Esteve]. *Criterio Libertario.* Biblioteca Buena Semilla. Barcelona: Tipografía de la Vda. de José Miquel, 1905.

———— *La Revolución de julio en Barcelona.* 1 ed.: Barcelona: Editorial Toribio Tabedicer, n.d. [1909?]; 2 ed.: Barcelona: Editorial B. Baure, 1923.

Borjás Ruíz, Angel de. *El Fin de una leyenda: España ante el proceso Ferrer.* Biblioteca de "La Rebeldía," folleto 1. Barcelona: Sociedad Anónima, "La Neotipia," 1907.

Brissa, José. *La Revolución de julio en Barcelona: Su Represión, sus víctimas, el proceso de Ferrer. Recopilación completa de sucesos y comentarios, con el informe del Fiscal y del Defensor Sr. Galcerán.* Barcelona: Casa Editorial Maucci, 1910.

Buenacasa, Manuel. *El Movimiento obrero español: 1886–1926. Historia y crítica.* Barcelona: Impresos Costa, 1928.

"C" [pseud. of José Comaposada], "Sucesos de Barcelona," *El Socialista* (Madrid), October 29–December 24, 1909. 9 articles. Issued in book form under the title *La Revolución de Barcelona.* Barcelona: Biblioteca Acción, 1909.

Canals, Salvador. *El Proceso de Ferrer ante las Cortes.* Madrid: Imprenta Alemana, 1911.

———— *Los Sucesos de España en 1909: Crónica documentada.* Madrid: Imprenta Alemana. Vol. I: 1910; Vol. II: 1911.

Carqué de la Parra, E., ed. *El Terrorismo en Barcelona: Lo que dicen los prohombres de todos los partidos.* Barcelona: Casa Editorial, "Mitre," 1908.

Casañas, Salvador, Cardenal. *Carta pastoral del Emmo. y Rdmo. Sr. Cardenal Casañas, Obispo de Barcelona, sobre las escuelas de estudios populares que proyecta el Excmo. Ayuntamiento de esta ciudad: 24 febrero 1908.* Barcelona: Imprenta de Eugenio Subirana, 1908.

Le Comité de Défense des Victimes de la Répression Espagnole. *Un Martyr des prêtres. Francisco Ferrer: janvier 1859–13 octobre 1909.* Paris: Librairie Schleicher Frères, n.d. [1909?].

Corazón de Jesús, Madre. "Carta-relación de la Rdma. M. Corazón de Jesús, Superiora de esta casa, a la Rdma. Madre Superiora General," Crónica de la Casa de Barcelona: Instituto de las Esclavas del Santísimo Sacramento y de la Caridad (Adoratrices). Quinta parte: 1908–1922. Vol. I: 165–72. (Mimeographed chronicle of the Barcelona chapter.)

del Rosal, Amaro. *Los Congresos obreros internacionales en el siglo XIX: De la "Joven Europa" a la Segunda Internacional.* Mexico, D.F.: Editorial Grijalbo, S.A., 1958.

Díaz-Plaja, Fernando, ed. *La Historia de España en sus documentos,* vol. IV: *El Siglo XX.* New series. Madrid: Instituto de Estudios Políticos, 1960.

Escarrá, M. Eduardo. *Développement industriel de la Catalogne.* Bibliothèque du Musée Social. Paris: A. Rousseau, 1908.

Fabra Rivas, Antonio. See Vidal y Ribas, Magin.

────── *El Socialismo y el conflicto europeo. El Kaiserismo: He ahí el enemigo! Debe España intervenir en la guerra?* Prologue: Vicente Blasco Ibañez. Valencia: Prometeo, Sociedad Editorial Germanías, F.S., 1915.

Ferrer: Páginas para la historia. Barcelona: Publicaciones de la Escuela Moderna, 1912. Contiene Consejo de Guerra: acusación, defensa y sentencia. Consejo Supremo de Guerra y Marina: Providencia decretando la irresponsabilidad civil y devolución de los bienes.

Ferrer Guardia, Francisco. *La Escuela Moderna: Póstuma explicación y alcance de la enseñanza racional.* Edited, with a prologue, by Lorenzo Portet. Barcelona: Editorial Maucci, n.d. [1911?].

────── *The Modern School.* New York: Mother Earth Publishing Association, n.d.

────── *The Origins and Ideals of the Modern School.* Trans. from the Spanish by Joseph McCabe. New York: G. P. Putnam's Sons, 1913.

Ferrer Sanmartí, Sol. *Le véritable Francisco Ferrer d'après des documents inédits, par sa fille.* Paris: L'Ecran du Monde, Editions Les Deux Sirènes, 1948.

────── *La Vie et l'oeuvre de Francisco Ferrer: Un Martyr au XXᵉ siècle.* Preface: Charles August Bontemps. Paris: Librairie Fischbacher, 1962.

The Francisco Ferrer Association. *The Rational Education of Children.* New York: Mother Earth Publishing Association, n.d.

Frollo, Claudio [pseud. of Ernesto López Rodríguez]. *Cataluña.* Publicaciones de "España Futura." Madrid: Est. tip. de Juan Pérez, 1909.

Hernández Villaescusa, Modesto. *La Semana Trágica en Barcelona: Hechos, causas, y remedios.* Barcelona: Herederos de Juan Gili, editores, 1909. 2 ed. rev. and enlarged.

La Revolución de julio en Barcelona: Hechos, causas y remedios. Barcelona: Herederos de Juan Gili, editores, 1910. (Note: this second edition varies from the first only in the addition of a chapter on the Ferrer demonstrations in Europe, a chapter entitled "La 'España consciente.' ")

Herreros, Tomás. *Alejandro Lerroux tal cual es. Historia de una infamia relatada por el mismo obrero que ha sido víctima de ella.* Barcelona: Tipografía El Anuario de la Exportación, 1907.

La Huelga General en Barcelona. Verdadera relación de los sucesos desarrollados con motivo del paro general en Barcelona, durante la octava semana de este año, 1902, por un testigo ocular. Barcelona: Imprenta de Pedro Toll, n.d. [1902].

Hurtado, Amadeo. *Quaranta Anys d'advocat: Historia del meu temps,* vol. I: *1894–1915.* Mexico, D.F.: Editorial Xaloc, 1956.

Jaurès, Jean. *Acción socialista.* Trans. from the French by M. Ciges Aparicio. Biblioteca Sociológica Internacional. Barcelona: Imprenta de Henrich y Comp.ª en c., Editores, 1906. 2 vols.

La Cierva y Peñafiel, Juan. *Notas de mi vida,* 2 ed. rev. Madrid: Instituto Editorial Reus, S.A., 1955.

—— *The Case of Ferrer.* Speeches delivered by the Ex-Cabinet Minister Excmo. Sr. D. Juan de La Cierva in the Chamber of Deputies during the sessions of the 31st Mach [sic] and 5th of April 1911. Madrid: Imprenta Alemana, 1911.

Leroy, Constant [pseud. of Miguel Villalobos Moreno]. "Campaña humanitaria: Por la Verdad — Por la justicia," *El Correo Español* (Mexico, D.F.), December 27, 1912–February 28, 1913.

—— *Los Secretos del anarquismo.* Prologue: E. Guardiola y Cardellach. Mexico, D.F.: n.p., 1913.

—— *Los Secretos del anarquismo: Asesinato de Canalejas y el caso Ferrer.* Prologue: E. Guardiola y Cardellach. Mexico, D.F.: Librería Renacimiento, 1913. (Note: there is not any substantive difference between this text and the one cited above, but they were not printed from the same plates and therefore the pagination varies. This is the text cited in the footnotes.)

Lerroux y García, Alejandro. *Al Servicio de la república.* Madrid: Javier Morata, editor, 1930.

—— *De la Lucha.* Prologue: Nicolás Estévanez. Barcelona: F. Granada y C.ª, Editores, n.d. [1909?].

—— *Ferrer y su proceso en las Cortes.* Barcelona: Tipografía El Anuario de la Exportación, 1911.

—— *La pequeña Historia: España, 1930–1936. Apuntes para la historia grande, vividos y redactados por el autor.* Buenos Aires: Editorial Cámera, 1945.

—— *Las pequeñas Tragedias de mi vida: Memorias frívolas.* Madrid: Editorial Zeus, 1930.

—— *Mis Memorias.* Madrid: Afrodisio Aguado, S.A., 1963.

Lorenzo Asperilla, Anselmo. *La Anarquía triunfante,* vol. II of Biblioteca Liberación. Barcelona: Imprenta de J. Ortega, 1911.

—— *Evolución proletaria: Estudios de orientación emancipadora contra todo género de desviaciones.* Prologue: Fernando Tarrida del Marmol. Barcelona: Publicaciones de la Escuela Moderna, n.d. [1914?].

———— *El Proletariado militante: Memorias de un Internacionalista.* Vol. I. Barcelona: Imprenta de la Campana y la Esquella, n.d. [1902?].

Maura y Gamazo, Gabriel, Duke of Maura. *La Cuestión de Marruecos desde el punto de vista español.* Madrid: M. Romero, 1905.

———— *Memoria: Jurados mixtos para dirimir las diferencias entre patrones y obreros y para prevenir o remediar las huelgas.* Madrid: Imprenta del Asilo de Huérfanos del Sagrado Corazón de Jesús, 1901.

———— *Recuerdos de mi vida,* in the series Confesiones de Nuestros Tiempos. Madrid: M. Aguilar, 1934.

———— and Melchor Fernández Almagro. 2 ed. *Por qué cayó Alfonso XIII? Evolución y disolución de los partidos históricis durante su reinado.* Madrid: Ediciones Ambos Mundos, S.L., 1948.

Maura y Gelabert, Juan, Bishop of Orihuela. *La Cuestión social: Pastorales.* Madrid: Imprenta de Ricardo Rojas, 1902.

———— *La Democracia Cristiana: Pastorales.* Barcelona: Gustavo Gili, 1919.

Maura y Montaner, Antonio. *Treinta y cinco Años de vida pública. Ideas políticas, doctrinas de gobierno y campanas parlamentarias.* Editor: José Ruíz-Castillo Franco. Prologue and epilogue: the Duke of Maura. Madrid: Biblioteca Nueva, 1953.

Memoria que han escrito los maestros públicos de Barcelona acerca de la conversión de los auxiliares en escuelas. Barcelona: Imprenta de F. Badía, 1906.

Miquel, P. *Alejandro Lerroux. Epígrafes. Cuatro palabras. Lerroux político. Meetings a los que ha asistido. Su campaña en la prensa.* Barcelona: n.p., n.d. [1903?].

Morote, Luis. *Los Frailes en España.* Madrid: Imprenta de Fortanet, 1904.

———— *La Moral de la derrota.* Madrid: Estab. tip. de G. Juste, 1900.

Navarro, Emilio, ed. *Historia crítica de los hombres del republicanismo catalán en la última década: 1905-1914. Resúmenes históricos por Emiliano Iglesias y Juan Arderius Baujo.* Barcelona: Artega y Artis, Impresores, 1915.

La Neotipia: Societat anònima. Institució obrera. Introduction: Juan Maragall. Barcelona: Sociedad Anónima, "La Neotipia," 1908.

Ossorio y Gallardo, Angel. *Antonio Maura.* Salamanca: Imprenta de Nuñez, 1928.

———— *Barcelona, julio de 1909: Declaración de un testigo.* Madrid: Imprenta de Ricardo Rojas, 1910.

———— *El Sedimento de la lucha: Vida e ideas,* in the series Confesiones de nuestro tiempo. Madrid: M. Aguilar, n.d. [1933?].

———— *Mis Memorias.* Buenos Aires: Editorial Losada, S.A., 1946.

———— *Visita a Arenys de Mar: Mayo 1909.* Barcelona: Imprenta del Gobierno Civil, n.d. [1909].

———— *Visita a Mataró: Marzo 1909.* Barcelona: Imprenta del Gobierno Civil, n.d. [1909].

Padilla, Rafael. *España actual.* Madrid: Imprenta José Blas, 1908.

Padilla Serra, A. *Constituciones y leyes fundamentales de España: 1808-1947.* Prologue: Luis Sánchez Agesta. Granada: Universidad de Granada, 1954.

Palau, Gabriel, S.J. *Acción social del sacerdote: La Preparación del porvenir,* 2 ed. Conferencia dada . . . Barcelona, 19 junio de 1910. Barcelona: Acción Social Popular, 1911.

—— *Deberes sociales de la mujer en las cuestiones obreras.* Conferencia dada . . . Barcelona, el día 30 de noviembre de 1910. Barcelona: Imprenta de Pedro Ortega, n.d.

—— *El Problema de la eficacia de la acción social católica en las grandes ciudades* . . . conferencia en el Centro Católico de Estudiantes de Buenos Aires, el día 15 de mayo de 1917. Buenos Aires: Librería Católica "Alfa y Omega," n.d.

—— *La Acción social del sacerdote: Un Campo de acción.* Conferencia . . . 16 de enero y 20 de febrero de 1907. 1 ed.: Barcelona: Gustavo Gili, Editor, 1907; 3 ed.: Barcelona: Librería Plaza de Santa Ana, 1908.

Peray March, Joseph de. *Barcelona en 1908: Nueve impresiones.* Barcelona: Imprenta de F. Altes, 1909.

Pérez Baro, Alberto. "El Profesor Antonio Fabra Rivas ha muerto," *Revista de la Cooperación* (Buenos Aires), 14 (January 17, 1958), 3–6; 16 (May–June 1960), 81–82.

Prat de la Riba, Enrique. *Memoria endreçada á la diputació de Barcelona pel seu President. Obres públiques, cultura, beneficencia, hisenda provincial, según periode de sessions de 1910.* Barcelona: Imprenta de la Casa Provincial de Caritat, 1910.

—— *La Nacionalidad catalana.* Trans. from the Catalan by Antonio Royo Villanova. Valladolid: Imprenta Castellana, 1917. (Note: published originally in Barcelona, in Catalan, in 1906.)

Prat, José. *Orientaciones.* Biblioteca de Tierra y Libertad. Barcelona: Imprenta "Germinal," 1916.

El Proceso Ferrer en el Congreso: Recopilación de los discursos pronunciados durante el debate. Del "Diario de las Sesiones." Barcelona: Imprenta Lauria, 1911.

Reparáz Rodríguez, Gonzalo de. *Aventuras de un geógrafo errante.* Vol. I: *Soñando con España: Acompañan a la narración un epistolario político español, cartas del General Polavieja, documentos secretos relativos á Marruecos.* Berne: Casa editorial Ferd. Wyss, 1920. Vol. II: *Trabajando por España: A la Conquista de Tánger.* Barcelona: Linotipia Moderna, 1921. Vol. III: *Trabajando por España: La Derrota de la penetración pacífica, 1907–1911.* Barcelona: Librería Sintes, 1922.

—— *Del Paralelo al Rif.* Barcelona: 1909.

—— *Política española en Africa.* Madrid: Sáenz de Jubera, Hermanos, 1907.

Riera, Augusto. *La Semana Trágica: Relato de la sedición e incendios en Barcelona y Cataluña.* Barcelona: Editorial Hispano-Americano, 1909. This is a fifteen-page pamphlet summarizing his book, *La Semana Trágica: Reseña de las causas que originaron los sucesos ocurridos en Barcelona en los últimos días del mes de julio del corriente año.* Barcelona: E. Albacar, 1909.

Riu, Marcel. *Clar y Catalá. Rectificació dels falsejaments historichs, y refutació de las calumnias y falsas apreciaciones, que respecte al Catalanisme y a la Solidaritat Catalana, conté l'article "Mi evangelio" de D. A. Lerroux.* Barcelona: Imprenta de Joaquín Horta, 1906.

—— *Contra la Mentida, el terrorisme y el matonisme. Refutació de las falsas acusacións fetas por el diari* El Progreso, *rectificació y aclaració del fets relatius al terrorisme y matonisme y descobriment de sos autors.* Barcelona: Imprenta de Ignaci Xalapéira, 1907.

—— *La Rematada. Follet que conté íntegre l'article "Yo y la Solidaridad" d'en*

A. Lerroux y l'anàlisis y refutació dels seus falsos conceptes. Barcelona: Imprenta carrer Archs de Junqueras, 1907.

Rivas, Francisco. *Los Pecados capitales o Lerroux en escenario.* Barcelona: Tipografía Nuñez, 1915.

Rodríguez de la Pena, José. *Los Aventureros de la política: Alejandro Lerroux. Apuntes para la historia de un revolucionario.* Barcelona: Casa Editorial Ciencias y Letras, n.d. [1911?].

Rovira y Virgili, Antonio. *El Nacionalismo catalán.* Barcelona: Editorial Minerva, n.d. [1917?].

Royo Villanova, Antonio. *Cuestiones obreras.* Prologue: Gumersindo de Azcárate. Valladolid: Imprenta Castellana, 1910.

———— *El Problema catalán: Impresiones de un viaje a Barcelona.* Madrid: Victoriano Suárez, 1908.

Salillas, Rafael. "La Celda de Ferrer," *Ateneo: Revista Mensual* (Madrid), 2 (June 1907), 457–79.

Salmerón, Nicolás. "The Downfall of Spain," *The International* (London), 6 (August 1909), 22–24.

Sánchez de Toca, Joaquín. *Discurso del Excm. Sr. D . . . en apoyo de la letra B del proyecto de ley de Servicio militar obligatorio. Sesión del Senado: 16 de noviembre y 10 de diciembre de 1910.* Madrid: 1910. (Note: this is an offprint of his speech in the Senate.)

———— *El Movimiento antimilitarista en Europa. Discurso en la Real Academia de Ciencias Morales y Políticas, el 19 de noviembre de 1907.* Madrid: 1910.

Sardá y Salvany, Félix, Padre. *L'Anarquisme contemporani y sos factores. Conferencies donades durant la present quaresma de 1910 en la Academia Católica de Sabadell.* Barcelona: Tipografía Católica, 1911.

Sastre y Sanna, Miguel. *La Esclavitud moderna: Martirología social. Relación de los atentados y actos de "sabotaje" cometidos en Barcelona, y bombas y explosivos hallados desde junio de 1910 hasta junio de 1921.* Prologue: Angel Ossorio y Gallardo. Barcelona: Editorial Ribó, 1921.

———— *Las Huelgas en Barcelona y sus resultados durante el año. Acompañado de numerosos e importantes datos estadísticos sobre otros asuntos relacionados con la cuestión social obrera en Barcelona.* 8 vols.: 1903–1914. *Año 1903:* Barcelona: Establecimiento tipográfico de Ramón Pujol, 1904. *Año 1904:* Barcelona: Tipografía "La Industria" de Manuel Tasis, 1905. *Año 1905:* Barcelona: Est. tip. "La Hormiga de Oro," 1906. *Año 1906:* Barcelona: Est. tip. "La Hormiga de Oro," 1907. *Año 1908:* Barcelona, Est. tip. de Valls y Borrás, 1910. *Año 1909:* Barcelona: Acción Social Popular, 1911. *Años 1910 al 1914 ambos inclusivo:* Barcelona, Imp. Editorial Barcelonesa, S.A., 1915.

———— *Rasgos fisonómicos del problema social,* 2 ed. Barcelona: Imprenta Ribó, 1920.

La Semana Sangrienta. Sucesos de Barcelona: Historia, descripciones, documentos, retratos, vistas, etc. Barcelona: Editorial Ibero-Americana, n.d. [1910?].

Shaw, Rafael. *Spain from Within.* London: T. Fisher Unwin, 1910.

Simarro, Luis. *El Proceso Ferrer y la opinión europea,* vol. I: *El Proceso.* Madrid: Editorial Arias, 1910.

Soldevilla, Fernando. *El Año político,* vols. XIII–XVI: *1907–1910.* Madrid: Imprenta de Ricardo Rojas, 1908–1911.

Solidaridad Obrera: Confederación Regional de Sociedades de Resistencia. *Estatutos.* Barcelona: Imprenta J. Ortega, 1909.

Tato y Amat, Miguel. *Sol y Ortega y la política contemporánea.* Madrid: Imprenta Artística Española, 1914.

Torres, José María, ed. *Lerroux y la gran tragedia.* Barcelona: Talleres Gráficos, 1915.

―――― *Lerroux y sus enemigos.* Barcelona: Talleres Gráficos, 1912.

Uña y Sarthou, Juan. *Las Asociaciones obreras en España: Notas para su historia.* Madrid: Estab. Tip. de G. Juste, 1900.

Urales, Federico [pseud. of Juan Montseny], *Mi Vida.* Barcelona: Publicaciones de la Revista Blanca, n.d. 3 vols.

Vidal y Ribas, Magin [pseud. of Antonio Fabra Rivas].

―――― "La Révolte ouvrière en Espagne," *L'Humanité* (Paris), August 12, 1909.

―――― "Les Préliminaires de la grève générale," *ibid.,* August 13, 1909.

―――― "Barcelone en grève," *ibid.,* August 14, 1909.

―――― "En pleine Révolution," *ibid.,* August 15, 1909.

―――― "Vue d'ensemble," *ibid.,* August 16, 1909.

―――― "A Sabadell," *ibid.,* August 17, 1909.

―――― "Réponse a des calomnies," *ibid.,* August 18, 1909.

―――― "Contre les militares," *ibid.,* August 19, 1909.

Villaescusa, Modesto H. See Hernández Villaescusa, Modesto.

Villalobos Moreno, Miguel. See also, Constant Leroy.

―――― "Por la Verdad," *El País* (Madrid), November 2, 1909.

―――― "Le Mouvement de Barcelone," *Les Documents du Progrès* (Paris), (November 1909), 360–64.

Zancada, Práxedes. *El Obrero en España: Notas para su historia política y social.* Prologue: José Canalejas. Barcelona: Casa editorial Maucci, 1902.

IV. THE MOST IMPORTANT HISTORICAL ACCOUNTS

Alzina Caules, Jaime. "Investigación analítica sobre la evolución demográfica de Cataluña," *Cuadernos de Información Económica y Sociológica* (Barcelona). 4 parts: June 1955; December 1955; July 1956; December 1956.

Andrade y Uribe, Benito Mariano. *Maura y el partido conservador.* Burgos: Hijos de Santiago Rodríguez, Impresores, 1910.

Arrarás, Joaquín. "Hace cincuenta Años: Preparación y pretexto de la Semana Trágica de Barcelona," *ABC* (Madrid), July 26, 1959.

―――― "Hace cincuenta Años: La Semana Trágica," *ibid.,* July 28, 1959.

―――― "Hace cincuenta Años: El Inductor y responsable de la Semana Trágica," *ibid.,* July 29, 1959.

Aúnos, Eduardo. *Discurso de la vida: Autobiografía.* Madrid: Sociedad Española General de Librería, 1951.

Aznar, Severino. "El Padre Vicent," *Revista Social Hispano-Americana* (Barcelona), 11 (March 1912), 193–201.

Bau, Calasanz, Padre, and Padre José Poch. *Historia de las Escuelas Pías en Cataluña. Homenage a la provincia escolapia catalana en el lucentario de su canónica elección: 1751–1951*. Barcelona: 1951.

Belloc, H. H. P. *The Ferrer Case. The Motive Force*. Philadelphia Diocesan School Board of the Roman Catholic Church, Educational Brief no. 30. Philadelphia: 1910.

Benet, Josep. *Maragall i la Setmana Tràgica*, 3 ed. rev. Collecció a l'abast, núm. 15. Barcelona: Edicions 62, 1965. (Note: published originally in Barcelona in 1963, by the Institut d'Estudis Catalans, as vol. XXIII of Memòries de la Secció Històrico-Arqueològico.)

Boix, José M. "Sindicalismo católico: Su Actuación en Barcelona," *Revista Social Hispano-Americana* (Barcelona), 11 (March 1912), 209–19.

Buylla, Adolfo, Luis Morote, and Adolfo Posada. *El Instituto del Trabajo: Datos para la historia de la reforma social en España*. Madrid: Est. Tip. de Ricardo Fé, 1902.

Casanovas, Ignacio, S.J. *Nuestro Estado social: Comentario a la revolución de julio*. Barcelona: Gustavo Gili, 1910.

Castillejo, José. *Education and Revolution in Spain. Being three Joseph Payne lectures for 1936 delivered in the Institute*. London: Oxford University Press, 1937.

—— *Wars of Ideas in Spain: Philosophy, Politics and Education*. With an introduction by Sir Michael Sadler. London: J. Murray, 1937.

Comás, Casimiro. *Un Revolucionario de acción: Francisco Ferrer. Su Vida y su obra destructora. Justicia de su condena*. Barcelona: A. Suárez, 1910.

Comín Colomer, Eduardo. *La Semana Trágica de Barcelona*, no. 28 of Temas españoles. 2 ed. Madrid: Publicaciones Españolas, 1956.

Dommanget, Maurice. *Francisco Ferrer*, in the series Grandes Educateurs socialistes. Paris: Editions S.U.D.E.L., 1952.

Ebenstein, William. *Church and State in Franco Spain*. Research Monograph No. 8: Center of International Studies, Woodrow Wilson School of Public and International Affairs, Princeton University. Princeton, New Jersey: 1960.

Escofet, Domingo. *La Escuela Moderna. La Obra de su fundador, Francisco Ferrer Guardia y sus alumnos ante el momento actual*. Barcelona: Imprenta Industrial, 1931.

Fernández Jiménez, Miguel. *El Problema obrero y los partidos españoles: Estudio de la política contemporánea*. Prologue: Eduardo Dato. Granada: Tip. Lit. Paulino Ventura Traveset, 1904.

Gaziel [pseud. of Agustí Calvet]. *Tots els Camins drien a Roma. Historia d'un destí, 1893–1914*. Barcelona: Editorial Aedos, n.d. [1958?].

Inmaculada Concepción, Instituto de religiosas misioneras de la. "Reseña histórica de la fundación y desarrollo del instituto en el siglo XIX." Barcelona: 1944. (Mimeographed)

Jesús-María, Instituto de religiosas de. *Fundación y noticia del Instituto*. Barcelona: A. López Robert, 1906.

Jiménez Fraud, Alberto. *Ocaso y restauración: Ensayo sobre la universidad española moderna*. Centro de Estudios Literarios de El Colegio de México. Mexico, D.F.: El Colegio de México, 1948.

Kaspar, Jean-Jacques. *Pour la revision du procés Ferrer: Etude juridique d'après les pièces publiées par le gouvernement espagnol. Réponse des intellectuels français à S.M. Alphonse XIII.* Paris: Imp. Berger et Chausse, n.d.

La Iglesia y García, Gustavo. *Caracteres del anarquismo en la actualidad,* 2 ed. rev. Barcelona: Gustavo Gili, 1907.

Lamberet, Renée. *L'Espagne: 1750–1936,* in the series *Mouvements ouvriers et socialistes: Cronologie et bibliographie,* eds. Edouard Dolléons and Michel Crozier. Paris: Les Editions Ouvrieres, 1953.

Llorens, Montserrat. "El Padre Antonio Vicent, S.I.: 1837–1912: Notas sobre el desarrollo de la acción social católica en España," *Estudios de Historia Moderna* (Barcelona), 4 (1954), 395–439.

Lugan, Alphonse. *Un Précurseur du bolchevisme: Francisco Ferrer. Sa Vie et son oeuvre: Etude critique.* Paris: Procure générale, 1921.

Maitron, Jean. *Histoire du mouvement anarchiste en France: 1880–1914.* Paris: Société Universitaire d'Editions et de Librairie, 1951.

Malato, Charles. "Ferrer et son oeuvre," *Documents du Progrès* (Paris), (November 1909), 365–67.

Maristas de la Enseñanza, Hermanos, o Hermanitos de María. *Constituciones del Instituto.* Barcelona: Editorial F.T.D., 1923.

Marvaud, Angel. *La Question sociale en Espagne.* Paris: Félix Alcan, Editeur, 1910.

—— *L'Espagne au XXᵉ siècle: Etude politique et économique,* 2 ed. rev. Paris: Librairie Armand Colin, 1915.

Maurín, Joaquín. "El Movimiento obrero en Cataluña," *Leviatán* (Madrid), (October 1934), 15–23.

McCabe, Joseph. *The Martyrdom of Ferrer, being a True Account of his Life and Work.* Issued for the Rationalist Press Association, Ltd. London: Watts & Co., 1909.

Montseny, Federica. *Los Precursores: Anselmo Lorenzo: El Hombre y la obra.* Barcelona: Ediciones Españolas, 1938.

Normandy, Georges, and E. Lesueur. *Ferrer: L'Homme et son oeuvre. Sa mort. Castille contra Catalogne. Portraits, documents inédits, lettres originales.* Paris: A. Merícant, 1909.

Orts-Ramos, Antonio, and Francisco Carravaca. *Francisco Ferrer y Guardia: Apóstol de la razón. Vida, obra y doctrinas del famoso martir español.* Barcelona: Casa Editorial Maucci, 1932.

Pabón, Jesús. *Cambó: 1876–1918.* Barcelona: Editorial Alpha, 1952.

Peirats, José. *La CNT en la revolución española,* vol. I. Buenos Aires: Ediciones C.N.T., 1955.

Pouget, Emile. *La Confederación General del Trabajo en Francia.* Barcelona: Publicaciones de la Escuela Moderna, n.d.

Ramus, Pierre [pseud. of Rudolf Grossman]. *Francisco Ferrer: Sein Leben und sein Werk. Nachauthetischen Quellen und Materialen, insbesondere nach den dokumentarischen Veröffentlichungen des "Comité de Défense des Víctimes de la Répression espagnole."* Paris: Verlag "Die Freie Generation," 1910.

Ryan, John Augustine. *Francisco Ferrer, criminal conspirator. A reply to the articles by William Archer in McClure's Magazine, November and December 1910.* St. Louis: B. Herder, 1911.

Sagrada Familia, El Instituto de la. *Album conmemorativo en el septuagésimo quinto aniversario de su fundación, 1859-1934.* Barcelona: Editorial Balmes, S.A., 1935.

Sanahuja, Pedro, O.F.M. *Historia de la Seráfica Provincia de Cataluña.* Barcelona: Editorial Seráfica, n.d. [1956?].

Sangro y Ros de Alano, Pedro. *La Sombra de Ferrer: De la "Semana Trágica" a la guerra europea.* Madrid: Sobrinos de la sucesora de M. Minuesa de los Ríos, 1917.

Sevilla Andrés, Diego. "La Semana Trágica," *Gaceta Ilustrada* (Madrid), October 3, 1959, pp. 43-50.

Sirera, María José, A.C.J. "Obreros en Barcelona: 1900-1910," unpublished thesis for the degree of *licenciatura.* College of Philosophy and Letters, University of Barcelona, July 1959.

Ward, George Herbert Bridges. *The Truth about Spain,* 2 ed. rev. London: Cassell & Co., 1913.

V. OTHER WORKS CONSULTED

This bibliography does not include all works consulted for background material, but only those which are cited in the text.

Abad de Santillán, Diego. *Contribución a la historia del movimiento obrero español: Desde sus Orígenes hasta 1905.* Puebla (Mexico): Editorial Cajica, 1962.

———— and E. López Arango. *El Anarquismo en el movimiento obrero.* Barcelona: Ediciones "Cosmos," 1925.

Acomb, Evelyn M. *The French Laic Laws (1879-1889): The First Anti-Clerical Campaign of the Third French Republic.* New York: Columbia University Press, 1941.

Aguado Bleye, Pedro, and Cayetano Alcazar Molina. *Manual de historia de España,* vol. III, 7 ed. rev. Madrid: Espasa Calpe, S.A., 1956.

Albornoz, Alvaro de. *El Partido republicano. Las doctrinas republicanas en España y sus hombres. La Revolución del 68 y la República del 73. Los Republicanos después de la Restauración. La Crisis del republicanismo.* Madrid: Biblioteca Nueva, 1918.

Anderson, Eugene N. *The First Moroccan Crisis, 1904-1906.* Chicago: University of Chicago Press, 1930.

Arrarás Iribarren, Joaquín, ed. *Historia de la Cruzada Española,* 2 ed. rev. Madrid: Ediciones Españolas, 1940.

Ashmead-Bartlett, Ellis. *The Passing of the Shereefian Empire.* New York: Dodd, Mead, 1910.

Aznar, Severino. *Las grandes Instituciones del Catolicismo. Ordenes monásticos. Institutos misioneros.* Madrid: Imprenta de Gabriel López del Horno, 1912.

Ballesteros y Beretta, Antonio. *Historia de España y su influencia en la historia universal,* vol. XI. 2 ed. rev. by Manuel Ballesteros-Gaibrois. Barcelona: Salvat Editores, S.A., 1956.

Bayle, Constantino, S.J. *El segundo Marqués de Comillas: Don Claudio López Bru.* Madrid: Administración de "Razón y Fe," 1928.

Bedoya, José María. *Don Antonio Maura, ministro de la Gobernación: 1902-1903.* Madrid: Afrodisio Aguado, S.A., 1940.

Bennett, John Coleman. *Christians and the State*. New York: Charles Scribner's Sons, 1958.

Borkenau, Franz. *The Spanish Cockpit: An Eyewitness Account of the Political and Social Conflicts of the Spanish Civil War*. London: Faber & Faber, Ltd.

Bourgeois, Emile. *History of Modern France: 1853–1913*, vol. II. Cambridge [England]: The University Press, 1919.

Brenan, Gerald. *The Spanish Labyrinth. An Account of the Social and Political Background of the Civil War*, 2 ed. rev. Cambridge [England]: The University Press, 1950.

Carr, Raymond, "Spain: Rule by Generals," *Soldiers and Governments: Nine Studies in Civil-Military Relations*, ed. Michael Howard, pp. 133–48. Bloomington: Indiana University Press, 1959.

Carretero, José María. *Las Responsabilidades de A. Lerroux: Opiniones de un hombre de la calle*. Madrid: Ediciones Caballero Audaz, 1932.

Castro, Américo. *The Structure of Spanish History*. Trans. Edmund King. Princeton: Princeton University Press, 1954.

Chorley, Katherine. *Armies and the Art of Revolution*. London: Faber & Faber, Ltd., 1943.

Cole, G. D. H. *The Second International, 1889–1914: A History of Socialist Thought*, vol. III. London: Macmillan & Co., Ltd., 1956.

Comín Colomer, Eduardo. *Historia del anarquismo español: 1836–1948*. Madrid: Editorial R.A.D.A.R., n.d.;

Enciclopedia Universal Ilustrada Europeo-Americana. Barcelona: Hijos de J. Espasa, 1905–1930. Articles on "Desamortización," vol. XVIII, 361–70; "Francmasonería," vol. XXIV, 1085–87; "Masonería," vol. XXXIII, 718–50.

Fernández Almagro, Melchor. *Historia del reinado de Alfonso XIII*. Barcelona: Montaner y Simon, S.A., 1933.

—— *Política naval de la España moderna y contemporánea*. Madrid: Instituto de Estudios Políticos, 1946.

—— *Historia política de la España contemporánea*. Madrid: Pegaso, 1959.

Ferrater Mora, José. *Les Formes de la vida catalana. Seguit de, Reflexions sobre Catalunya, El llibre del sentit, Homenatges*. Barcelona: Editorial Selecta, 1955.

—— *Unamuno, a Philosophy of Tragedy*. Trans. Philip Silver. Berkeley: University of California Press, 1962.

Fuentes Quintana, Enrique, and Juan Velardes Fuertes. *Política económica*. Madrid: Doncel, 1959.

García Carrafa, Arturo, and Alberto. *Lerroux*, in the series: Españoles ilustres. Madrid: Imprenta de Antonio Marzo, 1918.

—— and Luis Antón del Olmet. *Maura*, vol. III of the series Los grandes Españoles. Madrid: Imprenta de "Alrededor del Mundo," 1913.

García Escudero, José María. *De Cánovas a la República*, 2 ed. rev. Madrid: Ediciones Rialp, S.A., 1953.

García-Nietro París, Juan N., S.J. *El Sindicalismo cristiano en España: Notas sobre su origen y evolución hasta 1936*. Bilbao: Instituto de Estudios Económico-Sociales, Universidad de Deusto, 1960.

García Venero, Maximiano. *Antonio Maura: 1907–1909.* Madrid: Ediciones del Movimiento, 1953.

—— *Historia de las Internacionales en España,* vol. I. Madrid: Ediciones del Movimiento, 1956.

—— *Historia del nacionalismo catalán: 1793–1936.* Madrid: Editora Nacional, 1944.

—— *Historia del nacionalismo vasco: 1793–1936.* Madrid: Editora Nacional, 1945.

—— *Melquiades Alvarez: Historia de un liberal.* Prologue: Azorín. Madrid: Editorial Alhambra, 1954.

—— *Vida de Cambó.* Prologue: Gregorio Marañon. Barcelona: Editorial Aedos, 1952.

Georges, Bernard, and Denise Tintant. *León Jouhaux: Cinquant Ans du syndicalisme,* vol. I: *Des Origines à 1921.* Paris: Presses Universitaires, 1962.

Harris, Walter B. *France, Spain and the Rif.* London: Edward Arnold & Co., 1927.

Headings, Mildred J. *French Freemasonry under the Third Republic,* vol. 66 of the Johns Hopkins University Studies in Historical and Political Science. Baltimore: 1948.

Hennessy, C.A.M. *The Federal Republic in Spain. Pi y Margall and the Federal Republican Movement, 1868–1874.* Oxford: Clarendon Press, 1962.

Hernández Villaescusa, Modesto. *Un Apóstol de las Uniones Profesionales: Padre R. Rutten,* 2 ed. Barcelona: Imprenta de Francisco J. Altes, 1908.

Horowitz, Daniel L. *The Italian Labor Movement.* Cambridge, Massachusetts: Harvard University Press, 1963.

Jackson, Gabriel. "The Origins of Spanish Anarchism," *The Southwestern Social Science Quarterly,* 36 (September 1955), 135–47.

Joaniquet, Aurelio. *Alfonso Sala Argemí, conde de Egara: Visión de una época. Debelación del nacionalismo catalanista. Luchas entre librecambistas y proteccionistas. Progreso de la técnica textil.* Madrid: Espasa Calpe, S.A., 1955.

Joll, James. *The Anarchists.* London: Eyre & Spottiswoode, 1964.

—— *The Second International: 1888–1914.* London: Weidenfeld and Nicolson, 1955.

Jutglar, Antoní. *L'Era industrial a Espanya.* Barcelona: Edicions Nova Terra, 1962.

Kapsner, Oliver L., O.S.B., ed. *Catholic Religious Orders. Listing Conventional and Full Names in English, Foreign Language and Latin. Also, Abbreviations, Date and Country of Origin, and Founders,* 2 ed. rev. Collegeville, Minnesota: St. John's Abbey Press, 1957.

Kiernan, V. G. *The Revolution of 1854 in Spanish History.* Oxford: Clarendon Press, 1966.

Klinger, Wallace Richard. "Spain's Problem of Alliances: Spanish Foreign Policy from the Conference of Madrid 1880 to the Mediterranean Agreement of 1907," unpublished dissertation. University of Pennsylvania, 1946.

Laín Entralgo, Pedro. *La Generación del Noventa y Ocho.* Madrid: "Diana Artes Gráficas," 1945.

León y Castillo, F. de. *Mis Tiempos,* vol. II. Madrid: Editorial Sucesores de Hernando, 1921.

Lorwin, Val R. *The French Labor Movement.* Cambridge, Massachusetts: Harvard University Press, 1954.

Mankeiwicz, Frank. "An Explanation of Community Development As It is Practiced by the Peace Corps in Latin America." Publication of the Peace Corps: GSA PC 66-2814. Washington, D.C., 1966.

Martí, Casimiro. *Orígenes del anarquismo en Barcelona*. Prologue: Jaime Vicens Vives. Barcelona: Editorial Teide, 1959.

Maura y Gamazo, Miguel. *Así cayó Alfonso XIII*. Mexico, D.F.: Imprenta Mañez, 1962.

Maurín, Joaquín. *La Revolución española: De la Monarquía absoluta a la revolución socialista*. Madrid: Editorial Cenit, S.A., 1932.

Melía, Juan A. *Pablo Iglesias: Rasgos de su vida íntima*. Madrid: Ediciones Morata, 1926.

Mola Vidal, Emilio. *Obras completas*. Valladolid: Librería Santarén, 1940.

Monroe, Paul, ed. "Modern Education" and "Francisco Ferrer," articles in *A Ciclopedia of Education*. New York: The Macmillan Company, 1911.

Montero Moreno, Antonio. *Historia de la persecución religiosa en España: 1936–1939*. Madrid: Biblioteca de Autores Cristianos, 1956.

Morató, Juan José. *Pablo Iglesias Posse: Educador de muchedumbres*. Bilbao: Espasa Calpe, S.A., 1931.

Morayta y Sagrario, Miguel. *Masonería española: Páginas de su historia. Ampliaciones y refutaciones de Mauricio Carlavilla*. Madrid: NOS, 1956. (Note: this is a much edited version, intended for Franco Spain, of the book first published in 1915 by Morayta, Grand Master of the Grand Spanish Orient.)

Niebuhr, Reinhold. "A Plea for Tolerance," *The Atlantic*, 210 (August 1962), 72–77.

Orts-Ramos, Antonio, and Francisco Carravaca. *Historia ilustrada de la revolución española: 1870–1931*, second part: *Desde la Coronación de Alfonso XIII hasta la Segunda República*. Barcelona: Editorial Iberia, 1932.

Payne, Stanley. "Spanish Nationalism in the Twentieth Century," *Review of Politics*, 26 (1964), 403–22.

Paulis, J. and F. de Sorel. *Maura ante el pueblo*. Prologue: Angel Ossorio. Madrid: Librería Española y Extanjera, 1915.

Peers, E. Alison. *Spain: The Church and the Orders*, 2 ed. London: Burns, Oates & Washbourne Ltd., 1945.

Pestaña, Angel. *El Sindicalismo: Qué quiere y a dónde va?* Barcelona: Biblioteca Selección, 1933.

Poderosa Fuerza secreta: La Institución Libre de Enseñanza. San Sebastián: 1940.

Prieto, Indalecio. *Cartas a un escultor: Pequeños Detalles de grandes sucesos*. Buenos Aires: Editorial Losada, S.A., 1961.

Ramos Oliveira, Antonio. *Politics, Economics and Men of Modern Spain*. Trans. Teener Hall. London: Victor Gollancz, 1946.

Regatillo, Eduardo F., S.J., (Postulador de la causa de la beatificación del marqués). *Un Marqués modelo. El Siervo de Dios, Claudio López Bru, el segundo marqués de Comillas*. Santander: Sal Terrae, 1950.

Rucabado, Ramón. *Santa Mónica de la Rambla y otras páginas de sangre. Una Página inédita de julio 1936, escrita en 1941 y publicada en 1959. Seguida de otras páginas de sangre*. Barcelona: Editorial Balmes, S.A., 1959.

Sagarra, Josep María de. *Memories*. Barcelona: Editorial Aedos, 1954.

Salomone, Arcangelo William. *Italy in the Giolittian Era. Italian Democracy in the Making: 1900–1914.* Intro: Gaetano Salvemini. 2 ed. Philadelphia: University of Pennsylvania Press, 1960.

Sánchez, José M. *Reform and Reaction: The Politico-Religious Background of the Spanish Civil War.* Chapel Hill, North Carolina: The University of North Carolina Press, 1964.

Sevilla Andrés, Diego. *Antonio Maura: La Revolución desde Arriba.* Prologue: Melchor Fernández Almagro. Barcelona: Editorial Aedos, 1953.

Silió y Cortés, César. *En torno a una Revolución.* Bilbao: Espasa-Calpe, S.A., 1933.

——— *Vida y empresas de un gran español: Maura,* vol. XXXIX of Vidas españolas e hispano-americanas del siglo XIX. Madrid: Espasa-Calpe, S.A., 1934.

Solana y Gutiérrez, Mateo. *Miguel Maura y la disolución de las ordenes religiosas en la constitución española.* Mexico, D.F.: Imprenta Cooperativa Mexicana, 1934.

Soldevila, Fernando. *Historia de España,* vols. VII, VIII. Barcelona: Editorial Ariel, 1959.

———, ed. *Un Segle de vida catalana: 1814–1930,* vol. II. Barcelona: Editorial Alcide, 1961.

Soriano, Rodrigo. *La Revolución española, 1931: Ayer y hoy.* Madrid: Ediciones Claridad, 1931.

Taxonera, Luciano de. *Antonio Maura: La gran Figura política de una época de España.* Madrid: Editora Nacional, 1944.

Termes Ardévol, José. *El Movimiento obrero en España: La Primera Internacional, 1864–1881.* Barcelona: Publicaciones de la Cátedra de Historia General de España, 1965.

Thomas, Hugh. "The Balance of Forces in Spain," *Foreign Affairs,* 41 (October 1962), 208–21.

——— *The Spanish Civil War.* London: Eyre & Spottiswoode, 1961.

Trend, J. B. *The Civilization of Spain,* 2 printing. London: Oxford University Press, 1963.

Turin, Yvonne. *L'Education et l'école en Espagne de 1874 à 1902: Liberalisme et tradition.* Paris: Presses Universitaires de France, 1959.

Turmann, Max. *El Desenvolvimiento del Catolicismo social desde la encíclica "Rerum Novarum." Ideas directrices y carácteres generales.* Trans. Severino Aznar. Madrid: Sáenz de Jubera, Hermanos, Libreros-Editores, n.d. [1909?].

Vergés Mundó, Oriol. *La I Internacional en las Cortes de 1871.* Prologue: Carlos Seco Serrano. Barcelona: Publicaciones de la Cátedra de Historia General de España, 1964.

Vicens Vives, Jaime. *Aproximación a la historia de España,* 2 ed. rev. Series A: Estudios, Centro de Estudios Históricos Internacionales, Universidad de Barcelona. Barcelona: 1960.

——— *Cataluña en el siglo XIX.* Trans. from the Catalan by E. Borrás Cubells. Prologue: Emilio Giralt y Raventós. Madrid: Ediciones Rialp, S.A., 1961.

——— and Jorge Nadal Oller. *Manual de historia económica de España.* Barcelona: Editorial Teide, 1959.

———, ed. *Historia social y económica de España y América*, vol. V: *Burguesía, industrialización, obrerismo.* Barcelona: Editorial Teide, 1959.

Vigón, Jorge. *Historia de la artillería española*, vol. III. Madrid: Consejo Superior de Investigaciones Científicas, Instituto Jerónimo Zurita, 1947.

Vilar, Pierre. *Historia de España.* Trans. from the French by Manuel Tuñon de Lara. Biblioteca Club de Bolsillo. Paris: Librairie des Editions Espagnoles, 1960.

Woodcock, George. *Anarchism: A History of Libertarian Ideas and Movements.* Harmondsworth (England): Penguin A622, 1963.

Zuyazagoitia, Julián. *Pablo Iglesias: Vida y trabajos de un obrero socialista.* Madrid: Ediciones Españolas, 1938.

NOTES

INTRODUCTION

1. For the ideas of Alejandro Pidal y Mon, see his letters to Antonio Maura published in Gabriel Maura y Gamazo and Melchor Fernández Almagro, *Por qué cayó Alfonso XIII? Evolución y disolución de los partidos históricos durante su reinado*, 2 ed. (Madrid, 1948), pp. 65, 410, 412–13, 461–63.

2. For the definitive work on Unamuno's philosophy, see José Ferrater Mora, *Unamuno: A Philosophy of Tragedy*, trans. Philip Silver (Berkeley, 1962).

3. For example, Nicolás Salmerón, "The Downfall of Spain," *The International* (London), 6 (August 1909), 22–24, subsequently reprinted in *La Publicidad* (Barcelona), September 21, 1909.

4. Josep Benet, *Maragall i la Setmana Trágica*, 3 ed. (Barcelona, 1965).

5. See Severino Aznar, *Problemas sociales de actualidad: 1914. La Conquista del proletariado. Para la historia del Catolicismo social en España. Hecho y criterios sociales* (Barcelona, 1914), and *Impresiones de un demócrata cristiano* (Madrid, 1931).

6. José María García Escudero, *De Cánovas a la República*, 2 ed. (Madrid, 1953), pp. 192–95.

7. See, for example, Magin Vidal y Ribas [pseud. of Antonio Fabra Rivas], "Réponse a des calomnies," *L'Humanité* (Paris), August 18, 1909.

CHAPTER I: THE NATIONAL CRISIS

1. For a concise statement on the position of the workers in this period see Jaime Vicens Vives, ed., *Historia social y económica de España y América, V: Burguesía, industrialización, obrerismo* (Barcelona, 1959), 384–85.

2. Antonio Cánovas del Castillo, *Estudios sobre el reinado de Felipe IV* (Madrid, 1888), I, 91.

3. For the economic interests represented in Restoration politics, see Antonio Ramos Oliveira, *Politics, Economics and Men of Modern Spain*, trans. Teener Hall (London, 1946), pp. 106–11. Joaquín Maurín, *La Revolución española: De la Monarquía absoluta a la revolución socialista* (Madrid, 1932), pp. 35–44.

4. Enrique Fuentes Quintana and Juan Velardes Fuertes, *Política económica* (Ma-

drid, 1959), pp. 136–37, 236–37. Jaime Vicens Vives and Jorge Nadal Oller, *Manual de historia económica de España* (Barcelona, 1959), pp. 666–68.

5. For the Spanish republican movement, see C. A. M. Hennessy, *The Federal Republic in Spain: Pi y Margall and the Federal Republican Movement, 1868–1874* (Oxford, 1962), ch. 11; Alvaro de Albornoz, *El Partido republicano* (Madrid, 1918); and Rodrigo Soriano, *La Revolución española, 1931: Ayer y hoy* (Madrid, 1931).

6. The classical studies of the cacique are Joaquín Costa, *Oligarquía y caciquismo* (Madrid, 1903), and Valentí Almirall, *L'Espagne telle qu'elle est* (Barcelona, 1886). For brief discussions see Fernando Soldevila, *Historia de España*, VIII (Barcelona, 1959), 186–93, and Gerald Brenan, *The Spanish Labyrinth: An Account of the Social and Political Background of the Civil War*, 2 ed. (Cambridge, 1950), pp. 5–11, 19–21.

7. Quoted in Vicens, *Historia social*, V, 378.

8. Quoted in Antonio Royo Villanova, *El Problema catalán: Impresiones de un viaje a Barcelona* (Madrid, 1908), p. 12.

9. The best biography of Iglesias is Juan José Morató, *Pablo Iglesias Posse: Educador de muchedumbres* (Bilbao, 1931). See also the biography by Iglesias' stepson, Juan A. Melía, *Pablo Iglesias: Rasgos de su vida íntima* (Madrid, 1926). For Spanish socialism see G. D. H. Cole, *The Second International, 1889–1914: A History of Socialist Thought*, III (London, 1956), part II, passim. As a survey Cole's study is of value, although it errs in fact and, in my opinion, in interpretation.

10. Angel Marvaud, *La Question sociale en Espagne* (Paris, 1910), p. 68.

11. Renée Lamberet, *L'Espagne: 1750–1936*, in the series *Mouvements ouvriers et socialistes: Chronologie et bibliographie*, eds. Edouard Dolléons and Michel Crozier (Paris, 1953), pp. 71, 74.

12. For the Spanish labor movement in this period see Manuel Buenacasa, *El Movimiento obrero español, 1886–1926: Historia y crítica* (Barcelona, 1928); Diego Abad de Santillán, *Contribución a la historia del movimiento obrero español: Desde sus Orígenes hasta 1905* (Puebla, Mexico, 1962); Maximiano García Venero, *Historia de las Internacionales en España*, I: *1868–1914* (Madrid, 1956), pp. 255–445; Amaro del Rosal, *Los Congresos obreros internacionales en el siglo XIX: De la "Joven Europa" a la Segunda Internacional* (Mexico, D.F., 1958); and Antonio Royo Villanova, *Cuestiones obreras* (Valladolid, 1910). For background see José Termes Ardévol, *El Movimiento obrero en España: La Primera Internacional, 1864–1881* (Barcelona, 1965); Práxedes Zancada, *El Obrero en España: Notas para su historia política y social* (Barcelona, 1902); Adolfo Buylla, Adolfo Posada, and Luis Morote, *El Instituto del Trabajo: Datos para la historia de la reforma social en España* (Madrid, 1902); and Juan Uña y Sarthou, *Las Asociaciones obreras en España: Notas para su historia* (Madrid, 1900).

13. See statement by Iglesias in May 1908, as quoted in Morató, *Iglesias*, p. 158. For an anarchist's charge that Iglesias' participation was an attempt to divide, and thereby weaken, the working class, see Leopoldo Bonafulla [pseud. of Juan Bautista Esteve] *Criterio libertario* (Barcelona, 1905), pp. 9–11.

14. For the best survey of Spanish anarchism see George Woodcock, *Anarchism: A History of Libertarian Ideas and Movements* (Harmondsworth, England, 1963), pp 335–75. For an excellent study of the origins see Casimiro Martí, *Orígenes del anarquismo en Barcelona* (Barcelona, 1959). See also Eduardo Comín Colomer, *Historia*

del anarquismo español: 1836-1948 (Madrid, n.d.). An undocumented work, the latter does contain much information, some from Buenacasa's invaluable study, some possibly from police files (Comín is chief of the Brigada Social de la Dirección General de Seguridad). Of some value for the period under study are Gustavo La Iglesia y Garcia, *Caracteres del anarquismo en la actualidad,* 2 ed. (Barcelona, 1907), and Federica Montseny, *Los Precursores: Anselmo Lorenzo: El Hombre y la obra* (Barcelona, 1938). Of less value than Woodcock's study is James Joll, *The Anarchists* (London, 1964).

15. For the Catalan labor movement see Joaquín Maurín, "El Movimiento obrero en Cataluña," *Leviatán* (Madrid), (October 1934), pp. 15-19. See also Jaime Vicens Vives, *Cataluña en el siglo XIX,* trans. E. Borrás Cubells (Madrid, 1961), pp. 217-60.

16. Vicens Vives, *Cataluña en el siglo XIX,* p. 256.

17. The organization of trade unions, including the election of officers and the payment of dues, is reported in the annual publication of Miguel Sastre Sanna, *Las Huelgas en Barcelona y sus resultados,* 1903-1914 (Barcelona, 1904-1915). The Barcelona typesetters' union, in its *Boletín del Arte de Imprimir,* makes continual references to dues. Fees of three céntimos per person per month are stipulated in Article X of the published statutes of Solidaridad Obrera: La Confederación Regional de Sociedades de Resistencia (Barcelona, 1909). For an account of textile unions unwilling to share their mutual funds see *La Internacional* (Barcelona), January 1, 1909.

18. Buenacasa, *Movimiento obrero,* pp. 280-85. Federico Urales [pseud. of Juan Montseny], *Mi Vida* (Barcelona, n.d.), I, passim. Vicens Vives, *Cataluña: Siglo XIX,* p. 259, and *Historia social,* V, 224.

19. Urales [Montseny], *Mi Vida,* II, 72. For further details on the labor federation see García Venero, *Las Internacionales,* I, 408-09, 447-48. La Iglesia, *Anarquismo,* p. 426. Marvaud, *Question sociale,* pp. 49-52. Abad de Santillán, *Historia del movimiento obrero,* pp. 488-90.

20. For anarcho-syndicalism see Jean Maitron's excellent analysis in, *Histoire du mouvement anarchiste en France: 1880-1914* (Paris, 1951), pp. 245-306. See also Val R. Lorwin, *The French Labor Movement* (Cambridge, Mass., 1954), pp. 15-46. Anarchosyndicalist treatises were translated into Spanish by Francisco Ferrer's publishing firm, as for example, Emile Pouget, *La Confederación General del Trabajo en Francia* (Barcelona, n.d.).

21. Fuentes Quintana, *Política económica,* p. 137.

22. Vicens Vives, *Historia social,* V, 206. Vicens made this assertion largely on the careful work of his student, María José Sirera, A.C.J., "Obreros en Barcelona: 1900-1910" (unpubl. thesis for the degree of *licenciatura,* College of Philosophy and Letters, University of Barcelona, 1959), pp. 22, 34, 48-50.

23. For Ruíz Zorilla and his contacts with army officers, see Hennessy, *Federal Republic,* pp. 152, 208. Alejandro Lerroux, *Mis Memorias* (Madrid, 1963), pp. 92, 148, 514-16. Pedro Sangro y Ros, *La Sombra de Ferrer: De la "Semana Trágica" a la guerra europea* (Madrid, 1917), pp. 75-76. Pedro Aguado Bleye and Cayetano Alcázar Molina, *Manual de historia de España,* 7 ed. rev. (Madrid, 1956), III, 761.

24. On Spanish Freemasonry, see Miguel Morayta y Sagrario, *Masonería española: Páginas de su historia,* published in 1915; the only readily available edition is that edited by Mauricio Carlavilla for publication in Franco Spain (Madrid, 1956). See also Sangro,

Sombra de Ferrer, pp. 185-204; Lerroux, *Mis Memorias,* pp. 516-18; "Francmasonería," *Enciclopedia Universal Ilustrada Europeo-Americana* (Barcelona, n.d. [1905-1930]), XXIV, 1085-87; "Masonería," *ibid.,* XXXIII, 718-750 (especially, 722 and 741-47); and Mildred J. Headings, *French Freemasonry under the Third Republic,* The Johns Hopkins Studies in Historical and Political Science, 66 (Baltimore, 1948), 67.

25. Vicens Vives, *Historia social,* V, 180-87. Melchor Fernández Almagro, *Historia política de la España contemporánea,* II (Madrid, 1959), 36.

26. Marvaud, *Question sociale,* pp. 9-10, and Fernández Almagro, *Historia política,* II, 162-65. For the viewpoint of a young army officer in this period see Emilio Mola Vidal, *Obras completas* (Valladolid, 1940), pp. 934-35, 963-65. In 1905 Unamuno warned of the danger for the nation if the King identified himself with the Army. See Unamuno, "La Crisis actual del patriotismo español," *Ensayos* (Madrid, 1916), VI, 131-56.

27. Katherine Chorley, *Armies and the Art of Revolution* (London, 1943), p. 178. For the nineteenth-century background of workers' opposition to conscription, see *ibid.,* pp. 104-05, and Hennessy, *Federal Republic,* pp. 109-10, 116, 130.

28. For the draft system, see Joaquín Sánchez de Toca, *Discurso . . . en apoyo de su enmienda a la base 1.ª de la letra B del proyecto de ley de Servicio militar obligatorio* (Madrid, 1910), passim; General Arsenio Linares, Minister of War, October 20, 1909, in *Diario de las Cortes,* pp. 74-78; Salvador Canals, *Los Sucesos de España en 1909: Crónica documentada,* I (Madrid, 1910), 124-27; Rafael Shaw, *Spain from Within* (London, 1910), pp. 199-211; and "Por qué van los reservistas a Melilla," *Las Noticias* (Barcelona), July 24, 1909.

CHAPTER II: THE CLERICAL ISSUE AND THE POLITICIANS

1. For the responsibility of religious orders in the Philippine Islands see Luis Morote, *La Moral de la derrota* (Madrid, 1900), passim; Morote, *Los Frailes en España* (Madrid, 1904), pp. 20, 63-64; and Angel Marvaud, *L'Espagne au XXᵉ siècle: Etude politique et économique,* 2 ed. (Paris, 1915), p. 168.

2. Shaw, *Spain from Within,* p. 202.

3. Evelyn M. Acomb cites this as one of the root causes of anticlericalism. See Acomb, *The French Laic Laws* (1879-1889): *The First Anti-Clerical Campaign of the Third French Republic* (New York, 1941), p. 41.

4. For the importance of clerical interests as a political issue in the Second Republic, see José María Sánchez, *Reform and Reaction: The Politico-Religious Background of the Spanish Civil War* (Chapel Hill, N.C., 1964).

5. For an excellent description of the merging of Catholicism and Spanish nationalism, see Américo Castro, *The Structure of Spanish History,* trans. Edmund King (Princeton, 1954).

6. For the disamortization of church property see "Desamortización," *Enciclopedia Universal Ilustrada,* XVIII 361-70; E. Alison Peers, *Spain: The Church and the Orders* (London, 1945); Fernando Soldevilla, *Año político,* XIV: *1908* (Madrid, 1909), 28-29, 36-39; *Boletín Oficial Eclesiástico* (Barcelona), 1446 (January 1910), 12-21; V. G.

Kiernan, *The Revolution of 1854 in Spanish History* (Oxford, 1966), pp. 140-48, 244-47; and Vicens Vives, *Historia social*, V, 88-95.

7. See Padres Calasanz Bau and José Poch, eds., *Historia de las Escuelas Pías en Cataluña: Homenage a la provincia escolapia catalana en el lucentario de su canónica elección: 1751-1951* (Barcelona, 1951), and Pedro Sanahuja, O.F.M., *Historia de la Seráfica Provincia de Cataluña* (Barcelona, n.d. [1956?]). These are detailed accounts of the dispersion of members after the disamortizing legislation, and of the re-establishment of the communities of their orders after the Restoration. Although legally exempted, many Piarists left the monasteries.

8. Hennessy, *Federal Republic*, passim.

9. Morote, *Frailes en España*, pp. 26-29. Soldevilla, *Año político*, XVI: *1910*, 391.

10. For an excellent study of the Spanish educational system until 1902 see Yvonne Turin, *L'Education et l'école de 1874 a 1902: Liberalisme et tradition* (Paris, 1959). For the period up to the Civil War see José Castillejo, *Wars of Ideas in Spain: Philosophy, Politics and Education* (London, 1937), and *Revolution in Spain* (London, 1937).

11. For the ideas of Francisco Giner de los Ríos (1839-1915) see his *Obras completas*, 19 vols. (Madrid, 1916-1928). For a study of the Institución and its influence, see José López-Morillas, *El Krausismo español* (Mexico, D.F., 1956). For a favorable view of Giner's Institución, see the book by Castillejo, *Wars of Ideas in Spain*. For criticism by a conservative see García Escudero (of Opus Dei), *De Cánovas a la República*, pp. 143-44.

12. See, for example, Pierre Vilar, *Historia de España*, trans. Manuel Tuñon de Lara (Paris, 1960), p. 109.

13. Vicens Vives, *Historia social*, V, 145-47. Abad de Santillán, *Historia del movimiento obrero*, p. 510.

14. Morote, *Frailes en España*, pp. 15-16, 25.

15. Royo Villanova, *Problema catalán*, p. 118. Sangro, *Sombra de Ferrer*, pp. 147-48.

16. Maurín, "Movimiento obrero," *Leviatán* (Madrid), p. 15. Shaw, *Spain from Within*, p. 15. Gabriel Jackson, "The Origins of Spanish Anarchism," *The Southwestern Social Science Quarterly*, 36 (September 1955), 136-37, 140-42.

17. Antonio Ballesteros y Beretta, *Historia de España y su influencia en la historia universal*, 2 ed. rev. by Manuel Ballesteros-Gaibrois (Barcelona, 1956), XI, 497. Fernando Díaz-Plaja, ed., *La Historia de España en sus documentos*, vol. IV: *El Siglo XX*, new series (Madrid, 1960), pp. 31-33.

18. Rafael Padilla, *España actual* (Madrid, 1908), pp. 129-38. Juan Ventosa, Lliga deputy, July 16, 1910, *Diario de las Cortes*, III, 686. Hermegildo Giner de los Ríos, Radical deputy, *ibid.*, III, 689. Letter from José Serrat defending the schools in the Ateneos Obreros of Barcelona, *La Publicidad* (Barcelona), October 29, 1909. Augusto Riera, *La Semana Trágica: Relato de la sedición e incendios en Barcelona y Cataluña* (Barcelona, 1909), p. 13.

19. Joaquín Aguilera, *La Revue* (Paris), 1912, as cited in Marvaud, *L'Espagne: XXe siècle*, p. 189.

20. See particularly speeches by Radical Republican politicians, July 1909, as reported by police in the military trial proceedings published by the Ministry of War, *Causa contra Trinidad Alted Fornet, Emiliano Iglesias Ambrosio, Luis Zurdo de Olivares y*

Juana Ardiaca Mas por el delito de rebelión militar. Ocurrió el hecho desde el 26 al 31 de julio de 1909. Dieron principio las actuaciones el 29 de julio de 1909. Terminaron el 5 de julio de 1910 (Madrid, 1911), I, 73–74, 75–84, 86–90 (Hereafter cited as *Causa: Rebelión militar*). Shaw, *Spain from Within*, chs. 5, 11, passim.

21. Shaw, *Spain from Within*, pp. 15, 287–96.

22. See the general instructions issued by Pope Leo XIII on the financing of new religious orders, on December 6, 1900, published in *Boletín Oficial Eclesiástico* (Barcelona), 1259 (February 1901), 59–70. See Leo XIII's recommendation on the role of religious in education and welfare, *ibid.*, 1268 (July 1901), 243–46.

23. See article on anticlericalism by Francisco Pi y Arsuaga (son of the distinguished President of the First Republic), quoted in its entirety in Leopoldo Bonafulla [pseud. of Juan Bautista Esteve], *La Revolución de julio en Barcelona* (Barcelona, n.d. [1909?]), pp. 65–73.

24. For the charge that clergy exploited their charity, see editorial, *El País* (Madrid), August 13, 1909. "C" [pseud. of José Comaposada], "Sucesos de Barcelona," *El Socialista* (Madrid), (November 19, 1909). *Las Noticias* (Barcelona), August 8 and 12, 1909.

25. Sirera, "Obreros en Barcelona," pp. 38, 49, 64.

26. See introduction by Pierre Waldeck-Rousseau, "La Política anticlerical: Una Definición," to Morote, *Frailes en España*, pp. 5–6.

27. Report by the Junta Diocesana Barcelonesa on the National Congress in Santiago, *Boletín Oficial Eclesiástico* (Barcelona), 1292 (August 1902), 388–94.

28. Letter from Pius X to the officials of the Italian Catholic labor movement, January 20, 1907, as printed in *Boletín Oficial Eclesiástico* (Barcelona), 1397 (July 1907), 250–54.

29. For the renewed Catholic labor activities, see Aznar, *Problemas sociales*, pp. 34, 44–49, 63–67, 119, 126–27, 279–82; Uña y Sarthou, *Asociaciones obreras en España*, pp. 333–44; Montserrat Llorens, "El Padre Antonio Vicent, S.J., 1837–1912; Notas sobre el desarrollo de la acción social católica en España," *Estudios de Historia Moderna* (Barcelona), IV: 395–439 (1954); Max Turmann, *El Desenvolvimiento del Catolicismo social desde la encíclica "Rerum Novarum": Ideas directrices y caracteres generales*, trans. Severino Aznar (Madrid, n.d. [1909?]), pp. 9–24, 94–99; and Juan N. García-Nieto, S.J., *El Sindicalismo cristiano en España: Notas sobre su origen y evolución hasta 1936* (Bilbao, 1960), pp. 12–14, 71.

30. On the workers' opinion that workers' circles were merely company unions, see Llorens, "Padre Antonio Vicent," *Estudios de Historia Moderna*, p. 433. See also letter from socialist members of the Institute of Social Reform, in *El Socialista* (Madrid), May 31, 1909, and José M. Boix, "Sindicalismo Católico: Su Actuación en Barcelona," *Revista Social Hispano-Americana* (Barcelona), 11 (March 1912), p. 216.

31. See Pablo Iglesias' reply to charge that he was a "clerical": Morató, *Iglesias*, p. 147. In a conversation, the Catalan labor spokesman Joaquín Maurín pointed out, in confirmation of this point, that the new history of the Spanish labor movement by Abad de Santillán barely mentioned anticlericalism (interview with Maurín, in New York City, on March 16, 1963). See also Claudi Ametlla, *Memòries polítiques, 1890–1917* (Barcelona, 1963), p. 164.

32. Angelica Balabanoff, "Anticlericalismo y socialismo," *La Internacional* (Barcelona), (February 5, 1909).

33. Reprinted in Soldevilla, *Año político*, XVI: *1910*, 204–06.

34. Morote, *Frailes en España*, pp. 64–65. G. Maura, *Por qué cayó Alfonso*, p. 36. Soldevilla, *Año político*, XIV: *1908*, 482.

35. Benito Mariano Andrade, *Maura y el partido conservador* (Burgos, 1910), pp. 51–52. It is of political significance that Maura's brothers-in-law were active in Catholic organizations: Maura's power base was the Gamazo faction which he took over at the death of his father-in-law. Trifino Gamazo was on the board of directors of Catholic Action (*Boletín Oficial Eclesiástico*, 1438 [September 1909], 311). Valentín Gamazo was associated with the ultraconservative Comité de Defensa Social (Soldevilla, *Año político*, XVI: *1910*, 31).

36. G. Maura, *Por qué cayó Alfonso*, p. 410. For the Nozaleda affair see also Diego Sevilla Andrés, *Antonio Maura: La Revolución desde Arriba* (Barcelona, 1953), pp. 230–44; G. Maura, *Recuerdos de mi vida* (Madrid, 1934), p. 70; Marvaud, *Espagne: XXᵉ siècle*, p. 168; Antonio Orts-Ramos and F. Carravaca, *Historia ilustrada de la revolución española: 1870–1931*, Second part: *Desde la Coronación de Alfonso XIII hasta la Segunda República* (Barcelona, 1932), p. 387; and Maximiano García Venero, *Antonio Maura: 1907–1909* (Madrid, 1953), p. 53.

37. Ballesteros, *Historia de España*, XI, 540.

38. Canals, *Sucesos de 1909*, II, 54–56. Jackson, "Origins of Spanish Anarchism," *Southwestern Social Science Quarterly*, p. 137.

39. The Ministry of Justice published almost the entire proceedings (testimony and judicial decisions) in *Causa por regicidio frustrado, 1906–1909. Atentado de 31 de mayo de 1906. Causa contra Mateo Morral, Francisco Ferrer, José Nakens, Pedro Mayoral, Aquilino Martínez, Isidro Ibarra, Bernardo Mata y Concepción Pérez Cuesta* (Madrid, 1911), 5 vols.

40. Sangro, *Sombra de Ferrer*, pp. 114–16. See also Padilla, *España actual*, pp. 132–33.

41. Soldevilla, *Año político*, XIII: *1907*, 10. Castillejo, *Wars of Ideas*, p. 116. Alberto Jiménez Fraud, *Ocaso y restauración: Ensayo sobre la universidad española moderna* (Mexico, D.F., 1948), pp. 206–86. For the persistence of the antagonism toward the Institución under the Franco Regime, see Anon., *Poderosa Fuerza secreta: La Institución Libre* (San Sebastián, 1940).

42. Soldevilla, *Año político*, XIII: *1907*, 81, 98, 103, 216–18.

CHAPTER III: REFORMS VERSUS "CLERICALISM" IN THE GOVERNMENT OF ANTONIO MAURA

1. For a concise, representative collection of Maura's ideas see *Antonio Maura: Treinta y cinco Años de vida pública*, ed. José Ruíz-Castillo, 3 ed. (Madrid, 1953). For invaluable letters see the appendix to the book by Maura's son and political secretary, Gabriel Maura, *Por qué cayó Alfonso*, pp. 401–533. The most recent and most complete biography is Sevilla Andrés, *Antonio Maura: La Revolución desde Arriba* (Madrid, 1953). For a good account of Maura's early career see Arturo García Carrafa and Luis Antón del Olmet, *Maura*, vol. III of *Los grandes Españoles* (Madrid, 1913). See also Luciano de Taxonera, *Antonio Maura: La gran Figura política de una época de España* (Madrid, 1944); Cesar Silió, *Vida y empresas de un gran español: Maura*, vol. XXXIX

of *Vidas españolas e hispanoamericanas del siglo XIX* (Madrid, 1934); and José María de Bedoya, *Don Antonio Maura, Ministro de la Gobernación, 1902–1903* (Madrid, 1940).

2. G. Maura, *Recuerdos*, pp. 109–12.

3. Stanley Payne, "Spanish Nationalism in the Twentieth Century," *Review of Politics*, 26 (1964), 403–22.

4. See "La Marina mercante," *Maura: Treinta y cinco años*, pp. 405–32, and Melchor Fernández Almagro, *Política naval de la España moderna y contemporánea* (Madrid, 1946), pp. 217–65. See summary of debates on the navy and the awarding of ship building contracts (awarded almost entirely to Comillas' Compañía Transatlántica) in Soldevilla, *Año político*, XIII: *1907*, 495–98, 502–06, 513; XIV: *1908*, 151–52, 470–71, 473–76, 480; and XV: *1909*, 68, 73–74, 118. For an attack on the inefficiency of the Transatlántica see Padilla, *España actual*, pp. 200, 241, 243–44.

5. G. Maura, *Por qué cayó Alfonso*, pp. 133–35. "Ante la Guerra: Lo que dice Linares," *España Nueva* (Madrid), July 25, 1909. Declarations of General Fernando Primo de Rivera to a French journalist, as reported in Soldevilla, *Año político*, XV: *1909*, 419–20.

6. Jesús Pabón, *Cambó: 1876–1918* (Barcelona, 1952), p. 304.

7. G. Maura, *Recuerdos*, p. 112.

8. For a thorough study of the Cambó-Maura negotiations, see Pabón, *Cambó*, ch. 6, passim.

9. Gaziel [pseud. of Agustí Calvet], *Tots els Camins drien a Roma: Historia d'un destí, 1893–1914* (Barcelona, n.d. [1958?]), p. 329. See also Eduardo Aúnos, *Discurso de la vida: Autobiografía* (Madrid, 1951), pp. 343–44.

10. Royo Villanova, *Problema catalán*, pp. 85, 121–23. For the importance of an expanded bureaucracy in republican politics, see Hennessy, *Federal Republic*, p. 249, and Acomb, *French Laic Laws*, pp. 42–43. Public school teachers zealously guarded their profession against political appointees; see *Memoria que han escrito los maestros públicos de Barcelona acerca de la conversión de las auxiliares en escuelas* (Barcelona, 1906).

11. Soldevilla, *Año político*, XIII: *1907*, 228.

12. *El Correo Catalán* (Barcelona), August 18, 1909.

13. For Maura and the sugar monopoly, see Shaw, *Spain from Within*, p. 291, and Soldevilla, *Año político*, XIII: *1907*, 304–06, 318–40, 348, 352. For the Vasco-Castellano railroad affair, see *Año político*, XIV: *1908*, 13, 20, 40–41.

14. Soldevilla, *Año político*, XIII: *1907*, 22–28, 36, 39–41. *Boletín Oficial Eclesiástico* (Barcelona), 1438 (September 1909), 318–20; 1446 (January 1910), 12–21. Vicens Vives writes that payment of the interest, suspended in 1862, was not renewed until 1948 (*Historia social*, V, 91).

15. For the Royal Order of September 12, 1908, and the Church's commentary on the order, see *Boletín Oficial Eclesiástico* (Barcelona), 1428 (February 1909), 80–84. For workers' reaction to cloistered nuns being buried within their convent, see, for example, "C" [José Comaposada], "Sucesos de Barcelona," *El Socialista* (Madrid), December 3, 1909.

16. García Carrafa, *Maura*, p. 396.

17. Benito de Pomés, Conde de Santa María de Pomés, May 21, 1908, as quoted in Soldevilla, *Año político*, XIV: *1908*, 175–76.

18. Albo (June 1908), *ibid.*, 222–23.

19. Melquiades Alvarez (December 1908), *ibid.*, 484.

20. Albo (December 1908), *ibid.*, 482.

21. Moret (February 1909) in Soldevilla, *Año político*, XV: *1909*, 87.

22. *Ibid.*, 83. G. Maura, *Por qué cayó Alfonso*, p. 127.

23. *El Socialista* (Madrid), June 25, 1909. See also *ibid.*, September 11, 1908; May 7 and 14, and June 4, 11, and 18, 1909. Morató, *Iglesias*, pp. 136, 139, 147.

24. Soldevilla, *Año político*, XIV: *1908*, 482.

25. For the Osera-Orense incident, see *El Socialista* (Madrid), May 7, 1909; *España Nueva* (Madrid), April 25–30, May 1, 14, and 23, and June 30, 1909; and Soldevilla, *Año político*, XV: *1909*, 171–72, 178–79, 185.

26. On the question of wages and prices, see Sirera, "Obreros en Barcelona," Charts 17 and 18. Marvaud, *Question sociale*, pp. 83–86, 89, 426.

27. Juan de La Cierva y Peñafiel, *Notas de mi vida*, 2 ed. (Madrid, 1955), pp. 119–22. Sangro, *Sombra de Ferrer*, pp. 179–80.

28. Díaz-Plaja, *Documentos: Siglo XX*, pp. 135–37.

CHAPTER IV: THE REGION AND ITS POLITICS

1. For an excellent study of Catalan nationalism up to 1909, see Pabón, *Cambó*, pp. 15–362. Royo Villanova, *El Problema catalán* (Madrid, 1908) is anti-Catalan, but very factual. For an objective analysis of the Catalan nationalist ideology, see José Ferrater Mora, "Flexions sobre Catalunya," *Les Formes de la vida catalana*, 2 ed. (Barcelona, 1955), pp. 125–36. See also the remarkably candid essay on Catalan industrialism by Emilio Giralt y Raventós, a prologue to Vicens Vives, *Cataluña en el siglo XIX*, pp. 9–26. Interesting, but undocumented, is García Venero, *Historia del nacionalismo catalán, 1793–1936* (Madrid, 1944). Less helpful is García Venero, *Vida de Cambó* (Barcelona, 1952).

2. Concerning the illiteracy in Barcelona, see Royo Villanova, *Problema catalán*, p. 119, and Soldevilla, *Año político*, XIV: *1908*, 297.

3. For housing conditions in workers' neighborhoods, see Sirera, "Obreros en Barcelona," Chart 7.

4. *Ibid.*, p. 30.

5. *Ibid.*, pp. 27–29.

6. *Ibid.*, Chart 23.

7. Ayuntamiento de Barcelona, *Anuario Estadístico de la Ciudad de Barcelona para el año 1905*, IV (Barcelona, 1906).

8. For a good discussion of journalism in Catalonia in this period, see Ametlla, *Memòries polítiques*, pp. 202–18.

9. For a general survey of Catalan industry in this period, see Ministry of Development [Fomento], General Directorate of Agriculture, Industry, and Commerce, *Memoria acerca del estado de la industria en la provincia de Barcelona* (Madrid, 1910), and M. Eduardo Escarrá, *Développement industriel de la Catalogne* (Paris, 1908).

10. For a description of the plight of workers in the Ter Valley, see speech by Alejandro Lerroux in the Cortes, on March 8, 1902, as quoted in Díaz-Plaja, *Documentos:*

Siglo XX, pp. 37–38. For the "Hunger Pact" of 1901, see "Nueva provocación patronal," *La Internacional* (Barcelona), May 28, 1909.

11. Boix, "Sindicalismo Católico," *Revista Social Hispano-Americana* (Barcelona), p. 211.

12. These figures and the following chart are from *Anuario estadístico de la ciudad de Barcelona: 1905,* vol. IV.

13. Sastre, *Huelgas: 1905,* p. 88.

14. Fernando Soldevila, ed., *Un Segle de vida catalana: 1814–1930* (Barcelona, 1961), II, 1320–21. For the General Strike of 1902, see Anon., *La Huelga General en Barcelona: Verdadera Relación de los sucesos desarrollados con motivo del paro general en Barcelona, durante la octava semana de este año, por un testigo ocular* (Barcelona, 1902); account by Francisco Manzano, Civil Governor of Barcelona in 1906, in E. Carqué de la Parra, ed., *El Terrorismo en Barcelona: Lo que dicen los prohombres de todos los partidos* (Barcelona, 1908), pp. 45–46; Abad de Santillán, *Historia del movimiento obrero,* pp. 492–93; and Montseny, *Anselmo Lorenzo,* pp. 27–29.

15. Manifesto dated February 8, 1903, reprinted in La Iglesia, *Caracteres del anarquismo,* pp. 427–29. Concerning socialist opposition to the 1902 General Strike, see article attacking socialist Toribio Reoyo, *El Progreso* (Barcelona), November 17, 1911; Abad de Santillán, *Historia del movimiento obrero,* pp. 494–97; and Díaz-Plaja, *Documentos: Siglo XX,* p. 55.

16. Sastre, *Huelgas: 1903,* pp. 63, 71, 77–78. *Huelgas: 1904,* pp. 87–88. *Boletín del Arte de Imprimir* (Barcelona), December 1907.

17. Sastre, *Huelgas: 1904,* p. 101. For a very blunt account of Foronda's campaign to break the streetcar workers' union, surprising because it is by a conservative author closely associated with Catholic circles, see Sastre, *Huelgas: 1903,* pp. 47–48; *Huelgas: 1904,* pp. 101–02; *Huelgas: 1909,* pp. 29–30; *Huelgas: 1912,* pp. 297–98. For the plight of streetcar workers, see also Soldevilla, *Año político,* XIII: *1907,* 140. José Brissa, *La Revolución de julio en Barcelona: Su Represión, sus víctimas, el proceso de Ferrer* (Barcelona, 1910), p. 35. Dalmacio Iglesias, Carlist deputy (citing report prepared by terrorist Juan Rull), July 14, 1910, *Diario de las Cortes,* III, 617.

18. Sastre, *Huelgas: 1904,* p. 77, and *Huelgas: 1909,* p. 37.

19. Angel Ossorio, *Visita a Arenys de Mar: Mayo 1909* (Barcelona, n.d. [1909]), pp. 3–5. Pabón, *Cambó,* pp. 137–40. Soldevilla, *Año político,* XIV: *1908,* 364.

20. *Boletín Oficial Eclesiástico* (Barcelona), 1310 (July 1903), 167–69, and 1397 (July 1907), 254–57.

21. See statement of principles issued by the Comité de Defensa Social in Barcelona on September 8, 1909, as reprinted in Bonafulla [Esteve], *Revolución de julio,* pp. 50–52.

22. Shaw, *Spain from Within,* p. 148. For the militant Carlist activity, see the comments of ex-Governor Ossorio, July 13, 1910, *Diario de las Cortes,* III, 588. Carlist deputy Pedro Llosas replied on July 14, 1910, *ibid.,* 614.

23. See Comillas' defense of these workers' circles, and his plea for funds to rebuild them after they were burned in 1909, *Boletín Oficial Eclesiástico* (Barcelona), 1438 (September 1909), 316.

24. García Nieto, *Sindicalismo cristiano,* pp. 63–64; 89–90. Severino Aznar of the

Catholic Action movement also advocated Catholic labor unions (instead of workers' circles): see Aznar, *Problemas sociales,* pp. 63–67, 279–82. For information on Father Palau and Popular Social Action, see *ibid.,* pp. 84–86. Sastre, *Huelgas: 1907,* 95–97.

25. Father Palau lectured with perception on the need for a dynamic program to attract the urban Catholic worker, and on the need to abandon the prevailing paternalistic attitude toward the worker. See *El Problema de la eficacia de la acción social católica en las grandes ciudades,* speech given in Buenos Aires on May 15, 1917 (Buenos Aires, n.d.); *La Acción social del sacerdote: Un Campo de acción,* speeches given in Barcelona, January 16 and February 20, 1907 (Barcelona, 1907); and *Accion social del sacerdote: La Preparación del porvenir,* speech given in Barcelona on June 19, 1910, 2 ed. (Barcelona, 1911).

26. On the decline in secular clergy, see the dramatic figures in Ebenstein, *Church and State in Franco Spain,* pp. 21–22. See also *Boletín Oficial Eclesiástico* (Barcelona), 1400 (September 1907), 317–20, and the editorial in *El Correo Catalán* (Barcelona), August 12, 1909.

27. Morote, *Frailes en España,* p. 26.

28. *Ibid.,* pp. 13, 22.

29. Ametlla, *Memòries polítiques,* pp. 155–56, 163–64.

30. For the *Cu-Cut* incident see *La Veu de Catalunya* (Barcelona), November 25, 1905, and Pabón, *Cambó,* pp. 254–269. As a result of this incident, Solidaridad Catalana was organized: for the details, see *ibid.,* pp. 269–78.

31. Pabón, *Cambó,* p. 310.

32. Amadeo Hurtado, *Quaranta Anys d'advocat: Historia del meu temps,* vol. I: *1894–1915* (Mexico, D.F., 1956), 125–48; 177–78. See also Royo Villanova, *Cuestiones obreras,* pp. 185–86.

CHAPTER V: PERSONALITIES AND FORCES FOR REVOLUTION

1. For the period prior to 1906, see Ferrer's autobiography in: *España Nueva* (Madrid), June 16, 1906. The most objective biography is William Archer, *The Life, Trial and Death of Francisco Ferrer* (London, 1911). See also the two books by Ferrer's daughter, Sol Ferrer y Sanmartí (who rarely saw her father before she was fourteen years old, and did not see him again after that time): most valuable is *Le véritable Francisco Ferrer d'après des documents inédits* (Paris, 1948). Far less detailed, and more idealized, is *La Vie et l'oeuvre de Francisco Ferrer: Un Martyr au XXe siècle* (Paris, 1962); this was a doctoral dissertation presented to the Faculté des Lettres et des Sciences Humaines of Paris, under the title "Francisco Ferrer: Pensée politique et sociale."

For a documented, albeit biased (pro-Ferrer) account of Ferrer's career, see *Un Martyr des prêtres: Francisco Ferrer, janvier 1859–13 octobre 1909,* prepared by a group of Ferrer's associates in Paris under the name Comité de Défense des Victimes de la Repression Espagnole (Paris, n.d. [1909?]). See also the extensive biographical data contained in the dictum on the Ferrer case prepared by the military judge advocate of Barcelona, General Ramón Pastor, *Causa contra Francisco Ferrer Guardia, instruída y fallada por la jurisdicción de Guerra en Barcelona: Año 1909* (Madrid, 1911), pp. 645–

68. Luis Simarro, *El Proceso Ferrer y la opinión europea,* I (Madrid, 1910) is extremely helpful because it summarizes all material published prior to 1910. Sangro, *Sombra de Ferrer* (1917), provides an excellent summary of the political ramifications of the Ferrer case.

For books attacking Ferrer which contain some material of historic interest, see Casimiro Comás, *Un Revolucionario de acción: Francisco Ferrer. Su vida y su obra destructora. Justicia de su condena* (Barcelona, 1910); Alphonse Lugan, *Un Précurseur du bolchevisme: Francisco Ferrer. Sa vie et son oeuvre: Etude critique* (Paris, 1921); and John Augustine Ryan, *Francisco Ferrer: Criminal Conspirator,* a reply to the articles by William Archer in McClure's Magazine . . . (St. Louis, 1911).

For books eulogizing Ferrer, see Joseph McCabe, *The Martyrdom of Ferrer, being a True Account of his Life and Work* (London, 1909); Georges Normandy and E. Lesueur, *Ferrer: L'Homme et son oeuvre. Sa mort. Castille contra Catalogne.* Portraits, documents inédits, lettres originals (Paris, 1909; despite the subtitle, this book contains no new documents); Maurice Dommanget, *Francisco Ferrer,* in the series Grandes Educateurs socialistes (Paris, 1952); and Antonio Orts-Ramos and Francisco Carravaca, *Francisco Ferrer y Guardia: Apóstol de la Razón. Vida, obra y doctrinas del famoso martir español* (Barcelona, 1932).

2. Lerroux published several books of memoirs but they are vague at best, sometimes erroneous. See for example his explanations of his early anticlericalism in *Mis Memorias* (published posthumously in 1963), pp. 611–26. A valuable source for Lerroux's ideas is his collection of editorials written during the period under study, *De la Lucha,* with a prologue by Nicolás Estévanez (Barcelona, n.d. [1909?]). For an acceptable biography of Lerroux during the period under study, see Alberto and Arturo García Carrafa, *Lerroux,* in the series Españoles Ilustres (Madrid, 1918). For an interesting account of Lerroux's career, and of his relations with Ferrer, see Archer, *Life of Ferrer,* pp. 49–190, passim.

Among Lerroux's later writings, of some value for the period under study is his collection of essays, *Al Servicio de la república* (Madrid, 1930). Of less value are *Las pequeñas Tragedias de mi vida: Memorias frívolas* (Madrid, 1930), and *La pequeña Historia: España, 1930–1936* (Buenos Aires, 1945).

For pamphlets eulogizing Lerroux's work in Barcelona, see P. Miquel, *Alejandro Lerroux. Epígrafes. Cuatro palabras. Lerroux político* (Barcelona, n.d. [1903?]), and José María Torres, *Lerroux y sus enemigos* (Barcelona, 1912). Of some interest for the period 1900–1910 is José María Carretero, *Las Responsabilidades de A. Lerroux: Opiniones de un hombre de la calle* (Madrid, 1932).

3. Lerroux, "Rebeldes! Rebeldes!," published September 1906, and reprinted in *De la Lucha,* p. 121.

4. Letter from Ferrer to José Nakens, May 31, 1906, *Causa por regicidio frustrado,* I, 486–87.

5. Letter from Lerroux to Ferrer, December 1, 1899, *Causa contra Ferrer,* p. 400.

6. See charges made by Catalan deputies in the Cortes, June 27 through July 3, 1907, summarized by Soldevilla, *Año político,* XIII: 1907, 302–04, 311–15. Urales [Montseny], *Mi Vida,* 146–48.

7. Many years later Lerroux would defend the extreme ideas exemplified in the editorials in *De la Lucha,* on the ground that they were the only means to resurrect "that corpse," meaning the general electorate (*Mis Memorias,* pp. 357, 423).

8. José Prat, *Orientaciones* (Barcelona, 1916), p. 11.

9. For the growth of the Radical centers, see Lerroux, "A la Opinión," published May 1907 and reprinted in *De la Lucha,* p. 257. Lerroux, *Mis Memorias,* pp. 434, 554. Lerroux, July 15, 1910, *Diario de las Cortes,* III, 648. Lerroux, *Al Servicio de la república,* p. 58.

10. For example, in the by-elections of December 1908, the Radicals won three out of four deputy seats by a margin of only 1,500 votes (Soldevilla, *Año político,* XIV: *1908,* 460).

11. Luis Bertrán, *"Yo Acuso": El Testamento de Ferrer* (Barcelona, 1911), pp. 6–7. See also Claudio Frollo [pseud. of Ernesto López Rodríguez], *En Cataluña* (Madrid, 1909), pp. 23–26, and Lerroux, "Los Cocodrillos," published April 1904 and reprinted in *De la Lucha,* pp. 73–82.

12. Lerroux, July 15, 1910, *Diario de las Cortes,* III, 646. Lerroux, *Mis Memorias,* 353, 423.

13. Lerroux, "Rebeldes! Rebeldes!," September 1906, *De la Lucha,* p. 122.

14. Lerroux, *Mis Memorias,* pp. 519–21. Archer, *Life of Ferrer,* pp. 154–56.

15. Ametlla, *Memòries polítiques,* p. 249. Soldevilla, *Año político,* XIII: *1907,* 68–69, 102–03.

16. Lerroux, "El Alma en los labios," *De la Lucha,* p. 96.

17. Lerroux' statements are quoted from the account of the Unión Republicana assembly, held in Madrid from June 23 through June 26, 1907, in Soldevilla, *Año político,* XIII: *1907,* 288–302; 323. The dissolution of Unión Republicana was announced on June 11, 1908 (*Año político,* XIV: *1908,* 207). For Lerroux's account, see his articles, "Antes de la Asamblea," and "En la Asamblea," published July 1907 and reprinted in *De la Lucha,* pp. 259–65; 269–303, and *Mis Memorias,* pp. 430–38.

18. Francisco Rivas, *Los Pecados capitales o Lerroux en escenario* (Barcelona, 1915), pp. 8–9.

19. Testimony of Iglesias, July 30, 1909, *Causa: Rebelión militar,* I, 37–38. See also biographical sketch of Iglesias in Emilio Navarro, ed., *Historia crítica de los hombres del republicanismo catalán en la última década: 1905–1914. Resúmenes históricos por Emiliano Iglesias y Juan Arderius Baujo* (Barcelona, 1915), pp. 279–86. In later years Lerroux turned against Iglesias (*Mis Memorias,* pp. 328, 396, 589–90, 633, 647).

20. *El Progreso* (Barcelona), July 4, 1909. *Solidaridad Obrera* (Barcelona), January 15, 1917.

21. Testimony of Emiliano Iglesias, July 31, 1909, *Causa: Rebelión militar,* I, 34. But one year later Lerroux bragged that he had enrolled not only the workers of Catalonia, but their wives and children, July 15, 1910, *Diario de las Cortes,* III, 648. See the statutes of the Damas Radicales, dated January 1, 1909, *Causa: Rebelión militar,* I, 368–73, and of the Damas Rojas, May 5, 1909, *ibid.,* I, 374–80.

22. See, for example, Rivas, *Los Pecados capitales;* José Rodríguez de la Pena, *Los Aventureros de la política: Alejandro Lerroux. Apuntes para la historia de un revo-*

NOTES TO PAGES 92–97

lucionario (Barcelona, n.d.); Tomás Herreros, *Alejandro Lerroux, tal cual es: Historia de una infamia relatada por el mismo obrero que ha sido víctima de ella* (Barcelona, 1907); and Urales [Montseny], *Mi Vida*, II, 14.

23. Herreros, *Lerroux, tal cual es*, pp. 12–13. Marcel Riu, *La Rematada: Follet que conté integre l'article "Yo y la Solidaridad" d'En A. Lerroux y l'análisis y refutacio dels seus falsos conceptes* (Barcelona, 1907), p. 13. Frollo [López Rodríguez] *En Cataluña*, pp. 25–26.

24. Lerroux, "Revolución y república," published January 1905 and reprinted in *De la Lucha*, p. 23.

25. Canals, *Sucesos de 1909*, II, 138. Cristobal Litrán, "Fragmento de un libro inédito," *El Progreso* (Barcelona), October 13, 1910.

26. Lugan, *Précurseur du bolchevisme*, p. 52. For Ferrer and Freemasonry, see Sangro, *Sombra de Ferrer*, pp. 186–258, passim; Sol Ferrer, *Véritable Ferrer*, pp. 21–22, 59, 86; and Constant Leroy [pseud. of Miguel V. Moreno], "Campaña humanitaria," *El Correo Español* (Mexico, D.F.), January 10, 13, and 17, 1913. For the charge that Ferrer was subsidized by the Masons, see statement by representative of the ultra-conservative Comité de Defensa Social in Orts-Ramos, *Ferrer*, p. 271. See also Casimiro Comás, *Revolucion de acción*, pp. 22–24, 117. The accusation was revived fifty years later by Joaquín Arraras, "El Inductor y responsable de la Semana Trágica," *ABC* (Madrid), July 29, 1959.

27. On the educational theories of Ferrer, and their origins, see Dommanget, *Francisco Ferrer*, pp. 3, 7–10, 37. Leonard D. Abbott, ed., *Francisco Ferrer: His Life, Work and Martyrdom. With messages written especially for this brochure by Ernst Haeckel, Maxim Gorky. Published on the first anniversary of his death* (New York, n.d. [1910]), p. 70.

28. Dommanget, *Francisco Ferrer*, pp. 10–11. For the charges that Masons subsidized anarchists, especially in Catalonia, see Comín, *Anarquismo español*, pp. 100, 127–28, 131.

29. Woodcock, *Anarchism*, pp. 295, 331.

30. Ferrer, *La Escuela Moderna: Póstuma explicación y alcance de la enseñanza racional*, ed. Lorenzo Portet (Barcelona, n.d. [1911?]). This book was translated into French by Charles Malato, and into English by Joseph McCabe under the title, *The Origins and Ideals of the Modern School* (New York, 1913). Ferrer's daughter writes that he left an unpublished manuscript, "Principes de morale scientifique," on which she bases her assertion about Ferrer's intellectual distinction (Sol Ferrer, *Ferrer: Martyr*, p. 87).

31. Sol Ferrer, *Véritable Ferrer*, p. 74. Note emphasis on Ferrer's domestic affairs in all accounts critical of his activities.

32. Autobiography of Ferrer, *España Nueva* (Madrid), June 16, 1906. See also Sol Ferrer, *Véritable Ferrer*, p. 120 and 155. The calculation of the value of Mlle. Meunie's estate is from Constant Leroy [pseud. of Miguel V. Moreno], *Los Secretos del anarquismo: Asesinato de Canalejas y el caso Ferrer* (Mexico, D.F., 1913), pp. 60, 78. For Ferrer's stock in Fomento de Obras y Construcciones, S.A., see *Causa: Regicidio frustrado*, II, 136–37, 231–33; V, 441–88. Lerroux talked openly about the relationship between Ferrer's stocks and the expansion of municipal public works at the time of

Ferrer's trial: "Campana pro Ferrer," published in July 1906 and reprinted in *De la Lucha*, pp. 309–10. By 1908 a conservative city councilman estimated that 14 million pesetas had been invested in sewer and street construction (Ramón Albó y Marti, *El Pressupost extraordinari de cultura del Ayuntament y les escoles d'enseyenassa primaria que en el mateix es proposar* [Barcelona, 1908], p. 6).

33. Letter from Odón de Buen published in Canals, *Sucesos de 1909*, II, 54.

34. Letter from Ferrer to José Prat, December 6, 1900, published in *ibid.*, II, 53. See also Hurtado, *Quaranta Anys d'advocat*, I, 97. Ametlla, *Memòries polítiques*, pp. 144–45.

35. Sol Ferrer, *Véritable Ferrer*, p. 106. Claudi Ametlla reports Rodríguez Méndez, Rector of the University, gave lectures at the Escuela Moderna, one among many prominent professors to do so (*Memòries polítiques*, p. 144).

36. Bertrán, "Yo Acuso," pp. 10–11. Sol Ferrer, *Véritable Ferrer*, p. 108. *Diario Universal* (Madrid), June 5, 1906.

37. Sol Ferrer, *Véritable Ferrer*, p. 130. Canals, *Sucesos de 1909*, II, 123–24, 136, 141. The figures for the growth in enrollment are from a brochure, "La Escuela Moderna: Enseñanza racional y científica. Quinto año escolar: 1905–1906"; and Abbott, *Ferrer*, pp. 32–34.

38. Lerroux, July 15, 1910, *Diario de las Cortes*, III, 648. For an attack on these schools, see Lliga Deputy Ventosa, July 16, 1910, *ibid.*, III, 686. For the importance of Ferrer in organizing these schools, see the brief prepared by officer defending Ferrer in military trial of 1909 (Captain Francisco Galceran), *Causa contra Ferrer*, p. 607; Dictum of the Chief Military Judge Advocate, General Ramón Pastor, *ibid.*, pp. 655, 666.

39. For the importance of these texts, see Bertrán, "Yo Acuso," pp. 11–12; Archer, *Life of Ferrer*, p. 60; McCabe, *Martyrdom of Ferrer*, pp. 48–49; Dictum of General Pastor, *Causa contra Ferrer*, pp. 653, 655–57; and Ametlla, *Memòries polítiques*, pp. 145–46.

40. Archer, *Life of Ferrer*, p. 61. Comité de Défense, *Martyr des prêtres*, p. 23.

41. Bertrán, "Yo Acuso," p. 27. Article by anarchist Soledad Gustavo, in *España Nueva* (Madrid), June 5, 1907. Sol Ferrer, *Véritable Ferrer*, p. 135.

42. *Causa: Regicidio frustrado*, IV, 401.

43. Sol Ferrer, *Véritable Ferrer*, p. 154.

44. Pío Baroja, "Memorias desde la última vuelta del mundo: Final del siglo XIX y principios del XX," *Obras completas* (Madrid, 1949), VII, 780.

45. See pamphlet by Angel de Borjas Ruíz (of Lerroux' Radical party) attacking republicans for failing to defend Ferrer: *El Fin de una leyenda: España ante el proceso Ferrer* (Barcelona, 1907). Urales tried in vain to find a prominent republican lawyer to defend Ferrer ([Montseny], *Mi Vida*, III, 17–19, 22–30). See article by Rafael Salillas, a prominent republican, deprecating Ferrer: "La Celda de Ferrer," *Ateneo* (Madrid), 18 (June 1907), 457–79.

46. See series of articles by Lerroux, "Campaña pro Ferrer: Justicia: La Verdad en marcha, "published in *El Progreso* in 1907 on July 11, August 26, September 14 and 23, and reprinted in *De la Lucha*, pp. 306–40.

47. See comments of Miguel de Unamuno, as cited in Pabón, *Cambó*, pp. 337–38.

Castillejo, *Wars of Ideas*, p. 21. Sol Ferrer, *Véritable Ferrer*, p. 86, and *Ferrer: Martyr*, pp. 44, 237.

48. Sol Ferrer, *Véritable Ferrer*, pp. 153, 159. La Cierva, *The Case of Ferrer: Speeches delivered by the Ex-Cabinet Minister . . . in the Chamber of Deputies during the sessions of the 31st Mach* [sic] *and 5th of April 1911* (Madrid, 1911), p. 65. Dictum of the Legal Advisor to the Military Tribunal hearing the case of Ferrer (Enrique Gesta y García), *Causa contra Ferrer*, p. 627.

49. Article by Bidegain, *L'Eclair* (Paris), cited in Sangro, *Sombra de Ferrer*, p. 191. Comín, *Anarquismo*, pp. 135–36. For documents related to the Lodge ("Siete Amigos"), see *Causa: Rebelión militar*, I, 496–97. After the repression of Masons in 1909, Lerroux's newspaper, *El Progreso*, on July 13, 1911, urged Masons to revive their organization. In *Mis Memorias*, pp. 516–18, Lerroux states that he prefers to remain silent about his associations with Freemasonry.

50. *Solidaridad Obrera* (Barcelona), March 26, 1909. Canals, *Sucesos de 1909*, II, 141.

51. Interrogation of Ferrer, *Causa contra Ferrer*, p. 189. Letters to Ferrer from his business manager, Juan Colominas, May 21 and June 21, 1908, *ibid.*, pp. 400–04. Herreros, *Lerroux tal cual es*, p. 8. Sol Ferrer, *Véritable Ferrer*, p. 162. See also police report on Ferrer's activities, including his contacts with Radicals, June 1907 to July 1909, in *Causa: Rebelión militar*, I, 257–62.

CHAPTER VI: THE GOVERNOR AND THE TERRORISTS

1. Ossorio frankly discusses his personality in his memoirs (which often err in fact): *El Sedimento de la lucha: Vida e ideas*, in the series Confesiones de nuestro tiempo (Madrid, n.d. [1933?]); *Mis Memorias* (Buenos Aires, 1946); and *Barcelona, julio de 1909: Declaración de un testigo* (Madrid, 1910).

2. Emiliano Iglesias used the term "viceroy" to describe Ossorio in his discussion of the La Cierva-Ossorio feud (July 6, 1910, *Diario de las Cortes*, III, 403). For La Cierva's complaint see his *Notas de mi vida*, p. 132.

3. For La Cierva's version of the feud, see *ibid.*, pp. 101–03, 131–34. For Ossorio's version, see *Mis Memorias*, pp. 89–90.

4. Ossorio, *Visita a Mataró: Marzo 1909* (Barcelona, n.d. [1909]), and *Visita a Arenys de Mar: Mayo 1909*. See also Ossorio, *Mis Memorias*, pp. 74–79, and García Venero, *Maura*, pp. 190–92.

5. Memoirs of Charles Arrow published in *The Evening News* of London in August 1910, and summarized by Ramiro de Maeztu in *El Progreso* (Barcelona), August 17, 1910. See also Marcel Riu, *Contra la Mentida, el terrorisme, y el matonisme: Refutació de las falsas acusacións fetas por el diari* El Progreso, *rectificació y aclaració dels fets relatius al terrorisme y matonisme y descobriment de sos autors* (Barcelona, 1907); and Miguel Sastre, *La Esclavitud moderna: Martirologio social. Relación de los atentados y actos de "sabotaje" cometidos en Barcelona, y bombas y explosivos hallados desde junio de 1910 hasta junio de 1921*. Prologue by Angel Ossorio (Barcelona, 1921).

6. For the anarchist movement in Barcelona in this period, see Bertrán, *"Yo Acuso,"* pp. 8, 19. *El País* (Madrid), August 28, 1909. Carlist deputy Dalmacio Iglesias, citing

report of terrorist Juan Rull, July 14, 1910, *Diario de las Cortes,* III, 617–18. Report by Barcelona police official, Muñoz Rodríguez, *Causa: Rebelión militar,* I, 12.

7. See police report of search of the premises of *Tierra y Libertad* in August 1909, *Causa: Rebelión militar,* I, 547–50.

8. E. Carqué de la Parra collected all interpretations of terrorism in *El Terrorismo en Barcelona: Lo que dicen los prohombres de todos los partidos* (Barcelona, 1908). The only one he missed concerned cases such as that of Captain Morales of the Civil Guard who planted bombs in order to collect the reward for detecting them (Ossorio, July 16, 1910, *Diario de las Cortes,* III, 685).

9. Statement by the Count of Santa María de Pomés, representative of the Comité de Defensa Social of Barcelona, in Soldevilla, *Año político,* XIV: *1908,* 175–76. See also *Año político,* XVI: *1910,* 26, 31.

10. For charges of "industrial terrorism," see Lerroux, July 15, 1910, *Diario de las Cortes,* III, 644; Radical City councilman Luis Zurdo, July 9, 1908, "Actas del Ayuntamiento" (Barcelona), IV, folio 209; testimony of terrorist Juan Rull, reported in Carqué, *Terrorismo,* pp. 22; 120–23; and Soldevilla, *Año político,* XIV: *1908,* 6.

11. Charges of terrorism subsidized by the 'central government,' or by the Liberal party, lodged by left Catalan deputies in the Cortes, June to July 1907, as reported in Soldevilla, *Año político,* XIII: *1907,* 302–19, passim.

12. For charges that terrorism was subsidized by religious orders, see José Ferrándiz (a former priest), "No olvidemos al Loyola," in Carqué, *Terrorismo,* pp. 29–38; Lerroux interview in 1908, reported in *ibid.,* p. 27; Lerroux, July 15, 1910, *Diario de las Cortes,* III, 644; Shaw, *Spain from Within,* pp. 182–85; and Soldevilla, *Año político,* XIII: *1907,* 314, 321.

13. On Rull's execution see Soldevilla, *Año político,* XIV: *1908,* 275–78. The memoirs of Juan Rull are used by Spanish historians as the authority on anarchism and terrorism in the decade 1900–1910. Before his execution, Rull gave one version to newspaper reporters (Carqué, *Terrorismo,* pp. 97–136). Essentially the same version was read into the legislative record by Dalmacio Iglesias, Carlist deputy, member of the ultra-conservative Comité de Defensa Social, and a lawyer for one of the Rull band (July 14, 1910, *Diario de las Cortes,* III, 616–22). Enrique Pujol, an anarchist associated with the Radical party, declared that the "Rull memoirs" were only a recapitulation of memoirs prepared by anarchist Alfredo Picoret under police direction while imprisoned ca. 1905 (*El Progreso* [Barcelona], August 15, 1910). For background on the Rull case, see Carqué, *Terrorismo,* pp. 75–83; Soldevilla, *Año político,* XIII: *1907,* 317, 321–22, 366–67; and *Año político,* XIV: *1908,* 122–26, 131–37.

14. *Año político,* XIV: *1908,* 278.

15. *Año político,* XV: *1909,* 220–21.

16. Hermegildo Giner de los Ríos, April 14, 1909, speaking in the Cortes, as quoted in Soldevilla, *Año político,* XV: *1909,* 148.

CHAPTER VII: THE STRUGGLE FOR THE MASSES

1. *La Publicidad* (Barcelona), July 26, 1907. Even men not sympathetic with Solidaridad Obrera respected its original intent to create an effective labor movement;

see Ramón Albó, *Barcelona: Caritativa, benéfica, y social* (Barcelona, 1914), II, 216–17, and Gabriel Palau, S.J., *Deberes sociales de la mujer en las cuestiones obreras* (Barcelona, n.d. [1910]), pp. 7–8.

2. Vicens Vives, *Cataluña: Siglo XIX,* pp. 241–45.

3. Official statement by the Central Committee of Solidaridad Obrera, *La Internacional* (Barcelona), February 5, 1909.

4. Manifesto as quoted in Boix, "Sindicalismo Católico," *Revista Social Hispano-Americana* (Barcelona), pp. 214–15. On the founding of Solidaridad Obrera, see also *España Nueva* (Madrid), June 8, July 5 and 24, August 1, 4, 23, 29 and 31, 1907; Lamberet, *Mouvements ouvriers,* pp. 74–75; Buenacasa, *Movimiento obrero,* pp. 47–48, 287; *Boletín del Arte de Imprimir* (Barcelona), August, October and November 1907. Sirera, "Obreros en Barcelona," p. 95. *La Internacional* (Barcelona), February 5, 1909. Comín, *Anarquismo,* pp. 121–22.

5. Letter from Arturo Gas, *El Socialista* (Madrid), March 18, 1910. Some socialists opposed this policy on the ground that syndicalism was merely a new name for "communist anarchism" (letter from J. González Nieto, *ibid.,* September 4, 1908).

6. Ossorio, *Visita a Mataró,* pp. 4, 5, 79. Concerning the charge that Ossorio protected the socialists, see Garcia Venero, *Maura,* pp. 190–92, and *El Progreso* (Barcelona), November 4, 1911.

7. Letter from Enrique Pujol, *El Progreso* (Barcelona), March 9, 1909. *El País* (Madrid), August 22, 1909.

8. Antonio Badia Matemala, "Deshaciendo injurias. La Novela de protesta de *El Progreso,*" *La Internacional* (Barcelona), January 1, 1909.

9. *Boletín del Arte de Imprimir* (Barcelona), December 1907.

10. On the preparation of the Labor Congress, see "Circular Num. 4 del Consejo Directivo de Solidaridad Obrera," cited in *Boletín del Arte de Imprimir* (Barcelona), June 1908; Lamberet, *Mouvements ouvriers,* pp. 103, 116: Buenacasa, *Movimiento obrero,* pp. 48–49; 288–89.

11. Sastre, *Huelgas: 1908,* p. 114. On the proceedings of the Labor Congress see also *ibid.,* pp. 111–16. Canals, *Sucesos de 1909,* I, 152–53. Ernesto Bach, "A propósito del Congreso obrero: El Sindicalismo en Cataluña," *La Publicidad* (Barcelona), September 8, 1911. Leroy [V. Moreno], *Secretos del anarquismo,* pp. 261–62. Comín, *Anarquismo,* p. 126.

12. The statutes were published as a pamphlet by Solidaridad Obrera (*Estatutos de Solidaridad Obrera: Confederación Regional de Sociedades de Resistencia* [Barcelona, 1909]).

13. For the members of the Central Committee of Solidaridad Obrera as registered with the police on April 8, 1909, see *Causa: Rebelión militar,* I, 69. This list differs from that of the officers elected on December 29, 1908, as reported in *La Internacional* (Barcelona), January 1, 1909.

14. For biographical data on Fabra Rivas see Alberto Pérez Baro, "El Profesor Antonio Fabra Rivas ha muerto," *Revista de la Cooperación* (Buenos Aires), 14 (January 1958), 3–6, and "Antonio Fabra Rivas," *ibid.,* 16 (June 1960), 81–82; and the prologue by Vicente Blasco Ibañez to Antonio Fabra Rivas, *El Socialismo y el conflicto europeo. El Kaiserismo: He ahi el enemigo! Debe España intervenir en la guerra?* (Valencia,

1915), pp. vii–xiv. For his ideas, see Fabra Rivas, "La Acción societaria y la acción política," *El Socialista* (Madrid), March 10, 1910.

15. Ametlla, *Memòries polítiques,* p. 264. Emiliano Iglesias, "Uno que huye," *El Progreso* (Barcelona), December 4, 1910.

16. See prologue which Jaurès wrote for the Spanish edition of his book *Acción socialista,* trans. M. Ciges Aparicio (Barcelona, 1906), pp. 1–2. For struggle between two factions within the Spanish Socialist party, see Marvaud, *Question sociale,* pp. 413–14.

17. *El Socialista* (Madrid), September 4, 1908. See also *ibid.,* June 12, August 7 and 28, and October 2, 9 and 13, 1908. *La Internacional* (Barcelona), December 11, 1908; February 5, 1909.

18. Badía Matemala, "Deshaciendo injurias; La Novela de protesta de *El Progreso,*" *La Internacional* (Barcelona), January 1, 1909, and "Discusiones bizantinas," *ibid.,* May 28, 1909. Letter from Anselmo Lorenzo to Ferrer, September 13, 1908, reprinted in *Causa contra Ferrer,* pp. 47–48. Report to police from Tomás Herreros, October 1908, *Causa: Rebelión militar,* I, 258.

19. Quoted by Badía, "Deshaciendo injurias," *La Internacional* (Barcelona), January 1, 1909. See also *El Socialista* (Madrid), October 17, 1908, and *Solidaridad Obrera* (Barcelona), March 26, 1909.

20. For the Ayxelá strike, see Sastre, *Huelgas: 1908,* pp. 15–22, and J. Paulis and F. de Sorel, *Maura ante el pueblo,* prologue by Angel Ossorio (Madrid, 1915), pp. 210–11.

21. Police report in *Causa: Rebelión militar,* I, 258. See also *Causa contra Ferrer,* pp. 82, 465–66.

22. *Solidaridad Obrera* (Barcelona), March 26, 1909. For details of the strike, see "Historia de la huelga de *El Progreso,*" a supplement to *Boletín del Arte de Imprimir* (Barcelona), November 1908; Joaquín Bueso, "*El Progreso* y los obreros," *La Internacional* (Barcelona), January 1, 1909; and Lamberet, *Mouvements ouvriers,* pp. 5–6.

23. As quoted in *La Internacional* (Barcelona), February 5, 1909.

24. *Ibid.,* January 1, 1909.

25. Prat, *Orientaciones,* pp. 11–12.

26. For charge that Ferrer, at the instigation of anarchists, founded Solidaridad Obrera, see La Cierva, July 12, 1910, *Diario de las Cortes,* III, 563; Sangro, *Sombra de Ferrer,* p. 20; Canals, *Sucesos de 1909,* II, 139–42; and Comín, *Anarquismo,* p. 122.

27. Sol Ferrer, *Véritable Ferrer,* p. 154.

28. For an excellent account of the anarchist congress at Amsterdam, based on the official transcript of the proceedings, see Maitron, *Mouvement anarchiste,* pp. 412–16. For a proanarchist, antisyndicalist point of view, see Diego Abad de Santillán and E. López Arango, *El Anarquismo en el movimiento obrero* (Barcelona, 1925), pp. 160–61, 199–200.

29. For Ferrer's enthusiasm for syndicalism, see Sol Ferrer, *Véritable Ferrer,* pp. 115, 118, 158–59; Leroy [V. Moreno], *Secretos del anarquismo,* pp. 154–66; Dommanget, *Ferrer,* pp. 10–11, 21–22; Cristobal Litrán, "Fragmento de un libro inédito," *El Progreso* (Barcelona), October 13, 1910; and "Ferrer's Syndicalism," in Abbott, *Work and Martyrdom,* pp. 42–43. For a detailed report of Ferrer's attempts to influence Soli-

daridad Obrera leaders, see Leroy [V. Moreno], *Secretos del anarquismo*, 154–238, passim.

30. For Ferrer's relation with Lorenzo, see Montseny, *Anselmo Lorenzo*, p. 28; Canals, *Sucesos de 1909*, II, 137–38; and police report, *Causa contra Ferrer*, pp. 258–59.

31. This was the only evidence of Ferrer's association with Solidaridad Obrera, and as such was exploited by government prosecutors in 1909; see comment by the army officer defending Ferrer in 1909, *Causa contra Ferrer*, pp. 606–07.

32. Pablo Iglesias, July 12, 1910, *Diario de las Cortes*, III, 552.

CHAPTER VIII: MOUNTING TENSION: PLANS FOR A GENERAL STRIKE

1. For the recession in Catalonia, see Ossorio, *Visita a Mataró*, pp. 9–13; and Soldevilla, *Año político*, XV: *1908*, 154.

2. For background on the 1908–1909 recession in Catalonia, see Escarrá, *Développment industriel*, pp. 163–74; Ministry of Development, *Memoria*, pp. 188, 195–96; *La Internacional* (Barcelona), December 11, 1908; and *El Progreso* (Barcelona), July 8 and 20, 1909. For the limited ability of Catalan industry to expand, see Vicens Vives, *Cataluña: Siglo XX*, pp. 114–20.

3. Ministry of Development, *Memoria*, p. 196.

4. For the organization of textile syndicates and of the federation, see *La Internacional* (Barcelona), December 11, 1908 and January 1, 1909; Sastre, *Huelgas: 1905*, pp. 11–14; *Huelgas: 1906*, pp. 22, 28–29; *Huelgas: 1907*, pp. 21–23, 56; *Huelgas: 1908*, p. 118; and *El Socialista* (Madrid), June 11, 1909.

5. For the Alcalá del Valle case, see Abad de Santillán, *Historia del movimiento obrero*, pp. 502–03; Ballesteros, *Historia de España*, XI, 510–11, 522; Lerroux, *Mis Memorias*, pp. 527–28; and Lamberet, *Mouvements ouvriers*, p. 103.

6. Buenacasa, *Movimiento obrero*, pp. 48–49.

7. Lerroux, *Mis Memorias*, p. 462.

8. Ametlla, *Memòries polítiques*, p. 147.

9. Sol Ferrer, *Véritable Ferrer*, p. 159. Cristobal Litrán, "Fragmento de un libro inédito," *El Progreso* (Barcelona), October 13, 1910.

10. Report by Tomás Herreros to police, October 1908, *Causa contra Ferrer*, pp. 465–66. For further details on Clapes' relation with Ferrer, see *Causa por regicidio frustrado*, I, 341–44; and Leroy [V. Moreno], *Secretos del anarquismo*, pp. 243–44; 263–65.

11. Article published by Ferrer in a newspaper in southern France, in the fall of 1908, which he ordered Litrán to translate and publish in Barcelona (*El Progreso*, December 29, 1908). The article was reprinted on the first anniversary of Ferrer's execution (*ibid.*, October 13, 1910).

12. Report in *Causa: Rebelión militar*, I, 261–62.

13. Leroy [V. Moreno], *Secretos del anarquismo*, pp. 225–29; 246–62, passim. The Paris police informed Barcelona police of the contacts between Ferrer and the French labor organizations; see *Causa: Rebelión militar*, I, 261. See also statement by Barcelona police chief, Díaz-Guijarro, *Causa contra Ferrer*, p. 21.

14. Bernard Georges and Denise Tintant, *Léon Jouhaux: Cinquant Ans de syndicalisme,* vol. I: *Des Origines à 1921* (Paris, 1962), 19-27.

15. For Miguel Villalobos Moreno see prologue by E. Guardiola y Cardillac to Leroy [V. Moreno], *Secretos del anarquismo,* pp. 7-10; Canals, *Sucesos de 1909,* I, 153, and II, 140; *El Progreso* (Barcelona), February 8, 1912; and article from *Il Secolo* (Milan) reprinted in *La Publicidad* (Barcelona), July 19, 1910.

16. *España Nueva* (Madrid), April 16 and 19, 1909. For further details on the Alcalá del Valle campaign, see *ibid.,* April 12, 15 and 25, and May 16, 1909. (*España Nueva* was a newspaper that was very sympathetic to Francisco Ferrer, even during his first trial).

17. Angel Pestaña, *Historia de las ideas y las luchas sociales en España,* as cited in Sevilla Andrés, *Revolución desde Arriba,* p. 351.

18. *Causa: Rebelión militar,* I, 261. *Causa contra Ferrer,* p. 186. Sol Ferrer, *Ferrer: Martyr,* pp. 130-31. Canals, *Sucesos de 1909,* I, 216-17; II, 148-49.

19. For the royal pardon see Soldevilla, *Año político,* XV: *1909,* 216; Leroy [V. Moreno], *Secretos del anarquismo,* pp. 260-63; *El Progreso* (Barcelona), May 8 and June 19, 1909; and *El Socialista* (Madrid), July 2, 1909.

20. The agenda for the second labor congress of Solidaridad Obrera was printed in *El Socialista* (Madrid), July 2, 1909. See also *El Progreso* (Barcelona), June 30, 1909.

21. *La Publicidad* (Barcelona), July 21, 1909. *El Progreso* (Barcelona), July 10, 11, 12, 17, and 19, 1909. *Solidaridad Obrera* (Barcelona), July 16, 1909. For Ferrer's part in the reception, see Ossorio, July 13, 1910, *Diario de las Cortes,* III, 592; Report of Ferrer's police escort, *Causa contra Ferrer,* pp. 81; and *Causa: Rebelión militar,* I, 259.

22. On the lockout in Manlleu see *La Internacional* (Barcelona), May 28, 1909; and letter from officials of textile unions, *El Progreso* (Barcelona), July 10, 1909.

23. *La Publicidad* (Barcelona), June 6, 1909. *El Socialista* (Madrid), June 11, 1909. See also the statement of José Román, Secretary General of Solidaridad Obrera, as quoted in *La Internacional* (Barcelona), May 28, 1909, and *El Progreso* (Barcelona), July 8 and 20, 1909.

24. *El Progreso* (Barcelona), July 13, 15, 16, and 18, 1909. *La Publicidad* (Barcelona), July 12-19, 1909.

25. Circular, Consejo Directivo de Solidaridad Obrera, dated July 2, 1909, and printed in *El Progreso* (Barcelona), July 6, 1909.

26. Report of meetings on July 10 and 11 in Granollers, furnished by Solidaridad Obrera to *El Progreso* (Barcelona) and published on July 15, 1909.

CHAPTER IX: PUBLIC OPINION AND THE "MOROCCAN ADVENTURE"

1. José Ortega y Gasset, "Vieja y nueva Política," *Obras completas,* 2 ed. (Madrid, 1950), I, 271-75. For Maura's cautious foreign policy, 1907-1909, see Soldevilla, *Año político,* XIII: *1907,* 97-98, 254-56, 356-57, 391-93, and *Año político,* XIV: *1908,* 6-10, 48-49, 69, and 311; also Canals, *Sucesos de 1909,* I, 42-79.

2. For Spain's foreign policy during the decade 1900 to 1910, see Gonzalo de

Reparáz Rodríguez, *Política española en Africa* (Barcelona, 1907), and *Aventuras de un geógrafo errante* (Barcelona, and Berne, Switzerland, 1920–1922), 3 vols.; Wallace Richard Klinger, "Spain's Problem of Alliances: Spanish Foreign Policy from the Conference of Madrid 1880 to the Mediterranean Agreement of 1907," unpublished dissertation (University of Pennsylvania, 1946); Walter B. Harris, *France, Spain and the Rif* (London, 1927); E. Ashmead-Bartlett, *The Passing of the Shereefian Empire* (New York, 1910); and Gabriel Maura, *La Cuestión de Marruecos desde el punto de vista español* (Madrid, 1905).

3. Canals, *Sucesos de 1909*, I, 120–21. Charge is repeated again in a rally on July 15, 1909, *Causa: Rebelión militar*, I, 79. For further details of the Merry del Val mission, see Reparáz, *Geógrafo errante*, II, 393–94; Ballesteros, *Historia de España*, XI, 550; Soldevilla, *Año político*, XV: *1909*, 187–94, 205–11.

4. Canals, *Sucesos de 1909*, I, 73–77. For reports on the investment of Eusebio Güell and the Marquis of Comillas in the Beni-bu-Ifrur mines in the Rif (the basis for the later charge that Maura agreed to the Moroccan campaign because of pressure from Comillas), see Soldevilla, *Año político*, XIII: *1907*, 375, 471–73, 487–500. Canals, *Sucesos de 1909*, I, 68–70.

5. For the Liberals' antiwar campaign, see "Las Acusaciones de Villanueva," *El País* (Madrid), July 24, 1909; "Declaraciones de Romanones," *ibid.*, July 26, 1909; Bonafulla [Esteve], *Revolución de julio*, pp. 3–9; Soldevilla, *Año político*, XV: *1909*, 240; and Canals, *Sucesos de 1909*, I, 67–69, 112–14.

6. For the newspaper antiwar campaign, see G. Maura, *Recuerdos*, p. 68; Sevilla Andrés, *Revolución desde Arriba*, pp. 182–84, 237–38, 352–54; and Canals, *Sucesos de 1909*, I, 107–41; II, 463–66, 469.

7. For editorials pointing out the discrepancy between the numbers of troops and Maura's policy of limited objectives, see "Los Responsables," *El Socialista* (Madrid), July 16, 1909, and *España Nueva* (Madrid), July 23, 1909.

8. *El País* (Madrid), July 24, 28, and 29, 1909.

9. Letter from Pablo Iglesias to Belgian socialist Clerbaut, August 17, 1909, and reprinted in Canals, *Sucesos de 1909*, I, 176–77.

10. For the antiwar activities of the Spanish Socialist party, see Fabra Rivas, *Socialismo y el conflicto europeo*, pp. 28–32; Morató, *Iglesias*, pp. 180–82; Soldevilla, *Año político*, XIV: *1908*, 413–14; García Venero, *Las Internacionales*, I, 431–32. See also James Joll, *The Second International: 1888–1914* (London, 1955), pp. 133–40.

11. Pablo Iglesias, July 7, 1910, *Diario de las Cortes*, II, 434–35.

12. Later Pablo Iglesias would try to explain away this threat of armed rebellion; see July 12, 1910, *ibid.*, III, 550. For the socialist campaign against the war, see *El Socialista* (Madrid), May 21–July 30, 1909; Brissa, *Revolución de julio*, pp. 14 and 25; and Soldevilla, *Año político*, XV: *1909*, 215–16, 236–37; 247–48.

13. Ametlla, *Memòries polítiques*, pp. 264–65. For Jaurès position see Joll, *Second International*, pp. 131–40.

14. A detailed account of the proceedings of the congress appears in *La Publicidad* (Barcelona), July 20, 1909. See also *El Poble Català* (Barcelona), July 20, 1909; Simarro, *Proceso Ferrer*, I, 46; and *El Socialista* (Madrid), July 16, 1909.

15. Catalans constituted a majority in the Cazadores, the Reus, and the Estrella

battalions; see *El País* (Madrid), July 17, 1909; *El Progreso* (Barcelona), July 15 and 18, 1909; and Canals, *Sucesos de 1909*, I, 189.

16. Bonafulla [Esteve], *Revolución de julio,* pp. 10-13. For accounts of the events on July 18, see *El Progreso* (Barcelona), July 19 and 20, 1909, and Brissa, *Revolución de julio,* p. 11.

17. For the distribution of these medals as a major irritant see Anselmo Lorenzo, "Revolución y solidaridad," *El Socialista* (Madrid), October 22, 1909; Pablo Iglesias, as quoted in *El País* (Madrid), July 15, 1909; and "Pera les Dames blanques," *El Poble Català* (Barcelona), July 20, 1909.

18. *El Poble Català* (Barcelona), July 6, 10-22, 1909. For the anticlerical orientation of this group, an important factor in subsequent developments, see Ametlla, *Memòries polítiques,* pp. 149, 155-56, and Aurelio Joaniquet, *Alfonso Sala Argemí, conde de Egara: Visión de una época* (Madrid, 1955), p. 164. The anticlerical orientation was so forceful that Cardinal Casañas, Bishop of Barcelona, prohibited Catholics from reading *El Poble Català,* in a pastoral letter dated July 31, 1908, in *Boletín Oficial Eclesiástico* (Barcelona), 1417 (August 1908), 235-36.

19. Ametlla, *Memòries polítiques,* p. 263. See also *El Poble Català* (Barcelona), July 15, 1909.

20. Ametlla, *Memòries polítiques,* pp. 263-64. Article by R. Noguer Comet, *La Forja* (Barcelona), July 30, 1910.

21. *La Rebeldía* (Barcelona), July 22, 1909.

22. León Roch, "Guerra a la guerra," *ibid.,* July 16, 1909.

23. Police report of meeting, *Causa: Rebelión militar,* I, 77-78. See also *El País* (Madrid), July 16, 1909.

24. Ossorio, *Julio de 1909,* pp. 13-14.

25. Gaziel [Calvet], *Tots els Camins,* p. 331. For assertions that the "conjunción lerrouxista-anarquista" encouraged and guided the events of July 1909 see the following: declaration of Barcelona police chief, Díaz-Guijarro, *Causa contra Ferrer,* pp. 19-23; Dalmaico Iglesias, Carlist deputy, July 6, 1910, *Diario de las Cortes,* II, 421. Frollo [López Rodríguez], *En Cataluña,* pp. 8, 26-27; interview with Ossorio as reported in *La Epoca* (Madrid), August 4, 1909; *La Publicidad* (Barcelona), November 11, 1909; and Marvaud, *Question sociale,* pp. 402-03.

26. The police inspector assigned to the Casa del Pueblo submitted a list of the most active, extremist leaders: *Causa: Rebelión militar,* I, 255-56. On Bertrán, see Bertrán, *"Yo Acuso,"* passim. *Causa: Rebelión militar,* I, 49.

27. On Ignacio Claría San Romá see *Solidaridad Obrera* (Barcelona), January 14, 1917; *El Progreso* (Barcelona), August 7, 1911; police report, *Causa: Rebelión militar,* I, 255-56; Leroy [V. Moreno], *Secretos del anarquismo,* p. 163; and Lerroux, *Mis Memorias,* pp. 395-96, 646.

28. On Juan Colominas Maseras see *Causa contra Ferrer,* pp. 196-97; Navarro, *Historia crítica,* pp. 206-07; *Causa: Rebelión militar,* I, 62, 261; and *El Progreso* (Barcelona), June 16, July 23, 1909.

29. On Lorenzo Ardid Bernal see Miquel, *Lerroux,* pp. 5-6; Navarro, *Historia crítica,* p. 151; *Solidaridad Obrera* (Barcelona), January 20, 1917; and *Causa: Rebelión militar,* I, 256, 334-35.

30. On José Ulled Altamir see *Causa: Rebelión militar,* I, 256, 319–20, 359, 517; II, 154–55.

31. For Ossorio's unpopularity, see Ossorio, *Mis Memorias,* pp. 83–84, 91; La Cierva, *Notas de mi vida,* pp. 120–26, 133–34, 142; Emiliano Iglesias, July 6, 1910, *Diario de las Cortes,* II, 403; and Brissa, *Revolución de julio,* p. 30.

32. Letter from Ossorio to Maura, quoted in G. Maura, *Por qué cayó Alfonso,* p. 139. La Cierva, *Notas de mi vida,* pp. 135, 142.

CHAPTER X: FROM STREET DEMONSTRATIONS TO GENERAL STRIKE

1. Ossorio, *Julio de 1909,* pp. 33–34.

2. The general narrative is based on contemporaneous Barcelona newspaper accounts: *El Progreso, El Poble Català, La Publicidad, Las Noticias, La Vanguardia,* and *La Veu de Catalunya,* July 19–25, 1909.

3. Juan Caballé, Catalan republican deputy, March 30, 1911, *Diario de las Cortes,* II, 486.

4. *El Progreso* (Barcelona), July 21, 1909. See Ossorio's comment on the dichotomous Radical policy, July 13, 1910, *Diario de las Cortes,* III, 591.

5. *El Progreso* and *El Poble Català* (Barcelona), July 20, 1909. Emiliano Iglesias, July 6, 1910, *Diario de las Cortes,* II, 404.

6. *La Publicidad* (Barcelona), July 19, 1909. *El Poble Català* (Barcelona), July 21, 1909. For the importance of the Catalan Nationalists in fomenting the protest see declaration of Barcelona police chief, Díaz-Guijarro, *Causa contra Ferrer,* p. 22, and declaration of Ossorio, *Causa: Rebelión militar,* I, 97.

7. The Solidaridad Obrera antiwar rally was first announced on the front page of *El Poble Català* (Barcelona), on July 21, 1909. On July 22 it was announced by *El Progreso* and *Las Noticias.*

8. Ossorio, *Julio de 1909,* pp. 29–30. Ossorio declaration, *Causa: Rebelión militar,* I, 97.

9. Juan Ventosa, Lliga Deputy, July 15, 1910, *Diario de las Cortes,* III, 687.

10. The translation of the Tarrasa resolution is from the text in Simarro, *Proceso Ferrer,* I, 47–48. For further details on the Tarrasa rally, see *La Publicidad* and *El Poble Català* (Barcelona), July 23, 1909; Canals, *Sucesos de 1909,* I, 151–52; and Ossorio, *Julio de 1909,* pp. 31–32.

11. La Cierva, October 19, 1909, *Diario de las Cortes,* pp. 58–59, and *El País* (Madrid), July 26, 1909.

12. La Cierva, *Notas de mi vida,* pp. 93, 136. Ossorio, *Julio de 1909,* pp. 43–44.

13. Ossorio, *Julio de 1909,* pp. 39–40. *El Progreso* (Barcelona), July 23, 1909.

14. *La Publicidad and El Progreso* (Barcelona), July 23, 1909.

15. Ossorio, *Julio de 1909,* pp. 46–47; *El Poble Català* (Barcelona), July 24, 1909; and Brissa, *Revolución de julio,* p. 32.

16. For the socialist plans, see Pablo Iglesias (who states that the initiative for a national general strike came from the Barcelona socialists), July 7, 1910, *Diario de las Cortes,* II, 434–36. See also *La Internacional* (Barcelona), July 23, 1909, as reprinted in Sangro, *Sombra de Ferrer,* pp. 18–19; Brissa, *Revolución de julio,* p. 32; *La*

Publicidad and *El Poble Català* (Barcelona), July 23, 1909; Morató, *Iglesias*, pp. 182–83; and lecture by Mariano García Cortés of the Socialist party's National Committee, as reported in Simarro, *Proceso Ferrer*, I, 145.

17. For the attempts to subsidize the conscripts' families through private philanthropy, see *La Publicidad* (Barcelona), July 22, 1909, and *Las Noticias* and *El Correo Catalàn* (Barcelona), July 23–24, 1909. For the Radicals' scornful denunciation of such efforts, see *El Progreso* (Barcelona), July 24, 1909.

18. Report by police agent in attendance in *Causa: Rebelión militar*, I, 90–91.

19. For the activities of Solidaridad Catalana politicians, see Joaquín Salvatella, Catalan republican deputy, April 5, 1911, *Diario de las Cortes*, II, 551; *El Poble Català* (Barcelona), July 21–25, 1909. *El Noticiero Universal* (Barcelona), July 23–25, 1909.

20. For the Solidaridad Obrera antiwar rally, see *El Poble Català* (Barcelona), July 24 and 25, 1909; *Las Noticias* (Barcelona), July 24, 1909; Interview with R. M. (identified as a Solidaridad Obrera official), *El País* (Madrid), August 13, 1909; Unidentified exile interviewed in France by José Reig, *El Mundo* (Madrid), August 9, 1909; *España Nueva* (Madrid), July 28, 1909; Miguel V. Moreno, "Por la Verdad," *El País* (Madrid), November 2, 1909; Testimony of Federico Arnall, *Causa: Rebelión militar*, I, 109; Brissa, *Revolución de julio*, p. 32; and Ossorio, *Julio de 1909*, p. 49.

21. Bonafulla [Esteve], *Revolución de julio*, p. 14.

22. Ossorio, *Julio de 1909*, pp. 49–50.

23. Emiliano Iglesias, July 6, 1910, *Diario de las Cortes*, II, 403–04.

24. *La Vanguardia* and *El Noticiero Universal* (Barcelona), July 25, 1909. *La Publicidad* (Barcelona), July 24 and 25, 1909.

25. Ossorio, July 13, 1910, *Diario de las Cortes*, III, 592.

26. On the formation of the Committee for the Strike, see V. Moreno, "Por la Verdad," *El País* (Madrid), November 2, 1909. Juan Colominas, "Veinte años después," *El Progreso* (Barcelona), July 31, 1929. Letter from R. M. (identified as a Solidaridad Obrera official), *El País* (Madrid), August 13, 1909. For the statement that Solidaridad Obrera did not officially sponsor the strike see Pablo Iglesias, July 12, 1910, *Diario de las Cortes*, III, 552. For the Committee's activities on Saturday night, see Emiliano Iglesias, April 5, 1911, *ibid.*, II, 563; Article by 'Domingo Rompecabezas,' *La Publicidad* (Barcelona), November 28, 1909; Interview with an unidentified trade union official not affiliated with Solidaridad Obrera, *Las Noticias* (Barcelona), August 7, 1909.

27. Letter from R. M., *El País* (Madrid), August 13, 1909. V. Moreno, "Por la Verdad," *ibid.*, November 2, 1909.

28. For the Committee's negotiations with the socialists, see V. Moreno, "Le Mouvement de Barcelone," *Les Documents du Progrés* (Paris), November 1909, p. 362; Magin Vidal [Fabra Rivas], "Les Préliminaires de la gréve génèrale," *L'Humanité* (Paris), August 13, 1909; Article by Magin Vidal [Fabra Rivas] in *Acción* (Toulouse), July 6, 1910, as reprinted in *El Diluvio* (Barcelona), August 5, 1910; Amparo Marti, "Los que prepararon los sucesos de julio," *España Nueva* (Madrid), July 17, 1910.

29. Eusebio Corominas, July 13, 1910, *Diario de las Cortes*, III, 582.

30. V. Moreno, "Por la Verdad," *El País* (Madrid), November 2, 1909.

31. Interview with R. M., *ibid.*, August 13, 1909.

32. Noguer, writing in *La Forja* (Barcelona), July 30, 1910.

33. For the Committee's activities Saturday night–Sunday, see V. Moreno, "Por la Verdad," *El País* (Madrid), November 2, 1909; V. Moreno, "Mouvement de Barcelone," *Documents du Progrés* (Paris), p. 362; Brissa, *Revolución de julio*, p. 33; *El País* (Madrid), August 13, 1909; and "C" [José Comaposada], "Sucesos de Barcelona," *El Socialista* (Madrid), November 5, 1909.

34. Juan Bacón [Cristobal Botella], "Los Revolucionarios," *La Epoca* (Madrid), October 24, 1909. See reply by V. Moreno in "Por la Verdad," *El País* (Madrid), November 2, 1909.

35. Noguer, *La Forja* (Barcelona), July 30, 1910.

36. For the socialist charge that V. Moreno was maneuvering to turn the movement over to the Radicals, see Letter from socialist Miguel Serrador Pérez, *El Diluvio* (Barcelona), August 6, 1911; *El Progreso* (Barcelona), August 1 and 7, 1911, and July 26, 1912.

37. Interview with trade union official not affiliated with Solidaridad Obrera, in *Las Noticias* (Barcelona), August 7, 1909.

38. For the Committee's contacts with newspapers, see Emiliano Iglesias, April 5, 1911, *ibid.*, II, 563; *Las Noticias* (Barcelona), August 2, 1909; *El Progreso* (Barcelona), July 26 and 27, 1914; *La Publicidad* and *El Poble Català* (Barcelona), July 26, 1909.

39. Letter from socialist Serrador, *El Diluvio* (Barcelona), August 6, 1911.

40. Emiliano Iglesias, July 9, 1910, *Diario de las Cortes*, II, 494. On the editorial "Remember," see Ossorio, July 13, 1910, *ibid.*, III, 591. On the parliamentary immunity conferred by Giner de los Ríos, see *El Progreso* (Barcelona), July 24, 1909, and *Causa: Rebelión militar*, I, 102–04.

41. Baldomero Bonet informed military interrogators of the meeting, then subsequently denied all knowledge (*Causa: Rebelión militar*, I, 469–73; II, 18–19; see also *ibid.*, I, 105, 536–37).

42. Magin Vidal [Fabra Rivas], "Préliminaries," *L'Humanité* (Paris), August 13, 1909. For this first meeting, see *El Progreso* (Barcelona), August 7 and 11, 1911; also Emiliano Iglesias, "Preguntas y respuestas: Para los nacionalistas y para un socialista," *ibid.*, July 27, 1911, and "Uno que huye," *ibid.*, December 4, 1909.

43. For the preparations for the strike, see "C" [Comaposada], "Sucesos de Barcelona," *El Socialista* (Madrid), November 5, 1909; Magin Vidal [Fabra Rivas], "Préliminaires," *L'Humanité* (Paris), August 13, 1909; Juan Colominas, "Veinte años después," *El Progreso* (Barcelona), July 31, 1929; V. Moreno, "Por la Verdad," *El País* (Madrid), November 2, 1909; Letter from R. M., *ibid.*, August 13, 1909; Brissa, *Revolución de julio*, pp. 32–33; and Bonafulla [Esteve], *Revolución de julio*, p. 14.

44. Letter from socialist Serrador, *El Diluvio* (Barcelona), August 6, 1911. The account of this meeting is based on the following: Interview with Fabra Rivas published in *Acción* (Toulouse), July 26, 1910, and reprinted in *El Diluvio*, August 5, 1910; Letter from Fabra Rivas, *El Diluvio*, August 13, 1911; and Emiliano Iglesias, April 5, 1911, *Diario de las Cortes*, II, 563, and "Preguntas y respuestas," *El Progreso* (Barcelona), July 27, 1911. See also *El Progreso*, July 28, August 1, 7, and 13, 1911.

45. For the importance of neutralizing the middle class in a general strike, see Chorley, *Armies and the Art of Revolution*, pp. 78–79.

46. Noguer, writing in *La Forja* (Barcelona), July 30, 1910. See also *El Poble Català* (Barcelona), July 28, 1911.

47. For the Sunday evening rally to vote on the general strike plans, see V. Moreno, "Mouvement de Barcelona," *Documents du Progrès* (Paris), p. 362; Magin Vidal [Fabra Rivas], "A Sabadell," *L'Humanité* (Paris), August 17, 1909; *El Poble Català* (Barcelona), July 28, 1911; Ossorio, *Julio de 1909*, p. 50; Paulis, *Maura ante el pueblo*, pp. 221–22; *Las Noticias* (Barcelona), August 2, 1909; and Brissa, *Revolución de julio*, pp. 33–34.

48. Report of Police Inspector Salagaray, based on information from the president of the teamsters' syndicate, in *Causa: Rebelión militar*, I, 26–27. Ossorio, July 13, 1910, *Diario de las Cortes*, III, 592. Salagaray was Ossorio's regular contact with Solidaridad Obrera and labor leaders, as Radical party member Enrique Pujol had sarcastically pointed out in a front page letter in *El Progreso* (Barcelona), March 9, 1909.

49. Ossorio, interview in *La Epoca* (Madrid), August 4, 1909, and July 13, 1910, *Diario de las Cortes*, III, 591–92.

50. Orts-Ramos, *Historia de la revolución española*, p. 430.

51. La Cierva, October 19, 1909, *Diario de las Cortes*, p. 59. La Cierva, *Notas de mi vida*, pp. 136–37. Ossorio, *Julio de 1909*, pp. 49–50.

52. Ossorio, *Julio de 1909*, p. 50. Ossorio, July 13, 1910, *Diario de las Cortes*, III, 592.

CHAPTER XI: EVENTS: JULY 26 THROUGH AUGUST 1, 1909

Monday, July 26

1. Ossorio, *Julio de 1909*, p. 52. The narrative of the week's events is based largely on the following account: "Versión de varios representantes de la mayoría de los periódicos en Barcelona y hecha de acuerdo con instrucciones de censura militar," published by Barcelona newspapers on August 2, 1909. See also independent versions in *Las Noticias* and *El Correo Catalán* (Barcelona), August 2, 1909; *El País* (Madrid), July 28, 1909; *El Progreso* (Barcelona), July 26, 1911; and Magin Vidal [Fabra Rivas], "Barcelone en grève," *L'Humanité* (Paris), August 14, 1909.

2. Ossorio, July 13, 1910, *Diario de las Cortes*, III, 593. One Catalan deputy praised the factory owners for "acceding to the workers' desires" (Joaquín Salvatella, Catalan Federal Republican deputy, April 5, 1911, *ibid.*, II, 550). See also *Almanaque del Diario de Barcelona* (Barcelona), 1909, p. 83.

3. On the newspapers, see *El Correo Catalán* (Barcelona), September 19, 1909, *La Publicidad* (Barcelona), September 20, 1909, and Brissa, *Revolución de julio*, p. 37.

4. Concerning the lack of leaflets (either for information or for propaganda), see Benet, *Maragall i la Setmana Tràgica*, p. 52; *La Forja* (Barcelona), July 30, 1910; *El Progreso* (Barcelona), July 26, 1910; and Shaw, *Spain from Within*, p. 168.

5. Sol Ferrer, *Véritable Ferrer*, pp. 180–81 and *Ferrer: Martyr*, p. 136. One policeman reported he had seen Ferrer in Barcelona during the weekend of July 24–25 (*Causa contra Ferrer*, p. 81).

6. Sol Ferrer, *Véritable Ferrer*, pp. 181–82.

7. As told to Archer by V. Moreno; see Archer, *Life of Ferrer*, pp. 143–44. See also

V. Moreno, "Por la Verdad," *El País* (Madrid), November 2, 1909; Sol Ferrer, *Ferrer: Martyr,* p. 136; and Simarro, *Proceso Ferrer,* I, 77.

8. Testimony of Ferrer, corroborated by witnesses, of business activities, in *Causa contra Ferrer,* pp. 51–52, 62–67, 69, 146–47. Cristobal Litrán, "Alrededor de Ferrer: Intimidades," *El Progreso* (Barcelona), July 20, 1910.

9. *La Publicidad* (Barcelona), November 3, 1909. *Las Noticias* (Barcelona), September 11, 1910.

10. Concerning the anarchists' activity, see report of the Auditor General, General Ramón Pastor, in *Causa: Rebelión militar,* I, 540–41. Report of the Auditor de División, *ibid.,* II, 135. For the arrests of the anarchists, see *ibid.,* I, 19–20, 24–26, 256, 303–05; II, 26.

11. Reported in a speech by Emiliano Iglesias, printed in *El Progreso* (Barcelona), January 23, 1911. On the limited power of the anarchists, see report of the Auditor de División, *Causa: Rebelión militar,* II, 134. Castellote's wife reported visiting the newspaper offices on Friday and Saturday: *ibid.,* I, 113–14.

12. Report of a police official in the Atarazana district, in *Causa: Rebelión militar,* I, 256–57.

13. Ossorio, *Julio de 1909,* p. 51. For the progress of the strike to this point (10 A.M.), see *La Tribuna* (Barcelona), July 14, 1910, and *El Progreso* (Barcelona), July 26, 1911.

14. *El Progreso* (Barcelona), July 26, 1911.

15. *El Correo Catalán* (Barcelona), August 2, 1909.

16. Hurtado, *Quaranta Anys d'advocat,* I, 152–53.

17. On the importance of women in organizing the General Strike, see Minister of War (General Arsenio Linares), October 20, 1909, *Diario de las Cortes,* 77; testimony of Francisco Ferrer, *Causa contra Ferrer,* p. 59; Memorial of Javier Ugarte, Attorney General (*Fiscal*) of the Supreme Court, September 17, 1909, as reprinted in Modesto Hernández Villaescusa, *La Semana Trágica en Barcelona: Hechos, causas, y remedios* (Barcelona, 1909), p. 60; Republican Senator Sol y Ortega, in an interview published in *El País* (Madrid), August 4, 1909; and declaration of Hermegildo Giner de los Ríos, in *Causa: Rebelión militar,* I, 103.

18. On María Llopis, see report by police official in *Causa: Rebelión militar,* I, 257; *La Publicidad* (Barcelona), November 12, 1909, March 10, 1910; and *El Poble Català* (Barcelona), November 13, 1909. María Llopis was condemned to die, a sentence later commuted to perpetual exile; this was one of the most severe sentences imposed by the courts.

19. Sirera, "Obreros en Barcelona," Charts 7, 23, and 25. On Pueblo Nuevo see also *Causa: Rebelión militar,* I, 70–71, 227–28.

20. Magin Vidal [Fabra Rivas], "Barcelone en grève," *L'Humanité* (Paris), August 14, 1909. For the importance of the Pueblo Nuevo group in the attack on the streetcars, see Ugarte memorial in H. Villaescusa, *Semana Trágica,* p. 59. Brissa, *Revolución de julio,* p. 35. For the streetcar encounters see: "C" [Comaposada], "Sucesos de Barcelona," *El Socialista* (Madrid), November 5, 1909, and *El Progreso* (Barcelona), July 26, 1911.

21. Emiliano Iglesias, July 6, 1910, *Diario de las Cortes,* II, 403–04. On Ossorio's determination to restore order at any cost in the afternoon of Monday, July 26, see letter

from Ossorio to Juan Maragall, dated October 20, 1909, as quoted in Benet, *Maragall i la Setmana Trágica*, pp. 266–67. See also Ossorio, interview in *La Epoca* (Madrid), August 4, 1909, and Ossorio, July 13, 1910, *Diario de las Cortes*, III, 593.

22. The conflict between Ossorio and La Cierva was commented upon by the Radical newspaper on the morning of the strike (*El Progreso* [Barcelona], July 26, 1909).

23. For events in Sabadell, see Ossorio, *Julio de 1909*, pp. 32, 52, 60; Magin Vidal [Fabra Rivas], "A Sabadell," *L'Humanité* (Paris), August 17, 1909; Canals, *Sucesos de 1909*, I, 167; and Brissa, *Revolución de julio*, pp. 187–88.

24. Ossorio, July 13, 1910, *Diario de las Cortes,* III, 593. Ossorio, *Julio de 1909*, pp. 59–60. Juan Ventosa of the conservative Lliga, and Eusebio Corominas of the Catalan republicans both supported Ossorio's contention that he could have restored order better than could an army officer (July 13, 1910, *Diario de las Cortes*, III, 576, 582).

25. Ossorio, *Julio de 1909*, p. 60.

26. The account of the meeting is based primarily on Ossorio, *Julio de 1909*, pp. 61–65. This is corroborated by the official account, signed by the three principal participants: Simarro, *Proceso Ferrer*, I, 5–6. See also La Cierva, October 19, 1909, *Diario de las Cortes*, p. 60. For an amusing version see Magin Vidal [Fabra Rivas], "Barcelone en grève," *L'Humanité* (Paris), August 14, 1909.

27. La Cierva, *Notas de mi vida*, p. 138.

28. Ossorio, July 13, 1910, *Diario de las Cortes*, III, 594.

29. General Santiago's report to the War Ministry was sent to the Cortes, and entered in the legislative record: "Copia de las comunicaciones del capitán general de la 4.ª región dando cuenta de los sucesos ocurridos en Cataluña durante los días 26 al 31 de julio de 1909," dated August 20, 1909, fourteen pages, entered as Appendix 1 to the fourth session (October 19) of the 1909 Legislature, *Diario de las Cortes*.

30. Juan Ventosa, Lliga deputy, July 13, 1910, *Diario de las Cortes*, III, 576–77, and Pedro Corominas, July 13, 1910, *ibid.,* III, 582–83.

31. General Linares, October 20, 1909, *Diario de las Cortes*, p. 77. La Cierva, *Notas de mi vida*, p. 140.

32. Pedro Corominas, July 13, 1910, *Diario de las Cortes*, III, 582–83. The complete text of Santiago's proclamation was published in *El Correo Catalán* (Barcelona), August 2, 1909.

33. Concerning this embarkation, see report by General Santiago, p. 1 of Appendix 1 to October 19, 1909, *Diario de las Cortes,* and trial of Federico Artiga, *El País* (Madrid), October 17, 1909.

34. Concerning the roll of the women, see *El País* (Madrid), July 28, 1909; General Linares, October 20, 1909, *Diario de las Cortes,* p. 77; and Dalmacio Iglesias, Carlist deputy, July 6, 1910, *ibid.,* II, 420. For a photograph of the women see Joaquín Arrarás, *Historia de la cruzada española*, 2 ed. (Madrid, 1939), I, 44.

35. For Esteban Roig see *La Publicidad* (Barcelona), October 25, 1909, and *El País* (Madrid), October 26, 1909. For the incident on the Calle Valencia, see *Las Noticias* (Barcelona), August 2, 1909.

36. Sastre, *Huelgas: 1909*, p. 31.

37. For the Calle Aribau incident see Bonafulla [Esteve], *Revolución de julio*, pp. 15–16; Emiliano Iglesias, July 6, 1910, *Diario de las Cortes*, II, 404; and *El Progreso* (Bar-

celona), Julio 26, 1911. For Foronda's activities, see his letter of appreciation to his employees for their loyalty during the week in *El Correo Catalán* (Barcelona), August 14, 1909. See also the letters from a streetcar employee protesting the discipline during the week, in *El Progreso* (Barcelona), December 25 and 27, 1909.

38. *El Progreso* (Barcelona), July 26 and 27, 1914.

39. For the attack on the police station in Clot-San Martín, see report by police chief, *Causa: Rebelión militar,* I, 499; *Las Noticias* and *El Correo Catalán* (Barcelona), August 2, 1909. For the participation of Carmen Alauch, see police report, *Causa: Rebelión militar,* I, 418.

40. For the incident on the Paseo de Colón, see report by General Santiago, p. 1 of Appendix to October 19, 1909, *Diario de las Cortes*; Republican Senator Sol y Ortega, April 8, 1911, *ibid.,* II, 661; *El País* (Madrid), July 28, 1909; Bonafulla [Esteve], *Revolución de julio,* p. 22; and "C" [Comaposada], "Sucesos de Barcelona," *El Socialista* (Madrid), December 24, 1909.

41. The account of Ferrer's visit to the Casa del Pueblo is based on the testimony of Lorenzo Ardid in *Causa contra Ferrer,* pp. 369–71; the statement by Ardid, "Hoja extraordinario: El Calvario de un partido," as reprinted in Simarro, *Proceso Ferrer,* I, 354; Sol Ferrer, *Véritable Ferrer,* p. 232; Emilio Junoy, "Pequeña Tribuna: Alrededor del Proceso Ferrer," *La Publicidad* (Barcelona), March 28 and April 3, 1911. In his first two interrogations, Ferrer did not mention his visit to the Casa del Pueblo and in fact stated that he had not been in the Casa del Pueblo for some time; even after Ardid testified on September 10 about Ferrer's visit, Ferrer denied it. When forced to confront Ardid, Ferrer admitted the visit but said it was only to find his business manager, Cristobal Litrán. (See *Causa contra Ferrer,* pp. 50–62, 183–93, 417–18, 433–34).

42. Testimony of Emiliano Iglesias, *Causa: Rebelión militar,* I, 35, and Emiliano Iglesias writing in *El Progreso* (Barcelona), July 27, 1914.

43. Testimony of Ardid, *Causa contra Ferrer,* p. 370. For Ferrer's conversation with other Radical leaders, see Junoy, "Pequeña Tribuna," *La Publicidad* (Barcelona), March 28, 1911.

44. See comment of Civil Guard cavalry commander, Lieutenant Colonel Adolfo Riquelme, *Causa: Rebelión militar,* I, 334–35.

45. *El Progreso* (Barcelona), January 23 and August 13, 1911; July 26, 1912; and July 27, 1914.

46. Report from Police Inspector Moises Zapatero, *Causa: Rebelión militar,* I, 24.

47. On the activities in the Casa del Pueblo on Monday afternoon, see the testimony of Emiliano Iglesias, *Causa: Rebelión militar,* I, 33–34; report of Captain Pablo Riera of the Civil Guard, *Causa contra Ferrer,* p. 41; Emiliano Iglesias, writing in *El Progreso* (Barcelona), July 27, 1914; *La Metralla* (Barcelona), January 21, 1911. See also testimony of Republican Deputy Giner de los Ríos, *Causa: Rebelión militar,* I, 104–05. For evidence that the Casa del Pueblo had been entered during the week, see police report, *ibid.,* I, 177–79.

48. Emiliano Iglesias, "Detalles inéditos," *El Progreso* (Barcelona), July 26, 1912. See also *ibid.,* July 27, 1914.

49. On the meeting of newspaper editors, see May 7, 1910; August 7 and 13, 1911;

July 26, 1912; *El País* (Madrid), July 28, 1909; and *El Diluvio* (Barcelona), August 13, 1911.

50. For Emiliano Iglesias' activities on Monday night, see Iglesias, *Solidaridad Obrera* (Barcelona), January 9, 1917; Testimony of Iglesias, *Causa: Rebelión militar*, I, 477, 537; Iglesias, *El Progreso* (Barcelona), August 13, 1911; and Magín Vidal [Fabra Rivas], "Barcelone en grève," *L'Humanité* (Paris), August 14, 1909.

51. For the report that some labor leaders wanted strike to end, see Canals, *Sucesos de 1909*, I, 172, and Eduardo Comín Colomer, *La Semana Trágica de Barcelona*, No. 28 of Temas Españoles, 2 ed. (Madrid, 1956), p. 19.

52. Chorley, *Armies and the Art of Revolution*, p. 153. For the Strike Committee's deliberate policy of applauding the Army, see V. Moreno, "Mouvement de Barcelone," *Documents du Progrés* (Paris), p. 363; Magín Vidal [Fabra Rivas], "Barcelone en grève," *L'Humanité* (Paris), August 14, 1909; and Juan de La Cierva, July 8, 1910, *Diario de las Cortes,* II, 466.

53. For the offer of reinforcements from Sabadell, see "C" [Comaposada], "Sucesos de Barcelona," *El Socialista* (Madrid), November 12, 1909; and Magín Vidal [Fabra Rivas], "Barcelone en grève," *L'Humanité* (Paris), August 14, 1909.

54. Magín Vidal [Fabra Rivas], "Barcelone en grève," *L'Humanité* (Paris), August 14, 1909.

55. Concerning this manifesto, two witnesses for the state implied that Ferrer had prepared the manifesto (Francisco Domenech Munté, *Causa contra Ferrer*, p. 24, and Radical party official Juan Puig, *ibid.*, pp. 31–32). Two individuals sympathetic to Ferrer said that Moreno prepared it and Ferrer agreed to sign it (Sol Ferrer, *Véritable Ferrer*, pp. 233–34, and Archer [possibly on the basis of information from Moreno, with whom he had talked], *Life of Ferrer*, p. 208). Emilio Junoy also reported that Ferrer was willing to act as a revolutionary leader ("Pequeña tribuna," *La Publicidad* [Barcelona], March 28, 1911). At his trial, Iglesias denied having seen Ferrer for nine months prior to the insurrection (*Causa contra Ferrer*, pp. 360–62). Later (free of possible prosecution) he affirmed he had met with Ferrer and advised him to stay at home (April 5, 1911, *Diario de las Cortes*, II, 564. See also, "Campaña revisionista: Lo que *no* dijo Emiliano Iglesias," *El Progreso* [Barcelona], March 26, 1911.)

56. Testimony of two soldiers on guard duty, *Causa contra Ferrer*, pp. 483–86. Simarro, *Proceso Ferrer*, I, 76–77.

57. Sol Ferrer, *Véritable Ferrer*, pp. 233–34. Archer, *Life of Ferrer*, p. 208.

58. For Ferrer's activities on Monday evening, see testimony of Francisco Domenech in *Causa contra Ferrer*, pp. 24–25, 27–28; testimony of Ferrer, *ibid.*, pp. 52–55; statement by Cristobal Litrán, *España Nueva* (Madrid), November 17, 1909; and Emiliano Iglesias, *El Progreso* (Barcelona), July 27, 1914.

59. The account of the Monday evening meeting with Radical leaders is based on testimony of Iglesias, *Causa: Rebelión militar*, I, 34; Emiliano Iglesias, *El Progreso* (Barcelona), March 26, 1911; Enrique Tubau, *ibid.*, July 26, 1914; Magín Vidal [Fabra Rivas], article in *Acción* (Toulouse) as reprinted in *El Diluvio* (Barcelona), August 5, 1910; and *Solidaridad Obrera* (Barcelona), January 12, 1917.

60. Navarro, *Historia crítica*, p. 284.

61. Emiliano Iglesias in *El Progreso* (Barcelona), July 27, 1914.

62. Emiliano Iglesias in *ibid.*, August 7, 1911. Iglesias, April 5, 1911, *Diario de las Cortes*, II, 564. Magín Vidal [Fabra Rivas], "Barcelone en grève," *L'Humanité* (Paris), August 14, 1909.

63. Emiliano Iglesias, *El Progreso* (Barcelona), August 13, 1911, and July 26, 1912. Magín Vidal [Fabra Rivas], interview in *Acción* (Toulouse) as reprinted in *El Diluvio* (Barcelona), August 5, 1910.

64. Iglesias, April 5, 1911, *Diario de las Cortes,* II, 564. Iglesias in *El Progreso* (Barcelona), July 27, 1914. Testimony of Domenech, *Causa contra Ferrer,* p. 24.

65. Testimony of Domenech in *Causa contra Ferrer,* pp. 24–25, 27–28.

66. Cristobal Litrán, "Alrededor del Proceso Ferrer," *El Progreso* (Barcelona), July 20, 1910.

67. In later years Emiliano Iglesias confessed many facts that he had denied during his trial. However, he steadfastly denied that Ferrer played any role in Barcelona after Monday, July 26 (*El Progreso* [Barcelona], March 26, 1911, and July 27, 1914; see also his letter to *Solidaridad Obrera* [Barcelona], January 6 and 11, 1917. In addition, see Rafael Salillas, republican deputy, March 31, 1911, *Diario de las Cortes*, II, 502, and Joaquín Salvatella, Catalan republican deputy, April 5, 1911, *ibid.*, II, 555–56).

68. Eusebio Corominas, July 13, 1910, *Diario de las Cortes*, III, 582.

69. Canals, *Sucesos de 1909*, II, 373–74. Liberal party leader Moret taunted Maura by pointing out that despite all the favors bestowed upon them, Barcelona citizens had not aided his government to restore order (October 18, 1909, *Diario de las Cortes,* p. 27). On the failure of citizens to aid the government see General Linares, October 20, 1909, *Diario de las Cortes,* pp. 77–78, and Pablo Iglesias, July 7, 1910, *ibid.*, II, 437.

70. Emiliano Iglesias, July 6, 1910, *Diario de las Cortes,* II, 404–05. See also Eusebio Corominas, July 13, 1910, *ibid.*, III, 582.

71. Magín Vidal [Fabra Rivas], "Réponse a des calomnies," *L'Humanité* (Paris), August 18, 1909.

72. In Pueblo Nuevo it was public knowledge that the burning of convents was being planned in this Radical center (testimony of Mariano Bordas, *Causa: Rebelión militar,* I, 346).

73. H. Villaescusa, *Semana Trágica,* pp. 33, 36, 39–40. For the director, Brother Lycarion, see Ramón Rucabado, *Santa Mónica de la Rambla y otras páginas de sangre* (Barcelona, 1959), p. 173.

74. Santiago López y Díaz de Quijano, Marquis of Casa Quijano, was reported to be the sole sponsor of the school, by H. Villaescusa (*Semana Trágica,* p. 19) and by Joaquín Arrarás ("La Semana Trágica de Barcelona," *ABC* [Madrid], July 28, 1909). But in November 1961 an elderly priest in Pueblo Nuevo, who had been in Barcelona during the Tragic Week, told me that the benefactor was the Marquis of Comillas, and that the workers' antagonism was directed against him. See a similar report in Benet, *Maragall i la Setmana Tràgica,* p. 50.

75. For José Robles see Leroy [V. Moreno], *Secretos del anarquismo,* pp. 232–33; *Causa contra Ferrer,* p. 464; and Pablo Iglesias, July 12, 1910, *Diario de las Cortes,* III, 553.

76. For the commission for rationalist education, see *Boletín de la Escuela Moderna:*

Enseñanza científica y racional, second series (July 1909); Bertrán, *"Yo Acuso,"* pp. 11–12; and *El Progreso* (Barcelona), June 5, 1909.

77. *El Progreso* (Barcelona), July 23, 1909. *Causa: Rebelión militar,* I, 62.

78. *El Progreso* (Barcelona), June 16, 1909.

79. *Las Noticias* (Barcelona), August 3, 1909. Report by General Santiago, p. 2 of Appendix 1 to October 19, 1909, *Diario de las Cortes.*

80. *El Progreso* (Barcelona), July 2, 1912, and July 27, 1914. One report states that Ferrer remained in Barcelona until he was certain the convent had been burned (Comás, *Revolucionario de acción,* p. 84).

81. *Las Noticias* (Barcelona), August 12, 1909.

Tuesday, July 27

1. For the destruction of railroad lines, telephone, and telegraph, see statement by La Cierva to newsmen in Madrid, *España Nueva* (Madrid), July 28, 1909. See also statement quoted in Soldevilla, *Año político,* XV: *1909,* 265–66; Ossorio, *Julio de 1909,* pp. 53–54; Magin Vidal [Fabra Rivas], "En pleine Révolution," *L'Humanité* (Paris), August 15, 1909; and Juan de La Cierva, July 8, 1910, *Diario de las Cortes,* II, 466.

2. La Cierva, *Notas de mi vida,* pp. 138–39, 141. *El País* (Madrid), August 24, 1909.

3. The police inspector assigned to the Casa del Pueblo, Antonio Andrade, provided a list of twenty-one particularly active Radical extremists: *Causa: Rebelión militar,* I, 255–56. For pressure exerted on Monday night, see testimony by Narciso Verdaguer, Lliga councilor, *Causa: Rebelión militar,* I, 462; Carlist Deputy Manuel Senante, July 11, 1910, *Diario de las Cortes,* II, 517; article by Francisco Colldeforms, *El Siglo Futuro* (Madrid), August 9, 1909; and Ametlla, *Memòries polítiques,* p. 269.

4. For the attack on the Marists and the death of Brother Lycarion, see *Las Noticias* (Barcelona), August 3, 1909; H. Villaescusa, *Semana Trágica,* pp. 39–40; and *Bulletin de l'Institut des Petits Frères de Marie,* I (1909), 256–57. Brother Adaulfo Abaurrea of the Marist house in Barcelona was most solicitous in his efforts to obtain more data, but reported that because the Marist buildings were burned again in 1936 there are no records in Barcelona or in the central house in Saragossa.

5. *La Publicidad* (Barcelona, a republican but anti-Radical paper), November 15, 1909, defended the slaying of Brother Lycarion and promised to provide the full details as soon as it was free to do so. I was unable to locate the reference, if it ever was published.

6. Testimony of Bravo Portillo, *Causa: Rebelión militar,* I, 19–21.

7. Bonafulla [Esteve], *Revolución de julio,* p. 21. See also "C" [Comaposada], "Sucesos de Barcelona," *El Socialista* (Madrid), November 15, 1909.

8. Trial of José Bel Pla, *El País* (Madrid), October 11, 1909; see also *La Publicidad* (Barcelona), October 8, 1909. Trial of Salvador Lloret, *ibid.,* November 9, 1909. See also trial of Francisco Ramírez, *ibid.,* October 8, 1909; *Las Noticias* (Barcelona), August 27, 1909; and *El País* (Madrid), October 9 and 11, 1909.

9. Report by General Santiago, p. 1 of Appendix 1 to October 19, 1909, *Diario de las Cortes.*

10. Soldevilla, *Año político,* XV: *1909,* 269–70, 479–80. For an account of the battle, see Díaz-Plaja, *Documentos: Siglo XX,* pp. 171–75.

11. La Cierva, *Notas de mi vida*, p. 139. See also La Cierva, October 19, 1909, *Diario de las Cortes*, p. 63. La Cierva's statement to the Madrid press corps on July 27 in Soldevilla, *Año político*, XV: *1909*, 265-67. For the adverse effect of La Cierva's charge on Catalan politicians, see Salvatella, April 5, 1911, *Diario de las Cortes*, II, 554, and Hurtado, *Quaranta Anys d'advocat*, I, 156. For its adverse effect on the socialists' plans for a national general strike, see "C" [José Comaposada], "Sucesos de Barcelona," *El Socialista* (Madrid), November 26, 1909.

12. Gaziel [Calvet], *Tots els Camins*, p. 331; letter from Pablo Iglesias to Belgian socialist Clerbaut, August 17, 1909, in Canals, *Sucesos de 1909*, I, 176; Magin Vidal [Fabra Rivas], "Barcelone en grève," *L'Humanité* (Paris), August 14, 1909; Ferrer statement to Juan Puig, *Causa contra Ferrer*, pp. 32, 617; editorial, *El Correo Catalán* (Barcelona), July 28, 1911.

13. Emiliano Iglesias, "Detalles inéditos," *El Progreso* (Barcelona), July 26, 1912, and July 27, 1914.

14. Sol y Ortega, April 8, 1911, *Diario de las Cortes*, II, 662.

15. *El Poble Català* (Barcelona), July 22, 1911.

16. Tato, *Sol y Ortega*, pp. 479-80. Republican Senator Odón de Buen told a newspaperman that the popular protest had been converted into a "serious republican movement," even to the extreme of organizing a "junta revolucionaria," but it collapsed when it was learned that the republic had not been proclaimed elsewhere (see newspaper article reprinted in *Causa: Rebelión militar*, I, 165). When questioned, de Buen denied having made the statement (*ibid.*, II, 57-58).

17. Emiliano Iglesias, July 6, 1910, *Diario de las Cortes*, II, 410.

18. Navarro, *Historia crítica*, p. 284.

19. *Solidaridad Obrera* (Barcelona), January 12, 1917. According to a letter from Lorenzo Ardid, he was accused of being "the director of the movement" and of "leading the groups of incendiaries" (*El País* [Madrid], September 30, 1909).

20. *Causa: Rebelión militar*, I, 517; II, 154.

21. Juan Colominas, "Veinte Años después," *El Progreso* (Barcelona), July 31, 1929. For background information see Navarro, *Historia crítica*, pp. 206-07; Leroy [V. Moreno], *Secretos del anarquismo*, p. 242; *Causa contra Ferrer*, pp. 12, 181-82, 188-89, 196-98, 400-02; and Sangro, *Sombra de Ferrer*, p. 43.

22. Navarro, *Historia crítica*, p. 284. For the rebels' use of Red Cross armbands, see trials of Rafael Guerra del Río, Radical youth leader (*La Publicidad* [Barcelona], November 5, 1909), Enrique García and Daniel Villanueva (*ibid.*, October 15, 1909), and Felipe Novales (*ibid.*, September 25 and October 23, 1909). For the "lists," see account of the burning of the Salesian school, in *El Correo Catalán* (Barcelona), August 30, 1909; account of the burning of the asylum of the Sisters of Charity, *ibid.*, August 28, 1909; memorial of Javier Ugarte, Fiscal of the Supreme Court, as reprinted in H. Villaescusa, *Revolución de julio*, p. 60; and La Cierva, October 19, 1909, *Diario de las Cortes*, p. 59.

23. Ignacio Casanovas, S.J., *Nuestro Estado social: Comentario a la revolución de julio* (Barcelona, 1910), pp. 17-18. See also Dalmacio Iglesias in *Diario de las Cortes*, II, 420.

24. Military interrogators tried but failed to prove that Dr. Ricardo Jaussens, a Radi-

cal city councilman, warned the Hospital de Santa Cruz it would be burned (*Causa: Rebelión militar,* I, 506–07, 515–16, 531–32). The Adorer Sisters reported that they were warned (*El Correo Catalán* [Barcelona], August 7, 1909). So did the Conceptionist Sisters (*Las Noticias* [Barcelona], August 16, 1909). For reports on instructions not to kill, see José Puig y Cadalfach, *La Epoca* (Madrid), November 17, 1909; "C" [Comaposada], "Sucesos de Barcelona," *El Socialista* (Madrid), November 19, 1909; and Magin Vidal [Fabra Rivas], "En pleine Révolution," *L'Humanité* (Paris), August 15, 1909.

25. Statement by José Negre, Secretary General of Solidaridad Obrera in 1910, *La Publicidad* (Barcelona), April 13, 1910. See also trial of Juan Crespo, *El Progreso* (Barcelona), January 16, 1912; and reports on the burning of the Piarist buildings (*Las Noticias* [Barcelona], August 14, 1909), the convent of the Hieronymites (*ibid.,* August 17, 1909), and the convent of the Capuchinesses (*ibid.,* August 11, 1909). For the accusation that the incendiaries and the looters were one and the same, see statement of a nun of the Sacred Family in *Las Noticias,* August 15, 1909.

26. See statement by Moret, Liberal party chief, as quoted in Soldevilla, *Año político,* XV: *1909,* 287–88. For the importance of the rumor that arms were stored in convents, see H. Villaescusa, *Semana Trágica,* p. 45; letter from Eduardo Dato to Antonio Maura in G. Maura, *Por qué cayó Alfonso,* p. 142; and interview in France with an unidentified socialist, *El Mundo* (Madrid), August 9, 1909. See also the trial of Simeón Puñorrosa, *La Publicidad* (Madrid), November 1, 1909.

27. Dictum of the Chief Military Advocate of Barcelona (General Pastor) in *Causa: Rebelión militar,* II, 304.

28. Testimony of Narciso Verdaguer, *Causa: Rebelión militar,* I, 462. For the details of this meeting, see testimony of Emiliano Iglesias, *ibid.,* I, 35, and testimony of Trinidad Monegal, *ibid.,* I, 456; II, 245.

29. Letter from Emiliano Iglesias in *Solidaridad Obrera* (Barcelona), January 11, 1917. For the incident on the barricades, see letter from Francisco Sánchez, *El Progreso* (Barcelona), August 10, 1910. Also for this incident, see *Causa: Rebelión militar,* I, 449–50, 535; II, 27–30, 58–59, 242–43, 249–51.

30. Magin Vidal [Fabra Rivas], interview in *Acción* (Toulouse), reprinted in *El Diluvio,* August 5, 1910. Editorial in *Solidaridad Obrera* (Barcelona), January 12, 1917.

31. For Emiliano Iglesias' account of this meeting, see *El Progreso,* August 6, 1910, and August 13, 1911; and Iglesias, April 5, 1911, *Diario de las Cortes,* II, 564.

32. Letter from Fabra Rivas to *El Diluvio* (Barcelona), August 13, 1911.

33. Magin Vidal [Fabra Rivas], interview in *Acción* (Toulouse), reprinted in *El Diluvio* (Barcelona), August 5, 1910.

34. *El Progreso* (Barcelona), August 6, 1910.

35. *Ibid.,* August 13, 1911.

36. "C" [Comaposada], "Sucesos de Barcelona," *El Socialista* (Madrid), November 12, 1909.

37. *El Poble Català* (Barcelona), April 7, 1911.

38. For details of this meeting, see Joaquín Salvatella, Federalist Republican deputy, April 5, 1911, *Diario de las Cortes,* II, 550–52. See also Hurtado, *Quaranta Anys d'advocat,* I, 151–57.

39. Hurtado, *Quaranta Anys d'advocat,* I, 153.

40. *Ibid.,* 154.

41. Salvatella, April 5, 1911, *Diario de las Cortes,* II, 551.

42. Hurtado, *Quaranta Anys d'advocat,* I, 156. See also "C" [Comaposado], "Sucesos de Barcelona," *El Socialista* (Madrid), November 17, 1909.

43. Salvatella, April 5, 1911, *Diario de las Cortes,* II, 551.

44. Hurtado, *Quaranta Anys d'advocat,* I, 156.

45. Salvatella, April 5, 1911, *Diario de las Cortes,* II, 551.

46. Hurtado, *Quaranta Anys d'advocat,* I, 156. For the same conviction see Juan Caballé, Catalan republican deputy, as quoted in *El Socialista* (Madrid), November 5, 1909.

47. The Provincial Superior of the Piarists in 1909, Father Antonio Mirats, had fought as a colonel in the Carlist army after he was ordained a priest. When the war ended in 1877, he received absolution from the Bishop of Perpignon "from the censures which he might have incurred for the spilling of blood," and he returned to his religious duties. (Bau, *Historia de las Escuelas Pías,* pp. 463–64; see also statement by Pedro Llosas, Carlist deputy, who described the rector of the Piarist school as "mi querido amigo," July 14, 1910, *Diario de las Cortes,* III, 614.)

48. Bau, *Historia de las Escuelas Pías,* pp. 472–73.

49. For the attack on the Church of San Pablo, see *Las Noticias* (Barcelona), August 14 and 27, 1909; *El Progreso* (Barcelona), December 16 and 17, 1909; *El Correo Catalán* (Barcelona), August 27, 1909.

50. For accounts of this incident, see trial of José Gomís Montells, *La Publicidad* (Barcelona), February 7, 1910; *El Correo Catalán* (Barcelona), August 11, 1909; Orts-Ramos, *Historia de la revolución española,* p. 432; and Brissa, *Revolución de julio,* p. 46.

51. *Las Noticias* (Barcelona), August 14, 1909. For the burning of the Piarist schools, see also *El Correo Catalán* (Barcelona), August 2, 20 and 21, 1909.

52. Interview with Father Riera, *Las Noticias* (Barcelona), August 14, 1909. See also Pedro Llosas, Carlist deputy, July 14, 1910, *Diario de las Cortes,* III, 614.

53. Interview with Father Enrique Serraima, Rector of the Escuelas Pías de San Antón, in Barcelona, on December 5, 1961. See also Carlist Deputy Pedro Llosas, July 13, 1910, *Diario de las Cortes,* III, 584; and Soldevilla, *Año político,* XV: 1909, 286.

54. For Antonio Villanueva see his trial, *El Progreso* (Barcelona), July 6, September 14, 1910. See also *El Poble Català* (Barcelona), January 4 and July 6, 1910; and *La Publicidad* (Barcelona), December 21, 1909.

55. For the attack on the Hieronymite convent, see *El Correo Catalán* (Barcelona), August 13 and 31, 1909; *Las Noticias* (Barcelona), August 17, 1909; and trial of Raimundo Surroca, Francisco Albad, and Jaime Vivern, *El Progreso* (Barcelona), December 31, 1909.

56. *Las Noticias* (Barcelona), August 17, 1909. See *El Correo Catalán* (Barcelona), August 11, 1909, for a partial list of the stocks missing from the convent: included are municipal bonds and railroad and bank stocks, but not speculative or commercial stocks. See also *El Correo Catalán,* August 18, 1909. In December 1961 a young parish priest in Barcelona told me that the Hieronymite Nuns were still reputedly the wealthiest order in that city. For persons accused of selling the Hieronymites' stocks, see trial of

Rosa and José Pages, *La Publicidad* (Barcelona), September 25, 1909, and trial of Juan Cardó, *ibid.*, December 21, 1909.

57. For the attack on the school of the Franciscan Sisters, see *Las Noticias* (Barcelona), August 12, 1909, and *El Correo Catalán* (Barcelona), September 10, 1909.

58. For the attack on the parish church of Santa Madrona la Nueva, see *El Correo Catalán* (Barcelona), August 14, 1909, and *Las Noticias* (Barcelona), August 25, 1909. For the attack on the Christian Brothers' school, see *El Correo Catalán* (Barcelona), September 13, 1909. For the attack on the parish church of Santa Madrona la Antigua, see *Las Noticias* (Barcelona), August 10, 1909.

59. For the attack on the convent of the Assumptionist Sisters, see *Las Noticias* (Barcelona), August 10, 1909, and *El Correo Catalán* (Barcelona), August 16, 1909.

60. Interview with Mother Superior, *Las Noticias* (Barcelona), August 8, 1909. The Sisters of Charity denied that any goods were made by the children for commercial sale, and declared that expenses were paid by benefactors under the presidency of the Marquise of Alella, wife of an ultraconservative Catalan senator (*Las Noticias* [Barcelona], August 8 and 10, 1909). For further details on this burning, see *El Correo Catalán* (Barcelona), August 26, 1909.

61. For the attack on the school of the Sisters of the Sacred Heart, see *El Correo Catalán* (Barcelona), August 14, 1909; and "C" [Jose Comaposada], "Sucesos de Barcelona," *El Socialista* (Madrid), November 12, 1909. See also the trial of Ramón and Antonio Guralons, alleged participants, in *La Tribuna* (Barcelona), August 30, 1909. For Antonio Comallonge see *La Publicidad* (Barcelona), December 7, 1909, and *El Progreso* (Barcelona), December 8 and 22, 1909.

62. For the attack on the convent of the Arrepentidas, see *La Tribuna* and *El Liberal* (Barcelona), May 7, 1910; *El Correo Catalán* (Barcelona), August 18, 1909; *Las Noticias* (Barcelona), September 3, 1909; and Anon., *La Semana Sangrienta: Sucesos de Barcelona, Historia, descripciones, documentos, retratos, vistas, etc.* (Barcelona, n.d. [1910?]), p. 94.

63. Testimony of Mariano Bordas, *Causa: Rebelión militar*, I, 346.

64. For the attack on the Church of Santa María del Taulat, see *El Correo Catalán* (Barcelona), August 7 and September 1, 1909.

65. For the attack on the school of the Franciscan Sisters, see *El Correo Catalán* (Barcelona), September 13, 1909, and *Las Noticias* (Barcelona), August 12, 1909.

66. For the death of Father Riu, see *El Correo Catalán* (Barcelona), August 7, 1909. Rucabado, *Santa Mónica de la Rambla y otras páginas de sangre,* p. 174.

67. Trial of Francisco and Salvador Segarra, Pedro Ramón, and others, *La Tribuna* (Barcelona), May 3, 1910. For the attempt to destroy police records, see La Cierva, *Notas de mi vida,* p. 140.

68. Trial of Enriqueta Sabeter and Rosa Esteller, *La Publicidad* (Barcelona), December 3, 1910.

69. For the barricade in Clot-San Martín, see police reports in *Causa: Rebelión militar,* I, 418, 499–50. For charges against Carmen Alauch, see *ibid.,* I, 168, 213–14. The chief military advocate decided that Carmen Alauch should be prosecuted for armed rebellion, and orders were issued to gather evidence, but no disposition of her case appears in the published transcript (*ibid.,* II, 135 and 142).

70. Trial of Gregorio Baltrina, *La Publicidad* (Barcelona), December 16, 1909. For the attack on the church of San Martín, see *El Correo Catalán* (Barcelona), September 7, 1909; and Brissa, *Revolución de julio*, p. 102.

71. For the attack on the school of the Sisters of the Holy Child Jesus, see Brissa, *Revolución de julio*, pp. 91-92, and *El Correo Catalán* (Barcelona), August 29, September 20, 1909.

72. For the attack on the Franciscan residence and the killing of Father Usó, see the following: trial of Luis Alferez, his son Francisco, and Buenaventura Mateu, *La Publicidad* (Barcelona), January 26, 1910; *El País* (Madrid), January 27 and 29, 1909. See also *El Correo Catalán* (Barcelona), August 25, 1909; H. Villaescusa, *Semana Trágica*, p. 38; *La Rebeldía* (Barcelona), November 25, 1909; Rucabado, *Santa Mónica de la Rambla*, pp. 176-77; and *La Rebeldía* (Barcelona), November 25, 1909.

73. *El Poble Català* (Barcelona), July 24 and 26, 1909.

74. For the attack on the residence of the Oratorian Fathers, see *Las Noticias* (Barcelona), August 26, 1909, and *El Correo Catalán* (Barcelona), September 4, 1909.

75. *Causa: Rebelión militar*, I, 100-01, 104, 337.

76. Trial of Esteban Sala Bonnany, *La Publicidad* (Barcelona), April 5, 1910.

77. Trial of José Alvarez and accomplices, *El Poble Català* and *La Publicidad* (Barcelona), October 4, 1909; *El País* (Madrid), October 5 and 14, 1909. Trial of Ramón Ballonga, *La Publicidad*, October 11 and 13, November 4, 1909. Trial of Modesto Jaume, *ibid.*, May 8, 1910.

78. For an account of the battle in Gracia, see report by General Santiago, p. 2 of Appendix 1 to October 19, 1909, *Diario de las Cortes; Las Noticias* (Barcelona), August 4, 1909; *El Progreso* (Barcelona), July 27, 1911; and letter from cavalry officer, *Las Noticias* (Barcelona), August 21, 1909.

79. Letter from cavalry officer, *Las Noticias* (Barcelona), August 21, 1909.

80. Tato, *Sol y Ortega*, p. 478. For details of this meeting, see *Las Noticias* (Barcelona), August 2, 1909; *La Veu de Catalunya* (Barcelona), August 8, 1909; Juan Ventosa, Lliga deputy, April 8, 1911, *Diario de las Cortes*, II, 666; declaration of Trinidad Monegal, Nationalist Republican councilor, *Causa: Rebelión militar*, I, 456-57, and declaration of Narciso Verdaguer, *ibid.*, I, 462.

81. Reported by Pedro Milá Camps, Lliga deputy, April 8, 1911, *Diario de las Cortes*, II, 666.

82. Declaration of Trinidad Monegal, *Causa: Rebelión militar*, I, 457.

83. Letter from Fabra Rivas to *El Diluvio* (Barcelona), August 13, 1911.

84. The account of the role of cutting off food supplies in rebel planning has been pieced together from sources cited in note 80, *supra*, and from the following: testimony of Emiliano Iglesias, *Causa: Rebelión militar*, I, 36; Navarro, *Historia crítica*, p. 284; Emiliano Iglesias, "Detalles inéditos," *El Progreso* (Barcelona), July 26, 1912; and *ibid.*, August 13, 1911.

85. Article by Enrique Tubau, Radical party official, *El Progreso* (Barcelona), July 26 and 27, 1914. For the events that occurred in the plaza outside the city hall before and during the Council session, see *Las Noticias* (Barcelona), August 12, 1909; letter from Enrique Pujol and Ramón Homedes, *ibid.*, August 8, 1910; and trial of José Pérez Rosas and Marcelino Saavedra Fernández in *La Publicidad* (Barcelona), October

11, 1909. For the Radicals' attempts to organize the City Council as a revolutionary junta, or convention, see letter to Maragall from José Pijoan, July 31, 1909, as quoted in Benet, *Maragall i la Setmana Tràgica,* p. 64, and Lliga Deputy Francisco Cambó, speaking in the Cortes on November 20, 1916, as quoted in Sangro, *Sombra de Ferrer,* pp. 21-22; and Magin Vidal [Fabra Rivas], "En pleine Révolution," *L'Humanité* (Paris), August 15, 1909.

86. *La Forja* (Barcelona), July 30, 1910.

87. For Coll y Pujol's remark, see the official minutes, July 27, 1909, in "Actas del Ayuntamiento," (Barcelona), IV, folio 208. For the report of the entire session see *ibid.,* folios 207-13. See also the account in *Las Noticias* (Barcelona), August 2 and 12, 1909, and *El Correo Catalán* (Barcelona), August 4 and 21, 1909.

88. *El Progreso* (Barcelona), August 6 and 8, 1910.

89. Letter from Fabra Rivas to *El Diluvio* (Barcelona), August 13, 1911. For the events of late Tuesday night, see also the interview with Magin Vidal [Fabra Rivas], published *ibid.,* August 5, 1910. *El Progreso* (Barcelona), August 6 and 8, 1910, and August 13, 1911.

90. Letter from Fabra Rivas to *El Diluvio* (Barcelona), August 13, 1911.

91. "De la Revolución de julio," *El Progreso* (Barcelona), August 6, 1910. See also letter from Enrique Pujol and Ramón Homedes, *ibid.,* August 8, 1910.

92. For the meeting late Tuesday evening of the Catalan republican deputies, see Salvatella, April 5, 1911, *Diario de las Cortes,* II, 551-52, and Ametlla, *Memòries polítiques,* pp. 269-70.

93. Hurtado, *Quaranta Anys d'advocat,* I, 155.

94. The words of Fabra Rivas and of Carner are quoted from the account in Ametlla, *Memòries polítiques,* pp. 269-70. See also, for the same idea, Salvatella, April 5, 1911, *Diario de las Cortes,* II, 551.

95. Hurtado, *Quaranta Anys d'advocat,* I, 155.

96. Salvatella, April 5, 1911, *Diario de las Cortes,* II, 551-52. For a bitter commentary on the failure of the deputies to be "truly heroic" during this week, see letter to Maragall from José Pijoan quoted in Benet, *Maragall i la Setmana Tràgica,* p. 64.

97. Interview with Magin Vidal [Fabra Rivas], published in *El Diluvio* (Barcelona), August 5, 1910. Fabra Rivas said he was not free to reveal the name of the "eminent person." From the account in Ametlla it seems quite probable that the person was Carner. In a letter to the author from Ametlla (June 6, 1966), Ametlla agreed that it was quite probably Carner, given the "great respect" Fabra Rivas had for him. See also the article by Mariano Garcia Cortes, of the National Committee of the Socialist party, referring to contacts between Fabra Rivas and "various republican deputies of the Nationalist group," in *España Nueva* (Madrid), November 2, 1909.

98. On the plans for a national general strike, see Pablo Iglesias, July 12, 1910, *Diario de las Cortes,* III, 550, and July 7, 1910, *ibid.,* 436-37. Juan de La Cierva, July 8, 1910, *ibid.,* II, 462-63; *El Socialista* (Madrid), July 30, 1909; Magin Vidal [Fabra Rivas], "Vue d'ensemble," *L'Humanité* (Paris), August 16, 1909; speech by Pablo Iglesias in Bilbao, as reported in *El Progreso* (Barcelona), July 25, 1911; Morató, *Iglesias,* p. 183; and Garcia Venero, *Las Internacionales,* I, 450.

99. Report by police inspector Moíses Zapatero, *Causa: Rebelión militar,* I, 24.

100. Magin Vidal [Fabra Rivas], "En pleine Révolution," *L'Humanité* (Paris), August 15, 1909. Fabra Rivas told Joaquín Maurín that he was the "man in the straw hat," reported as having been seen everywhere in Barcelona on Tuesday night and popularly identified as Francisco Ferrer (interview with Maurín in New York City, on March 16, 1963).

101. *Las Noticias* (Barcelona), August 16, 1909.

102. For the defense of the Adorer convent-school, see "Carta-Relación de la Rdma. M. Corazón de Jesús, Superiora de esta casa, a la Rdma. Madre Superiora General," *Crónica de la Casa de Barcelona. Instituto Esclavas del Santísimo Sacramento y de la Caridad* (mimeograph), I, 160–76. *El Correo Catalán* (Barcelona), August 7 and 12, 1909; *El Progreso* (Barcelona), September 1, October 9, 1911; Albó, *Barcelona, Caritativa*, I, 84–86; and *Las Noticias* (Barcelona), August 2, September 1, 1909.

103. For the attack on the convent of the Sisters Magdalenes, see *Las Noticias* (Barcelona), August 2 and 6, 1909, and *El Correo Catalán* (Barcelona), August 11, 1909.

104. For the attack on the convent of the Servants of Mary, see *El Correo Catalán* (Barcelona), August 7 and September 8, 1909; and testimony of José Llorens, *Causa: Rebelión militar*, I, 450–51.

105. Brissa, *Revolución de julio*, p. 115. See also *El Correo Catalán* (Barcelona), August 30, 1909.

106. For the attack on the residence of the Capuchin Friars, see *El Correo Catalán* (Barcelona), September 5, 1909; and Brissa, *Revolución de julio*, pp. 43–44, 96–97. For background on this order, see Severino Aznar, *Las grandes Instituciones del catolicismo: Ordenes monásticas, institutos misioneros* (Madrid, 1912), pp. 255–60.

107. For the attack on the residence of the Camillian Priests, see *El Correo Catalán* (Barcelona), August 2 and September 6, 1909, and Brissa, *Revolución de julio*, pp. 43, 47, 135.

108. For the attack on the Church of San Francisco de Paula, see García Venero, *Nacionalismo catalán*, p. 572, and *El Correo Catalán* (Barcelona), August 2, 1909.

109. For the attack on the Chapel of Marcus, see *El Correo Catalán* (Barcelona), August 30 and September 19, 1909.

110. For the attack on the Church of San Cucufate, see Brissa, *Revolución de julio*, pp. 54, 122–23; Albó, *Barcelona: Caritativa*, II, 121–22; and *El Correo Catalán* (Barcelona), August 4, 19, and 29, 1909.

111. For the attack on the Church of San Pedro de las Puellas, see *El Correo Catalán* (Barcelona), August 17 and 21, 1909; *Las Noticias* (Barcelona), August 9, 1909; Pedro Llosas, Carlist deputy, July 14, 1910, *Diario de las Cortes*, III, 614; and Albó, *Barcelona: Caritativa*, II, 120–21.

112. *El Correo Catalán* (Barcelona), September 3, 1909.

113. Captain José Roca Navarra, defense lawyer for Luis Zurdo Olivares, in *Causa: Rebelión militar*, II, 284–85. See also letter to Maragall from José Pijoan, July 31, 1909, quoted in Benet, *Maragall i la Setmana Tràgica*, p. 63.

114. Magin Vidal [Fabra Rivas], "Réponse a des calomnies," *L'Humanité* (Paris), August 18, 1909.

115. Anon., *Semana Sangrienta*, p. 137. For the attack on the Vincentians' residence, see *ibid.*, 135–37, and *El Correo Catalán* (Barcelona), September 3 and 5, 1909.

116. For the attack on the Montesión convent, see *El Correo Catalán* (Barcelona), August 20 and 24, 1909. For the attack on the residence of the Sacred Heart Priests, see *ibid.*, August 13 and 20, 1909.

117. For the attack on the school of the Conceptionist Sisters, see *Las Noticias* (Barcelona), August 16, 1909. For Bonet's participation, see *Causa: Rebelión militar*, I, 469, 471-73. Trial of Bonet, Fabregas, and the Torrents brothers, *La Rebeldía* (Barcelona), May 6, 1910; *Tierra y Libertad* (Barcelona), October 13, 1910; and *El Liberal* and *La Tribuna* (Barcelona), May 3 and 4, 1910.

118. For the attack on the convent-school of the Beatas Dominicas, see *El Correo Catalán* (Barcelona), August 29, 1909; *Las Noticias* (Barcelona), August 21, 1909; and Brissa, *Revolución de julio,* p. 68.

119. *Las Noticias* (Barcelona), August 7, 1909. See also protest of the Gremi de Profesors particulars de Catalunya about this fact in *El Correo Catalán* (Barcelona), August 11, 1909.

120. Sol y Ortega, April 8, 1911, *Diario de las Cortes,* II, 663. See also report by General Santiago, p. 3 of Appendix 1 to October 19, 1909, *Diario de las Cortes.* Ten years earlier, the Marquis of Comillas had personally directed the defense of the Jesuit residence against an attack by a group of workers (Eduardo F. Regatillo, S.J., *Un Marqués modelo: El Siervo de Díos, Claudio López Bru, el segundo marqués de Comillas* [Santander, 1950], pp. 199-200).

121. Canals, *Sucesos de 1909,* II, 304-05. On Sol's involvement see also Soldevilla, *Año político,* XV: *1909,* 375, and XVI: *1910,* 21-22. See also letter from N.O.B.: *Causa: Rebelión militar,* I, 166-67.

122. For the attack on the Jesuit residence, see *Causa: Rebelión militar,* I, 508-13; II, 64-65, 66-68, 71-72; *Las Noticias* (Barcelona), August 3, 1909. Brissa, *Revolución de julio,* pp. 48-50; Sol y Ortega, April 8, 1911, *Diario de las Cortes,* II, 663; and Orts-Ramos, *Historia de la revolución española,* p. 431.

123. Testimony of Angela Santiago, *Causa: Rebelión militar,* I, 414-15. She said the incident occurred Monday night; Juana Ardiaca, who admitted making the statement, said it occurred on Tuesday night (*ibid.,* I, 417-18). For further testimony, see *ibid.,* I, 414-21; 425-30, 438-39; II, 151-53, 169, 294-95.

124. For the attack on the Church of San Pedro el Pescador, see *El Correo Catalán* (Barcelona), September 11, 1909. For Father Barguño's work, see Albó, *Barcelona: Caritativa,* II, 81-82.

125. *El Correo Catalán* (Barcelona), August 28, 1909. For the attack on the asylum of the Sisters of Charity, see also Brissa, *Revolución de julio,* pp. 92-93, and Anon., *Semana Sangrienta,* pp. 81-82. For the work of these sisters see Albó, *Barcelona: Caritativa,* I, 13-17.

126. Trial of Antonio Eudaldo Plácido, *La Publicidad* (Barcelona), October 23, 1909. For the attack on the convent-school of the Piarist Sisters, see *El Correo Catalán* (Barcelona), September 19, 1909.

127. Trial of Rafael Climent and others: *El Progreso* (Barcelona), October 4 and 5, 1910. For the attack on the residence of the Minims, see also *El Correo Catalán* (Barcelona), September 9, 1909.

128. For the attack on the Church of San Juan Bautista, see *El Correo Catalán* (Bar-

celona), August 28, 1909, and *Las Noticias* (Barcelona), August 9, 1909. For the attack on the convent-school of the Discalced Carmelites, see *El Correo Catalán,* August 23, 1909, and Brissa, *Revolución de julio,* p. 103. For the attack on residence of the Oratorians see *El Correo Catalán* (Barcelona), September 4, 1909.

129. For the attack on the Paulist Sisters' asylum, see *El Correo Catalán* (Barcelona), September 12, 1909.

130. For the attack on the school of the Sons of the Holy Family, see *Las Noticias* (Barcelona), August 15, 1909; trial of Juan Carnicer and Ramón Pérez, *La Publicidad* (Barcelona), September 21, 1909.

131. For the attack on the school of the Sisters of the Holy Family, see *La Publicidad* (Barcelona), January 30, 1909; *El Correo Catalán* (Barcelona), August 4 and 17, 1909; and *Las Noticias* (Barcelona), August 4 and 15, 1909.

132. For Luis Alferez, see *Causa: Rebelión militar,* I, 255-56; *El País* (Madrid), January 27 and 29, 1910; and *La Publicidad* (Barcelona), January 26, 1910.

133. *Las Noticias* (Barcelona), August 11, 1909. For the attack on the convent of the Capuchin Nuns, see also *El Correo Catalán* (Barcelona), August 4, 15, and 23, 1909. For the trial of Francisca Norat and others (defended by Radical extremist lawyers Rafael Guerra del Río, Puig de Asprer, and José Ulled), see *El Progreso* (Barcelona), November 16 and 17 and December 31, 1910; also *La Tribuna* (Barcelona), November 15, 1910. An indignant Barcelona resident cites this case as the most flagrant example of the exoneration of persons accused of serious crimes, in *El País* (Madrid), November 19, 1910.

Wednesday, July 28

1. The calculation that 30,000 men, women, and children participated in the rebellion is from Frollo [López Rodríguez], *En Cataluña,* p. 13.

2. For the tacitly agreed upon, early morning truce, see Gaziel [Calvet], *Tots els Camins,* p. 328 and Hurtado, *Quaranta Anys d'advocat,* I, 157. For the early morning activities, see "Versión acordada," *Las Noticias* (Barcelona), August 2, 1909, and *El Progreso* (Barcelona), July 28, 1911.

3. Report by General Santiago, p. 4 of Appendix 1 to October 19, 1909, *Diario de las Cortes.*

4. Magin Vidal [Fabra Rivas], "En pleine Révolution," *L'Humanité* (Paris), August 15, 1909.

5. Interview with Alberto Pérez Baro, in Pueblo Nuevo (Barcelona), on July 28, 1960.

6. For the text of this proclamation, see *El Correo Catalán* (Barcelona), August 2, 1909.

7. Magin Vidal [Fabra Rivas], "En pleine Révolution," *L'Humanité* (Paris), August 15, 1909, and "Vue d'ensemble," *ibid.,* August 16, 1909.

8. Magin Vidal [Fabra Rivas], "Vue d'ensemble," *L'Humanité* (Paris), August 16, 1909.

9. The Radical party had been planning an elaborate welcome (testimony of

Hermenegildo Giner de los Ríos, *Causa: Rebelión militar*, I, 104-05). For details of Lerroux' voyage home, see Lerroux, *Mis Memorias*, pp. 318-22.

10. Letter from José Pijoan to Juan Maragall, July 31, 1909, as quoted in Benet, *Maragall i la Setmana Tràgica*, p. 63.

11. Trial of Mariano Portoles, *La Publicidad* (Barcelona), November 3, 1909. For other armed men arrested on Wednesday afternoon, see trial of Francisco Ortega, *ibid.*, October 12, 1909; Augusto García Moret, *ibid.*, October 14, 1909; Juan Martí Parés, *ibid.*, October 16, 1909; Amadeo Minguell Mas, *ibid.*, October 18, 1909; Eugenio Casado Bargalló, *ibid.*, October 25, 1909; Manuel Ribas Pla, *ibid.*, October 25, 1909; José Salvador Alvarez, *ibid.*, October 26, 1909; and Pedro Guardiola Carbó, *ibid.*, October 28, 1909. For the opinion that a small group of marauders was able to maintain the tension, because the streets were empty of peaceful citizens, see Eusebio Corominas, July 13, 1910, *Diario de las Cortes*, III, 582-83.

12. Report by General Santiago, p. 4 of Appendix 1 to October 19, 1909, *Diario de las Cortes*. On the meeting of the Consuls, see also Brissa, *Revolución de julio*, p. 71; *España Nueva* (Madrid), August 12, 1909; and Soldevilla, *Año político*, XV: *1909*, 272.

13. Trial of Esteban Roig, *La Publicidad* (Barcelona), October 25, 1909. On Roig see also *El País* (Madrid), October 26 and 30, 1909.

14. Report by General Santiago, p. 3 of Appendix 1 to October 19, 1909, *Diario de las Cortes*.

15. For the fighting on these barricades, see report by General Santiago, p. 3 of Appendix 1 to October 19, 1909, *Diario de las Cortes*. For Josefa Prieto and Encarnación Avellaneda, see report of Police Inspector Bravo Portillo, *Causa: Rebelión militar*, I, 20-21; trial of Prieto, Avellaneda, Domingo Ruíz, and Rafael Fernández, *La Publicidad* (Barcelona), October 30, 1909. Rafael Fernández was tried separately for the burning of the Church of San Pablo (*El Progreso* [Barcelona], December 16 and 17, 1909); he was defended by Radical officials Guerra del Rió and Ulled.

16. Official estimate of damages by a municipal official, *La Publicidad* (Barcelona), November 4, 1909.

17. For Eugenio del Hoyo, see *El Correo Catalán* (Barcelona), August 26, 1909; *El País* (Madrid), August 28, September 6 and 9, 1909; *El Progreso* (Barcelona), September 13, 1910; Brissa, *Revolución de julio*, pp. 163, 206; Soldevilla, *Año político*, XV: *1909*, 315; and Emiliano Iglesias, April 5, 1911, *Diario de las Cortes*, II, 569.

18. For the case of Lieutenant Izquierdo, see *La Publicidad* (Barcelona), August 25, 1909. For the case of Tomás Rodríguez, see *ibid.*, August 26, 1909; also *El Correo Catalán* (Barcelona), August 28, 1909, and *El País* (Madrid), August 29 and September 25, 1909.

19. For the low salaries, and the police complaint about this, see *El Progreso* (Barcelona), July 23, 1909.

20. Trial of Santiago Guillén, *La Publicidad* (Barcelona), October 13, 1909, and *El País* (Madrid), October 14, 1909. See also the case of Sinforiano Sánchez, *ibid.*, October 8 and 10, 1909; *La Publicidad*, August 25, October 7, 1909; and *El Correo Catalán* (Barcelona), August 26, 1909.

21. Letter from Manuel Carrillo, *El Progreso* (Barcelona), September 13, 1910.

See also *El País* (Madrid), October 22, 1909, and *La Publicidad* (Barcelona), August 25, 1909.

22. "C" [José Comaposada] "Sucesos de Barcelona," *El Socialista* (Madrid), November 26, 1909.

23. Report by General Santiago, pp. 3 and 4 of Appendix 1 to October 19, 1909, *Diario de las Cortes*. For the attack on the Veterans' headquarters, see *Las Noticias* (Barcelona), August 7 and 14, 1909.

24. For José Ginés Perea, see *La Internacional* (Barcelona), January 1, 1909. For reports of his trial see *La Publicidad* (Barcelona), October 4 and 20, 1909; Bonafulla [Esteve], *Revolución de julio*, p. 224, and V. Moreno, "Por la Verdad," *El País* (Madrid), November 2, 1909. For the trial of Ginés, Natividad Rufo, Concha Ortíz, Inocencio Emperador, Carlos Pasalamar, and Eugenia Ruíz, see *La Publicidad* (Barcelona), October 4 and 5, 1909, and *El País* (Madrid), September 22 and October 4, 6, and 8, 1909.

25. *El País* (Madrid), October 8, 1909. For Natividad Rufo Sánchez, see *ibid.*, October 6, 1909; V. Moreno, "Por la Verdad," *ibid.*, November 2, 1909; and *La Publicidad* (Barcelona), October 5, 1909.

26. For a remarkably candid account of the assault, see Manuel Andrés (a "white collar" Radical party member who participated in the assault), in *El Progreso* (Barcelona), July 26, 1913. This account is the source of quotations in the paragraphs describing this assault and the attack on the police station. For a glorified account, see "C" [Comaposada], "Sucesos de Barcelona," *El Socialista* (Madrid), November 26, 1909.

27. For a photograph of the men marching with the captured rifles on their shoulders, see Navarro, *Historia crítica*, p. 110.

28. Report by General Santiago, p. 3 of Appendix 1 to October 19, 1909, *Diario de las Cortes*. After the Tragic Week, the Maura government dissolved the organization of the Veteranos de la Libertad throughout the country in order to prevent a recurrence of this incident: *El Correo Catalán* (Barcelona), August 29 and 31, 1909.

29. "C" [Comaposada], "Sucesos de Barcelona," *El Socialista* (Madrid), November 26, 1909.

30. Report by General Santiago, p. 3 of Appendix 1 to October 19, 1909, *Diario de las Cortes*.

31. For the attack on the school of the Claretians, see *El Correo Catalán* (Barcelona), August 2, 17, 23, and 28, 1909, and Brissa, *Revolución de julio*, pp. 129–30. For background on the Claretians, see Aznar, *Grandes Instituciones del Catolicismo*, pp. 191, 357–58, 361, 368.

32. For the attack on the school of the Teresian Sisters, see *El Correo Catalán* (Barcelona), August 7 and 24, 1909.

33. *Las Noticias* (Barcelona), August 24, 1909.

34. For the attack on the Seminary, see *El Correo Catalán* (Barcelona), September 5, 1909. Anon., *Semana Sangrienta*, pp. 89–90. For the Ulled brothers' alleged participation, see *Causa: Rebelión militar*, II, 154. For Ardid's alleged participation, *El País* (Madrid), September 25, 1909.

35. Emiliano Iglesias, July 6, 1910, *Diario de las Cortes,* II, 407. For details of this incident, see also Dalmacio Iglesias, Carlist deputy, *ibid.,* II, 422; interview in France with unidentified socialist exile, *El País* (Madrid), August 13, 1909; "C" [Comaposada], "Sucesos de Barcelona," *El Socialista* (Madrid), December 3, 1909; Magin Vidal [Fabra Rivas], "Réponse a des calomnies," *L'Humanité* (Paris), August 19, 1909; and H. Villaescusa, *Semana Trágica,* p. 25.

36. From the account of *El País* (Madrid), October 2, 1909. For Ramón Clemente Garcia's activities, see also *Solidaridad Obrera* (Barcelona), January 11, 1917, and *El País* (Madrid), September 8 and 15, 1909.

37. For the attack on the residence of the Salesian Priests, see *Las Noticias* (Barcelona), August 24, 1909, and *El Correo Catalán* (Barcelona), August 30, 1909.

38. For the attack on the school of the Salesian Sisters, see *Las Noticias* (Barcelona), August 26, 1909; *El Correo Catalán* (Barcelona), September 17, 1909.

39. For the attack on the orphanage of the Sisters of the Holy Family of Bordeaux, see *El Correo Catalán* (Barcelona), August 29, 1909.

40. For the attack on the convent of Santa María de Valdoncella, see *El Correo Catalán* (Barcelona), September 1, 1909; *Las Noticias* (Barcelona), August 5, 1909; *El País* (Madrid), August 8, 1909; and Brissa, *Revolución de julio,* p. 146. For Manuel Santamaría and the nuns, see *Causa: Rebelión militar,* II, 9.

41. For the attack on the monastery of Nuestra Señora de Jerusalén, see *El Correo Catalán* (Barcelona), September 16, 1909. The monastery is also called Santa María de Jerusalén, and on one occasion San Juan de Jerusalén (*ibid.,* August 29, 1909).

42. Report by General Santiago, pp. 4 and 5 of Appendix 1 to October 19, 1909, *Diario de las Cortes.*

43. *El Correo Catalán* (Barcelona), August 28, 1909.

44. For the attack on the workers' circle in Clot, see *Las Noticias* (Barcelona), September 4, 1909, and Anon., *Semana Sangrienta,* pp. 97–99. For a description of the circle and its activities see Albó, *Barcelona: Caritativa,* II, 29–35.

45. *La Tribuna* (Barcelona), February 12, 1910.

46. For a description of Luis Zurdo's activities, see testimony of Luis Plaguina, *Causa: Rebelión militar,* I, 408–09, and testimony of Luis Zurdo Olivares, *ibid.,* I, 440–43. See also *ibid.,* I, 332–33. Joaquín Maurín recalls that Zurdo Olivares was described in Barcelona labor circles as "el del quema de los conventos" (interview in New York City on March 16, 1963). Zurdo had been prosecuted for antiwar articles which appeared in *El Progreso,* on July 13 and 19, 1909; for details see report in *La Publicidad* (Barcelona), October 26, 1909. For Zurdo's antiwar speeches during the month of July, see *Causa: Rebelión militar,* I, 74, 80, and 87.

47. Report by a police official, *Causa: Rebelión militar,* II, 23.

48. Testimony of Joaquín Beltri, *ibid.,* I, 394.

49. Testimony of Emilio Escoda, *ibid.,* II, 62–63.

50. The account of the attack on the residence of the Marist Brothers is based on the following: interview with Marist Brother Adaulfo Abaurrea, in Barcelona on October 31, 1961; *El Correo Catalán* (Barcelona), August 12, 1909; *Las Noticias* (Barcelona), August 19, 1909; and Anon., *Semana Sangrienta,* pp. 68–73.

51. Interview with an elderly priest of the Congregation of the Fathers of the Sacred Heart, in their residence in San Andrés (Barcelona), on October 24, 1961. Brissa also reports shots were fired from the Marist residence, in *Revolución de julio,* p. 86.

52. For early developments in San Andrés, see *El Progreso* (Barcelona), September 28 and 29, 1909; *El País* (Madrid), September 2, 1909; and *Las Noticias* (Barcelona), August 25, 1909.

53. *El Correo Catalán* (Barcelona), August 24, 1909.

54. Account by Pedro Corominas, writing in *El Poble Català* (Barcelona), April 29, 1911. For José Miquel Baró's activities on Wednesday afternoon, see *El Progreso* (Barcelona), September 28 and 29, 1909; *El Correo Catalán* and *Las Noticias* (Barcelona), August 24, 1909; and La Cierva, *Case of Ferrer,* pp. 94–95. For background on Miquel Baró and his political affiliation, see *El País* (Madrid), August 23, 1909; *Las Noticias* (Barcelona), August 21, 1909; and Brissa, *Revolución de julio,* pp. 163, 202–04. For the burning of the Church of San Andrés (for which 8 men were tried), and the burning of the Marist residence (for which 4 men were tried), see the detailed reporting of the group trial in *El Progreso* (Barcelona), September 27–30, 1909.

55. For the attack on the school of the Christian Brothers, see *El Correo Catalán* (Barcelona), September 20, 1909, and trial of José Llansá, *El Progreso* (Barcelona), August 10, 1910.

56. For the episode of the hospital, see interview with Prior Lorenzo González, *Las Noticias* (Barcelona), August 7, 1909. The Prior did not tell exactly the same story to military authorities, in *Causa: Rebelión militar,* I, 170–71; however, his interview in *Las Noticias* is corroborated by a letter from Friar Andrés Ayucar in *El País* (Madrid), August 8, 1909.

57. Letter from Friar Andrés Ayucar in *El País* (Madrid), August 8, 1909.

58. Letter to Maragall from José Pijoan, July 31, 1909, as quoted in Benet, *Maragall i la Setmana Tràgica,* p. 64.

59. Article by Emiliano Iglesias in *Solidaridad Obrera* (Barcelona), January 12, 1917. For the laxative, see testimony of Iglesias, *Causa: Rebelión militar,* I, 36.

60. The expression, "el heroe de la purga," appears in a letter from Fabra Rivas to *El Diluvio* (Barcelona), August 13, 1911. For opponents' sarcasm that Iglesias' fear was so great that it led to excretory problems, see *Solidaridad Obrera* (Barcelona), January 15, 1917; *La Forja* (Barcelona), July 30, 1910; socialist Mariano García Cortés, quoted in *La Metralla* (Barcelona), January 21, 1911; and Ricardo Soriano, March 29, 1911, *Diario de las Cortes,* II, 457.

61. Barcelona Police Inspector Ferreiro declared that the Radicals were responsible for extending the protest throughout Catalonia (*Causa: Rebelión militar,* I, 119), and the official Radical party history acknowledges its role (Navarro, *Historia crítica,* p. 284).

62. *El Progreso* (Barcelona), August 13, 1911.

63. *Ibid.,* August 13, 1911, and July 26, 1912.

64. *Solidaridad Obrera* (Barcelona), January 15, 1917. See also testimony of Emiliano Iglesias, *Causa: Rebelión militar,* I, 36.

65. Letter from Ferrer in prison to Charles Malato in Paris, dated October 1, 1909, reprinted in Comité de Défense, *Martyr des prêtres,* p. 55. For a version of the events

in Masnou and Premiá based primarily on Ferrer's letters, see *ibid.*, pp. 35–47, and *Causa contra Ferrer*, pp. 57–58, 189–93, 407–08. See his confrontations with his accusers, *ibid.*, pp. 453–60. See also Sol Ferrer, *Véritable Ferrer*, pp. 186–89, and *Ferrer: Martyr*, pp. 139–40.

66. Testimony of Juan Puig Ventura, "El Llarch," *Causa contra Ferrer*, p. 30. Authorities charged Puig as well as Ferrer with being the "authors" of the rebellion in Premiá and Masnou, but dismissed the charges against Puig after he testified against Ferrer (*ibid.*, pp. 29–32, 89–91, 105–18).

67. Declaration of Lieutenant Colonel Leoncio Ponte Llerandi of the Civil Guards, *Causa contra Ferrer*, p. 34.

68. Declaration of Juan Alsina, *ibid.*, pp. 91, 284.

69. Testimony of the waiter, Francisco Calvet, *ibid.*, p. 98. Sol Ferrer, *Ferrer: Martyr*, pp. 139–40.

70. Testimony of Juan Puig, *Causa contra Ferrer*, p. 32. Brief prepared by officer defending Ferrer, Captain Francisco Galcerán Ferrer, *ibid.*, pp. 617–18.

71. Sol Ferrer, *Véritable Ferrer*, p. 189.

72. Testimony of Domingo Casas, Mayor of Premiá, *Causa contra Ferrer*, pp. 35–36, 86–88, 121–24, 155–56, 306–15.

73. For the activities of Leopoldo Iglesias, see *ibid.*, pp. 25–26, 124, 162, 263–70, 473.

74. Testimony of Esteban Puigdemont, *ibid.*, p. 473. For further charges of Ferrer's direction of Leopoldo Iglesias, see *ibid.*, pp. 25, 91, 123, 366, 587.

75. Declaration of Juan Alsina, *ibid.*, p. 91.

76. *Ibid.*, pp. 123, 135, 267.

77. For events outside Catalonia, see Soldevilla, *Año político*, XV: *1909*, 268–69; Magin Vidal [Fabra Rivas], "Vue d'ensemble," *L'Humanité* (Paris), August 16, 1909; and "Hace un año," *La Publicidad* (Barcelona), July 26, 1910.

78. *El Correo Catalán* (Barcelona), July 29, 1911.

79. La Cierva, *Notas de mi vida*, p. 142. Concerning events in Valencia see also Magin Vidal [Fabra Rivas], "Vue d'ensemble," *L'Humanité* (Paris), August 16, 1909, and Navarro, *Historia crítica*, p. 284.

80. For La Cierva's statement to newsmen see Soldevilla, *Año político*, XV: *1909*, 267. See also La Cierva, July 8, 1910, *Diario de las Cortes*, II, 462–66.

81. *España Nueva* (Madrid), July 29, 1909. For Nougués' letter summoning republican deputies see *Las Noticias* (Barcelona), July 26, 1909.

82. Letter to Belgian socialist Clerbaut, from Pablo Iglesias, dated August 17, 1909, published in *Le Peuple* of Brussels on August 22, 1909, and reprinted in Canals, *Sucesos de 1909*, I, 176–77.

83. "El Partido Socialista en 1909," *El Socialista* (Madrid), December 31, 1909.

84. For La Cierva's success in preventing a national general strike, see Pablo Iglesias, July 7, 1910, *Diario de las Cortes*, II, 435 and *ibid.*, pp. 434–37; Juan de la Cierva, July 8, 1910, *ibid.*, II, 461–62; Pablo Iglesias, July 7, 1910, *ibid.*, II, 435–36, and July 12, 1910, *ibid.*, III, 550–52; *El País* (Madrid), July 30, 1910; and La Cierva, *Notas de mi Vida*, p. 142.

85. Magin Vidal [Fabra Rivas], "Vue d'ensemble," *L'Humanité* (Paris), August 16, 1909.

86. Ametlla, *Memòries polítiques,* p. 270.

87. *El Progreso* (Barcelona), August 13, 1909; "Detalles inéditos," *ibid.,* July 26, 1912.

88. *El Poble Català* (Barcelona), July 31, 1911.

89. Emiliano Iglesias, April 5, 1911, *Diario de las Cortes,* II, 565. See also E. Iglesias' commentary on a speech by socialist leader Pablo Iglesias, *El Progreso* (Barcelona), July 25, 1911. Moreno first accused Fabra Rivas of treachery in his article, "Por la Verdad," *El País* (Madrid), November 2, 1909; he claimed that the socialist had exalted his role through the articles in *L'Humanité* and had defamed the Radicals. Fabra Rivas demanded a hearing before a joint meeting of anarchists and socialists in the Paris offices of *La Guerre Sociale.* For a general account of the meeting, see *El Socialista* (Madrid), November 19, 1909; *El País* (Madrid), November 21, 1909; and letter from Fabra Rivas to *La Publicidad* (Barcelona), December 2, 1909.

90. Testimony of Emiliano Iglesias, *Causa: Rebelión militar,* I, 100.

91. Francisco Colldeforns identified him as "alma de la Casa del Pueblo, redactor jefe de La Rebeldía" (*El Siglo Futuro* [Madrid], as reprinted in *El Correo Catalán* [Barcelona], August 13, 1909). Just a few weeks earlier, the Radical newspaper had identified Juan Colominas as the "director," that is, managing editor of the youth movement's *La Rebeldía* (*El Progreso* [Barcelona], July 23, 1909).

92. Ametlla, *Memóries polítiques,* p. 271. See also Gaziel [Calvet], *Tots els Camins,* p. 331, and Dalmacio Iglesias, July 6, 1910, *Diario de las Cortes,* II, 420–21.

93. Eusebio Corominas, July 13, 1910, *ibid.,* III, 582.

94. See for example, anarchist Bonafulla [Esteve], *Revolución de julio,* p. 33, and "C" [Composada], "Sucesos de Barcelona," *El Socialista* (Madrid), November 26, 1909.

Thursday, July 29

1. For events on Thursday morning, see Bonafulla [Esteve], *Revolución de julio,* p. 31; *Las Noticias* (Barcelona), August 2, 1909; report by General Santiago, pp. 4–5 of Appendix 1 to October 19, 1909, *Diario de las Cortes;* and *El Correo Catalán* (Barcelona), August 2, 1909.

2. For the Aragonese sniper, see *El Progreso* (Barcelona), July 29, 1911, and Brissa, *Revolución de julio,* p. 74.

3. Bonafulla [Esteve], *Revolución de julio,* p. 33.

4. For the importance given to the destruction of this liqueur factory, belonging to a Carlist, see interview with Sol y Ortega, *El País* (Madrid), August 4, 1909; Magin Vidal [Fabra Rivas], "Réponse a des calomnies," *L'Humanité* (Paris), August 18, 1909; Shaw, *Spain from Within,* pp. 165–67.

5. From the account in *El Progreso* (Barcelona), July 29, 1911. See also *ibid.,* August 2, 1909. For the trial of Domingo Ferrer March, see *La Publicidad* (Barcelona), November 17, 1909; see also *El Progreso* (Barcelona), July 20, 1910. Factory owner Antonio Tortrás denied that there was a passageway to the Piarist school; when antagonism continued in the neighborhood, he asked for an official inspection to disprove the rumor (*El Correo Catalán* [Barcelona], August 15, 1909).

6. Magin Vidal [Fabra Rivas], "Vue d'ensemble," *L'Humanité* (Paris), August 16,

1909. For details of the troop reinforcements see report by General Santiago, p. 4 of Appendix 1 to October 19, 1909, *Diario de las Cortes.* See also Brissa, *Revolución de julio,* pp. 58–60; *El País* (Madrid), August 6, 1909; and "C" [José Comaposada], "Sucesos de Barcelona," *El Socialista* (Madrid), November 26, 1909.

7. *El Progreso* (Barcelona), July 29, 1911.

8. *El Progreso* (Barcelona), August 13, 1911. See also V. Moreno, "Por la Verdad," *El País* (Madrid), November 2, 1909.

9. Navarro, *Historia crítica,* p. 284.

10. For activity in Manresa and Igualada, see Brissa, *Revolución de julio,* pp. 175–94 passim; Canals, *Sucesos de 1909,* 1, 167–69; report by General Santiago, p. 14 of Appendix 1 to October 19, 1909, *Diario de las Cortes;* and Ossorio, *Julio de 1909,* pp. 52–53.

11. Trial of Juan Castells, *La Publicidad* (Barcelona), September 20, 1909. *El Correo Catalán* (Barcelona), September 21, 1909.

12. Trial of Ramón Caballé, *La Publicidad* (Barcelona), September 21, 1909. See also *El Progreso* (Barcelona), July 16 and 20, 1910, and February 23, 1911.

13. Trial of Victoriano Segués, *El País* (Madrid), September 23, 25, 27, and 28, 1909.

14. For events in Pueblo Nuevo on Thursday, see *Las Noticias* (Barcelona), August 3, 1909, and report by General Santiago, p. 5 of Appendix 1 to October 19, 1909, *Diario de las Cortes.*

15. For events in the Atarazana district, and for General Santiago's strategy, see his report, p. 5 of Appendix 1 to October 19, 1909, *Diario de las Cortes.*

16. Bonafulla [Esteve], *Revolución de julio,* p. 32.

17. "De la Revolución de julio," *El Progreso* (Barcelona), August 6, 1910.

18. Concerning the popularity of General Germán Brandeis, see Emiliano Iglesias, July 6, 1910, *Diario de las Cortes,* II, 405; Sol y Ortega, April 8, 1911, *ibid.,* II, 661; *El Progreso* (Barcelona), August 17, 1910; "C" [Composada], "Sucesos de Barcelona," *El Socialista* (Madrid), December 24, 1909; and Pabón, *Cambó,* p. 257.

19. For the attack on the Church of San Andrés de Palomar, see *El Correo Catalán* (Barcelona), August 24, 1909; *Las Noticias* (Barcelona), August 25, 1909; and *El País* (Madrid), August 28, 1909.

20. See testimony of Marist Brother Benefoix in the trial of José Benedicto, *El Progreso* (Barcelona), September 28, 1910. See also the account in *Las Noticias* (Barcelona), August 19, 1909; Brissa, *Revolución de julio,* pp. 84–86; Anon., *Semana Sangrienta,* pp. 68–73.

21. For the attack on the Marist residence, see trial of José Benedicto, Domingo Valls, Pedro Duaso, Francisco Queralt, Francisco Villarroel, and six others, *El Progreso* (Barcelona), September 27–30, 1910; *El Liberal* (Barcelona), May 6, 1910; and *La Tribuna* (Barcelona), September 26, 1910. The case of José Miquel Baró was detached from this general case, and was prosecuted summarily.

22. Testimony of a municipal official, Clemento Porto, *Causa: Rebelión militar,* II, 56.

23. Report by General Santiago, p. 5 of Appendix 1 to October 19, 1909, *Diario de las Cortes.* On the fighting in Clot, see also *Las Noticias* (Barcelona), August 2 and 3, 1909, and H. Villaescusa, *Semana Trágica,* p. 22.

24. Soldevilla, *Año político*, XV: *1909*, 271–72. See also *El País* (Madrid), July 31, 1909.

Friday, July 30

1. Report by General Santiago, p. 6 of Appendix 1 to October 19, 1909, *Diario de las Cortes*.

2. Trial of Ramón Escuder Villas, *La Publicidad* (Barcelona), November 1, 1909. For the embarkation, see also Brissa, *Revolución de julio*, p. 58.

3. For the military supervision of the Atarazana district and the resumption of normal activities there, see *El País* (Madrid), July 31, August 6, 1909; *El Correo Catalán* (Barcelona), August 2, 1909; H. Villaescusa, *Semana Trágica*, p. 23; and Soldevilla, *Año político*, XV: *1909*, 286.

4. H. Villaescusa, *Semana Trágica*, p. 23.

5. Hurtado, *Quaranta Anys d'advocat*, I, 159.

6. Testimony of garden attendant, Ramón Villegas: *Causa: Rebelión militar*, I, 401–03.

7. H. Villaescusa, *Semana Trágica*, p. 23.

8. Trial of Antonio Terradés Caballé, *La Publicidad* (Barcelona), October 22, 1909.

9. Report by General Santiago, p. 5 of Appendix 1 to October 19, 1909, *Diario de las Cortes*. Interview with ex-Governor Ossorio, *La Época* (Madrid), August 4, 1909.

10. "C" [Comaposada], "Sucesos de Barcelona," *El Socialista* (Madrid), November 26, 1909. For the problem of the hidden snipers and the charge that they were priests in disguise, or financed by clergy, in order to incite the Army into carrying out a harsh rebellion, see Bonafulla [Esteve], *Revolución de julio*, p. 74; also Emiliano Iglesias, July 6, 1910, *Diario de las Cortes*, II, 405, and April 5, 1911, *ibid.*, II, 565. Even cautious Republican Senator Odón de Buen made the charge against the clergy, in *El Noticiero Universal* (Barcelona), August 4, 1909. When interrogated, Buen insisted a priest bearing arms had been arrested (*Causa: Rebelión militar*, II, 58). See also article by José Reig, *El País* (Madrid), August 8, 1909, and Rafael Shaw, *Spain from Within*, pp. 165–67.

11. Magin Vidal [Fabra Rivas], "Vue d'ensemble," *L'Humanité* (Paris), August 16, 1909.

12. For the incident on the Calle Aribau, see *La Tribuna* (Barcelona), July 29, August 1 and 3, 1910, and *El Correo Catalán* (Barcelona), July 30, August 4 and 5, 1909. For the incident on the Calle Aragon, see police report in *Causa: Rebelión militar*, I, 256.

13. For the incident in Pueblo Seco, see *El País* (Madrid), August 7, 1909, and Bonafulla [Esteve], *Revolución de julio*, p. 74.

14. *El Correo Catalán* (Barcelona), August 5, 1909. See also Dalmacio Iglesias, Carlist deputy, *Diario de las Cortes*, II, 421.

15. For discussion of the effects of the sniping, see Ametlla, *Memòries polítiques*, pp. 270–71, and article by José Reig, *El País* (Madrid), August 8, 1909.

16. Trial of Rafael Guerra del Río, *La Publicidad* (Barcelona), November 5 and 6, 1909.

17. *El Progreso* (Barcelona), August 13, 1911.

18. Letter from Emiliano Iglesias to *Solidaridad Obrera* (Barcelona), January 11, 1917.

19. *El Progreso* (Barcelona), August 13, 1911.

20. Testimony of Emiliano Iglesias, *Causa: Rebelión militar,* I, 36–37. Declaration of Trinidad Monegal, *ibid.,* I, 457.

21. For the attack on the convent-school of the Sisters of Jesus and Mary, see *El Correo Catalán* (Barcelona), August 15, 23, and 31, 1909, and *Las Noticias* (Barcelona), August 22, 1909. For background material, see Jesús-María Instituto, *Fundación y noticia del Instituto de Religiosas de Jesús-María* (Barcelona, 1906).

22. For the attack on the school of the Sons of the Holy Family, see *El Correo Catalán* (Barcelona), August 29, 1909, and *Las Noticias* (Barcelona), August 15, 1909.

23. For the attack on the asylum of the Sisters of the Holy Family of Urgel, see *Las Noticias* (Barcelona), August 22, 1909. For background on this order see Sagrada Familia Instituto, *Album conmemorativo en el septuagésimo-quinto aniversario de su fundación, 1859–1934* (Barcelona, 1935) provides background on this order. See *ibid.,* pp. 100 and 149 for events during the Tragic Week.

24. *El Progreso* (Barcelona), August 17, 1910. See also report by General Santiago, p. 6 of Appendix 1 to October 19, 1909, *Diario de las Cortes.*

25. Police search of the Fraternidad Republicana of Horta, *Causa: Rebelión militar,* I, 93–94. The Radical officials all fled from Horta to escape arrest.

26. For Ramón Font Garrliga, see Sangro, *Sombra de Ferrer,* pp. 403–04; also *El Progreso* (Barcelona), August 6, 1910, January 23, 1911, and January 14, 1913.

27. Interrogation of rebels from Horta, *Causa contra Ferrer,* pp. 445–51. See also *Causa: Rebelión militar,* I, 93–94. For the trial of the 49 individuals from Horta (17 of whom were tried in absentia, and 22 of whom were condemned to prison), see Soldevilla, *Año político,* XVI: *1910,* 26. See also *El Progreso* (Barcelona), December 24, 1909; August 16, 18 and 21, September 4 and 7, October 14, and December 20, 1910, and January 21, 1911; *La Publicidad* (Barcelona), January 26, and February 18, 24, and 25, 1910; and *El Poble Català* (Barcelona), February 14, 1911.

28. For the attack on the Church of San Juan, see *El Correo Catalán* (Barcelona), September 14, 1909.

29. For the attack on the school of the Dominican Sisters, see *ibid.,* September 15, 1909.

Saturday, July 31

1. For the text of the edict, see *El Correo Catalán* (Barcelona), August 2, 1909.

2. H. Villaescusa, *Semana Trágica,* p. 25. For the actual number of troops in Barcelona, see report by General Santiago, p. 6 of Appendix 1 to October 19, 1909, *Diario de las Cortes,* and Brissa, *Revolución de julio,* pp. 58–60. For events in Barcelona on Saturday morning, see "C" [Comaposada], "Sucesos de Barcelona," *El Socialista* (Madrid), December 3, 1909, and H. Villaescusa, *Semana Trágica,* pp. 24–25.

3. For the visit of the tourists, see *El País* (Madrid), August 2, 1909, and *Las Noticias* (Barcelona), August 2, 1909.

4. For the incident at the San Agustino barracks, see H. Villaescusa, *Semana Trágica,* p. 24 and Amado, Carlist Deputy, July 13, 1910, *Diario de las Cortes,* III, 568. For the continued firing from the Vincentian residence, see Anon., *Semana Sangrienta,*

p. 136. For the burning of the Church of Santa Madrona, see Almanaque, *Diario de Barcelona: 1910*, p. 95.

5. For the incident at the convent-school of the Beatas Dominicas, see "C" [Comaposada], "Sucesos de Barcelona," *El Socialista* (Madrid), December 3, 1909; the report by General Santiago, p. 6 of Appendix 1 to October 19, 1909, *Diario de las Cortes*; Bonafulla [Esteve], *Revolución de julio*, p. 34; and *El Correo Catalán* (Barcelona), August 2, 1909.

6. "C" [Comaposada], "Sucesos de Barcelona," *El Socialista* (Madrid), December 3, 1909.

7. Testimony of Councilor Francisco Puig y Alfonso, *Causa: Rebelión militar*, I, 500–01. For further details of the meeting, see *ibid.*, I, 36–37, 457–58, 463.

8. Testimony of Narciso Verdaguer, *ibid.*, I, 463.

9. *Solidaridad Obrera* (Barcelona), January 12, 1917. For the arrest see *Causa: Rebelión militar*, I, 37.

10. Testimony of Emiliano Iglesias on July 31, 1909, *Causa: Rebelión militar*, I, 31–38.

11. For the meeting of the "corporations" and their recommendations see Canals, *Sucesos de 1909*, I, 201; Orts-Ramos, *Historia de la revolución española*, p. 436; report by General Santiago, p. 6 of Appendix 1 to October 19, 1909, *Diario de las Cortes*; and "Versión: Censura militar," *Las Noticias* (Barcelona), August 2, 1909.

12. Trial of Alfonso Monreal Cotrina, *El Poble Català* (Barcelona), February 19, 1910, and *La Publicidad* (Barcelona), February 18, 1910.

13. *El Correo Catalán* (Barcelona), August 2, 1909.

Sunday, August 1

1. For events on Sunday morning, see *El País* (Madrid), August 2 and 3, 1909; *La Publicidad* (Barcelona), August 2, 1909; *El Correo Catalán* (Barcelona), August 2, 1909; and Brissa, *Revolución de julio*, pp. 66–67.

2. Ossorio, *Mis Memorias*, p. 95.

3. Constant Leroy [V. Moreno], "Campaña humanitaria," *El Correo Español* (Mexico, D.F.), January 7, 1913. For Ferrer's hiding place, see Sol Ferrer, *Ferrer: Martyr*, p. 141.

4. For report that the "miserable" sum of money disgusted them, see Emilio Junoy, "Pequeña Tribuna," *La Publicidad* (Barcelona), March 28, 1911. For details of Moreno's escape, see interview with V. Moreno, in *Il Secolo* (Milan), as reprinted in *ibid.*, July 19, 1910, and Constant Leroy [V. Moreno], "Campaña humanitaria," *El Correo Español* (Mexico, D.F.), January 7, 1913.

5. *El País* (Madrid), August 4, 1909.

6. Brissa, *Revolución de julio*, pp. 66–67. Report by General Santiago, p. 7 of Appendix 1 to October 19, 1909, *Diario de las Cortes*.

CHAPTER XII: THE TALLY SHEET

1. Trial of Ramón Baldera Aznar, *El Correo Catalán* (Barcelona), August 24, 1909.

2. On Governor Crespo, see Soldevilla, *Año político*, XV: *1909*, 289; Pabón, *Cambó*, pp. 341-42; and Benet, *Maragall i la Setmana Tràgica*, pp. 130-37.

3. Ugarte's report is reprinted in H. Villaescusa, *Semana Trágica*, pp. 58-60. See also *El Correo Catalán* (Barcelona), August 28 and 29, September 3, 17, and 28, 1909; also *Las Noticias* (Barcelona), August 11, 1909. Luis Simarro, a psychology professor active in republican politics, accused Ugarte of being "a salaried Catholic," of being an instrument of the Comité de Defensa Social in its successful efforts to have the Maura government close secular schools and to convict Ferrer (*El Proceso Ferrer y la opinión europea*, I, passim; see also Lerroux, *Ferrer y su proceso en las Cortes* [Barcelona, 1911], pp. 51-53).

4. *El Correo Catalán* (Barcelona), August 24 and 26, 1909.

5. *Ibid.*, August 7, 1909. Ugarte report as reprinted in H. Villaescusa, *Semana Trágica*, p. 59. Sirera reports there was a significant number of French workers in Barcelona, and that they were highly resented by Catalan workers ("Obreros en Barcelona," p. 27).

6. Santiago's figures can be found, for example, in *Las Noticias* (Barcelona), August 28, 1909, and *El Correo Catalán* (Barcelona), August 29, 1909. For Laureano Miró's protest against the implication of Catalan regionalism, see *La Publicidad* (Barcelona), August 3, 1909. Socialist Fabra Rivas denied that the rebellion was in any way a Catalan separatist movement ("Vue d'ensemble," *L'Humanité* [Paris], August 16, 1909, and "Réponse a des calomnies," *ibid.*, August 18, 1909).

7. Ricardo, Obispo de Eudoxia, Vicario Capitular, on August 9, 1909, as reported in *Boletín Oficial Eclesiástico* (Barcelona), 1435 (August 1909), 233-34.

8. Protest sent to Maura by the Vicario Capitular, dated August 6, 1909, printed in *ibid.*, 1436 (August 1909), 255.

9. Summary of report by the Liberal government of Canalejas on April 27, 1910, in Soldevilla, *Año político*, XVI: *1910*, 130.

10. *La Rebeldía* (Barcelona), May 6, 1910.

11. Katherine Chorley points out that although this type of fighting gives the rebel, who is fighting on friendly territory, an initial advantage over soldiers, it does not permit him to defeat an Army; see *Armies and the Art of Revolution*, p. 21.

12. For the figures on the Red Cross, and praise for its services during the week, see *La Publicidad* (Barcelona), August 2, 1909, and *Las Noticias* (Barcelona), August 6 and 8, 1909.

13. Report by la División Tercera, Urbanización y Obras, *Causa: Rebelión militar*, I, 491. See also report from same office in *Las Noticias* (Barcelona), August 27, 1909. The municipal archives in Barcelona has an excellent collection of photographs of the Tragic Week. See also the photographic review, *La Actualidad* (Barcelona), August 28, 1909.

14. La Cierva, July 8, 1910, *Diario de las Cortes*, II, 458, 462. See also *ibid.*, II, 517-18.

15. Concerning the municipal employees who participated, see La Cierva, July 8, 1910, *Diario de las Cortes*, II, 468, and Soldevilla, *Año político*, XV: *1909*, 285.

16. Trial of Antonio Capdevila Marques, reported in *El País* (Madrid), August 27, 1909; *La Publicidad* (Barcelona), October 30, 1909, and March 13 and April 1, 1910.

17. For the events in San Vicente de Castellet, and for the participation of Santiago

Alorba, see *Causa: Rebelión militar*, I, 313. For the trial, see *El Correo Catalán* (Barcelona), August 24, 1909. For Timoteo del Usón's relationship with Ferrer, see Constant Leroy [V. Moreno], *Secretos del anarquismo*, p. 163. A Santiago Alorda is reported as being vice president of the Committee for the Defense of Expatriated Spaniards (*El Poble Català* [Barcelona], June 19, 1910).

18. For the case of José Miquel Baró, see *El Correo Catalán* (Barcelona), August 24, 1909; *Las Noticias* (Barcelona), August 24, and September 15, 1909; and La Cierva, *Case of Ferrer*, 94–95. For background on Miquel Baró, see Orts-Ramos, *Historia de la revolución española*, 441; Brissa, *Revolución de julio*, pp. 163, 201–04; *El Poble Català* (Barcelona), April 29, 1911; and *El País* (Madrid), August 23 and 31, 1909.

19. *El Progreso* (Barcelona), August 17, 1910.

20. For the case of Eugenio del Hoyo, see *El País* (Madrid), August 28, September 6 and 9, 1909, and the editorial on the anniversary of his execution in *El Progreso* (Barcelona), September 13, 1910.

21. Soldevilla, *Año político*, XV: *1909*, 315.

22. For the case of Antonio Malet Pujol, see *El Correo Catalán* (Barcelona), August 16, 24, and 29–31, 1909; Brissa, *Revolución de julio*, pp. 163, 182, 204–05; *El País* (Madrid), August 29 and 31, and September 5, 1909; and Emiliano Iglesias, April 5, 1911, *Diario de las Cortes*, II, 567.

23. For the exchange between La Cierva and Corominas, see La Cierva, *Case of Ferrer*, p. 93.

24. Brissa, *Revolución de julio*, p. 209. Pedro Corominas, Nationalist Republican deputy, interrupted La Cierva to point out the difference in social class between Clemente and the three clerks who were acquitted (*Case of Ferrer*, p. 96).

25. For the charge that the Maura government did not dare to pardon Clemente because of the Ferrer case, see *La Forja* (Barcelona), October 8, 1910 and Emiliano Iglesias, July 6, 1910, *Diario de las Cortes*, II, 407.

26. For the charge that Nationalist Republicans, anarchists, and Radicals had organized the events, see report of Francisco Pedro y Méndez, Division Legal Advisor (Auditor de División), November 2, 1909, *Causa: Rebelión militar*, II, 133; declaration of Barcelona police chief, Enrique Díaz-Guijarro, *Causa contra Ferrer*, pp. 19–23; report of ex-Governor Angel Ossorio, *Causa: Rebelión militar*, I, 95–98; report of a captain of the Civil Guards, Vicente Tudela Fabra, *ibid.*, I, 337–38.

27. For the case against the anarchists, see Dictum of the Chief Military Advocate, General Ramón Pastor, September 21, 1909, *Causa: Rebelión militar*, I, 540–42; dictum of the officer in charge of the entire proceedings related to the leaders of the armed rebellion (Juez Instructor), Major Vicente Llivina y Fernández, October 22, 1909, *ibid.*, II, 119; report of the legal advisor, Francisco Pego y Mendez, *ibid.*, II, 133–35. The case of the anarchists was formally transferred to the civil courts on November 9, 1909 (see order in *ibid.*, II, 137).

28. On the disposition of the case against Juana Ardiaca Mas, see *Causa: Rebelión militar*, II, 216–17, 292–95, 298, 301, 307–09, 312, 341.

29. On the disposition of the case against Trinidad Alted Fornet, see *Causa: Rebelión militar*, II, 212–13, 291–92, 298, 301, 309–10, 312, 341.

30. "Protesta elevada por el Ilmo. Sr. Vicario Capitular al Excmo. Sr. Presidente del Consejo de Ministros," August 6, 1909, *Boletín Oficial Eclesiástico* (Barcelona) 1436 (August 1909), 256. For the charge that the Army stood passively by, see also Pedro Llosas, Carlist Deputy, July 13, 1910, *Diario de las Cortes,* III, 584, and July 14, 1910, *ibid.,* III, 614, and Joaquín Salvatella, Federal Republican Deputy, April 5, 1911, *ibid.,* II, 554.

31. Emiliano Iglesias, July 6, 1910, *Diario de las Cortes,* II, 410.

32. General Angel Aznar, Minister of War, July 6, 1910, *ibid.,* II, 417.

33. Testimony of Emiliano Iglesias, *Causa: Rebelión militar,* I, 98–99.

34. Instructions contained in a general telegram sent out by Major Llivina, in charge of the entire proceedings, on August 13, 1909, *Causa: Rebelión militar,* I, 327. See also *ibid.,* I, 21, 118, 256, 508–13, 539.

35. *El Correo Catalán* (Barcelona), August 28, 1909. *La Publicidad* (Barcelona), August 27, 1909.

36. Instructions contained in the telegram sent by Major Llivina, *Causa: Rebelión militar,* I, 327.

37. Request for evidence of Ulled brothers' participation, dated November 17, 1909, *Causa: Rebelión militar,* II, 154–55.

38. Interview with Estévanez, *La Rebeldía* (Barcelona), November 25, 1909. In the same issue, Ulled protested the police search of his home, declaring that it was undoubtedly the result of *police* obsession and that it had not been authorized by *military* authorities.

39. *La Rebeldía* (Barcelona), November 25, 1909. Dalmacio Iglesias, Carlist deputy, told the Cortes that in Barcelona the *lerrouxistas* had bragged of their part in the Tragic Week and had used it as an election weapon; he dared them to say the same things to the Cortes (speech on July 6, 1910, *Diario de las Cortes,* II, 421). Juan Ventosa, Lliga deputy, pressed the issue and demanded that Lerroux state explicitly which acts he "approved" of those occurring during the Tragic Week, and which he did not approve (July 16, 1910, *ibid.,* III, 687).

40. Dictum of the military officer in charge of the entire proceedings related to the leaders of the armed rebellion, Major Vicente Llivina y Fernández, summarizing all the evidence, October 22, 1909, in *Causa: Rebelión Militar,* I, 115–32. For the case against Emiliano Iglesias and Luis Zurdo Olivares, see the indictment prepared by Major Julián Santa Coloma Olimpo, January 24, 1910, *ibid.,* II, 213–16; the dictum of military advocate Ramón de Viala, March 4, 1910, *ibid.,* II, 296–98; sentence handed down by the military tribunal, March 4, 1910, *ibid.,* II, 300–02.

41. Pío Baroja, "Juventud egolatría," *Obras completas,* V, 220. For Emiliano Iglesias' account of how he suborned a principal witness (the porter of Solidaridad Obrera), see *Solidaridad Obrera* (Barcelona), January 9, 1917.

42. *Causa: Rebelión militar,* II, 310, 314–27, passim.

43. The military prosecuting officer, Enrique Gesta y García, acknowledged Radical help in the conviction of Ferrer (*Causa contra Ferrer,* p. 638). The officer defending Ferrer, Francisco Galcerán, protested the Radical action (*ibid.,* pp. 606–07).

44. For the testimony of Francisco Domenech Munté, on August 7 and 12, 1909,

see *Causa contra Ferrer*, pp. 23–26, 27–29. Archer writes that Domenech was given money, to pay off military service and to go abroad, by the Catholic Comité de Defensa Social (*Life of Ferrer*, p. 218).

45. Testimony of Domingo Casas Llibre, Mayor of Premiá, on August 16, 21, 28, 30 and 31, and September 12, 1909, *Causa contra Ferrer*, pp. 35–36, 86–88, 100–02, 121–24, 155–56, 306–15. Testimony of Juan Puig y Ventura, "El Llarch," on August 27 and September 1 and 22, 1909, *ibid.*, pp. 89–91, 113–15, 451–53.

46. Testimony of Emiliano Iglesias, September 16, 1909 (that is, after Ferrer had been arrested), *Causa contra Ferrer*, pp. 360–63. Testimony of Manuel Jiménez Moya, *ibid.*, pp. 41–42. Testimony of Baldomero Bonet Ancejo, September 18 and 22, 1909, *ibid.*, pp. 371–74.

47. Testimony of Alfredo García Magallanes, September 24, 1909, *ibid.*, pp. 467–68, 478–79.

48. Testimony of Lorenzo Ardid Bernal, September 10, 1909, *ibid.*, pp. 369–71.

49. *La Publicidad* (Barcelona), November 27, 1909. Ferrer reportedly said these words after he had been convicted.

CHAPTER XIII: FRANCISCO FERRER: "AUTHOR AND CHIEF OF THE REBELLION"

1. Dictum of the Chief Military Advocate, General Ramón Pastor, *Causa contra Ferrer*, pp. 660, 665.

2. Joaquín Salvatella pointed out that police should have known Ferrer's activities (April 5, 1911, *Diario de las Cortes*, II, 553). For reports that Ferrer eluded his police escort by going in a car, see *Causa contra Ferrer*, pp. 183, 467.

3. Pascual Zulueta, *La Epoca* (Madrid), August 4, 1909. See also Simarro, *Proceso Ferrer*, pp. 143–44, and Canals, *Sucesos de 1909*, I, 247. In a book for which ex-Governor Ossorio wrote the introduction, Paulis declared that Ferrer took the money from the bank and that it was distributed in the Radical Casa del Pueblo on the Sunday before the Tragic Week (*Maura ante el pueblo*, pp. 221–22). See also report of money circulating in Casa del Pueblo on July 25, in *ABC* (Madrid), August 4, 1909.

4. Letter from Ferrer, in hiding, August 1909, to Charles Matato, printed in Comité de Défense, *Martyr des prêtres*, p. 44.

5. Canals, *Sucesos de 1909*, I, 254.

6. *Causa contra Ferrer*, p. 625.

7. Police report, from confidant Tomás Herreros, *ibid.*, p. 466.

8. *Causa: Rebelión militar*, I, 106–07; II, 247–49.

9. Testimony of García Magallones, August 18, 1909, *Causa contra Ferrer*, p. 38. See also testimony of Lorenzo Arnau in Premiá, *ibid.*, p. 303; testimony of Jaime Font, *ibid.*, p. 521; and testimony of the mother of Soledad Villafranca (Ferrer's mistress), *ibid.*, pp. 351–53.

10. *Causa contra Ferrer*, p. 549. *Causa: Rebelión militar*, II, 73–74, 81–82, 86, 248–49.

11. For the relationship between Ferrer and Moreno, see indictment prepared by the army prosecutor, in *Causa contra Ferrer*, pp. 580–81, and dictum of the Chief Military Advocate, *ibid.*, pp. 660, 665. See also Emiliano Iglesias' statements in *El Progreso* (Bar-

celona), March 25 and 26, 1911. For 'Captain Moreno' and the barricades, see La Cierva, *Case of Ferrer*, pp. 78, 107, and the account of José Regás and others at the Calle San Pablo barricades, in *El País* (Madrid), October 8, 1909.

12. Letter from Serrador, a socialist, *El Diluvio* (Barcelona), August 6, 1911.

13. *El Progreso* (Barcelona), August 1, 1911.

14. Sol Ferrer, *Véritable Ferrer*, pp. 181, 233, and *Ferrer: Martyr*, pp. 136–37.

15. Litrán, "A los Amigos de Ferrer," *El Progreso* (Barcelona), November 11, 1910. Friends in Montevideo, Uruguay, were unable to locate the article to which Litrán refers.

16. Constant Leroy [V. Moreno], "Campaña humanitaria," *El Correo Español* (Mexico, D.F.), January 29, 1913, and *Secretos del anarquismo*, pp. 47, 56. For Moreno's activities, see Archer's account, based on his interview with Moreno, *Life of Ferrer*, pp. 143–44, 208; interview with V. Moreno in *Il Secolo* (Milan) as reprinted in *La Publicidad* (Barcelona), July 19, 21, and 27, 1910; V. Moreno, "Por la Verdad," *El País* (Madrid), November 2, 1909; *El Socialista* (Madrid), November 19, 1909, and Simarro, *Proceso Ferrer*, I, 76–77.

17. Constant Leroy [V. Moreno], *Secretos del anarquismo*. I am grateful to Dr. Manuel Alcalá, Director of the National Library of Mexico, who reported in a letter dated April 18, 1963, that no second volume was published.

18. For books eulogizing Ferrer as a martyr for secular education in Spain, see Simarro, *Proceso Ferrer* (Madrid, 1910); McCabe, *The Martyrdom of Ferrer* (London, 1909); Georges Normandy and E. Lesueur, *Ferrer: L'Homme et son oeuvre* (Paris, 1909); and Leonard D. Abbott, ed., *Francisco Ferrer: His Life, Work and Martyrdom* (New York, n.d. [1910?]).

19. La Cierva, *Case of Ferrer*, p. 109.

20. Urales [Montseny], *Mi Vida*, III, 80.

21. *El Progreso* (Barcelona), July 27, 1914. Iglesias bragged of not having confessed details of his own meetings with Ferrer: "Lo que *no* dijo Emiliano Iglesias," *ibid.*, March 26, 1911.

22. Laureano Miró, as quoted in Sangro, *Sombra de Ferrer*, p. 429. See also Rafael Salillas, republican deputy, March 31, 1911, *Diario de las Cortes*, II, 502.

23. *El Progreso* (Barcelona), March 25, 1911.

CHAPTER XIV: NATIONAL CONSEQUENCES OF THE TRAGIC WEEK

1. Maragall, "Ah! Barcelona . . . [sic]," published October 1, 1909, and reprinted in Benet, *Maragall i la Semana Tràgica*, p. 104.

2. For accounts of the events abroad which influenced Spanish deputies, see particularly *ABC* (Madrid) and *El País* (Madrid), October 14–20, 1909. See also documents in Sol Ferrer, *Ferrer: Martyr*, pp. 173–209. Sangro provides a comprehensive, albeit extremely biased account of the international protest in the Ferrer case, 1909 to 1917, in *Sombra de Ferrer*, pp. 231–364.

3. Only two republican deputies, both from Valencia, Felix Azzati Descalzi and Julio Cervera petitioned for a pardon for Ferrer (*Sombra de Ferrer*, pp. 70–73). For the later attempts of Catalan republicans to explain their silence, see Juan Caballé,

March 30, 1911, *Diario de las Cortes,* II, 486; Joaquín Salvatella, April 5, 1911, *ibid.,* II, 555-56; and Hurtado, *Quaranta Anys d'advocat,* I, 161.

4. Shaw, *Spain from Within,* pp. 170-77. *La Petite Marseilles* on August 7, 1909, reported that the Carlists had tried to use the disorders of the Tragic Week, or the repression that followed, as an occasion for the establishment of a Carlist dynasty. Miguel Yunyent, a Carlist leader in Catalonia, found the accusation sufficiently important to deny it officially in *El Correo Catalán* (Barcelona), August 15, 1909.

5. Miguel de Unamuno, *En torno al Casticismo* (1895), 5 ed. (Madrid: Colección Austral, 1961), pp. 87-88, 127-29.

6. As quoted in Fernández Almagro, *Historia del reinado de Alfonso XIII* (Barcelona, 1933), p. 154.

7. Maura, October 19, 1909, *Diario de las Cortes,* pp. 55-56.

8. La Cierva, October 19 and 20, 1909, *ibid.,* pp. 52, 82.

9. Vicens Vives, *Historia social,* V, 399-400.

10. G. Maura, *Por qué cayó Alfonso,* pp. 154-56. See also García Escudero, *De Cánovas a la república,* pp. 167-70.

11. For this crisis in the political career of Antonio Maura, see G. Maura, *Por qué cayó Alfonso,* pp. 204-70.

12. *Ibid.,* p. 156.

13. Pablo Iglesias, speaking on June 13, 1914, in the Cortes, as quoted in Sangro, *Sombra de Ferrer,* pp. 179-80. He expressed the same sentiments in his first speech to the Cortes, on July 7, 1910, *Diario de las Cortes,* II, 433-34.

14. "El Fracaso de la Conjunción," *La Justicia Social* (Reus), May 7, 1914. See also García Venero, *Las Internacionales,* I, 447-52.

15. Ametlla, *Memòries polítiques,* pp. 277-98. See also Hurtado, *Quaranta Anys d'advocat,* I, 177-78.

16. Benet, *Maragall i la Setmana Tràgica,* p. 170. See also Moret, October 18, 1909, *Diario de las Cortes,* p. 27, and Pablo Iglesias, July 7, 1910, *ibid.,* II, 437. Maura reportedly was bitterly disappointed by the failure of regionalists to aid his government (*Las Noticias* [Barcelona], August 12, 1909). After the Tragic Week, the merchants of Almería tried to enforce a national boycott of all Catalan goods (Canals, *Sucesos de 1909,* I, 203-04).

17. The Lliga almost completely dominated the Mancomunidad during its existence, 1914-1924 (Ametlla, *Memòries polítiques,* pp. 312-34).

18. *Causa contra Ferrer,* pp. 465-66, 592-93, 606. For assertions that Solidaridad Obrera refused to sponsor the strike, see V. Moreno, "Por la Verdad," *El País* (Madrid), November 2, 1909; *La Forja* (Barcelona), July 30, 1910; Pablo Iglesias, July 12, 1910, *Diario de las Cortes,* III, 552; and Magin Vidal [Fabra Rivas], "Les Préliminaires de la Grève Générale," *L'Humanité* (Paris), August 13, 1909.

19. On José Román, see V. Moreno, "Por la Verdad," *El País* (Madrid), November 2, 1909, and *La Publicidad* (Barcelona), November 11, 1909.

20. *El Progreso* (Barcelona), December 20, 1909.

21. Prat, *Orientaciones,* p. 7. See also José Peirats, *La CNT en la revolución española* (Buenos Aires, 1955), I, 17, and the article by 'Domingo Rompecabezas' in *La Publicidad* (Barcelona), November 28, 1909.

22. *El Progreso* (Barcelona), December 20, 1909.

23. Prat, *Orientaciones,* p. 7. Concerning the lack of class spirit among Catalan workers, see speech by Fabra Rivas to Solidaridad Obrera, on July 3, 1909, as reported in *La Publicidad* (Barcelona), July 5, 1909. See also speeches made during his socialist propaganda campaign in the Balearic Islands reported in *El Socialista* (Madrid), July 23, 1909.

24. On the decision of the socialists to abandon Solidaridad Obrera, see "Acuerdo de la asamblea de la Agrupación Socialista de Barcelona," *El Socialista* (Madrid), December 9, 1910. See also the editorial praising Fabra Rivas for having participated in Solidaridad Obrera, in contrast with the later socialist action (*Solidaridad Obrera* [Barcelona], December 2, 1910).

25. "Justo Recuerdo," *Solidaridad Obrera* (Barcelona), October 7, 1910. See also Boix, "Sindicalismo cristiano," *Revista Social Hispano-Americana* (Barcelona), p. 215. For the sessions of the Second Labor Congress (October 30 through November 1, 1910), see *La Publicidad* (Barcelona), October 30–November 3, 1910; García Venero, *Las Internacionales,* I, 454–58; and Vicens Vives, *Historia social,* V, 228.

26. For the sessions of the CNT's first congress in 1911, see *La Publicidad* (Barcelona), September 8–11, 1911. See also E. Bach, "A propósito del Congreso Obrero. El Sindicalismo en Cataluña," *ibid.,* September 8, 1911; Buenacasa, *Movimiento obrero,* pp. 51–53; and García Venero, *Las Internacionales,* I, 458–59.

27. Lerroux, as quoted in Sangro, *Sombra de Ferrer,* p. 39, and *El Progreso* (Barcelona), February 4, 1912. For the 1911 General Strike, see also Constant Leroy [V. Moreno], "Campaña humanitaria," *El Correo Español* (Mexico, D.F.), January 2–4 and 16, 1913, and *Secretos del anarquismo,* pp. 31–34.

28. Buenacasa, *Movimiento obrero,* pp. 52–56.

29. Hugh Thomas, "The Balance of Forces in Spain," *Foreign Affairs,* 41 (October 1962), 221. See also Buenacasa, *Movimiento obrero,* p. 53.

30. *El Correo Catalán* and *Las Noticias* (Barcelona), August 11, 1909.

31. General Pastor, Auditor General, charged that the leaders of the rebellion were often teachers appointed by Ferrer to the schools in Radical centers (*Causa contra Ferrer,* p. 666). The specific school in point was the one in the Radical center in Premiá de Mar, with which Ferrer had maintained close contact (for this school, and its teacher, Jose Folch Dalmau, who participated in the uprising, see *ibid.,* pp. 108–09, 111–12, 125–27, 225–27, 246–47, 207–08).

32. La Cierva, *Notas de mi vida,* p. 144. The church hierarchy were almost unanimous in their statements that the events of the Tragic Week had been caused by secular schools and an uncensored press; see *Boletín Oficial Eclesiástico* (Barcelona), 1435–1438 (August–September 1909). For the clearest expression of this viewpoint, see the joint statement sent by the prelates to Canalejas on April 6, 1910, *ibid.,* 1460 (July 1910), 377–382.

CHAPTER XV: THE FUNCTION OF ANTICLERICALISM IN SPANISH POLITICS

1. The works most helpful in writing these conclusions were: an article by Juan Caballé, writing in *El País* (Madrid), November 3, 1909; Anselmo Lorenzo, "Revolu-

ción y solidaridad," *El Socialista* (Madrid), October 22, 1909; "C" [José Comaposada], "Sucesos de Barcelona," *ibid.*, November 19, 1909; article by Francisco Pi y Arsuaga, quoted in its entirety in Bonafulla [Esteve], *Revolución de julio,* pp. 65–73; and Shaw, *Spain from Within,* Chs. 3, 4, 6.

2. John C. Bennett, *Christians and the State* (New York, 1958), p. 258.

3. "Hace un Año: Remembranzas," *La Publicidad* (Barcelona), July 9, 1910.

4. Maurín, "Movimiento obrero," *Leviatán* (Madrid), p. 19.

5. Ossorio, *Julio de 1909,* pp. 13–14.

6. "La Huelga contra Rusiñol," *El Socialista* (Madrid), October 22, 1909.

7. Caballé, in *El País* (Madrid), November 3, 1909.

8. "C" [Comaposada], "Sucesos de Barcelona," *El Socialista* (Madrid), November 19, 1909.

9. On this struggle between political patronage and subsidies to clerical institutions, see editorial, "La Infancia abandonada," *El Correo Catalán* (Barcelona), August 12, 1909; Marvaud, *Question sociale,* p. 406; and Albó, *Barcelona: Caritativa,* I, 225, 227. See also the bitter exchange over the Radical patronage in the Barcelona municipal government when the Lliga deputy called it "la lista civil de la democracia radical" (Juan Ventosa on July 16, 1910, *Diario de las Cortes,* III, 686).

10. Lorenzo, "Revolución y solidaridad," *El Socialista* (Madrid), October 22, 1909.

11. Maragall, "Ah! Barcelona . . . ," as quoted in Benet, *Maragall i la Setmana Tràgica,* p. 104.

12. Letter from Maragall to Francisco Cambó, October 9, 1909, as quoted in *ibid.,* p. 114. On the egotism of the bourgeoisie see also Padre Casanovas, *Estado social,* pp. 95–96; and Pablo Iglesias, July 7, 1910, *Diario de las Cortes,* II, 437. See also, as background, the prologue by Emilio Giralt y Raventos, to Vicens Vives, *Cataluña: Siglo XIX,* pp. 17–21.

13. Benet, *Maragall i la Setmana Tràgica,* pp. 165–72.

14. Frank Mankeiwicz, "An Explanation of Community Development As It Is Practiced by the Peace Corps in Latin America," Publication of the Peace Corps: GSA PC 66-2814 (Washington, D.C., 1966), p. 12.

15. Vicens Vives believes that anticlericalism may have served the same function in the eighteenth century, when the failure of the agrarian reform movement was covered over by the expulsion of the Jesuits (*Approximación a la historia de España,* 2 ed. rev. [Barcelona, 1960], pp. 177–78).

Index